Freedom, Racism, and Reconstruction

Freedom, Racism, and Reconstruction

COLLECTED WRITINGS OF
LaWanda Cox

EDITED BY DONALD G. NIEMAN

The University of Georgia Press   *Athens*

Paperback edition, 2016
© 1997 by the University of Georgia Press
Athens, Georgia 30602
www.ugapress.org
All rights reserved
Set in New Caledonia by G&S Typesetters, Inc.

Most University of Georgia Press titles are
available from popular e-book vendors.

Printed digitally

The Library of Congress has cataloged the
hardcover edition of this book as follows:

Cox, La Wanda C. Fenlason.
Freedom, racism, and Reconstruction : collected writings of
La Wanda Cox / edited by Donald G. Nieman.
xviii, 425 p. : ill. ; 24 cm.
Includes bibliographical references (p. 319–425).
ISBN 0-8203-1901-5 (alk. paper)
1. African Americans—History—1863–1877. 2. Reconstruction
(U.S. history, 1865–1877). 3. African Americans—Southern States—
Economic conditions. 4. Land tenure—Southern States—
History—19th century. 5. African Americans—Civil rights—
Southern States—History—19th century. 6. Freedmen—Southern States—
Social conditions. 7. Southern States—Race relations.
I. Nieman, Donald G. II. Title.
El85.2.C76   1997
973'.0496073—dc21   97-20517

Paperback ISBN-13: 978-0-8203-5158-2

CONTENTS

Acknowledgments   vii

Introduction   ix

PART ONE   Land and Labor

CHAPTER ONE
Tenancy in the United States, 1865–1900: A Consideration of the Validity of the Agricultural Ladder Hypothesis
3

CHAPTER TWO
The American Agricultural Wage Earner, 1865–1900: The Emergence of a Modern Labor Problem
16

CHAPTER THREE
The Promise of Land for the Freedmen
41

PART TWO   The Politics of Equal Citizenship

CHAPTER FOUR
Lincoln and Black Freedom
63

CHAPTER FIVE
Andrew Johnson and His Ghost Writers: An Analysis of the Freedmen's Bureau and Civil Rights Veto Messages
76

CHAPTER SIX
Civil Rights: The Issue of Reconstruction
94

CHAPTER SEVEN
Negro Suffrage and Republican Politics: The Problem of Motivation in Reconstruction Historiography
125

PART THREE Southern Reconstruction: A Doomed Commitment?

CHAPTER EIGHT
General O. O. Howard and the "Misrepresented Bureau"
149

CHAPTER NINE
The Perception of Injustice and Race Policy: James F. McGogy and the Freedmen's Bureau in Alabama
172

CHAPTER TEN
Reflections on the Limits of the Possible
243

PART FOUR The Second Reconstruction and the Changing Historiography of the South

CHAPTER ELEVEN
Ella Lonn: Pioneer Woman Historian of Civil War and Reconstruction
281

CHAPTER TWELVE
From Emancipation to Segregation: National Policy and Southern Blacks
288

Notes 319

ACKNOWLEDGMENTS

I owe many persons special thanks for helping bring this project to fruition. Malcolm Call of the University of Georgia Press believed in this book from the beginning and has performed all manner of tasks large and small to move it from an idea to a finished product. He also did his best—not always successfully—to keep the volume's editor on track. Kim Cretors did a fine job of copyediting the manuscript, and Kristine Blakeslee has shepherded it through the production process with efficiency and good humor. Clemson University and the Policy History Program at Bowling Green State University provided generous support for this project. Without their assistance, its completion would not have been possible. Dirk Karrenbauer and Charles Morrisey provided assistance in checking sources and proofing the final text. Mary J. Farmer gave the introductory essay a careful reading and made a number of suggestions that improved the final product. Barbara Welter and Shelley Trefousse, two good friends, took time from their busy lives to provide wise, patient, and informed editorial assistance as the project neared completion. Finally, LaWanda Cox herself was always ready to provide information and offer suggestions on matters of substance and style. I am especially grateful to her for providing me with information on her personal and professional life that I used in writing the introduction.

The following are the original citations to the previously published works that appear in this volume. All are used with the permission of the publishers.

LaWanda Fenlason Cox, "Tenancy in the United States, 1865–1900: A Consideration of the Validity of the Agricultural Ladder Hypothesis," *Agricultural History* 18 (July 1944): 97–105.

LaWanda F. Cox, "The American Agricultural Wage Earner, 1865–1900: The Emergence of a Modern Labor Problem," *Agricultural History* 22 (April 1948): 95–114.

LaWanda Cox and John H. Cox, "General O. O. Howard and the 'Misrepresented Bureau,'" *Journal of Southern History* 19 (November 1953): 427–56.

LaWanda Cox, "The Promise of Land for the Freedmen," *Mississippi Valley Historical Review* 45 (December 1958): 413–40.

LaWanda Cox and John H. Cox, "Andrew Johnson and His Ghost Writers: An Analysis of the Freedmen's Bureau and Civil Rights Veto Messages," *Mississippi Valley Historical Review* 48 (December 1961): 460–79.

LaWanda Cox and John H. Cox, "Civil Rights: The Issue of Reconstruction," in *Politics, Principle, and Prejudice, 1865–1866: Dilemma of Reconstruction America* (New York: Free Press, 1963), 195–232. © 1963 by The Free Press. Reprinted with permission of The Free Press, an imprint of Simon and Schuster.

LaWanda Cox and John H. Cox, "Negro Suffrage and Republican Politics: The Problem of Motivation in Reconstruction Historiography," *Journal of Southern History* 33 (August 1967): 303–30.

LaWanda Cox, "Ella Lonn: Pioneer Woman Historian of Civil War and Reconstruction," *Southern Studies* 20 (Summer 1981): 102–10.

LaWanda Cox, "Reflections on the Limits of the Possible," in *Lincoln and Black Freedom: A Study in Presidential Leadership* (Columbia: The University of South Carolina Press, 1981), 142–84.

LaWanda Cox, "From Emancipation to Segregation: National Policy and Southern Blacks," in *Interpreting Southern History: Historiographical Essays in Honor of Sanford W. Higginbotham,* John B. Boles and Evelyn Thomas Nolen, eds. (Baton Rouge: Louisiana State University Press, 1987), 199–253. © 1987 by Louisiana State University Press.

LaWanda Cox, "Lincoln and Black Freedom," in *The Historian's Lincoln: Pseudohistory, Psychohistory, and History,* Gabor S. Boritt, ed. (Urbana: University of Illinois Press, 1988), 175–88.

INTRODUCTION

In the 1950s and 1960s, a talented group of revisionist historians rewrote the history of Reconstruction. Challenging conventional wisdom, they demonstrated that emancipation and civil rights were the real issues of Reconstruction rather than a smokescreen employed by Republican leaders to advance sectional political and economic interests. These historians and their scholarship not only transformed our understanding of Reconstruction, but recognized the centrality of race in American history. While today that might seem unremarkable, it was a truth that had eluded most white historians, for whom race and African Americans were peripheral if not entirely out of the picture. By placing race at the heart of the Reconstruction drama, revisionists also encouraged a reexamination of the postemancipation African American experience.

LaWanda Cox stands out among the remarkable group of scholars responsible for this historiographical revolution—a group that included such notables as William Brock, David Donald, John Hope Franklin, Harold Hyman, Eric McKitrick, Willie Lee Rose, Kenneth Stampp, and Hans Trefousse. In articles published in the 1950s, Cox developed many of the themes and arguments that later came to define this new understanding of Reconstruction. Subsequently, in *Politics, Principle, and Prejudice, 1865–1866* (coauthored with her husband, John H. Cox, and published in 1963), she clearly identified civil rights as the crucial issue of Reconstruction. In doing so, Cox established the central tenet of revisionism, a position on which there is scholarly consensus more than thirty years later.[1] Indeed, in the mid-1990s, *Politics* remains part of the Reconstruction canon. It is required reading (or rereading) for specialists and one of a handful of books on the subject listed as suggested reading in virtually every introductory U.S. history textbook.

Among the reasons for the staying power of Professor Cox's scholarship is its solid grounding in archival research. In the 1930s, when she began doctoral study at the University of California at Berkeley, the archival sources available to students of American history were expanding dramatically.

She eagerly exploited these new materials, tirelessly mining the manuscript sources. As a result, she built her interpretations on a solid foundation. Indeed, her research was so thorough and so thoroughly honest that it was not subject to displacement by subsequent researchers who discovered sources she had neglected or who revisited those she had used.

Cox's career was guided by intellectual honesty and rigor, willingness to pursue leads suggested by careful reading of the sources, and determination to find the truth. She never set out with a preordained thesis that she was determined to support. Rather, she went to the sources, read them carefully and intelligently, and followed the evidence where it led. That approach often took her in directions that were wholly unanticipated but were exciting and remarkably fruitful. As LaWanda Cox once remarked with characteristic modesty, "I got into everything through the back door."[2] If that statement suggests luck, it is misleading. Like other creative minds, she made her own luck by going to the sources and asking the right questions.

The endurance of Cox's scholarship is also attributable to her analytical skills. Part of a generation of historians who insisted that history move beyond narrative and placed an especially high value on analysis and nuanced interpretation, she crafted powerful, compelling interpretive arguments. She also possessed the ability to define issues precisely. Thus while some revisionists confused Reconstruction-era Republicans' support for civil rights measures with a commitment to the twentieth-century goal of racial equality, Cox was always clear that Republicans' commitment had been to the more limited goal of civil equality. Her ability to define issues precisely and to craft well-reasoned interpretations—like her careful attention to archival sources—assured that her analyses would remain as fresh and powerful to subsequent generations of scholars as they were to her contemporaries.

Although intensely interested in politics and social issues (among Cox's fondest memories is dining at the home of Lincoln Steffens and Ella Winter on her wedding day in 1935), Cox insisted on separating politics and scholarship. While she realized that historians are inevitably influenced by their times and personal convictions, in her view scholarship would be discredited if it eschewed the pursuit of objectivity even in the interest of economic and civil rights for the oppressed. While these views may be out of fashion in a postmodern world, they give her writing an enduring quality.

Born in Washington state in 1909, LaWanda Fenlason grew up in Oregon. Nurtured in childhood by dinner table conversation among, as she describes them, an articulate, maverick exsocialist father, a conservative Republican older brother, and a skeptic mother who argued that reform should begin at home (her home), early on Cox developed a concern for social justice. That concern would be evident in her intellectual odyssey as a scholar.

After graduating from the University of Oregon with a B.A. in history, she headed East in the fall of 1931 to accept a graduate fellowship at Smith College. There she pursued her M.A., working under the direction of Merle Curti, a pioneering social historian whose concern for social justice reinforced and helped crystallize her own. Curti asked Cox to be his full-time assistant during the following year, when he would take leave to work on a grant from the American Historical Association to study the social ideas of American educators.[3] Cox's salary was paid with money intended for a typist; Curti told her that he could type, what he needed was a research assistant. They became close, lifelong friends. Cox considers Curti "the most resolutely and consistently democratic person I've ever known well, both in his personal conduct and intellectual concerns."[4] It was an example that would guide her own personal and professional life, as dozens of younger scholars who benefitted from her openness and encouragement as graduate students or freshly minted Ph.D.s will attest. Over the years Curti remained an intellectual confidant; not surprisingly *Politics* is dedicated to him.

During their research in Washington, D.C., Curti introduced Cox not only to archival research but also to southern-style racism. John Hope Franklin arranged a meeting for them with a group of Howard University historians; Cox never forgot her shock and outrage when a white taxi driver refused to take her and Curti to the meeting because it was located in a black neighborhood. If the encounter with the driver was disturbing, the introduction to Franklin was decidedly more auspicious. It began a friendship that spanned the next sixty years.

Cox moved back to the West Coast and in the fall of 1934 began doctoral study at the University of California at Berkeley, where her future husband, John H. Cox, was already enrolled. (The romance had begun in the stacks of the University of Oregon library when the two were undergraduates. The couple would marry in 1935, after Cox's first year at Berkeley.) The Great Depression had aroused not only her concern but her curiosity about the history of past depressions. She had hoped to change her major from history to economics but abandoned the idea when she learned that would have cost her a tuition waiver. She quickly became involved in the campus debate that crackled between communists and democratic socialists, with the former trying but ultimately failing to win her support.

Her arrival in Berkeley also coincided with rising concern over the rural proletariat being driven to California from the South, the Midwest, and the Great Plains by the dust bowl, the depression, and the mechanization of agriculture. Cox originally planned a dissertation on colonial trade, which was suggested by her history advisors because new sources had recently become available. However, her choice was criticized by Paul Schuster Taylor, an economist with whom she was taking a course. Taylor had joined with photographer Dorothea Lang to document the plight of the migrants, a collaboration that led to the powerful photo essay *An American Exodus: A Record of Human Erosion*.[5] Taylor challenged Cox to write on the history of migratory farm labor, although he asserted that it had no history before 1900. Cox promptly accepted the challenge but defied the time limitation, in 1941 completing an impressive dissertation entitled "Agricultural Labor in the United States 1865–1900, with Special Reference to the South."

By the time she completed her dissertation, Cox had once again crossed the country. In 1941, she settled in New York City with her husband after both had spent a year teaching at Northeast Missouri State Teachers College in Kirksville—his being a full-time appointment, hers part time and temporary. The drive from Missouri to New York in the summer of 1941, begun as a visit to Merle Curti, resulted in an appointment for John Cox as Assistant Professor at City College. Cox spent the fall completing her dissertation; she defended the work in Berkeley the day after Pearl Harbor.

In New York, as throughout the country, Cox found that a Ph.D. was no automatic ticket to academic employment—especially for women. While women were not uncommon in graduate programs—almost one in five Ph.D.s in history awarded by U.S. universities in the 1930s went to women—significant barriers existed to academic employment and opportunities for professional advancement were limited. Most men's colleges and coeducational institutions openly discriminated against women, and women Ph.D.s knew that their best hope for employment was in women's colleges.[6] Cox was no exception.

In early 1942, she accepted a temporary position at Hunter College, the city's women's college. The pay was low ($2,450) and the teaching load heavy, but it began a long relationship with Hunter that spanned most of her professional career. For two years (1944–46), while her husband was in the military and stationed overseas, Cox left Hunter to accept an appointment as Assistant Professor at Goucher College. Although Goucher offered her tenure and a promotion, she declined, leaving Baltimore in 1946 to rejoin John Cox when he returned to City College. Fortunately, a reappointment to the

Hunter faculty enabled her to resume her career as an educator. Teaching there until her retirement in 1971, she earned a reputation among undergraduates as a demanding but caring professor, and a number of her students went on to distinguished academic careers. When the City University of New York opened its graduate center in 1964, Cox received a joint appointment to its faculty and played an important role in shaping its Ph.D. program in history.

In New York, Professor Cox had returned to her work on agricultural labor, although heavy teaching loads and the temporary move to Baltimore slowed her progress. The dissertation—still highly regarded by scholars—yielded two influential articles that offered probing, original, and strikingly revisionist accounts of agricultural labor in the decades following the Civil War.[7] The articles convincingly refuted the widely accepted agricultural ladder hypothesis, which posited that during the nineteenth century, tenant farmers and agricultural laborers were young men on the road to becoming independent landowning farmers. In earlier accounts opportunity and social mobility had characterized nineteenth-century rural America; the South, with its heritage of slavery, sharecropping, and rural poverty, was an aberration. Cox's work told a different story. Focusing on the growth of commercial truck farming in the East, the bonanzas of the Dakotas, the great commercial farms of California, and the vast ranches of the Southwest, as well as the southern plantation, she demonstrated that the decades following the Civil War witnessed the emergence of a rural proletariat regarded by landowners as little more than a commodity necessary for production. Even the hired men ubiquitous on the farms of the Midwest found that their wages, far from enabling them to set aside money to purchase farms of their own, fell behind those of industrial workers, prompting an exodus from the countryside to the cities. During a period long regarded as the golden age of U.S. agriculture, Cox concluded, propertyless laborers were a fixture of the United States' rural landscape and "farm labor was rapidly approaching the essential nature of industrial labor."[8]

In the late 1940s, as she pursued her research on agricultural labor, Cox's career took an unexpected but propitious turn. Seeking archival sources that would illuminate the transition to free labor in the post–Civil War South, she turned to the vast records of the Freedmen's Bureau, which the National Archives had recently opened to researchers. The bureau records not only provided a wealth of information on southern agricultural labor, but, when subjected to careful reading by an open-minded historian, suggested a highly revisionist view of Reconstruction and Republican politics, a subject to which Cox turned her attention.

At the time she began this new endeavor, conventional wisdom held that Republican leaders had cynically championed the rights of the former slaves in order to cement their hold on the national government and enact legislation that would serve the interests of northern bankers and industrialists. In this view, President Andrew Johnson, a staunch Unionist and champion of the southern yeomen, followed Lincoln's policy in a courageous stand on behalf of constitutional principle and speedy restoration of the Union, but was thwarted by a group of unscrupulous Radical Republicans who pushed through Congress a self-serving and disastrous program of Reconstruction. It devastated an already prostrate South and left a legacy of bitterness that poisoned southern race relations for generations. Most scholars also believed that race and civil rights had little to do with Reconstruction except to provide a convenient rationale for Radical greed and vindictiveness.

Beginning with her 1953 article, "General O. O. Howard and the 'Misrepresented Bureau,'" Cox challenged this interpretation and began to construct a new paradigm to replace it.[9] After examination of the bureau records, in which her husband joined, she recognized that creation of the Freedmen's Bureau had been a wise decision, fully necessary if slavery were to be effectively ended and freedom established. Far from being a tool of the Radicals, she concluded, the bureau's commissioner and most agents made a genuine, if flawed, effort to build a system of free labor on the ruins of slavery. It was a task of staggering dimensions, she argued, but it had been complicated by the intransigence of southern whites and the racism of Andrew Johnson. Indeed, she suggested that it had been these factors rather than Republican vindictiveness that had driven congressional Republicans to adopt more radical measures.

Long concerned about the plight of agricultural laborers, Cox also investigated Republicans' efforts to provide former slaves with land.[10] Tracing the evolution of legislation that created the Freedmen's Bureau, she called attention to its provisions for making available to former slaves land seized from supporters of the Confederacy. The essay identified the land issue as critical, an insight fundamental to subsequent scholarship.[11] It also pointedly broke with the prevailing view of congressional Republicans as pawns of northern capital. Instead, Cox argued that, while they were by no means free of racial prejudice, Republicans were guided by a "commitment to freedom and equality inherent in the American heritage."[12]

While this essay, which appeared in 1958, returned to some of the themes of her dissertation, it clearly reflected Cox's growing preoccupation with Reconstruction politics and policy. Even before the Freedmen's Bureau article was published in 1953, she had begun research in the Johnson Papers at the Library of Congress, the Edwin D. Morgan Papers at the New York State Library, and the Thurlow Weed and William Henry Seward Papers at the University of Rochester. This led her to a reassessment of the break between congressional Republicans and Andrew Johnson and the significance of civil rights in postwar politics.

Although her thesis had crystallized by the time the Supreme Court decided the *Brown v. Board of Education* case in 1954, publication in its fully developed form waited until 1963, when *Politics, Principle, and Prejudice* appeared. Here she boldly argued that by the end of the Civil War, congressional Republicans—moderates as well as Radicals—had come to support equality before the law as vital to securing substantive freedom for African Americans. While the moderates who dominated party councils wished to avoid a break with President Johnson and repeatedly offered to compromise, they ultimately refused to abandon their commitment to civil equality short of suffrage. It was Andrew Johnson, Cox argued, driven by virulent racism and narrow partisanship, who rejected compromise with Republicans. He refused to accept any form of national intervention on behalf of the former slaves, insisted that white southerners be allowed to define the status of the freedpeople, and openly appealed to white racism. Cox concluded: "By standing adamant against a federally enforceable pledge of minimum civil equality for the Negroes as a prerequisite to restoration of the secession states, Johnson precipitated a great issue of moral principle central to the battle over Reconstruction; and he brought upon himself unparalleled humiliation."[13]

During the years following publication of *Politics*, Cox remained an influential voice in Reconstruction scholarship. Intrigued by the role of presidential leadership in Reconstruction, an important theme in *Politics*, she turned her attention to Johnson's predecessor. The results appeared in *Lincoln and Black Freedom* (1981), a powerful revisionist examination of Lincoln, emancipation, and wartime Reconstruction policy.[14] While not denying the role African Americans played in their own liberation, Cox offered a powerful argument for restoring Lincoln's reputation as the "Great Emancipator." Challenging the reigning scholarly consensus, she argued with characteristic persuasiveness that Lincoln had provided skillful leadership on the issue and that his policy had been driven by principle rather than expedience. Historians had been misled by Lincoln's circumspect and indirect style of leadership, she insisted, as well as by his public statements justifying emancipation on grounds of expedience—statements calculated to win political support for black freedom from a populace in which racism was dominant.

Lincoln and Black Freedom closely examined Lincoln's Reconstruction policies as they affected occupied Louisiana. Because the permanence of emancipation remained uncertain until late 1864, Cox pointed out, Lincoln's Reconstruction policies were driven by a determination to ensure permanent freedom not only for slaves affected by his proclamation but for all. Moreover, she demonstrated that by 1864 Lincoln had come to support civil equality and limited suffrage for all African Americans. Cox argued that had Lincoln escaped the assassin's bullet the history of U.S. race relations might have been far different. Rather than ending in failure, with African Americans powerless, impoverished, and under the boot heels of southern whites, a second Lincoln administration might well have resulted in a Reconstruction settlement that provided a firmer foundation for black freedom.

Long interested in issues of causation and motivation, Cox also focused on the failure of Reconstruction. As scholars struggled to explain the nation's failure to fulfill Reconstruction's promise of equality, she cautioned against monistic interpretations that offered simple answers to a complex problem. To those who placed the blame on northern whites' racism, she pointed out that northern attitudes were far from monolithic, insisting that there were significant differences between Republicans and Democrats. Moreover, Cox reminded scholars that the Republican commitment to civil equality resulted in an unprecedented use of federal power on behalf of civil rights that persisted well into the 1890s. More important than northern racism, she contended, was resistance by white southerners. This resistance, she perceptively argued, could not simply be overcome by force; success required a program that deftly combined force with initiatives that elicited consent, however grudging, from a significant number of white southerners. This, she suggested, was a tall order for even the most astute political leader.[15]

Cox also took issue with those who dismissed Republicans' preoccupation with civil rights as largely irrelevant to the impoverished former slaves and attributed Reconstruction's failure principally to Republicans' failure to fulfill the promise of land for the freedmen. She recognized the importance of providing African Americans economic independence; indeed, her own early work had identified the centrality of the land issue. Nevertheless, she pointed out that acquisition of land by former slaves in the South and plantation societies elsewhere had not been a panacea. She also insisted that legal rights and access to political power were crucial if African Americans were to escape white hegemony. Cox cautiously suggested that the Reconstruction experience showed that former slaves eagerly used their newly won civil rights to good advantage.[16] In this respect, her work anticipated Eric Foner's argument in *Reconstruction: America's Unfinished Revolution, 1863–1877* (1988), now widely regarded as the standard treatment of the period.

Cox's research led her to question the adequacy of Reconstruction as a concept. While recognizing that any sort of periodization is problematic, she concluded that Reconstruction, defined by historians as beginning during the Civil War and ending with the Compromise of 1877, was especially inappropriate. It made far more sense, she argued, to take the longer view and look at the forty years from the outbreak of the Civil War through the turn of the century as the age of emancipation. She pointed out that the meaning of freedom for African Americans was a critical issue throughout this period, one that remained quite fluid and was subject to intense debate through the 1890s. Although we await synthetic works incorporating this insight, Professor Cox's suggestion offers a promising conceptual framework for integrating the rich scholarship of the past two generations.[17]

This broader periodization was the inspiration for the Symposium on Emancipation and Its Aftermath, which Cox conceived, organized, and ran after retiring from Hunter. Sponsored by the City University of New York, the symposium met annually for a decade (1979–1989), bringing together approximately forty scholars to hear and discuss papers by colleagues on work in progress. It served as an incubator for a number of important studies that appeared in the 1980s and early 1990s. It also provided an opportunity for those working in the field to join an ongoing conversation about critical issues in the field. A model of scholarly exchange, the symposium owed its existence and success to Cox's vision and persistence.

The necessity of stretching the boundaries of Reconstruction also guided Cox's own research. In the mid-1980s, she began an ambitious project designed to examine a tentative hypothesis that would help explain the rise and decline of the nation's post–Civil War commitment to civil equality. Drawing on the work of social psychologists and anthropologists, she had come to see the perception of injustice as a deeply rooted characteristic in human nature that possibly played a determining role in Reconstruction civil rights policy.

It did so, first, by overcoming many northern whites' racial prejudice, and then by weakening their support for equal citizenship when they came to believe that Republican government in the South appeared inequitable and illegitimate. Cox planned a series of case studies examining the genesis of the perception of injustice among northern whites, the ways in which it shaped policy, and why it dissipated in the decades following 1875. Although she threw herself into the research and completed the first of the case studies, failing vision forced her to halt work on the project in 1989.

Professor Cox has produced a remarkable body of work. While some of her contemporaries published more, few produced scholarship that equaled hers in its originality, analytical power, and historiographical significance. Few historians of any period can equal the crisp lucidity of her style. Certainly no one did more to shape our understanding of the age of emancipation. By publishing this collection, which includes the previously unpublished case study, the University of Georgia Press offers those familiar with Cox's writings the opportunity to revisit them, and provides a new generation of students with an introduction to a body of scholarship that remains required reading for anyone who wishes to understand the age of emancipation and the historian's craft.

PART ONE

Land and Labor

CHAPTER ONE

Tenancy in the United States, 1865–1900

A Consideration of the Validity of the Agricultural Ladder Hypothesis

The intention of this study is to challenge the widely accepted hypothesis that the agricultural ladder was the dominant and most significant pattern in the rural life of the United States during the period, 1865–1900.[1] The progression from farm laborer to tenant to owner as a basic pattern is simply too neat a formula to explain complex historical phenomena. Its essential accuracy is open to question from several points of attack. Its utility is even more questionable, for the prevailing acceptance of this hypothesis has tended to discourage rather than to provoke detailed and careful historical investigation. Its basic assumptions, deep rooted in American tradition, as to ownership and opportunity for economic advancement, are value judgments which may, or may not, be justified. It is, therefore, important to examine the historical functioning of these assumptions.

Scholars in fields other than history have been chiefly responsible for the formulation of the agricultural-ladder doctrine and have utilized it more consciously than historians. Nevertheless, the work of the historians has been influenced by an acceptance of the formula.

The treatment of tenancy in histories of American economic development illustrates the influence of the ladder concept. One textbook speaks of the widespread alarm over the extent of tenancy revealed by the 1880, 1890, and 1900 censuses, but concludes that "Tenancy indicated the endeavor of ambitious farm laborers and persons of small means to make themselves independent rather than the fall of unsuccessful owners to the rank of tenants."[2] Similarly a second text attributes the increase in tenancy in part to the inability of the poor man to meet the costs of expensive machinery and higher-priced land but adds: "On the other hand, it should be pointed out that the growth of tenancy may be an encouraging sign, for to many men tenancy is a step toward ultimate ownership."[3] After a more extensive survey of farm tenancy development and of sectional differences in its growth, a third text repeats the familiar explanation in respect to the growth of tenancy in the wheat and corn belts before 1920. "Tenants were so only in transition. Some were brothers, sons, or other relatives who would step into the property when the owner died; others were accumulating the money necessary to make the final payments on the farm; most were young men who would become owners when they were older. In brief, there was a tenure ladder which led upward."[4]

To cite these passages is not to point the finger of criticism. They merely illustrate the fact that historians have been influenced by the formulations and explanations which have been set forth often and elaborately by the agricultural economists and rural sociologists. The truth of the matter is that except in respect to the South there is a dearth of historical studies on farm tenancy. Of the forty-eight items on farm tenancy and rural population listed in Everett E. Edwards' *Bibliography of the History of Agriculture in the United States* not one appeared in a historical journal, and the neglect of the field by the historical profession has not been substantially remedied since the publication of that excellent guide. Notable exceptions, of course, are the pioneering studies by Paul W. Gates. In all fairness, it should be pointed out that agricultural economists have shown a very real awareness of and interest in the historical roots of tenancy. They have proposed its historical investigation in their formulations of needed research, and they have frequently analyzed contemporary tenancy problems with the nineteenth century as a point of departure.[5] Their studies include material helpful and suggestive to historians, but they are based too extensively, indeed in many instances exclusively, on census figures to constitute a substitute for intensive historical research.

That the historian's neglect has been due to an acceptance of the hypothesis of the agricultural ladder is not, of course, a proposition susceptible of absolute proof. Yet no one who delves into the history of tenancy in the last decades of the nineteenth century will find it easy to deny the inference. Particularly is this true in the light of the wealth of material on the economic basis of the movements of farm protest during the period, materials which one would expect to have piqued the historian's curiosity.

It was not the historians, then, who marshaled the evidence to show the workings of the agricultural ladder. Although the idea was already common currency as a reassurance to those who had been alarmed by the extent of tenancy revealed in the 1880 and subsequent census statistics—figures which seemed to belie the American faith in opportunity for economic advancement upon the land—the documentations of the ladder hypothesis did not begin to appear until the second decade of the twentieth century.[6] The agricultural economists in that decade and in the twenties were disturbed by the obstacles which confronted the young farmer who desired to attain farm ownership. They attributed his difficulties largely to the increased cost of land and compared his opportunities unfavorably with those that were available to farm laborers and tenants in earlier decades.

The very circumstances in which these early studies appeared should evoke the caution of the historian. In other words, the hypothesis was crystallized in a period when agriculture, being in a relatively advantageous condition as compared to industry, was in a very different relationship to the rest of the American economy than it had been earlier. Agricultural prices and wages in the first two decades of the twentieth century were outdistancing the advances in industrial prices and wages, whereas in the period after the Civil War and before the turn of the century, the farmer and farm wage earner had been at a disadvantage. The drastic drop in farm prices during the earlier period is well known; the money wages of farm laborers declined more precipitously than did those of nonfarm workers after the close of the Civil War, and the gains in real wages for farm labor lagged behind those for industrial labor.[7] The agricultural economists, however, were concerned not with the problems confronting the ambitious young farmers of earlier decades, but with those that seemed to menace their contemporaries. It ought to occasion no surprise if their backward glance should be shown to have been distorted by the roseate hue that so commonly tends to obscure the realities of the past.

It is not the intent of this paper to deny that there were tenants who did acquire the status of farm owner nor to determine the number of those who succeeded in making the transition. Its purpose, rather, is to arouse a spirit of critical inquiry as to the assumptions of the ladder hypothesis and to cast suspicion upon its validity as applied to the last half of the nineteenth century. The proponents of the theory must be faced in their home territory, the corn and wheat belt of the North. That the agricultural ladder did not work in respect to the cotton plantation regions and the freedmen is, of course, a fact well known and readily accepted. However, the South cannot be summarily dismissed. At the time of emancipation, the idea of advance to ownership through tenancy was not prevalent—for Americans were yet to be made aware of tenancy by the census figures of 1880—but the assumption of the desirability and easy achievement of farm ownership was common. This belief was an important factor in the failure of the national government to adopt a program to assist Negroes in acquiring land ownership. At the inception of Reconstruction, the Negro's northern friends believed that his economic problem would be readily solved if only he were given "a fair chance"—that is to say "just rights of person and property" and "a fair and equal administration of justice."[8] Many confidently expected that the freedman would pull himself up to the status of farm owner with the savings from his wages. Officials of the Freedmen's Bureau and northern friends showered the Negro with admonitions to work industriously and to save as the best way to achieve land ownership.[9] When the antislavery leaders added the demand for suffrage, they characterized it as the "one vital issue. . . . All other questions are unimportant or will easily settle themselves."[10] This contention was made despite their own slogan of "land, education, and the ballot." When they finally marshaled their forces behind a constructive and nonvindictive proposal for government aid in financing land ownership for Negroes, they met opposition even from liberals and humanitarians based upon the belief that all the freedman needed was "manly self-reliance and a spirit that asks help of no man and no treasury."[11] These were the words of Horace Greeley, confident of the opportunities in the West. To the land proposal he raised the answering cry "Root, hog, or die"; and his conviction could not be shaken even by the bitter retort of Wendell Phillips that he would like to "strip HORACE GREELEY, and put him out upon the prairie, and say to him 'Root, hog, or die.'"[12] In the 1860s the tendency to view American economic life as one of opportunity, which would yield wealth and security in just proportion to a man's diligence, was instinctive and widespread. This assumption in respect to American agricultural life prior to the opening of the twentieth century (and the concept of the agricultural ladder is but a variant of this faith) has been persistent and almost unchallenged. That it should have played an important role in determining the policy which was to fasten tenancy upon the South suggests the need for careful appraisal of the idea as a functioning historical force.

There is no need to belabor the point that tenancy in post–Civil War cotton areas did not prove to be a rung on the agricultural ladder, since this fact has been generally recognized and most students have been careful to except the section in their generalizations about the ready advance through tenancy to ownership. However, one aspect of tenancy development in the old plantation Black Belt casts doubt that need not be sectionally delimited upon a refinement of the theory. According to the ladder formula, transition from share to cash tenancy is an intermediary step up the ladder. Analysis of tenure statistics for selected counties in South Carolina, Georgia, Louisiana, and Mississippi which have been the heart of the antebellum cotton plantation economy and whose population remained predominantly Negro even after the turn of the century discloses a remarkable increase in the number and percentage of money tenants between 1890 and 1900. For example, according to the Census, in seventeen Georgia counties there were 5,672 farms operated by money tenants in 1890; in 1900 they numbered 9,047—an increase from 30 to 48 percent of the number of all farms. The number of share-tenant (or sharecropper) farms dropped from 12,614 to 9,605 during the decade. Similarly eleven central Alabama counties gained 17,186 farms operated on money tenure and lost 2,867 share-tenant farms. This would seem to indicate an advance for large numbers of Negro farm workers, yet the economic condition of tenant farmers in the 1890s was desperate. They sank farther and farther into debt. Cotton prices were extremely low, falling even below five cents a pound. For large numbers of producers cotton was being raised at cost or below. In the significant understatement of one planter, when cotton sold at four, five, or six cents a pound "the tenants had to live very hard."[13] In 1899, the year that marked an upturn in cotton prices, the average value of products on Negro farms in Georgia not fed to livestock was $328 and in Alabama $286.[14]

The change in tenure accompanied the low prices of the 1890s because landowners, including new purchasers from the ranks of the local merchants or cotton factors, and operating plantation owners of the 1880s, who moved to town in search of an occupation to supplement their farm incomes, made it a policy to lease their lands for a fixed money rental.[15] They were pushing the farm laborer nominally up the agricultural ladder in order that he might absorb a greater share of the risk and losses incident to cotton production. Land operated by sharecroppers and share tenants represented a greater risk—probably a financial liability—than land which brought a fixed money rental. When higher prices again made cotton production profitable in the decade from 1900 to 1910, the tendency was to displace renters with share tenants, croppers, and hired laborers. The relationship between share and money tenure must be studied in its historical setting before these so-called rungs of the agricultural ladder can be given any meaning in terms of the status of the operating farmer.

What of the tenant farmer in the northern corn and wheat states during the decades of the 1870s, 1880s, and 1890s? Was he advancing steadily upward? Certainly farm conditions were not propitious for his ascension. The period was one of falling prices and hard times, conditions that bred the Granger movement, the Greenback agitation, and the Populist revolt. The Illinois Board of Agriculture estimated that farmers had received a profit on corn in only ten of the twenty-four years from 1870 to 1893 and that they had lost money on wheat in more than half of the fifteen years from 1880 to 1894.[16] The cost of producing wheat in Kansas and the Dakotas was reported to have been above the average selling price for nine of the ten years preceding 1894. In 1884 Dakota farmers were complaining that wheat prices were 20 percent below the cost of production.[17] Of the 1,015 Iowa farmers who made returns to the state bureau of labor statistics in 1890, 860, or 85 percent, reported that the local market price of farm produce from January 1885 to January 1890 had been below cost; 6 percent reported the market price to have been at cost; and only 9 percent stated that it had been above production costs.[18]

High interest rates and inadequate credit facilities plagued the western farmer. These were important considerations for the tenant struggling to lay something by or contemplating the venture into mortgaged ownership. In the newer regions particularly, interest rates reached usurious heights; they were as much as 24 percent even on real estate mortgages, and nominally moderate rates were augmented by penalties and bonuses. Chattel mortgages brought consistently high returns to lenders. The connection between the Granger movement and the credit problem has been well established. In the lean years of the 1870s and again in those of the late 1880s and the 1890s, farmers found it difficult to obtain advances at any rate of interest, and the easy credit thrust upon them by the representatives of eager eastern investors in the years of good prices and rising land values of the early 1880s was no unmixed blessing. The heavy weight of indebtedness bore down upon the borrowers when the bad years came.[19]

Indeed, the shift from tenancy to ownership can be realistically evaluated only in terms of permanent ownership. The fact that the agricultural ladder operated in the reverse direction has been all too summarily noted and put aside by those who deal with the ladder hypothesis. Historical studies of the economic conditions of the western farmer suggest that backsliding may have been a major factor in many localities. Grasshopper plagues, droughts, the downward spiraling of prices, the periods of general depression—all broke the hold of many a man upon his land. In the 1870s, hundreds of debt-ridden Iowa farmers left their lands and frequently were mistaken for vagabonds.[20] The situation was worse in Kansas and Nebraska where, in the words of one authority, frontier counties "felt this depression more severely than older ones because there was no considerable store of accumulated savings with which to meet it."[21] Even in Wisconsin, farmers whom the panic had found in debt lost their farms and moved on.[22] Mortgage foreclosures and forced sales in great numbers accompanied the crop failures and falling prices of the late 1880s and 1890s. Kansas is said to have lost nearly 180,000 persons between 1887 and 1891.[23] According to one student, half the population of the western part of the state trailed eastward between 1888 and 1892.[24] A contemporary estimated that two-and-a-half settlers occupied Nebraska homesteads before one came who was able to stay.[25]

Stories of failure came out of the recently settled areas beyond the Mississippi; but to the aspiring tenant in the older states of the Midwest farm ownership may well have appeared less readily attainable at home than farther west. At home, land was no longer cheap. Expensive machinery or other large investments, as for dairying, were increasingly necessary for successful farming. In 1885 an Illinois crop correspondent wrote: "The farm work is mostly done by expensive machinery, and those unable to own such machinery, being unable to compete with the others, find it more profitable to hire out than to farm on their own account."[26] After 1880 the rural population of Michigan decreased, intensive farming increased, and by 1885 it was recognized that there existed "an absence of facilities for advancing in the 'profession.'"[27] In Iowa the eighties witnessed what one historian of the Populist movement termed an "agricultural transformation," with farming "becoming more and more a matter of capital, business and scientific methods."[28]

If tenancy in this period was—as many have held—primarily a healthy medium through which the farm worker could acquire sufficient funds to meet the increasing cost of land and equipment, it might be expected to recede gradually before the advance up the agricultural ladder in the areas where it was concentrated. However, in areas where tenancy was high in 1880 or 1890 it tended to remain high. Thus, of the seven Iowa counties with the highest rate of tenancy in 1880, every one had a still higher percentage of tenants in 1900; and in that year (and also in 1910) all save one had a tenancy rate well above the average for the state as a whole. Similarly the ten Illinois counties with the highest percentage of tenant farms in 1890 showed an increase of tenancy from 47.8 to 54.2 percent during the decade, an increase of 6.4 points as compared to 5.3 (from 34 to 39.3 percent) for the state.[29] In just one of the Illinois counties was there a slight drop in the percentage of tenancy. Obviously, tenancy was not preparing the way for ownership in these areas.

When writers compare the tenancy trends before and after 1900, they generally point to the availability of free or cheap lands in the earlier period and the ease with which the young tenant in the more settled areas who had no prospect of an inheritance could settle upon the public domain. If they searched the records they could undoubtedly find many instances of such migration and settlement to buttress their point. Their generalizations, however, fail to take into account two factors—the difficulties of maintaining a foothold on the public lands of the last frontiers and the extent to which good agricultural lands were held by railroads and speculators. Historical studies, such as the article by Paul W. Gates on "The Homestead Law in an Incongruous Land System," have called attention to the fact that much of the public domain was never accessible to the homesteader.[30] Fraudulent practices, huge land grants to railroads and states, continuance of cash sales, issuance of large quantities of land scrip, and persistent activity of land speculators consumed great tracts of the best arable public lands of the Mississippi Valley before 1880. Poor home seekers were often faced with the alternatives of paying a good price for speculatively held lands, becoming tenants, or seeking homesteads upon inferior lands. The study of farm conditions in Harrison Township, Hall County, Nebraska, published by Arthur F. Bentley in 1893, convincingly documents the thesis that purchase from railroads or land speculators was a tremendous handicap to those seeking to maintain farm ownership. The average debt per acre of those farmers who had purchased their lands from individuals was $9.38; for those who had acquired their holdings from railroads it was $7.80 an acre. In contrast, the debt of settlers who had taken government lands was only $3.09 per acre. Bentley expected that some of the second group would be able to extricate themselves but that most of the first group would have to give up their holdings within a short time.[31]

In a series of convincingly documented studies Paul W. Gates has pointed out the intimate relationship between the growth of tenancy in the prairie states of Indiana, Illinois, and Iowa and the activities of land speculators, loan sharks, large-scale farmers, and persons selling landed estates.[32] Nonoperating owners in some instances introduced tenancy deliberately as a permanent or temporary policy. Even where this was not the case, the higher cost of land and the onerous debt burden incident to their activities turned the sod for the seeds of tenancy. Although these activities were concentrated in certain localities, they cannot be dismissed as exceptional and incidental. A study of the land policies in Nebraska, the state west of the Mississippi with the highest percentage farm tenancy in 1900 (Illinois had the highest percentage of any state to the east) discloses that fully half of the public domain was "given or granted to railroad corporations, land speculators, and bogus entrymen with no purpose of permanent settlement."[33] Moreover, after the depression of the 1870s, speculators were busy picking up bargains.[34] The roles of the speculator and money lender have not been recognized by those who view nineteenth-century tenancy as an easy road to farm ownership, and it is difficult to see how their importance can be accepted without major qualification of the ladder hypothesis.

Tenancy statistics in themselves should give pause to those who regard the period under consideration as a golden age for aspiring farm tenants. In 1880, the first year for which these statistics are available, more than 20 percent of the farms of the East North Central states (Wisconsin, Michigan, Illinois, Indiana, and Ohio) and the West North Central states (the Dakotas, Kansas, Nebraska, Missouri, Minnesota, and Iowa) were operated by tenants. The rate of tenancy was 31.4 percent in Illinois and 18 percent in Nebraska. In the decade between 1880 and 1890, the number of tenant farmers in the West North Central states increased 49.9 percent. In the 1890s, the increase in numbers was 43.4 percent. In the East North Central states the percentage increases were 14.4 and 29.4 percent. Here, in the 1890s, the greatest increases in tenants per thousand farmers came in the age group of those 45 to 54 years old.[35] Of all Illinois tenants almost 26 percent were 45 years of age or over in 1890. A considerably greater number, 37 percent of the total, were 40 or older.[36]

The formulators of the agricultural-ladder theory relied heavily upon the census data concerning the age of tenants as compared to the age of owners. The tabulations disclosed that whereas the percentage of tenants among farm operators under twenty-five years of age was extremely high, it diminished with each successive age group until tenants became a small proportion of farm operators 65 years of age and over. According to W. J. Spillman and E. A. Goldenweiser in the Department of Agriculture *Yearbook* for 1916, these figures showed clearly that "tenant farming represents a step toward ownership," and unquestionably indicated that "by far the greater proportion of young men who start out as tenants succeed in becoming owners."[37] Actually, these figures only show that the older men left on the farm were predominantly owners. They do not take into account the possibility that many former tenants may have failed to establish themselves as owners, slipped down the ladder to the status of farm laborers, sought a brighter future in the cities, or been eliminated otherwise. The authors of subsequent studies were more cautious in drawing conclusions from these statistics but continued to use them as evidence of the functioning of the agricultural ladder.[38]

The number of tenants who succumbed to the lure of the metropolis will never be known, but the migration from country to city in the 1880s and 1890s is an important historical fact. Throughout those decades, there was constant complaint that those who had formerly worked for hire upon the farms were departing to seek jobs in industry. A survey of Wisconsin farmers disclosed that the great majority of native farm wage earners desired to leave the farm for the city even in the depression years of the 1890s.[39] After 1880 the city was functioning as the safety valve for farm labor—not the farm for city labor.

Another imponderable that casts doubt upon any sweeping generalizations based upon the tenant age statistics is the number of new farm owners during the period who acquired their lands without serving an apprenticeship as tenants. The investigations made in the 1920s and later as to the route by which farm owners acquired their holdings are an inadequate and technically questionable basis for conclusions concerning the 1880s and 1890s. However revealing this type of inquiry may be of present farm-ownership patterns, the findings cannot be transferred back to an earlier period; the conditions of twentieth-century agriculture differed too greatly from those of previous decades. To suggest one possible approach to the problem, there is no study to indicate how many of the immigrant families who settled on the land in the 1880s purchased farms from savings brought with them from abroad or stored up during previous periods of employment in the cities. Statistics indicating a substantial increase in the total number of farm owners, in themselves, prove nothing.

Agricultural economists have made extensive use of the data reported by farm owners as to their previous experience as tenants.[40] From this material some drew the conclusion that the step from tenancy to ownership was quicker and easier in the earlier decades than after the turn of the century. These data, like the age figures, are selective and distorted because they are based solely upon the experience of those tenants who succeeded in becoming owners. Further, they are vitiated by the factor of mortality; that is to say, the records of those who in earlier decades climbed slowly to ownership were eliminated in undue proportion because they had died by the time the surveys were made. This factor of error was early and vigorously pointed out;[41] and by the 1930s prospective investigators of the agricultural ladder were being warned that distortions due to death or to departure for other occupations had not been satisfactorily eliminated from this type of data and that the earlier assumptions as to contemporary trends had not been proved.[42] Nevertheless, the fact needs emphasis that conclusions drawn from these inquiries into the working of the agricultural ladder are as invalid in interpreting the past as in interpreting the present. Moreover, these statistics of farm experience together with those on the age of owners and tenants have been the chief evidence offered by the formulators of the ladder hypothesis.

Implicit in the theory of the agricultural ladder is the assumption—indeed it is often clearly stated as a fact—that the tenant enjoyed the same social status as the farm owner. The democratic equalitarian nature of the process has often been pointed to as adequate reassurance for those troubled by the tenancy statistics. Yet suggestive of other and contradictory implications is the fact that farm wage labor and farm tenancy have so generally been regarded as transitional and as necessarily inferior to farm ownership. Even in small farm communities with relative equalities may not this attitude have resulted in subtle social distinctions between renters and owners? The tendency to attribute permanent tenancy to lack of ability or to lack of ambition warrants suspicion that in respect to tenants in the older age group such distinctions were not always subtle.

There is evidence to indicate that immigrant folk who struggled to obtain farm ownership in the 1880s and 1890s were not always accepted on terms of equality by their neighbors. Foreign-born farmers in the North Atlantic states—Poles, Italians, and Portuguese—frequently made the climb to land ownership by means of a standard of living conspicuously lower than that of their neighbors. A New Jersey farmer in 1888 described the process. "After years of working by the month and day and saving one or two hundred dollars they rented or bought a low priced farm, a team, some stock, and a few implements, and then commenced in earnest to get up in the world. Father, mother and children are working hard, early and late; spend little or nothing for luxuries, clothing, churches, schools, or public improvements. Whenever an opportunity is afforded they work out by the day; every dollar that can be saved goes towards paying off the mortgage on the place, or adding to the bank account."[43] Even from the Midwest came reports which suggest a similar method of advance. State officials in Ohio, Illinois, Michigan, and Nebraska were agreed in attributing the greater success of foreign-born farmers, particularly Germans, not to superiority in their methods of cultivating the land, but to their manner of living. These newcomers were described as thrifty and economical, willing to begin at the bottom while the Yankee was not; and "As a general thing their standard of living is lower than that of the American."[44] It would be interesting to try to discover whether a similarly inferior class status was attached in the earlier years of the period to immigrants who came to the more settled lands of the Midwest. At least in respect to farm laborers there was a tendency in the 1870s to distinguish between the native and foreign born.[45] Furthermore, the remarks of the New Jersey farmer quoted above bring into view a broader consideration—the likelihood that an inferior economic and social status tagged even some of the hardworking folk who acquired farm ownership.

Certainly, the foregoing considerations weighed collectively raise doubts as to the validity of the ladder hypothesis. However, this paper is not meant to be a springboard for further inquiry and controversy concerning the working of the agricultural ladder. It has attacked the thesis in order to clear the way for new roads of inquiry. No constructive purpose would be served by searching the records for those who made their way upward and those who did not. The important historical fact is not that certain individuals, even though a numerous group, could and did change their status from that of tenant to owner, but that the institution of tenancy itself was growing. Consider the state of understanding of industrial labor if the recorders of its history had been concerned primarily with showing that many wage earners had become employers and captains of industry. In other words, the impetus for this discussion has been a conviction that the ladder concept is a sterile one. It has not promoted historical research. It has stifled curiosity concerning the conditions that surrounded tenancy. It has tended to exalt farm ownership as the prized goal, the pot of gold at the rainbow's end, irrespective of whether ownership brought any real advantage to the operating farmer, irrespective of the precariousness of the owner's economic status or the circumscription of his way of life.

Future historical work will benefit if students are aware of the pervasive and subtle hold of the ladder concept. A definite effort is being made by agricultural economists to put aside the emotional colorings wrapped about ownership and tenancy. Historians can assist this healthy departure. They can turn a more searching light upon tenancy in the past; they can scrutinize the effect upon historical events and relationships of the American ideal of land ownership and the American faith in its attainability. There is need for more knowledge of the historical facts of tenancy—its origin, the divergent patterns of its development (or disappearance) in various sections of the country and in differing areas within the sections, its interrelationship with land policies, speculation, farm prices, land values, credit facilities, sizes of farm, types of crop, conditions of inheritance, and the attitudes of immigrant folk toward the land. There is need to know more about the manner of life of farm tenants, particularly of those who remained renters in their forties and fifties. Such inquiries will be of the greatest possible value only if those who undertake them are on guard against an unconscious acceptance of the ladder theory and all that it implies.

CHAPTER TWO

The American Agricultural Wage Earner, 1865–1900
The Emergence of a Modern Labor Problem

A weight of evidence that can be ignored but cannot be denied has established the presence in contemporary American agriculture of a farm-labor problem, a problem distinct from that of the employing farmer in search of labor or from that of the laboring farm owner in pursuit of a secure and comfortable living.[1] It is as much a social problem as were the conditions of employment in the early nineteenth-century factories of England and America. In terms of status, personal relationships, and opportunity for economic independence, a gulf exists between the traditional hired man and large numbers of the present farm-labor force comparable to that between the medieval apprentice and the country weavers of the putting-out system.

The activities of the Industrial Workers of the World in the second decade of the twentieth century and the disclosures of the Commission on Industrial Relations during World War I brought some awareness of the problem of casual farm labor, but widespread public attention was first aroused by the wave of farm strikes in the mid-1930s and by the vivid pages of John Steinbeck's *The Grapes of Wrath*. Subsequent waning of interest has been due in part to the alleviation brought by war and post-war full employment. Yet the report of the Federal Interagency Committee on Migrant Labor issued in March 1947 is evidence that the social problem remains; and the first convention of the American Federation of Labor's National Farm Labor Union (the successor of the Southern Tenant Farmers' Union) suggests that it will increasingly be approached as essentially a *labor* problem.

The roots of the contemporary farm-labor situation, therefore, are of more than historical interest. And in fact, it has been the men seeking present-day solutions who have initiated the historical study of the agricultural wage earner.[2] Except for California, however, there are available only patchwork pieces of the story. Moreover, problems of farm labor as distinguished from those of agriculture generally have frequently been assumed peculiar to the twentieth century. The question raised here is the importance of the period between the Civil War and the opening of the twentieth century to the development of characteristics of farm-labor employment that do not square with the traditional hired-man–farm-operator relationship. This question leads to an inquiry as to whether casual labor and other atypical patterns of farm employment were established characteristics of American agriculture during those years; and if so, whether such patterns had already given rise to the social problems and conflict of economic interest associated with them in contemporary society. It also requires an examination of the status of the monthly wage earner on the grain or nonspecialty farm to determine whether in any respects even the "typical" pattern of farm labor more nearly resembled industrial employment rather than the tradition of the hired man on his way toward metamorphosis into family-farm operator.

One guide to the presence of laborers whose way of life contrasts with that of the hired man is the amount of money spent on a farm for wages. The characteristic family farm is worked by the farmer-operator and his sons with help at harvest time or with a hired man employed for most of the year. Areas where this type of farming predominates may have large aggregate labor bills, but the per-farm expenditures will not tend to rise above the national average. High per-farm expenditures mark divergent labor patterns. To determine whether marked wage variations existed during the period under consideration, use was made of the county census statistics for 1869 and 1899 that give aggregate labor expenditures as well as the number of farms in each county. Average labor expenditures per farm were computed, and all counties where the average was three (or nine) times the national average were indicated on maps, one for 1869 and one for 1899.[3]

In the earlier year, 226 counties appear on the map; at the end of the century there were 272. More than half of the high-wage counties of 1869 were in the South, most of them concentrated in the cotton areas of the Black Belt of Georgia and Alabama, in northern Florida, and along the Mississippi River. This irregular pattern of cotton counties completely disappears from the wage map of 1899. Both maps, however, point to southeastern Louisiana (sugar and rice), to areas along the Atlantic coast, to most of the Rocky Mountain states or territories, and to California. Between 1869 and 1899 these areas of high-wage expenditures, except Louisiana, show a notable expansion, and to the borders of the western group are added extensive areas of western Texas and eastern Oregon and Washington. On the 1899 map the Red River Valley region also is prominent; otherwise, only a few scattered counties appear in the great agricultural Midwest.

A comparative glance at a contemporary map marking high-wage counties discloses an interesting resemblance between the general pattern now and in 1899.[4] The twentieth-century expansion of truck, fruit, sugar beet, and western cotton production has not made as marked changes in the wage map as might have been expected. New counties have appeared, especially in Florida and in the irrigated lands of southern Arizona and California's Imperial Valley; but the general configuration is similar.

The appearance on a wage map of cotton counties in the deep South across which great plantations had extended in antebellum days is in some respects startling. Even when allowance is made for distortions due to inconsistencies and errors in collecting statistics during the confusion of Reconstruction, the expenditures in this region suggest the need for a careful reevaluation of the role of wage labor in the transition from slavery to tenancy. On the other hand, the continuing divergence of the post–Civil War cotton South from the northern family-farm–hired-man pattern of agriculture is well established though sometimes minimized by citation of statistics showing the increased numbers of small farms. In regions where Negroes were most highly concentrated in the days of slavery, tenancy has not proved a transition to ownership. Many large landholdings have survived in fact if not in farm census figures, and sharecroppers together with large numbers of other tenants have not enjoyed the independence or status of northern farm operators.

Generalizations about American farm labor are not accurate unless they give due weight to southern workers. This is true even if one wishes to distinguish the money wage earner from such other nonindependent farm labor as the sharecropper and certain tenant farmers. Of the 2,885,996 farm laborers so classified in the Census of 1870, 947,283 lived in six states of the deep South; and the entire South held 1,708,513 or 59 percent of all. Even in 1900 when tenancy was fully established, the South had 47 percent of the nonfamily workers, 55 percent of all persons classified as farm laborers.[5] The men, women, and children whose lives centered in the cotton fields undoubtedly have been the largest single segment of American farm labor in contrast to the hired man.

Personal relationships between employer and employee are not usual in nonfamily farm agriculture, but they survived slavery in the South. The relationship, however, was not one between social equals as in the case of hired hand and farmer. Nor did it eliminate evidences of conflicting economic interests that generally characterize agriculture that is carried on primarily as an industry for profit rather than as a personal way of life. True, attempts on the part of Negro field labor to strike and organize were infrequent after Reconstruction. There exists, however, an interesting account of a strike for higher wages by Negro workers on Louisiana sugar plantations in 1880. The Negroes went from plantation to plantation getting others to join them. The state militia was sent out, and the ringleaders were arrested, tried, and imprisoned for trespass. Petitioning the governor for pardon, they stated that they had thought it within their rights to go where other laborers were working, even though on the property of an individual, and induce those laborers to join them. They now understood this to be a violation of the law. "When laborers differ with their employers hereafter about the price of their labor," the petition read, "it will be in a peaceable manner and with law always on their side." They were released and "quiet was restored."[6] Except for the petition, the incident might have occurred in California during the 1930s. Conflict between southern laborer and landowner took forms other than overt clashes. Most notable was the continued bargaining throughout the period over wages, shares, or cash rentals, with each party trying to obtain whichever arrangement would assure him the largest income.

Southern staple crops had seasonal labor peaks, but most southern farm laborers were year-round residents rather than seasonal or casual workers. But the need for casual labor, both in the South and North, developed with the expansion of vegetable, berry, and fruit production. Part of the increased production went into the rapidly developing canning industry; in 1899 no less than 213,739,992 cans of tomatoes found their way to grocery shelves. Large quantities of the "most delicate of garden products" were destined not for tins but for the tables of northern cities.[7]

Market gardening antedated the Civil War, but during the following decades it graduated into the status of truck farming, that is the growing of fresh produce for distant markets. Developments in transportation stimulated its growth. The modern refrigerator car was in an experimental stage from the late sixties through the 1880s, but during those years shipments were made by small refrigerator chests, box cars, stock cars, and special ventilated fruit cars equipped with springs and wire netting. The success of refrigerator cars assured the permanence of the truck industry, and by 1900 there were an estimated 60,000 cars in service in the United States, Canada, and Mexico.[8]

Truck farming had not waited upon rail transportation. Northern markets were supplied by fast sailing vessels and steamboats from Maryland's eastern shore and south along the Atlantic coast. Norfolk, the earliest important center, shipped north a million dollars worth of tomatoes, peas, potatoes, strawberries, and other fresh products in 1869. Before 1900 the industry stretched southward through the older centers of Wilmington, Charleston, and Savannah, around the tip of Florida to Mobile and Galveston. Florida growers were finding truck produce their most profitable crop in the mid-1880s, and less hazardous than orange culture. They were not yet competing with the hot beds near Boston and New York in the extremely perishable crops; but by 1899, when rapid freight connections were well established, Florida had more acres in lettuce than any other state in the Union.[9]

Rail, rather than water, transportation found markets in St. Louis, Chicago, and Cincinnati for Georgia peaches and for the potatoes, strawberries, and tomatoes grown in Mississippi, Louisiana, Texas, Arkansas, and Tennessee.[10] When in 1888 refrigerator cars were first used to rush California fruits to New York City, the state's citrus products were already known in eastern cities; and by the end of the century the annual shipment was more than 6,000 carloads.[11] The increased demand for fruits and vegetables also profited areas nearer to the great cities, southern Illinois and Michigan, New Jersey, Long Island, the lower Hudson Valley, and New England.

Fruits and vegetables often brought their growers very considerable cash incomes. The New England crop in 1870 was reported to have yielded "handsome returns."[12] Gross receipts on truck farms near New York ranged from $300 to $2,000 an acre in 1865, and an 80-acre New Jersey farm, with most of its acreage in regular field crops, netted $6,000 just from tomatoes, potatoes, and peas.[13] A company-operated peach orchard in Maryland made an annual profit of from $20,000 to $30,000 in the early 1870s.[14]

All along the Atlantic coast, fruit and truck crops created a need for greater numbers of agricultural wage earners; and in the North Atlantic states where old staple crops were particularly hard hit by western competition, other specialties, notably Connecticut Valley tobacco, added to the labor demand.[15] In the decade of the 1880s, the proportion of farm laborers in the nationwide farm population dropped from 43 to 35 percent, but the proportion of farm workers to farmers increased in Massachusetts, Rhode Island, New York, and

New Jersey. In the other North Atlantic states the decrease was not nearly so great as for the country as a whole, and in New York the increase was small. In the South the need for labor was supplied in large part by Negro workers whose bonds with the plantations had been loosened by the Civil War. White workers were also recruited from the cities for the seasonal demands of nearby fields. Around Norfolk in 1885 from 2,560 to 3,200 Negro hands were employed just to gather the strawberries.[16] In the 1890s nearly 22,500 workers were employed in this area during the six peak weeks of the season. Some of the men, women, and boys and girls came from Richmond, from other interior cities of Virginia, and from North Carolina.[17]

Farther north, immigrants were an important source of the needed labor. Workers were often recruited from new arrivals in the cities or directly from Castle Garden, the Ellis Island of the period. As a New England farmer phrased it, "A farmer sends there and orders his help, and they are shipped to him."[18] First the older immigrant stock, Irish, Germans, and Swedes, took to the fields, then came the Italians and Poles. By the 1890s, padrones were rounding up Italian families in Philadelphia for harvest work in New Jersey. Before the end of the decade, Polish people had replaced the Irish as the most important group of foreign-born farm labor in Massachusetts.[19]

In his report for 1870–1871 the chief of the labor bureau of Massachusetts devoted considerable attention to the condition of farm labor in his State. He pointed out that a great change had occurred in New England through "the substitution of ignorant and unskilled foreign labor, for the intelligent, school-taught labor of the former era of our agriculture. . . ." Very rarely, he reported, was there to be found an active and intelligent person of American parentage employed as a hired farm laborer. The educational condition of farm laborers he found to be even lower than that of factory operatives; a large percentage of them could neither read nor write. Although the labor of women in the fields had "not yet been generally adopted," investigation disclosed that in Worcester County women did a great deal of farm work such as hoeing, shoveling, and raking; that in Franklin County they were employed in weeding tobacco, and that in Middlesex, Norfolk, and Essex counties women picked fruit and did weeding, hoeing, and haying. Irish women were said to labor extensively on land of their own but to work for others only in cases of emergency, at which times they received two-thirds of a man's pay. Boys were used chiefly in the cultivation of tobacco. The report predicted that if the demand for cheap labor continued, "Mammon will say to farmers, as it has to manufacturers, 'take the children' . . ."[20]

The report for the following year took notice of the employment of women of foreign nationality in the weeding and picking of small fruits and peas and beans and in the harvesting of potatoes and the stripping of tobacco plants. Commenting on the use of children in the lighter work of the fields, the labor chief called attention to the deficiencies in their education. Although schools were everywhere open to all, "these privileges are not universally and continuously made use of, and the compulsory educational law on the statute book is, as a general thing, *wholly neglected and inoperative.*" The nationality of farm laborers was estimated at 50 percent Irish, 15 percent French-Canadian, 10 percent Nova Scotian, 5 percent German, and 20 percent native.[21]

The Massachusetts census for 1875 put the number of farm laborers in the state at 35,488. Nearly 3,000 of these were girls and boys under fifteen, and over 7,500 were women. The total number of persons engaged in agriculture was listed as 70,945. The apparent fact that one-half of the persons engaged in agriculture in the state were paid laborers aroused public attention and concern. Carroll D. Wright, who had taken office as chief of the labor bureau in 1873, felt it necessary to point out that the women and children included in the number of farm laborers had not for the most part been reported in the number of those engaged in agriculture, so that the proportion of laborers to farmers was not so great as it seemed.[22]

Northern farming, unlike southern agriculture, had developed according to the family-farm–hired-man pattern. The shift in crops and in the composition of the labor force brought a distinct change in the relationship between the northern farmer and his help. The farmer came to look upon the laborer not as a temporary member of his household but as an important item in the cost, and consequently in the profit, of his business enterprise. After analyzing the problems that confronted him, a Massachusetts farmer in 1870 concluded: "What is needed to improve the farming interest is more and cheaper help. *Let the Asiatic come.* Ireland has almost run out, and those now here are getting too much Americanized to be very efficient help,—the best working for themselves and buying farms and the others earning their wages as easily as they can."[23] The chief of the labor bureau in summarizing the 1870 returns from questionnaires sent to farmers stated that "The price of labor is of as much importance to the farmer as it is to the manufacturer, and both alike look to cheap labor as their only relief."[24]

Two years earlier a speaker before a public meeting of the Massachusetts Board of Agriculture, in an address entitled "How To Make Farming Profitable," emphasized the need of employing more labor on the farm. He quoted a potato and small fruit grower as saying: "'I get more returns, better returns, for the money I invest in labor than from that which I invest in manure, in land, or anything else.'"[25] In the early 1880s, Maine farmers were receiving similar counsel. They were told: ". . . provided we are able to make our labor pay its way and pay a profit on the enterprise, the more labor we employ on the farm the greater the profits. No manufacturer ever built up a fortune on the employment of one laborer, or on the employment of his own hands alone. It is the employment of many laborers and in the accumulated profits of those many laborers that he builds up his income. It is precisely so in farming."[26]

The impersonal way in which immigrant labor was often recruited encouraged the business attitude toward farm workers. During a discussion of the labor problem at a Connecticut farmers' convention in the winter of 1887, a market gardener who hired men through a New York agent and got them "low enough" offered some interesting advice. "If you hire this class of men," he said, "there is one thing you must not do. Don't go into the field with them to work."[27] In 1891 a Massachusetts farmer succinctly summarized the changed status of farm wage earners: "The old-fashioned term, 'help,' has been dropped, and the word 'labor' used, with a peculiar significance."[28] A student of Massachusetts agriculture explained in 1900 that many farmers preferred foreign laborers because they worked for lower wages and were "satisfied to be regarded as servants."[29]

By 1900 New York farms had instituted a system of time cards, and wages by the day even for those regularly employed were becoming common.[30] Agricultural leaders in Massachusetts were by then of the opinion that the wide-awake farmer hired all the help he could with profit, but "When profits cease he will be the first to discharge help which he does not need."[31] Even in Pennsylvania, which was much less affected by agricultural changes than were the neighboring states, the new employer consciousness of the farmer had become apparent. Investigating the complaint of farmers in the mid-1880s that wages were much too high in comparison with the price of farm products, the secretary of the State Board of Agriculture reported: "Some claim that if the present proportions between the relative price of farm labor and farm products is maintained, the battle between capital (agricultural) and labor must soon take on a new phase."[32] And some years earlier a Pennsylvania farm laborer complained that employers cared nothing for the welfare of their employees and that there was "too much *extreme* social proscription."[33]

There were some farmer protests against the change in attitude, but such protests were in themselves an indication of the passing of the traditional hired man. One Connecticut farmer questioned the new standards in the following words: "Why then the laborer himself should receive so little true consideration from those who employ him upon the farm, I am at a loss to explain. It would seem, in numerous instances, as though he was from the beginning to the end of his service nothing more than a free slave, a drudge, to be fed and lodged, and worked to the limit of his ability."[34] A Maine farmer insisted that a good employer was "not a man who looks upon a laborer as a mere machine. . . . He does not show by his habitual bearing that he is conferring a favor by tolerating the presence of the workmen in his fields."[35]

Such admonitions would have found a more chill reception in California than in New England. Long before the Joads troubled the conscience of the nation, the storied land of gold and sun had marked those who labored over its crops as an inferior class of mankind, the value of which varied inversely with the cost of its services.[36] These attitudes predated the expansion of orchards, vineyards, the fields of hops, berries, and sugar beets that began in the 1870s and gathered momentum in the 1880s. They had existed in the days of the great wheat ranches when the methods of mass production and the enormity of the yields, and of the profits, attracted national attention.[37] Their historical roots go back to the large landholdings of the Spanish period and the early days of the American cattle ranchers, when the pattern of large-scale agriculture was established. In the 1870s, California land monopoly was under attack by those who wanted to see it replaced by the small-farm pattern of the Midwest. They declared it "contrary to the genius of our institutions" and stated that the fertile valleys of the state were "as effectually locked up to the indigent emigrant as are the deer parks and rabbit pastures of the English lord."[38]

The attack continued, but so did the large-scale commercial character of California agriculture. It depended upon an abundance of cheap labor that appeared when it was needed and then departed, and "how they afterwards maintain themselves is not known."[39] In 1869, the 159 farms of Merced County in the San Joaquin Valley had an average annual payroll of $1,129, nine times the national average. In 1899, the farms had increased to just short of a thousand, and the average wage bill had dropped below its level in the post–Civil War years of inflation; yet computations based on the census reports show that it was eleven times as large as that of the country as a whole.

A revealing picture of the condition of farm labor in the state is presented in the testimony taken in 1876 by the congressional committee investigating

Chinese immigration. By that date a large proportion of the field work was done by Chinese, particularly in the vineyards and orchards.[40] They were customarily hired in gangs through a "boss Chinaman" or contractor. For $1.00 a day, Chinese workers boarded themselves. Their usual sleeping accommodations were "a little crib" and their customary cooking equipment "a little place" where they could dig a hole, build a fire, and put on a big pan that served both as cooking pot and communal serving dish.[41]

Witnesses defended the Chinese on the ground that the fruit and vegetable crops of the state could not be harvested without them. Some maintained that even cheaper labor was a necessity.[42] According to one large grower, "... the Chinese should be allowed to come until you get enough here to reduce the price of labor to such a point as that its cheapness will stop their coming." The Chinese were described as "these mud-sills ... at the bottom of our success...."

The treatment of farm labor as servile and a thing apart from the operating farmer was not restricted to the Chinese.[43] White workers were not infrequently labeled "bummers." When a San Mateo farmer was asked whether he objected to hired white boys and girls eating at his family table, he replied: "... these eastern gentlemen must remember it is somewhat different here from what it is in the East. A farm-hand will come along looking for a day's or a month's work; you do not know who he is, and you do not want to bring him into your family. You generally have beds up-stairs in the granary and they furnish their own blankets. We generally have mattresses for them, with straw, and let them furnish their own beds."

With the restriction of Chinese immigration by congressional legislation in 1882, there was agitation in California to provide better living quarters and longer employment for labor so that desirable white immigrants would be attracted to the state. The State Agricultural Society was told that "our nomadic herds of farm hands must have all the year employment and an abiding place with their work; they must be fed and housed as civilized men should be fed and housed; they must be encouraged to save their earnings; the wide gap between the employed and the employer must be closed...."[44] One spokesman who urged the establishment of model villages declared: "The proprietors of large estates have been content to herd their workmen as they would their cattle. Isolated planters have depended upon contract labor. All these conditions must soon change...."[45]

But the conditions did not change. Chinese were still numerous and easily available throughout the 1880s. By 1889 California industries were in a period of depression that extended through the 1890s, making a great supply of cheap white labor available for the harvests.[46] By the mid-1890s, "another pest in the shape of cheap labor" was making a place for itself in the hop, beet, and fruit lands.[47] The Japanese, like the Chinese, worked in organized gangs with one of their own number as boss or spokesman. In some instances, this system developed into the double exploitation of worker, by employer and "boss," as commonly has happened under all contract systems for field labor. On the other hand, the Japanese "boss" frequently acted as an effective agent for collective bargaining in the interest of his fellows. During the depression 1890s Japanese gang labor was generally cheap and docile, but shortly thereafter the Japanese were using walkouts, or threats of them, to force higher pay from growers when the harvest was underway. Employers lamented the passing of the more tractable Chinese, but many preferred either of the Asiatic peoples to white workers. A Pajaro Valley fruit grower in 1902 discouraged efforts to attract laborers from the eastern states. "Now, to come to the point. Of course you understand that a certain class of labor has been degraded by the Chinese to a certain extent, and to-day white labor will not perform it. If you get white laborers from the East they may work part of the season, but will finally take the course that all white labor does—they will want to boss the job."[48]

The white laborer from the East was apt to be equally enthusiastic about the prospect of working for the California growers. A farmer recently arrived from Minnesota told of a young hired man who had left for California and soon returned with the report that he had "not been treated much better than a dog by his employers in California."[49]

The impersonal profit-dominated relationships between employer and employee in California agriculture brought only a few sporadic small-scale strikes before the close of the century. White workers developed no organized opposition to grower interests comparable to that of the Japanese. Yet by 1902 there were a number of ineffective local unions, and the American Federation of Labor in its national convention of that year voted to place an organizer among the agricultural workers in California.[50] It is interesting to note how long ago a need for unionism in agriculture was officially recognized, especially in view of the long subsequent record of neglect and failure.

The expansion of fruits and vegetables was the most readily recognizable development in post–Civil War American agriculture that nurtured a type of farm labor distinct from the hired man. But by far the most extensive areas of high labor costs revealed by the wage map of 1899 were in the cattle country. The cowboy, whose services necessitated those expenditures, was in fact just another variant among those who labored for wages in American agriculture. His kinship to others at work on the land and to all wage earners has not generally been recognized. Romance set him apart; and the very business of cattle raising with its swift growth to the stature of a large-scale industry has been accepted as something distinct from the agriculture of the country, an agriculture very generally identified with the family farms of the Midwest. Yet the large plantations of the South, the truck gardens of the East, the bonanza farms of the Dakotas, and the agricultural enterprises of California have also differed from the accepted norm.

When the cowboy has been classed with agricultural labor, he has been distinguished as the "aristocrat of all wage earners"; and his scorn for the hired man has been proverbial.[51] Only a few studies throw light upon the cowhand as wage earner and his relations with the men who hired him. Certain facts are suggestive. The cowboy often worked with an outfit whose monthly wage bill ran from $500 to $1,000, or even to $8,000. Unless he were a trail driver or a foreman, his usual wage was $25 or $30 a month. From one-half to three-fourths of these men could expect to find employment for only eight months of the year.[52] Resentment against employer occasionally found written expression,[53] but more often it took the form of discourteous treatment of a visiting absentee owner or the theft of cattle. Among rustlers it was a point of honor never to touch the cattle of a poor man or of a small owner. Cattlemen's associations took stringent measures to control theft, including an extensive and rigidly enforced black list of suspected cowhands. In some instances cattlemen denied employment to any hand known to own cattle of his own.[54]

The intimations of employer-employee antagonism are confirmed by a recent study that has uncovered a strike of approximately 325 cowboys employed on seven large Texas ranches in 1883. To force an increase in wages, they quit work before the spring roundup and stayed out until their money was exhausted. Texas rangers as well as economic necessity came to the support of employer interests, but the cowhands gained some wage increases. The strikers were motivated not only by wage consciousness but also by resentment of the impersonal treatment and the loss of status and of opportunity to become independent ranchers that accompanied the expansion of absentee corporate ownership.[55]

In the days of the open range, the economies of large-scale operation tended to squeeze out the small rancher.[56] There had been a chance in the very early days of the industry for the enterprising cowboy to brand on shares, acquire stock of his own, pasture them on the public lands, and himself become a large operator.[57] A number of cowhands continued to own a few head of cattle, but as a group they were not on their way up the economic ladder. Even the limited opportunity for small owners was further circumscribed by the advent of barbed-wire enclosures and the exclusion of small cowboy owners from the annual spring roundup upon the insistence of the large ranch companies.[58] On the other hand, the benevolence of individual employers staked a few hands to small ranches during the late 1880s when the cattle industry tended to break up into smaller units under the impact of reverses.[59] But the smaller enclosed ranches represented more capital than the average cowhand was apt to be able to command; land had to be acquired, fences built, and wells sunk in arid regions at great cost.[60]

The literature of the cowboy suggests that more times than not he readily accepted his status of wage earner and harbored few ambitions. The cowboy was a notoriously easy spender. His paycheck vanished quickly during his occasional splurges in town and disappeared almost as soon on horses, spurs, saddles, and sombreros. His pride centered in his prowess in the saddle.[61]

With the shift from the open range to the enclosed ranch, the wage-earner aspect of the cowboy became more and more apparent. Much of his labor consisted of the routine duties necessary for the cultivation of a feed farm. The famous Spur Ranch in northwestern Texas employed an average of forty men a month from 1885 to 1908; but significantly its records held no mention of the "cowboy," only of the "hands."[62]

Sheep as well as cattle were raised on the western grazing lands that figure so prominently on the wage map of 1899. Since 1860 their numbers in the western states and territories had increased tenfold, from less than 10 percent of the nation's flocks to more than half. In expanding westward, sheep raising, like cattle raising, took on the character of a specialized commercial enterprise.[63] An average sheep ranch with its flock of 5,000 woollies represented an investment of about $15,000.[64] The "sheep baron" might have a herd that was ten, or even twenty, times as large and might employ as many as seventy-five regular men plus twice that number at shearing time.[65] Yet, as compared to the cattle industry, there was a secure place for the small operator;[66] and the humble herder, unless he were Mexican, had a fair chance of becoming a sheep owner, despite his wage of $10 or $15 monthly.[67] Even as late as 1900, large numbers of sheep were grazed on the public domain, eliminating the necessity for a large land investment;[68] and one herder could tend a flock of from 1,250 to 4,000.[69]

The shepherd was an isolated figure, but the sheep shearers worked in bands. They constituted a skilled group of seasonal workers who migrated regularly over vast stretches of the Rocky Mountain country from New Mexico to Canada. By the 1880s shearing was the regular occupation of many an itinerant worker. In the early years of the industry, the shearers were largely Mexicans, but many nationalities established themselves in the strenuous but well-paid trade.[70] Essential to the sheep man, equipped with a skill that set them apart particularly in the days before machine shearing, and working together as a cohesive group, shearers were more likely material for organization than the herders of the sheep or most casual workers. As early as the 1890s they organized a number of local unions. From these beginnings developed the first stable union movement among the nation's agricultural workers, the Sheep Shearers Union of North America.[71]

The great wheat fields of North Dakota, eastern Washington, and eastern Oregon, as indicated on the wage map of 1899, provided yet another variant from the American family farm with its hired man. The wheat production of the Red River Valley aroused much contemporary comment, and has received considerable study.[72] The bonanza farms of that area had their beginning in 1875 when an able Minnesota wheat grower, Oliver Dalrymple, contracted to establish and manage the production of wheat on a vast block of land that had been acquired at low cost by former bondholders of the Northern Pacific Railroad. The topography of the country lent itself to large-scale farming with the use of the latest mechanical equipment, such as the gang plow, the broadcast seeder, the Marsh harvester with binder attached, and the steam engine and separator for threshing.

The big farms made money even when the small farmers were taking losses.[73] According to the report of a Senate committee in 1894, "On these immense plantations farming is conducted with as much business tact and attention as a great manufacturing establishment or railway corporation."[74] The expansion of the bonanza farms continued through the 1880s; by the early 1890s the outlook was no longer so bright. Droughts, the fall in wheat prices, and the financial panic of 1893 combined to diminish their huge profits. The price of land, however, continued to climb as undeveloped agricultural lands grew scarce, and holders of great tracts found it profitable to sell land.[75]

Small armies of single or footloose men performed the labor of the great farms. Indeed, except for a ready supply of transient labor the establishments could never have been operated with success. On one twenty-thousand-acre tract a crew of 350 to 400 men were employed in harvesting and an even greater number in threshing.[76] These men were drawn from the lumbering regions of Minnesota and Wisconsin, the cities of St. Louis, Omaha, St. Paul, Chicago, and Milwaukee, and the homesteads and poorer farms of the region.[77] The railroads, which reached this territory in the 1880s, facilitated their arrival. The big farms were said to "ship their men in and ship them out" just as they shipped in their supplies and shipped out their wheat.[78]

To the permanent residents of the Dakotas these men were "hoboes," "tramps," "bums," or individuals who had "outrun the sheriff."[79] Local authorities were urged to take precautions against trouble and to provide additional police protection against the "tramp nuisance."[80] On the other hand, a shrewd observer of the American scene, William Allen White, declared them to be "steady, industrious men with no bad habits, and small ambitions."[81] The methods of the bonanza farms were thought by one Dakota farmer to eliminate "all the individuality and independence of these men" and to prevent their having little homes of their own. In his words, "It unAmericanizes them."[82]

Many of the men who worked on the bonanza farms had followed the wheat harvest north from Oklahoma.[83] They were part of an important and regular migratory movement of labor that characterized the entire western wheat country of the Great Plains until tractors and combines replaced them in the 1920s.[84] Perhaps the movement began as early as the 1870s;[85] it was well established by the 1880s. The role of the migratory harvest hands in American agriculture was widely recognized by the turn of the century, when they were described as "a peculiar product of the great wheat-raising districts, moving in crowds from south to north as the grain ripens, and returning to the cities for such casual employment as may be had in winter, or to hibernate, or bed, or go as vagrants to workhouses."[86] In the Pacific states these transient laborers were also known. An abundance of labor was reported in southeastern Washington in 1892 because "crops south of us ripen and are harvested first, so that we get hands from that direction when the harvest is over there."[87]

This survey of the characteristics of farm-labor employment in the areas of high-wage expenditures revealed by the wage maps of 1869 and 1899 has established the fact that many variants from the hired-man pattern had been established or greatly expanded on the American land during the thirty-five years before the opening of the twentieth century.[88] It also suggests that these diverse patterns gave rise to most of the problems and attitudes of which the general public has been aware only since the 1930s. And further examination substantiates this conclusion.

There was the migrant. The harvest hands, the sheep shearers, the California "bindle stiff," and his Asiatic competitors were the most conspicuous migratory laborers of the period, but there were others. Transient labor was important in the Atlantic-coast fruit, berry, and truck districts.[89] Some of these laborers were recruited directly from urban centers,[90] but others followed regular routes of travel. Each summer Negro workers from Virginia and Maryland, with recruits from North Carolina, moved northward into southeastern Pennsylvania, New Jersey, southeastern New York, across Connecticut, and into Rhode Island.[91] This Negro migratory labor was of importance in New Jersey at least as early as 1889.[92] In 1900, it was estimated that from two thousand to four thousand such laborers came into the state each year.[93] Itinerant strawberry pickers probably were already following the harvest up the Mississippi Valley.[94] Even the old-fashioned general farms of Vermont made use of migratory laborers; they were the habitants of Quebec and other French Canadians from Nova Scotia who came south to help in the harvests. "The summer over, they return with almost the only money they ever see, and which is too often all exhausted before they reach home."[95] From the St. John River region their countrymen came to dig the potatoes of Aroostook County, Maine. Farther west, other Canadians crossed the border to aid in the North Dakota harvests.[96] From Kentucky, American migrants moved north across the Ohio River to work in the truck and fruit farms of southern Illinois.[97] Farther south, in Louisiana, Italian workers from the central and northern states, and even from Italy, arrived in numbers to cut the sugar cane.[98] There was also another less regular type of migratory laborer who had proved useful in American agriculture. He was the penurious homesteader or small frontier farmer who turned eastward at harvest time to obtain some cash income in the more settled regions.[99]

Women and children were at work on the American land. To be certain, the day of family labor in California agriculture had not yet arrived; at the turn of the century single men predominated in the migratory labor force.[100] In the South, however, the labor of Negro women and children was taken for granted, even as it had been in pre–Civil War days, despite the fact that freedmen in the first years of their freedom tried to keep their women from the fields.[101] Wherever there were berries, fruit, or vegetables to be gathered, women and children were employed.[102] By 1900 flatcars and steamboats carried thousands of women and children from Chicago and Detroit to the berry fields.[103] A few years later, a special report of the U.S. Department of Agriculture extolled the beneficial effects upon the health and habits of city children of work in nearby beet districts.[104]

Apparently there was more labor of women and children on the general farms of the Mississippi Valley in those years than in recent times. This work was more apt to be on the home farm than for wages elsewhere. The Iowa Bureau of Labor Statistics in 1891 estimated that 40 percent of the farm children from 8 to 16 years of age were kept from school to do farm labor, thereby losing an average of 54 days of schooling each year.[105] The Missouri commissioner of labor statistics in 1880 published returns showing that women and children were at work in the fields throughout the state. He commented: "It would scarcely be supposed in the absence of facts that so large a proportion, nearly one-fourth of farmers' wives are employed in field labor." Although some parents required only chores of their children, "many others, it must be confessed, compel their children to perform the labor of an adult." The schooling available to Missouri farm children averaged four to five months in the year; but as a result of the work that the children had to do in good weather and the difficulties of transportation in bad weather, the average length of attendance was only two or three months.[106]

Although the foreign-born constituted a negligible percentage of all farm workers throughout the country,[107] in a number of localities their cheap labor was of utmost importance in the cultivation and harvesting of the crops.[108] Now and then, in the years when labor was scarce, farmers consciously promoted the coming of foreign laborers. The withdrawal of farm labor during the Civil War prompted the legislature of Wisconsin to memorialize Congress to encourage emigration to the United States. "The wages of those whom the agriculturist must employ, or lose his crop, have increased more than a hundred per cent, and the consequent tax upon the net receipts . . . has brought down the profits of the farmer to a minimum beyond which he cannot afford to have them reduced."[109] The American Emigrant Company in 1865 was busily engaged in importing young men of seventeen to twenty-one for farm laborers and wished Congress to make enforceable in the courts the contracts entered into with these minors.[110]

The movement in the early 1870s to import Chinese laborers for agriculture was sponsored by southern plantation owners,[111] but it received endorsements from farmers in the North Atlantic states.[112] In 1873 Pennsylvania farmers were securing Swedish immigrant laborers by an advance of $50 or $60 paid to an association in Wilmington, Delaware, but subtracted from the $10 to $12 a month wages of the workers.[113] About the same time, families from England and Ireland were encouraged to come to Ohio and New York by advance payment of their passage, and one farm journal reported that agricultural associations might soon be able to take part in "an organized plan for the introduction of skilled farm labor from England."[114] The supply of home labor after the depression struck in the mid-1870s made importation of foreign workers unnecessary and uneconomical.

Upon farm workers who varied from the hired-man norm, there was bestowed an opprobrium that did not offend the sensitivities of the nation until several decades later. The disparaging terms of "tramp," "bum," "riffraff," and "undesirable labor" were applied to farm workers not only in the wheat belt and on the Pacific coast, but in most any locality where they were unemployed, or where they had taken to the road in search of jobs, or where they constituted a racial group distinct from that of the employing farmers.[115] Their low social status reflected both economic changes and community prejudice. Even J. R. Dodge of the U.S. Department of Agriculture, the one man during this period who could be considered a government expert in the field of farm labor, cast a stigma upon these workers. At the turn of the century he contrasted the hired man with "a class less efficient and desirable, with inferior training in rural occupations, whose rate of compensation is less, and whose condition, from lack of economy and judgment more than deficiencies of compensation, is not so good, and whose lives and aims are not on so high a plane." There was no mistaking the workers to whom he referred when he said: "The annual inundation of grain fields in harvest time, hop yards in picking season, fruit picking in districts of extensive market orchards, and similar harvest seasons requiring large numbers of hands for a short time, has a demoralizing effect on farm labor, reducing its efficiency in those lines. Such employments demand little skill; the requirements of each are simple and easily satisfied. They constitute a low order of farm labor, if worthy to be classed with it at all, and are excrescences upon its fair face."[116]

Impersonal employer-employee relationships and an antagonism of economic interest accompanied the loss of status for increasing numbers of farm workers. As yet there was not much in the nature of organized activity by either laborers or farmers in defense of their pecuniary interest; but there were intimations of such developments. Evidence has been noted of some strikes and union organization during the period. In the opposite camp, there already existed convenient vehicles for implementing concerted labor policies in the associations organized among cattlemen, fruit growers, and sugar planters. There is some indication that community pressure was exercised against farmers who offered more than the going wage.[117]

Although there is reason to suspect that the growing impersonality of employment had some effect upon the position of the American-born hired man, other types of farm workers were the focus of the new problems and attitudes. However, the hired man shared with all farm wage earners certain disadvantages—the constriction of opportunity for attaining farm ownership,[118] low wages, and the hazards of unemployment. These disadvantages affected his standing in society. Though related to the problems facing American farm operators during these years, they tended to undermine the hired man's apprentice status. It is significant that at the turn of the century the U.S. Industrial Commission recognized farm labor as a group with interests distinct from those of farmers generally.

Sponsors of the Industrial Commission evinced no special interest in agricultural labor, but when topics were formulated to guide the inquiry, an entire section was devoted to the conditions and wages of farm labor. The conclusions and recommendations of the commission in this section of its report showed little discernment and marked complacency. The testimony taken might have suggested less optimism despite the failure to give farm workers themselves a day in court. The Assistant Secretary of Agriculture, a man of long-standing prominence in grange activities, was questioned about the opportunity for ambitious young men to become farm owners. "A great many of them do," he replied, "the industrious, saving men do. . . . A good many men who are good workers do not save money; they spend it as fast as they get it. . . . There are a great many men who start in on the farm and are good workers and continue as farm hands all their life."[119] Eugene Davenport, dean of the College of Agriculture of the University of Illinois, testified that twenty-five years earlier a man worked upon the farm to get money enough to buy land for himself but that now "there seems to be a decided tendency for the farm laborer, if he is unmarried, to work for money without a very definite object, and this money is likely used for whatever his fancy dictates, most likely for a horse and buggy of his own." The trouble was that the farm laborer's wages, though higher than a generation earlier, would not buy so much land. "It can not secure the opportunity for a man that it could 25 years ago."[120]

Whether or not a farm laborer could advance to the position of farm owner had been a question of discussion and controversy for some years before the Industrial Commission opened its inquiry. In 1891 Ohio farmhands were told that, although farmhands considered their monthly wages inadequate, they still could save enough to get a start in the world.[121] A woman farmer of Iowa in 1898 denied the assertion she heard made by young and old that "no man can start out penniless and become possessor of 160 acres of $50 land." She attributed the lack of advancement on the part of farmhands to their extravagant spending.[122]

There could be no controversy over the fact that farm laborers in ever greater numbers were turning to the cities in search of opportunity. Throughout the 1880s and the early 1890s there was constant complaint that those who had formerly worked for hire upon the farms were leaving to seek jobs in industry.[123] The movement to the cities continued even in the depression years of the 1890s. Of more than five hundred Wisconsin farmers who were asked in 1895 whether the tendency among unmarried farm laborers was to acquire a farm or to go live in the city, 75 percent answered that farm laborers desired to go to the city, 20.6 percent indicated that laborers desired to stay on the farms, and 4.4 percent replied that both tendencies were evident. A number of farmers distinguished between foreign laborers, who tended to stay on the farm, and Americans, who preferred the city. One return bore the comment, "Never can save enough to buy a farm."[124]

The preference for city employment was in part a reflection of the discrepancy between industrial and farm wages. Statistical data on wages in this period is not complete nor precisely comparable, but it is sufficient to indicate general levels and trends. To be certain, the value of prerequisites to farm workers, a perennial matter for dispute, cannot be definitely determined. Yet it is safe to assert that farm labor was the lowest paid major type of American labor. For the country as a whole, the average monthly wage with board in 1899 was $13.90, without board it was $19.97; for the North Central states, the region of the hired man, the comparable rates were $17.36 and $24.75. And in 1899 wages were higher than they had been for most of the years since 1866.[125]

Available statistics indicate that the trend of farm wages, as well as the amount, compared unfavorably with wages in industry. The wage trend has often been presented as more advantageous to farm labor than was actually the case for the simple reason that the 1912 report of the U.S. Department of Agriculture, which is the most authoritative source for this data, recomputed the actual wages for the years 1866 to 1878 into their equivalent in gold, a practice that has not been followed with nonagricultural wages. Though farm wage rates can be corrected in respect to this distortion, they are available only for irregular time intervals since 1866.[126] However, a continuous yearly record from a much earlier date has been carefully assembled for Vermont.[127]

Money wages of farm labor at the turn of the century were actually less than they had been at the close of the Civil War. During that conflict, farm labor had made very considerable wage gains, an increase roughly estimated at 50 percent.[128] By the end of the 1870s a severe drop in rates had wiped out much of this advance. There was some recovery in the 1880s and early 1890s, but another dip followed in 1893. Higher rates in 1898 and 1899 marked an upward movement of farm wages, which was to continue through the years of World War I.[129] Of course, wages in the 1860s and 1870s were paid in currency, and their purchasing power was restricted by the prevailing high prices. Although money wages did not again reach the heights of 1866 until 1902, real wages—that is, wages in terms of purchasing power—did increase because of the general downward trend in prices.

A general comparison of farm and nonfarm wage trends can be made from Table 1, which places in juxtaposition an index of hourly rates for nonagricultural labor with an index of money wages based on various types of farm rates.[130] A comparison of the two indices discloses the fact that farm labor, much more than industrial labor, lost its Civil War gains during the depression years of the 1870s.[131] For a short time in the early 1880s farm labor made wage gains at a more rapid rate than did city labor, but this trend was reversed by 1888. During the depression following the financial crisis of 1893, farm wages dropped much farther than did industrial wages.

The same trends are indicated in Table 2 where the index of farm wages is converted into an index of real wages and compared with an index of real wages for nonagricultural labor.[132] Whereas only one point separates the two indices of real wages in 1866, there is a fifteen-point difference by 1879, which narrows to four points by 1882 and then again widens to seventeen points in 1894.

For the Vermont wage study there has been computed an index of real earnings based upon a cost of living index constructed specifically for the state's farm laborers. This index is consistently higher than the above approximate national index until the year 1898. However, as compared with real wages in industry, it confirms the unfavorable position of farm workers. By 1899 the Vermont index is only seventeen points higher than for 1866, as against a fifty-five-point gain for nonfarm labor. Furthermore, the Vermont index shows no substantial gains in the real income of farm labor during the entire period of this study as compared with the wage level of the late 1850s. The early level of real earnings was not again reached until the 1880s and

Table 1. Indices of Farm and Nonfarm Wages

Year	Farm Wages	Nonfarm Wages
1866	78	61
1869	74	66
1874/5	67	67
1877/9	56	61–60–59
1879/80	59	59–60
1880/1	62	60–62
1881/2	65	62–63
1884/5	65	64
1887/8	66	67
1889/90	66	68–69
1891/2	67	69
1893	67	69
1894	61	67
1895	62	68
1898	65	69
1899	68	70

Table 2. Indices of Real Farm and Nonfarm Wages

Year	Farm Wages	Nonfarm Wages
1866	50	49
1869	59	66
1874/5	62	75
1877/9	65	80
1879/80	70	81
1880/1	70	76.5
1881/2	73	77
1884/5	80	88
1887/8	84	92
1889/90	83	93
1891/2	88	98.5
1893	88	99
1894	84	101
1895	88	104
1898	94	107
1899	94	104

1890s; and in only six of the entire thirty-five years between 1865 and 1900 was the index number higher than in 1859—in twenty-six years it was lower, in the other three years it was identical.[133]

Many factors affected the rate of farm pay. Daily wages for harvest labor decreased much more sharply than rates for other types of farm labor because of the increase in the use of ever more efficient machinery for harvesting and threshing. Day wages with board for harvest work in the North Central states dropped from $1.59 in 1881 to $1.28 in 1894 and recovered by 1899 only to $1.37, although by that date the rates for other types of farm labor were higher than they had been in 1881. Living costs were reflected in the marked divergence of sectional wage rates. From county to county, wages varied in accordance with transportation facilities, the distance to markets, or the competition of factories, mines, lumber camps, or public works for men.[134] Both the prices of farm products and the demand for industrial labor influenced the general ups and downs of farm rates. In the late 1880s wages did not fall as sharply as farm prices because the supply of available labor was lessened by the demand for men in industry. Conversely, the unemployment in the cities after 1873 and again after 1893 sent men back to the farms, increasing the supply of farm labor and helping to depress wages. But in the early 1880s, when agriculture was prospering, farm wages rose more rapidly than did industrial wages.[135]

The income of the farm worker was not a simple matter of wage rates. The amount of employment he could obtain was of utmost importance. Seasonal unemployment was a well-established characteristic of farm work, even of that performed by the hired man. Although some farmhands were kept through the winter months, at times with board and room the only pay, a majority were without work unless they were lucky enough to get jobs in the cities or lumber camps. The report of the Missouri commissioner of labor in 1880 indicated that nearly half of the farmhands at work in the summer were left stranded in the winter, swelling the "already over-stocked labor market" of the cities or becoming "tramps." When "their few dollars are spent" they became "inmates of soup houses, for their scant earnings during the summer season are insufficient to carry them through the winter."[136] Reports from other states confirm the prevalence of winter unemployment. The length of the working season varied greatly. Even average employment in the Midwest ranged from four to nine months.[137]

Winter unemployment was a serious matter for farm laborers, but the chronic unemployment during periods of depression was apt to be even more damaging to their security and their financial resources. Moreover, farm workers had to face the competition of the industrial unemployed during depression years. This competition was most disastrous to casual workers, but it also affected more permanent farm labor. Tenants and farm owners who had slipped back down the agricultural ladder added to the scramble for jobs. Contemporary evidence documents the flooding of the countryside during the depression years of the 1870s and 1890s. The job seekers were often greeted with suspicion or antagonism, and when they did find work the compensation was meager.[138] Both after 1873 and 1893 farm wages dropped more drastically than did industrial wages.[139]

In the boom years of industrial activity during the 1880s and early 1890s, farm labor did not make wage gains comparable to the losses sustained during the depression years. There were a number of contributing factors in addition to the low farm prices, which in certain of these years affected the farmer's ability to pay. Increased use of machinery cut the farm demand for labor and lowered the pay for harvest work.[140] The influx of German, Swedish, and Norwegian immigrants created an oversupply of labor in some sections even when it was scarce elsewhere.[141] Homesteaders with little money made labor abundant in some western counties, while crop disasters coupled with low prices compelled poor farmers "to offer their labor for hire on the farms of their wealthier neighbors."[142] Low farm prices in the 1880s caused many farmers who were accustomed to hiring labor to do their own work, exchanging labor at harvest or rearranging their crops.[143]

The years between 1865 and 1900 pushed American farm labor into an increasingly disadvantaged position as compared with other workers or with the hired hand of an earlier period. Even the most privileged of the farm labor force faced low wages, job insecurity, and the loss of farmer-apprentice status. Seasonal workers, the least privileged, swelled the ranks of women and children at work in the fields and confronted problems of transportation, community hostility, inadequate housing, and lack of educational facilities for their families. Worker-employer relationships were changing. Farmers increasingly looked upon wage earners in their fields as a factor in the cost of production; and production costs increased in importance as farming became more commercialized, with its produce destined for distant and highly competitive markets, and dependent for transportation and distribution upon facilities over which the farmer had little control.

The decline in the average farm wage bill from $116 in 1869 to $64 in 1899 suggests that the proportion of farms hiring little or no help was increasing.

The drop in the rate of wages was not large enough to explain this decrease. New machinery was enabling the family farm operator to dispense with hired help at the same time that expansion of crops such as fruits, vegetables, and livestock created a greater demand for wage labor.[144] The trend had begun toward concentration of farm labor on larger and more commercial agricultural enterprises. In 1899 farms with crops worth $2,500 or more were only 2.7 percent of all farms, but hired nearly one-third of the man hours of farm labor and paid an average wage bill of $786.[145] Managers operated 59,213 of the nation's farms, which accounted for nearly 12 percent of the total wage expenditure. Farms of 1,000 or more acres spent an average $1,059 for labor while those of 100 to 175 acres spent $60, and those of 50 to 100 acres only $33. Nearly 150,000 large farms of 500 acres or more were reported by the census enumerators, an increase of 43 percent in the two decades since 1880.[146] In other words, at the end of the period as compared to its beginning, a relatively larger proportion of farm wage earners were hired by farm operators who were entrepreneurs with incomes dependent to a very considerable extent upon managerial functions, capital investments, and the employment of others rather than upon their own work on the land.

Not only were there established by the twentieth century diverse patterns of farm labor with attendant social problems and economic conflicts, but between 1865 and 1900 the nature of farm-labor employment, even for the "typical" farm wage earner, had departed significantly from the apprentice status of the traditional hired man. Farm labor was approaching the essential nature of industrial labor. Moreover, as wage earners, farm workers found themselves in a disadvantaged position as compared to their fellow wage earners in industry. Detailed study of the farm-labor problem since 1900, however, may reveal some temporary reversals of the trends here delineated.

CHAPTER THREE

The Promise of Land for the Freedmen

What might have been one of the momentous decisions in the annals of the U.S. Congress was finally made in the closing midnight session of the Thirty-eighth Congress, March 3, 1865.[1] The House and Senate agreed with the report of their second conference committee on the Freedmen's Bureau bill that from the abandoned and confiscated lands of the South forty acres should be assigned to "every male citizen, whether refugee or freedman" at rental for three years and then for purchase from the United States with "such title as it could convey."[2]

Only a few weeks earlier the members of Congress by their approval of the Thirteenth Amendment had agreed that henceforth the Negro was to be a free man, never again a slave; now they took action to put him on the road to economic independence of the type traditional to free men in the nineteenth-century agrarian Republic, namely, ownership of the land that he tilled. Implicit in the decision was the acceptance of the fact that the freedman would not be colonized abroad, as Lincoln and many others less concerned with the Negro's welfare had wished,[3] nor even colonized in designated areas within the home boundaries,[4] but that he should remain a basic economic and social element in his southern homeland.

Historians have asked why Radical Republicans did not provide land ownership for the emancipated slave. The more historically valid and perceptive query might well be a dual one. How was it that such a crucial decision for land ownership was taken? And having been made, why was the legislative decision never translated into effective policy? It is to the first of these questions that this article is addressed.

On first study, the legislative history of the Freedmen's Bureau bill leaves the origins of the land provisions of the final law an enigma. The bill as brought before the House in the winter of 1863–64 by its sponsor and author, Thomas D. Eliot, Republican from Massachusetts, held no promise of permanent land ownership for the freedmen. In fact, its land provisions were ambiguous. The officials of the proposed bureau, with the approval of the Secretary of War, under whose jurisdiction the agency was to function, were empowered to *permit* freedmen "to occupy, cultivate, and improve" all land that had been abandoned and all real estate to which the United States might acquire title within the rebel states.[5] Such disposal of the land was not made mandatory; the terms under which the Negroes should occupy or cultivate the lands were not specified. In the same section, indeed in the same sentence of the bill, the bureau officers were directed to aid and advise the freedmen and when needful "to organize and direct their labor, adjust with them their wages, and receive all returns arising therefrom." It is significant, however, that an earlier provision of the bill that would have empowered the bureau commissioner to execute all laws providing for the colonization of freedmen had been eliminated.[6]

The House debates on the measure only compound the ambiguity. They leave the reader in doubt as to the expectations of the bill's framers and as to its probable consequences. Opponents of the measure attacked it as a device to "set apart for the sole benefit of the freedmen" the vast domain "paid for by the blood of white men." They saw its provisions as an invitation for cotton cultivation under government direction and control, a possibility they stigmatized as entailing a "species of servitude worse than slavery" and governmental activity of a "socialistic, Fourieristic, Owenistic, erotic" nature.[7] At the same time, they charged that the bill would promote the moneymaking schemes of northerners at the expense of the black race, a charge that implied that southern lands would be leased to northern speculators. In reply Eliot and his Republican colleague on the committee, William D. Kelley of Pennsylvania, argued that the bill was not for the exclusive benefit of the Negro but that it would also aid the poor white man of the South, who might rent from the government a farm as large or as small as his means might justify.[8] Whether or not the lands were to be cultivated as government plantations, or leased to northern entrepreneurs, or to poor southern whites, or to freedmen—or disposed of by a combination of all these methods—one thing is clear: no promise of a permanent homestead for the freed Negro was implied in the House bill.

In the Senate, the bill was completely rewritten by Charles Sumner's Committee on Slavery and Freedom, despite the slim majority of two votes by which the bill had passed the House on March 1, 1864. The most conspicuous change in the Senate's substitute measure was the shift of the bureau from the War Department to the Treasury, but the section dealing with abandoned lands underwent a basic modification.[9] It did not move closer to the promise of land ownership embodied in the finally enacted law, but rather seemed to face in the opposite direction. The Senate version directed bureau officials to rent or lease the land "or in case no proper lessees can be found, then to cause the same to be cultivated or occupied by the freedmen," on terms to be determined by the bureau's commissioner,[10] provided only that no freedmen might be held to service except according to voluntary, written contracts. The bureau's commissioner and local superintendents were to act as "advisory guardians, to aid the freedmen in the adjustment of their wages, or where they had rented plantations or small holdings, in the organization of their labor." They were to see that the freedmen did not suffer from ill treatment or failure of contract on the part of others and that the freedmen on their part performed their duty on the premises. The latter provision was first changed by amendment to read "their duty under any contract entered into by them," and later entirely omitted.[11] In other words, the Senate measure indicated an expectation that the freedmen's relation to the land would be primarily that of laborers under contract. Private enterprise (white) was given a preferred status over government plantation projects, but government agents were to exercise an intermediary role between freedmen and entrepreneur. Henry Wilson of Massachusetts complained that the section dealing with the lands looked "very much as though it were to take care of the plantations instead of the freedmen."[12]

The discrepancies between the House and Senate bills resulted in a conference committee, on which Sumner sat as undoubtedly the dominant member for the Senate. Eliot and Kelley, together with a Democratic colleague, represented the House. The conference committee was formed by the second session of the Thirty-eighth Congress in December 1864, and its report was presented to the House on February 2, just two days after the Thirteenth Amendment had finally been approved, and to the Senate on February 13, 1865. The new bill created an independent Department of Freedmen and Abandoned Lands, and the land provisions were restated in a manner that Eliot described as a "material modification" of the Senate bill.[13] They directed the commissioners to rent or lease to freedmen all real estate abandoned by disloyal persons and all to which the United States had title or possession, or to permit these lands to be cultivated under such terms and regulations as should be mutually agreed upon between commissioner and freedmen. Only if the lands and the property on them were not "required for freedmen" were they to be rented or leased to other persons. No freedman was to be employed on these lands except under a voluntary, written contract certified by the assistant commissioner or local superintendent.[14]

Most significant, as compared to the finally enacted law, was the provision that no lease or contract or permission to occupy should be for more than one year. In short, as Sumner explained, the freedmen as lessees were to have first preference on the abandoned and confiscated southern lands that they had "fertilized . . . with their sweat" for "weary generations," but with no expectation of permanent possession. "The time has come," he stated, "when they *should enjoy the results of their labor at least for a few months.*"[15] However, there was one curious aspect of the conference bill that might have provided freedmen with permanent homesteads. Unlike earlier versions, it referred to all lands not already appropriated for other uses to which the United States "had title." This would have included the public domain in the seceded states, lands excluded from the Homestead Act of 1862. Whether the new wording was deliberate or mere chance is not clear; but the fact that it might reserve all public lands for freedmen was pointed out in the Senate debate.[16]

The House accepted the conference report by a narrow margin but the Senate rejected it on February 22, 1865, by a vote of fourteen to twenty-four. The Democrats were solidly arrayed against the measure, as they had been against the earlier version of the bill, but in addition fourteen Republican or Union senators joined the opposition. Only two of these had voted against the Senate bill of June 1864. The chief spokesmen for the Republican opposition were James W. Grimes of Iowa, Henry S. Lane of Indiana, and John P. Hale of New Hampshire, all antislavery men who feared that the supervision provided for the freedmen might lead to their abuse. As the New York *Herald* reported with some satisfaction, the Freedmen's Bureau bill "was killed by its friends," a display of independence toward Sumner that the paper found "quite refreshing." The Massachusetts senior senator was reported as "much excited," almost losing his temper, and when the vote was finally taken as appearing "in utter despair."[17] The congressional session was within a few days of its closing deadline and both friend and foe thought the freedmen's bill was lost.[18]

It was in a burst of final activity, so hurried that neither the press nor members of Congress could follow the proceedings in detail, that a second conference committee was named, its six members hammered out "an entirely new bill,"[19] and Congress enacted the remodeled version into law. There was very little discussion in either the House or the Senate, none touching the new land provisions. The law, in contrast to the earlier bills, was a brief measure; it covered white refugees as well as freedmen and placed the bureau under the War Department. All provisions were dropped that suggested supervision of the freedmen either by way of arranging employment contracts or directing their labor. Its wording contained nothing that might be construed as a directive to organize government-operated plantations or to lease lands to any whites other than loyal southerners. It did not even directly instruct bureau officers to act as mediators between Negro laborers and their employers. The law simply stated in general terms that the bureau would have "control of all subjects relating to refugees and freedmen." Aside from administrative details and a section providing relief for the destitute, the only specific provision was for the forty-acre land allotments. The language identifying the lands for allotment was rephrased apparently to preclude an interpretation that would cover the public domain of the South; the new formulation read: "such tracts of land within the insurrectionary States as *shall have* been abandoned, or to which the United States *shall have* acquired title by confiscation or sale, or otherwise."[20] Whether the addition of acquisitions made *by sale* was significant no one explained and no one asked.

Neither congressional debates, contemporary news accounts, nor manuscript collections yield a ready explanation of the Thirty-eighth Congress's extraordinary action.[21] In the final days of its session, without debate, and without precedent in earlier versions of the bill that had been lengthily examined and argued, Congress made in effect a promise of land ownership to the freed slave. And it made the commitment, arousing the expectation of the freedmen, despite the fact that any title the United States might obtain to rebel lands would be limited, in accordance with the joint resolution accompanying the Confiscation Act of 1862, to the lifetime of southern owners. The limiting resolution had been rushed through both houses in order to forestall a presidential veto of the confiscation measure.

Here, indeed, is a major enigma, and a series of minor puzzles as well. Why was the Thirty-eighth Congress not content to offer the freedmen a guarantee of fair treatment as wage laborers and the temporary use of abandoned lands? Was the promise of land ownership mere chance, an improvisation of hurried, last-hour legislation; or did it represent a serious, considered effort to create a new independent status for the former slave? Did it spring from altruism, or from less lofty interests? Having made the decision for land ownership, why did the second conference committee not recommend homesteads on the public domain? Why did it provide for the sale of lands to which the United States had only an uncertain expectancy of full title, a title that in fact was never acquired? And since the committee asked Congress to offer so much that it did not possess, why did it not recommend an outright gift of a homestead rather than payments from the penniless for rental and purchase? How did it happen that there were no specific directives in the final bill for benevolent supervision of the freedmen in their new economic role? And, in a measure built to bridge the chasm between slavery and freedom, why were white "refugees" included in the benefits meant primarily for Negroes? The answers are not obvious; but there are clues.

For one thing, the legislative record of the Freedmen's Bureau bill suggests that congressional decision was affected by the changing fortunes of war and politics, and by the crystallization of northern opinion in respect to emancipation. The bill was introduced and the first votes taken in the House and Senate at a time when the problems of war were uppermost, the outcome of conflict inscrutable, and the future of the institution of slavery the subject of bitter contention in the North. True, Lincoln had already issued the Emancipation Proclamation, but it was not until the June convention of the Republican party that president and party were committed to the extinction of slavery by constitutional amendment. The Democratic opposition, on the other hand, was not committed at all, was bitterly attacking the president for prolonging the war in order to free the slaves, and had high expectations of winning the presidential election in November. When the Thirty-eighth Congress opened its second session in December 1864, the Republicans, with a platform promising the end of slavery, had triumphed at the polls. The victory for freedom, however, was not automatic; not until January 31, 1865, did the House reverse its action of the previous June and give the amendment the requisite two-thirds endorsement, a victory made possible only by the abstention of eight Democrats from the vote. By that time, too, military victory and the end to warfare were in sight. All this suggests that the second conference committee report may be viewed as the culmination of a process that shifted the focus of the Freedmen's Bureau bill from wartime military problems of southern Negroes and southern lands behind northern lines, to the great peacetime question of the Negro's future status. The encouragement to land ownership was undoubtedly intended to translate emancipation into substantive freedom, to rule out any halfway station between freedom and slavery.

The arguments during the debates on the bill and the nature of the changes it underwent also indicate that the transmutation of its provisions evolved from an earnest effort to assist the former slaves in their transition to free men and to safeguard them against abuse and exploitation. Except for the Senate substitute version in the first session, each change in the provisions respecting land and supervision of labor looked toward strengthening the bill in the interests of the freedmen. Even Sumner's proposal, while weakening the land provisions, added passages designed to protect the Negro's civil rights. Sumner explained in private correspondence that he and one other senator on his committee favored the House bill but that a majority of the committee opposed it.[22] His key role in drafting the first conference committee's report and his championing of it in the Senate provide further evidence that Sumner's first concern was the freedmen's welfare. Unmistakably, the House framers of the original bill desired a law that would protect the Negroes from northern speculators, whom Eliot called "white blood hounds . . . whose pursuit is for gold." "Humanity," not "the greatest revenue," he emphasized, should determine policy.[23] They wished to ensure fair wages, promptly paid, and they anticipated that at least a portion of the former slaves would become owners of land, purchased either with their savings from wages or their earnings as lessees. The desire of the Negro to remain in his homeland and to become the owner of land they considered not only proper, but convincing "proof of manhood."[24] In other words, the sponsors of the bill did not intend to freeze the former slaves into a lowly position of hired laborers on the land, but hoped to encourage them to attain substantial economic status.

In struggling with the difficult problem of shaping the freedman's future, legislators could look to the results of a considerable body of wartime experience in dealing with southern Negroes and southern lands. Since early 1862 a notable experiment had been under way in the occupied Sea Islands off the coast of South Carolina. There the planters had fled at the approach of Union forces, leaving behind large numbers of slaves who labored for them in the production of the islands' valuable long staple cotton. Secretary of the Treasury Salmon P. Chase had sent to the islands as special agent with instructions to investigate and prepare a plan of labor a Massachusetts man and friend of Senator Sumner, Edward L. Pierce. Like Chase and Sumner, Pierce was opposed to slavery and eager to demonstrate the fallacy of the southern contention that Negroes would labor effectively only under slavery and that cotton could not be produced by free labor. His strong concern for the Negroes led him to condemn proposals "to lease the plantations and the people upon them," for he held that not even the best of men should be placed in a position where they would be torn between humanity and self-interest. He recommended that superintendents be appointed for each large plantation, who would enforce a paternal discipline without coercion and would prepare their charges for unsupervised freedom. As fast as possible, Pierce wished the Negroes to be dismissed from the system and allowed any manner or place of employment they might choose.[25] With Chase's blessing and under his authority, Pierce inaugurated his plan with the enthusiastic cooperation of the northern freedmen's aid associations. Within a few months the experiment passed under the jurisdiction of the War Department and the supervision of Gen. Rufus Saxton, who carried on the work in the manner and spirit that Pierce had introduced.

The Sea Islands experiment was hailed with great interest by northern friends of the Negro, including both lowly teachers and "eminent citizens" of the business community, and the results vindicated Pierce's faith in free Negro labor. However, disposition of the lands came under the control of a special commission charged with enforcement of the direct tax act of June 1862, and the tax commissioners proceeded to sell the lands. By the end of 1864 the experiment of government-operated plantations had come to an end.[26] Furthermore, this operation had not been without fault; wages were frequently woefully in arrears and there had been military interference aimed to promote army enlistments of the able-bodied Negro workers. Early in 1863 the most influential of the supervisors, Edward S. Philbrick, Boston businessman and humanitarian, shifted his role from that of superintendent to private entrepreneur when the tax commissioners' sales in St. Helena Parish made possible his purchase of a considerable number of choice plantations. Philbrick thought government supervision inefficient and anticipated substantial profits for himself and his New England associates, but he also justified the new departure on the ground that private employment would save the Negroes from a hand-to-mouth existence and bring them greater benefits than they had enjoyed under government management.[27]

Congressional debates show suspicion and hostility toward government control of Negro labor. Critics attacked it as an improper activity for the national government and as a guardianship system that might prove worse than slavery for the freedmen. Although some of this criticism was but a smoke screen for those who shared southern racist views and opposed any national program for the freedmen, in part these objections represented the apprehensions of men sincerely interested in the Negroes' future as free men. It was no mere chance that the final legislation establishing the Freedmen's Bureau omitted any provision that might encourage or authorize government-operated plantations.

Nor was it sheer accident in the final rush of legislation that the second conference committee eliminated provisions of the earlier bills that looked toward the leasing of southern lands to northern entrepreneurs and toward supervision of labor relations between Negroes and their former masters.[28] In Louisiana Gen. Benjamin F. Butler, and following him Gen. Nathaniel P. Banks, had struggled with the problem of stabilizing the relationship between Negro laborers and old planters, who for the most part had remained on their plantations. In January 1863, Banks established a yearly contract system of labor with detailed regulations that were further elaborated in February 1864. Many provisions were meant to benefit and protect the Negroes, including those for rations, clothing, quarters, medical attention, schools, care of the disabled, small lots for independent cultivation, and the establishment of a savings bank. Ten hours of labor in summer and nine in winter were declared due employers. A wage scale was established beginning at $10 a month for foremen and $8 for first-class hands, with at least half the wage payments ordered withheld until the end of the year. One-fourteenth of the net proceeds of the crop might be substituted for wages by mutual consent. Laborers could choose their employers but were held to a year's service. Provost marshals were to enforce penalties for indolence, feigned sickness, disobedience—penalties that included labor upon public works without pay. This disciplinary measure operated also against all "unemployed persons of color, vagrants, and camp-loafers." Banks set forth the premise that labor was a public duty and a law of God, idleness a crime.[29]

The Banks labor system encountered many difficulties and aroused much criticism, private and public. Although Banks's work on the whole deserved commendation and although the general defended it vigorously to his New England antislavery friends, still his system was suspect.[30] The most devastating, and probably the most influential, criticism of freedmen's affairs in the lower Mississippi Valley was made by James McKaye, a member of the American Freedmen's Inquiry Commission, in a supplementary report presented to the public in pamphlet form apparently in July 1864.[31] It was entitled "The Mastership and Its Fruits; The Emancipated Slave Face to Face with His Old Master." McKaye reported that subordinate army officials, often without conscious intent, had become instruments of employers in perpetrating great injustice and ill treatment on Negro laborers. He reported that provost marshals did not interfere with the use of the whip on many plantations. He condemned the system of fixed wage rates and practice of compelling the laborer to remain with his employer for a year as wrong in principle and liable to abuse. And McKaye stated that the old planters desired to maintain control over laborers either directly or through military supervision that would compel the Negroes to labor. He interpreted this as a survival of the spirit of slavery, and feared the danger of a "system of serfdom" developing out of the temporary regulations of the Banks system.

Disposition of lands and indirectly of Negro labor through treasury agents to northern lessees brought forth even greater condemnation than direct military supervision. Leasing of lands and private employment of Negroes by new masters played a minor role in the lower Mississippi, and a more important one farther north along the river in the area under General Grant's control. The investigations of James E. Yeatman for the Western Sanitary Commission late in 1863 revealed shocking exploitation and abuse of freedmen working the leased plantations.[32] Attempts during 1864 to remedy the abuses resulted in confusion and conflict of authority between army officers and treasury agents.[33] General Grant had placed the Negro refugees, who flocked in great numbers behind his lines, under the jurisdiction of Chaplain John Eaton, a transplanted New England educator who labored tirelessly to aid and protect his charges. In June 1864, Eaton was writing President Lincoln with bitter words in respect to "the money interests of the unprincipled," "the old prejudice among officers and soldiers," and "the customs of masters."[34] His persistent hostility was directed at the subordination of the freedmen's interests to treasury revenue and private profit, and he used his very considerable influence with government officials, freedmen's friends, and members of Congress to discredit treasury control.[35] Public attention was directed to the failings of treasury agents and the leasing system by the reports of newspaper correspondents in the South who sent accounts of abuses and fraud, and even of the conviction of certain officials in charge of leasing plantations near Natchez.[36]

There can be no doubt but that these varied wartime experiences, together with the criticism and publicity they evoked, affected Freedmen's Bureau legislation. They make clear what the framers of its final version were attempting to avoid, namely, operation of plantations by the government, exploitation of Negro labor by northern speculators, abuse and rigorous control of freedmen by southern planters whether in violation of military directives or in collusion with military personnel, even the minute paternalistic regulations drawn to safeguard the freedmen that might lead to a permanent "pupilage." The position of the influential American Freedmen's Inquiry Commission had anticipated that of Congress. Its preliminary report, issued in June 1863, had regarded with favor, as temporary measures, government-operated plantations and government supervision over the hiring of freedmen to lessees and loyal owners. The final report in May 1864 emphatically stated that "the freedman should be treated at once as any other freeman," subject to no compulsory contracts, no regulation of wage rates, no interference between hirers and hired. The report recognized that some aid was needed, but held that all supervision should be provisional and advisory, for "as much danger lay in doing too much as in doing too little."[37]

Wartime experience also helps to explain the solution that Freedmen's Bureau law proposed—the simple forty-acre allotment with provision for rental, then purchase. Independent land ownership as the ultimate goal for the emancipated slave was a remarkably pervasive concept among northerners interested in his freedom.[38] Perhaps not so remarkably, for land ownership had been the historic trademark of American democracy, the country's approaching industrial greatness had not yet much affected popular concepts, and the traditional goal must have appeared peculiarly appropriate for a class that had been intimately linked with southern agriculture. The problem posed by the land allotment provisions of the Freedmen's Bureau law is not, however, simply that of the origin of the goal of *ultimate* ownership but more particularly the origin of the decision to provide for *immediate* independent cultivation of the land. In part, as has been shown, the decision was a negative one, the subtraction of alternate possibilities leaving this as the remainder. But there were also positive forces that influenced the decision. They came in considerable measure from those closest to the freedmen's wartime problems, including the Negro himself.

General Banks had set aside small lots for the freedmen's use and encouraged them to raise cotton, sugar, and rice, and to save the money earned for the purchase of land. In the antislavery press Banks made known his rancor toward the treasury men who ordered an end to the cultivation of commercial crops on the ground of theft.[39] John Eaton's concern to see the freedmen transformed into independent cultivators was even greater. He recommended that all Negroes able to conduct independent enterprises as lessees should have small farms. Those capable, but without the means of carrying on independently, should receive the needed assistance from benevolent individuals and societies or receive subsistence and incidental aid from the government.[40] Experience convinced him that both groups would be able to make a success of their efforts. A number of Negroes under his jurisdiction were operating as completely independent lessees, and others, some two thousand including the members of their families, were working plantations financed by government subsistence until their crops could be sent to market. Eaton took special interest and pride in the Negro settlement at Davis Bend and successfully battled treasury agents who sought to lease the land to whites.[41] According to a close associate, Eaton desired that "small tracts of land for independent tillage should be assigned to each black family so far as they desired it," and believed "in the early ability of the black to take care of himself," if he were set "on his feet, with land under them." Although Eaton later characterized the bureau law a "make-shift," the only measure on which Congress could agree, his convictions may well have been a factor in the final formulation of its land allotment provision.[42]

Even greater impetus came from the South Carolina coastal region. Gen. Rufus Saxton on the Sea Islands had fought fiercely since December 1862 to gain preemption privileges for the freedmen under his charge. The government's claim to the available lands was based on the nonpayment of direct taxes assessed upon southern as well as northern states by the act of June 7, 1862, and a special tax commission had authority over their disposition. Saxton was never able to win over a majority of the commission, who were intent upon selling the lands at auction. The embattled general marshaled support from Secretary of War Stanton, Secretary of the Treasury Chase, Senator Sumner, and even from President Lincoln himself. At one time, under authority of Lincoln's instructions, Saxton succeeded in helping the freedmen stake out preemption claims that covered almost all the lands in the district. But the tax commission refused to recognize the claims or accept the Negroes' proffered payments; and in the end the commission's will prevailed. By 1865 only a fraction of the Negroes desiring to make land purchases had obtained land ownership.[43]

On December 30, 1864, General Saxton sent a trenchant and bitter review of the Sea Islands developments to Secretary of War Stanton. Some two weeks later, on January 16, 1865, Gen. William T. Sherman after consultation with Stanton issued the famous Field Order No. 15. It was meant to solve the perplexing problem of providing for the numerous bands of Negroes who had followed his army in its march across the South to the Atlantic coast. The order set aside the Sea Islands from Charleston south and the rice lands along the rivers for thirty miles inland for the exclusive use of the Negroes, and provided for their allotment, lease, and sale in forty-acre "homesteads."[44] The freedmen were to be protected in the use of these lands until Congress should regulate their title. Sherman afterward maintained that only temporary provision for the Negroes was intended, and technically provision was made for only a possessory title.[45] But the freedmen quite naturally anticipated permanent possession; and Saxton later testified that he had begged not to be charged with carrying out Sherman's order if the freedmen's expectations were once again to be broken, and that he had received assurances from Secretary Stanton that the Negroes would retain possession of the land.[46]

A most interesting aspect of General Sherman's action was its direct origin in the desires of the Negroes. On January 12, 1865, just four days before his order was issued, Sherman and Stanton met with twenty Negro representatives, ministers, and church members in Savannah. According to the minutes of this meeting, the Negroes were asked how the freedmen could best care for themselves and aid the government in maintaining their freedom. Their spokesman replied: "The way we can best take care of ourselves is to have land, and turn it and till it by our own labor." All the Negro leaders present, except one, preferred separate Negro communities because, in the words of their spokesman, "there is a prejudice against us in the South that will take years to get over." Henry Ward Beecher, who later read from his pulpit the detailed report of the meeting, quoted Stanton as saying that this was the first time in the history of the nation that government officials had gone to the Negroes and asked them what they wanted for themselves.[47] Stanton told Charles Sumner that the order would "electrify the country."[48]

General Sherman's action came during the last stages in the formulation of the Freedmen's Bureau bill. It met approval from both the moderate and the radical press. Even the New York *Herald* called it an "excellent plan," that would prove whether or not the Negro had "any capacity for self-government, any innate industry, any desire to rise in the world."[49] The order, which itself invited congressional action to regulate the land titles, undoubtedly influenced the report of the second conference committee. The distinguished historian of Reconstruction, Walter L. Fleming, in fact refers to the Freedmen's Bureau Act as legalizing Sherman's order.[50] It may well have been a determining factor in the endorsement of a land program by the freedmen's associations, whose members exerted powerful influence upon Congress and were particularly active in lobbying to save the bill after the defeat of the first conference report on February 22.[51] The annual meeting of the National Freedmen's Association overflowed the hall of the House of Representatives on the evening of February 26. The annual report presented to the gathering raised objections to the Freedmen's Bureau bill because it would place too much power in the hands of one man and insisted that the "black man wants no such paternal care, he has had too much protection; all that he asks is justice."[52] This, of course, reflected the same reaction against abuse and excessive control of Negro labor that had been evident in the final report of the Freedmen's Inquiry Commission and in congressional debates. In addition, however, the conference adopted a resolution from the floor that held that permanent relief for the freedmen and their families would be found "in opening large facilities for their occupation and cultivation of the soil in the South."[53]

The final version of the Freedmen's Bureau bill cannot be fully understood without recognizing that during 1864 there was not only widespread concern for the future of the Negro in freedom but also considerable pressure to break up once and for all the large scale agriculture characteristic of the antebellum South. The outstanding exponent of this view in Congress was George Washington Julian, representative from Indiana, who reflected with great intensity the agrarian equalitarianism and hatred of "land monopoly" characteristic of many westerners. Julian had taken an important part in the passage of the Homestead Act, and in Congress he acted as watchdog of the public domain, an inveterate foe of railroad lobbyists and land speculators.[54] In March 1864, he brought before the House a bill to place all confiscated or forfeited lands of the South in the public domain, divide them into forty-acre tracts, and make them available under the Homestead Act on terms that would give preference to men who had served the Union forces, including Negro laborers. His intent was unmistakable.

> The rich lands of the South [he said] have been cursed by this evil land monopoly from the beginning, and without the interposition of Congress the system will be continued and vitalized anew by falling into fresh hands. . . . Of what avail would be an act of Congress totally abolishing slavery, or an amendment of the Constitution forever prohibiting it, if the old agricultural basis of aristocratic power shall remain. Real liberty must ever be an outlaw where one man only in three hundred or five hundred is an owner of the soil.[55]

Julian's southern homestead bill passed the House on May 12, 1864, by a vote of 75 to 64; in the Senate it was reported from committee without amendment but did not come up for discussion before the session ended in July.

Julian's opposition to the continuance of large landed holdings in the South, whether of old planters or of northern capitalists, was shared by others, both in and out of Congress. One of the latter was William Whiting, solicitor of the War Department. His influence is attested by the fact that both Julian in drafting the southern homestead measure and Eliot in framing the original Freedmen's Bureau bill sought Whiting's suggestions.[56] Indeed, a Democratic opponent of the bureau bill named the solicitor as the man responsible for its land provisions and called him "the reservoir of all the Republican heresy and legislation proposed in the House," including the confiscation measures.[57] Whiting was a Massachusetts man with a hatred of the Old South's aristocratic land pattern, and he fervently believed that unless the large estates were broken into small farms the South would develop a semifeudal system based on the hired labor of Negroes and poor whites. A more widely publicized attack upon the plantation system was that of James McKaye made in his report for the American Freedmen's Inquiry Commission. McKaye, like Whiting and Julian, feared the emergence of a system of serfdom and called for a "social reconstruction of the Southern states" that would overthrow the "whole scheme and tenure of the mastership." "No such thing as a free, democratic society can exist," he wrote, "in any country where all lands are owned by one class of men and cultivated by another."[58]

Permanent confiscation of large southern plantations was implied both by Julian's southern homestead bill and by the act establishing the Freedmen's Bureau. This expectation, although never realized, was by no means fanciful in 1864. Provision for forfeiture of rebel real estate was embodied in law by the Confiscation Act of 1862, but had been limited to the natural lifetime of the owner by the accompanying joint resolution. A drive to nullify this limitation won approval both in the House and in the Senate. In February 1864, the House voted to amend the joint resolution so that it would read no forfeiture "contrary to the Constitution," with the expectation that the Supreme Court would uphold a permanent forfeiture.[59] The Senate did not agree to the House bill changing the resolution; but on June 28, by a vote of twenty-three to fifteen, it accepted an amendment made by Sen. Lyman Trumbull of Illinois to the Freedmen's Bureau bill that repealed the joint resolution in its entirety.[60] The Senate action, like that of the House, marked a victory for the policy of permanent confiscation, subject to judicial consent. The Trumbull amendment was retained by the first conference committee, whose report, it will be recalled, was approved by the House but not by the Senate. There is even evidence to suggest that President Lincoln, whose objections had been responsible for the limiting resolution, was then willing to approve its repeal. Eliot so stated during the House debate; and according to Julian's printed recollections, Lincoln told him in July 1864 that he "thought" he would now sign a bill striking at the fee simple.[61] When the Senate's rejection of the conference report made it appear that no Freedmen's Bureau legislation would be enacted before the end of the session, the House rushed through a separate bill repealing the joint resolution. It was carried by a one-vote majority on February 24, 1865.[62]

This action of the House helps to explain a part of the puzzle still unresolved: namely, that the Freedmen's Bureau Act provided for the *sale* of forty-acre allotments and yet at the same time recognized that the United States might never have permanent title to the lands allotted, and specified that they were to be sold with "such title as it could convey." The passage by the House of the separate confiscation bill afforded the final conference committee an opportunity to drop the confiscation section from the Freedmen's Bureau bill, thereby ensuring a unanimous report and strengthening the bill's chance of passage. Four members of the committee had earlier voted for unrestricted confiscation, two members—neither friendly to the Freedmen's Bureau—had voted against it; all six members signed the committee report.[63] It was dated February 28, 1865; just the day before, the Senate Committee on the Judiciary had reported the House bill on confiscation adversely.[64] The wording of the final freedmen's bill suggests that while the minority of the conference committee could take satisfaction in the elimination of the confiscation provision, the majority still hoped that confiscation would become a reality. It is even possible that the inclusion of the phrase, lands acquired "by sale," represented hedging in order to provide a possible means of fulfilling the promise of land should confiscation fail. The last session of the Thirty-eighth Congress ended without a Senate vote on the House-approved confiscation measure.

Senate approval of the Trumbull amendment together with the affirmative House votes, three on confiscation and a fourth on Julian's southern homestead bill, also suggest that a number of the voices approving the Freedmen's Bureau bill were voting not only for the freedmen's future but also against the survival of the plantation system. To say that all who supported the final bill believed they were inaugurating a program of fundamental social-economic reorganization of the agricultural economy of the South would be manifestly false. To deny that such an intent was a factor of some importance would be myopic.

The relation of business and political interests to the Freedmen's Bureau Act deserves attention. A study of the bureau concludes that the purpose behind the law was as much to aid Radical politicians seeking power and northern businessmen seeking profits in the South as to assist the freedman in his transition from slavery.[65] One of the obvious reasons for the change from a *department* to a *bureau*, however, was to minimize the possibility of creating a vast patronage machine, and in practice the bureau was not so operated.[66] The law, moreover, was not a "Radical" measure. The Radicals at this time were identified by their support of full civil rights including voting privileges for the Negro. The more extreme spokesmen of the antislavery movement used the slogan of land, education, and the ballot, but the possibility of national legislation to obtain land ownership for the freedmen was at the time practically ignored by both the Garrison and the Wendell Phillips forces.[67] On the other hand, the idea of land ownership for the freed slave had very general approval; even Sherman's dramatic action had been hailed by moderates. The congressional history both of the Freedmen's Bureau law of 1865 and that of 1866 gives evidence that support of the Freedmen's Bureau was quite as much a mark of moderate as of "Radical" Republicanism.

The land allotment program probably was expected to meet objections based upon the cost to the Treasury of legislation in aid of the freedmen. Democrats were preparing to make the financial question a major political issue, and many Republicans as well were concerned with the country's financial stability in view of the unprecedented wartime expenditures. Rental and sale of southern lands would provide funds to finance the bureau's activities without cost to the taxpayers. Significantly, the Thirty-eighth Congress made no appropriation for the Freedmen's Bureau; it was expected to be self-sustaining.

Although it is reasonable to conclude that congressional decision was influenced by the desire for economy in governmental expenditures, a concern prevalent in the business community but one by no means limited to that group, the narrow economic self-interest that some northern entrepreneurs undoubtedly had in legislation concerning southern lands and laborers was clearly repudiated. The act was designed deliberately to eliminate northern speculation in southern lands and the abuse of Negroes by northern lessees. This should not obscure, however, the important fact that the legislation was not in conflict with the primary interest of northern business, whether mercantile, financial, or manufacturing. The primary interest was the restoration and expansion of cotton culture—more and cheaper cotton.

More and cheaper cotton would give New England manufacturers a share in the markets of India and China and larger sales at home; more and cheaper cotton meant that the United States could recapture control of the world market for raw cotton, a predominance endangered during the war by expanded production in Egypt, Asia Minor, Brazil, and, particularly, India. Cotton exports would build up favorable foreign exchange that would enable payment of the public debt held abroad, would finance increased imports, would support specie payment and deter inflationary currency schemes at home. A prosperous free cotton economy would restore and extend the market for northern products in the South.[68]

Some northern capitalists undoubtedly believed that cotton production required the survival of the plantation and the rigorous control of Negro labor. Others, however, welcomed the breakup of the plantation system and the prospect of land ownership for the Negroes. This was true of Edward Atkinson, Boston cotton manufacturer and humanitarian. In 1861 he had written an influential little pamphlet entitled *Cheap Cotton by Free Labor*. He argued that slavery had limited cotton production and kept cotton prices high, that with free labor cotton would be produced more cheaply and its cultivation extended to large areas of unimproved land in the southern states.[69] Another even more prominent Massachusetts capitalist, John Murray Forbes, took a keen interest in the Sea Islands experiment and urged that the Negroes be provided with land.[70] While not averse to small land holdings for the freedmen, these men envisaged a reorganized cotton culture based predominantly upon either small white freeholdings or benevolent northern enterprise.

Such men as Atkinson and Forbes were not disregardful of the warnings that the freed slave, unused to the expectation of profits, would have little incentive to produce more than the corn and vegetables that would keep him alive. But they had great faith in the effect of schools and education; and they rejoiced at the reports sent from the Sea Islands of the eagerness with which the freedmen purchased northern merchandise. They anticipated that the opportunity to achieve independent cultivation and ownership of land would be a powerful incentive to industry. There is no evidence of the direct influence of northern business leaders in the final formulation of the Freedmen's Bureau Act, but the desire for abundant cheap cotton helps to explain why Congress did not make a *gift* of land to the freedmen. Rental and the opportunity to purchase would provide a powerful incentive for the freed slave to produce the much-wanted cotton. If this served northern businessmen, it certainly did not indicate congressional capitulation to any narrow capitalistic self-interest. Cotton production would serve the interests of the freedmen, the South, and the nation.

Indeed, the rental and purchase provision of the act can be viewed not only as a concession to the economy-minded and to those concerned lest cotton production languish but also as a vindication of faith in the freedmen. His friends had insistently maintained that, given a fair chance, the Negro would show as much capacity as the white man to make his own unaided way. At the time, moreover, the cultivation of cotton was generally assumed to be so profitable an enterprise that it would afford ready access to the higher rungs of the agricultural ladder. True, some believed that the Negro was entitled to southern land in compensation for past exploitation, but there existed as yet little or no apprehension that freedom and opportunity were insufficient guarantees for the Negro's economic future. The possibility of his obtaining a free homestead on the public domain in the South, it should be noted, was not ruled out by the Freedmen's Bureau Act. The whole matter of opening this land for settlement was simply deferred, left for consideration by the next Congress. Thus the controversial question of what preference, if any, should be given former slaves over white settlers was removed—as was the equally controversial matter of permanent confiscation—from the final freedmen's bill.

This suggests a further aspect of the Freedmen's Bureau Act that challenges consideration. It is indicated by the formal title of the bureau, a bureau of *refugees*, freedmen, and abandoned lands, and by the land allotment provision, forty acres to be assigned to "every male citizen, whether *refugee* or freedman." White refugees were included only in the final version of the bill. The report of the first conference committee had been criticized in the Senate, by those very friends of the measure and of the Negro whose votes had killed it, on the ground that it made no provision for loyal white refugees. More particularly, they objected to the possibility that all lands, both abandoned property and public domain in the South, might be bestowed upon freedmen.[71] A decisive number of the Republican senators who voted against the bill on February 22, 1865, were from the agrarian Northwest.[72] There is no evidence to prove beyond doubt that in rejecting the proposal they were mindful of the prejudice of race so widespread among their constituents; yet such a conclusion appears to be a reasonable one.[73] The final version of the act avoided a decision in respect to preferential treatment for freedmen on the public domain in the South, and it opened confiscated lands to settlement by whites as well as by Negroes. And what measure more persuasive than the promise of land could have been taken to forestall an influx of freed Negroes to the North, an influx feared by large numbers of race-conscious eastern laborers and western farmers? What could more effectively answer the charges of extravagance, corruption, and exchanging slavery for government serfdom—all charges used repeatedly by those unfriendly to emancipation and opposed to any government assistance to the freed Negro?

True, the inclusion of whites within the bureau's jurisdiction had its humanitarian aspect. Benevolent organizations had brought to the attention of Congress the plight of the destitute whites who had fled from their homes in the Mississippi Valley, from Atlanta, from the valley of the Shenandoah, from East Tennessee, to miserable places of refuge within the Union lines.[74] During the last days of the congressional session, the president of one of these organizations, the American Union Commission, was lobbying actively in Washington. Shortly thereafter he wrote a most interesting account of the passage of the Freedmen's Bureau Act. He explained that the bill drawn by the first conference committee "was strongly objected to by many because it proposed to create a new *department,* in the *civil* service, with leeway for abuses, and also because it was exclusively for the blacks." The final version "drew to its support many Democratic members, because it was not exclusive. This accounts for the naming of refugees first; and but for this combination no bill for freedmen could have passed the last Congress."[75]

Whether or not the enactment of the Freedmen's Bureau law with its promise of land for the freedman was made possible only by a concession to the "prejudice of race," the decision to put the freed slave on the road to land ownership was essentially a victory not for prejudice, not for self-interest, but for that commitment to freedom and equality inherent in the American heritage. Approval of the forty-acre allotment program, though given hurriedly in the last hours of the Thirty-eighth Congress, grew out of a deliberate legislative search for a plan that would aid the Negro without compromising his new status as free man, would safeguard him against abuse, would foil the selfish designs of northern speculators, and would transform the social-economic organization of the South from a plantation economy to an economy of small, family-owned farms.

PART TWO

The Politics of Equal Citizenship

CHAPTER FOUR

Lincoln and Black Freedom

A central challenge of Reconstruction history can be defined by two questions: first, how did it happen that a racist, white North freed black slaves and made all blacks the equal of whites before the law and at the ballot box? Second, what went wrong? *Lincoln and Black Freedom* focuses on pieces of the puzzle: the actual and potential roles of the presidency, specifically of Lincoln as president; and then, on the limits of the possible—the opportunity, if any, for Republican leaders in the 1860s to have established firmly in practice the equality that they made the law of the land. The focus required a reexamination of Lincoln's presidential record in respect to the status of southern blacks. Lincoln emerged as a consistent, determined friend of black freedom, but a friend whose style of leadership obscured the strength of his commitment—and still does.[1]

In the popular mind the image of Lincoln as Emancipator may endure. Scholarship, though divided on the issue, has cast serious doubt upon its historical validity. More than that of any other historian the work of J. G. Randall, for two decades the leading academic authority on Lincoln, in stripping emancipation of its "crust of misconception" (Randall's phrase) discredited the Emancipation Proclamation and Lincoln as emancipator. His Lincoln acted against slavery without enthusiasm, forced by political and military necessity to issue a paper pronouncement that set no slave free. Though recognizing Lincoln's strong moral judgment against slavery, Randall portrayed Lincoln as more deeply committed to gradualism, compensation, and colonization than to emancipation itself. Randall's views reverberated across college campuses in the arresting prose of two distinguished historians, Richard Hofstadter and Kenneth M. Stampp. According to Hofstadter, the proclamation "had all the moral grandeur of a bill of lading." In Stampp's words, "If it was Lincoln's destiny to go down in history as the Great Emancipator, rarely has a man embraced his destiny with greater reluctance than he." Richard N. Current, who completed Randall's *Lincoln the President* after Randall's death and became a leading authority in his own right, found justification for the title of Emancipator in Lincoln's support for the Thirteenth Amendment, but he let stand Randall's view that expediency had pushed Lincoln the president into an actively antislavery policy. As more recent historical writing increasingly, and validly, presents blacks as active participants in achieving emancipation, Randall's interpretation is implicitly accepted, Lincoln's role diminished, and the popular image of the Emancipator overtly attacked as robbing blacks of credit "for setting themselves free."[2]

The term freedom as I have used it encompasses more than the absence of property rights in men. It includes as well release from the bondage of discrimination imposed by white prejudice through law. More than the reassertion of Lincoln's claim to the title of Emancipator, the conclusion that Lincoln was a friend of black civil and political rights is controversial. Here again the persistence of Randall's influence has been significant. Hostile to abolitionists and Radicals, Randall found and commended contrasting qualities in Lincoln: prosouthern empathy, generosity toward the vanquished, an unqualified priority for speedy restoration of the Union, respect for states' rights, willingness to let the southern people (i.e., white southerners) "solve their own race problem."[3]

Historians writing in the spirit of the civil rights revolution of our time repudiated Randall's prosouthern, anti-Radical bias but generally accepted his characterization of Lincoln's policy. One wrote regretfully that it was difficult to reconcile Lincoln's role "with our own consciences."[4] Current found a way. He enlisted Lincoln on the side of civil rights by holding him up as an example of "man's ability to outgrow his prejudices," citing as evidence the respect with which Lincoln as president treated blacks, notably Frederick Douglass.[5] This was limited reassurance. Other historians discovered a bond between Lincoln and the Radicals, in goal if not in method. A few went so far as to hold that at the time of his death Lincoln was about to align himself with the Radical policy of a broad enfranchisement of southern blacks. That view has not been generally accepted. Indeed, Lincoln's racial attitudes have attracted closer scrutiny than his racial policy.

For a time in the 1960s and 1970s, particularly after Lerone Bennett's charge in *Ebony* that Lincoln was a white supremacist, the Lincoln image seemed in danger of being transformed into a symbol of white America's injustice to black America. Even sympathetic scholarly replies left Lincoln sadly wanting in moral indignation at the racial discrimination that permeated American society, North and South. He was also faulted for lack of thoughtful concern for the future of the freed slaves. By the 1970s another development compromised the Emancipator. Writings on Reconstruction had become sharply critical of federal policy toward southern blacks and traced back to the war years what were seen as its fatal flaws in the postwar era. Lincoln was not the focus of these studies but by implication, and at times by direct accusation, he was held responsible.

The vulnerability of Lincoln's reputation as friend of black freedom in his day, and in the historiography of ours, derives in considerable part from his style of presidential leadership. In dealing with matters affecting the status of blacks it left his purpose and his resolve open to understandable doubt. On occasion he acted boldly. More often, however, Lincoln was cautious, advancing one step at a time, and indirect, exerting influence behind the scenes. He could give a directive without appearing to do so, or even while disavowing it as such. Seeking to persuade, he would fashion an argument to fit the listener. Some statements were disingenuous, evasive, or deliberately ambiguous.

Examples of Lincoln's less than forthright style are familiar, though not always recognized as such. Best known is his response to those urging emancipation during the weeks when he had decided to issue the proclamation but was awaiting a propitious moment. He gave no public indication of his intent, he questioned the efficacy of an executive order, and he wrote the famous reply to Horace Greeley. That letter was skillfully fashioned to deflect criticism from both Radicals and their opponents, but principally the latter. Lincoln stated that what he did, or did not do, about slavery and "the colored race" was determined by what he believed would help save the Union. Later he acknowledged that even as he issued the proclamation he had been uncertain whether it would do more good than harm. The same action might not have been taken by another president, equally committed to saving the Union but of lesser moral conviction that all men everywhere should be free.

Lincoln's decision on the proclamation was not his first decision as president to move against slavery. His earlier offensive also is illustrative of his presidential style. It was behind the scenes in late 1861 that he pressed Delaware to enact a plan of emancipation, drafting alternative bills to guide the state legislature. More open was the initiative that followed in March 1862 when he sent Congress a special message asking passage of a joint resolution promising financial aid to any state that would adopt gradual abolishment of slavery. More open, but not altogether open. He had worked three months on the message—"all by himself, no conference with his cabinet."

Shortly thereafter he confided to Wendell Phillips that he meant slavery "should die," that the message, like the drink slyly requested by the Irishman in legally dry Maine, contained "a drop of the crathur . . . *unbeknown to myself*"; that is, the message was stronger than it appeared to be.[6] A passage therein characterizing the resolution requested of Congress as "merely initiatory" and expressing hope that it "would soon lead to important practical results" had suggested as much but ambiguously.[7] Seeking implementation of the proposal, Lincoln attempted to persuade border-state representatives with assurances and arguments that strain credulity. His basic argument, though fervent, was unrealistic: compensated emancipation by Union slave states would discourage the enemy and shorten the war. If such action were taken, Lincoln told their congressmen, he would countenance no coercive measure against slavery by the federal government. This assurance must not be made public lest it force a quarrel with the Greeley Radicals.

Lincoln followed his initial request with two additional ones to Congress. A special message in July presented the draft of a bill to compensate any state that abolished slavery "either immediately or gradually." In December his annual message included the text of a constitutional amendment to the same end—giving the states until 1900 to act. Ostensibly conservative and deferential to the rights of the states, the proposed amendment held more than a single "drop of the crathur." One provision stated that all slaves "who shall enjoy actual freedom by the chances of war" would be "forever free." Note that for a not inconsiderable number (many slaves were already fleeing to Union lines), freedom would be legalized not by state action but by constitutional amendment. Only loyal owners would be compensated. Although Lincoln expressed, and would continue to express, the judgment that gradual rather than sudden emancipation would be better for all, the amendment he drafted would have sanctioned immediate emancipation. Here was antislavery medicine of stronger proof than its label. A comparable stratagem was embodied in the preliminary Emancipation Proclamation. It offered, or seemed to offer, protective immunity to slavery in the Confederate states if they returned to the Union. The likelihood that any would do so within the one-hundred-day grace period between the two proclamations was practically nil. This was not the only product of Lincoln's pen that appeared to offer more protection to slavery than he was prepared to give.

With the final Emancipation Proclamation issued, Lincoln in early 1863 turned his antislavery effort to occupied Louisiana, again acting indirectly and discreetly. An earlier effort at restoration had led to the election of two

Unionists as congressmen, and they were briefly seated during the last days of the Thirty-seventh Congress. Lincoln made it a point to cultivate them. As Benjamin F. Flanders, one of the two, later reminded Lincoln: "You took me by the hand and said there was a strong effort to break down your administration and asked me to support you. . . . I did it then to the extent of my influence and have ever since."[8] Lincoln used Flanders and his colleague Michael Hahn as conduits to encourage local Union leaders to take an antislavery stance. He dispensed patronage as Flanders, Hahn, and the local Free State leader, Thomas J. Durant, considered necessary in order to carry the state for freedom. Through Sec. Salmon P. Chase, Lincoln not only dispensed such patronage but sought to neutralize the influence of proslavery Unionists. One of their number was appointed to the important post of collector of the New Orleans customhouse with the understanding that his brother-in-law, the owner and editor of an influential proslavery newspaper, would change its editorial policy to one of support for emancipation.

All this, and more, Lincoln did in such a way as to keep an appearance of neutrality and of respect for the right of Louisianians (white) to decide freely the slavery issue. He so adroitly rejected an overture from proslavery Unionists to return Louisiana to the Union with the old slave constitution that their first reaction was disbelief—surely, Lincoln would not refuse readmission to a state because of slavery! They continued to expect that he would make proslavery concessions; so did some Free State leaders. Even to Gen. Nathaniel P. Banks, who had taken over command from Benjamin F. Butler, Lincoln expressed his objective—that is, to end slavery by state action before readmission—as only a wish, something he would be "glad" for Louisiana to do. He admonished, however, that reorganization as a free state be "pushed forward" and completed by the time Congress met in December 1863.[9]

Lincoln acted directly to obtain his goal only when the leader of the Free State movement, and registrar, wrote him in the fall of 1863 that it would not be possible to complete the work of reorganization before Congress met, that public sentiment in occupied Louisiana could not by then be brought to support emancipation. Durant gratuitously added that no harm would come of delay, a conclusion incompatible with Lincoln's fear of political defeat in 1864 with incalculable consequences for the advancement of emancipation. Thereupon Lincoln turned to Banks as commanding general, making him "master of all."

Lincoln's Proclamation of Amnesty and Reconstruction was similarly precipitated by the situation in Louisiana. Its purpose was to hasten the return of Louisiana and other occupied territory as *free* states by removing the condition Lincoln had been understood as desiring, namely a broad geographic and electoral base for reorganization. Now, in order to obtain emancipation, he would accept reconstruction by a small minority, a mere one-tenth of prewar voters. Yet the requirement that slavery be abolished, instead of being explicitly stated in the proclamation, was so worded that Richard Current has recently concluded that "it did no such thing."[10] Lincoln had obfuscated his purpose even while pushing it forward. Yet there is no question but that he was determined to insist on the destruction of the institution of slavery as a prerequisite to readmission. His approval of General Banks's plan to destroy slavery by using military authority to set aside the slavery provisions of the old state constitution and *then* obtaining the consent of voters for the fait accompli—a policy of "consent *and* force"—makes Lincoln's purpose unmistakable.

There is even evidence strongly suggesting that General Banks, with the president's approval, was prepared to set aside the confirming election if won by candidates identified as proslavery. Lincoln's approval of high-handed military action to obtain state sanction of slavery's demise was not limited to Louisiana. He directed Gen. Frederick Steele to follow a similarly manipulative procedure in Arkansas, but there the plan was overtaken by the course of local events.

My favorite example of Lincoln's elusive style is the note he wrote that ensured passage of the Thirteenth Amendment through the House of Representatives on January 31, 1865. The Democratic opposition had been assiduously and secretly undermined by Lincoln's promises of patronage and by Secretary of State William H. Seward's mobilization of an extraordinary lobby, but opposition to the amendment gained last-minute strength from rumors that southern commissioners were on their way to Washington for peace talks. When James Ashley, in charge of the measure on the floor of the House, feared the vote would be lost without a denial of the rumor direct from the president, Lincoln sent a one-sentence response: "So far as I know, there are no peace commissioners in the city, or likely to be in it."[11] Peace commissioners, as he well knew, were on their way—not to "the city" but to Fortress Monroe.

The style of presidential leadership that characterized Lincoln's effort on behalf of freedom is only partially explained by his skill as pragmatic politician. It derived as well from the nature of the man, the goal he sought, and the obstacles to its attainment. The goal and the man were integrally related.

Holding to the principle that all men are created equal and entitled to certain inalienable rights, Lincoln's goal was to realize that principle, to use his own words, "as nearly . . . as we can." The qualification is as critical to an understanding of Lincoln's role as is the objective: "So I say in relation to the principle that all men are created equal, let it be as nearly reached as we can."[12] The words carry no expectation for perfection, no demand for immediate fulfillment. By temperament Lincoln was neither an optimist nor a crusader. Human fallibility, of which he was keenly aware, did not lessen his conviction that in a self-governing society a generally held feeling, though unjust, "can not be safely disregarded."[13] Lincoln would accept what he saw as "necessity," that is, a limitation imposed by realities. He did not, however, submit to necessity with complacency. Characteristic was his query: "Can we all do better?"[14] He stood ready to do more when more could be accomplished.

As Lincoln advanced the nation toward freedom for all, the direction he set was steady; the pace was determined by his political judgment, his sense of timing, and his acute awareness of the constraints under which he labored. Those constraints were formidable. There was the need to preserve the Union and the duty to uphold the Constitution, a constitution that recognized and protected slavery. Both obligations were those of solemn oath and of deep conviction. There was the practical imperative of keeping power out of the hands of an opposition party that would sustain slavery and the political hazard of any step toward equality for blacks in view of the intractable racism pervasive among whites. Fully alert to the force of racial prejudice, Lincoln met it by maneuver and sapping rather than by frontal attack.

War, and the participation of blacks as soldiers, made it possible to "do better." And Lincoln did. Keeping political support intact, he moved from his prewar advocacy of restricting slavery's spread to a foremost responsibility for slavery's total, immediate, uncompensated destruction by constitutional amendment. To borrow the terms used by James MacGregor Burns, Lincoln's presidential leadership was both "transactional" (i.e., a matter of exchange, compromise, deference to majority sentiment) and "transforming" (i.e., a moral leadership that helps achieve needed social change). The title of Emancipator is validated by the consistency of direction evident throughout his presidency, not alone by the Emancipation Proclamation and/or the Thirteenth Amendment, and validated by his skill in seizing the opportunities war opened. Lincoln was not pushed into antislavery action by military and political expediency. He was no reluctant emancipator.

To recognize Lincoln's role as "transforming" leader in no way diminishes that of others—of the forthright abolitionist, the outspoken Radical in Congress, the slave fleeing to precarious freedom, the black soldier fighting with spade and arms (with arms less often than he wished). All were essential participants in the process that led to slavery's destruction. To credit Lincoln is a reminder, however, that presidential leadership can be critically important in effecting social change. It also constitutes recognition of "transactional" skill added to moral purpose as an essential of effective presidential statesmanship. The demise of an entrenched, evil social institution, even after it has become an anachronism, does not automatically follow upon an appeal to conscience; nor did death for the South's peculiar institution follow with inevitability the outbreak of civil conflict.

There is less evidence of Lincoln as friend of black rights than of Lincoln as Emancipator. That evidence, however, conforms to the pattern of Lincoln's style and purpose in dealing with emancipation, and thereby carries weight. Its significance is further enhanced by recognition that Lincoln's first priority was the destruction of slavery, an objective that could be jeopardized by open support for the rights of free blacks. From the distant perspective of a century, victory over slavery may appear to have been inevitable and Lincoln's priority misplaced. To contemporary antislavery spokesmen the outcome as late as mid-1864 was frighteningly uncertain, contingent upon the success of Union forces on the battlefield and of the Republican party in the political arena. Frederick Douglass held that a victory for the Democratic party in 1864 would have been "a fatal calamity," leaving slavery "only wounded and crippled not disabled and killed."[15] Lincoln's concern that slavery be "killed" continued even after passage of the abolition amendment through Congress. His apprehension that the amendment might not be ratified is evident in his very last public address.

Once Lincoln's style and the priority he gave emancipation are recognized, there is no mistaking the fact that he considered the unequal treatment of free blacks an injustice. "Not a single man of your race is made the equal of a single man of ours," he bluntly stated to a group of black leaders upon whom he was urging colonization. He added: "It is a fact, about which we all think and feel alike, I and you."[16] The interpolation has been generally overlooked, for which Lincoln may have been as responsible as the historians who have deleted it. Whether or not he had arranged the interview in order to use colonization as a means of diffusing opposition to emancipation, as many historians now believe, Lincoln's purpose certainly was not the disclosure of his racial attitude. Yet as he indicated to his black audience, Lincoln's emotions as well as his sense of justice were stirred by the inequality to which white prejudice subjected blacks. His feelings are evident in the sardonic response he ordered sent to the man who wrote him that "white men is in class number one and black men is in class number two & must be governed by white men forever." The reply asked whether the writer was a white man or a black one "because in either case you can not be regarded as an entirely impartial judge. It may be that you belong to a third or fourth class of yellow or red men, in which case the impartiality of your judgment would be more apparent."[17] Similarly, Lincoln responded with indignation on learning of the exploitation of freed slaves by lessees of abandoned plantations in the Mississippi Valley. Only matters of utmost import loosened the tight rein Lincoln kept on a display of emotional reaction.

Although the uncertainty of slavery's destruction, the political hazard posed by white racism, and the multitude of wartime demands necessarily left decisive action to the future, Lincoln took steps toward equal status for blacks where he felt it possible to do so. His initiative brought the official diplomatic recognition of two black nations, Haiti and Liberia. In urging colonization upon black Americans, and in directing efforts to find suitable places, he sought assurance from governments that black colonists would be made citizens, legal "equals of the best." Through an official opinion of the attorney general, the Lincoln administration quietly repudiated the Dred Scott dictum that blacks were not citizens and had no rights as such under the Constitution. That opinion was made available to the military governor of Louisiana in August 1863 when, on the president's instruction, he was authorized to register all loyal citizens, an encouragement, though not a directive, to enroll as voters the free blacks of New Orleans. With issuance of the Reconstruction Proclamation in December 1863 Lincoln appeared to rule out black voting in the reorganization of seceded states; in fact, he did not. Publicly he indicated only in general terms that variants from the procedure outlined would be accepted; privately through Secretary Chase he again gave approval for the registration of blacks. Lincoln's actions were generally unknown, discreet, and indirect. Until a free state was established, he left to others the initiative in respect to black enfranchisement.

Louisiana was the one state that provided Lincoln relative freedom to push for more than emancipation. The plan General Banks put into effect was highly irregular and rested upon the military to an extent Lincoln had hoped to avoid, but it gave Louisiana a reorganized, elected government that Lincoln could and did recognize as a free state—that is, one with slavery abolished—before a state convention met to rewrite the prewar constitution. This was not the case in Arkansas or Tennessee. Nine days after the inaugural of Michael Hahn as Free State governor, Lincoln sent him a mere "suggestion"—that the upcoming Louisiana constitutional convention admit some blacks to the franchise, mentioning specifically "the very intelligent," and "those who have fought gallantly in our ranks." Marked "private," the letter was not made generally public, though Governor Hahn used it behind the scenes. Both he and General Banks recognized Lincoln's "mild and graceful" suggestion (Hahn's phrase) for what it was, a directive.[18] Neither man had previously looked with favor on black enfranchisement, at least so soon, yet they pressured members of the convention. Their effort did not succeed in fulfilling Lincoln's wish, but by changing at least twenty votes it reversed a majority decision to forbid ever giving the vote to blacks and in its place obtained a constitutional provision authorizing black enfranchisement on the basis of military service, taxation, or intellectual fitness (the latter an extremely elastic qualification) by simple act of the Louisiana legislature. This limited but not insignificant advance unmistakably was due to Lincoln. Governor Hahn after Lincoln's death (and B. Gratz Brown while Lincoln still lived) attributed the provision to the president. Hahn also credited to Lincoln's influence other constitutional provisions favorable to blacks, the education of all children without distinction of color and the enrollment of all men, black and white, in the state militia. Lincoln's desire that blacks share public education is well documented.

The framing of the Louisiana constitution did not mark the end of Lincoln's interest and influence. He helped mobilize support for ratification of the document by letting "the civil officers in Louisiana, holding under me, know this is my wish," and implied discipline for those who did not "openly declare for the constitution."[19] When Louisiana's representatives came knocking at the doors of Congress, Lincoln privately assured Radicals reluctant to seat them that the administration's influence was being exerted for enfranchisement. William D. Kelley, the Pennsylvania Radical, was among those convinced. Extension of suffrage to blacks "was not a mere sentiment with Mr. Lincoln. He regarded it as an act of justice to the citizens, and a measure of sound policy for the states."[20] Working with Lincoln for Louisiana's admission in the fall and winter of 1864, Banks too gave private assurances. And in his public speeches in New England, the general interpreted the authorization in the Louisiana constitution as "under the circumstances . . . a command."[21] Back in New Orleans, Republican leaders of the Lincoln-Banks faction, both white and black, openly supported black enfranchisement.

Of utmost significance was Lincoln's insistence that Banks return to New Orleans for the express purpose of "advancing the new state government." His return was with "plenary power," to use Secretary of War Edwin M. Stanton's phrase. Lincoln further strengthened Banks's hand by stating publicly in his last address his own desire for qualified suffrage, and did so in such a way as to leave open the possibility of a broad enfranchisement. By the time Banks reached New Orleans Lincoln had been assassinated. At a memorial mass meeting Banks directly assured blacks in the audience that "Abraham Lincoln gave his word that you will be free, and enjoy all the rights invested to all citizens," and that the last day of fulfillment "was not far distant."[22] Listeners recognized that the general was promising enfranchisement. Apparently he expected to succeed by ruthless removals of Conservatives from office (which he began) and by influencing the next elections. He informed Lincoln's successor, Andrew Johnson, that "we can carry an election triumphantly at any time if we are not disturbed [i.e., not disturbed in ousting hostile officeholders]." Even the question of Negro suffrage, he stated, would then be settled "without involving the Administration in any trouble, and satisfactorily to the country."[23] President Johnson did not leave General Banks undisturbed. Instead of sustaining the general, Johnson dismissed him from command.

Lincoln's support for black suffrage is sometimes minimized as limited to suffrage for only the black elite. This was not the case. Lincoln recognized, and used, military service as the most persuasive argument for extending the franchise. Most black privates could not sign their names. Nor did Lincoln restrict his encouragement for black suffrage to Louisiana. Chase did not understand as limited to that state the presidential approval for black voting during the process of reorganization. Banks believed Lincoln meant enfranchisement in Louisiana to be a model for other states. B. Gratz Brown cited Lincoln's pressure on Louisiana as an argument for extending suffrage to blacks in Missouri. Moreover, we now know that in December 1864 Lincoln was ready to accept Reconstruction legislation that would admit Louisiana with its 1864 constitution but require other returning states to include black suffrage in theirs. Although the extent of enfranchisement Lincoln desired is a matter of some uncertainty, my conclusion is that he was ready to go at least as far as the majority in Congress. With the Radicals unable to obtain any such legislation by the time Congress adjourned in March 1865, Banks's mission indicates Lincoln's intent to use executive power to obtain whatever was possible at the state level. In short, Lincoln was still looking to realize the principle of equality "as nearly . . . as we can."

No student of history can with confidence fault Lincoln's political judgment of what was attainable in the 1860s, or how best he could achieve the maximum possible. The distance between the dominant racial sentiment of Lincoln's day and that of our own is too great. As late as October 1864 the electorate of Maryland, except for the soldier vote, would have rejected emancipation and celebrated not the end of slavery but the "Death Knell of Abolitionism."[24] The best that could be obtained from Unionist Missouri in 1863 was emancipation as of July 4, 1870, with continuing servitude for those over forty during their entire lifetime and for those over twelve until they reached twenty-three. Immediate and unconditional emancipation was established in Missouri only after Lincoln's death, in June 1865. In the free North white opposition to equal status for blacks suffered erosion during the course of the war, but remained tenacious. In August 1862 Illinois voters rejected a new constitution as a whole but overwhelmingly approved provisions that would have enshrined in the state's constitution prohibitions against any Negro migrating into the state and against any resident Negro voting or holding office. Before the war only four states, all in New England, provided equal suffrage. No others extended this right to blacks during the war years. In the fall of 1865 Republican attempts to do so in Connecticut, Wisconsin, and Minnesota failed in referendum voting.

The time has come to disengage Lincoln from the present and let the historic record speak for itself. To do so will diminish neither the man nor the tasks that remain before us to attain racial justice. Without hazard we can relinquish Lincoln as a mirror of the present and beacon to the future, whether of guidance or of warning. Grant that his circumspect style of presidential leadership as an instrument to reach equality irrespective of race offers no acceptable model for the present, since forthright advocacy from the oval office can now mobilize a national consensus to this end. Grant that the achievements beyond abolition that Lincoln nurtured, though essential, are insufficient for the 1980s. But let us take care to recognize that Lincoln's record as friend of freedom is impressive—that it was no reluctant concession to the pressures of a grim war, or the expediency of politics.

To summarize: Lincoln let war come rather than retreat on the expansion of servitude. Within a year of the war's beginning he determined that slavery "should die." Nine months later he boldly proclaimed as a war measure emancipation for the slaves of loyal and disloyal alike in areas of rebellion. He did so though uncertain whether the Emancipation Proclamation would strengthen, or weaken, the Union war effort. By mid-1863 he was ready to deny readmission to any state unwilling to abolish the institution. In order to force state action in occupied territory he boldly employed the power of patronage plus that of military authority—the latter without the covering justification of military necessity. Refusing to let freedom rest solely upon the precarious authority of presidential proclamation and congressional legislation, or upon the uncertainty of state action, Lincoln succeeded in obtaining passage of the abolition amendment. Meanwhile he had officially recognized blacks as citizens and used the weight of his high office in an effort to set former slaves on the road to equality through access to the ballot box.

On the most divisive issue this nation has ever faced, the status of black Americans, Lincoln's presidential record stands without need of myth, apology, or transformation into symbolism. The preeminent meaning of Lincoln the president lies in the historic substance of his role as a friend of black freedom. It is a meaning sufficient for all time.

CHAPTER FIVE

Andrew Johnson and His Ghost Writers
An Analysis of the Freedmen's Bureau and Civil Rights Veto Messages

No other decisions of Andrew Johnson's political career held such momentous consequences for himself and for the nation as did his first two presidential vetoes. His rejection of the Freedmen's Bureau bill on February 19, 1866, and of the civil rights bill on March 27, marked the beginning of a conflict between president and Congress that was to prove irreconcilable. The bitter consequences did not end with the spectacle of impeachment nor even with the tragic years of struggle over Reconstruction and restoration in the defeated South. One of the central issues, the question of the Negro's civil rights, was to pass unresolved to twentieth-century America. In the 1860s the nation lost an opportunity to establish a firm foundation for equal citizenship with moderation and a minimum of rancor. The manner in which Johnson took action against the two bills—the advice he accepted and the advice he rejected—is of paramount importance in understanding the conflict that ensued and the failure to achieve an early solution of the civil rights problem.

Johnson had the help of a number of counselors. In the manuscript messages of the Johnson Papers, deposited with the Library of Congress more than half a century ago, there are five draft papers for the first veto message, four for the second veto. No analysis of these working papers, no attempt to identify their origins, has hitherto been made; this is true despite the startling discovery by William A. Dunning long ago that Johnson's first annual message was written by the eminent scholar and Democrat, George Bancroft.[1]

Knowledge of Bancroft's role, however, was not the impetus that led us to trace the authorship of the several drafts of the veto messages. The point of departure was a disturbing sense of the familiar about some of the manuscripts. The familiarity lay not in the script, for the writing was obviously in the hand of a copyist, and more than one; it was rather in the type of paper and the distinctive manner of its use. One of the drafts for each of the two veto messages—and for Johnson's annual messages as well—was written on long, lined, legal-type paper, often with a small hole in the upper left corner as for a file or ring. The copyists had used the sheets with lavish extravagance, leaving wide margins and skipping every other line, apparently with a view to facilitating emendations. The corrections were in a different handwriting; indeed, in more than one variant from the copyists' script.

These were characteristics seen before—at the University of Rochester Library, in the collection of manuscripts of William H. Seward. A check of other evidence corroborated Seward's authorship. At least some of the changes written between the copyists' lines were unquestionably made by Seward's own hand. Interestingly, these particular drafts were filed first or second among the working papers for each message, a not unnatural priority for the suggestions of the Secretary of State. Furthermore, the substance of the December 1865 draft in the Johnson Papers at the Library of Congress corresponded with that of a less-finished draft in the Seward manuscripts at Rochester. A final confirmation of Seward's authorship was the emphasis upon foreign affairs in his versions of the 1865 and 1866 annual messages.

This discovery quickened our curiosity with respect to the other working papers for Johnson's first two veto messages. Would it be possible to identify the men other than Seward whose counsel Johnson had welcomed during the critical period of the president's break with Congress? The search for handwriting specimens that would correspond with each of the seven unidentified veto papers was exciting, and exhausting. In the end, all but one were identified. The identifications were made on the basis of handwriting, but in a number of instances additional evidence supported the findings.

For the nine papers, there proved to have been seven authors. Secretary of the Navy Gideon Welles, like Secretary Seward, had furnished a draft for each of the vetoes.[2] Two of the drafts, both for the Freedmen's Bureau message, had come from loyal Republican supporters of President Johnson in the Senate: James R. Doolittle of Wisconsin and Edgar Cowan of Pennsylvania.[3] Another of the papers, a digest of the civil rights bill rather than an argument for its veto, came from Sen. Lyman Trumbull of Illinois, the author of both bills. These identifications are not surprising in view of the position of each man, though it was curious to find Senator Doolittle supplying arguments for the veto of a bill that he had supported in the Senate.[4] More surprising was the identification of Henry Stanbery as the author of a draft message for the second veto. An able Ohio attorney and former Whig conservative, Stanbery at the time of the Civil Rights veto had not yet become identified with Johnson's administration. He had been called to Washington, however, to help represent the government in the famous Milligan case that was argued before the Supreme Court during the second week of March, and by mid-March he was being recommended confidentially for the cabinet post of Attorney General by Johnson's close political adviser, Thomas Ewing, with whom Stanbery as a young man had begun the practice of law.[5]

With the papers identified, except for one draft of the Freedmen's Bureau veto, we began a comparison of the drafts with the final versions of the two messages. For the Freedmen's Bureau veto there were the drafts written by Secretary Seward, Secretary Welles, Senator Doolittle, Senator Cowan, and the unidentified draftsman. In addition to these five, we considered another statement of objections to the bill, filed not in the volume of messages but with the president's incoming mail. It had been sent by young Gen. Joseph S. Fullerton of the Freedmen's Bureau, as his accompanying note makes clear, in reply to the president's "verbal request."[6]

Secretary Seward's draft for the Freedmen's Bureau veto is written in the first person, as if it were meant to be used verbatim for the official message. Although seventy-four pages long, it is relatively brief in substance. Much of its length is accounted for by the widely spaced lines of the writing and the extended summary of both the original act establishing the bureau and the proposed law to continue and extend it. Seward's objections to the content of the bill are limited, and much of his argument is devoted to the point that the new legislation is unnecessary. Secretary Welles's paper is headed "Objections," and in four pages it enumerates and expounds six arguments against the bill. For the most part, it is a criticism of the bill's provisions for trials before bureau officers. Senator Doolittle's contribution, "Suggestions of Objections to the Freedmen's Bureau Bill," fills fourteen pages with a lengthy exposition of numerous objections. Several printed clippings are inserted, particularly to buttress its legal arguments. Senator Cowan's objections, nine in all, are more succinctly stated in three pages of small, neat writing. The unidentified draftsman, as Seward had done, used the first person pronoun, and, like Seward, incorporated lengthy extracts from the bill. But the arguments he proposed against the measure in his fifteen-page exposition are more numerous and varied than those proposed by the Secretary of State. Unlike the other papers, this draft deals extensively with the status of the Negro under freedom and with the rights of the states.

A careful textual comparison of each of the six papers with Johnson's veto message on the Freedmen's Bureau bill shows that sentences and passages have been lifted virtually intact from two of the drafts, those of Seward and Welles.[7] The borrowings from Secretary Welles appear in the first part of the message and condemn trials before Freedmen's Bureau officials as lacking in regular judicial procedure and constitutional safeguards for the protection of the innocent. Selections from Seward's draft, some limited to a few phrases and others consisting of extensive passages, appear in various parts of the message. In the two longest, Seward argued that there was no need for new legislation since the existing Freedmen's Bureau law was still in effect and gave the bureau powers adequate for the protection of freedmen and refugees. About twice as much wording was taken from Seward as from Welles.

These verbal borrowings, though noteworthy, constitute only a small part, roughly a fifth, of the substance of the message. A quite different proportion of borrowing, however, is evident in the argument, as distinguished from the wording, of the official message. Most of the basic ideas can be found in one or more of the working papers, although the elaboration of the ideas in the final message often varies considerably. In fact, there is not one of the papers that might not have been used to fashion some part of the official version.

Specific examples of parallel arguments in the working papers are numerous. The argument that trials by other than the regularly constituted judiciary are unconstitutional in time of peace appears not only in Welles's draft but also in those of Senator Cowan, Senator Doolittle, and the unidentified draftsman. Interestingly, the constitutional aspect was not raised by Seward, though he did question the policy of using military tribunals "except on occasions of imperative and absolute necessity" raised by present or imminent war, invasion, or rebellion. The argument that the bill provided for a permanent or indefinite special agency to protect the freedmen, an objection technically correct but misleading, appears in four of the drafts. Senator Cowan and the unidentified draftsman held that there existed in the federal government no power to purchase or rent lands for the benefit of freedmen. The latter, together with General Fullerton, emphasized the class nature of the legislation. Fullerton, Doolittle, and Seward all called attention to the great expense that the bill would impose upon the national government. The first two also pointed with alarm to the immense patronage that the bill allegedly would place in the hands of the president. The unidentified draftsman also used the argument that the freedman would find protection in his value as a laborer and in his right to change residence freely. Five of the writers, Seward only excepted, made a special attack against section 5 of the bill, which extended for three years the right of freedmen to occupy land on the coast and adjacent islands of South Carolina and Georgia, which they held under a wartime order of Gen. William T. Sherman. All these points were incorporated into the president's message; they do not exhaust the parallels between the drafts and the official message, but they are sufficient to indicate Johnson's indebtedness.

The official message did not, of course, include all the suggested arguments, and the omission of some is of particular interest. Johnson did not adopt the argument by the unidentified draftsman, denying unequivocally the power of the national government and asserting the exclusive authority of the states in the area of natural rights, civil rights, race relations, education, and relief. Except to prohibit slavery and insure freedom to change residence, according to this argument, the federal government had no right to extend special protection to the freedmen; it could not compel states "to give to all people equal rights either over the law or under it"; it could not provide relief, schools, or asylums. Senator Doolittle's exposition was more restrained, but he argued similarly that by the Thirteenth Amendment the states had not granted to Congress any power over "their cherished and sacred right of exclusive government over their own citizens in all matters of domestic concern." Senator Cowan objected to the bill's placing the "negroes upon the same footing precisely as the whites as to all *civil rights and immunities*," and to this end overriding all state laws. There is good reason to assume that President Johnson privately shared the opposition to federal enforcement of civil rights and the solicitude for the reserved powers of the states. These arguments, however, were not used in the message.

One explanation is suggested by the fact that there are no similar arguments in the Seward draft. In fact, the Secretary of State recognized a responsibility on the part of the federal government. It was his opinion that "Freedmen who were emancipated by the nation as a means of suppressing the civil war are entitled to national protection until the country shall have resumed its normal and habitual condition of repose." Indeed, his draft would have the president promise to support in the future a new bill to continue the Freedmen's Bureau beyond the time limit set by existing law if its extension should prove necessary for the protection of the freedmen, an objective that Seward referred to as a "proper" one. The secretary's attitude was a very mild version of the opinion that predominated at that time among moderate as well as Radical Republicans. We can only speculate that the influence of this cautious and conciliatory Republican helped to restrain Johnson from embodying in the official message statements that would have been offensive to the Republican congressional majority.

References in the president's message to the subject of federal enforcement of civil rights appear to have been carefully worded. The president shared "with Congress the strongest desire to secure to the freedmen the full enjoyment of their freedom and property, and their entire independence and equality in making contracts for their labor." But he expressed no desire to share the congressional intent to establish a federal guarantee for these rights, or to interpret them as including *all* rights, exclusive of suffrage, belonging to white persons. He observed that the bill would subject white persons who violated its civil rights provisions to punishment "without, however, defining the 'civil rights and immunities' which are thus to be secured to the freedmen." Although the bill had not attempted to make a definitive statement of civil rights, it had specified a long list of rights as included within the phrase "civil rights or immunities belonging to white persons." Those named were: "the right to make and enforce contracts, to sue, be parties, and give evidence, to inherit, purchase, lease, sell, hold and convey real and personal property, and to have full and equal benefit of all laws and proceedings for the security of person and estate, including the constitutional right of bearing arms [and of not being] subjected to any other or different punishment, pains, or penalties, for the commission of any act or offence than are prescribed for white persons."[8]

The President did not comment on this impressive listing. As for the respective power of the states and of the nation, the message stated that "Undoubtedly the freedman should be protected, but he should be protected by the civil authorities, especially by the exercise of all the constitutional powers of the courts of the United States and of the States." There was no clarification of what President Johnson considered "the constitutional powers" of the federal courts. His later argument that the southern states had a right to participate in legislation affecting them, and that with southern representatives present Congress would still have "full power to decide according to its judgment," may imply that the president believed that federal authority was adequate to legislate concerning civil rights for Negroes. On this point, however, the message was conveniently indefinite.

Another significant feature of the message was the omission of any statement that might be considered a commendation of the past services of the Freedmen's Bureau. Secretary Seward's draft was explicit in recognizing the "usefulness" of the bureau, that it had been "administered with becoming care and fidelity," and that the original act establishing the bureau had been "just, wise and conformable to public law." His draft included a promise to accept and even recommend a new Freedmen's Bureau bill if circumstances should necessitate the continuance of its functions. Seward expressly interpreted the wording of the original law, which stated that the bureau was to function during the war "and for one year thereafter," as meaning that the bureau would be in operation for a full year after the war had been terminated legally by formal announcement. Since neither Congress nor the president had yet issued such a proclamation, Seward's draft insured to the bureau at least twelve more months of operation. Johnson's message merely stated that the act establishing the bureau "has not yet expired." The omission of this part of the Seward draft was probably a concession to the Democracy and the South, since the president's Democratic supporters, North and South, viewed the bureau as an odious agency and were demanding its swift and irrevocable termination.

Decisions to omit, like decisions to include, specific material from the drafts reveal an awareness of political expediency, as well as considerable political astuteness. Clearly a very competent hand other than that of the authors of these drafts had a large measure of responsibility for the organization, elaboration, and phrasing of the veto. The message was no mere scissors-and-paste montage of the six papers. To know with certainty Johnson's own role in the final formulation of the message is not possible, but there is substantial basis for speculation. During his presidency, Johnson seldom used pen or pencil; in the vast collection of manuscripts he preserved there is little more than a few brief endorsements in his own hand. This reticence has been attributed to a broken arm that Johnson suffered in an accident in 1857; it may also have arisen from a sense of inadequacy due to his late and labored mastery of the skill of writing.

Whatever the explanation, there is nothing to suggest that Johnson sat down with paper and pen to compose this or other messages, and there is considerable evidence to the contrary. He had intrusted to George Bancroft the writing of the critically important first annual message to Congress. Some other evidence exists, also, about presidential papers prepared subsequent to the first two veto messages. According to the shorthand diary of his private secretary, Maj. William G. Moore, the veto of the District of Columbia Negro suffrage bill of January 1867 "was entirely prepared in the office." The final paragraph, which "the President had prepared," was replaced by one written by Henry Stanbery, then Attorney General, and "revised by the President." The veto of the first Reconstruction act was the work partly of Jeremiah S. Black, the influential Pennsylvania Democratic politician, partly of the Attorney General. According to the same source, Johnson asked Secretary of State Seward to prepare a general amnesty proclamation in July 1868, then carefully scrutinized Seward's draft with his private secretary, asked the advice of the prominent Democratic senator Reverdy Johnson, of Secretary of the Navy Welles, and of Attorney General Orville H. Browning, consulted again with Seward and with his private secretary, and finally directed Moore to make certain changes.[9]

As all this suggests, Johnson did not personally write his official papers, but they were very much his own. That he took particular care in preparing the Freedmen's Bureau message is quite evident. It was his first veto, and he delayed the message until almost the end of the period constitutionally permitted for presidential consideration. In the interval he had obviously invited opinions from a number of sources. A second seven-page letter from General Fullerton answering a request for additional information with respect to bureau costs is evidence of Johnson's special interest in that aspect of the argument.[10] Shorthand notations on the draft by Secretary Welles indicate that Johnson went over at least that paper with his private secretary, but there is no evidence to suggest that he actually dictated the content of the final version. The most likely assumption is that he turned over the six drafts to his office staff, or to some trusted intimate of more stature, with oral instructions for deletions, modifications, and additional objections. We can be reasonably certain that not only the major arguments but even the most oblique passages received his scrutiny and approval.

Some significant passages in the message appear in no one of the six drafts, and they may reflect in a special sense Johnson's own attitudes and position. One such passage is the argument against those sections of the proposed law that authorized grants to the freedmen for the relief of suffering, the rental and purchase of land for their benefit, and the building of schools and asylums. Johnson's opposition to the proposal is less revealing than are some parts of his argument, particularly the phrases we have italicized:

> It [Congress] has never deemed itself authorized to expend the public money for the rent or purchase of homes for *the thousands, not to say millions of the white race, who are honestly toiling from day to day for their subsistence.* A

system for the support of indigent persons in the United States was never contemplated by the authors of the Constitution; nor can any good reason be advanced why, as a permanent establishment, it should be founded for one class or color of our people more than another.

Here is either a deliberate appeal to race prejudice and to the self-interest of whites against the grant of special federal assistance to Negroes, or an unwitting reflection of racial antipathy on the part of the president. Subsequent passages argue not only that the freedmen are capable of taking care of themselves because of the demand for their labor, but that the provisions of the bill would keep them "in a state of uncertain expectation and restlessness," and that such treatment for the freed Negroes would be "a source of constant and vague apprehension" to "those among whom he lives." Johnson also expressed the opinion that freedmen should establish and maintain "their own asylums and schools." That is to say, not the entire population of local southern communities but the Negroes themselves were expected to pay for the education of their children and the support of their aged and poor. Thus the friendly interest in protecting the freed Negro and insuring his future, which the president explicitly stated in the message, was delimited in a manner that reflected the prejudice of race and the self-interest of whites. In the unborrowed passages of the final version, the turn of a phrase here and there significantly affected the generally restrained tone and unemotional arguments of the message. Such changes, either in phrasing or in the elaboration of the argument, may have reflected both the inner tension with which Johnson faced the race problem and an acute sensitivity to the political implications of racial attitudes. Without directly challenging those who believed in equal civil status for the Negro and national responsibility for its attainment, the message seems designed to allay the fears of friendly southerners and northern Democrats to whom racial equality or national guardianship of the freedmen was anathema.

The one major objection to the Freedmen's Bureau bill that was distinctively the president's own contribution is found at the end of the message. The essential argument was that under the Constitution all states are entitled to a voice in legislation, that southern states were not represented in Congress at the time of discussion of the bill, and—an obiter dictum—that the authority of Congress to judge the qualifications of its members "cannot be construed as including the right to shut out, in time of peace, any State from the representation to which it is entitled by the Constitution." The obiter dictum constituted a challenge to the Congress, a virtual declaration of war. Secretary Seward's draft, it is true, had raised the issue of restoration and many of Seward's phrases and sentences are incorporated in this part of the text. Seward undoubtedly favored the speedy restoration of the South, but his draft did not challenge the constitutional authority of Congress to "shut out" southern representation. Johnson's own imprint can be seen here in his use of the phrase "no taxation without representation," a principle he had explicitly stated a few days earlier during an interview with a delegation from the Virginia legislature.[11] In other words, Johnson rather than any of the six advisers was directly responsible for the most explosive part of the veto message. But this is not to say that the denial to Congress of any right to set conditions preliminary to the readmission of the southern states was at all original with the president. This view had for months been the position of Democratic spokesmen and their party press. In the Freedmen's Bureau veto, however, Johnson officially adopted it, expounded it at length, and in effect held it to be the only tenable principle with respect to Reconstruction.

It is significant that no one of the president's major Republican consultants in the group of identified draftsmen, nor even the unidentified draftsman (whose party affiliation is unknown, although he was clearly a strong supporter of state rights) had suggested for inclusion in the veto so sweeping a challenge to congressional authority. It is even possible that Seward's version indicated an effort on the part of the Secretary of State to modify Johnson's intentions. The relationship between the two was of so constant and intimate a nature that it is altogether likely that Johnson had discussed his ideas for the message with Seward before the secretary began his writing. Seward's draft presented the president's view of the right of the seceded states to be represented in Congress, but presented it without denying to Congress the right to a differing opinion. The bombshell that Johnson exploded in the concluding paragraphs of his veto, and that precipitated a disastrous war between Congress and the executive, was not designed in accordance with the principles and desires of the party in power but followed instead those of the government's "loyal opposition."

Johnson also added a strong statement about presidential responsibilities and an implied challenge to Congress to take the issues raised by the veto to the voters of the country for decision. He described the president's role in the following passage: "The President of the United States stands towards the country in a somewhat different attitude from that of any member of Congress. Each member of Congress is chosen from a single district or State;

the President is chosen by the people of all the States. As eleven States are not at this time represented in either branch of Congress, it would seem to be his duty, on all proper occasions, to present their just claims to Congress." This is a curious statement to come from a chief executive who had been elected not to the presidency but to the vice-presidency, and at a time when the eleven southern states had no political voice in the national government because of their own decision to reject its authority. The statement suggests not the role that history had cast for the Tennessee president but the position of national leadership to which he aspired. The implied challenge to Congress appeared in the conclusion of the message: "I return the bill to the Senate, in the earnest hope that a measure involving questions and interests so important to the country will not become a law, *unless upon deliberate consideration by the people it shall receive the sanction of an enlightened public judgment.*"[12] The italicized passage again suggests Johnson's desire to supplant the Republican Congress in the role of spokesman for the national interest.

One of the most important conclusions that emerges from the identification and examination of the drafts for the Freedmen's Bureau veto is that, despite a loyal personal and political relationship and agreement upon a general policy of conciliation, a marked difference of political approach existed between Secretary of State Seward and President Johnson. In his draft of the presidential message, Seward ignored or minimized constitutional issues, he included nothing that suggested an acceptance of or an appeal to race prejudice and refrained from criticizing provisions of the bill intended to aid the former slave in adjusting to his new economic status. He had an appreciative word for the Freedmen's Bureau, assured to it a further year of existence, and left open its possible continuance thereafter. With respect to Congress and its role in Reconstruction, Seward offered conciliation, Johnson demanded surrender. Although he used what Seward had written in this connection, Johnson shifted the order and emphasis, creating a message of a very different tone from that of the Seward draft. A comparison of the following passages illustrates the difference.

Seward	*Johnson*
I am pleased to see that the bill contemplates a full restoration of the several states which heretofore were in rebellion in all their constitutional relations to the United States but is	I would not interfere with the unquestionable right of Congress to judge, each house for itself, "of the elections, returns and qualifications of its own members." But that authority

vague and uncertain in defining the conditions which will be accepted as evidence of that full restoration. It is hardly necessary for me to inform the Congress that in my own judgment most of those states so far at least as depends upon themselves have already been thus fully restored and are to be deemed as entitled to enjoy their constitutional rights as members of the Union. Since Congress now proposes to make so important a proceeding as the prolongation of the Freedmen's Bureau dependent upon a restoration in some sense which differs from the one entertained by the Executive Department it would seem to be important that Congress and the President should first agree upon what actually constitutes such restoration. . . .

Without trenching upon the province of Congress I may be permitted in explaining my own course on the present occasion to say that when a state however insubordinate insurgent or rebellious its people may have been at some previous time comes not only in an attitude of loyalty and harmony but in the persons of representatives whose loyalty cannot be questioned under any existing constitutional or legal test that in this case they have a claim to be heard in Congress especially in regard to projected laws which bear especially upon themselves.

cannot be construed as including the right to shut out, in time of peace, any State from the representation to which it is entitled by the Constitution. . . .

I hold it my duty to recommend to you, in the interests of peace and the interests of union, the admission of every State to its share in public legislation, when, however insubordinate, insurgent, or rebellious its people may have been, it presents itself not only in an attitude of loyalty and harmony, but in the persons of representatives whose loyalty cannot be questioned under any existing constitutional or legal test. . . .

The bill under consideration refers to certain of the States as though they had not "been fully restored in all their constitutional relations to the United States." If they have not, let us at once act together to secure that desirable end at the earliest possible moment. It is hardly necessary for me to inform Congress that in my own judgment most of those States, so far at least as depends upon their own action, have already been fully restored, and are to be deemed as entitled to enjoy their constitutional rights as members of the Union.

Seward loyally supported the president in the veto; but had the president adopted his draft, the message would have been a document of considerably greater political finesse.

Congress was not sufficiently united against Johnson in February 1866 to override his veto. The next month, however, Congress passed a new measure, the civil rights bill, which he vetoed and thereby consolidated Republican opposition. Once again Johnson had advice in the preparation of his veto message. The working papers for this message are easier to collate and compare with the final message than in the case of the earlier veto. There are but four such papers, and the one written by Sen. Lyman Trumbull contains no material in support of a veto but presents merely a digest and explanation of the bill. It is significant chiefly as an authoritative statement of the intent of Congress to protect all citizens, especially Negroes, against hostile local legislation, but not to bestow the right of voting or of officeholding. It also corroborates the generally recognized fact that Senator Trumbull in sponsoring the measure sought the cooperation of the president. The other three papers are arguments against the bill. They are the work of Secretary Seward, of Secretary Welles, and of Henry Stanbery. The Ohio attorney, not at the time a member of the president's official family, was four months later to replace James Speed as Attorney General. Unlike the Freedmen's Bureau veto, most of the civil rights message—something more than 80 percent of the writing—was lifted verbatim from the working papers with only minor editing. About 12 lines were taken from Secretary Welles's paper, approximately 135 from Seward's, and some 240 from that of Stanbery. Only two passages of any length and consequence in the final version were newly prepared.

The extant drafts by Seward and Stanbery, both written in the presidential first person, contain numerous penciled markings on the margins and the body, as well as minor changes in phraseology inserted above the lines. These markings are easy guides to the manner in which the two papers were edited and pieced together to form the finished message. Much more of Stanbery's contribution was incorporated than of Seward's—roughly, 60 percent of the former and somewhat better than a third of the latter. Interestingly, shorthand notations appear between the lines of Seward's draft in the midst of passages that were not included in the presidential veto. They indicate that even those parts of Seward's paper that the president finally rejected had received his close scrutiny and consideration.

As with the earlier veto, the most significant conclusion reached from a comparison of the drafts with the official message is that Secretary Seward and President Johnson differed notably in their approach toward the proposed legislation. Indeed, the difference is considerably greater than on the earlier measure. Despite his extensive borrowings from the secretary, Johnson rejected the essence of Seward's recommendations with respect to civil rights legislation. Unlike Seward's draft, the whole tone of the president's message was not conciliatory, but hostile, as were the drafts prepared by Welles and Stanbery.

Seward's draft explicitly approved the general policy or object of the bill, "to secure all persons in their civil rights without regard to race or color." He made clear his opposition to the discriminations that the bill sought to make illegal. Objecting to certain aspects of the enforcement provisions, Seward in effect invited Congress to reframe those sections, but in a manner that would still provide effective review by the federal judiciary to enforce, within the states, civil equality for the Negro. He tried to put at rest the apprehension that the bill would jeopardize state control over suffrage and officeholding qualifications; these matters would be "left precisely as if the bill were not enacted into law." In support of congressional action on civil rights, exclusive of suffrage, Seward found a firm constitutional basis in the privileges and immunities clause of the original Constitution and in the enforcement clause of the Thirteenth Amendment. He approved of the passage that declared all native-born Americans to be citizens of the United States, although he found no express power vested in Congress for such a declaration. The courts, Seward confidently anticipated, would sustain this definition of citizenship for the Negro either by upholding the congressional declaration or by finding it to have been unnecessary. If the latter, "no harm will have been done"; if the former, the declaration would prove both "wise and useful."

In contrast, President Johnson raised a "grave question" as to the desirability of bestowing citizenship upon the emancipated slaves. In a long passage that appears in none of the drafts, he questioned whether the newly emancipated freedmen possessed "the requisite qualifications to entitle them" to citizenship and stated, in effect, that a bestowal of citizenship upon the Negro would constitute a discrimination in favor of black men as against "large numbers of intelligent, worthy and patriotic [presumably, white] foreigners."

With respect to equal civil rights, Johnson's message followed Stanbery's draft. Without directly repudiating the goal of civil equality, the passage upholds the practice and the right of states to pass discriminatory legislation and interjects the emotion-laden question of mixed marriages. It raises the politically explosive subject of Negro voting, by arguing that if Congress had authority, as assumed in the bill, to override local and state legislation it also had the power to declare who should be juror, judge, and voter. Again using Stanbery's words, Johnson declared that "the distinction of race and color is, by the bill, made to operate in favor of the colored and against the white race."

In short, Johnson, unlike Seward, expressed an attitude on racial issues in conflict with that embodied in the bill, one congenial to the feeling of northern Democrats and southerners. A brief shorthand notation beside a passage in Seward's draft suggests that the president's attitude was in part a conscious propitiation of racial prejudice. Seward had written that it belonged to Congress "to provide by legislation proper measures, when necessary, to secure to citizens of the United States anywhere, the rights which the Constitution guarantees." The shorthand, apparently a jotting down of Johnson's comment, reads "inexpedient."[13]

The message, again following Stanbery's draft, stated that the president did "not propose to consider the policy of this bill." The whole tenor of the veto, however, belied the assertion and offered strong evidence of Johnson's lack of sympathy for the basic objectives of the bill. Although he did not directly analyze the question of constitutional authority for congressional civil rights legislation, Johnson interpolated near the end of the veto an incisive passage from Secretary Welles's draft, one completely at variance with Seward's position. It condemned the bill's provisions as contrary to state rights and the nature of the federal Union. According to Johnson the bill meant "an absorption and assumption of power by the general government which, if acquiesced in, must sap and destroy our federative system of limited powers, and break down the barriers which preserve the rights of the States. It is another step, or rather stride, towards centralization, and the concentration of all legislative powers in the national government."

In the closing paragraphs of his veto, Johnson also incorporated a passage from Seward's draft, somewhat edited, that pledged cooperation with Congress in any measure to protect the civil rights of freedmen through judicial process and impartial laws in conformity with the Constitution. The passage is obviously inconsistent with the general tone of the message. Its presence is perhaps explained by an urgent note, unsigned and undated, but in Seward's handwriting, preserved among the presidential papers. It reads: "If you can find a way to intimate that *you are not opposed to the policy of the bill* but *only to its detailed provisions*, it will be a great improvement and make the support of the veto easier to our friends in Congress. I think a passage to this effect can be found in my notes heretofore sent."[14] Thus Johnson's civil rights veto was not a straightforward, consistent argument against the bill. It was a contradictory composite designed to attract political support among both Republicans and Democrats.

The identification of the drafts for Johnson's first two vetoes, together with a comparative study of the official messages, is revealing of much more than the process of message writing and the president's indebtedness to others. It provides new insights for an understanding of Johnson and his advisers. The generally accepted picture of Johnson as courageous, stubborn, forthright, and correct in his dealings with Congress needs qualification in view of the evidence of evasive contradictions, racist attitudes, and concessions to political expediency.

Secretary Welles emerges as an influential adviser, despite the fact that the president borrowed much less from his draft than from those of Seward and Stanbery. Welles's relatively brief opinions were sharply unequivocal in opposition to both the Freedmen's Bureau and the civil rights bills; Johnson's messages were less incisive but in substantial agreement with the secretary's position.

The significance of Henry Stanbery's large role in formulating the second veto is not clear. It may have indicated either the ascendancy of a new influence with the president or simply Johnson's discovery of a skilled advocate to whom he could intrust the exposition of his own views. The latter assumption is the more likely one. Stanbery's reputation was that of an attorney interested primarily in his profession rather than in office seeking. In acknowledging his nomination to the Supreme Court in April 1866, he characterized the honor as one "conferred spontaneously, and without the pressure of political or personal influence."[15] With the Ewings he had close ties, and they were urging that he be appointed attorney general; yet his first large service to the president in connection with the civil rights veto was apparently undertaken without their foreknowledge or counsel.[16] His later acceptance of the office of attorney general was thought to have been given with some hesitation and reluctance as a response to an unsolicited call to public duty.[17] We know that Johnson, at least by the close of his administration, was of the firm conviction that the office of attorney general had never been filled "by any one who was so smart as a man or a lawyer" as Stanbery.[18] This evidence, though inconclusive, suggests that Stanbery was an instrument rather than an originator of policy.

Stanbery's part in the formulation of the civil rights veto had another aspect of considerable historical interest. It may have cost Stanbery a place upon the Supreme Court and possibly was a decisive factor in the Senate's action in July 1866 to reduce the number of Supreme Court justices. Three weeks after the veto message went to Congress, on April 16, Johnson nominated Stanbery, who was not then a member of the cabinet, for a vacancy on the court. A bill to reduce the number of justices by one had already passed the House but had not been acted on in the Senate. The vacancy thus existed in April when Johnson made the nomination. But in July the Senate proposed to reduce the number of justices by two. When the House agreed to the Senate version of the measure, the *Independent*'s Washington news column reported that it "defeats the nomination of Mr. Henry Salisbury [*sic*] of Ohio, to the bench as a reward for his *ex parte* opinion against the Civil Rights act."[19]

At the time of the veto, a report had circulated, and had also been denied, that Stanbery had prepared that part of the message embracing the legal objections to the civil rights bill.[20] A month later, while Stanbery's nomination was still before the Senate, the New York *Times* reported that Radical senators who believed that he had either prepared or approved the legal objections to the bill viewed his act as a "heinous offence." According to this report, Stanbery's "fate would seem to be sealed," though the Senate would probably "avoid the question by passing the House bill" to reduce the number of judges.[21] About the same time, Thomas Ewing, Jr., wrote to his father from Washington that it was "very doubtful whether Stanbery will be suffered to become Sup Judge—though it is conceded he can not be directly rejected. The plan proposed, as you have doubtless seen, is to pass the House bill now pending in the Senate abolishing Judge Catron's circuit."[22] Thus it is quite possible that the *Independent* was correct in linking the passage of the court bill with congressional hostility toward the veto message and its suspected draftsman. Even before final House action on the court bill the president sent Stanbery an offer of the position of attorney general.[23] The Senate's ready confirmation of Stanbery for the cabinet post suggests that the opposition to the Ohio attorney was not so much a personal matter as a concern to protect congressional civil rights legislation against adverse Supreme Court decision. Conversely, Johnson desired to appoint a man who, from the presidential view, was "right on fundamental constitutional questions." Stanbery, the president told Welles, was such a man and "is with us thoroughly, earnestly."[24]

Finally, a comparative study of the drafts and the official messages suggests a new perspective upon the relationship existing between Seward and the president, and upon the post–Civil War failure to resolve the nation's racial dilemma. Johnson appears to have given to the Secretary of State, his most intimate and eminent link with Lincoln's administration and with the Whig wing of the Republican party, a measure of deference and respect while at the same time rejecting critical parts of his secretary's advice. The president's decision to discard Seward's explicit and unequivocal approval of national protection for the Negro's civil rights, and to substitute an ambiguity more pleasing to numerous southerners and northern Democrats, destroyed a unique opportunity to initiate a firm national policy. In such a policy the South might then have acquiesced. The vetoes nurtured a hope and a determination to settle the Negro's new status not with a view to preponderant opinion in the North but in accordance with local sentiment in the South. The course that Johnson chose alienated large numbers of moderate Union men and proved politically disastrous to himself, to Seward, and to the nation. It is just possible that a greater deference to Seward's political acumen and his sensitivity to Republican racial attitudes might have spared the president, the secretary, and the country a tragic experience.

CHAPTER SIX

Civil Rights

The Issue of Reconstruction

In April 1866, Andrew Johnson chose to renew warfare with Congress with a battle over federal protection for the basic civil rights, not including suffrage or office holding, of the slaves now made free men by the Thirteenth Amendment. The veto of the civil rights bill, officially entitled "An Act to protect all persons in the United States in their civil rights, and furnish the means of their vindication," reopened the conflict between Executive and Congress. The second veto, like the first, can be viewed as an accommodation to the sentiment of the South and of the northern Democracy.[1] Not one Democratic vote had been cast for the bill in either House. A few days after its passage, George W. Morgan, the Democratic candidate for governor defeated by Jacob D. Cox in Ohio the previous fall, sent the proceedings of a pro-Johnson meeting and the message: "We are looking for another veto."[2] The elder Frank Blair wrote Johnson a letter with four pages of argument against the bill. His objections were all directed to the heart of the matter: under the bill, as Blair saw it, the states would be able to make "no discrimination between *Whites* & Black," a result he considered disastrous. "No man can advocate an amalgamation of the white & black races and so create a mongrel nation. . . . The policy of the country must therefore be a gradual segregation of the Races. This will be attempted by the legislation of the States now filled by negroes." These states must retain such rights, for example, as that to send black convicts to penal colonies outside the country while retaining white convicts in local workhouses. They must be able to induce manufacturing companies into the South by educating the rising generations of the white race while restricting the blacks "to the ruder trades and to the producing of the raw material." Blair concluded the long letter:[3] "An infinite variety of municipal regulations grow up in the economy of states to advance the interest of the Race who made the Govt & to whom it belongs by making discriminations Congress forbids. Has it a right to do it?" Although stated with typical indiscretion, Blair's position represented widespread opinion at the South and among the Northern Democracy.

In contrast, eminent Republicans who had supported the president after the Freedmen's Bureau veto, ardently desired presidential approval of civil rights legislation. Henry Ward Beecher, invoking the privilege of one who had "suffered, as being a friend of President Johnson," urged Johnson to sign Trumbull's civil rights bill. The *"thing itself* is desirable," it would harmonize feelings, strengthen "your friends' hands," frustrate those who had tried to create the impression "that you have proved untrue to the cause of liberty," and meet the prevailing "deep tide of moral feeling."[4] Governor Cox wrote from Ohio pleading for approval, even if it meant that the president must *"strain a point."* The people looked to the purposes of the bill: namely, to give the freedmen "the same rights of property and persons, the same remedies for injuries received and the same penalties for wrongs committed, as other men—This they approve, and they know that you and I and all true Union men have constantly desired this result." Though many of the provisions for enforcement were objectionable, Governor Cox argued that they were still *"civil* provisions . . . not the unrestrained despotism of military power which was embodied in the Freedmen's Bureau bill." If the southern people would "do right themselves," by breaking down "the distinctions between classes," the law would be of little "practical moment . . . a dead letter." Executive approval of a bill, the Ohio governor counseled, "by no means implies full assent to a measure," only that its objectionable features are not so "gross" as to make it an executive duty to interpose. The long letter made an appeal based upon practical politics. Cox had found the Ohio Democracy hypocritical in their support of the president; inasmuch as they had no disposition "to abandon their organization as a party," no real help could come from them except "as we convert *individuals."* Approval of the civil rights bill would make Johnson with "our Western people," "fully master of the situation," would remove any possibility of opposition in Union ranks to other administration measures, and would greatly assist in "holding together our State organizations, but this is a consideration I would not feel like urging upon you."[5]

On the eve of the veto, aware of its imminence, Thurlow Weed wrote Seward a letter meant for the president's eye. If the civil rights bill were to be vetoed, the president must make a point of his long-standing "paternal regard for a race whose changed condition" required such legislation. "If he manifests a desire that the Negroes shall be protected in all that concerns his personal rights and material welfare the People will go with him."[6] Seward himself sent a hurried and unsigned note to the president: "If you can find a way to intimate that *you are not opposed to the policy of the bill* but *only to its detailed provisions,* it will be a great improvement and make the support of the veto easier to our friends in Congress."[7]

As in the case of the earlier Freedmen's Bureau bill, Secretary Seward's attitude toward the civil rights bill is revealed in a draft message prepared for the president.[8] Once again, Seward was conciliatory where Johnson was hostile. He objected at length to certain aspects of the bill, "rather questions of form than questions of substance," particularly the enforcement provisions; but in effect, Seward invited Congress to frame a new bill that would eliminate objectionable features yet effectively safeguard civil equality for the Negro through the federal judiciary. The object of the bill, "to secure all persons in their civil rights without regard to race or color," received Seward's explicit approval, as did the status of citizenship for the freedmen. So far from challenging the right of Congress to pass such legislation, he pointed to a constitutional basis for the bill in the enforcement clause of the Thirteenth Amendment and in the privileges and immunities clause of the original Constitution. He tried to counter apprehensions that a guarantee of civil rights would open the door to congressional legislation granting suffrage to the Negro. Qualifications for voting and office holding, according to Seward, would be left with the states, "precisely as if the bill were not enacted into law."[9]

In all these aspects, Seward's attitude was in sharp contrast to the position taken by Johnson in the official message. This is true despite the fact that the president borrowed liberally from Seward's draft.[10] Johnson challenged the assumption that the newly emancipated slaves were qualified for citizenship.[11] By indirection, he defended discrimination by state law on the basis of race. He raised the objection that if Congress had the power to abrogate state discriminations in respect to certain civil rights, it would also have the power to decide who should be juror, judge, and voter. He affirmed that Congress had no power over states, as it did over territories "'to make rules and regulations' for them."[12] The weight of argument in the president's message, as this quotation indicates, was against the position that Congress possessed authority to pass civil rights legislation; it implied that such legislation would be an invasion of the reserved rights of the states. The message, however, did not squarely face the basic question of congressional authority. At one point, the president referred to the enforcement clause of the Thirteenth Amendment as presumably the authority by virtue of which the bill gave federal courts exclusive jurisdiction over cases involving discrimination. Without agreeing or disagreeing with that presumption, he continued, "It cannot, however, be justly claimed that, with a view to the enforcement of this article of the Constitution, there is at present any necessity for the exercise of all the powers which this bill confers."[13] Toward the close of the message, the president included a strong states'-rights statement drafted by Secretary Welles. This passage condemned the bill's provisions generally as an interference with municipal legislation that would destroy the federal system of limited powers and intrude upon the reserved rights of the states.

Seward had ended his draft with a presidential promise to approve "any bill that should provide, in harmony with the convictions I have expressed, for the protection of the civil rights of all classes of persons throughout the United States by judicial process in conformity with the Constitution of the United States." In a slightly more qualified version, Johnson added Seward's conclusion to his own veto. In the context of the message as a whole, however, it was a meaningless concession.

Despite the ambiguous concluding promise, Johnson's message when compared with Seward's draft clearly indicates that presidential opposition to civil rights legislation was a matter not of form but of substance. In fact, Johnson refused to make any substantive concessions to moderate Republicans, Seward included, who desired a federally enforceable status of civil equality, short of voting and office holding, for the former slave. Conclusive evidence can be found in the letters of Sen. Edwin D. Morgan. Senator Morgan, it will be recalled, was closely associated with Seward and Weed. He had voted to uphold the Freedmen's Bureau veto; even after the veto of the civil rights bill, he counseled against hasty condemnation of the president and made known his desire that "the great body of those with whom I am politically associated will continue acting together, and acting with the President."[14] He refused to bend before the pressure of "the malcontents," insisting that "the President means to do right."[15]

Morgan was ill during this period, but he was much concerned about the civil rights measure and kept in touch with Seward. On March 26, the day before the veto, he sent an urgent note to Seward requesting information. "I am all in the dark as to what is going on and I want much to know more than I do concerning the Veto which it is said will be sent to the Senate perhaps today."[16] Secretary Seward sent Morgan's plea to the executive mansion with the notation: "Have the President please read and enable me to answer Gov. Morgan." The penciled reply to Seward read: "It will not go in before tomorrow—Mr. Moore will be over to see you."[17] The president's secretary, however, apparently did not appear. He wrote Seward that the president had directed another copy of his message to be made and expected that "it would be prepared in time for your examination this evening. He finds, however, that but little progress has been made, and fears that if he arrests the work he will not be able to obtain a correct copy in time for the Cabinet meeting tomorrow morning. He therefore directs me to say that it will be ready for you at any hour in the morning that you may designate."[18] This correspondence suggests not only Morgan's apprehensions and his desire to act in harmony with the president, but also a presidential reluctance to discuss the message privately with Seward on the very eve of its release. In view of what we now know of Seward's position and its variance with that of the president's, the report of the cabinet meeting next morning, March 27, which Welles noted in his diary, is of special interest. Welles wrote, "Seward said he [had] carefully studied the bill and thought it might be well to pass a law declaring negroes were citizens, because there had been some questions raised [on that point] though there never was a doubt in his own mind."[19] This passage suggests that Seward made a final, but ineffectual, plea for a major modification of the position Johnson had taken.

Between the veto and the vote upon it in the Senate, Sen. Morgan conferred with the president in an attempt to secure "an understanding in relation to a new 'Civil Rights Bill,' free from Constitutional objections, and that will afford all necessary protection." He was convinced that this would achieve "harmony, in the party; and unity in the Nation."[20] At first he was hopeful. Thurlow Weed, whom Morgan kept informed of his position and activities, sent words of encouragement and counsel. Morgan's statement of his support of the president had quieted apprehensions among friends in New York and Albany. "Pray do not let the Friends of the Administration be kept in a negative position," Weed continued. "You need *affirmative* ground to stand on. The president can be invincible if to wisdom he adds calmness and *tact.*"[21]

On April 6, in a dramatically close vote, the Senate overrode Johnson's veto of the civil rights bill. Senator Morgan, to the applause of the galleries, cast his vote for the bill and against the president. Two days later he sent Thurlow Weed an explanation. He had made "most earnest efforts with Mr. Fessenden and with the President to have a compromise bill agreed upon and passed. It looked hopeful at one time but failed. The difficulty really was the President's objections to the *first* section of the bill. It was then *this* bill or *nothing.* . . . It is unfortunate perhaps that the bill was not signed. But if it had been returned with the President's objections to the second section *only* we could have got along with it very well and maintained ourselves which is a matter of *some* consideration." Morgan argued that with the issue out of the way in the elections, the president would be in a better position than if the bill had been defeated.[22] The first section of the bill, to which Morgan referred as crucial in the negotiations with the president, was the section granting Negroes citizenship and equal civil rights.

Other personal letters of Morgan repeated and elaborated his explanation to Weed. Had the president disavowed objections to the "*Principle* and pointed out the defects of the *details,* the Senate would have amended and passed the bill without any break or serious trouble, as we all knew that the *second* section was objectionable. But the first section declaring the Blacks Citizens, we could not and would not give up."[23]

When the civil rights bill was returned to the Senate, Lyman Trumbull rose to voice the conclusion of a moderate man who felt a profound obligation to the newly freed Negroes of the South: "Whatever may have been the opinion of the President at one time as to 'good faith requiring the security of the freedmen in their liberty and their property' it is now manifest from the character of his objections to this bill that he will approve no measure that will accomplish the object."[24] Ironically, the *Herald* agreed. Ten days earlier its editorial columns had characterized the bill as "a practical, just and beneficent measure," in no way conflicting with the "declared opinions and policy of President Johnson";[25] now it jubilantly greeted the veto as the signal of a political revolution: "The objections submitted against the first section of the bill, however, are those which mark the impassable barrier between him and the ruling radicals of Congress. He is opposed to the recognition at present, by law, of the blacks as citizens of the United States, and he is opposed to any further legislation by Congress affecting the domestic affairs of the several States. . . ."[26] Just after the veto, the conciliatory Henry L. Dawes, who had harsh words for the president's extreme opponents, wrote his wife that Johnson had deprived "every friend he has of the least ground upon which to stand and defend him."[27]

No oratory of Charles Sumner, no lash of Thaddeus Stevens' tongue nor of his reputed political whip, could drive the Republican majority in Congress into sustained open warfare with the president. This accomplishment was Johnson's own. By refusing presidential support to any program that would effectively secure equality before the law to the four million slaves whom the national government had made free, he fatally alienated the reasonable men who wished to act with him rather than against him. For some, the principle of equal status was decisive; for others, the prospect of repudiation by their Republican constituencies may have been sufficient reason. Johnson might have called for modified civil rights legislation or asked for a constitutional amendment to put beyond question the right of Congress to secure for the freedmen civil equality.[28] He did neither.

By giving countenance to the Democratic claim that the Civil Rights Act was unconstitutional, Johnson helped to destroy any possibility that the civil rights issue, as Senator Morgan had hoped, would be removed from the political arena. When Congress subsequently formulated its own amendment, with the vital section one on citizenship and equal rights, Johnson might have accepted it in whole or in part, or he might have used it as a point of departure for compromise. Instead, the president made clear his disapproval of any constitutional amendment whatsoever before the South had been fully restored to a voice in national affairs.[29] It was obvious at the time, as it is evident in retrospect, that no civil rights amendment could have received the requisite two-thirds vote of both Houses of Congress with the South fully represented. Neither in March of 1866, nor later, did Andrew Johnson give to the moderates of the party that had elected him any alternative with which they might spare the nation a dread conflict between Congress and the chief executive.[30]

In declaring war upon the Radicals, Johnson chose to make as well an issue with moderate Republicans. His action on the civil rights bill, like that on the Freedmen's Bureau bill, cannot be explained on the sole basis of Radical provocation or constitutional principles. It must be viewed in the context of pressures from the Democracy, North and South, and of plans to precipitate a reorganization of national parties that would result in a new or transformed Union party under his personal leadership. Yet a new or transformed Union party would be only the Democracy in disguise unless it could command the support of moderate men in the Republican ranks. Whether Johnson wished the substance or only the appearance of a new amalgam, we cannot know. If the former, his unyielding attitude on the civil rights issue was a major blunder. He may have been blinded by his own racial attitudes or by his victory in the battle over the Freedmen's Bureau bill. Contemporary evidence, however, should have made unmistakably clear the near unanimity of Republican public opinion on behalf of some national guarantee of equal civil rights for the freedmen.

The advice of Henry Ward Beecher, of Governor Cox, of Thurlow Weed, and of Secretary Seward indicated the importance of the civil rights issue to continued support from rank-and-file Republicans. Even Senator Cowan in advising the second veto cautioned the president to "Be careful to put it distinctly as a question of *power*—not of policy—indeed it might be recommended to the States with propriety."[31] It will be recalled that John Cochrane, who had labored so diligently to prepare the way for a Johnson party centered about the War Democrats, had sent similar advice. He had cautioned Johnson that in the approaching conflict with his "disguised enemies" it would be essential that the line of presidential policy could not be interpreted as unfriendly to the Negro. "That concession to public opinion" would enable Johnson to carry the North.[32] R. P. L. Baber, a diligent Johnson political lieutenant, wrote from Ohio both before and after the veto to Senator Doolittle, Secretary Seward, and the president about the strategy needed for success in the approaching congressional elections. A central requisite was "Some effective and Constitutional law to enable the Freedmen to enforce in the Federal Courts, rights denied them in the State Courts, as to the protection of person and property."[33] Russell Houston, an old personal friend who had acted as an intermediary between Johnson and the New York Democracy, wrote Johnson from Kentucky advising that the president's supporters in Congress take the lead in advocating a civil rights bill that would not be unconstitutional or inappropriate. "It is important to you and to the country, that when the issues now being made, shall go before the people, you should appear as you are and have been the advocate, the friend and the promoter of the freedom of all the people of our Country whether of one race or another. . . . Under ordinary circumstances, I might say that no legislation on the subject was necessary, but under present circumstances, I think differently."[34] A New Jersey representative wrote the president to explain that his vote on the civil rights bill did not indicate any desire to desert the administration. "Whilst a different course would not have sustained you practically it would have been a violation of my own sense of right, and in decided contravention of the will of our friends whose opinion I have ascertained by personal observation during my stay at Trenton last week. They strongly desire protection to the freedmen and fear the States would be slow to accord it."[35]

Private letters to Secretary Seward and to Senator Morgan bear eloquent testimony to the importance of the civil rights issue. Seward's public defense of the Freedmen's Bureau veto evoked from an old friend and political supporter words of harsh but sorrowful repudiation.

> Had any one predicted even a single year ago you would in so brief a period be found side by side with the Hoods, Vallandigham, Pearce, Buchanan, Voorhees,

Brooks, Davis and other aiders and abetters of the rebellion, I should have deemed him as a libeller. . . . [Your friends] have the painful mortification of seeing you co-operating with your life-long enemies and the enemies of Freedom, Justice, Humanity and the Union, to fasten upon the country a system of slavery ten times more odious and cruel than that which the Army of the Republic has destroyed.[36]

After the second veto, another former admirer wrote: "Your former friends are all deserting you. . . . Your reconstruction policy is believed by the people fatal to the true interests of liberty and the life of the Nation. Justice to the loyal whites of the South and the Freedmen is justice to the nation, so the people believe."[37] The pastor of New York's Trinity Church wrote to commend Morgan for sustaining the civil rights bill. "That Bill seemed to us to be the necessary Legislation to give vitality to the late Amendment to the Constitution of the United States and to make freedom a real thing to the emancipated. . . . It is high time to assert by Legislation, the Union and Nationality of this great Country, and to maintain the citizenship of every native born American."[38] Another minister expressed satisfaction in the passage of the law for much the same reasons: "If our people are not to be protected by national law in the Civil Rights that are secured even in the empires of Europe, with what face can we stand up among the free nations of the world?"[39] A New York banker succinctly stated the issue: "The Freedmen's Bureau Bill involved a question of expediency about which earnest Union men might differ—the Civil Rights Bill however stood upon a different basis. The people whose rights as Citizens are sought to be protected by the Bill, were entitled to receive from the Government a law that would secure to them the practical enjoyment of those rights."[40] A New York lawyer congratulated Morgan upon his vote: "I am not radical but I am confident you will never regret the aid you gave to common humanity in sustaining that bill."[41]

The response of the press also indicated that Republican opinion was committed to some form of civil rights action. Republican papers were much more united in their support of Congress than had been the case after the first veto. Bryant's *Evening Post,* which had supported the president earlier, now regretfully dissented. The moderate and conciliatory editor of the Springfield *Republican* reluctantly concluded that the civil rights bill must be passed over the president's veto "or the hope of any special legislation for the protection of the freedmen must be abandoned."[42] A few days later, at the very time when Senator Morgan was seeking compromise, Bowles wrote an extended analysis of the political situation. The president's purpose, according to the Springfield *Republican*'s editor, had been to drive off from the Republican party a small faction of extreme radicals and consolidate the mass of Republicans with War Democrats of the North and loyalists of the South into a powerful party that would bring the Union "peace and prosperity" and "give him a triumphant re-election." Even after the February 22 speech, the president might have held half the Republicans, "led Congress to his plan of reconstruction," and gained a larger power with the country than he had ever before possessed. The veto of the civil rights bill, however,

> instead of driving off from him a small minority of the republican party, or even the half of it, drives off substantially the whole of it. There is but one voice among republicans on this point. . . . If Mr. Johnson is to stand by the doctrine of that document, he must inevitably part company with all the great body of his old supporters, and rely for his friends upon the northern democrats and the reconstructed rebels of the South. . . . For though they might give up everything else; waive universal suffrage, concede the admission of southern Congressmen, abolish the test oath, grant general amnesty, they cannot give up national protection to the weak and minority classes in the South.[43]

The *Democrat and Free Press* of Rockland, Maine, gave a similar warning. "Mr. Johnson is mistaken if he supposes that fanaticism is at the bottom of the movement to give the negroes the rights of free men. It is not fanaticism, but cool judgment; it is not sustained by the few, but by the great mass of those who fought down the rebellion."[44] The Columbus, Ohio *Journal* commented that by the veto, the president "had done more to strengthen the supporters of Congress and to determine the policy of the wavering, than months of argument."[45]

Even the Republican papers that remained friendly in their attitude toward the president made clear their own support for some form of national guarantee of the freedmen's rights. A few reconciled their own attitude with that of the president by pointing to his concluding promise, the one Johnson had incorporated from Seward's draft, and insisting that the president was not opposed to federal protection. Most of the Republican press, however, saw the veto as drawing a sharp line between the position of the president and that of their party.[46]

What had been taking place in the Republican party since the close of the civil conflict was a gradual metamorphosis, similar to the one that had taken place during the war. The war years transformed the Republicans, a political amalgam originally united on the principle of opposition to the extension of slavery, into a party committed to the destruction of slavery. This objective had been formally embodied in the party platform of 1864. The platform, however, had not included a plank supporting equal legal status for the freed slaves, despite the fact that such a plank was offered and considered. By the winter of 1865, Republicans generally had expanded their repudiation of slavery into a condemnation of legal discriminations, which by then seemed to them the last vestiges of slavery. Important elements within the party held that the freedmen's rights must include an equality of suffrage, but on this more advanced position, Republicans were not yet agreed. They had, however, come to identify Republicanism with a defense of basic civil rights for the freed slave.[47] Sometimes this identification of Republicanism with the principle of equal status before the law was stated explicitly; sometimes it was expressed through generalizations that invoked liberty, freedom, or humanity. A characteristic argument, advanced by one Republican paper, was that if the position on equal civil rights embodied in Johnson's veto message were correct, then "all the principles of democracy and freedom upon which our creed of Republicanism rests are false and we must recant them."[48] When Republicans accused Johnson of treachery to the Republican party and Republican principles, or with greater forbearance simply asked that he give them some unmistakable evidence so that they might "continue to confide in him as a *Republican*,"[49] they were identifying their party with the principle of equality in legal status for all freedmen.

Thus what had once been an advanced, or "Radical," position within Republican ranks by 1866 had become accepted and moderate. To most opponents of equal civil status, however, the principle still appeared "Radical." Herein lies one clue to the confusion in the use of the term "Radical" that plagues any serious student of the period. The term is inescapable; yet a man labeled a "Radical" by one set of contemporaries or historians is often found designated a "moderate" by another group of contemporaries or historians. All would agree that Charles Sumner, Thaddeus Stevens, and Wendell Phillips, extreme men though not of one mind, were the prototypes of Radicalism. The term *radical*, however, has often been used to identify, and castigate, all Republican opponents of Andrew Johnson. Many of these men were almost as critical of Sumner, Stevens, and Phillips as were their Conservative adversaries. Few followed Stevens in his demand for confiscation; most were ready to abandon or drastically compromise Sumner's aim of Negro suffrage. Though they wished to proceed with caution, there was no strong desire among them for an indefinite postponement of restoration by reducing the South to the status of "territories" or "conquered provinces." In other words, many Radicals were moderate men. The Radical opponents of President Johnson were united in one demand—that of national protection for the freedmen. On other issues of Reconstruction they held widely divergent views.

It has sometimes been assumed that a common economic attitude united Radicals and marked them off from pro-Johnson men. This assumption is demonstrably false. Some were protariff men, some antitariff men; some advocated cheap money, some upheld a sound gold standard; some were spoilsmen, others were among the spoilsmen's bitterest critics.[50] In 1865 and 1866 substantial members of the business community were as often found in the ranks of the president's supporters as in those of the opposition.[51] John A. Dix, a key figure in the Johnson movement, was president of the Union Pacific. A twenty-thousand dollar reception and dinner at the famed Delmonico's, at the opening of Johnson's ill-fated Swing-around-the-Circle, was attended by many of the most powerful figures of New York business and finance.[52] As late as September 1866, the New York *Times,* in an editorial entitled "Business and Politics—the Conservatism of Commerce"—spoke of the "great unanimity of the commercial and business classes in supporting the conservative policy of the Administration, and in opposing with their might the schemes of the Radical Destructives."[53]

Nor were the Radicals distinguishable from the general run of Union men, as is often claimed, by vindictiveness toward the South or clamor for the heads of "traitors." Indeed, New York's outstanding Radical leader, Horace Greeley, was a leading figure in the movement for amnesty and forgiveness. Henry Wilson, Radical senator from Massachusetts, wrote to Johnson in support of a plea for the parole of Clement C. Clay of Alabama.[54] Even Thaddeus Stevens offered his services in the defense both of Clay and of Jefferson Davis.[55] The feeling against southern leaders of the rebellion, which found expression both in a stubborn indignation at the prospect of their speedy return to the halls of Congress and in an emotional demand for Jefferson Davis' trial and conviction, cut across the division between pro-Johnson and anti-Johnson men. Thus in December 1865, the House passed a resolution supporting the stringent Test Oath of July 1862 as binding without exception upon all branches of government. Only one Republican registered opposition.[56] A few days earlier, without a single dissenting voice, the House had declared treason a crime that should be punished; thirty-four Democrats joined the Republicans in voting "yea."[57] In June, after the break with the president, a resolution calling for the trial of Jefferson Davis passed by a vote of 105 to 19, with no Republican voting against it. Six of the seven Conservatives who had broken with the majority of their party to support Johnson in the civil rights veto, registered their approval of this demand.[58]

The only common denominator that united the Radicals of 1866, and the only characteristic they shared that could logically justify the term *radical*, was their determination that the rebel South should not be reinstated into the Union until there were adequate guarantees that the slaves liberated by the nation should enjoy the rights of free men.[59] It is true that Johnson's opponents believed Congress should have some voice in Reconstruction and that they were profoundly disturbed by the prospect of a restored South, united with the Northern Democracy, immediately controlling the destinies of the nation. They were also extremely sensitive to any patronage moves that might seem to indicate Johnson's support of the Democracy or an intent to punish Republicans for failure to agree completely with the president's position. These attitudes, however, can hardly be termed radical; and they were not decisive factors with most of the men who broke with the president after the veto messages. Possibly, without the civil rights issue, one of these points of friction might have generated warfare and become the dividing line between Johnson's opponents and his supporters; but this is extremely doubtful. The testimony of such men as Samuel Bowles, Thurlow Weed, Jacob D. Cox, and John Cochrane must be given weight. They believed that the president could achieve his goal of speedy restoration and renewed fellowship between North and South if only he endorsed some effective national guarantee of the freedmen's civil rights as citizens.[60] One of the most distinguished students of congressional Reconstruction, thoroughly sympathetic to Johnson, concluded that the moderate leadership in Congress desired just three conditions and would have settled for two: a guarantee of "the negroes' civil rights" and recognition of "the prerogative of Congress."[61] Since executive action alone could not guarantee the South's permanent acquiescence in the freedmen's newly gained rights, such security could be had only by way of the second condition, acceptance of some congressional action in the matter. In other words, the two conditions were inseparable; Johnson's consent to the first would have automatically fulfilled the second. Had Johnson come to terms with the moderates on the civil rights issue, the truly radical men of the party would have been clearly distinguishable from Republicans generally; and the true "Radical" would have faced the choice of compromise or defeat. Instead, except for a handful of Conservatives who totally accepted Johnson's leadership, "Republican" tended to become synonymous with "Radical."

The Democracy had a major responsibility for the blurring of distinction between the terms *Radical* and *Republican*. Even before the vetoes, they had tended to stigmatize the entire Republican leadership in Congress as "Radical"; after the vetoes, they delighted in maligning the Freedmen's Bureau bill and the Civil Rights Act as parts of a sinister Radical design to defeat Johnson's plan for speedy restoration. This was good political strategy. Political expediency and propaganda, however, are not a complete explanation. In the eyes of Democrats, North and South, the claim of "equality," in any form, for the newly freed Negro was indeed radical, an outrageous postwar version of prewar abolitionism. Both before and after the vetoes, one finds expressions in the Democratic press and in private letters of the period that indicate an unmistakable identification of "Radical" with "Abolitionist." Thus, a Tennessee judge, complaining about the interference of the military, started to write that this was "just what the abominable Abolitionis [sic]" desired, then crossed out "Abolitionist" and substituted the word "Radicals."[62] It is true that Northern Democratic spokesmen and responsible southerners at times urged upon the southern states full equality in civil proceedings; but they did so because this appeared to them not only an inescapable concession to Republican opinion but a necessary condition for presidential support as well. Moreover, so long as exclusive state authority were maintained, concessions made by state action before restoration could be undone by state action after restoration.

There is a certain validity in the Democratic equation that denied the historical differences between old-time Abolitionists, postwar extremists, and those moderate Republicans of 1866 who upheld equal civil rights for the Negro. Between pro-Johnson Conservatives and anti-Johnson Radicals— whether the latter were moderate or extreme—the dividing line was marked by a distinction in race attitude. Wide differences existed on each side of the line, and there were those who took their places in each camp for reasons primarily of political expediency and advantage. Yet by 1866 all Radicals accepted, indeed most held as an article of faith, a nationally enforceable equality of civil status, even though their attitudes might differ in respect to equality of suffrage and equality of social status for the Negro. The position of Johnson supporters varied from extreme racism to an uncomfortable accommodation to the probability that legal discrimination and inequitable treatment for the freed slave would follow upon an unrestrained local autonomy in race relations. The anti-Johnson side attracted men with a deep sense of concern and responsibility for the freed slave; the pro-Johnson ranks drew men who thought national responsibility had ended with the destruction of property rights in human beings. The latter preferred to base formal argument upon aversion to centralized government, a defense of states' rights, respect for the Constitution, and devotion to a reunited Union. But behind such arguments there most often lay some shade of that prejudice of race that still divides the nation.

The racist tendency among Northern Democrats hardly needs further demonstration. If evidence is desired, it can be found among the editorials with which the veto messages were greeted. Johnson does not believe, wrote one New England Democratic editor, "in compounding our race with niggers, gipsies and baboons, neither do we . . . [or] our whole Democratic people."[63] A Washington paper editorialized:[64] "The negro is to have full and perfect equality with the white man. He is to mix up with the white gentlemen and ladies all over the land . . . at all public meetings and public places he is to be your equal and your associate. . . . How long will it be if Congress can do all this before it will say the negro shall vote, sit in the jury box, and intermarry with your families? Such are the questions put by the President." The *Ohio Statesman* declared it was no crime for the president to "esteem his race as superior to an inferior race. In this hour of severe trial, when the President is endeavoring so to administer the government that the white man shall not be subordinated to the negro race, will not the white man stand by him."[65] The Radicals, commented a Pennsylvania paper with satisfaction, "now find that President Johnson regards this government as the White man's."[66] One set of huge headlines read:[67]

> ALL HAIL!
> GRAND AND GLORIOUS!
> GREAT VICTORY FOR THE WHITE MAN
> REJOICE, WHITE MAN, REJOICE!
> THE HOUR OF YOUR DELIVERANCE HAS COME
> SATAN IS BOUND
> RADICALISM REBUKED
> TAXPAYERS RELIEVED
> PRESIDENT JOHNSON TURNS OUT TO BE
> A FULL BLOODED WHITE MAN
> HAS VETOED THE FREEDMEN'S BUREAU BILL
> 'THE NEGROES HAVE TO WORK'

The limitations of Andrew Johnson's own benevolence toward the freedmen have already been explored.[68] A word more should be added as to the overtones of race prejudice apparent in his veto message. These may have been unintended expressions of his own bias or, more probably, deliberate appeals to the race prejudice of others. The first veto offended much less overtly than the second, although it called forth at least one protest against its appeal to "a low prejudice against color."[69] The offending passage was the argument that Congress could hardly appropriate moneys for relief, lands, and schools for the freedmen when it had never considered itself authorized "to expend the public money for the rent or purchase of homes for the thousands, not to say millions of the white race who are honestly toiling from day to day for their subsistence." The civil rights veto claimed that "the distinction of race and color is, by the bill, made to operate in favor of the colored and against the white race." It also raised the emotion-laden subject of intermarriage between whites and blacks, although the matter had little relevance to the president's argument. And in a passage clearly not intended as a compliment, it equated "the entire race designated as blacks, people of color, negroes, mullattoes, and persons of African blood" with Chinese, Indians, and "the people called Gipsies."[70]

The racist attitudes of the Blairs and of James Gordon Bennett, men whose influence with Johnson was very considerable, have already been sufficiently established.[71] The attitude of Conservative Republicans who stood with the president is less evident and requires examination.

Though not without criticism of the president, Gideon Welles agreed more completely with him than did any other member of the original cabinet. Welles alone thoroughly approved of the civil rights veto. What he criticized in Johnson's conduct of affairs was *too little* of the very qualities most other critics have thought the Tennessean had in excess—inflexibility and boldness. The fact is that Welles at one end of the Republican spectrum was at least as dogmatic and extreme as was Charles Sumner at the other. An old Jacksonian Democrat, Welles's narrow views of national power and states' rights were unaffected by his adherence to the Republican party. Qualified only by fading personal loyalties and a stout defense of the war effort, his sympathies throughout the postwar period were with the Democrats. A sanctimonious curmudgeon, whom history has largely taken at his own self-evaluation, Welles had kind words for few men. Even so, the sustained animus and distortion that he directed against the Radicals in his famed diary are particularly malicious.

With a record of having broken with the Democratic party over slavery and of having ordered the wartime navy to protect runaway slaves and to enlist Negroes, Welles's hostility toward the Radicals might be thought to have arisen entirely from his states'-rights views. This, however, was not the sole explanation. In the diary, Welles revealed a marked distaste for the "ingrained Abolitionism,"[72] which he thought motivated Johnson's opponents. He was also frank in stating that he was "no advocate for social equality, nor do I labor for political or civil equality for the negro. I do not want him at my table, nor do I care to have him in the jury-box, or in the legislative hall, or on the bench."[73] The Washington correspondent of the Springfield *Republican*, while unconvinced by rumors that Welles had told his Democratic friends in Connecticut that he was opposed to Negro suffrage just before the state was to vote upon the question, thought it quite likely that Welles, who "never was very radical on the slavery question . . . retains many of his prejudices against the colored people."[74] Welles agreed with Sumner that there was "a dreadful state of things South" and that "the colored people were suffering"; but his own concern was for the whites who had also passed through a terrible ordeal and had hardship enough without "any oppressive acts from abroad."[75] Sumner told Welles that he, New England's representative in the cabinet, misrepresented New England sentiment;[76] in this judgment, Sumner was most certainly correct.

Senator Doolittle of Wisconsin, the strongest pro-Johnson Republican in Congress, was not without compassion for the Negro, but his view of future race relations precluded any possibility of equality. Before and during the civil conflict, Doolittle had been acutely aware of the race problem and the difficulty of its solution. In his opposition to the extension of slavery, a key consideration was the desire to save the western lands for white settlers. He had been willing that the North should join in paying the expense of colonizing southern Negroes in Latin America, and he had developed a strong feeling of resentment against the Abolitionists.[77]

In the fall of 1865, Doolittle proposed as a solution of the Negro problem that a part of Texas, and perhaps of Florida as well, be ceded to the federal government for a segregated freedmen's territory. His object was to attract the entire Negro population of the South to these exclusively Negro territories by the offer of free homesteads. Only thus, in his view, could they "save themselves from being trodden under foot by the advancing tide of Caucasian emigration from Europe and from all the North."[78] Short of such a territorial haven, Doolittle apparently thought that the problem would be resolved only by the passing away of the Negro due to his excessively high death rate in freedom.[79] He believed that rather than the comprehensive freedom given by the Thirteenth Amendment, it would have been far better for the slaves had their emancipation been gradual, with those born after a certain date made free at twenty-one or even thirty years of age.[80] After the veto of the civil rights bill, the Wisconsin legislature instructed Doolittle, who had not voted on its original passage, to support the measure. When he refused to do so, the legislature called for his resignation.[81]

The draft argument of Sen. Edgar Cowan of Pennsylvania for Johnson's veto of the Freedmen's Bureau bill is revealing. In it there is no kind word for the freedmen nor for the bureau. Cowan viewed with distaste not only the military jurisdiction that the bill authorized but also the fact that it went "the whole length of putting the negroes upon the same footing precisely as the whites as to all *civil rights and immunities.*" He not only argued a want of power on the part of the federal government to purchase lands for the relief of destitute freedmen or to establish school buildings for their benefit, but added: "The people were willing to emancipate the slave in order that he might have a chance to take care of himself—but they will be very unwilling to pay for his maintenance and support out of the public purse—and they say justly that if he is unable to cope with his neighbors, in the battle for life—he must be content with the fate which awaits him and not expect them to feed him at the nation's expense."[82] After the first veto, it is clear that Cowan recognized that general opinion in the North was not altogether in accord with his own. He urged Johnson to veto the civil rights bill, but warned that the president's public opposition to the measure should not include an attack upon its principle of equal status.[83]

Cowan had been one of the three Republican senators voting against the civil rights bill on its passage in early February, before the first veto; the other thirty-three Republicans who voted supported the measure.[84] On the Freedmen's Bureau bill a few days earlier he had registered no vote, but in the course of discussion, when he had referred to himself as a friend of the Negro, Sen. Henry Wilson had sharply attacked his record. "Why, Sir, there has hardly been a proposition before the Senate of the United States for the last five years leading to the emancipation of the negro and the protection of his rights that the Senator from Pennsylvania has not sturdily opposed. . . . He has made himself the champion of 'how not to do it.'"[85] A sympathetic student of Cowan's public career quotes Wilson's speech at length, and then comments, "These were strong words yet underneath them there was much truth."[86] The following May, Cowan was arguing that the men who were repudiating the Union-Republican platforms of Chicago (1860) and Baltimore (1864) were not those who stood by the president, but those "who go away after false lights, who wander in dangerous places, who cook up Freedmen's Bureau and civil rights bills."[87]

About James Dixon of Connecticut, the third of Johnson's Republican supporters in the Senate, we have little evidence. In October 1865, he wrote the president that "the People desire justice to the Negro but they are tired of the perpetual reiteration of his claims upon their attention to the exclusion of all other interests. Moreover, as you will see by the recent vote of Connecticut on the question of extending suffrage to the colored population, there are grave doubts as to his fitness to govern the country, even *here*."[88] These words do not sound like those of a man with a deep concern for the Negro and his status. The same implication appears in an attack upon Senator Dixon by a fellow Connecticut Republican, who publicly accused him in 1863 of caring only for power. "I was forced to the conclusion that his [Dixon's] sympathies were not with his own section, but were with the Southern oligarchy. . . . That he hated republicanism for its humanity, and its self-sacrificing devotion to principle."[89]

The Thomas Ewings were among the most influential of Johnson's political counselors. Both father and son had a staunchly antislavery prewar record; yet the elder Ewing was known as a conservative Whig and Republican, not "as one of the 'earnest' or 'progressive' men of his time."[90] That the want of "earnestness" characterized his view of the Negro would seem evident from Ewing's notes for a public statement in 1867. In arguing against Negro suffrage in the South, he maintained that in the North "the popular mind cannot be excited to enthusiasm in favor of negro equality, social or political." Neither laborers, mechanics, nor professional men would admit a Negro man or woman on terms of equality to their parties, dinners, or dances, for the consequence would be mixed marriages. The feeling might be "vulgar prejudice, but if so, I am content to acknowledge myself therein essentially vulgar— I would be most unwilling to have a black daughter in law." According to Ewing, some Republicans thought that Providence would interfere and bring about Negro suffrage because it was founded on eternal justice, but God knew when he created man what was good for his creatures. "It is not probable that he will by a special miracle suddenly change his nature—his instincts, his prejudices and his passions, in order to adapt him to any man's or party's purposes."[91]

Two intimate associates of Ewing's were brought into Johnson's cabinet in 1866 on his recommendation, Henry Stanbery as Attorney General and Orville H. Browning as Secretary of the Interior. Though a Republican, Stanbery described himself to Democrats in 1868 as having been an "old guard" Whig who ceased to be one only when the party ceased to exist. Apparently he had not voted for Lincoln: "My last vote was given to that Party [Whig] in the Presidential contest of 1860."[92] He was the author of those passages in Johnson's civil rights veto that appealed to race prejudice by interjecting the question of mixed marriages.[93] According to Gideon Welles, Stanbery told cabinet members in 1867 that as a member of the Ohio legislature he had voted against Negro suffrage, and that he would do so again if he were in Ohio.[94] Before the Supreme Court in 1875, it was Stanbery who argued the famous case of *U.S. v. Reese*, thereby helping to set aside the Civil Rights Enforcement Act of 1870.[95]

Stanbery's colleague in the cabinet, Orville Browning, had been an antislavery man, but one of the most conservative variety, an outspoken opponent of Abolitionists.[96] During the war he deplored Lincoln's action in issuing the Emancipation Proclamation.[97] The Thirteenth Amendment, in Browning's opinion, merely gave the slaves personal freedom and did not confer other rights "not necessary incidents of personal liberty, and not necessary for its enjoyment"; and he was opposed to further legislation or constitutional amendment to secure additional liberties. "If the general government will take its hands off, and let the thing alone, it will soon adjust itself on a better and more satisfactory basis for all parties, than it can ever be forced to do by Federal interference."[98] Even after the ratification of the Fifteenth Amendment, Browning was numbered among those who opposed suffrage and nonsegregation for the Negroes in the conviction that, as an "inferior" race, their legal equality would threaten Anglo-Saxon institutions.[99]

Alexander W. Randall, who came into the cabinet along with Stanbery and Browning, had been a vigorous war governor of Wisconsin, and then as Assistant Postmaster under Lincoln had assisted effectively in mending the president's political fences in preparation for his reelection in 1864.[100] Retaining that politically strategic post under Johnson, Randall was soon recognized as an active political lieutenant of the new president. In the cabinet reorganization of 1866, he was raised to the rank of Postmaster General. While a young man in Wisconsin politics, Randall had helped prepare a proposal for Negro suffrage to be submitted for referendum in connection with the revision of the state constitution, an action that made him highly unpopular and kept him out of politics for some time.[101] Although associated with the Free Soil Democracy, he is said to have taken little part in its activities because of his opposition to the radical ideas of its leaders.[102] There is little evidence of his racial attitudes during the Johnson period. To judge from his position as reported by Gideon Welles, Randall was equivocal and politically minded rather than either prejudiced or deeply concerned in respect to matters touching equality for the freedmen.[103]

Hugh McCulloch, Secretary of the Treasury under both Lincoln and Johnson, believed firmly in the superior intelligence and energy of the white race.[104] He was reported to have said that "so far as the pretended equality of races was concerned," history showed that the Anglo-Saxon race in contact with an inferior one must "dominate or exterminate."[105] Like many another resident of Indiana, he was opposed to granting the vote to the Negroes even in the northern states.[106] Charles Sumner, who found it difficult to condone the position of Seward and Welles on the question of Negro suffrage in the South, was inclined to more charity toward McCulloch as one "imbued with the pernicious folly of Indiana."[107] McCulloch was aware that Johnson's veto of the civil rights bill, together with his February 22 speech, had "turned not only the Republican party but the general public sentiment of the northern states against him"; yet he had wanted the administration forces to make an open attack upon the proposed Fourteenth Amendment.[108] In his reminiscences written more than two decades after the struggle between Johnson and Congress, when the Reconstruction amendments were the law of the land, McCulloch characterized the Negroes as "an alien race" and held that the federal government should abstain "from all interference with local affairs" on their behalf. Once outside "interference" was discontinued and "colored people understand that the government, by their emancipation, had done for them all it can do, and that hereafter their welfare and elevation must depend upon their own efforts, the great problem of what is to be the political future of these states must be worked out by the joint action of the two races."[109]

Lewis D. Campbell, perhaps Johnson's most active personal political emissary in the West, was a man who had only scorn for the prewar Oberlin antislavery movement and its underground railroad activities.[110] An ardent opponent of Negro suffrage in Ohio as well as in the South, he held that in crushing secession, slavery had been only an incidental casualty and that there was no basis for the idea being promulgated by "wild one-idea fanatics" that the mission of the Union party was "to advance the interests of the black man and disregard those of the *white* man."[111] Campbell's perception was so limited that when Sumner, during a private interview with the president at which Campbell was present, expressed concern for the freedmen, the Ohioan saw in Sumner's attitude only the shedding of "crocodile tears."[112]

The support given to the president by Seward and by Raymond is of special interest. Neither man was a party to that prejudice of race so common among adherents of Johnson's cause. Raymond broke with the pro-Johnson movement during the campaign of 1866; Seward remained loyal to the president until the bitter end. A definitive historical understanding and evaluation of Seward, if ever one can be reached, must wait upon a comprehensive modern study of the man. His prewar national repute was based upon his public identification with the opposition to slavery as a moral wrong; he had rallied devotion to himself and to the Republican party by his appeal to "the higher law" and the "irrepressible conflict." Whatever part the pull of oratory or of political ambition may have played in calling forth Seward's ringing phrases, there is no reason to think that they cloaked hypocrisy or an antislavery stand concerned only with the interest of white men. Seward's ardor may have weakened since the days when his words stirred the nation. There had been the cruel defeat of his presidential aspirations, due in considerable part to the very effectiveness of his phrases; there was the death of his wife, which severed a close personal tie between Seward and the moral intensity of antislavery sentiment.[113] The uncertainty of conjecture is compounded because in the postwar years, as we have noted,[114] Seward did not wish to reveal even in private his innermost convictions and intentions. Yet he retained more than compassion for the former slaves. He believed in their right to citizenship and equal status before the law—even equality of suffrage— though for the attainment of the latter, in his characteristically sanguine way, Seward would rely upon some vague development of the future rather than upon federal authority.[115] It was Seward's adamant opposition that prevented an open attack upon the proposed Fourteenth Amendment, a position favored by the president, in issuing the call for the Philadelphia Convention to mobilize the pro-Johnson forces for the election battle of 1866.[116] After the Radical victory, the paper that Seward submitted as a basis for the president's message to Congress was conciliatory, leaving open an avenue for accommodation to congressional policy.[117] It was this draft message, its authorship unknown, which has been interpreted, erroneously, as evidence that Johnson in November 1866 first decided not to oppose the amendment further, then changed his mind, revived the quarrel with Congress and urged southern states not to reconsider their refusal to ratify.[118] Not Johnson, but Seward, sought conciliation; and there is nothing to suggest a change of mind on the part of the secretary of state.[119]

With these attitudes, why did Seward defer to Johnson? Why did he not like other moderates of similar sympathies break with the president? Why did he open himself to bitter repudiation by old friends and to political isolation, a fate that must at least have loomed as an ominous possibility by late spring of 1866?[120] Again, we cannot say with certainty; but a number of considerations come readily to mind. Seward believed that he had already made a major contribution to the cause of freedom by his part in the abolition of slavery and the treaty with Britain to suppress the slave traffic. With these great ends accomplished, and his always hopeful view of the future, perhaps he felt, as Weed had implied in explanation to an English friend's concern for the freedmen, that what "the Freedmen must suffer while the relationships arising between capital and labour are being adjusted" was a minor evil, to be borne with rather than publicly fought.[121] And the consequence of an open fight, the surrender of his post as Secretary of State without assurance of some other major position in national affairs, would have been a hard and selfless decision.

Since the days of battle for the Thirteenth Amendment, Seward had been committed to a reorganization of parties that would attract the support of southerners and of northern Democrats by a speedy and generous restoration of the secession states. He had undoubtedly been influential in directing Johnson toward that objective. Indeed, opinion in Congress in 1866 viewed him as the "head and front of the new party movement," though by the end of July he was thought to have given it up for "reconciliation between the President's particular friends and the body of the Union party."[122] And the president, while withholding full support for Seward's strategy as to both practical politics and basic policy, nevertheless deferred to him to an extent that would naturally have evoked Seward's loyalty and also his hope for a political victory that would renew his national influence and prestige. Then there was the secretary's concern with the record and the achievement of his stewardship of foreign affairs. These were delicately balanced in 1865 and 1866, and he may well have felt that his departure from the cabinet would lead to a dangerously adventuristic policy toward Mexico such as the Blairs had been urging. Or he may have been concerned lest any recognition on his part of basic disunity in the country weaken the nation's position abroad. In addition, Seward together with Stanton had become the symbol of Johnson's refusal to embrace the Democracy unconditionally.[123] To the secretary, this role may have appeared not mere symbol but substance. What other man in the cabinet could offset the full pressure of the Democracy? And if they were not kept at arm's length what might be the consequences? The possible result was a matter of patronage and party power, but not that alone. There were extreme programs of action in the air, defiance of Congress with a denial of its legitimacy, recognition of a national legislature with southern representatives seated by force if necessary. Contemporaries feared another civil war, more fratricidal than the first.[124] The possibility of such dire consequences may have stirred Seward's very real sense of devotion and responsibility to the nation.

Which considerations weighed with Seward, whether he viewed them as politician or statesman or something of both, we cannot know. But in his papers for 1868 there is an interesting passage, not revealing, but suggesting much. It appears in the draft of a response to an affectionate letter from a friend, a reply that was a far from modest affirmation of his historic role as "first secretary to the President." The passage reads: "The Government has been seriously endangered first by ambition on one side and the reckless passions on the other. I have been *felt* if not always *seen* in saving it from both. Only four months of trial remain, before the Government and the Constitution thus saved are in a constitutional way to be delivered into the keeping of a new administration when I shall be entitled to my discharge."[125]

Although Raymond voted to uphold Johnson's veto of the civil rights bill, his entire course shows a consistent concern to protect the basic rights of the freedmen. In the summer and fall of 1865, the New York *Times* editorials made this objective abundantly clear and identified it with the president's policy. Raymond's paper even found no difficulty in accepting the principle that color should not be a basis for exclusion from the voting franchise although it did not favor the national government's forcing Negro suffrage upon the South.[126] It had hoped that the president might sign the civil rights bill. The critical first section, with its "absolute equality of civil rights," was, according to the *Times*, "unquestionably just and right"; the objection was to the arbitrary enforcement provisions of the second section.[127] This position was very close to Senator Morgan's.[128]

Raymond was the administration leader in the House, chairman of the Union (Republican) National Executive Committee, and a close ally of Seward. These political commitments constituted a very formidable restraint upon his championship of equality for the freedmen. Yet in the House of

Representatives, the *Times* editor voted "yea" on the roll call for the Fourteenth Amendment. The fact that no enabling legislation accompanied the passage of the amendment, which would have made clear that its ratification was a condition for readmission of the rebellious states, helped Raymond reconcile his vote for the amendment with his support of the president, who publicly opposed any prerequisite to the return of southern representatives.[129] Raymond had considered the object of the Freedmen's Bureau bill of "utmost importance" and explained that he had not supported the civil rights bill because he, along with Bingham and others, thought that it was not warranted by the Constitution. He had introduced an alternate proposal to declare all persons born in the United States citizens, entitled to the privileges and immunities of citizenship. All the main principles of the Fourteenth Amendment he considered "eminently wise and proper."[130]

It was the desire to placate Raymond and to insure the support of the *Times* for the pro-Johnson movement that broke down the intent of Welles, Cowan, Doolittle, Browning, and McCulloch to include an open attack upon the proposed Fourteenth Amendment in their call for the Philadelphia Convention.[131] For that meeting, Raymond prepared an address that recognized the need for the enlargement of federal powers in respect to the freedmen's rights, and also the power of Congress and the states to make such amendments; but this part of his statement evoked sharp opposition and was deleted.[132] The resolutions adopted by the convention stated that it was the desire and purpose of the southern states that all inhabitants should receive "equal protection in every right of person and property," but omitted any statement that might be interpreted as acquiescence in federal authority over civil rights unless by amendment after the admission of the southern states and with their free consent.[133] This was the most that Raymond could achieve in his effort to gain southern agreement to the principle of "equal protection by law, and by equal access to courts of law, of all the citizens of all the states, without distinction of race or color."[134] He himself was ready to accept the provisions of the Fourteenth Amendment as the platform of the party, and he felt that the president had "made a great mistake in taking ground against those amendments."[135] Johnson's defeat in the fall elections of 1866 was interpreted by Raymond as a popular decision in favor of the principles of the amendment, particularly "the absolute equality of civil rights to all the people of the United States."[136]

Although Raymond's break with Johnson did not come over the civil rights issue, his defection to the opposition was consonant with his basic convictions in respect to equality of citizenship for the Negro. Most other key Republican moderates who took their stand against Johnson shared those convictions. Sen. John Sherman had long been troubled by the probability that freedmen would be oppressed if they had no share of political power. As for the civil rights bill, he wrote, "I felt it so clearly right that I was prepared for the very general acquiescence in its provisions both North and South. To have refused the negroes the simplest rights granted to every other inhabitant, native or foreigner, would be outrageous."[137] The veto was a major factor in Sherman's repudiation of Johnson, whom he had hitherto defended. "The President's course on the Civil Rights Bill and constitutional amendment was so unwise that I could not for a moment allow anyone to suppose that I meant with him to join a coalition with the rebels and Copperheads."[138] Senators Lyman Trumbull of Illinois, James Grimes of Iowa, and William Fessenden of Maine were all men of moderation and principle, able to withstand terrific pressures, as their votes against Johnson's conviction on impeachment charges later made amply clear; their principles included a commitment to basic civil rights for the freedmen. All three wished to work with the president rather than against him, but, to use Welles's characterization of the latter two men, "their natural tendency would I knew incline them to the opposition. They are both intense on the negro."[139] The same might be said for other moderates, for Gov. John Andrew of Massachusetts, for Henry Ward Beecher, for Samuel Bowles of the Springfield *Republican,* for John Bingham of Ohio, for Henry Dawes of Massachusetts, for James Hawley of Connecticut, and for Gen. O. O. Howard of the Freedmen's Bureau.

The case of the two influential midwestern governors, Oliver P. Morton of Indiana and Jacob D. Cox of Ohio, is not so clear. Both were chief executives of a citizenry much given to discrimination against the Negro and closely divided between Republicans and Democrats. Although Cox had strong convictions in respect to the evil of slavery and took great satisfaction as a military officer in freeing refugee "contrabands," he disappointed antislavery men who had hoped that his early Oberlin training and his close relationship to Charles G. Finney would bring support for Negro suffrage. Such support Cox refused, and instead issued a public statement proposing separation of the races in the southern states, with schools, homesteads, and full political privileges for the Negroes.[140] Later in advising Johnson to accept the civil rights bill, Cox stressed political expediency; but he also assumed that the president as well as himself and "all true Union men" believed in the principle of equality before the law—that it was "right."[141] While still supporting

Johnson, he accepted the Fourteenth Amendment, expressing privately his approval of all parts of the amendment except the disqualifying clause of the third section.[142] In the campaign of 1867 to amend the Ohio constitution, he argued for Negro suffrage since it had already been forced upon the South.[143]

Governor Morton was a political enemy of Radicals in Indiana; and his public opposition in September 1865 to making Negro suffrage a condition for southern restoration was widely publicized and enthusiastically received by pro-Johnson men. An examination of his speech discloses not an opposition to Negro suffrage as such but the argument that Indiana was in no condition to urge voting privileges for Negroes in the South when the state itself discriminated so grossly against the "many very intelligent and well qualified" colored people within its own borders. Morton pointed out the restriction not only upon their political power but also upon their testimony in court, their access to public schools, and, if they had come into the state since 1850, their legal right to make valid contracts. He spoke highly of the fighting record of the Indiana colored regiment and pointed to the ironic fact that half the men who composed it could not legally come back into the state. The tone of the address was not one of defending discrimination but one of gently criticizing his fellow Hoosiers. As for southern freedmen, Morton believed that they should have time to acquire property and obtain a little education, and then "at the end of 10, 15, or 20 years, let them come into the enjoyment of their political rights."[144] The governor was clearly in advance of state sentiment in advocating for Negroes the benefit of schooling and the right to testify in court. His sponsorship of the repeal of the state statute that excluded their testimony finally resulted in the elimination of that discrimination.[145] It was Morton who warned Johnson that a veto of the civil rights bill would separate the president and the Union-Republican party, that if he did not sign the measure the two men could not again meet in political friendship.[146] Morton's decision to oppose Johnson was no doubt essentially a political one, but his attitude toward the Negro was not identical with that of the president.[147]

Behind conciliatory Republican leaders whose personal attitudes might in other circumstances have enabled them to accept a solution that would leave the future status of the freedmen in the hands of southern whites, there was the pressure of mass Republican opinion. The overwhelming preponderance of Republican sentiment was behind a national guarantee for basic civil equality, short of suffrage, for the freedmen. This sentiment is unmistakable in newspaper editorials and private correspondence;[148] it was also reflected in the congressional vote on what was to become the Fourteenth

Amendment. In the Senate, Republicans divided thirty-three to four in its favor. The "nays" were those of senators Cowan, Doolittle, Norton of Minnesota and Van Winkle of West Virginia. Senator Dixon was absent and not voting. In the House, 138 Republican votes were cast for the amendment; not a single Republican voted against it.[149] This vote was taken before Johnson made clear his political intentions by issuance of the call for the Philadelphia Convention.

After the civil rights veto, Republican opinion had crystallized in a determination to set further conditions before accepting southern representatives back into the counsels of the nation, but not just any conditions.[150] The matters dealt with in sections two and three of the Fourteenth Amendment, namely the basis of future southern representation, the granting of suffrage to the Negro, and the degree of proscription of Confederate leaders, were negotiable; the question of equality before the law, federally enforceable, was no longer open to compromise. The issue of civil rights and national protection for the freedmen was not, as has sometimes been implied, the product of campaign propaganda and exaggeration, nor even of the shocking impact of the Memphis and New Orleans riots. The civil rights issue predated those developments.

Although in deference to Seward and Raymond the pro-Johnson leaders had attempted to evade discussion of the Fourteenth Amendment, it was generally recognized as being at stake in the ensuing campaign. After Radical victories in the states that voted in September and early October, pressure was put upon the president to accept the amendment. As early as September 19, Bennett in the *Herald* foresaw defeat unless the president would "take up" the proposed Fourteenth Amendment and "push it through all the still excluded Southern States as rapidly as possible" with the kind of pressure he had used in behalf of the Thirteenth Amendment. Bennett at last deplored the condition he had done so much to provoke, "the widening of his [Johnson's] conflict with the radicals to a conflict with Congress." He now viewed the amendment as "not a radical measure, but a measure of the republican conservatives of Congress."[151] When Samuel S. Cox asked the president about the rumors that he would modify his opposition to the amendment in keeping with "the poplar [sic] current," Johnson "got as ugly as the Devil. He was regularly mad. . . . There's no budge in him. Browning's letter is his view."[152]

S. L. M. Barlow's attitude toward the amendment's role in campaign strategy is pertinent. He was much opposed to the president's yielding unless the Johnson forces should suffer defeat in New York. In that event, he thought the president might be "compelled to yield on the Constitutional amendment, but to yield to the pressure now, before our election, would destroy him & be in gross bad faith . . . as we are making a good fight & cannot now change our course."[153] If faced with defeat in November, however, Barlow thought Johnson could say to the South, "While I have not thought the ratification of the amendment necessary . . . the Northern people have decided otherwise—You must be represented. . . . Ratify the amendment therefore." Barlow explained that Johnson could "be supported in this, if necessary, after November, not only here but by the ablest presses of the South in New Orleans, Mobile, Charleston & Richmond—To change now would deprive him, practically of every paper and every voter—The Radicals would not be won back to him and he would lose the whole power of the democratic party."[154]

Browning's letter, to which Representative Cox referred, is additional proof of the importance of the amendment as a campaign issue. It is also, and more importantly, added evidence that the opposition of the pro-Johnson forces to the amendment was not merely limited to a distaste for section three, which denied southern leaders state and national office. The heart of Browning's argument, approved by the president, was that section one, the civil rights guarantee, would restrict the states in functions properly their own. It would subject the "authority and control of the States over matters of purely domestic and local concern . . . to criticism, interpretation and adjudication by the Federal tribunals, whose judgments and decrees will be supreme."[155]

Johnson's refusal, despite great pressure and much advice, to capitulate on the Fourteenth Amendment after his election defeat cannot be attributed alone to his stubborn nature. The explanation that he decided for conciliation, then reversed course on the basis of the Radicals' behavior, is exploded by the identification of the early conciliatory draft message as the work of Seward.[156] Another factor entered into policy considerations, the hope of ultimate victory and the tactical advantage to be gained by encouraging extreme action on the part of the opposition with a view to ultimate popular reaction against it. Doolittle wrote Browning on November 8: "The elections are over and we are beaten for the present. But our cause will live. If all the states not represented refuse to ratify the amendment . . . the extreme Rads will go . . . for reorganizing the southern states on negro suffrage. . . . That will present the issue squarely of forcing negro suffrage upon the South and upon that we can beat them at the next Presidential election."[157] A short time later, Weed was writing Seward that he had rebuffed Senator Morgan's suggestion of an organization in Congress against "extreme men." Weed explained, "I think that if the pressure should be withdrawn the Radicals would hang *themselves*."[158] From Ohio the prediction reached the president that "if Congress resorts to rash and violent means to carry out the destructive purposes of the radicals, their own party will break to pieces."[159] From New York came more positive advice: "Are those proposed amendments to be adopted, changing the whole nature of our government. I trust not. I think a year or two of Radicalism more, will satisfy the country that the principles contained in that old instrument are too dear to us to be frittered away. . . . I believe that with you standing firmly on the ground you have assumed and each state organizing her conservative men on the Philadelphia platform, two years more will have seen the end of the Radical race."[160] Analysts of the 1866 election returns pointed out to the president that if the potential vote of the unrepresented South were added to the Conservative vote in the North, a large majority of the nation supported the president and opposed the amendment, and that ultimately the president must triumph.[161]

Raymond's editorials in the *Times* had urged the president to accept the decision of the people in favor of the amendment, and either to recommend its ratification by the southern states or to stand aside while they made a settlement with Congress upon the basis of its principles. By the end of December, however, Raymond had come to the conclusion that Johnson's opposition to the amendment was unyielding. The president, he explained, intended to hold to his earlier position in the conviction that his policy would ultimately prevail. Johnson believed that the Supreme Court would set aside any conditions Congress might impose upon the South or, failing such a resolution of the conflict, that the use of military power to enforce congressional policy would become so "expensive, odious and intolerable" that the voters would expel from power the party responsible for such a policy.[162]

The losses that the Radicals sustained in the state elections of 1867 seemed to justify the president's hope of victory and the strategy of no compromise. News of the defeat of the Radicals in Connecticut's April election of that year was received by Johnson as "the turn of the current" and by Welles as "the first loud knock which admonishes the Radicals of their inevitable doom."[163] Welles believed that the returns from Pennsylvania and Ohio in October indicated the "total overthrow of the Radicals and the downfall of that party."[164] In November 1867, Johnson celebrated the election results by a victory speech before a group of serenaders in which he held that "the people have spoken in a manner not to be misunderstood."[165] The president's "stubbornness" of the previous November seemed to have prepared the way for success in the presidential election of 1868. The hope proved an illusion; but the hope was present, and died hard.[166]

In refusing to accept the equal rights provisions of the Civil Rights Act or of the Fourteenth Amendment, Johnson won lasting gratitude from white southerners to whom the concept of equality between the races was anathema,[167] and this despite the ordeal of military government and immediate universal Negro suffrage, which they in all likelihood would have been spared had Johnson's course been different. But with this decision, the president lost the confidence and respect of moderate Republicans. Lyman Trumbull and John Sherman both felt a sense of betrayal in Johnson's veto of the civil rights bill. "Besides," confided Sherman to his brother, "he [Johnson] is insincere; he has deceived and misled his best friends."[168] The confidence in Johnson's assurances of justice for the freedpeople, which characterized Republican opinion, except that of extreme Radicals, in December 1865, turned to distrust. No longer were misgivings directed toward presidential policy alone; they came to embrace the president's intention and integrity, and corroded his public influence. "The truth is," Senator Fessenden wrote to Senator Morgan in mid-1867, "Mr. Johnson has continued to excite so much distrust that the public mind is easily played upon by those who are seeking only the accomplishment of their own purposes."[169] By standing adamant against a federally enforceable pledge of minimum civil equality for the Negro as a prerequisite to restoration of the secession states, Johnson precipitated a great issue of moral principle central to the battle over Reconstruction; and he brought upon himself an unparalleled humiliation.

CHAPTER SEVEN

Negro Suffrage and Republican Politics
The Problem of Motivation in Reconstruction Historiography

Republican party leadership of the 1860s was responsible for establishing the legal right of Negro citizens to equal suffrage, first in the defeated South by act of Congress and then throughout the nation by constitutional amendment.[1] Whether historians have condemned or applauded the grant of suffrage to Negroes in the post–Civil War years, they have more often than not viewed the motives behind this party action with considerable cynicism. The purpose of this article is to review their treatment and to raise for reexamination the question of what moved Republicans in Congress to such far-reaching action.

The earliest study of the origins of the Fifteenth Amendment was prepared by a scholarly lawyer from western Virginia, Allen Caperton Braxton, for presentation to the state bar association in 1903. The work is still cited, and a new edition was printed in the 1930s.[2] Braxton held that Negro suffrage was the result of "gratitude, apprehension and politics—these three: but the greatest of these was politics."[3] To Radical leaders of the Republican party, enfranchisement early appeared "a promising means of party aggrandisement"; it soon became "essential to the perpetuation of their power." In the struggle with President Andrew Johnson over Reconstruction, they had alienated "the entire white race of the South" for at least a generation to come. Once the southern states were restored to the Union and the white vote of the South added to the Democratic vote of the North, the Republicans would face hopeless defeat; the only means of escape lay through the southern Negro. In the legislation of March 1867 Radicals effected "a *coup d'etat* of the first magnitude," but it was not a stable foundation on which to build future political power. The law might be rescinded by Congress, overturned by judicial decision, or defied by the southern states after their readmission. Only a constitutional amendment could provide security. It would also mean votes from an increasing Negro population in the North as a potential balance of power in close elections.[4] A few footnotes and quotations, notably one from Charles Sumner, appear as illustrative, and there is a flat assertion that debates in Congress on the Fifteenth Amendment "leave no room to doubt" its political inspiration.[5] It is clear, however, that the author felt no need either to scrutinize or to document his interpretation; a primary relationship between Negro suffrage and party expediency appeared to him self-evident.

Braxton did examine in detail a thesis and the historic contradiction that it implied. "One may well question," he wrote in conclusion, "whether the popular will was executed or thwarted when negro suffrage was written into the fundamental law of this nation."[6] No reader would doubt that the author's answer was "thwarted." Despite some overstatement and minor distortions of fact, this thesis is sound history. The national guarantee of an equal vote to the Negro did not reflect a popular consensus, even in the North.[7] Braxton's attempt to explain how an unwanted policy became the fundamental law of the land, though less convincing, raised an important historical problem.

Despite his emphasis upon political expediency as the impelling causal element behind equal suffrage, the Virginia attorney might have considered Republican leaders who had imposed this result upon the nation, at least a few of their number, men sincerely concerned with the Negro's right to vote. References to "fanaticism," "bigotry," and "negrophiles" suggest that he did, though obviously without sympathy. This implication, however, is explicitly disavowed and with specific reference to Senator Sumner, Braxton found "shocking" evidence of insincerity in the fact that men who argued for the inalienable right of the Negro to vote agreed to exclude Indians and Chinese from the franchise.[8] He considered leaders of the party to be distinguished from the rank and file of northerners neither by principle nor by lack of prejudice. Unlike their constituents, congressmen were removed from personal competition with the Negro, and their national perspective made them aware of the dependence of Republican party power upon Negro enfranchisement. Braxton's indictment of Republican motivation showed charity on just one count. He granted that some leaders were moved neither by "malice toward the South" nor by "heartless political ambition." They had come to equate the life of the Republican party with the life of the nation and honestly feared a Democratic victory as a national disaster.[9]

The second study of the Fifteenth Amendment, by John M. Mathews, appeared in 1909 and was to remain the standard historical account for more than half a century. Originally prepared as a paper for a seminar in political science at Johns Hopkins University, it is a most unhistorical history in the sense that its author was more concerned to analyze concepts than men or events. He narrowly delimited the chronology and substance of his "legislative history" and showed special interest in the judicial interpretation of the amendment.[10] Neither the historic problem posed by Braxton's study nor the question of men's motives as individuals or as party leaders presented a challenge to Mathews; he did not even consider it important to identify with particular congressmen or with political parties the four elements in his analysis—the humanitarians, the nationalists, the politicians, and the local autonomists. Indeed, he explicitly stated that "These forces were primarily principles, rather than men or groups of men. They were not always separable except in thought, for the same senator or representative was often influenced by more than one of them at the same time."[11]

Yet the Mathews monograph does carry certain implications in respect to motivation. The statement that "There was little real difference of opinion among the leaders in Congress as to the desirability of enlarging the sphere of political liberty for the negro race" might be read as an assumption of genuine concern for the Negro on the part of the lawmakers. On the other hand, a quite different interpretation could be given to statements that "The politician was the initiator and real engineer of the movement," that he labored for a concrete objective "fraught with definite practical results," and that he was not altogether satisfied with the final form of the amendment "because it did not directly and specifically guarantee the African's right to vote" and hence might be evaded.[12] In this study so long considered authoritative, there is nothing to confirm Braxton's identification of equal suffrage with partisan advantage, but neither is there anything that would cause its readers to question that assumption.

The writings of William A. Dunning and of James Ford Rhodes, the two most influential scholars with accounts of Reconstruction published during the first decade of the twentieth century, did sound a warning.[13] To southerners it had been "inconceivable," Dunning pointed out, that "rational men of the North should seriously approve of negro suffrage *per se*"; hence they assumed that the only explanation was "a craving for political power."[14] Dunning was implying a fallacy in their understanding. Yet he himself attributed

Republican sponsorship of Negro suffrage in the First Reconstruction Act of 1867 to the "pressure of party necessity and of Sumner's tireless urging." In writing of the Fifteenth Amendment, Dunning assumed that he had established the motivation behind it. He cited an earlier paragraph as support for the statement: "We have already seen the partisan motive which gave the impulse to the passage of the Fifteenth Amendment." Any reader who took the trouble to turn back the pages would find a passage that, far from proving the contention, did not necessarily imply it. Dunning had written that after the presidential election of 1868 in which Democrats gained majorities in Georgia and Louisiana through the use of violence, moderate Republicans had no uncertainty as to "the policy of maintaining what had been achieved in enfranchising the blacks."[15]

Rhodes was more explicit in his warning and more direct in crediting to humanitarian feelings within Republican party ranks an influence in "forcing negro suffrage upon the South." He cautioned readers not to lose sight of the high motives involved "for it would be easy to collect a mass of facts showing that the sole aim of congressional reconstruction was to strengthen the Republican party."[16] Neither the statement quoted nor his account as a whole would stir to skepticism anyone who had assumed with Braxton the predominance of political expediency. He did not analyze or criticize the Braxton assumption but rather supplemented it. In Rhodes's view, there were men with "intelligence and high character" who were "earnest for the immediate enfranchisement of the freedmen," but they were "numerically small."[17] His writing at times carried an unintended innuendo. For example, he stated that the majority of Republicans in Congress when they reassembled after the Christmas holidays of 1866 did not favor the imposition of Negro suffrage upon the South, a policy that they sustained by a two-thirds vote a few weeks later. The explanation lay in "The rejection of the Fourteenth Amendment by the South, the clever use of the 'outrages' argument, the animosity to the President . . . which was increased to virulence by his wholesale removals of Republicans from office," factors that "enabled the partisan tyranny of Stevens and the pertinacity of Sumner to achieve this result."[18]

The ambivalence in Rhodes's treatment arose primarily from his strong conviction that the grant of suffrage to the Negro during Reconstruction was a major mistake in policy. This judgment was evident in a paper that he delivered before the Massachusetts Historical Society while writing his account of Reconstruction[19] and also in the volumes of his *History of the United States*, which appeared two years later. Suffrage had been an abysmal failure that "pandered to the ignorant negroes, the knavish white natives and the vulturous adventurers who flocked from the North" and "neutralized the work of honest Republicans. . . ."[20] Experience in the North, in his opinion, also discredited the grant of equal suffrage to the Negro—he had shown little political leadership, rarely identified himself "with any movement on a high plane," such as civil service, tariff reform, honest money, or pure municipal government, and "arrogantly asserts his right to recognition" because he is "greedy for office and emolument." All had not been the Negro's fault; he had been "started at the top" despite "all the warnings of science and political experience."[21] Rhodes believed that the findings of science were clear and they had been available to Sumner and his fellow advocates of Negro enfranchisement through the distinguished Harvard scientist Louis Agassiz, who was Sumner's friend.[22] He did not place all blame on Sumner, however, but indicated that the fault lay in our national character. "I think that England or Prussia would have solved the negro problem better"; they would have "studied the negro scientifically"; in the "age of Darwin and Huxley" Americans had made no attempt to do so.[23]

In discussing the problem with fellow historians, Rhodes revealed more sharply than in his writings his personal assessment of motivation: "From a variety of motives, some praiseworthy and others the reverse, we forced negro suffrage upon the South. . . . Party advantage, the desire of worthless men at the North for offices at the South, co-operated with a misguided humanitarianism."[24] The warning that he sounded, and the less explicit one from Dunning as well, reflected a conscientious desire on the part of these distinguished historians to be fair, restrained, and judicious. The assumption that most Republican members of Congress who voted for equal Negro suffrage did so primarily, if not solely, for reasons of political expediency, was an assumption they accepted; it apparently did not occur to either man that there was need for any careful scrutiny to establish the validity of this accusation.

For three decades, until the post–World War II years, few historians handled the question of Republican motivation with as much fairness as had Rhodes and Dunning. Ellis P. Oberholtzer, in his multivolume *History of the United States Since the Civil War*, wrote that "Just as the war had not been waged to free the negro from bondage" so the postwar strife "except to a few minds, had little enough to do with the improvement of the lot of the black man." He continued: "The project to make voters out of black men was not so much for their social elevation as for the further punishment of the Southern white people—for the capture of offices for Radical scamps and the intrenchment of the Radical party in power for a long time to come in the South and in the country at large."[25] The small but influential volume in the Yale *Chronicles of America* series written by Dunning's foremost student, Walter L. Fleming, made the indictment specific. The election of 1868, Fleming wrote, showed that Democrats could command more white votes than could Republicans "whose total included nearly 700,000 blacks." This prompted the Radicals to frame the Fifteenth Amendment, which, as it appeared to them, would not only "make safe the negro majorities in the South" but also add strength from Negroes previously denied the ballot in the North, thus assuring "900,000 negro voters for the Republican party."[26]

During the late 1920s and the 1930s, a period in Reconstruction historiography that saw the "canonization" of Andrew Johnson,[27] little charity was shown to those who had been Johnson's opponents. Claude G. Bowers developed the "conspiracy" approach to Negro suffrage, seeing it as the culmination of a plot hatched by Sumner and a few Radicals and dating back at least to the early days of 1865.[28] He quoted approvingly the Georgian, Benjamin H. Hill, who charged that Negro suffrage was a matter of knaves using fools "'to keep the Radical Party in power in the approaching presidential election, . . . to retain by force and fraud the power they are losing in the detection of their treason in the North.'"[29] George Fort Milton recognized that "The Radicals had mixed motives in this insistence on negro suffrage," but his lack of sympathy for the "old Abolitionists" led him to gibe at Sumner. From a letter of the senator, he quoted, "'We need the votes of all,'" then observed, "Could it be that practical political necessities moved him as well as lofty idealistic views?"[30] Milton did little more than mention the Fifteenth Amendment but could not resist using the opportunity to belittle its Republican sponsors: ". . . one or two Senators shamefacedly admitted that perhaps an intelligent white woman had as much right as an ignorant negro plowhand to determine the destinies of the nation. But there seemed little political advantage in women suffrage. . . ."[31] James G. Randall, whose substantial volume on the Civil War and Reconstruction served as a standard college textbook from the 1930s to the 1960s, handled the subject of Negro suffrage with restraint; yet in substance he accepted a mild version of Bowers' conspiracy thesis. Randall's variant was that "the importance of the Negro vote to the Republican party North and South caused leading Radicals to keep their eye upon the issue" although northern sentiment would not support nationwide Negro suffrage. Gradually, as the power of the Radicals increased, they moved toward their goal. "Step by step they were able to enact laws promoting Negro suffrage without an amendment, and finally to carry the suffrage amendment itself in the first year of Grant's administration."[32] This account was allowed to stand without modification when the volume was revised in 1961 by David Donald.[33]

The chronological limits of Howard K. Beale's study of the election of 1866, perhaps the most influential scholarly product of the pro-Johnson historiography, precluded an examination of the Reconstruction Acts of 1867 and the Fifteenth Amendment. However, there is a chapter devoted to Negro suffrage as a general issue.[34] Beale divided its Radical proponents into four groups—old abolitionists, who believed in the principle of equal suffrage; friends of the Negro, who saw the ballot as his only means of defense; men hostile to racial equality, who would use Negro suffrage to humiliate the defeated South; and, lastly, "a more numerous group" to whom "expediency was the motive."[35] Curiously, his classification had the same weakness as Mathews' disembodied analysis; it offered the reader no evidence that any one of the four "groups" was identifiable in terms of specific individuals. In fact, despite a deep personal commitment to Negro equality and intensive manuscript research, Beale added little new except to link the suffrage issue with his general thesis that Radical leaders were motivated by economic as well as political ends. "If the South could be excluded, or admitted only with negro suffrage," he wrote, "the new industrial order which the Northeast was developing, would be safe."[36]

Yet Beale did not dismiss the suffrage issue as summarily as had the Republicans in the 1866 campaign. His treatment suggests his interest in the subject, and particularly in the claim made during 1865 and after that the Negro would never be safe unless protected by the ballot. Beale considered it "a powerful [argument]" even though he looked with sympathy upon those who mistrusted a grant of unqualified suffrage to naive and uneducated freedmen. After struggling with the argument for several pages, he concluded that no one could say with certainty whether without the ballot the status of the newly freed slave among white southerners would have been shaped by "the fair-minded" or "the vicious." Then he added: "Few cared to know. Extreme Radicals wanted negro suffrage; outrages against the negroes, and an exaggeration of cruel codes would reconcile Northerners to it."[37] In other words, the "powerful argument" was essentially a propaganda device; its prevalence in the 1860s would not lighten the charges against the Republican Radical leadership.

Another election study, Charles H. Coleman's analysis of the Grant-Seymour campaign of 1868, was published in the 1930s and at once took its place as the standard, perhaps definitive, account. Coleman's discussion of the Negro suffrage issue in the elections of 1867 and 1868 is exceptionally fair and informative. Without raising the question of motivation or passing judgment, it yet provides considerable material pertinent to the problem.[38] Also, Coleman, like Walter Fleming, was interested in the importance of the Negro vote. He estimated that it had provided Grant with 450,000 of his total, without which the Republicans would not have gained a popular majority.[39] While Coleman believed that a majority of the white voters of the country favored the Democratic party in 1868 and implied that this remained true until 1896, unlike Fleming, he did not point to any connection between the 1868 election results and the movement immediately thereafter for an equal-suffrage amendment. The omission may have been due to his clear recognition that Grant's victory in the electoral college would have been secure without any Negro votes. The Democrats with better leadership, according to Coleman, might have contended with the Republicans on almost equal terms in 1868, but they did not lose the election "through the operation of the reconstruction acts."[40] Despite a generally careful and balanced presentation, in his opening paragraph Coleman made reference incidentally and uncritically to "Republican ascendancy" as the motive behind the Fifteenth Amendment.[41] He had not given thought to the relationship between his findings and the time-honored charges of Braxton and Fleming.

By the 1950s a new direction was evident in historical writings dealing with the Negro in nineteenth-century America, one that rejected the assumption of racial inferiority and cherished the quest for racial equality.[42] This trend, which reached major proportions in the 1960s, drew stimulus and support both from the contemporary social and intellectual climate and from interior developments within historical research. During the thirties revisionist articles dealing with so-called "black" Reconstruction in the South had anticipated postwar attitudes toward race relationships and had upset the negative stereotypes of "scalawags," "carpetbaggers," and "Radical" regimes.[43] In the forties the National Archives provided material for new departures in Reconstruction scholarship by making available the manuscript records of the Freedmen's Bureau with a useful checklist.[44] The extremes to which vindication of Andrew Johnson had been carried in the thirties, together with a program to assemble and publish his papers, led to reexamination of his record and that of his opponents.[45] Military confrontation with

Hitler stimulated a challenge to the "needless war" interpretation of the American civil conflict, redirecting attention to slavery as a moral issue.[46] Antislavery agitators became the focus of renewed interest and sympathy, the latter reinforced by a growing sophistication in the historian's borrowings from psychology and sociology.[47] Leadership of Negroes in the contemporary struggle for equality found a counterpart in an increased recognition of the role of Negro leadership during the nineteenth century.[48] Through new biographies and analytical articles, a beginning was made in reassessing the record and motives of leading Radicals.[49] Finally, the coincidence of the Civil War centennial with the great public civil rights issues of the 1960s quickened the pace of historical writings concerned with the status of the Negro.[50]

Out of these recent studies has come a new perspective on the post–Civil War grant of suffrage to the Negro, once widely regarded with dismay. The Fifteenth Amendment is now seen as a "momentous enactment." It included Negroes within "the American dream of equality and opportunity," gave the United States distinction as being the first nation committed to the proposition that in a "bi-racial society . . . human beings must have equal rights," and established an essential legal substructure upon which to build the reality of political equality.[51]

There has also emerged an explanation of political Radicalism during Reconstruction, even of Republicanism generally, in terms of ideas and idealism. The case has been subtly argued and dramatically summarized by Kenneth M. Stampp: ". . . radical reconstruction ought to be viewed in part as the last great crusade of the nineteenth-century romantic reformers." If anything, Radicals were less opportunistic and more candid than the average politician. "To the practical motives that the radicals occasionally revealed must be added the moral idealism that they inherited from the abolitionists."[52] The case for Radicalism has also been persuasively presented by the English historian William Ranulf Brock, who has written that the cement binding together the Radicals as a political group was "not interest but a number of propositions about equality, rights, and national power."[53] In fact, Brock does not limit this generous interpretation of motive to the Radicals, but includes moderate Republicans as well. He has gone even further and identified "the great moving power behind Reconstruction" with "the conviction of the average Republican that the objectives of his party were rational and humane."[54] The study by the present authors led to the conclusion that the moderates in Congress broke with the president in 1866 primarily because of their genuine concern for equal civil rights short of suffrage.[55]

With the ferment and new direction of Reconstruction historiography, the old Braxton-Rhodes-Fleming assumption of party expediency as the controlling motive behind support for Negro suffrage by Republican congressmen might reasonably be expected to meet one of three fates: it might be quietly replaced by the opposite assumption that congressional votes reflected in large measure the strain of idealism in Republicanism; it could be dismissed on the ground that there had been a fusion of principle and expediency so intimate and indivisible as to preclude further inquiry; or it could be subjected to an incisive, detailed, and comprehensive examination. At the present writing neither the first nor third alternative appears at all likely. As for the second, the problem of motivation deserves a better resolution, for it is important both to our understanding of the past and to our expectations of the future.

The "practical" view of Republican motivation is too casually accepted in historical writings and too consonant with prevailing attitudes toward politicians and parties to be in danger of just disappearing. Leslie H. Fishel, Jr., Emma Lou Thornbrough, and Leon F. Litwack in their sympathetic pioneering studies of Negroes in the North all assume that Republican politicians had little interest in the Negro except to obtain his vote.[56] In staking out the well-merited abolitionist claim of credit for having championed the cause of Negro equality during the Civil War and Reconstruction, James M. McPherson perpetuates the traditional attitude toward Republicans: the abolitionists provided moral justification, but party policies "were undertaken primarily for military or political reasons."[57] Indeed, McPherson condemns the whole North for a failure of conscience and belittles the public support given to equal rights as "primarily a conversion of expediency rather than one of conviction."[58] David Donald has attempted to bypass the "difficulty of fathoming ... motives" by disregarding individuals in favor of "objective behavior patterns" and "quantitatively measurable forces." His procedures and logic, however, start with the assumption that politicians wish either reelection or higher office and that this fact is controlling in presidential policy and congressional voting.[59] It is startling to read that Lincoln's policies could have been arrived at by "A rather simple computer installed in the White House, fed the elementary statistical information about election returns and programed to solve the recurrent problem of winning re-election. ..."[60]

Even Stampp, who restates the old hostile arguments regarding the political motivation of Radicals in order to challenge them, replies directly only with the observation that conservatives as well were thinking how best to keep the Republican party in power—to them Negro suffrage simply appeared an obstacle rather than an instrument of party unity and control. Stampp also strikes a disparaging note evident elsewhere in recent scholarship. This is the charge of "timidity" and "evasion" leveled against Republican politicians on the question of Negro suffrage.[61] There is irony in the shifting basis of attack upon the reputation of Republican politicians. Once berated from the right for plots and maneuvers to thwart the popular will and establish Negro suffrage, these whipping boys of history are now in danger of assault from the left for having lacked the boldness, energy, and conviction needed for an earlier and more secure victory.

There finally appeared in 1965 to supersede the Mathews monograph an intensive, scholarly work by a young historian, William Gillette, on the passage and ratification of the Fifteenth Amendment. Reflecting the modern temper in its rejection of caste and commitment to equality, the new study nevertheless represents a vigorous survival of the Braxton-Fleming tradition.[62] Gillette's thesis transfers to the North the emphasis formerly placed on the South, but political expediency remains the heart of the matter: "The primary object of the Amendment was *to get the Negro vote* in the North. . . ."[63] As revealed by the election results of 1868, "prospects for both northern and southern Republicans were not bright" and, according to Gillette, "Republicans had to do something." They were pessimistic about reliance upon the Negro vote in the South but alert to its potential in the North. This prospect motivated the framing of the amendment and accounted for ratification in the face of widespread opposition since it "made political sense to shrewd politicians. . . ."[64] In effect, Gillette accepts as his thesis the judgment pronounced in 1870 by the Democratic party-line newspaper, the New York *World,* that Republican leaders "'calculated that the Negro vote in the doubtful Northern states would be sufficient to maintain the Republican ascendancy in those states and, through them, in the politics of the country. It was with this in view that they judged the Fifteenth Amendment essential to the success of their party.'"[65]

In challenge to the dominant pattern of interpretation from Braxton through Gillette, we should like to suggest that Republican party leadership played a crucial role in committing this nation to equal suffrage for the Negro not because of political expediency but *despite* political risk. An incontestable fact of Reconstruction history suggests this view. Race prejudice was so strong in the North that the issue of equal Negro suffrage constituted a clear and present danger to Republicans. White backlash may be a recently coined phrase, but it was a virulent political phenomenon in the 1860s. The exploitation of prejudice by the Democratic opposition was blatant and unashamed.

The power base of the Republican party lay in the North. However much party leaders desired to break through sectional boundaries to create a national image or to gain some measure of security from southern votes, victory or defeat in the presidential elections of the nineteenth century lay in the northern states. With the exception of the contested election of 1876, electoral votes from the South were irrelevant—either nonexistent or unnecessary—to Republican victory. It was the loss of Connecticut, Indiana, and New York in 1876 and 1884, and of those states plus Illinois in 1892, which was critical; had they remained in the Republican column, Democrats would have waited until the twentieth century to claim residence for one of their own in the White House.[66]

What has been charged to timidity might better be credited to prudence. The caution with which Republicans handled the Negro suffrage issue in 1865, 1866, and again in 1868 made political sense. Had the elections of 1866 and 1868 been fought on a platform supporting equal suffrage, who could say with certainty, then or now, that Republicans would have maintained power?[67] In the state elections of 1867, when Negro suffrage was a major issue, the party took a beating in Connecticut, New York, Pennsylvania, and New Jersey, suffered losses in local elections in Indiana and Illinois, and came within 0.4 percent of losing the Ohio governorship despite the personal political strength of their candidate Rutherford B. Hayes. In Ohio the issue was clearly drawn, for, in addition to the nationwide commitment to Negro suffrage in the South made by the First Reconstruction Act of March 1867, the Republican party bore responsibility for a statewide referendum on behalf of equal suffrage at home. The proposed suffrage amendment to the state constitution went down to defeat with less than 46 percent of the votes cast. Democrats gained control of both houses of the state legislature, turning a comfortable Republican margin of forty-six into a Democratic majority of eight. Even judged by the gubernatorial vote, Republicans suffered a serious loss of support, for the popular Hayes gained 50.3 percent of the vote as compared to 54.5 percent won by the Republican candidate for secretary of state in 1866.[68]

There was nothing exceptional about Ohioans' hostility to Negro suffrage. In Republican Minnesota and Kansas equal-suffrage amendments also went down to defeat in the fall elections of 1867, with a respectable 48.8 percent of the vote in the former but with less than 35 percent in the latter despite the fact that Kansas Republicans in the 1860s constituted 70 percent of the electorate. From 1865 through 1869 eleven referendum votes were held in eight northern states on constitutional changes to provide Negroes with the ballot; only two were successful—those held during the fall of 1868 in Iowa and Minnesota. The Minnesota victory, gained after two previous defeats, has been attributed to trickery in labeling the amendment.[69] The issue was never placed before the white voters of Illinois, Indiana, Pennsylvania, or New Jersey; and this fact probably indicated a higher intensity of race prejudice than in Connecticut, New York, and Ohio, where equal suffrage was defeated.[70] These seven were marginal states of critical importance to the Republicans in national elections. The tenacity of opposition to Negro enfranchisement is well illustrated in New York, where one might have expected to find it minimal since Negroes had always voted in the state although subjected to a discriminatory property qualification since 1821. After a Republican legislature ratified the Fifteenth Amendment in April 1869, New Yorkers defeated a similar change in the state constitution, swept the Republicans out of control at Albany, and returned a Democratic majority of twenty, which promptly voted to rescind New York's ratification.[71]

In short, Republican sponsorship of Negro suffrage meant flirtation with political disaster in the North, particularly in any one or all of the seven pivotal states where both the prejudice of race and the Democratic opposition were strong. Included among them were the four most populous states in the nation, with corresponding weight in the electoral college: New York, Pennsylvania, Ohio, and Illinois. Negroes were denied equal suffrage in every one of these critically important seven and only in New York did they enjoy a partial enfranchisement. If Negroes were to be equally enfranchised, as the Fifteenth Amendment directed, it is true that Republicans could count upon support from an overwhelming majority of the new voters. It does not necessarily follow, however, that this prospect was enticing to "shrewd politicians." What simple political computation could add the number of potential Negro voters to be derived from a minority population that reached a high of 3.4 percent in New Jersey and 2.4 percent in Ohio, then diminished in the other five states from 1.9 to 1.1 percent, a population already partially enfranchised in New York and to be partially disenfranchised in Connecticut by the state's nondiscriminatory illiteracy tests; determine and subtract the probable number of white voters who would be alienated among the dominant 96.6 to 98.9 percent of the population; and predict a balance would ensure Republican victory?

The impact of the Negro suffrage issue upon the white vote might be softened by moving just after a national election rather than just before one, and this was the strategy pursued in pushing through the Fifteenth Amendment.[72] Yet risk remained, a risk that it is difficult to believe politicians would have willingly assumed had their course been set solely, or primarily, by political arithmetic. Let us, then, consider the nature of the evidence cited to show that Republican policy sprang from narrow party interests.

Since the days of Braxton, historians have used the public statements of public men, straight from the pages of the *Congressional Globe,* not only to document the charge of party expediency but also to prove it by the admission of intent. The frequency with which either Sen. Charles Sumner or Thaddeus Stevens has been quoted on the arithmetic of Negro enfranchisement might well have suggested caution in using such oral evidence for establishing motivation. As craftsmen, historians have been alerted against a proclivity to seize upon the discovery of an economic motive as if, to quote Kenneth Stampp, they then were "dealing with reality—with something that reflects the true nature of man." Stampp cites Sumner as an example of the fallacy ". . . when he argued that Negro suffrage was necessary to prevent a repudiation of the public debt, he may *then* have had a concealed motive— that is, he may have believed that this was the way to convert bondholders to his moral principles."[73] An equal sophistication is overdue in the handling of political motivation. With reference to the Reconstruction legislation of 1867, Sumner did state—frankly, as the cynically inclined would add—that the Negro vote had been a necessity for the organization of "loyal governments" in the South. He continued with equal forthrightness: "It was on this ground, rather than principle, that I relied most. . . ."[74] A man remarkably uncompromising in his own adherence to principle, Sumner obviously did not believe it wise to rely upon moral argument alone to move others. Thaddeus Stevens's belief in the justice of equal suffrage and his desire to see it realized were as consistent and genuine as Sumner's own, but Stevens was a much shrewder practitioner of the art of politics. It is worth noting, then, that Negro suffrage was not the solution to which he clung most tenaciously in order to guarantee "loyal governments" in the South; he looked more confidently to the army and to white disfranchisement. In the last critical stage of battle over Reconstruction policy, it was the moderate Republicans who championed an immediate mandate for Negro suffrage in the South while Stevens led the fight to delay its advent in favor of an interlude of military rule.[75]

All this suggests the need for a detailed analysis of who said what, when, in arguing that Negro suffrage, South or North, would bring Republican votes and Republican victories. Did the argument have its origin with the committed antislavery men or with the uncommitted politician? Was it used to whet an appetite for political gain or to counter fear of losses? Such a study might start by throwing out as evidence of motivation all appeals to political expediency made after the Fifteenth Amendment was sent to the states for ratification. By that time Republicans were tied to the policy and could not escape the opprobrium it carried; a leadership that used every possible strategem and pressure to secure ratification in the face of widespread opposition could be expected to overlook no argument that might move hesitant state legislators, particularly one that appealed to party loyalty and interest.

It has been implied that election results in the 1870s and 1880s were evidence of political motivation behind the Fifteenth Amendment. The logic is faulty. Consequences are not linked causally to intentions. Favorable election returns would not constitute proof that decision making had been dependent upon calculation, nor would election losses preclude the existence of unrealistic expectations. Yet it would be of interest to know the effect of the enfranchisement of Negroes upon Republican fortunes, particularly in the marginal northern states. Election returns might serve to test the reasonableness of optimistic projections of gain by adding black voters, as against the undoubted risk of losing white voters. If the end result of Negro enfranchisement in the North was one of considerable advantage to Republicans, we may have overestimated the element of political risk. If enfranchisement brought the Republicans little benefit, the case for a careful reexamination of Republican motivation is strengthened. Inquiry can reasonably be restricted to the results of presidential and congressional contests, since these were of direct concern to the Republicans in Congress responsible for the Fifteenth Amendment.[76]

Negro votes in the critical northern states were not sufficient to ensure victory in three of the six presidential elections following ratification of the Fifteenth Amendment in 1870.[77] For purposes of comparing the "before" and "after" vote, the election of 1872 is unfortunately of no utility. Horace Greeley proved so weak a Liberal Republican–Democratic candidate that in every one of the critical seven states Grant would have won without a single Negro ballot.[78] In the 1876 contest, which affords the best comparison with 1868, the Republican percentage of the vote dropped in every one of the marginal states, four of which were lost to the Democrats. Comparison of the number of Republican losses in the seven states for the three elections before 1872 with those for the three elections after 1872 shows four losses in the earlier period as against nine losses after Negro enfranchisement.[79] Of course, it could be argued that Republicans would have done even worse without the Negro vote and the politicians in 1869 could not have anticipated the depression of 1873. Politicians would have known, however, that Negroes in the North, outside the border states, were too few to constitute a guarantee of victory in the face of any major adversity. In 1880 and 1888, years of success, Republicans might have lost Indiana without the Negro, but they would not have lost the presidency. The only presidential contest in the nineteenth century in which Negro voters played a critical role was that of 1876, and the voters lived not in the North but in the South. Analysis of ballots in the 1870s and 1880s does not confirm the reasonableness of expectations for a succession of Republicans in the White House as the result of Negro enfranchisement.

As to Congress, Republicans could hope to gain very little more than they already held in 1869. Of thirty-six Democrats seated in the House of Representatives from the seven marginal states, only four came from districts with a potential Negro electorate large enough to turn the Republican margin of defeat in 1868 into a victory.[80] Of the four, Republicans gained just one in 1870, in Cincinnati, Ohio. Their failure to profit from the Negro vote in the Thirteenth District of Illinois, located at the southern tip of the state, is of particular interest. The district had gone Republican in 1866 and had a large concentration of Negro population. In 1868 the Republican share of the vote had been a close 49.1 percent; in 1870 it actually decreased with the Democratic margin of victory rising from 503 to 1,081. In the two counties with the highest proportion of Negroes to whites, more than 20 percent, a jump in the Republican percentage plus an increase in the actual number of Republican votes cast—unusual in a nonpresidential year—indicate that Negroes exercised their new franchise. However, this apparently acted as a stimulus for whites to go to the polls and vote Democratic. In three of the five counties in the district where Negroes constituted more than 5 percent of the population, more Democratic votes were recorded in 1870 than in 1868.[81]

The Republicans did better in holding seats won by slim margins in 1868 than in winning new ones. Eighteen congressional districts in the critical seven states had gone to Republicans by a margin of fewer than five hundred votes. Of these, Republicans retained fourteen and lost four to the Democrats in 1870.[82] Three of the four districts lost had a potential Negro electorate large enough to have doubled the Republican margins of 1868. The record of voting in congressional elections from 1860 through 1868 in the fourteen districts retained suggests that half might have remained Republican without any benefit of the Fifteenth Amendment.[83] It is doubtful whether three of the other seven, all districts in Ohio, would have been placed in jeopardy had Negro suffrage not been raised as an issue in 1867 both at home and in Washington, for the margin of victory dropped sharply from 1866 to 1868.[84] One of the remaining four, the Second District in Connecticut, consisted of two counties, Middlesex with a Negro population of 372 and New Haven with 2,734, the largest concentration of Negroes in the state. New Haven had gone Democratic in 1869 (Connecticut elected its congressmen in the spring) by 62 votes, though the Republican won the district; two years later, with Negroes enfranchised, the Democratic margin in New Haven actually increased to 270! Middlesex saved the day for the incumbent, who barely survived by 23 votes. This suggests that the district remained Republican not because of Negro enfranchisement, but despite it. Two seats, one in Pennsylvania and the other in New Jersey, were retained by an increase in the margin of victory larger than the number of potential Negro voters.[85] The last of the fourteen districts, the Eleventh of New York, consisting of Orange and Sullivan counties, may have been saved by Negro voters, although the election results there are particularly difficult to interpret.[86]

If we consider the total picture of the 1870 congressional races, we find that the Republican share of the vote decreased in five of the seven critical states, remained practically constant in Ohio, and increased in New Jersey. The party did best in the two states with the highest percentages of Negroes in their population, Ohio and New Jersey, netting one additional seat in each. However, in the seven states as a whole Republicans suffered a net loss of nine representatives. Democrats gained most in New York and Pennsylvania, almost doubling their congressional delegation in the latter from six to eleven out of a total of twenty-four. Republicans retained control in Congress but with a sharply reduced majority. In short, results of the northern congressional elections of 1870 suggest that Negro voters may have offset to some extent the alienation of white voters by the suffrage issue, that they did little, however, to turn Republican defeats into Republican victories, and that the impact of the Fifteenth Amendment was in general disadvantageous to the Republican party.

Election returns blanket a multitude of issues, interests, and personalities.

In an effort to relate them more precisely to the impact of Negro enfranchisement, we have identified all counties in the seven marginal states in which Negroes constituted a higher-than-average percentage of the population. Using 5 percent, we found thirty-four such counties.[87] An analysis of the number of Republican voters in 1868 as compared with 1870 and of the changing percentage of the total vote won by Republicans in 1866, 1868, 1870, and 1876 would indicate that Negroes did go to the polls and vote Republican in numbers that more than offset adverse white reaction, but this appears to have been the case in less than half the counties.[88] The net effect upon Republican fortunes was negligible, if not negative. Thus, in the first congressional election after Negroes were given the ballot, three of the thirty-four counties shifted from Democratic to Republican majorities, but another three went from the Republicans to the Democrats. The record was no happier for Republicans in the 1876 presidential election. Again, only six counties changed political alignment as compared with the 1868 balloting. Two were added to the Republican column, and four were lost!

From whatever angle of vision they are examined, election returns in the seven pivotal states give no support to the assumption that the enfranchisement of northern Negroes would help Republicans in their struggle to maintain control of Congress and the presidency. This conclusion holds for all of the North. Any hope that may have been entertained of gaining substantial strength in the loyal border states was lacking in realism. It failed to take into account the most obvious of facts—the intensity of hostility to any form of racial equality in communities recently and reluctantly freed from the institution of Negro slavery. Only Missouri and West Virginia had shown Republican strength in 1868; of the ten congressional seats that Republicans then won, half were lost in the elections of 1870. Kentucky had the largest Negro population in the North, but in seven of its nine congressional districts the Democratic margin of victory was so overwhelming that the state could not possibly be won by the Republican opposition, and, in fact, all nine seats remained Democratic in 1870. Although no Republican had won a seat from Maryland in 1868, there the odds were better. The outcome, however, was only a little more favorable. In 1870 Republicans failed to make any gain; in 1872 they were victors in two of the six congressional districts; these they promptly lost in 1874. The pattern of politics in Delaware was similar, consistently Democratic except in the landslide of 1872.

The lack of political profit from the Negro vote in pivotal states of the North reinforces the contention that Republican sponsorship of Negro suffrage in the face of grave political risk warrants a reexamination of motive. There is additional evidence that points to this need. Circumstances leading to the imposition of unrestricted Negro suffrage upon the defeated South are not consistent with an explanation based upon party expediency. Two detailed accounts of the legislative history of the Reconstruction Act of March 2, 1867, have recently been written, one by Brock and the other by David Donald; in neither is there any suggestion that the men responsible for the Negro suffrage provision, moderates led by John A. Bingham, James G. Blaine, and John Sherman, placed it there as an instrument of party advantage.[89] They were seeking a way to obtain ratification of the Fourteenth Amendment, which the southern states had rejected, and to restore all states to the Union without an indefinite interval of military rule or the imposition of more severe requirements.

The nature of the Fifteenth Amendment also suggests the inadequacy of the view that its purpose was to make permanent Republican control of the South. The amendment did not constitute a guarantee for the continuance of Radical Republican regimes, and this fact was recognized at the time. What it did was to commit the nation, not to universal, but to *impartial* suffrage. Out of the tangle of legislative debate and compromise there had emerged a basic law affirming the principle of nondiscrimination. A number of Republican politicians, South and North, who measured it in terms of political arithmetic, were not happy with the formulation of the amendment. They recognized that under its provisions the southern Negro vote could be reduced to political impotence by literacy tests and other qualifications, ostensibly equal.[90]

If evidence of Republican concern for the principle of equal suffrage irrespective of race is largely wanting in histories dealing with Negro enfranchisement, it may be absent because historians have seldom considered the possibility that such evidence exists. With the more friendly atmosphere in which recent scholarship has approached the Radicals of Reconstruction, it has become apparent that men formerly dismissed as mere opportunistic politicians—"Pig Iron" Kelley, Ben Wade, Henry Wilson—actually displayed in their public careers a genuine concern for the equal status of the Negro.[91] It is time to take a fresh look at the Republican party record as a whole. For example, let us reconsider the charge that Republicans were hypocrites in forcing equal suffrage upon the South at a time when northern states outside New England did not grant a like privilege and were refusing to mend their ways. Aside from disregarding the sequence of events that led to the suffrage requirement in the legislation of 1867, this accusation confuses Republicans with northerners generally. In the postwar referendums on Negro suffrage, race prejudice predominated over the principle of equality but not with the consent of a majority of Republican voters. Thus the 45.9 percent of the Ohio vote for Negro suffrage in 1867 was equivalent to 84.6 percent of the Republican electorate of 1866 and to 89 percent of the Republicans who voted in 1867 for Rutherford B. Hayes as governor.[92] In truth, Republicans had fought many lost battles in state legislatures and in state referendums on behalf of Negro suffrage.[93] What is surprising is not that they had sometimes evaded the issue but that on so many occasions they had been its champion. Even the most cynical of observers would find it difficult to account for all such Republican effort in terms of political advantage. What need was there in Minnesota or Wisconsin or Iowa for a mere handful of potential Republican voters? In these states, as in others, the movement to secure the ballot for Negroes antedated the Civil War and cannot be discounted as a mere maneuver preliminary to imposing Negro suffrage upon a defeated South.

Historians have not asked whether Republicans who voted for the Fifteenth Amendment were acting in a manner consistent with their past public records. We do not know how many of these congressmen had earlier demonstrated, or failed to demonstrate, a concern for the well-being of free Negroes or a willingness publicly to support the unpopular cause of Negro suffrage.[94] The vote in the House of Representatives in January 1866 on the question of Negro suffrage in the District of Columbia offers an example of neglected evidence. The issue was raised before a break had developed between President Johnson and Congress; it came, in fact, at a time when an overwhelming majority of Republicans accepted the president's decision not to force Negro suffrage upon the South, even a suffrage limited to freedmen who might qualify by military service, education, or property holding. In other words, this vote reflected not the self-interest but the conscience of Republicans. They divided 116 for the measure, 15 against, and 10 recorded as not voting.[95] In the next Congress, which passed upon the Fifteenth Amendment, support for that measure came from seventy-two representatives elected from northern states that had not extended equal suffrage to Negroes. Were these men acting under the compulsion of politics or of conscience? More than half, forty-four in all, had served in the House during the previous Congress. Every one of the forty-four had voted in favor of Negro suffrage for the District of Columbia. Why can they not be credited with an honest conviction, to use the words of a New York *Times* editorial, "that a particular color ought not of itself to exclude from the elective franchise... ?"[96]

The motives of congressmen doubtless were mixed, but in a period of national crisis when the issue of equality was basic to political contention, it is just possible that party advantage was subordinated to principle. Should further study rehabilitate the reputation of the Republican party in respect to Negro suffrage, it would not follow that the 1860s were a golden age dedicated to the principle that all men are created equal. During the years of Civil War and Reconstruction, race prejudice was institutionalized in the Democratic party. Perhaps this very fact, plus the jibes of inconsistency and hypocrisy with which Democrats derided their opponents, helped to create the party unity that committed Republicans, and through them the nation, to equal suffrage irrespective of race.

PART THREE

Southern Reconstruction: A Doomed Commitment?

CHAPTER EIGHT

General O. O. Howard and the "Misrepresented Bureau"

Gen. O. O. Howard, organizer and head of the Freedmen's Bureau throughout its bitterly assailed existence, was a man of great restraint.[1] Yet on occasion his indignation broke through his characteristic forbearance, particularly when subordinates in what he privately termed "this 'misrepresented bureau'" were charged with such offenses as playing "false to the govt & false to you," of being "hipocrites and scamps." "I emphatically declare," he wrote at a time when the major work of the bureau was nearing completion, "that the several Asst. Commissioners . . . are men of strict integrity and decided ability, men who will compare formally with any general and officers of their grade in our immense army." As to those holding the lesser offices, nine out of every ten had proved "efficient and true." Any who were dishonest or of bad habits, "drunken, licentious or profane," had been promptly removed as soon as the facts were discovered and proved.[2]

Coming upon these assertions after weeks of careful scrutiny of the papers of General Howard's office, we could not dismiss them as ex parte defense, for the records of the Freedmen's Bureau had already convinced us of the integrity and sound judgment of its commissioner.[3] They had also made evident the manner in which local resentment of functions entrusted to the bureau frequently found expression in bitter accusations against hapless officers, and disclosed gross distortion in charges against bureau officers made to the highest and most sympathetic nonbureau authorities, notably to President Johnson himself.[4] Indeed, our work in the bureau records had led us to the conclusion that even the most friendly studies of the bureau have exaggerated its weaknesses and minimized its strength.[5] This is understandable in view of the volume and animus of hostile contemporary criticism. The bureau was in many respects the symbol and substance of military occupation, a hateful or at best an unwelcome power of restraint to those under its shadow and to all men who believe in liberty. And at the vital core of the bureau's activities was the explosive and still unresolved problem of the nature of race relationships that should follow the forcible destruction of slavery. To these irrepressible sources of bias was added the novelty of the federal government's assumption of responsibility for the welfare of a large body of its citizens, a concept of national authority alien to the constitutional thought of the day. The intense emotional responses that these elements produced were fanned to white heat by the political conflict of the postwar years. Historical accounts have reflected in varying degrees the contemporary vilification of the institution, despite the very considerable recognition given to the bureau's constructive achievements. They have also, in our judgment, been distorted by questionable assumptions derived from the prevailing pro-Johnson interpretation of Reconstruction.

Of the specific indictments against the bureau, two are most common: first, that its good intentions were seriously compromised in performance by a significantly large number of unsuitable, often corrupt, lesser officials; and secondly, that the bureau was a partisan Radical Republican organization that degenerated into a mere political weapon used against Johnson and his supporters. The latter are generally presumed principled, compassionate, and uncontaminated by partisan or economic self-interest of any reprehensible character—virtues of which all but a minority of Radicals are held remarkably innocent. Other charges that evoke a considerable degree of credence are that bureau officials, as northerners with an inadequate understanding of the South, created distrust and hostility between Negroes and whites; that the bureau demoralized the freedmen by a lavish issuance of rations; and that General Howard as an administrator was lax and ineffective with the result that bureau records were defective and financial accounting loose, if not suspect.

The fact that the Freedmen's Bureau was primarily a *military* organization has far-reaching implications for an accurate appraisal of charges of corruption, incompetency, and disregard of official policy. Established in the War Department, the bureau was manned in positions of authority by army personnel. In its procedures the bureau followed standard army practices. This meant that there was a clearly defined chain of command and that its officers, including civilian agents, were subject to military discipline and held personally accountable for carrying out orders and for general good conduct. They were accountable not only to their bureau superiors but also to the department commanders of the army, "in the same manner as an officer of Engineers building a fort in the same Department, who reports directly to the Chief Engineer."[6]

Standard army procedures governed the bureau not only in matters of command and discipline but also in its records and accounting. "This Bureau being in the War Department," read the circular of basic directives, "all rules and regulations governing officers under accountability for property apply as set forth in the Revised Regulations of the Army."[7] Files of letters and reports received; copybooks of letters sent, orders, and circulars; registers and indexes of correspondence; accounts of supplies and funds, all attest the systematic manner in which orders were followed. The opportunity for official conduct contrary to directives, and particularly for fraud or self-enrichment, was narrowly circumscribed. It is true that the "accountability system" of the military sometimes proved too exacting and time-consuming for the overburdened local office, whose staff was consistently kept at or below minimum requirements and which on occasion even lacked essential office equipment such as desks and files. But only the sternest of historians would cavil at delinquencies in the office files of such an officer as the desperate captain who appealed without success for an assistant to aid him. "I am required to make 36 Reports & Returns—original duplicate and triplicate during the month—Enter every case upon the record and a recent order requires me to report half my cases to my Comd'g officer—My office is full from morning until night generally—I get nothing to eat from Breakfast until 5 or 6 o'clock P.M., and then comes camp duties—the outside duties of the office & these interminable Reports and Returns."[8]

The activities of bureau officers were subject both to the review of their immediate superiors and to that of inspectors sent from the Washington office, whose inquiries were not perfunctory but markedly critical.[9] Complaints against bureau officers on the grounds of negligent, offensive, or corrupt conduct were promptly investigated. Moreover, charges were freely invited by General Howard from all sources, including resident native southerners. Howard's only specification was that vague general complaints be accompanied by particulars. Assistant commissioners held and exercised summary powers, so that investigation and discipline were not limited to complaints that reached the Washington office.[10]

Both General Howard and his assistant commissioners consistently recognized that the difficulty and delicacy of the bureau's work required subordinates with high standards of personal and official conduct. They did their best to obtain the detail of sober, conscientious officers who were both sympathetic in their attitude toward the Negroes and also discreet and judicious. It was not always possible, of course, to obtain men of the character they sought. Much depended upon the cooperation of officers in charge of the local army posts, upon the nature and number of forces at their disposal, and upon the exigencies of a constant shifting of personnel due to the mustering out of volunteers and various reorganizations of the army as it settled into a peacetime status. The conduct of some officers did fall woefully short of the prescribed standards, but there was a constant alertness to the problem and a continuing effort to improve the personnel. For example, in August 1866, during an army reorganization that affected the bureau, General Howard directed the assistant commissioners, all themselves military officers of high rank, to use great care in recommending men to be retained. "Recommend none whose characters are not above reproach, and say no more about an officer than you are willing to be held responsible for, at any future time."[11] About the same time, he counseled the assistant commissioner for Texas: "You know this Bureau must be pure enough to withstand all sorts of accusations."[12]

Although we have not attempted to make a detailed study of bureau officials, we are convinced that the prominence given the weak and culpable has resulted in a major distortion of the bureau record. Emphasis upon the unfit, by contemporaries and by scholars, has tended to obscure the merits of hard-working, conscientious local agents. The bureau records hold abundant evidence that there were many such and that the schedule of a conscientious officer was almost unbelievably demanding—of physical energy, humanity, tact, and intelligence. Toward the colored people he must act as governor, judge, sheriff, jailer, and commissioner of the poor, and simultaneously "he should manifest an interest in their education and in their moral & religious culture." At nightfall he might be "obliged to sleep in his store house, with revolver in hand, to protect govt property," and daylight might find him dispensing justice to blacks and whites, "with a piece of pork in one hand, a measure of meal in the other, and a naked child by his side wanting to be clothed."[13]

Not only did General Howard insist upon remarkably high standards for his subordinates, in the broad areas of administrative decision and responsibility he demonstrated notable effectiveness. The criticism of General Howard as administrator is contradicted by unmistakable evidence of his skill and wisdom. In explanation, we can only suggest that the indictment on this count, which did not originate with historians but with contemporaries hostile to the bureau, was circulated because the man's known reputation for integrity and high purpose made it inexpedient for bureau opponents to charge him with more damaging offenses. Selected by Lincoln, though appointed by

Johnson, Howard was widely esteemed as a "Christian general." Henry Ward Beecher wrote the Secretary of War in urging the general's appointment that he "is, of all men, the one who would command the entire confidence of [the] *Christian* public.... Then, he is *pleasant* to work with, a gentleman, courteous, faithful & *cooperative*—He is very truly a Christian, & would give his whole strength to his duties disinterestedly without *second* thought either for himself—or any section, party, or sect."[14] Throughout the troubled years of the bureau's life, even when he as well as the institution was under the heaviest partisan attack, General Howard continued to command public respect and confidence throughout the North and West. This confidence and respect were warranted. The official and private records of this remarkable man confound the instinctive skepticism of the historian. When General Howard wrote a friendly but intemperate critic: "Whatever may be your opinion, I shall do in the future, as I have endeavored to do in the past, that is to stand firmly by my own convictions of what is right," his words can be accepted at their face value, as can the statement that followed: "Nothing irritates me more than the imputation of moral cowardice. I wish to assure you, my dear Sir, that I am not afraid of accusations."[15]

General Howard faced responsibilities unprecedented in American history, for the bureau was the "guardian" of four million "wards," entrusted by law with "the control of all subjects relating to refugees and freedmen." The bureau chief at once sought the counsel of those most experienced in the wartime problems of freedmen, and with their help formulated judicious and workable basic policies and procedures. He carefully selected as his assistant commissioners and members of his office staff men of character and experience, personally known to him or highly recommended. Then to these immediate subordinates he delegated power and discretion within the general framework of policy. Desirous of achieving the ends for which the bureau was established "in the most simple and practical way,"[16] he held orders and forms to a minimum, welcomed suggestions from the field, and stood ready to modify his directives. He inspired the confidence and respect of his assistant commissioners, and in return gave them his confidence and support. Never hesitant to review their activities or to reverse them for good cause, he worded his criticism and his directives clearly but courteously. Generally impersonal and devoid of sentimentality in official correspondence, General Howard could be intimate and confidential when occasion warranted. Although he acted consistently on the principle expressed in the postscript of a private letter: "I never will attempt to cover up the chicanery of villains,"[17] he brought rumor and hostile accusations squarely before the accused that they might present a defense, and was ready to reverse tentative adverse judgments when investigation discredited their basis. He would not permit the discrediting of loyal and trustworthy subordinates to appease opposition, even when his reticence in their defense would have been highly expedient.

General Howard's relations with army officers outside the bureau were conducted with as much skill as were his relations with subordinates. For the success of the bureau, there was need of close cooperation between bureau officers and army commanders in the South—and this Howard achieved to a remarkable extent, at times by his personal intervention. The constant danger of outright clashes of authority seldom materialized. Yet when military authority intruded, General Howard asserted the primacy of his jurisdiction over matters concerning freedmen with incisive force.[18] When in 1866 the policy was adopted of uniting in one person the position of assistant commissioner and of district commander, General Howard obtained the cooperation of the military high command in selecting men suitable for the work with the freedmen, and also gained their backing in his insistence upon direct responsibility and communication between the commander–assistant commissioners and himself in all matters pertaining to his authority. General Grant consistently supported and aided the commissioner, even in conflicts of authority between army and bureau.[19] This amicable relationship was a major achievement, particularly in view of the tendency of many army officers to treat the bureau and its work with contempt.

Most extraordinary of all was the fact that General Howard was able to ride out the storm of Reconstruction conflict without compromising the essential work of the bureau. Even in theory his position as head of the bureau was anomalous. As his adjutant general explained to one confused correspondent, "the Commissioner is not an elected officer, as are our Judges and other civil officers in many of the States; nor is he appointed to his position as are many civil officers; on the contrary he is an officer of the Army, of which the President is Commander in Chief. He holds his present position by virtue of an assignment, a direct order from the War Department, in obedience to which he must act, until he shall receive further orders from the same authority."[20] In practice Howard was accountable and his major decisions subject to the approval of President Johnson, Secretary of War Stanton, and General Grant, a trio whose basic aims in respect to the South were not infrequently at variance. In addition, his activities had to conform to the specific legislation of Congress, upon which he was dependent also for appropriations and necessary supplementary authority in a task central to the entire Reconstruction program over which the president and Congress quarreled disastrously.

General Howard was scrupulous in his adherence to legislation and in his obedience to superior authority. For example, to effect the essential work of the bureau in relieving want and promoting the rehabilitation of southern agriculture and industry, there was great need for the issuance of transportation orders. But the act establishing the bureau contained no specific provisions for transportation. The commissioner's general rule, in conformity with regular army orders, was that transportation should be supplied only to those freedmen who were destitute and dependent upon the government for support.[21] Aware of the uncertainty of his authority in this field, General Howard sought from Congress specific provision for the issuance of transportation.[22] Yet when President Johnson objected to sending into the South for employment the destitute freedmen who had collected in the Washington area, Howard promptly ordered an end to transportation for dependent able-bodied men and women, although he himself considered the original policy critically necessary and soundly administered.[23] Despite his eagerness to assist the poor Negro people congregated in overcrowded camps to establish themselves as homesteaders on the public lands in Florida, the commissioner refused a request for their transportation. He was "unwilling to risk specific exceptions to the general principle and recommend transportation till I shall have received written appropriation for it or the order of the President or Secretary of War."[24]

The greatest obstacle that General Howard had to face and parry in his administration of freedmen's affairs was the opposition of President Johnson. Johnson's opposition was not open, but covert; not stated as criticism of the general purpose of the bureau, but exemplified in sniping attacks upon its activities, its officers, and its public reputation.[25] The president was quite ready to besmear the bureau for his own political ends. An example of this, which should be notorious—and was in the eyes of contemporaries—is his appointment of generals J. B. Steedman and J. S. Fullerton to investigate the work of the bureau in April 1866, subsequent to his February veto of the Freedmen's Bureau bill and during the period when the congressional fate of a substitute bill was still in doubt. The purpose of the inspection was clear to them, to General Grant, and soon to his political opposition—their report was expected to discredit the bureau and prepare the way for its death.

Neither in the inception of the investigation nor during its progress was there consultation with the bureau's chief. Its highly impressionistic and distorted accusations were immediately released to the press, but the publication of findings that invalidated the partisan charges was suppressed until after the critical congressional elections of 1866.[26] Meantime the president utilized without scruple the discredit that the reports had cast upon the bureau as ammunition in his "swing around the circle" campaign oratory. "In fine," he stated in St. Louis, "the Freedmen's Bureau was a simple proposition to transfer 4,000,000 of slaves to the United States from their original owners to a new set of slavemasters. . . . Yes, under this new system they would work the slaves, and call on the Government to bear all the expenses, and if there were any profits left, why they would pocket them [laughter and cheers]." In reporting this incident, one of Howard's ablest and most conscientious assistant commissioners wrote: "I can not see how you or any other Bureau official can accomplish much good in the face of the President's most unjust and wicked attacks upon the Bureau and its officials—He loses no opportunity to misrepresent and defame us."[27] But General Howard and his bureau did continue to "accomplish much good." In his own words, "We are getting on very well, though all I can expect to do, is by the power of appropriation and social influence."[28] His former adjutant general, enjoying the pleasures of home and old friends, sent Howard a word of sympathy: "I . . . cannot resist the feeling of pity for you and others at Washington who are toiling away at Bureau problems and wondering what the President will do next."[29]

The charge that the bureau was a political arm of the Radical Republicans is an oversimplification that amounts to a major distortion. It completely disregards the efforts made by a number of the assistant commissioners in 1865 to further the president's policy of speedy readmission of the southern states by friendly advice and consultation with members of state conventions and legislatures.[30] Nor does it take into account the ultimate authority of the president, provided by law and exercised in practice, which included approval of bureau regulations and of the appointment of assistant commissioners. The indictment, moreover, ignores both the lack of scruple with which the opposition made political capital at the expense of the bureau and the extent to which the commissioner, consciously holding the bureau to its legitimate functions and its military character, refrained from utilizing it to make political capital for the Radicals—or for himself. It confuses with partisan self-interest functions of the bureau affecting political developments in the South that were legitimate, even mandatory, and places responsibility for the origin and consequences of the congressional Reconstruction legislation of

1867 upon those who were responsible only for its execution. Finally, in charging Radical partisanship historical accounts usually imply that only fanatics or unprincipled seekers for personal fortune or party advantage, including the safeguarding of predatory "big business" interests, could have supported the Radicals against Johnson.

President Johnson and his adherents, not the Radicals, made the bureau and its work a campaign issue in 1866. When Schuyler Colfax, the Republican speaker of the House, was stumping Indiana, he appealed to Howard: "My opponent talks every day about a trade of brown sugar for white sugar for freedmen in N. Ca. cutting kindling wood &c which I don't understand. Can you tell me how it is answered. I have never seen your report in reply to Steedman's."[31] General Howard replied with great restraint. He forwarded explanatory materials that had been previously released, but explained that he was not authorized to publish his reply to Fullerton and Steedman.[32]

The leaders of the Philadelphia Convention of southern loyalists and northern Republicans, held to counter the earlier pro-Johnson "National Union" convention, sent the following advice to Howard:

> They say "tell Howard to resign, or do better, take such decided grounds that the President will remove him." The whole country will make common cause with you and fight the battle of humanity, and equal justice & rights to all with your name as the rallying cry for the masses.... Everybody says, Can't Howard do battle for right & justice to his wards so vigorously that the President will remove him and shoulder the responsibilities of the hour? *This is the feeling*. The moment you are removed every gun in the radical camp will be trained upon the Bureau and its workings under the President. I know I have heard at least a hundred of the best men in this convention from all parts of the country say— "We'll take care of Howard, Tell him to fight vigorously and throw the responsibilities of the failure of the Bureau to protect the negro on the President."[33]

This report, incidentally, carries the significant implication that the Republican leaders did not view the bureau as a present or potential political arm but rather were quite willing to see it delivered completely into the power of pro-Johnson forces.

General Howard did not follow the Republican advice. On the one hand, he recognized, as he had written a friendly critic, that "no subordinate can be successful against his superior in making war upon him."[34] On the other hand, his private correspondence, though not his official action, indicates that he thought of asking to be relieved from his position, even of resigning from the army, in order to help arouse public opinion against the president's policy. The considerations that prompted the temptation were not partisan, at least not partisan in the sense that this word has been employed by the bureau's critics. His motivation was based upon principle, and his principles were rooted in a Christian concern for the well-being of the Negroes of the South. He wrote to the Rev. George F. Morgan: "I wish to do and to be just what God wills. The condition of the freedmen in many parts of the South is simply horrible. It is hard to believe that there exists so much downright murder in the human heart, as every day appears."[35] The political crisis was one that filled his heart with anxiety, "lest we may displease God by promoting or establishing some system of injustice."[36] He had fervently hoped that "our Father above would turn the heart and mind of Mr. Johnson to Himself."[37] When this did not happen, what he wished was to see "two things transpire—one is a great outpouring of the spirit of God upon the land—the other is the election which would grow out of such an event."[38]

Despite many rumors, public and private, General Howard did not resign and the president did not remove him. Apparently Johnson recognized that to do so would weaken rather than strengthen his cause in the fall elections. The president did show "a little pique," as Howard phrased it in a private letter, "by removing my brother Charles from a majority, and substituting an unknown man for him, after Charles had been recommended by General Grant and the Secretary." But, as Howard continued, "I shall never flinch from what I believe to be right, as long as God gives me the strength to act. Such is my purpose."[39]

And such was his conduct. His actions were guided by a concern to meet the high responsibility with which the bureau had been entrusted on behalf of the freed people. As its commissioner, he possessed the most extensive and objective factual information available on conditions in the South. The Christian organizations of the North looked to him for informed and moderate leadership, and his sense of responsibility would not permit him to evade the critical questions of the day. In October 1866, General Howard spoke in the North on "Our Christian Duty to the South." He wished "to avoid as much as possible in this inquiry anything of a partisan character," but, he declared, "each of us had a political duty to perform." There was a class among former Confederates who deserved to be "met half way" and to be "given immunity and pardon"; but he recognized reluctantly that there were other groups

> who combine openly & secretly to keep the negro in practical slavery, pay him reluctantly, do not treat him as a man entitled to a man's privileges, break their

labor contracts to deprive the laborer of his hire, attempt to govern with the pistol and the whip, hinder education, destroy schoolhouses, and in several of the States they killed freedmen's agents and maimed others for life; they murder and mutilate the freedmen and nothing can reach them but the vigorous, united arm of the Government, prepared to vindicate its laws and defend *all* its citizens.

It was a self-deception, he stated, to believe that the outrages of the past year, "the details of which were really upon record," were due alone to an irresponsible class of poor low whites. Without the acquiescence of a controlling majority who looked upon the Negro as an inferior and hated the "Southern Unconditional Union men," such outrages would not long continue. It did not follow that evil should be returned for evil, an eye for an eye and a tooth for a tooth; but hostility and injustice to the freed people should be firmly restrained by the hand of power. The "pledges and conditions" to be required for the protection of the freedmen he was willing to leave to the government, but he did not mean just "one department of Government." He himself saw "no violation of the Christian principle" in the proposed Fourteenth Amendment.[40]

General Howard might have attempted to make of the bureau a patronage plum for the Republicans with whose policies he sympathized. Instead he recommended to the Secretary of War that the position of assistant commissioner and military commander be combined in one person, and his directives to subordinates indicated his preference for army officers rather than civilians in lesser positions of authority. Both Howard and his immediate subordinates recognized that the prestige of the uniform aided the effectiveness of bureau work and that army men were more easily held to the required military discipline and responsibility than were civilians. In November 1867, when the rapid muster-out of officers meant the loss of army personnel and the need to replace them by civilian appointees, Howard requested Grant to urge upon President Johnson the retention of officers needed for bureau work.[41] Pending the president's decision, Howard directed assistant commissioners to ascertain whether officers "absolutely necesary" for the efficient administration of the bureau would consent to remain as civilian agents. A few weeks later he informed them that "all officers recommended by you will be retained as civilian agents after their muster out."[42] Furthermore, the commissioner insisted upon the strictest economy in the employment of personnel, both as to numbers and salary, despite a deluge of job applicants, many of them with endorsements from congressmen.

Had Howard desired the bureau to become an adjunct of the Republican party, he might have attempted to perpetuate its existence indefinitely; instead he consistently regarded it as a temporary organization and recommended its earliest practicable termination. "I believe none of us have wished to engraft the Freedmen's Bureau as a permanent institution upon our government," he explained in December 1868 to his assistant commissioner for Virginia, who had submitted a report urging the necessity of continuing the bureau. Although conceding that a continuation would in many respects be beneficial to the freedmen, Howard held that it was not "absolutely necessary" and that "its substantial removal can as readily be effected now as at any subsequent time."[43] The commissioner might have been jealous of any transfer of functions to other agencies, but such was not the case. "I am not wedded to a Bureau," he wrote in June 1866, "as the only means of accomplishing the good purposes of the friends of liberty and humanity. Yet for the present, something is necessary, as you know and feel."[44] He stood ready to transfer bureau activities to local officials, whether ex-Confederates or Union men, wherever justice was done to the freedmen.[45]

Most of the work of the bureau was terminated at the end of 1868. In the following year the bureau personnel was reduced to the insignificant number of 158, including 72 clerks; by October 1870, it was further reduced to a mere 88 officers, agents, and clerks. Had Howard's recommendations been followed, its only remaining functions, the promotion of education and the payment of bounty claims to Negro soldiers, would have been transferred to other branches of the government. On March 6, 1869, Howard asked to be relieved from duty in the bureau, but withdrew the request at the insistence of the Secretary of War and President Grant.[46]

On more than one occasion bureau officials were under attack because they would *not* be parties to the partisanship of Radical politicians. The assistant commissioner for Louisiana wrote Howard in May 1866 that "the only persons who complain of us are the N. O. Tribune people who are angry that I will not let the Bureau become involved by mixing it up in their political maneuvers."[47] A few weeks later, commenting on unfavorable reports about his agents, he explained that many intelligent Negroes were hostile to the bureau because they and "their particular friends amongst the whites" could not control the bureau "to advance their own personal political designs."[48] Charges against Gen. A. C. Gillem, the assistant commissioner for Mississippi, were published by T. W. Conway in a report to the Republican Congressional Committee in 1867. Howard forwarded the report to his subordinate with an explicit statement of his own confidence in him. In subsequent correspondence he assured Gillem that he "had nothing to do with Mr. Conway's mission," that he had never given much weight to such complaints for he "understood how they often arise," and offered to have published Gillem's official report answering Conway.[49]

Once Congress had given the vote to the freedmen, Howard quite properly considered it a function of the bureau to explain to the freedmen the nature and procedure of registration and voting, and to protect them in the exercise of the franchise against intimidation and reprisals. Southern efforts to deprive the new voters of their privilege were a violation of law to which bureau officials were in duty bound to refuse tacit consent. In the correspondence with General Gillem, he explained: "The Army cannot be a political machine; yet Congress has given the work of reconstruction into its hands and the law, like every other, must be executed by the Army with energy and good faith. The Freedmen's Bureau is a branch of the War Department and closely connected with the Army in this work."[50] The policy instituted in 1866 of uniting in the same person the position of assistant commissioner and of army general commanding, and in many cases of subordinate bureau and army posts, had been continued and adapted to the organization of military government under the Reconstruction acts of 1867. Although the officers holding dual posts were responsible to General Howard in matters pertaining to freedmen, and although he was careful to distinguish his proper authority from that assigned to army commanders, the close connection always existing between the two arms of the War Department was made even more intimate by the requirements of congressional Reconstruction. The law required army commanders in the South to "cause a registration to be made" of eligible voters. Both Grant and Howard interpreted this as a mandate not simply to provide the boards of registration but to make certain that the freedmen were not prevented from registering by ignorance, threats, or false rumors that registration was a device for taxation or military service. By law, army commanders appointed the registration boards from such men as could take the "ironclad" oath, which eliminated most southerners; and bureau agents were expected to serve when requested to do so. In the process of voting, the army and the bureau also had a responsible duty. When reports reached Howard of freedmen being threatened and actually discharged and left destitute "on account of their votes," he ordered "an effectual stop to this infamous conduct" and provisions "for those who suffer, at whatever cost." "It matters not which party is guilty of such contemptible measures as to make these unjust threats, the duty of the officers of the government is plain."[51]

There can be no doubt that the commissioner of the bureau insisted upon energetic measures to fulfill a duty in respect to the ballot. It is not at all evident, however, that it was a duty that he and his subordinates had sought. In retrospect, Howard wrote: "Though my officers and myself had no responsibility for the gift of suffrage, yet we had to bear no small part in its introduction."[52] Contrary evidence has been cited in the testimony before the Joint Committee on Reconstruction to identify officials of the Freedmen's Bureau with the movement to secure the ballot for the Negro.[53] But the hearings do not confirm this interpretation. Of fifteen bureau officials, or former officials, who testified, only three spoke in favor of Negro suffrage. Of the three, only one, J. W. Alvord, the bureau's general superintendent of education, was an officer of the bureau at the time of his testimony, and he merely agreed with his questioner as to the necessity for "the granting of civil and political rights to the black people."[54]

General Howard's own views as to Negro voting were so moderate, and so private, that he was under suspicion, even attack, by the advocates of the "right of suffrage" for the Negro. In defending him from such attack, a friendly coworker in the cause of the freed people pointed out that even Howard's critic had recognized that "on the suffrage question the Bureau has expressed no opinion because as here admitted it 'perhaps had no business to do so'."[55] Howard seems to have at first held views very similar to those publicly taken by President Johnson—that voting privileges should be gradually extended to the Negroes on the basis of education and property. He apparently came to accept the grant of suffrage to all freedmen because of the recalcitrant attitude of most southerners toward the granting of equal rights and equal justice in other spheres, and particularly the southern opposition to Negro education.[56]

In the troubled days of southern elections under congressional Reconstruction legislation of 1867, Howard took care to protect the freedmen as voters, but he also made it clear that the bureau's proper functions were of a political, not of a partisan nature. Rejecting a request of the chairman of the Republican state central committee of Arkansas for funds and direct assistance in organizing the Negro voters, the commissioner gave assurance of his hearty sympathy "in your efforts to elevate the colored race," but at the same time explained that officers and agents of the bureau understood that it was "their duty to instruct and protect the freedmen in all their rights and should explain to them their privileges under the franchise law, but should avoid partisan discussion."[57] Similarly he admonished a subcommissioner of the bureau stationed in Macon, Georgia, that it was his duty to instruct and protect the freedmen "but it is not proper to take those occasions for partisan addresses."[58] When Howard learned of charges that a Tennessee agent, a chaplain popular with the freed people, was using the influence of the bureau to promote his candidacy to Congress, he sent a trusted officer to investigate. Before his arrival, the agent had resigned his post, and the assistant commissioner had issued a circular to his subordinates calling their attention "to the impropriety of using their official positions to influence nominations in conventions." The investigating officer reported that "This seems to be satisfactory to all."[59]

An interesting example of the scrupulous avoidance of partisanship by bureau headquarters is the response to an urgent request made in July 1868 to Howard's adjutant general and inspector, Gen. F. D. Sewall, that he issue a history of the Freedmen's Bureau. "The whole Democratic party makes a direct attack on the Bureau as an issue—one of the most important of the day," ran the correspondent's argument. "I was greatly struck with the ignorance even among Republicans about the Bureau, what it really is and has done, while the Democrats regard it with a religious though insane horror—as a sort of fabulous monster." He felt that no one read the official reports, and that a popular resume would do great good, and even supply Republican speakers with material. General Sewall referred the matter to his chief with the comment that it might be wise for the Republican party to issue such a document but that he did not consider it a bureau matter. "I think the Bureau can stand a six mos. seige from copperheads with its present armament, garrison & supplies." Howard promptly directed that the request be refused.[60]

The line separating the proper from the improper political functions of bureau officers was not a sharp, easily definable one; and in this matter, as in most administrative policies, Howard left much discretion to his assistant commissioners in applying principle to specific situations. The following directives were sent in 1867 to the assistant commissioner for Louisiana:

> A few days ago, I saw your order forbiding your Agents to attend political meetings. While I agree with you fully as to the necessity of officers never mixing themselves up in politics, yet I think the officers ought to attend public meetings of every kind, whether political, judicious or religious, with a view of ascertaining everything possible with regard to the people with whom they have so much to do. Could you not write a simple letter privately to each agent or officer under your supervision, and caution him against becoming a candidate

for public office, or in any way mixing with politics, and at the same time, not forbid him absolutely from attending public meetings of a political character.

Many of the officers and agents you will doubtless make registers, with the sanction of General Sheridan. This will necessarily produce much political contact. I simply present this to you for your consideration.[61]

Another aspect of the problem is illustrated in the case of one G. Pillsbury of South Carolina, a devoted agent holding, to use his words, "the harmless and humble position" of superintendent of the Shaw Orphan Asylum in Charleston. Chosen a delegate to the constitutional convention, Pillsbury was summarily relieved of his position in the bureau. He appealed to General Howard for reinstatement or, at least, the transfer of the post to his wife because of the hardships that the sudden dismissal would mean for his family and the disorganization it would bring in the work with the orphan children. Howard left the decision to the conscience of his assistant commissioner, writing him that the intention of his instructions requiring the discharge of bureau agents elected to state conventions "had been to prevent officers from using their official position to lift themselves into power or position. I would as soon see our officers in good civil places as anybody else; but it will never do to encourage officers of the Freedmen's Bureau to seek office through their official strength. I refer particularly to officers of any considerable importance."[62] The assistant commissioner did not reinstate Pillsbury as head of the orphan asylum nor did he transfer the post to Pillsbury's wife. Shortly afterward, he wrote Howard that there was not in the state "a single salaried agent of the Bureau who is a candidate for office or is a member of the Union League, or any other organization of a political character."[63]

Howard never regarded office in the bureau as depriving himself or his subordinates of political rights and responsibilities. This led to apparent inconsistencies, just as did his large delegation of decision to assistant commissioners. For example, he gave his approval to an exceptionally strict policy pursued by one assistant commissioner of relieving from office subordinates who engaged in political activity. But subsequently he refused to sanction his assistant's action under this policy in removing an officer for the expression of political opinions. "If Capt. Gardner or any officer of this Bureau is elected to office or accepts nomination to any important office, he should of course resign his position as Bureau Agent. But expressing political opinions is not deemed a sufficient reason for the discharge of any one."[64] General Howard did not hide his own political convictions, and could not consistently penalize subordinates for expressing theirs. He disapproved the use of bureau influence to promote the candidacy of bureau officers, but he did not forbid the acceptance of nomination to local office.

The commissioner was perhaps more stern with bureau officials who campaigned for the Democrats than with those who erred on the side of the Republicans. He wrote confidentially to a captain in Alabama who was reported as advising Negroes not to trust Union men and to become Democrats: "I do not wish to control your politics, but know that the sympathy of the negroes at Mobile will be, if not already, alienated from you. I shall . . . advise a change of Station."[65] This should not be taken, however, to indicate that pro-Radical political activity was considered a recommendation for bureau office. On the contrary, there is evidence to suggest that participation in local Republican politics was viewed as disqualifying applicants for appointment as agents of the bureau.[66] Howard did not use his power and influence in appointments to create a Radical machine, but he did exert them to prevent active partisans of the president's policy from gaining positions in the bureau. He had considerable reason to fear that such men were poorly qualified to act as the guardians of the freedmen in the rights that Congress had bestowed upon them against the express wishes of the president.

Despite the restraints placed upon partisan political activity by bureau policy, there were bureau officials who entered the political battle, accepted nomination, and won office in southern elections. Historians have given much weight to evidence of such officeholding.[67] They have, moreover, accepted uncritically the derogatory insinuation of southern spokesmen that candidacy for office on the part of a bureau officer, or former officer, represented merely a yielding to the "great temptation" of making "his fortune" by virtue of being "the next friend of the Negro."[68] Furthermore, historians have tended to accept evidence of the pro-Republican sympathies of bureau officers as obvious and convincing proof of improper partisan use of their office.

The question of critical importance in passing judgment upon the undoubted predominance of Republican sentiment within the bureau, and upon such lapses from nonpartisanship as did occur, is: What motivated these men? Probably no altogether conclusive answer could be given even by a detailed and comprehensive study. But it is possible for the student of history to be certain that General Howard's own motives were above reproach. He did not covet office; he was not a politically-minded but an army-minded officer throughout his long career in the military service; deeply religious, loving

God and his fellow men, he did not seek revenge against the men or section he had faced in battle; upright in character, he sought neither for himself nor for others any avenue to financial profit through his official position; moderate and fair-minded, he consistently sought reliable factual information as the basis of judgment. Yet this wise and honorable man saw the election of 1866 as a contest between justice and injustice, and the defeat of Johnson's policy as evidence of the spirit of God moving the minds of men. This man wrote hopefully of the ultimate outcome under congressional Reconstruction policy and believed that the freedmen in 1867 and 1868 had exercised their new rights of discussion and suffrage in a manner that confirmed the wisdom of conferring upon them the privileges of full citizenship.[69] This man anxiously watched the results of the northern elections in 1868 with the conviction that the defeat of Seymour and the victory of Grant were of momentous importance to the security of just treatment for the freed slaves of the South.[70]

The hypothesis that Howard's subordinates, in large part, acted from motives similar to those that governed their chief is quite as tenable—in fact, we believe more tenable—than the usual assumptions of personal and party self-interest. The factual record systematically preserved in the files of the Freedmen's Bureau of outrages and murders, of the miscarriage of local justice, of local unwillingness to care for the Negro poor and dependent, of opposition to freedmen's schooling, of freed laborers denied due compensation, is a record of such a character as to have moved men to oppose the president's policy. The conscientious bureau officer, concerned with the future of the freed people, quite naturally looked for some way to remove the degrading barriers that stood between his wards and the fruits of that enterprise and responsibility in which he had attempted to instruct them. He might not necessarily regard the ballot as the best possible method. Yet there was logic in the argument that state and local officials who need look for the freedman's vote might be expected to maintain and enforce equality before the law, to promote schools for both black and white, to facilitate rather than obstruct the freed people's efforts toward economic advancement. The president's policy, on the other hand, offered no solution at all. Johnson would leave the problem of the Negro to white southerners, and he was never too sanguine of the outcome. This is not to assert that all bureau officers and agents who were partisan in thought or deed were men of moderation, character, and humanity. But, as shown above, high standards were continuously sought in appointing and discharging bureau personnel. The fanatic, the indiscreet, the negligent, the corrupt, and the prejudiced were passed over, or eliminated or disciplined wherever reliable evidence of these qualities came to the attention of General Howard and his assistant commissioners.

The ends that Howard set for the bureau were thoughtfully and clearly conceived, and the barriers he and his subordinates attempted to remove were neither ambiguous nor unmovable. The goal was the replacement of a slaveholding society by a free society, free without distinction as to color. If Howard be criticized as unrealistic or utopian or lacking in an "understanding of the South," it is pertinent to recall that his objectives were formulated in a period when southern society was in process of fundamental change. Howard was keenly aware that time was a necessary ingredient in the realization of these ends; what he attempted was to give direction to the changing pattern of southern life.

The controlling concept with which he vitalized the terse directives of the bureau statute was that the purpose behind the law was to aid the freedman "during the transition period from slavery to freedom by a United States Agency presumed to be free of local prejudice."[71] The most immediate tasks were to furnish food, clothing, and medical care, and at the same time to act as midwife in the birth of a free labor system that would enable the freed people to become self-supporting and the South speedily to reestablish a vigorous agricultural economy. This was a staggering assignment, without precedent in the life of the nation and without parallel until the 1930s. Into an economy shattered by war and demoralized by the overturn of its established labor relations, the bureau attempted to breathe life by promoting "simple good faith" and "free *bona fide*" agreements between worker and employer.[72] This was to be done in an agriculture characterized by large production units rather than the traditional family farm of the North, and in a time that preceded by generations the general practice and public acceptance of free labor bargaining supplemented by government mediation. In the face of widespread destitution, the necessities of life were to be furnished, but with prudent safeguards against abuse, permanent dependency, or extravagant expenditure and in such a manner as to guide and correlate the relief efforts of private freedmen's aid societies. The bureau ministered to the needs not only of freedmen and "refugees," but also to impoverished ex-Confederates under special congressional appropriations and by interpreting "refugees" as "liberally as possible to prevent starvation."[73]

The charges that the bureau demoralized labor by "supporting men in idleness" were largely partisan attempts to discredit the bureau. At the very start of his administration General Howard recognized and set about correcting the serious relief situation that had developed at various points where the army had been distributing rations. His early regulations regarding food rations enjoined "great discrimination," and strict accountability, to ensure that rations would be issued only to the "absolutely necessitous and destitute."[74] He and his officers made clear to the freed people their responsibility to become self-supporting, and his directives were so strictly enforced as to cause real hardship on occasion. The course General Howard pursued was prompted both by his New England belief in self-reliance and frugality and by the constant necessity to counter accusations of pampering freedmen or of exaggerating need merely "to put money into somebody's pocket."[75] In August 1866, goaded by such abusive charges from the president's supporters, he recommended to the Secretary of War, and the latter ordered, that all rations be discontinued after October 1, when crops would be harvested, except to dependents in hospitals and orphan asylums. Need was so great that the practical effect of the order was not to stop relief, but only to have its requirements attested by southern officials friendly to the president and critical of the bureau.[76]

The tremendous and unprecedented requirements of the emergency were joined with the responsibility, as Howard saw it, to guide and encourage the freed people in developing the habits, attitudes, and knowledge necessary for free men in a free society. These ranged from an attitude of respect and responsibility toward the marriage bond and family relationships to the habits of industry and thrift that guaranteed against dependence and held the promise of independent husbandry. The following selections from an early address of the assistant commissioner of Virginia to the freedmen in his charge are a pertinent illustration:

> The Government and charity will aid you, but this assistance will be of little advantage unless you help yourselves. To do this you must be industrious and frugal. . . . You have now no masters to provide for you in sickness and old age, hence you must see the necessity of saving your wages while you are able to work, for this purpose. . . . Schools as far as possible will be established among you, under the protection of the Government. You will remember, that in your condition as *freemen* education is of the highest importance, and it is hoped that you will avail yourselves, to the utmost of the opportunities offered you. In the new career before you each one must feel the great responsibility that rests upon himself, in shaping the destinies of his race. . . . Be quiet, peacable, law abiding Citizens.[77]

The barriers to a free society that the bureau attempted to eliminate are indicated by the powers that Bureau officers exercised when mutual good faith between whites and blacks was found wanting and mediation failed. Until southern laws eliminated distinctions based upon color and included the right of Negroes to testify in court, bureau officers maintained jurisdiction over cases involving freedmen; and where local justice met these requirements, officers were to watch court proceedings to safeguard against discriminatory treatment under cover of equal laws.[78] As guardians of the freedmen's children, they restored those apprenticed without their parents' consent and required good treatment for orphans bound out to service. Bureau officers were required to bring evidence of outrages to the attention of state and local authorities and empowered to order military arrest and imprisonment when murderers of Negroes remained at large. When an employer attempted to defraud laborers of their wages or shares, bureau officials could obtain court orders against the marketable crops. By the vigilance and authority of the bureau, protection was afforded freedmen who met hostile attempts to discourage their independent husbandry or ownership of land. Bureau officers did not at all times and in all places need to exercise these powers (and there were times when action was needed but officers could not or did not act), yet it is evident from the records of the bureau that the occasion for coercion was not incidental, but fundamental to the establishment of a free society in the South.

No aspect of the freedom that General Howard sought for the newly emancipated was quite so close to his heart as that of providing educational facilities. The original Freedmen's Bureau Act contained no specific provision respecting education, but Howard at once set about encouraging and coordinating the work of the volunteer organizations in providing teachers, books, and schoolhouses. He gave them all the protection and assistance within his power and saw to it that the bill extending the life of the bureau gave explicit authority to continue and enlarge this work. No indignity inflicted upon the freedmen in the South so kindled his indignation and strengthened his determination as the attacks upon teachers and the burning of schoolhouses. Education was the only means that he believed could be permanently effective in building a free society in the South, and his ultimate aim was a free common school system open to all southern children. Howard recognized that bureau influence and military authority could restrain but not rectify the "prejudice often amounting to hatred," which prevented the freedmen from obtaining justice in inferior courts and from exercising the rights of free men. "Through the schools we can reach the end we all seek more directly than in any other way."[79]

Convinced that continuing federal support was necessary for education in the South, Howard did his utmost to obtain legislative sanction for such a policy. His efforts were crystallized in a proposal to the president and Congress in November 1869. He desired a new department of education that would combine the educational work of the Freedmen's Bureau and that of the contemporary Department of Education (soon demoted to the status of a bureau). The department would be empowered to establish schools by cooperation with benevolent societies and state and local agencies and to incorporate as part of its organization the state superintendents of schools. This was to be done in such a manner as to safeguard the policy of community responsibility for schools. Howard concluded:

> If objections are offered to this proposition on the ground of its cost or of the tendency to centralization, it may be answered
>
> 1st That education is generally the very best possible investment that can be made in a free government: intelligent citizens, as every one knows, in all their varied occupations make constant returns to the government largely in advance of the money expended by it for their education.
>
> To the second objection it is sufficient to oppose the well known fact that the general education of the masses always tends to the procurement of the largest liberty consistent with good government, thus counteracting all centralizing tendencies.[80]

As the quotation above suggests, General Howard realized that the attainment of bureau objectives necessitated a new and enlarged concept of the proper function of the national government, a concept of government actively responsive to the needs of its citizens. In retrospect, he pointed out that the Freedmen's Bureau Act of 1865 had represented a new departure in government. "It was the exercise of benevolent functions hitherto always contended against by our leading statesmen." The bureau law had been a beginning in the transformation of American government from a "mere machine" into a nation "to love and cherish and to give forth sympathy and aid to the destitute."[81] Howard did not suggest the extent to which his own vision had given to the law this expansive meaning for the future.

Finally, in seeking to implement the general objectives of the bureau, whether in providing education or relief, whether in insuring fair trials at court or fair wages on the plantation, General Howard enjoined upon his subordinates conciliatory methods, understanding attitudes, and no recrimination for local abuse. "All the disturbing elements of the old system of industry and society are around you," he warned in his earliest general letter of advice to assistant commissioners. "Endeavor not to overdo, nor come short of duty. Do not forget in the discharge of your Governmental duties, that the less Government consistent with assured security of life and liberty and property, the better."[82] He advised and encouraged friendly consultation with the governors of the southern states and approved in a number of instances the entrusting of certain functions of the bureau to local magistrates and residents; and he did this in 1865 and 1866 when Johnson appointees and former Confederates controlled southern affairs.[83] In no state was public opinion more hostile to the bureau nor outrages against the freed people more shocking than in Texas, yet General Howard admonished his assistant commissioner there to do all that he could to "promote mutual good will among blacks and whites," by a "spirit of fairness," "great discretion," and the "broadest possible charity."[84] In this spirit, recognition was eagerly given where southern prejudice was subordinated to the requirements of uniform justice. Thus the assistant commissioner for Mississippi reported the case of a white man convicted for killing a Negro with the following comment:

> It is perhaps more than probable that the punishment awarded in this case [a year's imprisonment] was inadequate to the crime which was committed; but it is confidently trusted that the conviction in this case wholly on negro testimony and the excellent sentiments promulgated by Judge Campbell will be the *good seed* which will germinate at no distant day into the full fruition of perfect protection of the civil rights of the negro by the civil tribunals of this state.[85]

Under Howard's direction, bureau officers worked tirelessly, and with full consciousness that old attitudes die slowly, to help the South readjust from a slaveholding to a free society. They sought to promote mutual confidence between blacks and whites. But the mutual confidence and the free society for which they labored were to be based upon a concept of freedom alien to the heritage of race relationships under slavery.

CHAPTER NINE

The Perception of Injustice and Race Policy
James F. McGogy and the Freedmen's Bureau in Alabama

Prelude

My study of the relationship between the perception of injustice and postemancipation race policy was undertaken with a prefatory acknowledgment that it might be abandoned, be redirected in midcourse, or simply exhaust the explorer before it exhausted the terrain. The inquiry has in some degree been redirected and did, indeed, threaten to exhaust the explorer, but at an early stage it became apparent that the quest should not be abandoned as chimerical.

The genesis of the concept lies, if not in my very earliest research, in the first that resulted in a published volume.[1] I can recall the excitement of what was at the time a personal discovery and a startling departure from accepted historiography: namely, that something more was at issue in the quarrel between President Andrew Johnson and congressional Republicans than economic or narrowly partisan interests or Radical vindictiveness toward the conquered South. The title of the resulting book identified something as "Principle," but principle was not an adequate designation. A study of equal suffrage that was to have followed was aborted with the appearance of James M. McPherson's *The Struggle for Equality* and William Gillette's *The Right to Vote*, but resulted in our article on Negro suffrage and Republican politics as a problem of motivation in Reconstruction historiography.[2] The essay did not pretend to establish the mix or weight of motives behind the grant of suffrage to black Americans but it did sharply challenge the assumption that political expediency was the dominant impetus.

In the controversy that ensued, critics tended to posit a dichotomy and to identify it as one between interest or "expediency" and idealism. The term idealism seemed even less satisfactory than principle, and the adversarial duality unrealistic. As interest among historians shifted from the intent of Republican Reconstruction to explanation for its "failure," another dichotomy became dominant, that of a commitment to a racial equality versus race prejudice (or white racism). "Racial equality" struck me as distorting Republican intent to a larger degree than had "principle" or "idealism," and prejudice in the ranks of Republicans as a questionable taproot of failure.

Gradually I came to define the "something or other" as the perception of injustice, a broader common denominator of non-self-interest than principle, idealism, or commitment to racial equality. This coincided with increasing puzzlement over a related critical question brought to the fore by the outpouring of historical studies on racism "north of slavery."[3] They established a pervasiveness of prejudice that left untouched no segment of northern society, with the possible exception of a handful of abolitionists. How then did it happen that a racist white North imposed upon the South, and accepted for itself, equality of blacks before the law and at the ballot box?

Perception of injustice again seemed the answer, or rather an essential part of the answer, for the historic context precludes a monistic or static explanation. Could it not have evoked a response sufficiently strong, elemental, and ubiquitous to override prejudice? Might not our "sense of justice" as well, or better, be entitled "The Sense of Injustice"? One legal theorist has done so, seeing in it a primary spontaneous source of law "alive with movement and warmth."[4] The attribution of warmth is significant. Injustice, though ofttimes ignored or denied, when perceived as such, kindles and justifies strong emotion. In contrast, calm reason is indispensable to the process of justice and the defense of its outcome.

Theories, observation, and experiments in the behavioral sciences—though not without controversy and contradictions—warrant the conclusion that recognition of (and reaction to) justice-injustice is deeply rooted in human nature and nurture. Origins have been found in mutually satisfying exchange between infant and nurturing figure, in the social responses of infants, in the learning of early childhood, in identifiable stages of intellectual development that extend into adulthood.[5] The literature of psychology into which I had been drawn in pursuing a "sense of justice" promised no certainty that I had set forth upon an inquiry that would prove fruitful, but it did argue against abandoning an exploration of the perception of injustice as historical explanation.

If it could be established that a perception of injustice among northerners, at least among northern Republicans, had constrained racially discriminatory attitudes and behavior to make possible the *de jure* achievement of equal citizenship for blacks, critical questions would still remain. Why had response to that perception not been strong enough to translate the *de jure* victory into substantive reality? What had aroused a reaction to injustice of sufficient political power to reshape fundamental law, and what had reduced it to political impotence? Here the social psychologists' work on helping behavior and crisis intervention proved suggestive, and offered more than analogy.

The helping impulse is most closely associated with altruism or empathy, and some theorists would reject any identity between altruism and justice. Yet there is some convergence between the reaction to a stranger's distress and the perception of injustice. Each involves both sympathy and moral judgment. The bystander has been found more willing to help if he believes the plight of the stranger is not of his own making or, conversely put, the impulse to help may be neutralized if a victim is seen as responsible for his own distress. In other words, the observer makes an implicit judgment that the victim's predicament is either "just" or "unjust."[6]

Situations used or constructed by social psychologists who study helping behavior are models of simplicity as compared to the historical realities of the 1860s. Yet what is most striking is that their conclusions emphasize complexity. Action (or failure to act) depends on the person's awareness of what is happening, the degree to which his emotions are engaged, the clarity or ambiguity of the situation, how he interprets it, the extent to which he feels responsibility to act, and also his assessment of his own competence to help, of the degree of good that intervention can do the victim, of the harm that intervention can bring upon himself—this is but a partial list of the complexities that social psychologists have identified.[7]

Elements of their analysis paralleled a tentative hypothesis I had formulated based on the circumstances of the postemancipation years: namely, that a sense of injustice in order to have an important political impact required the arousal of public attention and indignation, a presumption that the injustice could be remedied, reenforcement by linkage to other concerns of party and nation, and a minimum of conflict with such interests.[8] Both point to awareness or immediacy, to emotional engagement, and to appraisal of the consequences of action. Two additional components of the behavioral analysis also appear relevant to post–Civil War decision-making—a sense of responsibility and the clarity or ambiguity of the situation.

Justice as a psychology of "entitlement," another focus of recent inquiry, offered an explanation more alien and less persuasive but not without potential for the inquiring historian: According to its theorists, the individual's need to maintain a "just" world illusion, to believe that he (and others) will obtain a fate "deserved" and deserve the fate received, leads to man's failure to perceive injustice, or if perceived his failure to alleviate or eliminate injustice. Injustice to others so threatens the individual's sense of security that he blames the victim or turns his back on the injustice.[9]

After my venture into the realms of psychiatry and psychology it was good to return to the familiar sources of history, to the specific circumstances and historically determined cultural context of the post–Civil War years. I did so hoping that my detour had left me better prepared to examine the role played by the perception of injustice as a victorious North struggled with the problem of establishing for the South and for the nation a race policy appropriate to freedom.

James F. McGogy and the Freedmen's Bureau in Alabama

James F. McGogy is missing from the pages of written history, as are most of the more than two thousand men, largely Civil War officers, who served as agents of the Freedmen's Bureau in the occupied South during the scant four years of its active existence. Yet he and his fellow agents, particularly the handful who like McGogy stayed with the bureau during most of those years, struggled to implement a national policy intended to reorder a slave society forcibly bereft of its slaves. Indeed, they gave specific content in the field to the general and often vaguely defined objectives of the bureau. Attitudes and reactions of individual agents, as certainly as directives from their superiors, shaped the northern effort to reconstruct southern race relations during a period of dramatic though tragically flawed social change.

There is little evidence of more than the outlines of McGogy's life and even less to disclose the convictions and prejudices with which he faced in 1865 a postwar challenge historic for the nation and intensely personal for James F. McGogy. The little that can be unearthed concerning his background and army career is not, however, without significance.

Raised in the essentially rural northern Indiana counties of St. Joseph and

LaPorte where smaller farms outnumbered those of more than a hundred acres almost three to one, he had been born on January 17, 1839, in South Bend and by 1850 was living in the neighboring town and county of LaPorte. South Bend was said to have been in 1836 a village of 800 inhabitants and 175 buildings, mostly one story houses. By 1860 it numbered somewhat more than thirty-eight hundred, about a fifth of the total population of the county, and included sixty-eight of its eighty-eight black residents. In that year LaPorte was larger but still a small town, just more than 5,000 with 56 of the county's 135 Negroes. The people of the two counties were overwhelmingly native-born Americans (more than 80 percent) though LaPorte had the larger number and proportion of foreign born. Although they constituted only a tiny minority of the population, just north in Cass County, Michigan, blacks had established one of the largest communities in the Midwest.[10]

McGogy's father, for whom he was named, had been born in Scotland, but his wife was a native of Connecticut. They had married in New York City, lived there for a time, then joined the movement to the Midwest via Buffalo and the Great Lakes. With two small children and still in their twenties, they arrived in Indiana in the fall of 1836. Fourteen years later, the 1850 census reported James an eleven-year-old student, the third eldest of seven children, and the second of five sons in the household of James and Mary "McGoggy." Family tradition identifies the father as "an educated engineer" who built the courthouse and jail in South Bend and installed a much admired staircase in the state capitol, a man who died while his children were still young, leaving his widow two farms and 280 acres of timber (of which she was defrauded by "an unscrupulous Priest"), plus a house in Walkerton, St. Joseph County. On the LaPorte census schedule of 1850 McGogy's occupation was recorded simply as that of carpenter and his real estate valued at five hundred dollars. Earlier records of St. Joseph County show that he had served as petit juror in 1840, was paid $19.12 in 1844 for shelving and other carpentry in the recorder's office, and some years before had been allowed 50¢ for repairing and hanging the jail gate. The senior James F. McGogy would seem to have left his namesake a legacy of westward mobility, industry, and aspiration—and of dry humor. A local historian mentions the father in passing as a man with a terrible impediment of speech who exemplified the wit and humor of the hotel barroom, the "social resort of the town" (South Bend). With an ingenious tale of a wager between himself and his companion he had outwitted its owner-bartender at a cost to the latter of two free grogs. The lack of any reference to McGogy's son James in accounts of either county is not surprising because the young man did not return to live in Indiana after his service in the army and the bureau.[11]

A few intimate glimpses of James McGogy before he entered the army are to be found in affidavits made years later to validate the claim of his fourth wife for a widow's pension. The day before Christmas 1859, a few weeks before his twenty-first birthday, James F. "McGogey" and Amelia M. Garlick, a young LaPorte lass, obtained their license to marry. After the ceremony they spent the winter in Walkerton, about sixteen miles from LaPorte, and then settled on a farm near Plymouth, seat of the adjacent county to the south. Tragically, Amelia lived to see only one wedding anniversary. By their second summer together the sickly bride was taken back to her father's home where she died in September 1861 of "consumption." On his way back from the funeral in LaPorte to the Plymouth farm, James stopped with his brother in Walkerton to raise money to cover the costs of her burial. About a month later, on the first day of November, he enlisted in Company D of the 48th Indiana Infantry. McGogy was twenty-two. He gave his occupation as that of "farmer"; his place of enlistment was variously reported, both as LaPorte and as Walkerton. Although army records give varying descriptions of his height and coloring, it is reasonable to picture the youthful widower as 5'6" or somewhat taller, with blue-grey eyes, dark brown hair, and a complexion either fair or dark depending upon the eye of the beholder.[12]

A brief biographical sketch published in 1880 credits McGogy with having "engaged in numerous battles during the [Civil] war, any one of which would reflect credit on his conduct." There is no reason to question the accolade though specific details are missing and major battles few. The men of the 48th had no role at Fort Henry, Fort Donelson, or Shiloh. On February 7, 1862, they had left Indiana for Paducah, Kentucky, arrived via Cairo three days later, received arms, and remained on duty there until May. Then they were sent south toward Corinth, Mississippi, where Confederate forces were concentrated after the bloody battle of Shiloh. Mid-September and early October found them engaged in the hard fought battles of Iuka and Corinth. The Union forces defeated the enemy but plans miscarried, losses were heavy, and the Confederates escaped the destruction Grant had intended. Luckier than many, McGogy had suffered no injury beyond a mild hernia when marching with his company on a hole-pocked road near Corinth in the dark of night.[13]

There followed for the Indiana regiment another less costly but more disheartening experience, the unsuccessful Yazoo Pass expedition, one of General Grant's futile attempts during the winter and early spring of 1863 to reach Vicksburg. With this episode at a dismal end, mid-April found the outfit encamped at Grant's headquarters at Milliken's Bend opposite Vicksburg in time to take part in the general's bold plan to cross the Mississippi farther south and attack the Confederate stronghold from the east. Soon McGogy's company was moving down through the already occupied bayou and plantation lands of northeast Louisiana to Smith's plantation, two miles from New Carthage—their original river destination, where for a few days Grant established his headquarters as had General Osterhaus and General McClernand before him. Then came unplanned detours to Perkins' plantation and Hard Times Landing, and after Admiral Porter's gunboats failed to silence the guns of Grand Gulf, on past "uninterrupted cornfields and the corn knee high" to the crossing of the great river at Bruinsburg on April 30, 1863.[14]

Across the river, the Indiana regiment won glory at Raymond, Champion's Hill, and the siege of Vicksburg, but Sergeant McGogy was not with them. He had been left behind on duty at Smith's plantation April 26, 1863. Six weeks later, and without having rejoined his company, McGogy was reported absent on detached duty with the 12th Louisiana Regiment, African Descent. On July 15 at Vicksburg, twelve days after its fall, he was formally discharged from the 48th Indiana and mustered into the black regiment.[15]

Army records do not disclose the nature of his assignment at Smith's plantation or whether it was a link to his reenlistment with the 12th Louisiana (later renamed the 50th U.S. Colored Troops). The plantation had been an important point on the line of communication from Milliken's Bend to the river crossing, a principal staging ground for Grant's final Vicksburg campaign. When Grant moved on, Smith's remained a depot for wagons, ambulances, and supplies left behind. These needed safeguarding as did numbers of freedmen, many destitute of food as well as protection. And there were livestock, grains, cotton to be foraged and wood to be cut in the Louisiana countryside. It was a time and place of uncertainty and confusion—of black liberation, black military recruitment, and raids by Confederate guerilla bands reported to include native whites who directed "a ferocity which only Comanches can equal" against the Negroes and Yankees whom they felt had driven them from their homes. Along the Mississippi that May and June it was also a time that saw the valor of raw black troops dramatically tested and not found wanting. To the south during the Union attack upon Port Hudson and then to the north in the defense of the camp at Milliken's Bend, the bravery of black men confounded prejudice and brought wide acclaim.[16]

From May to July while these feats were fresh in mind and Vicksburg lay besieged, the 12th Louisiana was being recruited and organized, its ranks filled largely by former slaves from nearby plantations and refugee camps. McGogy may have had a hand in the work for the records suggest the possibility that the decision to leave his fellow Hoosiers and accept a commission with black troops, formalized in July, had been made just before or very soon after his assignment to Smith's plantation. That April, Adj. Gen. Lorenzo Thomas, in the name of President Lincoln and at his direction, had been busy in the Mississippi valley recruiting black soldiers and white officers to help raise and command them. His speeches to white troops had included ones at Lake Providence and Milliken's Bend, where divisions of General McPherson's army corps were stationed, probably including McGogy's regiment.[17] According to official records, it was Lorenzo Thomas who recruited and commissioned McGogy; the date of his appointment was May 8, the place Milliken's Bend. After having served for a year and a half with the rank of sergeant, McGogy was being offered a first lieutenancy effective as soon as the new black regiment was raised.

Race prejudice among white men and officers in the valley was so pervasive that General Thomas' first task, as he saw it, was to persuade them to accept blacks as comrades-in-arms. His persuasion was not always gentle. He is said to have asked those who disagreed with the policy of arming Negroes to step out of ranks, and then ordered them to the guardhouse. Coercion, however, was not the usual or major inducement. In speech after speech, General Thomas appealed to the "patriotism, humanity, and self-interest" of the troops. While his authority to commission white officers, and only whites, to lead the new black regiments was a concession to prejudice and an offering to ambition, Thomas also made known his intent to select men of intelligence and proven ability who had their "heart . . . in the work." His early reports glowed with optimism that "prejudice in this army respecting arming the negroes is fast dying out," an expectation probably warranted if read to mean only that opposition to the enlistment of black soldiers dissipated as their potential contribution to a Union victory became increasingly apparent. It did not follow, however, that prejudice itself was fast dying. Almost two years later, at the end of 1864, Col. John Eaton, Jr., in charge of freedmen's affairs in the valley, reported to General Thomas that those assisting him were sneered at by their fellow officers as "'nigger men'" and "exposed to a test more severe to moral courage than the battlefield."[18]

It is impossible to establish with certainty what moved McGogy to join with the Colored Troops or what attitude toward blacks he brought to his new responsibility. In all likelihood he had responded to each aspect of General Thomas's appeal, and to specific circumstance as well; motives behind such decisions are most often complex. Unquestionably, he was a young man both patriotic and possessed of at least a normal desire for advancement, with the will and ability to achieve. Nor is there any reason to doubt his basic humanity. But neither is there any reason to believe that McGogy held racial convictions that set him apart from his fellow Hoosiers. Nothing uncovered in his life before or after his experience in the army and bureau, or during those years, suggests that he had entered the war with an atypical concern for blacks; nothing indicates that he began his wartime association with them from a sense of mission or a special commitment to freedom for those enslaved or to equality for those free.

The social environment of McGogy's childhood and early manhood was not one to invite such exceptionalism. Indiana during those years has been characterized as the most bigoted of the free states. State law denied blacks suffrage, militia duty, testimony in cases involving whites, and racial intermarriage. It also required Negroes settling from other states to register and post bond as guarantee of good conduct and self-support. Revision of the state constitution in 1850–51 made discrimination even more blatant. Article 13 of the revised constitution, approved by an overwhelming majority, more than five to one, forbad any Negro or mulatto to come into the state, made void contracts with those entering, mandated fines for all who encouraged or employed them, and directed that the fines collected be used to colonize abroad those Negroes already resident in the state.[19]

McGogy's home counties, St. Joseph and LaPorte, were situated too far north to be dominated by the extreme racial mores of transplanted southerners, but neither were they among the notable abolitionist, largely Quaker, centers of dissent from majority opinion. A Society of Friends had been established in the 1830s by a few pioneer settlers near the town of LaPorte, and in 1843 a representative from the county had attended a state meeting of the radical antislavery minority wing of the Friends. However, the community ceased to exist before 1860 "owing to the deaths that had occurred and the removal of others." Local histories make no mention of Quakers in St. Joseph County, though a scattering of dissenters resided there. In 1843, in the nearby town of Plymouth, Liberty party men included among their nominees a St. Joseph resident. But antislavery drew little political support in either county. During the campaign of 1840 in LaPorte County "a few . . .

boldly took upon themselves the then odious name of Abolitionist," but too few "to induce either party to court their favor. An abolitionist," continued the local historian, "was a political leper, whom it was dangerous to touch." In the presidential election of 1844, fifty-three Liberty party votes were cast for James G. Birney's "Abolitionist electors" in LaPorte and thirty-three in St. Joseph, 86 out of a total of 3,472. The two major parties dominated lively contests, with Whigs generally triumphant until 1852 when Democrats won decisive victories. Antislavery gained impetus as the Kansas-Nebraska issue took center stage, with Republicans in ascendancy by 1856, but it was directed against slavery's extension rather than against its perpetuation in the South or on behalf of equal treatment for Negroes in the North.[20]

Schuyler Colfax, who was to become St. Joseph's most eminent public man as Republican speaker of the House of Representatives and then Grant's vice president, held a position about as far beyond local consensus as a politically ambitious man could maintain. In beginning his career in September 1845 as editor of the Whig *St. Joseph Valley Register* he announced that the paper would take "the middle ground between the two dangerous extremes"— "Calhounism and Birneyism." He was "fixedly opposed to enlarging the boundaries of slavery even one inch" but would merely "hail with happiness the day when the Southern States, after calm examination, shall in a constitutional and legal manner adopt a feasible plan of emancipation!"[21]

Despite general acquiescence in the racial status quo, there existed in the area a leaven of elemental justice and humanity that on occasion could move the white community to action and its spokesmen to eloquence. In late September 1845, South Bend was the scene of a dramatic confrontation between judge, sheriff, local attorney, and townsmen on the one hand, and on the other a Kentuckian and his armed band who in the middle of the night had forcibly seized a family of former slaves in the black community of Cass County some thirty miles north, where they had established themselves as respected, hardworking landowners. Over a long weekend, from Friday noon through the following Monday, there was a flurry of legal maneuvers, writs, warrants, suits, and court hearings accompanied by a display of force on both sides, including the arrival of armed blacks from Cass County estimated to number from seventy-five to two hundred. Faced with an aroused white citizenry, armed blacks, and an initial adverse decision from the local probate judge, the Kentucky claimant retreated. On Monday the captive blacks went free without further contest. However, their South Bend attorney together with a number of local citizens were subsequently harassed with damage suits for aiding the Negroes to escape, suits that dragged on locally in the federal circuit court through the spring of 1851 and cost some defendants the loss of real estate to meet the judgment of $2,856 awarded the Kentucky master. During this sensational episode, the townspeople of South Bend had rallied to the support of the blacks, crowding the courtrooms and "without distinction of party, evinced the strongest feeling of sympathy for the oppressed." The defending attorney for the captives later spoke feelingly of the black mother's anguish. He justified his assistance on the ground of "higher law," quoting the biblical injunction: ". . . execute ye judgment and righteousness, and deliver the spoiled out of the hand of the oppressor."[22]

In 1851, while the repercussions of this highly publicized affair were still fresh in mind, the voters of St. Joseph and LaPorte nonetheless ratified the equally outrageous but less personal, more distant assault upon black dignity embodied in the Negro exclusionary Article 13 of the revised state constitution. To their credit, they did so by margins much less than those in the state as a whole, with a close vote in St. Joseph County, the locale of South Bend and the home of the rising political star, Schuyler Colfax.[23]

Young Colfax, a delegate to the constitutional convention of 1850, had spoken out with eloquence against the first version of the exclusionary provision, which not only forbad Negroes entry into the state but also had denied black residents the right to own property. Deprivation of such an elementary human right as property ownership Colfax condemned as "wanton injustice," "inexcusable tyranny," "unshielded even by popular prejudice," a provision "we shall burn with shame to see inscribed on the first page of our organic law. Let us do equal and exact justice, regardless of creed, race, or color. If we value liberty, let us not step beyond the Declaration of Independence, and declare its sublime truths a living lie." The property-owning proscription was dropped. Colfax's eloquence was not similarly directed against the exclusionary article as passed, but he did vote against each of its sections except the last, the provision to finance colonization—that vote was not surprising because Colfax had served as secretary of the St. Joseph County Colonization Society. In addition, he spoke up at the convention for the right of a radical wing of the Friends to petition for the abolishing of all distinctions "on account of color." Further, he argued, unsuccessfully, that the people by referendum—rather than the convention—should decide the question of Negro suffrage. These positions plus his eloquent appeal for equal justice and liberty might appear a forthright defense of black rights, but in fact they were not. During the debates, Colfax balanced uneasily between defiance of, and agreement with, popular prejudice, and his agreement went beyond a reluctant concession to political expediency. His concept of "equal and exact justice" was limited, his views of Afro-Americans uncomplimentary. He announced unequivocally that he would vote against extending the right of suffrage to Negroes; that he "would not propose to ingraft anything in the new Constitution that would invite them to immigrate into the State"; and that he hailed the colonization movement "as the most beneficent yet projected for the amelioration of the African, and at the same time, the relief of the people of the country from the evils of a black population in their midst."[24]

A few months later, Colfax began his first campaign for election to Congress. His Democratic opponent made political capital of the resounding words Colfax had spoken in the constitutional convention. During the contest Colfax maintained a conservative stance. He pledged not to favor the repeal of the compromise of 1850 or to interfere with slavery where it existed, not even in the District of Columbia unless the people of the district consented. Nonetheless, he lost the election. The continuing limits of Colfax's commitment to antislavery are suggested by his desire in 1858 to see Stephen A. Douglas, an exponent of white supremacy as well as of popular sovereignty, assume "the most commanding position of any statesman in the nation" and his neutrality during the historic Lincoln-Douglas senatorial contest of that year.[25]

The people among whom McGogy had been reared demonstrated in their politics, and in the South Bend incident, more moderation and more humanity than the state norm; yet they chose to perpetuate rather than to change the prevailing subordinate status of blacks. They sent their sons off to battle not for black freedom but for the Union. Only subsequently did they come to repudiate public measures of racial discrimination as "barbarous" and demonstrate in the sanguine words of their local historian (written in the mid-1870s) that they had "grown in the knowledge of the meaning of liberty, in the knowledge of human brotherhood, and of a genuine political manhood."[26] In choosing to link his wartime fortunes to those of a black regiment, it is safe to assume that with McGogy, as with his homefolk, patriotism outweighed brotherhood. It is equally reasonable to conclude that he had readily accepted, perhaps even welcomed, Lincoln's policy of wartime emancipation and the arming of blacks.

Records of the 50th U.S. Colored Troops reveal few glimpses of their activities and fewer clues to McGogy's personal relationships with the black recruits. Their first months in service during the summer of 1863 were grim. The men were kept on heavy fatigue duty without rest even on most Sabbaths; Company B was reported as suffering a vast amount of sickness and a great number of deaths. During one of the harsh hot months, McGogy was in command. A turn for the better came on October 1 when the men were issued arms. "The rapidity with which they learn and the precision with which they execute drill," according to the company report, "warrants the conclusion that they will make efficient soldiers." Thereafter more of their work presumably consisted of garrison duty and expeditions from Vicksburg into the countryside.[27] Those were chaotic days in occupied Vicksburg, rife with speculation, corruption, and crime. Black refugees by the thousands, many destitute and ill, flocked into the city whose white residents treated them as "escaped 'chattel.'" Doctors were few and incompetent, and there was only one hospital worthy of the name. Military guards and army facilities undertook essential roles in an effort to cope with the turbulent scene.[28]

After duty with his men for some seven months, Lieutenant McGogy was detailed to act as quartermaster, first for the army convalescent camp and then for all the hospitals of the Vicksburg command. His service came during a period marked by expansion and improvement in health care that benefited both black and white. More than a year later, on April 27, 1865, McGogy rejoined his company in Mobile, Alabama, where they were briefly stationed as occupying forces after having helped besiege under heavy fire, assault, and capture nearby Fort Blakely in the last infantry battle of the war. Within a month, McGogy was again detached from the colored troops to act as quartermaster elsewhere, this time with the Freedmen's Bureau in Alabama. It was an association that would continue for McGogy until the end of 1868, after March 1866 as a civilian agent. Although officially a member of Company B, 50th U.S. Colored Troops, until he and they were mustered out of service, McGogy had been physically present with his company for less than eight of the thirty-two months of his membership in the black regiment.

When in late May 1865 McGogy began at Mobile his more than three and a half years with the Freedmen's Bureau, the bureau's presence in Alabama was decidedly limited and ineffectual, awaiting the arrival of an assistant commissioner to take charge of the state. The man chosen, Gen. Wager Swayne, stopped in Mobile before moving on to establish—"practically alone"—bureau headquarters at Montgomery in late July. There he was without clerk or adjutant, but his minuscule staff did include the young quartermaster whom he had brought with him from Mobile. McGogy was to remain with General Swayne at headquarters for nearly a year, until mid-June 1866, attending not only to the routine duties of his office but as well to a variety of special assignments. Indeed, during his last months in Montgomery, McGogy, relieved as quartermaster, served as a special agent at the direction of the assistant commissioner.[29]

Within a few days of their arrival in Montgomery, General Swayne sent McGogy back to army headquarters in Mobile on the first of several missions. Orders for the journey directed McGogy to return as soon as possible with three employees, two horses, an ambulance, and such office furniture as he could procure; orders for subsequent trips to Mobile were not similarly specific. With urgent, often delicate, business needing attention, and normal channels of communication between the two cities frustratingly unreliable, McGogy was apparently being dispatched as a special courier with oral instructions from Swayne.

Another early assignment was inspection of the "home colony" located seven miles from Montgomery. McGogy's report, made the very day of his visit, was suffused with restrained indignation, his "suggestions" incisive. He had found eighteen hundred "destitute colored persons" living in a cluster of inadequate "buildings, or huts" while the army captain in charge, together with his thirteen noncoms and soldiers, were quartered a half mile away. Many of the freedmen he found "poorly clad," many sick. On the spot the lieutenant advised the captain that he should lay out the colony "formally" with streets at least "fifteen steps wide," erect new "good" buildings calling upon the quartermaster for tools and materials, locate several of his men in the immediate vicinity of the colony with orders to supervise the erection of buildings and visit every street and dwelling at least four times each day "to see that the inhabitants keep regular hours as regards labor, diet, sleep &c," and order clothing for his charges from the stores at army headquarters in Mobile! In addition, McGogy recommended to the assistant commissioner that "one good, energetic, efficient, Medical Officer" be sent immediately and a hospital be established "at a suitable distance . . . for in my opinion, (7) seven miles is too far distance between so many sick and any medical aid."[30] General Swayne had acquired a "good, energetic, efficient," and self-assured young staff officer.

There is no evidence to suggest the development of a close personal friendship between the lieutenant and the general (the latter only a few years older), but their working relationship was intimate. McGogy was one of only six officers at Swayne's headquarters after its organization was completed. It was McGogy whom Swayne chose to accompany him on a critical visit to Washington in late January and early February 1866, a period of imminent crisis for the bureau as its work became a central issue of conflict between the northern Republican majority in Congress and President Andrew Johnson, a border-state southerner who desired a speedy return of the secession states and in the interim so far as possible the preservation of state and local authority. Some months later, in asking to keep McGogy as a civilian agent, Swayne would commend him as "honest, energetic, sensible and good tempered," adding: "I regard him with affection and reliance."[31]

In the assistant commissioner, the lieutenant had a superior whose conception of his own responsibility to the freedmen reenforced McGogy's spontaneous response to their needs, and whose determined effort to obtain the cooperation of white southerners restrained any impulse to deal harshly with "rebels." Wager Swayne, unlike McGogy, was a deeply religious man born into an antislavery family of Quaker origins. Though he died an Episcopalian, a man of social prominence, and a highly successful corporation lawyer, until the last days of his life Wager Swayne was unstinting in his support of good government and philanthropic causes, and mindful of blacks. In 1901, on crutches and in pain from his loss of a leg during the war, he persuaded fellow members of New York City's Union League Club to reverse the decision of its house committee to fire the club's Negro servants. Also unlike McGogy, Swayne was well-trained and experienced in the law; before entering the army he had begun its practice with his father, Noah Swayne, whom Lincoln in early 1862 appointed to the Supreme Court.[32] Concern for the law fused with concern for humanity to give a distinctive character to General Swayne's stewardship of the bureau in Alabama, distinctive but thoroughly compatible with the goals and temper of his superior, O. O. Howard, the "Christian General" who headed the bureau. Both men, for reasons of expediency and of conviction, wished to attain their aims, so far as possible, by friendly persuasion rather than by force. Both sought the transformation of a slave South into a truly free society and realized how brief was the time allotted the bureau to facilitate so profound a change. Both "honestly desired to do what was best for all—the negro first."[33]

General Swayne began his work in Alabama with oral instructions received from Commissioner Howard at Washington to "'find out what there is to be done, and do it'" plus copies of two bureau directives. The first was Circular No. 5 consisting of rules and regulations for assistant commissioners and the second a less formal but printed letter of advice. The circular supplemented its generalities with some specifics, most notably authorization to assume jurisdiction over cases involving freedmen where civil courts did not allow Negro testimony. The exact wording of the authorization, a matter of considerable significance, read as follows: "In all places where there is an interruption of civil law, or in which local Courts by reason of old codes, in violation of the freedom guaranteed by the Proclamation of the President, and the laws of Congress, disregard the negro's right to justice before the laws, in not allowing him to give testimony...." The advisory letter admonished assistant commissioners to foster "liberty ... irrespective of color or rank," to promote "Virtuous intelligence [i.e., education] and industry," and to do their duty fearlessly but discreetly: "Endeavor not to overdo nor come short of duty.... The constraints and exactions of military law are neither normal nor congenial to the American spirit." It closed with an imperative injunction: "It is absolutely necessary to have officers above corruption and prejudice, who propose to do *simple justice*."[34]

The year of McGogy's close association with the assistant commissioner was one of endless challenge. Swayne struggled to protect the freedmen from abuse, stimulate education and industry, and meet the acute immediate needs of a people, black and white, who faced the ravages of war, the disruption of emancipation, and the natural vicissitudes of agriculture—struggled to do so without the requisite level or stability of officers and troops (the retention of trusted aides and the assignment of more cavalry were continuing and largely fruitless pleas), without adequate money, land, buildings, supplies of food and clothing and, in the face of local hostility, without the full support of the president who desired bureau cooperation with state authorities and did not share Swayne's view of the freedmen's rights. By October, the assistant commissioner was acutely aware that he was "requir[ed] ... to make bricks without straw."[35]

Swayne continued to try; and amidst the multiplicity of concerns that pressed upon him, he kept one goal paramount: to build for blacks an enduring foundation of "simple justice" that would include all the rights of whites, civil and "natural," a foundation he sought to create both in law and in practice. Swayne took this stand for equal rights without specific authorization, at a time when the status of freedmen had not been defined by congressional law or constitutional amendment. From late July 1865 through the following January, he cajoled and threatened local officials, Alabama's two governors (in accordance with the president's plan of Reconstruction, the first appointed and the second elected), delegates to the state's constitutional convention, and members of the subsequent legislative assembly. He advised them in the name of the president and Congress that readmission of the state and individual amnesty depended upon the institutionalization of equality before the law by statute and in judicial practice. He did so without equivocation though at the time he privately recognized that the requirement was one in which "I *hope* and believe," and later publicly acknowledged that there was no certainty "how far the rights of freedmen would be vindicated by the nation."[36]

A keen awareness of the injustices, gross and petty, to which blacks were subjected triggered Swayne's passionate commitment to equality of rights, and sustained it during his two and a half years as assistant commissioner. He believed an intrinsic causal relationship existed between outrages uncondoned by law and unequal treatment in law or in the courtroom. He did not, however, naively assume that equal laws would automatically result in equal justice or that, without a show of force, conciliation and sweet reason would bring the acquiescence of white southerners. Events during the first weeks of his tenure as assistant commissioner illuminate Swayne's attitudes and methods—that of the carrot and the stick, or in his words, "tact and firmness." They also suggest the atmosphere that must have prevailed at staff headquarters during McGogy's months as quartermaster and special agent.

On his arrival in Mobile Wednesday, July 19, anxious to get at "the real work," Swayne found a state of affairs that profoundly shocked him. Mayor Robert H. Slough, through the city court over which he presided, was daily inflicting upon freedmen what Swayne characterized as "the most shameless extortion and outrage . . . for nominal violation of the City Ordinances." The new bureau chief at once brought the matter to the attention of the commanding general and asked the local bureau agent to nominate a suitable officer and apply for jurisdiction over freedmen. He did not wait upon this action. Reaching Montgomery a few days later, Swayne paid his respects to Provisional Governor Lewis Parsons, left with him copies of Circular No. 5, and arranged an extended interview for the next Wednesday, July 26. That meeting was devoted almost entirely to the conduct of the mayor of Mobile and to the general question of jurisdiction over cases involving freedmen. Swayne urged the governor to order local judges and magistrates to accept Negro testimony. Parsons demurred, replying that beyond abrogating the slave code, he doubted his power to override state law. Swayne responded with a legal opinion so impressive that Parsons asked for it in writing. Swayne argued that the governor's power derived solely from the will of the president as commander in chief, that he had no responsibility to carry out local laws except as directed by the president, and that the president had denounced as a denial of justice the refusal to accept the testimony of Negroes "'by reason of *old* codes'" (quoting from General Howard's Circular No. 5). According to Swayne the circular constituted "a distinct and forcible expression of the will of the commander and actually an amendment to the laws of Alabama so far as their administration by the Provisional Governor is concerned"![37] It was an opinion that would have startled Andrew Johnson had he seen it.

At the interview, Governor Parsons had requested time to determine his course, a request Swayne "felt bound by your [Howard's] instructions" not to refuse. Though impatient for action, he felt obligated not to take jurisdiction generally or to act against Mobile's mayor before learning the governor's decision, promised for the following Tuesday, August 1. In his weekly letter to Howard, Swayne gave a full report of the exchange with the governor and a copy of his written opinion; he added that he would telegraph Parson's decision. When the week passed without word from the governor, Swayne pressed for an answer and on Friday, August 4, wired Howard that a reply had been promised for that evening. This time it arrived on schedule, "a negative answer, based on alleged grounds of political inexpediency." Swayne's reaction was incisive. That very night he issued General Order No. 7, which he succinctly summarized in a second telegram hurriedly despatched to Howard: "I have assumed jurisdiction under section seven Circular five the Judicial officers under provisional Governor are my agents to carry out the Laws without distinction of Color Martial Law in case of failure to accept or evident denial of Justice."[38]

Howard's Circular No. 5 upon which Swayne based his assumption of judicial authority had been formally approved by the president, but by any reasonable reading it said nothing about legal equality for blacks beyond the right to give testimony. Yet in the name of the president, and of justice, Swayne had set aside all provisions of Alabama law that discriminated on the basis of race. And he had, in effect, threatened to replace any judge or magistrate who failed to apply the same laws and procedures to blacks as to whites or otherwise denied them justice. Swayne's objective of equality before the law was one with which Commissioner Howard wholeheartedly agreed but President Johnson did not, though by August 1865 the president had publicly revealed only his opposition to equal suffrage, not his larger opposition to equality of civil status for blacks. Apparently Howard had a sufficient intimation of the president's position to have framed narrowly the authorization granted by Circular No. 5. It did not require state and local courts to recognize equality before the law; if they agreed to accept Negro testimony, they could exercise jurisdiction over freedmen. Swayne's order against all discrimination was far more sweeping than Howard's presidentially approved directive, and local judges after accepting Swayne's requirements remained his agents with authority derived from martial law, and subject to removal.[39]

The problem presented by Mayor Slough of Mobile was intimately interrelated with Swayne's assumption of jurisdiction by the order of August 4. He despatched a special courier to Mobile to hand the Mayor a copy hoping, expecting ("and determined") that Slough would *not* accept. Four days earlier, on receiving from the mayor complaints of the freedpeople's conduct together with a copy of the police order he had issued to arrest vagrants and put them to work on the roads unless they left the city, Swayne had written the governor "to ask your attention" to the mayor's course. The police order was "a violation of the rights of a free people" to peaceably assemble and choose where they would live and work. The colored people, Swayne caustically commented, had "at least as full and a better supported" bill of wrongs against the mayor than he against them. In "this crisis" of transition from slavery to freedom the mayor had violated their confidence; it was not likely to be restored. The letter included an appeal to the governor that revealed Swayne's own sense of history and of the historic moment: "May I add that those who are early and uncompromising like the precursors of the Revolution will be held for ages in exalted and affectionate remembrance."[40] Governor Parsons had not responded.

Mayor Slough answered the message of the special courier by telegram, one that did not disappoint Swayne's expectations; Slough rejected jurisdiction under the bureau. The assistant commissioner wired back: ". . . further exercise of jurisdiction in such cases [involving freedmen] would be at his [the Mayor's] peril as in violation of the order of the President." Then Swayne again wrote the governor. This time the indictment of Mobile's Mayor was detailed and damning. His police were arresting colored men out after ten P.M. and descending nightly "upon convivial and religious assemblies." Steamboat hands were being driven off without pay at the end of a trip, afforded no relief by the mayor's office, and left "to steal that they may live." Finally, the mayor had announced in a formal decision that "the negro cannot sue, though he can be sued, cannot testify, though he can be testified against, and that he had no greater civil rights than under the slave code." The "natural fruits" of the mayor's policy was "a state of quasi riot" with a church, a school, and an entire square of colored residences destroyed by incendiaries.[41]

"I can stop this and I will," Swayne concluded, but there was an alternative "much more conducive to complete order and that harmony . . . indispensable to the restoration of the State"—namely, the Governor could replace the mayor with an "honest and influential" man to whom Swayne would entrust jurisdiction over the freedmen as his agent, in effect a joint appointment. Swayne presented the alternative "confidently and respectfully . . . feeling that your own loyal sense of justice is, after all, the true refuge of this people." He did not, however, rely exclusively upon confidence in the governor's sense of justice for earlier in the letter he not only indicated that nonaction would threaten readmission but also flatly stated that the mayor's course "had been in progressive violation of the policy and order of the President of the United States."[42]

Governor Parsons graciously capitulated. With Swayne's general order a reality, he promised to endorse it and advise magistrates and judges to accept jurisdiction under bureau authority. He also agreed to appoint an "honest" man to replace Mayor Slough in Mobile. Decisive action followed swiftly. On the very afternoon of Swayne's respectful ultimatum, August 11, Parsons sent his adjutant to Mobile with commissions as mayor for two persons just in case the preferred choice would not accept. Swayne went along on the mission "to see it through." The first choice for mayor accepted, a man whom Parsons had been assured was "beloved by the colored people of Mobile" and would act "in kindness and good faith." The abbreviated weekly report that Swayne sent General Howard from Mobile before returning to Montgomery ended with an implicit apology, but not for the bold actions "which had time allowed I should have first submitted to yourself." "The use of crutches," wrote the one-legged general, "does not improve the handwriting."[43]

It was another week before Swayne fully explained to Howard his reasons for effecting the removal of Mayor Slough and for issuing General Order No. 7. There was the practical situation. When he took over the bureau he had found only "four feeble agencies for a negro population of 450,000"; officers and supporting troops were not available to establish military tribunals "on a sufficient scale and fit character to do the business." The course he had chosen, on the other hand, could make use of the vast judicial machinery the governor was fast restoring. And there were more fundamental considerations. Military jurisdiction over freedmen would unite public sentiment against the change of state law to eliminate distinctions based on race and would lead to misrepresentation and cries of outrage from whites. But if equal laws were administered by local officials they "could not be impugned by the people, being their own." Every judge who introduced Negro testimony would defend it. The upcoming constitutional convention would be "much more likely to incorporate into the organic laws what is already in full practice than to adopt what is rejected by their own courts and peculiar to military tribunals." At some point the colored people would be left to the civil courts; better to do so while the courts operated under the auspices of the bureau with its "power of removal." If civil jurisdiction followed that of the military, freedmen would be regarded as "protegees of a hostile jurisdiction" and themselves be the object of hostility.[44]

Swayne's was a powerful argument and his objective, though foredoomed to failure, essentially sound. He aimed to educate public sentiment, to develop a degree of acceptance of "simple justice" by white southerners sufficient to establish and make permanent for freedmen "those rights essential to security and well being," among which he included as axiomatic the right to nondiscriminatory laws and fair judicial proceedings. Swayne recognized from the start the hazard of empowering local judges to take jurisdiction over freedmen, reacted strongly to continuing instances of gross injustice, did not hesitate to use military authority, and supported the extension of the federal military presence in Alabama. But he also understood the limits of force.

In an official printed report of October 1866 he assessed the effect of his General Order No. 7:

> Practically, as concerned the administration of justice, this was found to be limited by the extent to which partisan bitterness, class-feeling, and the influence of particular electors, affected the conduct of judges, jurors, and the minor officers of the law. The result . . . was on the whole discouraging, though with many honorable illustrations of a different spirit. At that time, as at this day, the crying evil was not so much the wrongful administration of the laws, as their non-execution in behalf of freedmen, there being no public opinion by which this was rebuked, and no other accountability which freedmen could enforce. This difficulty was not to be fully met with troops, had their number been many times greater than it was.

Cautiously, but unmistakably, Swayne voiced his conclusion: above all, freedmen needed to be able to enforce "a stern accountability" upon "those who shall abuse their office in the Law, or shall ignore it. . . . But these are part and parcel of that hold upon the laws which they have who help make them. To give them this, as amply fit as many of them are, and many more becoming so, is duty, and humanity, and interest." He added defensively, "To omit this reference were to omit so far my duty."[45] It was a circumspect but courageous public statement from one whose favorable reputation and influence with white Alabamians and with the president depended upon a conciliatory approach. Black suffrage both to Andrew Johnson and to white southerners generally was the most unacceptable, indeed odious, of the freedman's claims to equality and justice.

Swayne had early recognized and was still struggling with the central dilemma of Reconstruction. The rights of blacks as free men could not be secured without force, but force without consent could not make "Liberty . . . complete."[46]

Whether Lieutenant McGogy, after a year working beside General Swayne and under his direction, fully comprehended the dilemma is problematic; but that he had gained an intimate knowledge of Swayne's administration of the bureau there can be little doubt: a knowledge of procedures, policy, problems—and most certainly of Swayne's formal instruction to agents that "A desire to secure justice without regard to color," together with a thorough knowledge of all orders, would "enable them to meet the requirements of humanity and duty."[47]

For McGogy, there are few revealing documents of his service while stationed at Montgomery. Apparently fellow officers thought well of him. His former superior officer, the chief army quartermaster in Mobile, without McGogy's knowledge, initiated an effort to obtain him a captaincy because he had "so faithfully, honestly served" and being so long detached from his regiment had lost a regular promotion. A brevet (an honorary rank that carries no pay increase) would not do "when board & lodging cost sixty dollars per month—it dont pay." Not that McGogy was without resources. Early in 1866, expecting to be soon mustered out of service, he decided to purchase a plantation of 387 acres near Montgomery at $12.50 an acre payable in three yearly installments, and persuaded his brother to help finance and take full responsibility for its management. When the propriety of such purchases came under scrutiny by the Steedman-Fullerton inquiry, initiated by President Johnson in an attempt to discredit the bureau and defeat a measure to extend its life and power, General Swayne endorsed the accuracy of

McGogy's explanatory statement that he had devoted "my undivided time and entire ability" to his duty as bureau agent. No issue was made of his ownership.[48]

Two reports by McGogy of special missions performed during the last weeks at his Montgomery station provide a tantalizingly incomplete but nonetheless revealing glimpse of his responsibilities and attitudes. A circuitous journey brought him at 2:45 on the afternoon of May 18, 1866 to the small town of Clayton, Barbour County, about fifty-five miles south and east of Montgomery. There he found, to use his own words, "a grave dug a rope tied and a large number of people collected to witness the Execution of Henry Witherby freedman which was to take place at 3 o'Clock, P.M. the prisoner was being brought from the jail when I arrived." As directed, and just in the nick of time, McGogy presented to the sheriff a reprieve from Governor Patton.[49]

The man about to be hanged had been convicted in the fall of 1865 of assault with intent to rape a little girl not nine years of age. A stranger in town, apparently of limited wit, he had been befriended by the girl's mother and allowed to sleep in their house. Some months after his conviction, his jailer and a number of townsmen, "high toned gentlemen" (to quote the jailer) petitioned for his release. The latter wrote the governor that the proceedings were rushed through at the end of the session and that the testimony against the freedman had been "too flimzy to deprive any human being of his life on." Witherby explained, when the jailer questioned him after the trial, that the child had fallen asleep and at the mother's request he had carried her to the bed and then "lay down across the foot of the bed as I suppose [the jailer reported] as near an idiot as he would do." Apparently Witherby's mental condition was indeed impaired though to what extent is not clear.[50]

McGogy's report did not indicate the nature of the crime nor the grounds for clemency, but did underscore the injustice that had narrowly been averted. "I was gratified to observe," he wrote (in his characteristically restrained manner) "that the Reprieve met with the hearty approval of nine-tenths of the large number of people who had assembled to see the same Henry Witherby hung and I learned from different reliable sources that it was generally believed throughout Barbour Co. that Henry Witherby was innocent of the crime for which he had been convicted and that false evidence and prejudice against the Freedmen had secured a verdict against an innocent man."[51]

That evening after having gathered what information he could of the general attitude of whites in Clayton toward the freedmen, and toward the government as well, McGogy went on to Eufaula, the other principal village of the predominantly black county, arriving late at night. The next day he met with a group of "Colored men" to explore the possibility of establishing a school for black children. McGogy was "soon convinced that with the assistance of Mr. R. Graves (Freedman)" it would not be difficult to establish a good school. "Mr. Graves" (the respect implicit in McGogy's reference is worthy of note) had located "a nice family" with whom the teachers could board, had secured a suitable building for a schoolhouse, and had compiled a list of 250 persons anxious to attend, most of whom would be able to pay at least a small sum, which would make the school self-supporting. McGogy visited the boardinghouse and school building, approved both as suitable, and also saw the mayor of the town who "kindly promised that the school should have all necessary protection." Further, he investigated other facilities for freedmen's children, finding two "select schools," one taught by "a lady of Eufaula, one by a freedwoman" both of whom admitted only those who could pay two dollars a month. McGogy's closing remarks indicate that this journey had not been his first such assignment: "I heard less disloyal sentiments in those places [Clayton, Eufaula, Union Springs in the state and Fort Valley in Georgia] than in any other part of the South which I have visited."[52]

The second McGogy report, some two weeks after his return to Montgomery, came from Elyton, the village in Jefferson County that preceded Birmingham, which was not founded until 1871. McGogy had apparently been sent to investigate reports of lawlessness, whether directed against freedmen, Union men, or both is not clear, and to take or instigate action. He was unable to find "any evidence sufficient to make an arrest" but intended to stay "as long as there is any prospect of my obtaining any information." Of that, however, he was not sanguine, reporting that people were opposed to violating the law "as a general theory" but "lack energy to prosecute." The civil officers, he stated bluntly, "in order to sustain popularity will cover-up the bad conduct of others."[53]

On this mission McGogy sought out local Union men and asked their opinion of one Dr. Thomas Houghey, a citizen of Elyton who had applied to the assistant commissioner for appointment as a U.S. commissioner under the Civil Rights Act of 1866. Houghey had written Swayne that he believed "impartial justice to the Freedman . . . an impossibility without the interposition of United States laws administered by United States officers." The applicant stated that his sentiments had always been antislavery, that he had opposed secession, had served three years as surgeon in the Union army, and also that he had diligently studied the common law. McGogy reported the doctor to be "very energetic & efficient" (from McGogy a high accolade of far-reaching implication); the Union men admired and would support him. McGogy urged an immediate appointment. If Houghey were "invested with the authority to arrest and try those offenders the law will be inforced at once."[54] It is evident that McGogy, like his chief, sought an effective means to counter the injustices in the local administration of justice.

During the ten months since Swayne's order of August 4, 1865, assuming legal jurisdiction over the freedmen and empowering local judges to exercise authority as his agents, the assistant commissioner's efforts to obtain equal laws, equal enforcement of the law, and respect for the black man's "natural rights" had been persistent—and discouraging. Despite brave words of hope, Swayne recognized the enormity of white resistance. His policy of "tact and firmness" had worked best at the top level of government, with Governor Patton as well as Governor Parsons responding helpfully, vetoing discriminatory legislation and acting on appeals for clemency. But at the community level, which Swayne tried to reach through local magistrates, his success was decidedly limited. It followed that state legislators reflected the prevailing white attitudes, "pandering [as Swayne wrote Howard] to low public sentiment."[55]

President Johnson's policy, with the priority it gave to state authority rather than federal responsibility for the freedmen, and his responsiveness to southern white opinion, was becoming more and more of an obstacle. Lack of presidential support had denied Swayne the victory he sought for equal law—law equal both in language and in effect. The limited concession he had wrung from the Alabama constitutional convention, which gave temporary recognition and support to his August 4 strategy against discriminatory laws and legal proceedings, terminated early in 1866 with adjournment of the first postwar general assembly. The assistant commissioner thereby lost authority over local magistrates, no longer his recognized agents subject to the threat of removal. Not that Swayne's influence with Alabama's lawmakers, and especially with the governor, had been without effect; it was largely responsible for the relative mildness of the black code enacted by Alabama's legislature. But President Johnson's mid-February 1866 veto of the congressional bill to extend and strengthen the bureau, a measure already diluted in deference to his views, dismayed Commissioner Howard and his lieutenants and bolstered white recalcitrance throughout the South, including Alabama.

National authority for equal rights, which the bureau bill would have conveyed, was delayed until the passage over a second veto of the Civil Rights Act in early April. With a hostile president given responsibility for implementing its judicial provisions, that act did not fulfill in practice McGogy's expectation that henceforth federal authority could and would arrest and try perpetrators of outrages (nor did the bureau bill finally enacted in July). Adding further to the uncertainty of the military's authority to act was the president's April 2 proclamation declaring the war at an end. Johnson assured Howard that the proclamation did not end martial law or affect the bureau, but an army order drawn up in the White House and promulgated May 1 denied commanders the right to convene military commissions to try civilians, the procedure used by the bureau for major offenses against freedmen. The clash in 1866 between the president's policy and the goals of the bureau culminated in a deliberate, unprincipled effort by Johnson to discredit the bureau through an investigation by commissioners who had no doubt as to what was expected of them. With their entourage of reporters the two commissioners, Generals Steedman and Fullerton, reached Alabama in June 1866, where Swayne was equally aware of the purpose of their mission and so bitterly resentful that he "could not help showing my teeth a little." Their official report commended Swayne's administration as discreet and cooperative with the civil authorities. A private letter from Steedman to the president damned Swayne as a Radical as fierce as Thaddeus Stevens himself. Radicals did not recognize Swayne as one of their own, nor does recent scholarship.[56]

In this beleaguered setting, with the bureau "the object of a prevalent malignity,"[57] attacked both for its support of the freedmen and for its alleged abuse of them, in mid-1866 McGogy (now a civilian) began a new phase of his bureau career. He was placed in charge at Greenville, Butler County, some forty miles south of Montgomery headquarters, with responsibility for one of the eight bureau districts into which the state had been divided. The assignment developed out of a special mission that followed close upon McGogy's return from Elyton, a joint one with Swayne's commissary of subsistence, Capt. W. C. Arthur. The two were sent to Greenville to deal with a problem not of violence or miscarriage of justice but of corruption.

Despite its relative proximity to headquarters, the bureau office at Greenville for some months before the arrival of Captain Arthur and McGogy had been a troubled outpost of Swayne's authority. Many of the complaints centered around the distribution of government rations for the needy, allocated under a complicated system of verification and distribution by local justices of the peace, county commissioners, probate judges, their designated agents, and for the town of Greenville by the mayor, known as the intendant. Allegations of corruption against the local bureau agent climaxed persistent and conflicting charges of favoritism and of neglect, both toward whites and toward blacks. The two most articulate critics were old-time Alabamians and respected leaders, both lawyers who had served in the state legislature and both soon to become notorious as the most prominent "scalawags" in the county yet in important respects opposites. William Seawell, an antebellum large slaveholder and ardent secessionist, was hostile to the bureau and bold enough to write the president directly. Benjamin F. Porter, an antisecessionist and Greenville's wartime and postwar intendant (i.e., mayor), supported the bureau and was so averse to what he considered unjustified handouts to whites that he brought down upon himself widespread animosity and the threat of bodily harm. Swayne considered Seawell a troublemaker; Porter enjoyed his confidence.[58]

The troubles in the Greenville district were not limited to the handling of food supplies. The inmates of the home colony at Garland, the bureau refuge for the temporarily unemployed and their dependents and for the unemployable—the young, the old, the disabled, and the ill—were without an attending doctor, were short on blankets and so lacking in clothing that some were reported to be in a state of nakedness. According to the intendant, blacks flocking into town were rented shanties at exorbitant rates, then encouraged to meet the cost by prostitution and theft; and freedmen in the countryside were being coerced or deceived into making inequitable contracts, with adjudication of disputes "utterly useless . . . before the Dogberrys of the different Beats, where ignorance or the influence of voters, hold the scales of justice." Porter recommended that all cases between freedmen and their employers be tried in the office of the bureau.[59] Butler County with forty percent of its population black was on the southern border of Alabama's plantation Black Belt.

Bad relations with the army post at Greenville had further compromised the effectiveness of the bureau. During the tenure of Thomas W. Mostyn, an army private, as subassistant commissioner, the lieutenant colonel commanding the post so constantly interfered with bureau affairs that Swayne had intervened with an order from army headquarters enjoining the post commander to cooperate with the bureau agent. Soon therefore Mostyn was demoted to superintendent of the Garland colony and a captain, F. O. Steinberg, chosen as his replacement. According to the captain, Mostyn, through a local grog dealer, began circulating false accusations to discredit his successor and regain the superior bureau appointment. For Captain Steinberg the army post was also a problem but with a difference: not its presence but an order for its removal threatened his effectiveness. Both he and intendant Porter thought the authority of the bureau would be undermined, unsustainable without at least some force, preferably mounted men. It was Porter who revealed that Steinberg had been threatened. He feared the captain would not press for troops lest it reflect upon his personal courage; Steinberg took care to report that he had no fear for his person, only fear of disrespect for the bureau.[60]

The mid-June investigation by Captain Arthur and McGogy focused on Captain Steinberg. They found damning evidence of his sale of pork, cornmeal, flour, and molasses—more than one hundred barrels, plus nearly twelve hundred pounds of bacon. Intendant Porter, who liked Steinberg, had not suspected the captain's guilt, which he compassionately attributed to the influence of designing men who had plied the captain with drink. Steinberg himself in an abject confession also attributed his "ruin" to bad company and intoxication, plus flattery and their argument that he would be committing no crime! Captain Arthur promptly arrested Steinberg and placed McGogy in charge, apparently following contingent instructions Swayne had given him orally. Steinberg was tried by court martial and convicted of embezzlement to the amount of two thousand dollars. Mostyn had also been implicated and arrested, but the charges were not proved. The episode, however, marked the end of his bureau career. Coming on the heels of the Steedman-Fullerton witch-hunt, the scandal at Greenville was especially embarrassing. Captain Arthur wrote Swayne that he had "endeavored to give as little publicity as possible to the object of my visit."[61]

It is reasonable to conclude that Swayne had chosen McGogy as the best possible man "for doing what can be done at Greenville."[62] McGogy was honest, efficient, energetic, discreet, experienced in hospital and quartermaster duties, familiar with bureau affairs throughout the state, aware of the diverse pressures originating from the nation's capital, and a trusted aide who knew well the policy objectives of the assistant commissioner whom he had served from the day eleven months earlier when Swayne, eager for "the real work" ahead, had assumed responsibility for the bureau in Alabama.

Although Swayne's instructions to officers in the field had stated that "much is necessarily left to the[ir] discretion," the bureau agent, in fact, despite his distinctive impact locally, had to function in accord with Swayne's policy of conciliation and in the context of a layered military bureaucracy that granted him little or no independent authority and demanded endless vouchers, receipts, estimates, accountings and reports. McGogy struggled manfully, working all day from 8 A.M. to 7 P.M. his second Saturday in Greenville and the following Sunday as well, to send off promptly monthly reports due within ten days of his taking office. With affairs in a state of confusion, and only one clerk to help with all his tasks, it proved impossible to complete them on time. McGogy asked forbearance and promised prompt compliance in the future as he would "hereafter be able to control my business." But bureaucratic obstacles intruded endlessly upon the performance of his "business": blank forms needed for returns were repeatedly exhausted and tardily replenished; rations received did not correspond with their invoices; how transportation costs should be paid and receipts given were matters of uncertainty or dispute that required Montgomery's intervention; scales on hand were worthless and new ones difficult to obtain, making it impossible to check quantities; some food stuffs were in short supply while others arrived in overabundance but no trades or borrowing could be done with local merchants even when advantageous or "necessary"; rations not issued had to be returned to headquarters as did empty cornmeal sacks; empty barrels were to be sold and the proceeds accounted for; payment for salaries, rent, and services arrived tardily, in bills too large for convenient distribution or in drafts difficult to cash. For McGogy at Greenville, the routine seems never to have become routine.[63] Nonetheless, he did not let it become all-consuming.

The home colony at Garland, more than twenty miles south and west of Greenville, was a matter of immediate and continuing concern for McGogy. A week after taking over the district, he was writing headquarters that the colony should be moved to a healthier location, one nearer his office where he could supervise it personally and save the services of one employee and "the trouble and expense of shipping rations from here." The curt response from headquarters was that he had better make some arrangement with the county commissioners to take charge of the indigent at Garland.[64]

McGogy obtained an oral commitment from the probate judge that the county would assume responsibility for the colony provided the bureau would continue to furnish rations, but McGogy protested the transfer with a vehemence that bespoke indignation. "I am confident," he wrote, "that the Judge of Probate and the County Commissioners have no sympathy for the destitute white people, much less for the Freedmen . . . and if said Colony is to be fed by the Bureau, I recommend that it be kept out of the control of a heartless class of men such as would eventually assume charge." Again McGogy urged that the colony be moved to Greenville, pointing out that he could then provide schooling for the children and short stays for persons in need of temporary shelter. His letter plus one of similar import from intendant Porter, which McGogy forwarded, brought grudging permission to look for a place near Greenville "at moderate rent for a term not more than two years" and a stern admonition that admission must be strictly limited to only those aged, decrepit, sick or too young to work. Within less than a week McGogy was reporting that he had found a suitable location, on high ground with good water, land suitable for gardens, and an abundance of wood that could be used to build comfortable log houses at no expense except that of the labor to build them—all for a rent of twenty-five dollars a month. He asked permission to employ two freedmen for a month, at twenty dollars each; together with the one freedman regularly employed he estimated that they could build one house a day. In addition he would need a requisition on the quartermaster for two or four mules. "In a few weeks," he wrote, "I will have the inhabitants of the 'asylum' comfortably situated in a healthy locality with a School house in their midst." On a visit to Montgomery a few days later he spoke personally with Swayne about the project and left anticipating authorization. Official approval never arrived. The colony remained at Garland, plagued with continuing inadequacies despite McGogy's constant attention. At the end of October it was providing shelter for seventy freedmen: five men, nineteen women, and forty-six children, plus five whites, three of them children.[65]

The records of McGogy's tenure at Greenville make evident a commitment to schooling for blacks which, like his concern for the destitute, sick, and helpless, transcended duty and was fueled by indignation. A school, for which his predecessor had rented and equipped a house, was to have opened the Monday of McGogy's arrival, but it did not. Its teacher was frightened off by a scurrilous threatening letter, which he brought to the new bureau agent. McGogy promptly forwarded it to headquarters, requesting instructions but leaving no doubt of those he desired. "If you will furnish me a few guards I will see that the school will open on Monday . . . should [we] now be compelled to abandon the enterprise it would be as well to discontinue all form of law, and acknowledge that the law both Civil and Military has failed to secure protection to its Citizens." Headquarters agreed that the school should be opened at once and promised to keep an armed force available as long as was necessary.⁶⁶

Classes began, and McGogy did not limit his oversight to their security. He discharged for "good reason" (unspecified) the assistant teacher, a black man, and hired another, a Mrs. Clancy, "a very respectable widow lady." Responsive to the complaints of black parents, like them McGogy was dissatisfied with Benjamin Hildreth, the teacher who ran the school, with his teaching methods, with his unwillingness to accept all who wished to attend, and with the fees he charged. All came under McGogy's censure in reports to the bureau's state superintendent of education. He also objected to the disparity of salary between Mrs. Clancy and Mr. Hildreth: "I am in favor of womans rights to such an extent that I am opposed to paying a man $50 per month, and a woman $30 per month for the same service especially when the woman is superior." Nor was he satisfied with the schoolhouse: one room was unsuitable for so many; the rent was unreasonably high; and the owners were "speculators" who "would dispossess us at any time they could make one dollar by so doing!" At a school meeting he called specifically for the purpose, McGogy asked, and obtained, from the black community a lot and the labor to build a new schoolhouse with bureau assistance. McGogy also started an evening school for adult freedmen whom he had encouraged to seek education, seeing it as a practical instrument of protection for black workers against the impositions of employers.⁶⁷

Though intendant Porter favored education for freedmen, white community sentiment did not. The sons of two of the country's most prominent citizens, one the probate judge and the other a state senator, were part of a gang that in early May had harassed freedmen in their homes and broken into the schoolhouse, smashing and burning its benches and desks. Seven months later McGogy bitterly pointed out to headquarters that no members of the group "have ever been tried." Publicly, through Porter, McGogy attempted to persuade the townsmen that the freedmen's school was "not intended as a malice or spite, nor [to] injure, or irritate the minds of any persons." Not white hostility but the difficulty of recruiting able teachers foiled McGogy's hopes and energetic initiatives. In November, thoroughly discouraged by Hildreth's incompetence and the unavailability of a satisfactory replacement, he suggested that the school be closed unless two good teachers could be found by the end of the month. The school survived, but the new schoolhouse was still incomplete when McGogy was reassigned at the end of January 1867. One of his last letters before leaving Greenville was a request for a hundred dollars "to enable us to complete said house at once." The "us" referred to the freedmen who were doing the building. They were "progressing finely," and he had been in hopes they would "be able to finish it by subscription"; but without assistance from the bureau the schoolhouse "will be delayed, perhaps for some time."[68]

One effort McGogy made to protect the freedpeople and further their interests, at least in the eyes of headquarters, overreached his authority and infringed upon their freedom. In late November, he reported that two colored ministers from Montgomery were holding meetings at which "they get up excitement and extort money from the colored people under the pretense of the money being for the 'Mission of Zion.'" McGogy had "quietly prohibited" church collections taken "for any purpose except for the benefit of the people in this community." He explained that he thought charity should begin at home and believed "no class of people are more in need of money than those in this place." By return mail, headquarters informed him that he could advise but he could not prohibit, "the colored people being . . . free and sole masters of their own money."[69]

An ever present atmosphere of menace surrounded bureau personnel, teachers, and freedmen. Very early in his tenure McGogy had canceled arrangements for a visit to Montgomery when reports reached him that the Fourth of July celebration planned by the colored people was "a thing [that] could not be done." He posted guards, appeared in person, and delivered a speech calculated to reassure whites as much as to encourage his audience of freedmen. They must not think that he was there to protect them "in an independence of law and good faith"; he could only claim for them "that the law shall be impartially administered. Your safety under the law, depends upon your own conduct." When the local newspaper reported the festive occasion with a ridicule and contempt that outraged McGogy's patriotism and humanity, he exploded in a report to headquarters that concluded: ". . . what kind of Justice do you think those freedmen would receive from a jury of men, who support such a paper, as the Advocate?" Swayne had just sent word that he wished to reassign the detail of soldiers still stationed at Greenville unless "actually needed." McGogy replied that it was necessary to allow at least a few to remain, citing threats, the danger of theft of bureau property, and the "many violent characters here who have no respect for themselves, or the law." As further justification, he added: "You must know that in my position there is a great difference between discharging my duty with a view to Justice, and discharging a duty with a view to pleasing [any] particular class of persons."⁷⁰ Six soldiers were left in Greenville, a number later reduced to three.

Notwithstanding McGogy's Fourth of July counsel to the freedmen and his deference to Swayne's policy of conciliation, he had little confidence in local justice. When hostility threatened to turn violent his impulse was to deal with it directly and forcefully. In August when a guard escorting the teacher home from night school reported that they had been followed by three menacing men with blackened faces, McGogy set off with the soldier to find the parties and "bring them into your presence by the first train with costume &c unchanged." Failing to find the men, he hoped still to meet up with them. At the same time he felt it necessary to assure headquarters "that I will do nothing to irritate the feelings of any person," and ask dutifully for instructions. Swayne's adjutant authorized McGogy to arrest the men if he could find them and bring them, not to Montgomery, but before the town intendant as suspicious persons.⁷¹

A less elusive outcome to an incident three weeks later brought from McGogy a burst of satisfaction, more attributable to the release of pent-up frustration than to justice achieved. A freedman working on the road to fulfill his tax obligation had brought along a gun to shoot some squirrels. A passing white, Peterson Harris, seeing the gun, seized and broke it in pieces, then snapped his own pistol at the unoffending black, who promptly reported the offence. He found McGogy very busy loading commissary stores into cars for transhipment, but not too busy to write a note for the freedman to present to the local prosecuting attorney. It stated with bluntness that "all men has the right to the highway and the law should protect the person, and property of all men regardless of color," and asked for an immediate investigation. The attorney declined to act, and the freedman returning to McGogy's office met Harris who threatened to kill him unless he dropped the matter. McGogy responded by sending his clerk to see the probate judge, who could not be found, and the prosecuting attorney who again refused to take any action, on the ground that Harris was a respectable man. Thereupon McGogy ordered his soldier guards to arrest Harris, resulting in a four-hour search that netted the man's horse while the culprit slipped out the back door of a friendly storekeeper's shop. Excitement among townsmen ran high, with some driving their buggies in and out of town, others galloping horses through the streets or running on foot, collecting in groups. A committee of three called upon McGogy, who read them Grant's General Order No. 44 when they questioned his authority to make the arrest. Issued in July 1866 at Commissioner

Howard's request, the order authorized the military to make arrests when civil authorities failed to do so. According to McGogy, the protesting committee agreed that he "had only obeyed orders," offered to see that Harris was punished if McGogy called off the guards, and brought him a confirming statement from the probate judge. Feeling triumphant and vindicated, McGogy ended the search, released Harris' horse, and sat down to record the happening for headquarters. "I tell you," he concluded, "that this was a great day in Greenville, it opened the eyes of many, and convinced them of the fact that the laws of the United States did afford protection to the persons, and property of all its citizens."[72]

Such satisfaction came rarely. Twelve days after the Harris affair some fifteen armed men more or less under the influence of liquor threatened "to chase the Yankees out of town." McGogy thought it best to ignore the provocation because they outnumbered three to one the combined force of soldiers and police in Greenville! Beyond in the countryside disguised armed men broke into freedmen's homes, demanding money, making off with guns, sometimes inflicting gunshot wounds. Local authorities made no effort to apprehend them or even to establish their identity; McGogy could do nothing. In a brutal hanging and whipping of a freedwoman accused of theft, and an assault upon her protesting husband, the vindictive employer and witnesses were identified, but the victims fled to parts unknown. Without them intendant Porter would issue no warrant for arrest. McGogy was convinced that if ever the case were brought to trial there was no juror in the county "but what would decide that the circumstancial evidence in reference to the theft would justify the man Pryor in assaulting, hanging, and killing the woman." Nonetheless, he thought Pryor should be apprehended under General Order No. 44; headquarters, though ready to act if a case could be established, apparently recognized the futility of an arrest. In another instance, that of a father and son responsible for repeated assaults on freedpersons, nothing could be done because witnesses were "afraid of their lives" should they make the affidavits required by the probate judge.[73]

When black men and women brought their grievances to the bureau office, more often than not McGogy's option was limited to sending a note, sometimes carried by the party aggrieved, to the appropriate local official—probate judge, justice of the peace, sheriff, prosecuting attorney, intendant—or to the offending employer. Reading those that have survived in the office files, one senses how difficult it was for McGogy to maintain a tone of polite deference. He certainly tried, and to local authorities generally succeeded. He would succinctly state the freedman's case, then ask for an investigation or a trial or an explanation, sometimes expressing a perfunctory confidence that the recipient would see that justice was done. But at times McGogy included a statement of principle or an admonition, formulated with considerable self-restraint, which nonetheless could have been read by the recipient as offensive. The arrest as a vagrant of a black mother who had come to town to report the wounding of her son by his employer brought from McGogy a caustic note to intendant Porter. "I have been informed," he wrote, "that the law of this City arrests all persons who have no visible means of support. I know of no persons being arrested except Freedman, notwithstanding there is many white persons who come equally under this law." As an Alabamian of atypical sensitivity to blacks' grievances, Porter may have shared rather than resented McGogy's quiet outrage; Porter's successor as intendant, however, responded to a similar protest from McGogy against vagrancy arrests with resentful defensiveness. McGogy held his ground, insisting that "the officers of the law should regardless of their knowledge of the Negro execute the law as it reads," but ended his reply with a feeble gesture of conciliation: "I trust our intercours may continue agreable."[74]

Probate Judge S. J. Bolling was another official who did not take kindly to McGogy's strictures. One exchange between the two men ended in a retreat that must have been painful for McGogy. Seeing two Negro men and one Negro boy brought into town fastened together by chains locked around their necks, he had written indignantly to Judge Bolling citing the equal punishment provision of the Civil Rights Act and commenting that it was "not the custom of this country to inflict such cruelty upon white prisoners, especially those of tender age." On receiving Bolling's reply, McGogy tried to propitiate the irate judge: he had not meant to imply that the case warranted a suit against those who had custody of the prisoners but rather "knowing the influence your Honor posseses" he had thought "a few words from you would to a great extent discontinue any similar proceedings"; he was "not familiar with the custom of this country" and if anything in his course had been improper, it was "an error of the head and not of the heart for I have all confidence that your Honor will discharge your whole duty and punish the offender for any offence that may come under your observation!"[75]

With nonofficials McGogy's tone was apt to be less conciliatory and more strident, though with them as well he struggled to be evenhanded. He invited more than one white against whom a freedman had registered a charge of mistreatment to present his version of the case, reassuring him that "I never form any opinion by hearing one side of a story." He added, however, an implied threat of a summons to appear before the U.S. commissioner at Montgomery if the offender did not respond promptly and satisfactorily.[76]

McGogy's sense of responsibility for "simple justice" extended to the plantation. In no uncertain terms he informed an employer who had ordered his workers to sell their share of the cotton or leave, that his action was "contrary to all law and justice," and to their contract. And he threatened to intervene whenever he heard of planters attempting "to take full control of the entire crop." "I will send guards to see that Freedmen have the benefit of their contracts." However, in the case of a freedman actually driven off the plantation without compensation for his year's labor, McGogy could not use direct action but only a strong letter to the local justice of the peace. "You must know," he wrote, "that Freedmen are not entirely blind to their own interest, and without the Law to afford them some assurance of protection, the Freedmen will have nothing to encourage them to labor and the now furtile fields of Alabama will soon be grown over with the native Oaks & Pines." The letter ended with a ritual expression of confidence that "from my knowledge of you" the recipient would "decide the case with a view to Justice."[77]

McGogy expected strict observance of contract terms from both planter and freedman; inequitable contacts presented him with a dilemma. In early January 1867 it was reported to him that planters were getting freedmen drunk immediately before signing a contract for the coming year, a contract from which some, on returning to a state of sobriety, wished to be released. McGogy succinctly stated the problem and asked headquarters what he should do. "I fear it will have a bad influence to advise the freedmen to disregard their contracts and on the other hand I know that it is unjust on the part of the Planter to obtain the labor of these people under such circumstances." The reply from Swayne's adjutant, O. D. Kinsman, informed McGogy that the common law does not recognize a contract made by a party "who from any cause whatever is in an unsound state of mind. It is therefore considered proper that the freedmen be advised that contracts made by them when in that condition, through their would be employer's means, are not binding."[78]

Undoubtedly McGogy followed instructions, to the discomfort of the planters. Their accumulated discontent apparently inspired an oblique attack upon McGogy's personal integrity that appeared in the January 11 issue of the *Daily Advocate*. Under the heading "Can it be so?" the local newspaper reported rumors that officers of the Freedmen's Bureau were advising freedmen and freedwomen not to hire for the present and requiring them to contract only through the bureau, and for a "consideration." McGogy sent the clipping on to headquarters along with a background account that began with events the previous September. A number of freedmen had then been summarily dismissed without compensation for their summer's work, and were saying they would never again work for any white man. On reviewing their contracts, McGogy found them so worded that there was no means of redress. Sensitive to the injustice of the situation, he yet felt that he could only advise them to avoid employers who had been "unmerciful to their hands." McGogy made a point of doing so, not only privately, but as well at a school meeting later in the month when many were present. At the same time he tried to impress upon them (so he informed headquarters when under attack the following January) that for those "entirely destitute of capital" it would be necessary to labor for others; there were good men as well as bad and they should seek out the former for employment. The advice may not have been necessary, the freedmen, as McGogy liked to put it, "not being entirely blind to their own interests." However great or small his influence with the black community, McGogy took satisfaction in the fact that it would be difficult for some men (i.e., "unmerciful" employers) to find labor. A few days before the January newspaper report, an exchange with "some gentlemen" who came to his office seeking laborers left no doubt as to whose interests came first with McGogy. They asked him to enforce the vagrancy law—against Negroes only. His reply was that he would "use my best endeavours *to prohibit the Vagrant law from being enforced at all.*" The "gentlemen" then asked, rhetorically, whether he did not think it wrong to allow the freedmen to become vagrants. The answer they received is best conveyed in McGogy's own words: "I said that it was not the purpose of the Government to exercise any compulsion against any one class of people and that in my opinion to compel the Freedmen as a vagrant law would do to enter into contracts with men who would take every advantage of them as they had last year the crime would be much greater than to allow a few vagrants, and under these circumstances there would be no inducement for those lawless characters to act with humanity towards the freedmen."[79]

McGogy concluded his letter to headquarters defiantly. He would not condescend to reply to the *Advocate*, "but if you have any fear that I have disregarded a strictly honest course in discharge of my duty I request that you send to this place at once an officer authorised to investigate the charges made against me." The answer from headquarters was one of unqualified support, even advising McGogy that he should under no circumstances reply to the article and if asked why, should state that he was "nowise responsible to them." "In conclusion," Kinsman wrote, "I would suggest that you call to mind the fable of the Moon and the cur, and that you remember that he that touches pitch becomes defiled."[80]

The policy of conciliation and restraint had evoked potentially explosive but still controlled anger both at the Montgomery office and at Greenville's. Swayne was trying to make justice more effective by finding a man for appointment in each county as U.S. Commissioner. McGogy reported that in Butler and the three adjoining counties he knew of no one suitable, despite an effort to study the past and present history of the people of his district. He could, however, recommend three persons in Lowndes county, two of them native New Yorkers turned planters.[81]

From McGogy's perspective the outlook for local justice remained grim, but not unrelieved, for another bittersweet episode had marked his last weeks at Greenville. One Saturday evening in mid-December when McGogy was in Montgomery, Enoch Hicks, the unpunished leader of the group that had pillaged the schoolhouse in May and continued to harass blacks, let loose his spleen upon the military and the bureau. A soldier and two townsmen got into a verbal altercation that had seemed settled when Hicks called upon the latter and others present to "kill the Yankee." With a large club he carried, Hicks himself struck down two men who tried to intervene, a Corporal Berry and the store's proprietor. He then set off with his companions for the bureau office, tried to draw his pistol on McGogy's clerk, and threatened to drive all the damned Yankees out of town and to burn down the bureau building. Hicks then returned to the store where the fracas had begun, breaking in the door and boasting of his threats. McGogy reported that when asked to bring Hicks to justice, intendant Porter stated that nothing could be done unless the military intervened because Hicks was the terror of the town and no jury would have the courage to convict him. Headquarters apparently agreed to take action. Hicks was arrested by the military and turned over to the civil authorities on the express condition that he be tried on the charges specified in the affidavit of arrest and punished if found guilty. A trial was held before Judge Bolling with Corporal Berry and Private Jones testifying for the prosecution. Within days of the incident, Hicks was convicted of assault and battery, fined fifty dollars and ordered to post one thousand dollars in bonds to keep the peace. Two days later, under the influence of liquor, he assaulted his bondsman who thereupon withdrew from the bond. McGogy could report to headquarters with satisfaction that "Hicks now quietly reposes in jail." The outcome of the case "had been rigid beyond the expectation of anyone here which is attributed to the example set by the military." The local press was not similarly happy.[82]

Despite the very real tensions that existed between bureau agent and the white community of Butler County, McGogy's tenure at Greenville was relatively peaceful and well received. At the end of December 1866, when there were reports that he would leave, Benjamin Porter hoped McGogy would remain "for his official and private course has been quite satisfactory to every fairminded man and he has been uniformly respectful and courteous." McGogy's departure at the end of January 1867 appears to have been unrelated to the fulminations of the *Advocate* over the Hicks case or to its charges of a fraudulent and misdirected labor policy. There was need at Talladega of a new man to head the bureau office, one of unquestioned efficiency and integrity and experienced in trouble shooting. Affairs there were in a state of disarray. As at Greenville when McGogy took over, the previous agent had been charged with the fraudulent sale of subsistence stores, arrested, and sent to Montgomery to await trial. Moreover, the Talladega office, in northeastern Alabama at a considerably greater distance from Montgomery than Greenville with attendant lapses in communications, had the responsibility in the hard winter of 1866–67 for reopening a major bureau hospital, undoubtedly another reason for the choice of McGogy.[83] For the former lieutenant, now brevet captain, the appointment was not only a mark of confidence and a challenge but also something of a promotion for he exchanged the title of "Agent" or "Assistant Superintendent" for that of "Sub-Assistant Commissioner." At Talladega, to judge from the incoming correspondence, McGogy was addressed as "Captain" though technically a civilian agent.

The new area of McGogy's responsibility was extensive and varied, nine counties of mountains, valleys and plateaus, of planters and of yeomen, of Unionists as well as Confederates. Blacks were a minority of the population of the district, in some counties a quite small minority but a substantial 41.9% in Talladega. Most of the sixteen months of McGogy's tenure in northern Alabama, from February 1867 to June 1868, coincided with the military control established by the Reconstruction Act of March 2, 1867, which also enfranchised southern blacks. Supplementary acts made the army command responsible for the registration of voters and the certification of elections (March 23) and confirmed military authority to remove and replace civil officers (July 19). All three acts were passed over the vetoes of President Johnson, and their implementation sharpened the conflict between him and the Republican majority in Congress over the status of former slaves and the protection of their rights as free men.

In Alabama, voter registration (the linchpin of Republican commitment to equal citizenship) began in July, elections for a state constitutional convention were held in early October, and in the following February there was a second round to ratify the work of the convention and to choose state officials. Gen. John Pope had been given command of the Third Military District of which Alabama was a part, with Swayne remaining as both state commander and bureau chief. The two men worked closely together, and until the February 1868 elections the reconstruction process fulfilled congressional expectations, resulting in widespread black participation and Republican victories. At the end of December 1867, however, President Johnson summarily removed both Pope and Swayne at the urging of his Conservative Democratic political allies. To the satisfaction of white Alabamians generally, their successors—generals George G. Meade and Julius Hayden—were officers, unlike Pope and Swayne, whom whites saw as "no negrophile[s]."[84] Indeed, Hayden was credited with Republican failure in the February referendum to obtain approval for Alabama's new constitution by the requisite majority of registered voters. The increasingly bitter local political scene of early 1868 had its parallel at the nation's capitol where on February 24 the House voted to impeach the president, with the trial itself extending from early March through late May. On June 25, two weeks after McGogy had left Talladega, Congress acted to permit the return of Alabama despite the February referendum; and in July military government in the state ended and Republican civilian control began.

The chaotic and changing political scene increased the scope and difficulty of McGogy's responsibilities but brought no compensating surcease from the vexations of bureau routine—indeed, those seem to have multiplied rather than diminished. Neither familiarity with procedures nor conscientious application to both the detail and the substance of duty spared McGogy the frustrations and humiliations that bureaucracy can inflict upon its victims.

A less resolute man might well have been overwhelmed by the exigencies McGogy faced in performing routine duties during his first three weeks in Talladega. On arrival he found himself without an office and urgently in need of "two mules harness ambulance horse & saddle" in order to oversee the hospital some two-and-a-half miles distant. Equally pressing was his need of "a good clerk" since the ability of the man temporarily filling the post was "very limited, further more he cannot take the test oath." Also lacking were letter paper, envelopes, pencils, pen and ink, blank forms and record books, and a file of the orders from headquarters that governed procedures. Inmates at the hospital, which housed the destitute as well as the ill, were without clothing, in need of soap, medicines, cooking utensils, "also tin plates, tin cups, iron spoons." There was no physician in attendance, in fact no one at all was in residence to take charge. Moreover, existing buildings were inadequate and in bad repair. In town, corn and flour were on hand, with conflicting directives as to their issuance and no storage facilities. The discrediting of McGogy's predecessor complicated an already cumbersome process of distribution and accounting for supplies. An accumulation of indebtedness had to be met, and drafts sent from headquarters were useless because they could not be cashed in Talladega. The temporary clerk expected to be paid, but there was no assurance that he would be. A sick woman some fifty miles distant needed hospitalization, but McGogy had no means of transporting her to Talladega. Six adult freedmen en route from Florida to Tennessee arrived in town "all broken out with the smallpox, not one cent of money and no means of support." The county could not provide for them.[85]

McGogy acted with characteristic energy in trying to meet the demands of the situation. The day of his arrival, after a fruitless search for suitable office space, he sent off letters to headquarters requisitioning needed supplies. The next day he succeeded in finding an office, executed a lease in triplicate, and sent it off for "the Genl['s] signature." He bought 130 yards of "osenburg" (osnaburg, a rough cotton cloth), intending to have clothes made for the women and children, at a price, then found three women at the hospital who could sew the garments ("by close watching"). A week later he reported that "I have already clothed the most needy" and would not need the twenty dollars estimated as the cost for "manufacture." To take charge at the hospital, McGogy located and employed at fifty dollars a month a Mr. George Miller, "an experienced gardener and in every respect a suitable person, being sixty-five years old, energetic and very sympathetic with the colored people and can take the test oath." Report of this action was accompanied by a request for a selection of medicines suitable for dispensing by a "man of no medical education" but "an experienced man in sickness," namely Miller, whom he assured headquarters was "very cautious." With such medicines at hand, as McGogy phrased it, he then "would not be inconvenienced for want of a physician."[86]

During those early weeks there were visitations from the chief surgeon and from General Swayne himself, whether to McGogy's comfort or discomfort is not evident from the records. Generally, response from Swayne's headquarters was supportive but not without delays, admonitions, and at times even reprimands. McGogy's relations with his successor as quartermaster appear to have become increasingly strained. Ten days after his initial requisitions and requests, feeling "in such great want I cannot wait longer," McGogy not only "respectfully" renewed his applications to Montgomery but also sent off a plea for help to the army quartermaster at Selma. Ten days later mules, horse, and ambulance arrived from Montgomery, but how to obtain forage for the animals was a continuing problem. In mid-April McGogy was protesting bitterly that the mules were suffering and could not survive long without forage. When none arrived, he resorted to borrowing, an unauthorized procedure that might make him liable for costs. His purchase of the osnaburg, also a financial risk, was approved but with a warning that no further expenditures of the kind were to be made. McGogy's requisition for men's clothing and blankets from the quartermaster's supplies, sent off six days after he arrived, was turned down on the basis that a similar request had been made three weeks earlier by his predecessor. Within a few days some clothing did reach Talladega but McGogy refused to sign a receipt because much of it was "entirely worthless . . . which leaves me quite as destitute as when I made the requisition." His arrangements for a resident supervisor at the hospital were reluctantly accepted as the best that could be done under the circumstances but "would not answer permanently"; if the surgeon who would shortly be sent determined that "an attendant" was required, Miller might possibly be retained "at the pay of such."[87]

Neither persistence nor plea produced an adequate supply of blank forms and stationery. Lack of the former was more than an incidental annoyance. For monthly returns, and other required documentation, no less than twenty-one varieties were required! And a wrong form, an irregularity in completing it, or delay in submission could—and did—bring censure. Similarly, McGogy's refusal to give receipts for supplies that had reached Talladega before he was accountable or were missing from subsequent shipments subjected him to reproof, including a threat to withhold his pay. Little wonder that his customary deference to authority was strained to the point of breaking. "It has ever been my purpose," he wrote Swayne's adjutant in early April, "to conform strictly to the regulations of the Department in which I am serving with a view of justice and harmony with my superior officers. My knowledge of the Q.M. Dept prompts me to insist that I am justifyable in returning said receipts for correction." As the end of June approached he sent off a more restrained but damning letter calling attention to "irregularities in the office of the Chf. Q.M. of this district" listing specific complaints: articles that were missing in shipments, promised replacements that never arrived, requisitions that brought no supplies, an unanswered request to be advised, if it were "impossible" to send blanks, "what course to pursue in making out my returns for the month of May." Vexing problems of supply and accounting continued throughout his long tenure of office at Talladega with McGogy from time to time asserting his grievances, including "the formality required by your office, [that] has greatly inconvenienced myself as well as unnessarily exposed many unclad persons in our Hospital, and County, to extremely disagreeable weather" and the "repeated letters I have written . . . without any reply."[88]

In the line of duty at Talladega McGogy suffered not only frustrations but the loss of a horse, a subject that appears and reappears in his official correspondence over a period of sixteen months. The records, despite their formality, vividly reveal the waywardness of bureau bureaucracy and the persistence of McGogy, a continuing encounter here joined over a very personal item, more often over matters McGogy saw as obstacles to duty, humanity, and justice.

In June 1867 McGogy along with other bureau district chiefs received orders to make certain that the newly appointed boards of registration, two whites and one black, had received all requisite registration books and instructions, and that freedmen be neither debarred from registering nor uninformed "as to the meaning and intent" of the process. Success of the congressionally mandated enfranchisement of blacks held a high priority with generals Swayne and Pope, a priority undoubtedly apparent to McGogy and probably one he shared. Directed to tour nine counties, he had planned to set out the first day of July. However, on the morning of the first he learned that registration for Talladega County would take place in town over several days beginning July 3. "I concluded that it would be best to remain here while the Board is registering," he advised headquarters, and then "at once proceed to comply with your instructions." On the sixth, he reported the results of the Talladega registration, adding that "no one will be denied his right to register in this County" and that he would leave the following morning on the inspection tour.[89]

As events developed, McGogy had "accomplished but a small portion of [his] journey" when the horse he was driving—army property—took sick and died. Horses were scarce and needed in the fields, so when he could not obtain another he returned to Talladega for his own "very fine horse," purchased three months earlier for $175, and again set forth on his assigned task. The first night out, "when seemingly perfectly secured," the horse was stolen, presumably by the "renowned outlaws" of the region. For a second time McGogy returned to Talladega. Before making his third attempt to fulfill his mission with a mule from the wagon team, he sent off two official letters, one to report in some detail that the registration boards were working well in the two counties he had visited, the other to relate "my recent misfortune and ask if there is any way by which I can be recompensed for a loss sustained while in the discharge of my official duty."[90]

The next ten days on the road must have taxed even McGogy's ample store of energy. He met with members of the registration boards whenever possible, made inquiries throughout the counties talking with both whites and blacks, personally checked whether handbills were posted, admonished board chairmen when sufficient notices had not been given or announced dates for registering not kept, arranged to have "an intelligent colored man" canvass portions of Calhoun county where he had found freedmen "quite indifrent as to registration having been influenced by corrupt men," and himself "instructed" freedmen on the benefits of being enfranchised. In addition, he found time to check on schools, to begin an investigation of a local official's dispersal of freedmen attending a political meeting, to gather information about a bureau agent unknown to him—or to the freedmen—concluding that the man "lacked the moral courage to faithfully discharge the duties of said office," and to send off a general report to headquarters![91]

Arriving back in Talladega on July 22, he vigorously attacked a formidable array of problems that had accumulated in his absence. Also awaiting him was a letter from headquarters that should have brightened his spirits. If he submitted a claim with an affidavit setting forth the facts in the loss of the horse, its cost, and its being used on official duty, the papers would be forwarded to Commissioner Howard with a favorable endorsement from General Swayne. Unhappily, McGogy's loss had become both more complicated and more costly. He had hired three "mounted detectives" who pursued the animal for four days without success (at five dollars a day per man), and also offered a reward of half the animal's value on recovery. Two "experienced" men took the challenge, and "after fourteen days untiring effort" found the horse but in so sorry a condition "owing to the extreme heat, and scarcity of food" that it could be sold only at half its original cost. McGogy's total loss, counting the money he had paid the "detectives," amounted to $190. Understandably, McGogy sought further advice from headquarters, writing to ask whether the recovery would bar reimbursement and whether a claim could be made for any part of the money spent in the effort to track the horse. Though cautioned that no assurances could be given, he was advised to send a full statement with expenses itemized and told it would be submitted to General Swayne when he returned from the North about August 20. McGogy responded with an affidavit recounting the incident and itemizing costs. It was duly forwarded to General Howard's adjutant general in Washington, by him to the bureau's chief quartermaster, by the quartermaster back to the adjutant, by the adjutant on order of General Howard back to Alabama headquarters. There, by order of General Swayne on September 10, affidavit and endorsements were returned to McGogy with "attention invited to endorsement of the *Chf Qr. Mr.* and *Commissioner*."[92]

In effect, the chief quartermaster had denied McGogy any compensation on the ground that "when officers and agents of the Bureau furnish their private horses for their own convenience and use them in the discharge of their public duties, it is at their own risk." However, there was an ambiguity. Before concluding that "the Bureau should not be called upon to make good any [such] loss," he cited authority for the only exception permitted: ". . . in cases of great emergency, and where a horse for temporary duty . . . could not be procured." General Howard, like Swayne, had "invited attention" to the quartermaster's endorsement adding ". . . the terms of which are approved." McGogy read the bureaucratic verbiage as rejecting his claim because he had not included in his affidavit the fact (stated in his letter of July 13) that he had tried and could not obtain a horse with which to continue on his assigned and urgent journey. He therefore returned the document on September 13 with the required explanation, asking that it be reforwarded to General Howard. Sometime in October McGogy was apparently informed that due to Swayne's absence reforwarding was delayed but that the papers would be approved and sent on to Washington. McGogy waited. Unbeknown to him, the document still reposed in Montgomery either by oversight or deliberate decision when General Swayne was removed from command. A last endorsement dated January 25, 1868, ten days after authority in Alabama had passed temporarily to General Hayden, read: "General thinks best not to forward."[93]

Soon thereafter, in early February during the third round of elections under congressional reconstruction, as we shall see, McGogy brought down upon himself the anger of General Hayden and a major crisis in his bureau career. It was probably no coincidence that mention of his horse does not reappear in the records until May 11, 1868, after headquarters had come under command of Gen. Oliver L. Shepherd, though ominously for McGogy with Hayden's adjutant remaining as such. McGogy then wrote the latter requesting that inquiry be made as to the fate of his resubmitted affidavit and such action be taken "as in your judgment the circumstances will merit." Either disapproval or inertia prevailed at headquarters; there is no record of a reply.[94]

Before McGogy again raised the issue (in a letter of September 11, 1868) four months had elapsed, with McGogy back in Greenville, and another change of assistant commissioner at Montgomery, and of his adjutant as well. Once more McGogy recounted the return of his original affidavit disapproved, his supplementary statement, and his request that the papers be reforwarded. He concluded: "Will you please ascertain and inform me whether said affidavit was ever received in the office of the Commissioner [General Howard] and if any action was ever taken in the same." This time he received a reply; it consisted of copies of the negative but ambiguous endorsements of September 1867! McGogy still did not give up. He sent back the letter and endorsements with still another endorsement of his own, again explaining his reforwarding request. At headquarters the four page exchange was marked "File."[95]

In late November with only a few weeks until his appointment and most bureau operations were scheduled to end, McGogy swore out another affidavit and asked that it together with Swayne's earlier endorsement be reforwarded. This second sworn statement did reach Washington. On December 6, it was returned to Alabama headquarters with "attention invited to the enclosed copy of previous action from records of this office upon this case."[96] The Washington bureaucracy had not relented. McGogy gave up, but he did so only in the face of an insurmountable obstacle. Similarly, in those final months of bureau service McGogy was forced to accept a much graver and less personal defeat.

In the spring and summer of 1867, however, as a Republican Congress took over the direction of Reconstruction from a southern president, McGogy's dogged determination to fulfill his trust was undeterred by personal loss, the fetters of bureaucracy, or the resistance of white southerners. In his monthly report from Talladega for July 1867, a single sparse, prosaic sentence summarized the preelection tour that had cost him grueling effort as well as a fine horse: "During the past month I have in person traveled through eight Counties looking after the interest of the colored people."[97]

For eighteen months at Talladega, as earlier and more briefly at Greenville, McGogy permitted no obstacle or personal concern to divert his attention or weaken his resolve "to look after the interests" of black men, women, and children at the hospital, in the schools, on the plantation, and before the law. He did so to the limits of his authority, and sometimes beyond, without the slightest trace of sentimentality. It was his duty.

McGogy's responsibility for the sick and the destitute, including the construction of additional facilities at the hospital, had not been eased by the arrival of a surgeon to take charge. Friction between the two men soon developed over a number of issues, including the hiring of a white woman as a cook and housing her at the hospital. McGogy strongly objected on the ground that women already resident there were willing and able to do the work. Further, if anyone were to be hired he maintained that preference should be given a "good faithful colored woman" because "the colored people of this country were the only one[s] who were accustomed to work." Shortly before leaving on his eight-county tour, McGogy learned to his dismay that patients at the hospital were receiving only two meals a day and that "disgraceful transactions [unspecified] are daily or nightly practised at the Hospital." He promptly issued an official order requiring three meals a day with hours specified and provision that those unable to come to the dining room be supplied meals in their wards. The order was followed by a demand for an accounting from Dr. King with the threat of an investigation unless it was satisfactory. Though McGogy accepted the doctor's explanation, it was with misgivings and an expressed "hope that this will be the last time that any discredit may be reflected upon any employee of the Bureau under my supervision."[98]

The misgivings, rather than the hope, were justified. While McGogy was absent, Dr. King was expelled from his hotel and refused board elsewhere because of his heavy drinking and outrageous conduct. The latter culminated in his riding double horseback with a known prostitute through the streets of the town. McGogy reported Dr. King's conduct as "humiliating the honor and dignity of the service," "a disgrace not only to the service but to civilization," and his "excessive intemperance" as rendering him "wholly unfit for the very responsible position he occupies." He feared for the safety of the patients, and grew increasingly concerned as weeks passed without so much as an acknowledgment from headquarters of his charges against Dr. King. After almost three months of waiting, he was instructed to discharge both the doctor and his steward, to see that the hospital was thoroughly cleaned and put in order, and to make temporary arrangements until another surgeon was sent. McGogy promptly complied, arranging that either he or his clerk, except during bureau office hours, would be present at the hospital because he felt there was no person in residence to whom he could entrust the keys to its commissary. Another physician did arrive before long, one whom McGogy could happily credit with "energy and ability in renovating the hospital and securing comfort to its inmates."[99]

For the rest of McGogy's tenure at Talladega affairs at the hospital proceeded without major incident. The institution survived a continuing bureau policy initiated in September 1867 to close hospitals wherever possible and elsewhere to limit admissions and reduce the number of inmates. At the end of December 1868, as the last remaining bureau hospital, it was finally transferred, not to county authorities, but to the state of Alabama. Just how much credit was due McGogy for its longevity and its assumption by the state is impossible to say but clearly his role was not insignificant. He had made the hospital haven an effective institution and given warning that not local authorities but only the state had sufficient resources to sustain it.

McGogy plunged with equal concern and vigor into the task of promoting education for the freedmen throughout his nine county district. And he kept a close watch on the local school. As parents bombarded him with complaints, he tried to maintain their confidence in the school but did not himself hesitate to call to account and report the head teacher for what he considered her arbitrary and self-interested actions. She was not "displaying the spirit of a true missionary," unlike many other teachers he knew who were "laboring faithfully and with consciencious motives to promote a noble cause." On his inspection tours, even in remote areas "where prejudice against colored schools is the strongest," McGogy urged black leaders to build and help sustain schools, promising that the Bureau would supply books and competent teachers. And he took pride in reporting that "I have made school matters a specialty."[100]

During the first two years of his command General Swayne had stretched bureau authorization in order to pay teachers and obtain supplies for them and the schools, but by the fall of 1867 bureau subventions were being curtailed and self-support urged upon black communities. McGogy pleaded with the bureau's state superintendent of education to sustain him in the promises he had made and "save me the humiliation of being compelled to disappoint any one. I can employ to good advantage in this Sub District from 15 to 18 good teachers." He assured Superintendent Buckley that money spent in employing and transporting teachers would not be lost, for in almost every instance "the colored people will be able to defray one half of the expense of the school." September had arrived, he argued, and to avoid delay in opening the new school was urgent. McGogy's pleas were to no avail. In mid-October "a worthy colored man" had come some seventy-five miles as representative of the freedpeople of Cherokee county, who had built a good schoolhouse, to ask that McGogy keep his promise. He could only urge the American Missionary Association (AMA) to send a teacher as "it is out of the question for the Bureau R.F. and A.L. to comply with my promise to these colored people."[101]

By December the AMA had superseded the bureau's authority over the schools and to McGogy's distress "desired each pupil to be taxed $1.00 a month" with no provision (contrary to bureau policy) for those unable to pay, some of whom had already withdrawn. Three months later McGogy had to report that "Out of nine counties of this Sub Dist. six are entirely destitute of schools." He was in touch with the AMA in an effort to increase the number. Its Talladega normal school for blacks, which had opened just six months earlier, was "Our main hope of accomplishing this work." This hope was not dashed, for he could report a month later that the normal school pupils "were rapidly acquiring the proficiency of teachers" and "the most competent" had already opened schools. He looked forward to a continuing increase in the number of schools.[102]

McGogy's satisfaction with the normal school, however, was not altogether unalloyed. Soon after assuming his post at Talladega, Swayne had given him responsibility for negotiations to obtain use of the former Baptist college as a "Colored people's College," and he had worked hard to speed the process and recondition the structure for a fall opening. The bureau had contributed four thousand dollars, half the cost, toward its acquisition by the AMA and had spent under McGogy's direction another two thousand dollars for repairs, plus large sums for the transportation of persons and freight. In May 1868, "feel[ing] a delicacy and yet a sense of duty," McGogy wrote headquarters of "what seems to me a misapplication of funds belonging to the General Govt." He charged that the AMA had made its day schools self-supporting by requiring tuition, which reduced the number of students, and that "a considerable proportion of the different expenditures [for the normal school] is appropriated in direct aid of a religious denomination." McGogy's letter was referred to the bureau's superintendent of education for investigation. He confirmed that the normal school "is tending toward denominationalism . . .

its influence being to further the interest of the Congregationalist Church, they having organized a church in connection with the school . . . while Govt has been assisting them wholly with the idea of establishing a *normal school.*" No mention was made of McGogy's objection to the AMA's tuition policy or its consequences.[103]

While more pressing responsibilities than the schools absorbed an increasing portion of McGogy's energy and time during the turbulent months of military authority over the reconstruction process, he continued to view education as a fundamental right of freedom. Literacy and knowledge he saw as essential if black workers were "to obtain justice in [i.e., through] the civil laws." And all around him, McGogy saw justice for the freedpeople under siege. Report after report voiced his indignation. "It seems impossible," he wrote, "for the people of this country to understand the rights which belong to a freeman when a laborer." Indeed, many "seem determined not to understand that a colored man poss[ess]es the rights of a freeman." Worse, "the civil officers manifest no interest in colored mans rights." The justices of the peace (of whom there were more than two hundred in McGogy's district) he held especially culpable. He saw them as a "great obstacle to securing Justice to the freed people" because of their incompetence and their "indisposition . . . to administer the law regardless of Color." In seeking a pardon for a Negro convict, McGogy bitterly characterized the sentence as having reflected the sentiment that "the rights of a freedman" included his being sent to the penitentiary "for the least shadow of offense."[104]

The 1867 congressional mandate that gave southern blacks the ballot and gave the army primacy over civil authority had seemed at last to provide instruments adequate to secure "simple justice." They had reinvigorated General Swayne's efforts to get on with "the real task" of reconstruction. Having come to the conclusion months earlier that black enfranchisement was a prerequisite for equal justice, he followed closely the progress of registration and the results of balloting. Bureau agents were expected to help implement General Pope's order that all those eligible to vote be given "all information concerning their political rights" and the opportunity to cast their ballots without hindrance from violence or any form of intimidation or interference. Moreover, Swayne felt the military had finally been empowered to displace recalcitrant local officials and to take action against the discriminatory effect of nominally equal laws. In early April he ordered the revocation of indentures of minors capable of self-support, forbad attempts to enforce the vagrancy law, and prohibited the use of chain gangs as a means of punishment.

In August General Pope directed that jurors be taken exclusively and "without discrimination" from the list of voters registered under the acts of Congress. In November Swayne issued orders to make more effective the laborers' lien on harvested crops.[105]

McGogy welcomed these measures, interpreted them broadly, and worked to make them effective. The tone of his dealings with local officials and with planters became increasingly incisive and assured. During an early tour of his district, he visited the probate judges of its various counties, personally checked to make certain that each had a file of military orders and would observe them, discussed particular cases, and obtained assurance of fair treatment for freedmen and prompt reports to his office. From Talladega when he could not take to the field, he sent letters that were in effect orders to sheriffs, county prosecutors, justices of the peace, and probate judges as well, asking for arrests, investigations, and explanations of what he considered derelictions of duty. They responded without protest. When they were helpful, McGogy was quick to acknowledge their cooperation with appreciation. His interventions were wide ranging—on behalf of a freedman whose mule had been borrowed then lost or stolen, for release of apprenticed children to their mothers, to obtain wages or crop share due a freedwoman or freedman, to spur actions against disguised raiders who had driven off a black family and appropriated their belongings, to keep a white assailant in jail without bond until it could be determined whether his colored victim would live or die, to investigate the murder of a black man whose white widow had sought safety at the bureau office against threats to her life. In the case of the murdered husband, the probate judge in replying to McGogy stated it "highly probable" that the murder was committed by relatives of the wife "outraged at her taking up with a Negro" or possibly by the neighbors to get rid of the couple though, he pointed out, they could have done so simply by obtaining a warrant for their arrest under a state law against intermarriage of Negro and white that carried a penalty of not less than two nor more than seven years of imprisonment in the penitentiary or hard labor for the county. The judge expressed himself satisfied that if local officials "knew who the guilty person was they would have him arrested and punished for his conduct."[106] It is reasonable to assume that McGogy was not equally satisfied.

Particularly in cases involving crop settlements, McGogy more often than not took direct action. When he arrived at Talladega, contracts for the year were already made and McGogy could only advise the freedmen to bring or send a copy to his office for filing. Few contracts arrived, but those that did in

McGogy's eyes were dismaying, "generally worded to bind the laborer in every particular, causing him to forfeit heavily . . . while his employer is left to act his own pleasure and pursue the most convenient and profitable course." McGogy refused to recognize such contracts. As crops were harvested he insisted that the planter deliver the laborers' share to them, threatening a trial for trespass if this were not done, ordered employers to report with their record books to his office, made it clear that overcharges for supplies furnished or time lost or deductions for supposed thefts would not be tolerated. He threatened to post guards to prevent any of the crop being moved before a fair settlement was determined, and requested from headquarters a small detachment of soldiers to do so on the plantations of "a few men" whom he thought "determined to swindle the colored men out of their dues." As late as March and April 1868, McGogy was supervising plantation settlements for the previous year "to the satisfaction of the colored people."[107]

McGogy recognized that the "confusion" and increasing distrust between laborer and planter was attributable in considerable part to the disastrous outcome of a season that had disappointed "the expectation of every person." Between drought, the "exorbitant" cost of provisions, and a very low price for crops, the year's farming was unprofitable. Many planters could not meet their expenses, he reported; freedmen were destitute; what work animals they owned were dying of starvation. It was the workers who received priority from McGogy. He interpreted Swayne's November orders as meant "to equalize the misfortune," "especially in favor of the laborer"; and he acted accordingly.[108] He did so though himself the owner of an Alabama plantation and facing financial disaster.

McGogy's concern and vigor in behalf of the freedpeople may have been exceptional, but there is no reason to believe that his attitudes toward blacks or toward free labor were atypical of those of his countrymen who had supported the war and the Republican party. When black workers in his bureau district tried to strike for higher wages, as McGogy saw it, "demand[ing] exorbitant prices during wheat harvest," he disapproved and effectively discouraged them. Although he thought confidence between the two races had been "entirely expell[ed] . . . for a long time," he yet believed that its restoration between employer and employee was essential. He sympathized with the freedmen's desire for economic independence, but did not plead his case for land ownership. McGogy's references to black men and women, regardless of status, were consistently respectful yet on one occasion he could express condemnation for an unscrupulous employer as one "who would take advantage of an inferior man."[109] For McGogy, freedom carried rights that must be observed; but his ringing denunciations of white injustice were a demand for just treatment, not an affirmation that the races were innate or potential equals.

Of greatest satisfaction to McGogy during his months at Talladega must have been the resolution of an incident that began with the theft from a widowed freedwoman in Clay County of forty-two bushels of corn, a large quantity of meat, and a gun. Learning that one Ingram and his sons were responsible, he "at once ordered" the local justice of the peace to cause their arrest. No action was taken. Further inquiry revealed that the justice had been too intoxicated to read McGogy's letter and that he as well as Ingram were "stilling spirits in violation of U.S. Int. Revenue Law." Moreover, the latter's sons were identified as members of "the Black Cavalry which caused so much terror to freedpeople in Clay, Randolph and Coosa counties."[110]

Without going through his own headquarters, McGogy appealed for military support from the army post at Jacksonville in neighboring Calhoun county. In Captain Hedberg, who commanded the cavalry there, McGogy found a soldier after his own self-image, one "ever ready to make any sacrifice in his power to enforce law and punish offenders and secure Justice to injured parties." Together they marched twenty miles "through swamps and over mountains exposed to inclement weather [it was late December]," found the two stills and the woman's property, arrested Ingram and his three sons, and brought them together with the captured stills and liquor back to Talladega for a hearing before the U.S. commissioner. The Ingrams were bound over to appear before the U.S. District Court on charges of violating the revenue law; on the black cavalry charge, however, evidence was apparently considered insufficient for further court action. Nonetheless, the outcome cheered McGogy, particularly since Captain Hedberg's appearance in Clay County "caused a remarkable change for the good," teaching the local citizens a needed lesson in respect to "the rights of others regardless of color" and enabling McGogy "to effect several satisfactory settlements for freedmen that had been pending for some time." Retroactively, headquarters gave its approval but cautioned McGogy against further such raids.[111] The episode occurred just after Swayne's removal, as General Hayden was taking command of the bureau and army in Alabama.

As a temporary appointee pending General O. L. Shepard's return from leave, General Hayden's tenure was brief, a mere two-and-a-half months from mid-January to the end of March 1868, but it came at a time of bitter political conflict with elections in early February to ratify the new Alabama constitution and to fill state offices. Whether ostensibly or naively above the battle, Hayden regarded his assignment as a mission to purge the bureau of politics, that is of agents who engaged in "partisan" behavior. In his view "an immediate purification was eminently necessary" if the bureau were not to be "a curse to white and black, instead of a blessing," and he began relieving civilian agents for political activity within forty-eight hours of taking office. He was undeterred by Commissioner Howard's gentle warning not to "lean over backward." Rather, in reply Hayden expounded his views at length. Bureau agents should attend only to "the moral education and material interests of the colored people" and leave their political education "to those most interested in securing his vote." Any other course Hayden saw as motivated by "self-aggrandizement," "a lust for office." A man could uphold the Constitution and the flag, he wrote, without "making himself stench in the nostrils of those who may be opposed to his way of thinking." The Negro's involvement in politics was generating ill will on the part of those upon whom he was dependent for employment. The new assistant commissioner would instruct bureau officers to express no opinions on divisive political issues; he would have them be patient, just, and merciful to the planters.[112] In sharp contrast to Swayne and the Republican congressional majority, Hayden evinced no conception of the ballot as a means by which freed slaves could protect their rights as men and citizens.

As he had under Swayne's direction during the July 1867 registration and the October balloting, McGogy kept a close watch over the February 1868 elections in his district. What was happening seemed to require immediate, decisive action. Employers were threatening to dismiss and turn out of their homes those who voted. The chairman of the Talladega election board was permitting clerks and others in the balloting room to speak contemptuously of the reconstruction acts and to insult freedmen who presented themselves to vote. McGogy sent off a sharp letter to the chairman suggesting that he exclude all persons from the room except proper judges and U.S. guards and that he prohibit from acting as clerk of election anyone "unable to withhold expressions of contempt for the laws of the United States." To counter the intimidation by employers he issued a formal order writing over his signature "By Command" of General Hayden, which stated that persons who attempted to obstruct the election or intimidate voters under pretext of violating a labor contract would be punished by military law. Copies of the admonition and order went promptly to headquarters together with a covering explanatory letter that concluded: "I trust the [Order] will meet your approval."[113]

Emphatically, headquarters did *not* approve. "No one in the Bureau," Hayden's adjutant wrote McGogy, "can have authority to issue orders for the Commanding General of the Military Sub-District, nor no one in the Military Department even, unless specially designated for that duty." McGogy was admonished to be careful and not to bring discredit upon his office, but he was also told that had his efforts "been directed in the proper channel [they] would have received commendation." The reassurance was somewhat less than candid. Three days later General Hayden forwarded McGogy's letters and order (but not the censure) to O. O. Howard in view of a telegram from Washington the day before that read by order of the commissioner: "Be careful to remove no agents without thorough investigation by order of Genl Howard." Clearly, Hayden had been on the point of relieving McGogy—and not for his having presumed to issue under the general's authority the order in question. His offense was "the interest taken by Mr. McGogy in the matter of the elective franchise." Hayden wanted to know whether it "was to be considered evidence of an undue interest in the political affairs of the people calculated to impair Mr. McGogy's usefulness as a 'Middleman' between the planters and the colored people, or as simply an exercise of his rights as a citizen."[114]

There can be no mistaking Hayden's own opinion, but that of General Howard was a quite different matter. "It is the duty of every officer," read the return endorsement, "to do all in his power to secure a just execution of the laws & to resist fraud of every kind. *Mr McGogy* is Commended for using his influence to preserve the purity of the elective franchise." The commendation was not forwarded from Montgomery to Talladega; the rebuff stood. Even added to the cool reception at headquarters of his joint raid with Captain Hedberg in January, it did not suppress McGogy's determination to fulfill what he considered his responsibility, but it may have restrained his impulse for direct action.[115]

Notwithstanding his intense gratification when forceful intervention had resulted in success, McGogy was not blind to the reality that such necessarily sporadic happenings were insufficient to secure for the freedmen protection and fair treatment. Moreover, he was well aware that his frequent intercessions with local authorities did not necessarily result in bringing white offenders to justice or in sparing black defendants harsh penalties; time after time his reports pointed to the inadequacy of the civil process. McGogy undoubtedly pondered the question of what might be done to make local justice a more effective instrument against injustice. Indeed, back in August 1867, McGogy had suggested a drastic solution: "a sweeping order requiring every officer, civil as well as military to take the test-oath." He had conceded that this would for a time create confusion in the machinery of local government (it would have meant widespread removals from office) but thought it would establish a government of "loyal men" who would see justice done. McGogy's remedy was too summary for generals Swayne and Pope, who were seen as proponents of removals but in practice used them sparingly.[116]

On the very day McGogy forwarded that bold proposal to headquarters, General Pope had issued the order to select jurors from the lists of registered voters, an action clearly intended to put an end to all-white juries. That result, however, did not necessarily follow. In Mid-March 1868 McGogy learned that for the entire county of Talladega only two blacks were included in the 108 names drawn for jury duty, though black registered voters outnumbered white. He demanded an explanation. The sheriff of Talladega County replied that he had argued for the force of the military order but had been overruled by the probate judge and the circuit clerk who by law shared with him responsibility for the jury list. They held the military order subject to state law, which provided that only such persons should be placed on the jurors list as the three officers considered competent to discharge the duties of grand and petit jurors "with honesty, impartiality, and intelligence and are esteemed in the community for their integrity, fair character, and sound Judgment." McGogy forwarded the sheriff's letter together with a terse endorsement: "You will see by the within report, that the civil authorities of this County disregard Genl Pope's Order No 53 in drawing jurors." With an uncharacteristic lack of deference, perhaps still smarting from the February reprimand, he added: "If you desire to have said order enforced you can act accordingly." The response from headquarters was another repudiation of Talladega's subassistant commissioner. It upheld unequivocally the probate judge and circuit clerk: "Negroes are not to be put upon juries simply because they are negroes . . . they are to enjoy equal rights with the white men, and nothing more . . . G.O. No 53 was simply to enforce this equality, and so negroes can only serve as jurymen when they can qualify as is required of white men."[117]

McGogy would not argue with a superior, but neither was he about to satisfy his concept of duty by a facade without a substantial structure to ensure equal treatment before the law. No more than a day or two after the sheriff's letter with the above endorsement arrived back on his desk, he came up with a fresh approach to the problem. "Permit me to suggest to you," he wrote headquarters, "what seems to me to be a very effectual method of vindicating the rights of the colored man" (namely): "If consistent to issue an order, allowing the Sub Asst Commer or Agent of the Bureau R&AL access at all times to the room of the Grand Jurors, while that body is in session; for the purpose of explaining various outrages, perpetrated upon the colored people, and suggesting suitable witnesses. There is no colored people chosen upon the Grand Jury, for the next term of Circuit Court in this County. The Jury is composed of men who have no sympathy for the colored man or his rights."[118]

The day after McGogy sent off this proposal "to vindicate the rights of the colored man," the office of assistant commissioner passed from Hayden to General Shepherd. By the latter's order, McGogy's letter was returned to him with an official endorsement that echoed the sterile logic of the reply he had received a week earlier at the direction of Hayden. It was "not deemed advisable" to issue such an order; "it would be giving to the colored man privileges that the white man does not enjoy."[119] The Hayden-Shepherd concept of equal rights disregarded the realities of local justice so evident, and distasteful, to McGogy.

The rebuffs from headquarters might well have dampened the efforts of another man. But not McGogy. During his last three months in Talladega, he carried on in the face of multiple obstacles—not only a military command with a view of "the interest of the colored people" considerably less expansive than his own, but as well a rising tide of white violence and a depressed agriculture that heightened distrust and antagonism between planter and worker. And he did so without diminution of vigor or initiative. To relieve destitution, he requisitioned supplementary supplies and saw to their distribution. In the month of April he supervised twenty, in May twenty-four, labor settlements with his usual concern for the freedmen's interest. By the end of March, as he reported, the "unsettled state of affairs, at the head of our Govt. [impeachment was underway at the nation's capital] has been inclined to develop an unusual large amount of lawlessness throughout this community." Shortly thereafter, he noted, "The band known as the Ku Klux Klan, created considerable excitement." McGogy had "to a great extent succeeded in allaying [the excitement]"; yet "many persons use every means at their command to harass and frighten the colored people without offending the law." In response he did what he could. He continued to use a mixture of persuasive advice and veiled threat to sheriffs and judges and at least on one occasion invoked army intervention (from nearby Jacksonville without prior clearance from Montgomery) in order to investigate atrocities, effect arrests, obtain testimony from intimidated witnesses, and make judges aware that their proceedings were under scrutiny. Notwithstanding all his efforts, "heartless outlaws" escaped capture and hearings before the justices of the peace were replete with "irregularities and prejudice."[120]

This was a situation that brought from McGogy fresh initiatives to make more effective the processes of local justice. He "made arrangements with competent legal council, to defend all the colored people, in the various courts, and to accept the obligations of the colored people for their services." And McGogy could take satisfaction in the results, at least in the case involving the largest number of black defendants—nine men, leaders of a group who had set out to avenge an attempted murder of one of their own, thereby precipitating a mass armed encounter between whites and blacks, with the whites forced to withdraw. The nine blacks were arrested and charged with riotous conduct, assault and battery, plus attempted murder. Counsel persuaded the judge, despite general "excitement and prejudice," to set aside the more serious charge and to reduce fines to a level at which the defendants could make bail.[121]

McGogy's most innovative effort was to request the probate judge of each of his counties, in cases involving freedmen, to take jurisdiction away from the justices of the peace. He found sanction for the procedure in Alabama's laws of 1865–66 establishing county courts of misdemeanor. His action was reported to headquarters after the fact. McGogy had other ideas as well. In early May he wrote General Shepherd's adjutant at length on the injustice perpetrated under Alabama's penal code (citing paragraph and page), which allowed probate courts to issue a warrant and bind the arrested party for appearance at the next term of court upon the filing of an affidavit by a plaintiff. The procedure, McGogy pointed out, was "equivalent to a denial of bail" for colored people unable to post bond. Frequently, he objected, they were held "weeks and perhaps Months [in] confinement and exonerated upon their first appearance in court." His concluding remark suggests a like comment upon his entire record of bureau service at Talladega: "Please pardon me for assuming to call your attention to this matter, but my observations have led me to believe that said act is in violation to Justice."[122]

In mid-June 1868 McGogy was relieved from duty at Talladega, ordered to report to headquarters, and assigned to a new district at Newton, a village in the southeast corner of Alabama from which the horseback mail arrived and departed only every seven days. The bureau agency there was short-lived, and McGogy's stay even briefer. He arrived June 29 and on July 21 was granted a twenty day leave on surgeon's certificate of disability. Before the leave expired, the Newton office was discontinued in order to curtail operations in view of the congressional decision of July 25 to end most activities of the bureau on January 1, 1869, and McGogy was reassigned to Greenville where a new subassistant commissioner was urgently needed. There he spent the final months of his bureau career. Whatever the reasons for McGogy's departure from Talladega, they are not revealed in the official records. His reassignment to Newton may merely have reflected the need of an experienced officer for a new post. His final destination, Greenville, may have been a tribute to his ability, a punitive measure, or sheer expediency. When he resumed charge of the bureau office, no bureau district in the state was more turbulent and potentially explosive; and it was a time when opposition to the bureau from native whites throughout Alabama had crested.

In Greenville, and Butler County generally, the focus of white animus was Samuel S. Gardner, the man from whom McGogy was taking over the bureau office, the very same agent who had replaced McGogy eighteen months earlier. Both men had been first assigned to the bureau while in the army and then continued bureau service as civilians. In their bureau careers each reacted strongly to what he saw as injustices to the freedmen. In his first assignment, at Selma, Gardner reported local justice for freedmen "a mockery"; in one of his last monthly accountings from Greenville he caustically commented that local magistrates "may generally be relied upon for unjust judgments against freedmen." As an example, he cited a colored man fined a hundred dollars and costs for beating his child, a sum "which will take nearly all his crop." Both men were courageous and persistent in their efforts to fulfill their responsibility toward the freedpeople, but Gardner had a deeper commitment and a greater courage. Born in Massachusetts and raised in Maine, as a youth he had been an outspoken abolitionist and after graduation from Bowdoin College and a few years of teaching he studied for the ministry, graduating in 1861 and accepting the pastorship of a Congregational church in Vermont. In the spring of 1864 he enlisted to serve as chaplain of a black regiment.[123]

The vicious white animosity Gardner encountered at Greenville that culminated in his suffering a series of brutal beatings, though not unrelated to the character of the man, primarily reflected local sentiment toward congressional reconstruction, a sentiment that quickly shifted from reluctant acceptance to bitter rejection as it became evident that blacks would not follow the political leadership of native whites. Gardner was both the local symbol and the chief instrument of national policy, not only vigorously implementing black enfranchisement—as had McGogy in Talladega—but as well taking an active role in politics. He had run successfully for the state constitutional convention of late 1867 and, with leave of absence from his bureau post, played a leading role in its deliberations, championing reforms too progressive for even that Radical body in respect to the financing of public education, the provision of university facilities for women, and the administration of justice. For the latter, he proposed that the state supply legal counsel for those unable to pay an attorney. Returning to Greenville and resuming his bureau duties, Gardner campaigned for ratification of the new constitution, challenging leaders of the Conservative Democratic opposition in open debate and taking a leading role in the formation of a Republican ticket for the local officials to be elected in February along with the referendum on the constitution. These activities made him in mid-January 1868 one of the first casualties of General Hayden's policy of separating the bureau from politics.

Gardner had vigorously protested his removal. He asked Hayden for a hearing to defend himself against the implication that he had used his office for personal and partisan ends, or if no censure were intended, requested some action to correct "the unintended wrong" that had brought him "humiliation and hardship." The request was denied in a bland reply purporting not to understand how Gardner could feel either censured or humiliated. "As the Asst Commissioner can see no wrong in what he has done," the letter concluded, "there is no wrong to be corrected" and he begs to be excused "for declining further consideration of the subject." A few weeks later, on March 2, a peremptory order from General Howard by telegram to Hayden restored Gardner to his bureau post. The explanatory letter that followed stated bluntly that Gardner appeared to have been relieved for expressing his views in favor of reconstruction under the laws of Congress and instructing colored people respecting their rights and duties as citizens. "Every officer and agent should use his influence in favor of law and not against it," it read, and "expressing political opinions is not deemed a sufficient reason for the discharge of anyone." Howard's instructions added that any bureau officer should, of course, resign if he were elected to office or accepted nomination to an important one. In the February election Gardner had run for the most important county office, that of probate judge, hoping to improve the quality of local justice for freedmen. Together with the entire Republican slate he won an overwhelming victory despite scurrilous attacks upon him in the local press—he was both ridiculed as "Possum" and maligned as self-seeking and incompetent. The Republican victory was made possible by black votes and a white boycott of the election meant to defeat the constitution and register opposition to the Reconstruction acts. Howard's support was undoubtedly gratifying to Gardner, and enabled him not only to resume control of the bureau in Greenville but to remain there until July 20; it would, however, provide little protection against the accelerating wrath of local whites.[124]

On July 31, a few days before McGogy's return, Gardner took over the office and records of probate judge. He did so without physical resistance but in the face of a strong verbal protest from his predecessor, Judge Bolling, who termed the Reconstruction acts unconstitutional and Gardner's election illegal. Gardner had also received an anonymous threat of assassination unless he left town. The incumbent sheriff, who had attacked one Republican-elect and declared his purpose "to assault all the Republicans in the place," had no intention of recognizing Gardner's authority or obeying his orders as probate judge. Indeed, he and his brothers (one of whom was a deputy sheriff) were leaders of the rowdy opposition. There was no military presence in town to which Gardner could turn, for despite the appearance of the Klan in March, repeated outrages against freedmen, and Gardner's warning while still bureau chief that the presence of troops was essential to prevent an outbreak, the squad of soldiers stationed there had incredibly been withdrawn just as he was to take office. Any call for a *posse comitatus* would be answered from the very crowds that gathered menacingly in the streets. On the night of Gardner's first day as judge, his office was broken into and smeared with filth.[125]

When McGogy arrived in Greenville in early August, Butler County was fast approaching a state of anarchy. Most of the men elected to local office on the Republican ticket refused to serve, publicly announcing (some accurately, others under pressure of public opprobrium) that their names had been placed upon the ballot without their consent. The one native son who might have had the prestige to moderate the local impulse to violence and the courage to accept office, former mayor and circuit judge–elect Benjamin F. Porter, had died early in June. William Seawell, the other prominent scalawag and only secessionist to seek office, was discredited in the local press as a "Judas," said to have admitted joining with the Republicans only for the solicitor's salary; in the eyes of "every specimen of his own proud race" he had become, according to the *Advocate*, "the public servant of the negroes and the dirty tool of Gardener." The elected sheriff, the incumbent sheriff, and the appointed acting sheriff each refused to act, leaving the county without a sheriff for some seven weeks. Renewed political activity by the Democratic Conservatives in preparation for the fall presidential election was adding fuel to the explosive situation. As early as August 10, they held a campaign meeting that generated talk in the streets that Gardner would be dragged out of bed and killed; and during the month there were an increasing number of assaults upon freedmen. In the understated words of McGogy's first monthly report, the vacancy in the sheriff's office made it "impossible to enforce the law."[126]

Gone were the days when McGogy could call upon the friendly commanding officer of a nearby post for help if local authorities failed to pursue offenders. Another change in Alabama's assistant commissioner had brought a separation of authority between the bureau and the army; the new assistant commissioner, unlike his predecessors, had no power to direct troops to troubled bureau outposts but could only make requests through the general in command of the state. Moreover, with the restoration of full civil government at the end of July, the apparent expectation was that the elected governor would assume primary responsibility for maintaining order, including the initiation of liaison with the military if federal troops were needed. Military intervention was in fact drastically curtailed and subject to impossibly ambiguous directives from Washington. General Meade, whose command included Alabama, was additionally constrained by his desire to avoid any appearance of abuse of military power.[127] Meade's concern was undoubtedly strengthened by his sympathy with the Conservatives in their opposition to the Radical constitution and to local officials placed in office by virtue of the boycotted elections of early 1868.

Judge Gardner and state assemblyman John A. Hart, another northerner formerly with the bureau who had won election in February, "earnestly solicited" McGogy to ask appointment as sheriff from the Republican governor, William H. Smith. First refusing to seek office, McGogy reluctantly agreed after the state auditor, a confidant of the governor, during a stopover at Greenville joined in their urgings, apparently arguing that a loyal man who would act forcibly was needed to prevent the political opposition from carrying the November election by intimidation. He wrote the governor that their friends in Butler County were despondent, feeling forsaken, and urged the prompt appointment of the men they were recommending for sheriff, justice of the peace, and mayor. He also reported that the governor's appointment of rebels to office had spread the word that he had "virtually gone over to the democratic party." All three appointments were made. The new mayor, though a native Alabamian and a Greenville merchant, was at once sabotaged, unable to retain or obtain the services of any police. After some delay, McGogy was bonded to act as sheriff but he, too, was powerless. On October 16, barely three weeks in office, he surrendered the barren title. Hart explained to the governor that, in the face of daily disturbances, McGogy resigned "conscious of his inability to perform the duties of his office without the cooperation or protection of the military." Gardner had forewarned the governor that "nothing, or very little" could be expected from McGogy or anyone else "without the aid of a stronger power than can be evoked from this demoralized and disorganized community"; and Hart believed he had the governor's assurance that at least a half company of troops would be forthcoming. Yet until the rioting of October 17, no steps were taken by governor or assistant commissioner to restation soldiers in Greenville.[128]

Although some local leaders publicly deprecated violence, with few exceptions even they shared the popular desire to force Gardner from office. When the judge did not capitulate to the threats and insults of August, he was subjected to physical attacks in his courthouse office and on the street. Certain that his assailants needed only an excuse to murder him, and confronted with pistols as well as fists, Gardner took the beatings without striking back. He was kicked, cut, his coat torn from his back, his face bloodied by an attempt to gouge his eyes. Crowds gathered, cheering on his assailants. Some local merchants were reported ready to contribute money to anyone who would finish off the job, and three men drew straws to see which one would attack Gardner on October 17.[129]

The violence of that day began in the early hours of the morning, just after midnight, when masked men in the nearby countryside burned a Negro schoolhouse and the home of its widowed white teacher. During the day ten or more armed men burst into the judge's office, where he was conferring with Assemblyman Hart. One William Payne, winner of the straw drawing, gave Gardner a fearful beating while his confederates held off Hart at gunpoint. The two victims managed to work their way to the courthouse yard and finally escape their attackers. The latter and their sympathizers were not content to let matters rest there. In the evening a lawless posse under the direction of former sheriff John T. Long, with arms freely supplied by a local merchant, set off for the railroad station in search of Gardner and Hart, and to "whip the damn niggers out." Two hours later when they were unable to find either man, some of the party started breaking down a door to the bureau quarters. Situated across from the station, the building was the residence as well as the office for McGogy and his clerk, Henry Booth. That morning McGogy had been called out of town to the Garland hospital but Booth, in bed asleep, was awakened by the noise and on assurance that he would not be harmed, lit a candle and opened the door. Two of the men entered, looked about, sat down, and made it plain that they wanted more than their hunted victims. The spokesman damned Booth as a liar and McGogy as "a damned lying thieving scoundrel," "as bad as the rest." He gave the bureau men ten days to get out of town. No further damage was done to bureau headquarters, but elsewhere in town fellow rioters broke into the homes of black men, seized guns and ammunition, and physically assaulted some. When McGogy returned by train from Garland at 2:00 A.M., armed men, some mounted, some on foot, milled excitedly about the station, searching through the cars with pistols in hand. Three hours later they were still on the hunt, but Gardner had managed to elude them and escape to Montgomery.[130]

The "possum" had fled Greenville, but he had not been intimidated into surrendering the office and powers of probate judge. These he continued defiantly to exercise at Montgomery with the consent of the state legislature after he had on November 2 again been attacked (and again escaped to the capital) when he returned for a meeting of the county commissioners. In January he reappeared in Greenville for a second time, and stayed on despite a night blast of buckshot fired through his bedroom window that struck but did not seriously injure him. His resignation came only at the end of November 1869 by which time tempers had generally cooled though there had been another assault upon the judge in September. The governor had responded to that attack with a threat of martial law—and a continuing policy of conciliatory appointments to local office that enabled native whites, who had swept the November 1868 elections, to consolidate their political dominance in Butler County. Gardner left office asserting that he had vindicated "principle" by outlasting public acquiescence in "assassination or brutal attack"; he added that no emoluments of office could compensate for "living in a community whose characteristics render possible such a struggle as has been forced upon me."[131] His courage had vindicated his integrity and faced down lawlessness but had not enabled Gardner to leave the freedmen of Butler County an enduring legacy.

McGogy and the bureau departed the battlefield almost a year earlier than did the parson from Maine. During the last weeks of McGogy's tenure bureaucratic detail—those of usual routine plus those of closing both the Garland hospital and the bureau office—had crowded upon him with relentless urgency. All such concerns, however, were dwarfed by McGogy's dismay at the collapse of civil order, at his inability as agent of the bureau to fulfill what he considered the elementary responsibility of government toward the freedpeople. His report for October succinctly limned the local scene. "I am at a loss for language," it began, "to express the present state of affairs in this Sub-district, especially in this county." McGogy continued

> The Judge of Probate has left this place to escape the violence of a mob. The machinery of civil government being disorganized there is little or no protection to persons or property. The Bureau R.F.& A.L. having discontinued the hospital . . . and in the absence of all charitable aid, some persons, both white and colored, will end their existence on earth, by starvation and neglect.
>
> On the night of the 17th of October an armed mob broke the door of my office, and entered my private room. A number of citizens of this county have organized themselves into a band known as the vigilance committee and patrol through the town and country every night.
>
> I will not enter into a detailed account of the various lawless acts, that are daily being committed, but suffice to say that in the absence of law many persons have lost all regard for order or humanity. Colored persons are daily being discharged by their employers, and imposed upon in the settlement for their year's service, and frequently assaulted without any means of protection or redress whatever.
>
> Owing to the demoralized state of affairs the colored schools are nearly suspended.
>
> It is to be hoped that the State or General Government will soon take steps to restore law and order, and protect the persons and property of the citizens of this country.
>
> Under these circumstances I would call your special attention to the unfortunate condition of the colored people, who are most invariably homeless, poor, and inexperienced, as well as destitute of the sympathy due them from the white people.
>
> Very Respectfully[132]

The tidal wave of troubles did not recede in Butler County after the presidential election. In late November McGogy felt it necessary to write both the assistant commissioner and Alabama's Secretary of State to let each know that matters were "growing fearfully worse in this county each day." Within four miles of Greenville a colored man had been murdered and others assaulted but "under the present state of affairs" it would not be safe for one man, or even two, to attempt to investigate the case. McGogy's last monthly report, written in early December, filled in the picture. A church and two schoolhouses used by freedmen had just been burned, and all black schools discontinued except one of twenty pupils in Greenville. The Negro destitute were being excluded from the poorhouse by express contract with the provider. Many inoffensive freedmen had been assaulted and robbed of their arms. No warrants issued for the arrest of offenders had been executed since the previous August. McGogy offered no remedy, voiced no plea, expressed no hope. There was a shattering finality in his summation: "The civil law has ceased to be any protection and *we have no claim upon the military authorities.*"[133]

All the energy McGogy had expended in "the interest of the colored people"—on the hospital and colony, on the schools, on the processes of local justice—had come to naught. Until the events of October 17 he could offer the freedman who came to him with a grievance some avenue of redress, usually referral to the judge of probate (Gardner); after that date McGogy recorded in his complaint book the nature of the grievance—nothing more. During the final weeks in Greenville there was little McGogy could do, but that little he did. For the destitute, black and white, he managed to obtain and issue 124 overcoats, 60 dress coats, and 20 pairs of shoes.[134]

At the end of December 1868, a few days short of McGogy's thirtieth birthday, most functions of the Freedmen's Bureau and McGogy's duty as bureau agent came to an end. The records of history reveal few glimpses of the purely private McGogy who stayed on in Alabama until 1871, then settled in Iowa for the rest of his days.

During the two postbureau years in Alabama, McGogy resided either on his plantation, in the rich bottom lands just north of Montgomery, or across the river in nearby Wetumpka, the seat of Elmore County. In August 1870 the U.S. Census enumerator listed him as living in a Wetumpka hotel or boardinghouse along with the proprietor's family of nine, a staff of three black adults with two children, and a dozen guests including a Maine farmer and his family, a physician, a dentist, a grocer, and a retired merchant. McGogy's occupation was reported as that of "revenue collector" and the value of his personal and real estate property as $7,000 and $3,200 respectively.[135]

That McGogy should have been worth some ten thousand dollars, a considerable sum for the time, appears puzzling at first glance. It is true that his personal or family resources had been sufficient in 1866 to finance the purchase and operation of the Montgomery County plantation, but the years that followed the war were disastrous for planters, northern newcomers as well as established southerners. There is no reason to believe that McGogy had prospered while others were being ruined. On the contrary, in early November 1868 shortly before the end of his bureau service, he had apologetically asked for a two-day leave of absence from Greenville to take care of his "business affairs" in Montgomery county where "my lessee is doing all he can to swindle me out of what little I have left." His brother, whom he had persuaded in 1866 to manage the plantation, had returned North, and for 1868 McGogy had leased the plantation to one M. J. Farrow.[136]

Though solvency was elusive in the postwar South, McGogy was a man who husbanded his resources. This was evident in the careful accounting and persistence with which he had tried to recoup his losses from the horse stolen during his 1867 inspection tour. It is also evident in the lease to Farrow. In almost incredible detail, that document was framed to safeguard his interests. In addition to a rent of $500 for the year, it provided that the lessee would pay 12.5 percent interest on livestock and equipment as assessed in an accompanying memorandum. The memo named forty-five items, from four mules at two hundred dollars each to four items at fifty cents apiece, one a "water keg." The list included two wagons, harnesses, curry combs, chains of various description, farm tools, hand tools, water bucket and rope, wooden bedsteads, and blankets. Total valuation was set at $1,397, interest at $174.65. By terms of the contract, Farrow was obligated to treat the livestock kindly, to give proper attention and protection to all property, and to return the items listed in as good a condition as when received, subject only to normal wear and tear. To repair fences he could cut timber from the pine woods but only from localities specifically designated by McGogy. For his personal use, McGogy reserved a bedroom in the main house and an additional room adjacent to the "quarters." As security he required a lien on the entire crop and specified that no part of it could be removed without his knowledge and consent.[137] With all these precautions, McGogy's balance sheet for the plantation year may not have been so dire as suggested by his lament.

Another example of McGogy's careful attention to profit and loss has survived in the record of a lien to secure a loan of ninety dollars made in early May 1870 and payable from the year's crop in "lint cotton of middling quality" delivered on or before October 15 at Wetumpka. Failure to fulfill the contract in any respect gave McGogy the right to sell the entire crop with the borrower waiving protection given by law for redemption or delay.[138] A man so prudent and concerned may well have managed to minimize "business" losses and to put aside some capital from his army and bureau pay. Not such savings, however, but rather the sale of his Montgomery County plantation accounts for most of McGogy's economic resources in 1870.

In mid-October 1869 Sancho Hails, member of a politically prominent local planter's family with extensive land holdings, had purchased the property for sixty-seven hundred dollars. The good cotton prices and crops of 1869 undoubtedly account for this otherwise unlikely purchase price. The 387-acre plantation, for which McGogy had paid $4,837, was valued for local tax purposes earlier in the year at $4,000; the 1870 federal agricultural census placed its cash value at only $2,000 but to that was added $80 for farm equipment, $900 for livestock, and $4,000 for farm production during 1869 (cotton, corn, and animals slaughtered), all of which had presumably been included in the sale. The 1870 figures amount to a total value of $7,280; Sancho Hails had received fair value. And McGogy had escaped the fate of most northerners who at war's end had invested their capital and labor in cotton plantations. They had departed in large numbers before 1869, "more or less cleaned out."[139] McGogy had been luckier than most, but his prospects in Alabama were not so promising as to wed his economic future to that of the South.

Sometime between January and July of 1871, probably during the spring, McGogy arrived in southwestern Iowa, where a younger brother had already settled. He acquired eighty acres of farmland in Fremont County adjoining the emerging town of Shenandoah, Page County, to which he moved two years later and established himself as owner of a livery stable. The following October 1874 he married a young widow, fourteen years his junior by whom he had five children, none of whom lived to reach the age of six. After nine years the marriage ended in a divorce that McGogy did not contest. His former wife, Emma, was awarded temporary custody of their only surviving child, a town lot, McGogy's ninety-day note for $50 and a ten-year note for $1,000 at 10 percent interest, plus $500 to cover court costs and attorney's fee. By then McGogy was numbered among Page County's "leading citizens," having rated a biographical sketch in the county history published in 1880. In 1888 he was again married, to a young woman of neighboring Clarinda, the county seat. When she had been born in 1865 McGogy, then a first lieutenant stationed in Mobile, was about to begin his service with the Freedmen's Bureau. McGogy died in 1904 at the age of 65 years, 10 months, and 11 days, leaving to his wife, Mae, and their fifteen-year-old son the Fremont County farmland, six town lots in Shenandoah, their home, a tenant house, bank deposits of $560, and eleven notes due him with interest, a total estate worth well more than $20,000. For the last fifteen years of his life, McGogy had been retired, spending many of his winters in the South. On the 1900 census schedule, his occupation was recorded as "Capitalist." He never held local office and his only recorded public philanthropy was a fifty-dollar contribution, more than most but by no means the largest, made to a fund raised by fellow townsmen in order to move the Western Normal College to Shenandoah. That he was a well-known and respected town father is beyond doubt. The "DEATH OF CAPT. McGOGY" made the front page and filled an entire column in the local Shenandoah *World*. A mason of longstanding, McGogy was buried with the honors of the lodge, as was his wish. His six pall bearers were founding fathers of Shenandoah. "He was regarded by all," concluded the *World's* account, "as one of our good men and there is general sadness over his death, even at the quite advanced age he has reached."[140]

Eight months before he died, McGogy wrote, signed, and sealed a brief statement "To whom this may concern" to be opened only ten days after his death. In the sealed letter he explained that he was disclosing a previous marriage in order to guard against the possibility of any question arising as to the property rights of his truly legal heirs, his wife and their son, James F. McGogy, Jr. During the last winter of his army life he had married a woman who, he stated, "was not what she pretended to be." Within a few months he had discovered his "mistake," they separated, and in 1870 at Wetumpka, Alabama, he sued for and was granted a divorce. McGogy asked that "the affair be kept a secret unless it should be necessary to use it to secure justice to innocent persons."[141]

Like those of the brief, unhappy marriage, one suspects that McGogy's experiences as bureau agent were banished from memory, sealed off from family and friends. His ardor to "protect the interest of the colored people," to secure for them the legitimate rights of free men and citizens—and his expectation that the national government would enable him to do so—had outlasted his passion for the woman "who was not what she pretended to be"; but there can be found no shred of evidence to indicate that McGogy carried from Alabama to Iowa a commitment to blacks. Indeed, what little evidence exists suggests the contrary.

Few blacks lived in Shenandoah during McGogy's lifetime, or since, but by the early 1870s there was an energetic community located close by in Clarinda, where McGogy was to wed and lose his third wife, and find a fourth. Largely former slaves who had fled Missouri during the war, the "colored people" of Page County numbered approximately 150 by the time of McGogy's arrival. In 1866 their leaders had inaugurated an annual emancipation celebration that continued well into the twentieth century, attracting hundreds even thousands of celebrants after the railroad reached Clarinda in the early 1880s. The morning parade started from "Africa" with band, wagons, and marchers, circled the town square, and then proceeded to a grove or fairground for speeches and a barbecue free to both whites and blacks. The local newspapers reported the numbers attending (in 1874 around two hundred blacks and a thousand whites) and the names of speakers. They made no mention of Captain McGogy.[142]

The biographical sketch in the 1880 history of Page County, undoubtedly based upon information obtained from McGogy or his family, omits any reference to his serving with the Freedmen's Bureau or with the 50th U.S. Colored Troops. Indeed, it erroneously states that his promotion to first lieutenant and then captain came in the same Indiana regiment in which he had enlisted. The 1895 Iowa State Census, which included questions on Civil War service, recorded McGogy as captain by brevet in the Indiana infantry, with no mention of the black regiment or of the bureau. The account of McGogy's life published in the Shenandoah *World* at the time of his death did state, though only in passing, that he was made captain in the 50th U.S. Colored Troops and that he had been an agent of the Freedmen's Bureau. What it highlighted in his Alabama experience, however, was that ". . . as acting assistant Quarter Master [he] had charge of the rebuilding of the streets of Mobile, Alabama, after the magazine had been blown up and the town almost destroyed, a very important and honorable position."[143]

The priority accorded by the *World's* account to McGogy's brief tour of duty at Mobile and its curiously defensive tone ("an honorable position") constituted a gross distortion of his Alabama service. It is one difficult to imagine had he revealed to family and friends in Iowa the commitment and concern with which for more than three years of turmoil in the wake of civil war and emancipation, he had striven to implement "simple justice." Perhaps in his dismay at the powerlessness that had marked the final days of the bureau's mission, a humiliation he undoubtedly felt and friends might have sensed, McGogy had downplayed his role as agent and magnified that of quartermaster in Mobile. It is also possible, despite the remarkable about-face Iowans had made in 1868 in favor of black voting rights, that there persisted a racism that demeaned agents of the Freedmen's Bureau, and kept McGogy mute.[144] What can be said with some certainty is that no recognition, no commendation, no award of honor awaited men of the bureau who had struggled against the odds to make secure for former slaves their basic human rights and their equality as citizens before the law and at the ballot box.

For McGogy, extant records leave many questions unanswered; some conclusions, however, are not in doubt. A humane, honorable, and prideful man, James F. McGogy in the compelling immediacy of the postwar situation had clearly recognized white injustice toward blacks and had wholeheartedly responded so long as the means to do so and the responsibility were his. But he was neither philanthropist nor reformer. An essentially private, practical, enterprising midwesterner, he would win the respect of his fellows as a successful small town entrepreneur. Yet during the aftermath of a shattering and liberating war, his energy, his wartime loyalties, his sense of duty as a bureau officer, and his perception of injustice had evoked a personal commitment to help realize the nation's first major effort to make justice color-blind.

CHAPTER TEN

Reflections on the Limits of the Possible

The identification of the southern policy of Andrew Johnson with that of Lincoln is no longer an unquestioned verity of Reconstruction historiography, but misconceptions of Lincoln's purpose and priorities tend to obscure the distance that separated the two presidential approaches to Reconstruction. The Louisiana story contradicts the assumption, commonly accepted, that Lincoln was prepared in the interest of reunion and reconciliation to return political power to the antebellum landed elite or that in the interest of either reunion or party he stood ready to sacrifice the freedmen. It confirms that the president and the radicals of his party shared an identification of purpose, if not of rhetoric and tactic, in seeking basic rights, citizenship, and political participation for former slaves.

From the Louisiana perspective, Lincoln's "Ten Percent Plan" can be recognized for what it was, not a policy of leniency but one of expediency, a means to precipitate an antislavery minority government. It reflected a first priority not, as generally assumed, for restoring an errant state as quickly as possible but priority for insuring freedom. Nor did Lincoln consider himself bound by the plan so often seen as defining his intentions. He did not view the December 1863 proclamation as a blueprint for the future. On the very day of the assassination he began with his cabinet a consideration of "the great question now before us"—Reconstruction—and urged deliberate and careful review of a proposal drawn up by Secretary Stanton. Four days earlier, on April 10, he had told Francis Pierpont, wartime governor of rump loyalist Virginia, "that he had no plan for reorganization, but must be guided by events." Stanton later testified that insofar as he knew Lincoln had not yet "matured any plan." In his carefully prepared public statement of April 11 on Reconstruction, Lincoln cautioned "that no exclusive, and inflexible plan can safely be prescribed."[1] The safety that Lincoln left undefined, for his fellow Republicans meant security for white Unionists, for freedmen, for party, and for the Union. Although he had not decided upon the best course to achieve them, there is no reason to believe that Lincoln differed from his party on basic objectives.

While Andrew Johnson might be expected to show concern for Union and for Union men, his commitment to the freedmen and to the Republican party was more tenuous. His appreciation of the need for flexibility in guiding Reconstruction was unlikely in view of the rigidity characteristic of his ideas and of his behavior. Moreover, he harbored a long-standing antipathy to antislavery Radicals that persisted despite his cooperation with them in late 1861 and early 1862 as a member of the congressional Joint Committee on the Conduct of the War. Both immediately before and immediately after, he publicly equated abolitionists and secessionists as disunionists, a term carrying an opprobrium that left no space for a measure of sympathetic tolerance.[2] In contrast to Lincoln, Johnson would never perceive Radicals as devils facing Zionwards. And notwithstanding Johnson's championship of "the people" and his assaults upon the planter aristocracy, as president he did more to resuscitate than to undercut the southern elite. It has been claimed that his goal was transfer of political power from landed wealth to plebeian and mechanic; if so, his presidential policy was ineffectual. Except in Alabama, where Sarah Wiggins has found that Unionists in 1865–1866 "had their day" at the political expense of Black Belt planters, and to a lesser extent in South Carolina, where Johnson men won from the 1865 constitutional convention a partial elimination of the political privilege enjoyed by the propertied, antebellum class leadership apparently had little difficulty in reestablishing its influence during Johnsonian restoration.[3] That this result was not entirely a matter of miscalculation or ineptness in exercising presidential power is indicated by Johnson's early decision with respect to Louisiana to sustain J. Madison Wells and Hugh Kennedy and to repudiate Gen. Nathaniel P. Banks. The new president had due warning of the consequences, but he was not deterred by the prospect of returning political power to the old planter establishment.

Johnson's interviews with Wells, Cottman, and Kennedy—and his decision—came within the first weeks of his administration. Draft proclamations of reconstruction and amnesty presented in cabinet by Secretary of War Stanton and Attorney General Speed were then, Gideon Welles noted in his diary, "in the hands of the President who will shape [them] right."[4] For Johnson this may have been a period of genuine indecision, which would help explain the expectation of Radicals that he would stand with them in desiring a stern settlement with the South, even Negro suffrage. If so, the Louisiana delegation may well have influenced the course of Reconstruction in general.

At Lincoln's last cabinet meeting, the president, according to Welles, characterized Stanton's proposal for initiating reorganization as "substantially, in its general scope," one previously "talked over in Cabinet meetings." Between then and Johnson's proclamations of May 29, the proposal underwent a series of significant changes. The result was an end product at variance in important respects with Stanton's original paper and inconsistent with Lincoln's objectives, his pragmatic approach, and his stance in Louisiana. The role Stanton envisaged for the military was diminished. Unlike his design, the final plan embodied in the North Carolina proclamation and all subsequent such proclamations provided for the appointment of provisional civilian rather than military governors. It omitted authorization for a special recruitment of volunteers "to preserve the peace and enforce the laws" as support for a corps of provost marshals. Both volunteers and marshals were to have been under the direction of the secretary of war. It added a new paragraph that undercut the primacy of military authority upon which Lincoln had insisted in Louisiana. The wording strongly suggests that Johnson was reacting to the protests against Banks' action in New Orleans made by the Louisiana emissaries. The military commander of the department and all officers and personnel were not only directed to "aid and assist" the provisional governor but also specifically "enjoined to abstain from in any way hindering, impeding, or discouraging the loyal people from the organization of a State government as herein authorized." To emphasize the civilian character of the president's plan, and his respect for the state as a continuing entity of self-government, the original heading "Executive Order to Reestablish the Authority of the United States, and Execute the Laws within the Geographical Limits Known as the State of North Carolina" was discarded in favor of simply "A Proclamation." Thus from its inception Johnson's version of presidential Reconstruction departed from Lincoln's insistence upon the military being "master," and despite Lincoln's warning it became one inflexible plan. Johnson's proclamations also closed the door that Lincoln had kept open for the use of national authority in extending suffrage to blacks as part of the Reconstruction process.

In his original paper Stanton had sidestepped the matter of who might be allowed to vote in initiating reorganization. Like Lincoln, he recognized that the party was divided on the suffrage issue and sought a basis for unity. At the urging of Senator Sumner, who with other members of Congress was in his office two evenings after Lincoln's assassination, he provided in the revised draft for suffrage by "loyal citizens," that is by blacks as well as whites. When the draft came before the cabinet on May 9, Stanton's wording was criticized as "equivocal, . . . vague and uncertain." President Johnson expressed a wish that there be no room for dispute or equivocation. Then the question of whether blacks should be authorized to vote was put to the cabinet, and the six members present divided evenly. Sometime after the cabinet meeting Johnson settled the issue in favor of white-only voting by substituting for Stanton's phraseology a provision that followed Lincoln's December 1863 proclamation. Later a passage was added that in effect disavowed any right on the part of president or Congress, even under the war powers, to require enfranchisement of blacks. It read that the state convention to amend the constitution, or the legislature meeting thereafter, "will prescribe the qualification of electors . . . a power the people of the several States composing the Federal Union have rightfully exercised from the origin of the Government to the present time."[5] No wonder that J. Madison Wells on returning home felt secure in assuring the Conservatives that Andrew Johnson would make no concession on the suffrage issue!

In New Orleans, more clearly than in the nation's capital, it was apparent that the decision Johnson made to oust General Banks and support Wells and Kennedy, a decision reached by May 17, foreshadowed the political substance of presidential policy to come. In the months ahead, to the surprise of Unionists, Johnson would generally support local officials in their clashes with the Freedmen's Bureau or the military. In doing so, he would take few precautions to protect antislavery men, white or black. Even more unexpected was Johnson's failure to use his influence as president to build political strength for Unionists generally. The course on which he had embarked by mid May broke with Lincoln's effort to implement through local political allies and the military an antislavery policy that extended beyond emancipation. And it failed to maintain Lincoln's stand that the commanding general must be "master."

The significance of Johnson's repudiation of Banks has eluded both contemporaries and historians. What motivated his Louisiana decision is an important question, the answer as varied and speculative as the many reasons scholars have offered to explain his subsequent break with the congressional majority. Speculation is not without some supporting evidence. From the letters extant it seems evident that the Louisiana delegation played upon Johnson's desire for presidential power in his own right, the culmination of a driving ambition now generally recognized as central to his character and career. Undoubtedly the three also appealed to his long-standing constitutional views as a states'-rights Democrat and to the concern for the primacy of civil over military authority that cut across party lines. In addition, Wells' letters suggest that Johnson as a southerner responded to the criticism of General Banks as an outsider, a Yankee attempting to impose alien values upon the South, and to charges that Banks and his associates were plunderers out to rob the state treasury. The letter of Wells to his wife, quoted earlier, makes it unmistakable that Wells also appealed to Johnson's racial prejudice.[6]

No historian can weigh with certainty the import of that prejudice upon Johnson's southern policy, or separate the conscious from the unconscious force of his bias.[7] To recognize these imponderables, however, is not to dismiss as inconsequential Johnson's attitude toward blacks. In considering the potential of presidential leadership for helping shape the future of the freed slave, whether by action or inaction, by positions publicly taken or by influence exerted behind the scenes, a comparison of the racial attitudes of Andrew Johnson and Abraham Lincoln is inescapable. From one perspective there was not much distance between the two men. Neither stood apart from his age, an age in which a pervasive racial prejudice cut across section, party, and class; an age to which was alien the concept of racial equality that a century later would give strength and ideological authority to those who fought racial injustice. Certainly Lincoln no more than Johnson championed equality of the races. Nor did Johnson's behavior, or even his rhetoric, as military governor or as president place him, any more than Lincoln, at the opposite extreme of the racial spectrum. Yet the difference between Lincoln and Johnson in racial attitude should not be minimized as a mere matter of degree. Philosophers recognize that a variation in degree (in quantity) can result in a significant difference in kind (in quality), though not necessarily discernible from every perspective or valid for every purpose.[8] Historians might well take note. Certainly in the context of an inquiry into the possibility of a different course and outcome of Reconstruction, the distinction between the racial views of Johnson and those of Lincoln is more importantly a matter of quality than a matter of degree.

Antebellum attitudes toward slavery helped shape postwar attitudes toward blacks and their future. On slavery, the distinction between Lincoln and the Tennessean who would become his successor in presidential office was unmistakable. In the prewar years Johnson had boasted of being as "sound" as any southern man on the question of slavery. He saw himself as its defender against abolitionists and black Republicans. He believed that "negro slavery was neither a moral, social or political evil, but was right"—"a blessing." As a spokesman for the common man he saw no contradiction between democracy and slavery: "our institution, instead of being antagonistical to democracy is in perfect harmony with it." He could "wish to God every head of a family in the United States had one [slave] to take the drudgery and menial service off his family." His own ownership of slaves was evidence of the opportunity that American democracy offered to climb "Jacob's ladder" from humble origin to status and achievement. Johnson was proud to be a slaveholder "not by inheritance, but by hard labour."[9]

The exigencies of war and politics, together with the gentle prodding of Lincoln, brought Johnson reluctantly and belatedly to embrace emancipation. Yet as late as March 1862, as Lincoln's military governor in Tennessee, he sought to reassure the citizens of Nashville and Davidson County that slavery was safe within the Union. According to Johnson, Lincoln was not waging war to free the slaves. "It is very easy to talk about Lincolnites. . . . I have repeatedly asked them if the war was being directed to the institution of Slavery. Their reply has always been, 'We've got more niggers at home that we want; d—n the niggers.'" Johnson's personal view was made clear: "I believe that slaves should be in subordination, and will live and die so believing."[10] Earlier that month Lincoln had sent to Congress his message urging support for gradual, compensated emancipation, and less than ten days after Johnson's address, Lincoln in the White House was trying to reassure Wendell Phillips, his specially invited guest and the most radical of Radicals, that unlike border-state senators and representatives who, he said, loved slavery and meant to perpetuate it, "he [Lincoln] hated it and meant *it should die.*"[11]

Unlike Lincoln, Johnson had never been tentative or qualified in his view of black men as not the equal of whites. He embraced white supremacy wholeheartedly; indeed, it is doubtful that he could conceive of a biracial society organized on any other basis. For Johnson, blacks were "not created equal in the very beginning. The distinction begins with the very germ itself." The Negro was "an inferior type of man, and incapable of advancement in his native country." Slavery had grown "necessarily out of the physical and mental structure of man." Johnson "had no hesitancy . . . upon the subject, believing and knowing, as he did, that the black race of Africa were inferior to the whiteman in point of intellect—better calculated in physical structure to undergo drudgery and hardship—standing, as they do, many degrees lower in the scale of gradation that expresses the relative relation between

God and all that he has created." When the author of the Declaration of Independence wrote that all men are created equal, "Mr. Jefferson meant the white race, and not the African race."[12]

The certainty and intensity of Johnson's racial view were part of his southern heritage. In assailing secession in the borderlands during the fall of 1861, he made clear his identification with section: "I am a Southern man, sharing the prejudices of my section, and I am no abolitionist." The depth of his prejudice may also have reflected, as David Bowen and William Riches have argued, an insecurity and defensiveness as son of a menial servant and apprentice to a tailor never totally accepted by the local elite, an insecurity reflected in his fierce attachment to democracy and the Jacob's ladder concept—for whites only. They have concluded that Johnson, in contrast to Lincoln, could not recognize blacks as human beings in the same sense as whites, even after his conversion to antislavery. A number of Johnson's public statements suggest that he tried. But his outbursts in private, characterized by his secretary as a display of morbid feelings against blacks, indicate that he could not escape his past. Frederick Douglass, "one of the most meritorious men in America" in Lincoln's view, was for Johnson "that d———d Douglass; he's just like any nigger."[13] The Tennessean who had climbed the heights of Jacob's ladder would, indeed, "live and die" believing that "slaves [and ex-slaves] should be in subordination." Lincoln could take pleasure and satisfaction in the achievement of a black man; Johnson felt uncomfortable in the presence of a black who was not "in his place."

Johnson's commitment to whiteness distorted his perception of reality and precluded the possibility that as president he would move his fellow southerners to accept and institutionalize a substantial measure of freedom and equality for blacks. This was the great historic challenge to the political leadership of the 1860s. Bound by his heritage of section and class, Andrew Johnson was incapable of perceiving it. He was further insulated from a sense of presidential responsibility for the future of freed slaves by his view of the proper constitutional limits of federal authority. Beyond freedom, he saw the status and condition of the black man as a matter for state, not national, decision. His drive for political power reinforced his inclination and his constitutional principles. The support of southerners and of the northern Democracy was welcome, perhaps essential, if the tailor's apprentice was to realize his ambition to be an elected president. They could not lightly be alienated. The Radicals, the old abolitionist wing of the Republican party, seemed politically expendable. An aggressive loner, stubborn, insecure, clinging to "right" principles and rejecting differing views as error or evil, Johnson could neither lead the nation nor accept the leadership of the Republicans in Congress. Whatever his conscious intent, the use Johnson made of the powers of the presidency—not only his vetoes but also his pardons, his appointments, his directives as commander in chief, his authority over the Freedmen's Bureau, erected barriers beyond which advance toward equal citizenship for blacks could be made only at the price of open and prolonged warfare between president and congressional majority.[14]

Lincoln had recognized the historic challenge. He was prepared to implement, so far as he would find practicable, "the principle that all men are created equal." The nature of presidential leadership helped shape events, and the leadership of Andrew Johnson and of Lincoln diverged markedly. Johnson lacked Lincoln's political skill, finesse, and flexibility; more important, he did not face in the same direction. Lincoln would expand freedom for blacks; Johnson was content to have their freedom contained. Both men held, to use Lincoln's words, that "important principles may, and must, be inflexible"; the operative principles of Lincoln and Johnson simply did not coincide. During his presidency, though not during his period as war governor, Johnson clung to a narrow concept of the powers of the national government as "right" principle. Lincoln's constitutional scruples, on the other hand, did not preclude the expansion of federal authority. He had exercised broadly the war powers of commander in chief, and his readiness to continue to do so in reconstructing the states was indicated both by his sending General Banks back to Louisiana and by his initiating cabinet consultations in preparation for making "some new announcement to the people of the South," after Congress had adjourned without agreeing upon a southern policy. Lincoln took to heart the warning of William Whiting, solicitor of the War Department, to which Phillip Paludan has called attention. He saw the danger in recognizing a doctrine of state existence that would enable "secessionists . . . to get back by fraud what they failed to get by fighting."[15] In his last public address, he carefully refrained from taking a stand on "whether the seceded States, so called, are in the Union or out of it." Also unlike Johnson and the Democrats, Lincoln indicated no aversion to the use of constitutional amendment to change the historic division of powers between state and federal government. Nor had he objected, as would they, that Congress had no authority to impose a provision in respect to suffrage upon the unreconstructed states. With enfranchisement, as with slavery, it is reasonable to view Lincoln's pressure for state action not as devotion to a narrow concept of states'-rights federalism but as a practical first step toward an ultimate solution. Given the differences in principle and prejudice between Lincoln and Johnson, Reconstruction history would have followed a different path both at the nation's capital and in the secession states of the South had Lincoln lived out his second term of office. Of that there can be no doubt.

At the nation's capital there would have been no war between president and Congress. Stubborn differences as to "mode, manner, and means of reconstruction" (to use Lincoln's characterization) would, of course, have persisted among Republicans and could not have been resolved easily, for unprecedented constitutional and practical problems were involved. Yet differences cut across congressional leadership and at some point surely would have been amenable to the legislative process. They would not have created a chasm between executive and legislature. With Lincoln as president, whenever a Republican consensus or compromise developed, executive agreement could be expected short of legislation that would force him to repudiate the Louisiana experiment while there was still hope of "hatching the egg." There is good reason to believe that president and congressional majority would have joined in an effort to insure that freedmen obtain at the very least equal standing before the law, schools, the right to bear arms, a measure of present and a more general prospective enfranchisement, plus governmental assistance in acquiring access to land. An eloquent passage in Lincoln's last address pointed to the general direction in which he intended to exert presidential pressure. He would not have the nation say to Louisiana blacks, and by implication to all others who had been slaves, "This cup of liberty . . . we will dash from you, and leave you to the chances of gathering the spilled and scattered contents in some vague and undefined when, where, and how."[16]

If in early 1865 there was a possibility of presidential conflict with Congress, it was not over ends. Nor was it over jurisdiction, for Lincoln had made clear his recognition of the right of Congress to a role in Reconstruction. Possibility for conflict lay in the use of military authority as means. Sending General Banks back to Louisiana indicated Lincoln's readiness to use, though not to acknowledge as such, what the general called "force" in order to obtain "consent" to the Reconstruction of states on a basis the president considered acceptable. It is difficult to believe that the issue would have been fateful in view of the reversal of roles on this question between Congress and President Johnson, and Lincoln's rationale that the military's function in establishing the Louisiana government was only one of "cooperation."[17] One of the unrecognized ironies of Reconstruction history is that Congress, by assigning primacy to the military in the legislation of 1867, in fact capitulated to the stand Lincoln had taken in Louisiana, one that helped bring down upon him in mid-1864 the denunciations of the Wade-Davis Manifesto.

War between Congress and President Johnson was precipitated by two issues: first, continuance and strengthening of the Freedmen's Bureau; and second, establishment of citizenship and basic rights for ex-slaves by national authority. There was a Republican consensus for both measures, and with Lincoln as president, there could only have been cooperation and concurrence. In the case of the civil rights legislation, should Lincoln have considered its constitutional validity questionable, presidential influence could have been expected on behalf of a covering constitutional amendment rather than against one, as with Johnson. As for the Freedmen's Bureau, Lincoln was not at all likely to have turned his back upon the recommendations of O. O. Howard, his choice to head the bureau. It is also worth noting that of the many reasons modern scholars have advanced to explain Johnson's break with Congress, none would have been operative with Lincoln—not the substance of the Freedmen's Bureau and civil rights bills, not states'-rights principles, not ambition, not identity with the South or misconception of Republican attitudes, certainly not susceptibility to flattery or the personalization of political differences.[18]

The fear that Johnson's policy aroused for the future of the Republican party, as well as for the security of freedmen and of the Union, could not have arisen under Lincoln. Lincoln might have continued into the postwar years the wartime coalition that joined Republicans and some Democrats under the Union party label, but such a development would have stirred few apprehensions of a Democratic takeover. Lincoln's identification with the party's past and his continuing role as party leader precluded suspicion of disloyalty; and he was not one to be taken in by professions of personal political support. As his handling of Bullitt, Cottman, and Kennedy in Louisiana makes unmistakable, Lincoln was adroit at using, rather than being used by, such allies. Johnson was less skillful at manipulating men; he also had less reason to be wary. As a Tennessee slaveholder and Democrat, he perceived neither a proslavery past nor a staunch Democratic party allegiance as signal for caution in matters of postwar political power.

Without the vetoes of the Freedmen's Bureau and civil rights bills, erase from history the events that followed. Erase the bitter contest of 1866 between president and the party that placed him in office; erase the clash over the Fourteenth Amendment and the overturn of presidential restoration by the legislation of 1867 with its reestablishment of primacy for military authority and its grant of suffrage to all blacks in the unreconstructed states; erase the subsequent presidential obstruction of congressional intent that stirred the passion and apprehension that culminated in the impeachment of a president. Erase the whole dramatic sequence of events, but with what effect upon the future of the freedmen? Could Lincoln and the Republican Congress working together have secured for the ex-slave a substantive freedom, one reflected in his economic as well as his legal status? Could they have established in the 1860s so firm a basis for equal citizenship that there would have been no turning back—no counterrevolutionary white "redemption," no "nadir" for blacks by the turn of the century?

Without conflict between president and Congress, whatever change Republicans agreed to impose upon the South would have enjoyed better odds for success than the settlement of 1867–1869. Both contemporaries and historians have noted the mood of acquiescence in the South that followed immediately upon the end of hostilities. Although it is unlikely that a pattern for Reconstruction would have emerged in time to capitalize on that mood, definitive requirements would certainly not have been delayed the two years that intervened between war's end and the Reconstruction legislation of 1867.

Even more important than the foreshortening of uncertainty would have been the minimizing of the false hopes, the confusion, and the resultant bitterness that arose from the president's course and its subsequent repudiation. Most white southerners believed from Johnson's conduct of the presidency that they would not have to make more than minimal concessions on the status of the ex-slave—none on suffrage and not even recognition of an absolute equality of traditional rights before the law. Although imposition of black civil and political rights finally was recognized as inescapable, delay fed a widespread reaction that to defeat was being added "dishonor." Had there been from the beginning a consistent southern policy that satisfied majority Republican opinion, it is reasonable to assume that compliance would have been greater and opposition less widespread and ruthless. Resistance had been encouraged by Johnson's stand and strengthened by a sense of injustice at the progressively severe and apparently open-ended peace terms demanded. The conflict between president and Congress fragmented a potential core of state leaders willing to cooperate in implementing the requirements of the victors. Some original supporters of the president became allied with the Conservative Democrats. Others looked to Congress and joined the Republican party. And under the rigidities of congressional Reconstruction even firm Unionists could find themselves ineffectual, barred from voting and officeholding because they had held minor office during the Confederacy. By 1868 southern white recruits to Republican ranks were discredited as traitors to section and to race. To this was added the opprobrium conveyed by the term "scalawag," which came into general use only with congressional Reconstruction. Otto Olsen has pointed out that the opponents of the Republican party in the South did not consider it a legitimate political entity with which to contest state elections, but an alien force to be destroyed.[19] In short, no stable political "nucleus" to implement national policy, such as Lincoln had tried to encourage, could cohere and expand while Johnson held presidential power. With Lincoln in office, odds for success would have been greater, but by no means assured. Nor would there have been any certainty that the white South's acceptance of Republican peace terms would enable blacks to gain a stake in the economy and a participation in the political process sufficiently large to realize the goals of the freedmen and their advocates.[20]

The victory for equal civil and political rights inaugurated by national legislation and the southern state conventions of 1868 was tragically temporary, but it should not be deprecated. Opportunities were opened to former slaves and antebellum free blacks for participation in political power, opportunities they pursued with vigor. However brief and episodic their role in political decision-making and their enjoyment of public facilities formerly denied them, free blacks had defied old taboos and left an imprint upon the institutions of the South—political, social, and economic—which the resurgence of white supremacy never completely annihilated.[21] Some native white southerners not only had supported them out of expediency or loyalty to the Union but had come to accept as valid concepts of racial equity alien to their own past. Yet there can be no question but that the equality of citizenship embodied in national and state law during the 1860s lay shattered and apparently unmendable as the South entered the twentieth century. Most former slaves and their children still lived in agrarian dependence and poverty, poorly educated, increasingly disfranchised and segregated, with little protection against a new surge of white violence.

All accounts of Reconstruction recognize the intensity of white southern resistance to the new status of blacks imposed by Republicans upon the defeated South. Curiously, in explaining the outcome, generally characterized by modern historians as the failure of Reconstruction (though with qualification and some dissent), they tend to place major responsibility not upon the South but upon "the North." By "the North" they usually mean the Republican party, which held national political power, and sometimes say as much. Their explanation is not free of moral stricture, often patently implicit when not expressly stated. Since the mid-1960s there has seldom been missing from accounts of the "First Reconstruction" the pejorative term "betrayal." Present-day scholars do not indulge in "moral discourse" on black slavery, for as David Donald observed "in the middle of the twentieth century there are some things that do not need to be said."[22] Even less likely is an echo of antebellum abolitionist strictures upon slaveholders as "sinners," though there has been lively debate as to whether or not planters harbored a sense of guilt about their peculiar institution. In terms of the moral judgment of history, the vanquished hold an advantage over the victors. Little restraint or understanding has been extended to the latter. Yet few historians would question the statement that those who won the military contest lost the peace. They have not considered the implications. To lose a battle is not to betray a cause; to retreat in the face of a seemingly weak but relentless and resourceful foe is not the equivalent of treachery; to put an end to a bruising fight that has been lost is not without a certain moral justification of its own. In a self-governing nation the will to persevere indefinitely in a just cause, subordinating all else both of interest and conviction, is beyond the realm of reasonable expectation. If Republican politicians and their constituencies of the 1860s and '70s have received little charity, the one professionally acceptable defense of the opprobrium cast upon them is that the political leaders had viable alternatives—viable in the sense that other policies would have changed the outcome, viable also in the sense that such measures could have been perceived and implemented.

An explicit and sweeping statement reflecting that assumption was made by the most distinguished and influential historian of the postbellum South, C. Vann Woodward, in a burst of eloquence that concluded a pathbreaking paper on comparative emancipations and reconstructions. When revised and republished, he did not allow the passage to stand unmodified. However, the original version is quoted at length because it reveals a premise quite generally held, though seldom openly stated or scrutinized. In the paper C. Vann Woodward had argued that postemancipation failure characterized all plantation America, the excesses of brutality, exploitation, and discrimination in the Caribbean and Brazil paralleling and even exceeding those in the South. Then he passed judgment:

> But failure, like most human experience, is a relative matter. It depends on expectations and promises, on *commitments and capabilities*. One man's failure is another man's success. And in a way *the American failure was the greatest of all*.

For in 1865 the democratic colossus of the New World stood triumphant, flushed with the terrible victories of Gettysburg, Vicksburg, Cold Harbor, and Appomattox. Its crusade for freedom had vindicated the blood shed by its sons, and in the full flush of power and victory and righteousness its leaders solemnly pledged the nation to fulfill its promises, not only of freedom but the full measure of democracy and racial equality. *The powers of fulfillment, sealed by the sacrifices of a victorious war, were unlimited.* And the federal government was no remote trans-Atlantic metropolitan parliament on the banks of the Thames or the Seine. It sat on the Potomac, with General Lee's Arlington Mansion in full view of the White House windows across the river, and its armies garrisoned the defeated states.

In the revision, the key sentence was changed to: "The powers of fulfillment, sealed by the sacrifices of a victorious war, were *seemingly* unlimited, *though of course they were not.*"[23]

A final paragraph, identical in both versions, introduces a note of ambiguity:

> Yet we know that, although the North won its four-year war against a fully armed, mobilized, and determined South when the issue was slavery, it very quickly lost its crusade against a disarmed, defeated, and impoverished South when the issue was equality. For on this issue the South was united as it had not been on slavery. And the North was even more divided on the issue of equality than it had been on slavery. In fact, when the chips were down, the overwhelmingly preponderant views of the North on that issue were in no important respect different from those of the South—and never had been.

The passage perhaps was meant to open the door, gingerly, to a shared culpability—or even a shared exculpation. Yet the two paragraphs in their final form render an unmistakably censorious verdict upon righteous leaders of a victorious North making pledges on the banks of the Potomac that they were unwilling to enforce against a defenseless South.

The verdict arises from the premise, qualified in the revision but still operative, that Republican leaders had power to force upon the white South equality between the races, a most questionable assumption. And the rhetoric in which it is stated blurs the factual record. With victory at hand, Congress had adjourned deadlocked over Reconstruction. The only leader who could and did speak with a measure of authority for the federal government was Abraham Lincoln. He did so from an upstairs window of the White House two days after Lee's surrender. Cautiously he revealed his hope for

Louisiana and the other states awaiting Reconstruction, a hope "to ripen" the changes already under way into "a complete success." Lincoln's statement was significant, potentially momentous had he lived, but it constituted no pledge on behalf of the nation to a "full measure of democracy and racial equality." The Republican commitment even at its peak never pledged "racial equality," a concept resting upon the conviction that there is no inequality in the innate endowment of races and carrying logical imperatives for personal and social conduct. The more limited commitment of the 1860s, and the demand against which the South proved far from "disarmed," was equality of civil and political rights irrespective of any inequality of race that might be thought to exist. There was also a promise, not legally binding but considered implicit in civil and political equality, that former slaves would not be held to an economic status of dependency and disguised servitude.[24] These were issues over which the postwar struggle was joined. And on these issues the preponderant view in the North did in fact differ from that in the South, even though its predominance there was far from overwhelming and had crystallized only under the pressure of sectional conflict.

The comparative approach to emancipation and Reconstruction might have led C. Vann Woodward to a charitable conclusion. What was attempted in the United States was of a magnitude and difficulty, and a daring, without equal in other emancipations, and in the body of his paper he made an impressive case for such a generalization. He pointed out the much greater number of slaves affected by emancipation in the South than in all the rest of the Americas, four million of an approximate six million. Despite their great number, blacks in the South, unlike those in most other areas of plantation America, were a minority who as free men faced a white nonslaveholding majority. As nowhere else, their freedom came as the result of a terrible war between whites, and came suddenly, without the transitional period characteristic of most emancipations. In comparative perspective, the situation in the United States was overwhelming. Yet to these elements of magnitude was added, as Woodward clearly states, an effort on an unparalleled scale to force upon white men the sharing of political power and office with blacks. Woodward even argues that the U.S. Congress, despite the constitutional restraints under which it functioned, was more tenacious in its effort to accompany freedom with radical reform than was the English Parliament in abolishing slavery in the West Indies. Similarly, in a comparative study of the response to emancipation, George Fredrickson characterizes the attempt to reconstruct the South as "the most radical departure from white supremacy attempted anywhere in the nineteenth century." And Peyton McCrary holds that until the twentieth century only the French Revolution "rivaled the magnitude of social transformation involved in the abolition of slavery in the United States."[25] In view of the dimensions of the undertaking it would seem fitting for historians of southern Reconstruction to mitigate judgment on the offense of failure.

A comparative approach to Reconstruction also suggests that there is an inherently stubborn difficulty to providing a road out of poverty for a dependent, subservient agrarian people, most especially for nonwhite laborers of a plantation economy. Even in Europe where race and plantation did not block advance, emancipation from the old servile order of the eighteenth century brought peasants escape from poverty and from social-political disadvantage only slowly, and then with major exceptions. In eastern Europe, where industrialization and urbanization lagged, the economic lot of most remained harsh far into the twentieth century. "The freeing of the [European] peasantry from the bonds of their servility" could be characterized by a responsible historian as late as the 1970s as a "still unfinished social revolution."[26]

In regions of plantation dominance, one searches with little success for examples of transformation that have raised the standard of living, except for the few, above a minimum essential for existence. A study of the economy of plantation areas published in 1972 appeared under the suggestive title *Persistent Poverty*. The author holds that plantation societies by their very nature perpetuate underdevelopment. "Rigid patterns of social stratification associated with race and color inhibit social mobility and severely restrict the participation of large groups of people in economic and political affairs. Plural societies pregnant with race conflict exhibit instability that is inimical to development. And the concentration of economic, social, and political power within the society prevents the emergence of a highly motivated population." With some emancipations, black workers largely escaped the plantation system, as in Jamaica and British Guiana. Their economic gains seldom proved sustained or substantial, even where change brought noneconomic satisfactions, crop innovations, and a lessening of the inequality of income distribution. In grappling with the problem of rural poverty, John Kenneth Galbraith in 1979 reminded his readers that "an end to injustice . . . is not necessarily or even usually an end to poverty."[27] And it is doubtful that any former slave society has completely eradicated economic or racial injustice.

One plantation area that might be expected to have offered the emancipated slave the economic substance of freedom is the São Paulo region of

Brazil, a country with little overt or blatant race discrimination.[28] Coffee production there in contrast to that of sugar and cotton elsewhere was a dynamic, expanding, and profitable agriculture in the 1880s at the time of emancipation, and continued to thrive with only a few short interludes of falling prices in the late nineteenth and early twentieth century. Profits from coffee remained largely in the region, helping to fuel urbanization and industrialization. The benefits of a remarkable economic development went not to the upper classes alone, but also to the propertyless men at the bottom. Yet few blacks gained a better livelihood. The jobs open to them remained the least remunerative and the most menial, and many were displaced even on the coffee plantations. Their role in the new order became more marginal than in the old. It was the white immigrants from Europe, predominantly Italian but also Portuguese, Spanish, and German, who took their places and then attained the status of landowners or seized the opportunities open to workmen and entrepreneurs in the bustling city of São Paulo. There occurred, as Florestan Fernandes has put it, not a transformation of freedmen into "free labor" but a substitution of white labor for black. Brazil, a nation that takes pride in a perception of its history as free from color prejudice or discrimination, has been found by modern scholars to nurture an illusion that masks the realities of thought and behavior rooted in its slavery past. They have concluded that Brazilian blacks and mulattoes are victimized without willful white intent, but victimized nonetheless. Men and women marked by color bear a disproportionately heavy burden of poverty, unemployment, underemployment, and low levels of schooling. And this failure of reconstruction occurred in a country that, in sharp contrast to the United States, enjoyed an historic tradition of racial tolerance and, to use Carl Degler's phrase, a "mulatto escape hatch" from the color line.[29]

If the success of Republicans in reconstructing the South rested upon the precondition of an absence of race prejudice, the limits of the possible were so narrow as to have foreordained failure. Modern scholarship has recognized and amply documented the pervasiveness and persistence of racial prejudice. In some form it contaminated almost all white Americans. Had mid-nineteenth-century America constituted a society utopian in its freedom from "racism," the obstacles to successful reordering of southern society would have been immensely lessened, though European experience suggests that they would not have been completely removed.[30] It does not follow, however, that race prejudice precluded an equality of civil and political rights. Differences in the quality and priority of prejudice, not only between individuals but between the two major parties, provided a significant opening for political action. By the 1860s many northerners who did not find objectionable discrimination against blacks in private and social relationships had come to view as unacceptable discrimination against blacks in public matters. Most of them were Republicans. Prejudices existed among Republicans, but they did not prevent the party from making equal citizenship the law of the land. To explain the breakdown of that law by pointing to the racial bias of Republicans is unconvincing unless one assumes that a commitment to civil and political equality can be met only by men who accept and seek to realize the more far-reaching twentieth-century concept of racial equality, a highly questionable premise.

Neither can it be taken for granted that a racism so strong as to reject an equality of basic rights is impervious to change. There is no question but that racial attitudes affect behavior, but it is also recognized that behavior affects racial attitudes, though more slowly. Furthermore, a belief in racial inferiority or an emotional revulsion against accepting one of a different race as an equal does not necessarily result in discriminatory action. That may be held in check by a whole range of countervailing forces—by self-interest or a common goal, by institutions such as law with courts that enforce the law, by perception of discrimination as unwarranted because it conflicts with other norms of societal behavior. And the experience gained by foregoing discrimination can result in changed views and changed emotional responses.[31] Even when it does not, nondiscriminatory practices may continue. Logically, equality may be indivisible; in practice, it has never been a seamless web.

Failure to enforce black civil and political rights in the South is often attributed to a lack of will on the part of Republican leaders and their constituencies due to their racial views. The explanation may not be susceptible of definite disproof, but it has not been proven and probably cannot be. Many factors entered into the abandonment of the cause of the black man in the South, and Republicans gave up neither quickly or easily. The voting record of regular Republicans in Congress through 1891 remained remarkably consistent and cohesive behind efforts to strengthen federal enforcement of Reconstruction legislation. Democratic party obstruction was equally consistent and created a major roadblock. Republicans enacted a drastic enforcement law in 1870 and another in 1871. For most of the twenty years after the elections of 1870 they did not have the power in Congress to pass additional legislation supportive of black rights but they kept the issue alive. It is true that as early as 1872 some Republicans, notably those who joined the Liberal

Republican movement, broke with the policy of national action in support of black rights. But race prejudice was neither a conscious nor a major determinant of their new attitude toward federal intervention in the South. Indeed, the Liberal Republican platform of 1872 tried to reconcile a policy of national retreat with loyalty to the Reconstruction amendments. When Republicans regained control of both houses of Congress in 1890–1891 by only a narrow margin, they passed in the House an enforcement bill to protect black voters but narrowly lost it in the Senate by the perfidy of a few who broke ranks to gain support for silver legislation.[32] On the local front in the northern states, in keeping with party tradition, the Republican record on black rights remained better than that of their opponents.

In 1877 when President Hayes withdrew federal troops and acquiesced to "home rule" for the South, racism was not the key to presidential decision. No critical causal connection has been established between the "betrayal" and race attitudes.[33] There is no doubt but that Hayes' action was related to a general lessening of northern support for intervention in the South. The erosion had been going on for several years, and for that there were a number of reasons. The will to continue the battle was undermined by growing doubt of the wisdom of immediate universal black enfranchisement, increasingly seen as the source of corruption. There was revulsion against the turmoil of disputed elections and the force used to settle them. Many Republicans were discouraged as state after state came under "Redeemer" control, or distracted by the pressure of problems closer at home. There was a general desire in the North for the peace and national reconciliation that Grant had invoked but could not attain as president. Whatever part race prejudice played in weakening Republican support for continuing military intervention, its role was peripheral rather than central.

In the face of persistent and successful resistance by the white South, President Hayes found a fragile hope. The southern conservative leadership that had returned to power appeared to be pledging its honor that "home rule" would protect black southerners in their civil and political rights. Republicans had not succeeded in forcing the South to accept blacks as equal citizens. Perhaps more could be secured by entrusting their rights to the section's own leaders. The agreement of 1877 has been characterized by C. Vann Woodward as a "honeyfugling" of the North. When Hayes recognized the deception, he tried to change course with means short of military force. They proved ineffectual.[34]

Race prejudice played a larger role in the obstructionist tactics of northern

Democrats than in weakening the will of Republicans. During and after the Civil War, appeal to the race prejudice of their constituencies was a standard procedure in election battles. Yet when it failed to yield decisive political profit, northern Democratic leaders changed tactics. By the mid-1870s they had retreated from public avowals to overturn Reconstruction. By the 1880s in northern states they were wooing black voters by helping to enact local civil rights laws and by giving blacks recognition in patronage appointments. Prejudice had bowed to political advantage. Within little more than a decade, an equal right to the ballot was accepted and institutionalized in both northern parties. Continuing support by northern Democrats in Congress for their southern colleagues in opposing federal enforcement of the right to vote rested upon party advantage in maintaining solidarity with the Democratic South.[35]

Racism linked to southern resistance was more politically formidable. As events developed after Congress repudiated Johnsonian Reconstruction and prescribed its own plan, the appeal to white prejudice was critically important. It enabled Democrats to recapture political ascendancy and to cripple the projected operational arm of congressional policy, the Republican party in the South, as an effective contestant for political power. To attain victory the "Redeemers" mobilized a racism whose many faces were evident about them—conviction that white superiority and black incapacity were nature's law, revulsion against accepting the black man on an equal basis in any capacity as both distasteful and insulting, umbrage at being confronted with violations of the race etiquette to which whites had been conditioned by slavery. Racial hostility was used to organize and to justify terror, intimidation, and fraud, particularly in election contests but also in more mundane activities when freedom led blacks beyond "their place."

Even so, racism alone does not explain southern intransigence. It was strongly reinforced by other factors—by the psychological need of white southerners to avoid "dishonor" in defeat, by fears of economic chaos and race warfare, by shock and outrage at the congressional peace terms of 1867, by a perception of Republican demand for black civil and political equality as punitive. Increased taxation at a time of economic stress helped inflame emotions. The result was resistance, sometimes open and sometimes covert, often violent but also subtle. A guerrilla warfare outmaneuvered and overwhelmed Republican forces in the South and gave way before federal military force only to regroup and strike again.[36] It was a resistance strengthened by a sense of right in safeguarding a social order in which blacks were subordinate to whites. If racism was a critical element in the failure to establish securely black civil and political rights, it was not because racial prejudice permeated both sections, both parties, and all classes. It was because prejudice in the South was deeply rooted, intrinsic to the social and economic structure, and effectively mobilized for political combat. To induce a change in southern white racial behavior to the extent of accepting the black man as an equal in the courts and at the ballot box and as a free laborer entitled to choose, to move about, to better his condition—that task was not in theory beyond the power of Congress and president but it was an uncertain undertaking that would have tested the political skill of any party and president. Fortuitous circumstances, both political and economic, may well have precluded success. Lincoln's assassination changed the direction of presidential policy, and the downward slide of the postbellum cotton economy of the South reinforced white resistance to change.

A critical question needs to be addressed. Could a greater use of force have brought white southerners to accept civil and political rights for blacks? Neither history nor theory can answer this question with certainty. A number of historians have implied that direct coercion could have effected a fundamental change, that Reconstruction was the nation's great missed opportunity. Few would go so far as Eugene Genovese, who has written that there was no prospect of a better future for blacks unless several thousand leaders of the Lost Cause had been summarily killed. Michael Perman would have had the political and economic power of the southern elite eliminated by means less Draconian and more nearly representative of recent historiographic opinion. He suggests an immediate "edict of the conqueror" enforced by occupying troops to exclude the elite from political power, give suffrage to blacks, confiscate plantations, and divide their lands among the freedmen. Far too good an historian to argue that such an edict had been a practical postwar possibility, he nonetheless believes that had it been possible, it would have worked. William Gillette has taken a more historically realistic approach to the problem. Recognizing that Republicans were not in a position to enforce their Reconstruction program until 1869 when they obtained control of the presidency as well as of Congress, he examines closely the southern record of the Grant years. While he comes to the conclusion that Republicans might have succeeded, or at least achieved a great deal, his analysis of the requirements for success is not reassuring. The skill he sees lacking but needed by Grant might have overtaxed even a Lincoln. According to Gillette, Grant should have been cautious where he was bold, bold where he was timid. He had to be both master politician and resolute soldier. The situation required his effective direction of an expert bureaucracy and an overwhelming military muscle, neither of which was at his disposal. Grant should have overpowered militarily southern white resistance yet come to terms with the fact that "in the long run coercion could not replace a sanctioned consensus." Given the nation's traditional commitment to civilian control and majority rule, "the use of force was self-defeating."[37]

Force *and* consent, how to achieve the one by use of the other, posed a dilemma that by the 1870s strained the bounds of the possible. The outcome would have been only a little less problematic had Reconstruction been formulated in early 1865 and backed by force, that is, by force alone. Particularly vulnerable is the assumption that by eliminating the power of the landed aristocracy, resistance would have been broken and a new order of equal rights for blacks securely established. There would still have remained for the South as a whole a white majority with prejudices and interests inimical to the advancement of blacks. A stunned acceptance in the despondency of defeat of such peace terms as Perman has outlined would have been no guarantee of their permanent observance by white southerners. Here theory is of some help to speculation. It lends support to Gillette's perception of the need to reconcile the seemingly irreconcilable. Historians have tended to approach the concepts of coercion/consent, or conflict/consensus, as coercion vs. consent or conflict vs. consensus, and not without precedent in political and sociological thought. There exist, however, theoretical analyses that see coercion and consensus as compatible, even complementary. They suggest that the problem, both in theory and practice, is one of interrelationship. Even theorists identified with the view that conflict and coercion are essential to the creation of a new and better social order seldom argue that force alone is sufficient to bring about the change desired. Nor do they overlook the danger that coercion can be self-defeating. The more consensus oriented see force as unable to operate alone over any length of time. The concern to identify "authority," to examine the sources of its "legitimacy," to distinguish authority from "power," to establish the noncoercive forms of power and the nonphysical forms of coercion—these continuing efforts indicate the importance attached to means other than direct force in effecting and maintaining social change. And there is a long tradition of political thought that admonishes caution in trying to force change contrary to traditional convictions lest it provoke deep and bitter reaction.[38] From an approach either through theory or history, it would seem reasonable to conclude that a policy of force *plus* some form and degree of consent—even if the consent, to borrow from P. H. Partridge, were only "a patchwork of divergent and loosely adjusted values, norms, and objectives"—would have had a better chance of success in reordering the South than force alone. Lincoln was capable of a "patchwork" design in implementing policy.

Certainly by the mid-1870s the use of coercion had intensified a deep and bitter reaction. Instead of passive resignation, coercion led to a "negative consensus" that rejected the legitimacy of national authority over the status of blacks, fed resistance, and united white southerners to an unprecedented degree. It is well to be reminded that the coercion used had been considerable. Whatever the formality of consent in the ratification of the Fourteenth Amendment, Congress had left the recalcitrant secession states no effective choice. In the initial enfranchisement of blacks, white southerners were allowed not even the formality of consenting; enfranchisement was mandated by Congress and implemented by military authority and presence. The military also intervened in the reorganization of the South's labor system and in the operation of its local courts. The presence of an occupying army preceded the interim period of military rule set up by Congress in 1867 and did not disappear with the restoration of state authority. Violent resistance to the new order was answered not only by the passage of drastic congressional legislation in 1870 and 1871 but also by the use under these laws of federal armed forces, notably in Mississippi, South Carolina, North Carolina, and Alabama. Troops helped make arrests, guarded prisoners, protected court proceedings, and maintained order at the polls. More than a thousand military arrests were made in three counties of South Carolina in 1871–1872. Federal attorneys obtained 540 criminal convictions in Mississippi in 1872–1873 and 263 in North Carolina in 1873. The district attorney for the northern and middle districts of Alabama obtained indictments of more than 350 persons from two grand juries, one in the fall of 1871 and the other in the spring of 1872. From 1870, when the first enforcement law was passed, through 1874, 3,382 cases under the acts were adjudicated in federal courts in the southern states. In addition, under Grant's direction federal troops in effect decided disputes over who rightfully held elective office in Louisiana, Arkansas, and Mississippi.[39]

The force employed in the 1870s was grossly insufficient for the task at hand. Too often local officials and courts sidestepped justice for blacks without interference. Troops stationed in the South were woefully inadequate in number to contain violent resistance wherever it erupted. Relatively few of the men arrested in South Carolina were brought to trial. In general, indictments were difficult to obtain and even in the federal courts many cases were dismissed. By the end of 1874 little vitality was left in the federal enforcement program. Southern resistance turned increasingly to intimidation and more subtle, less legally vulnerable means than the earlier violence. Democratic power in Congress deprived the executive of resources needed to enforce the laws and prevented legislative action to strengthen them.

Nonetheless, the direct coercion mobilized by the national government in the 1860s and 1870s was substantial, far greater than any similar action in support of desegregation and black voting in the 1950s and '60s. It was large enough to give strong support to the contention that a century ago the amount of force necessary to realize equal civil and political rights in the South was impossible to sustain in a nation whose democratic tradition and constitutional structure limited the use of power, exalted the rule of law, and embodied the concept of government by the consent of the governed. Neither national institutions nor public opinion could be expected to have sustained a military intervention of indefinite length and of sufficient strength to crush all local resistance. And by the mid-1870s, the issue at stake no longer appeared clear-cut, even to northern Republicans. Popular government in the South seemed to have become "nothing but a sham."[40]

Assumptions regarding the potency of national power to effect social change, largely valid for the "Second Reconstruction," may inadvertently have biased historical judgment concerning the earlier period. By the 1950s the capacity for resistance in the South, although still strong, was markedly less than in the post–Civil War decades. Race prejudice remained formidable, but in the wake of Hitler's holocaust and advances in the social sciences, psychology, and biology, prejudice could no longer command arguments of scientific or moral respectability. Despite shocking episodes of violence, white terror never reached the epidemic proportions of the 1860s and '70s. Apparently it was no longer condoned by majority white opinion in the South. Moreover, in the 1950s and '60s not Congress but the judiciary took the initiative in forcing change and remained a vital mechanism for implementing it. The aura of legitimacy created by supportive judicial decisions, lacking in the earlier period, greatly lessened the necessity for direct physical coercion. With a few exceptions, notably at Little Rock in 1957, federal enforcement of court decisions and civil rights legislation proceeded without a show of force. Nor were federal criminal prosecutions numerous. A total of only 323 criminal cases were filed by the newly established civil rights division of the Justice Department from 1958 through mid-1972, only a tenth of the number that had been brought by the attorney general's office in the first five years of the 1870s. Other methods of coercion were available, both more effective and more consonant with the traditional primacy of civil over military authority, of persuasion over force. Civil cases initiated or assisted by the Justice Department far outnumbered criminal ones, and the department was active in negotiating voluntary agreements of compliance and in community counseling. With the great increase in the functions undertaken by the federal government to meet the needs of a mature industrial society, there were at hand powerful monetary and administrative sanctions, and a bureaucracy to use them.

In contrast to the 1870s, during the "Second Reconstruction" votes and time were available to pass a whole array of acts, progressively more comprehensive in scope and more resourceful in their enforcement provisions. What made this achievement possible, according to authorities in the field, was the existence of a national consensus. Although it did not encompass majority white opinion in the South, elsewhere it found support in both major parties, quite unlike the situation in the Civil War era when consensus, on a much more limited program of black rights, existed only within the Republican party. Presidential leadership by the second President Johnson, in contrast to that of the first, was exerted to expand civil rights. In the creation of the national consensus of the 1950s blacks themselves played a key role beyond that open to them a century earlier. Their political influence in the North was considerable because of the numbers who had moved out of the South to fill northern labor needs. The distance from slavery allowed their leaders, South as well as North, to operate with formidable resources, skills, and organization and to present a case that could no longer be evaded by a show of scientific or social justification. They made inescapably visible to white America the injustices piled high during the postemancipation decades.[41]

In short, the "Second Reconstruction" is a false model from which to project in retrospect the limits of the possible a century earlier. As an analogy, however, it suggests the need for far more than direct force to attain success. Its loss of momentum by the 1970s also indicates the difficulty of sustaining a national moral purpose, even with a task recognized as unfinished. In November 1971, the United States Commission on Civil Rights wrote "that the American people have grown somewhat weary, that the national sense of injustice, which was the foundation on which the legislative victories of the 1960s were built, has dimmed." And a few years later other informed analysts agreed. They attributed the fuel for the engine of change during the two previous decades in part to the deceptive clarity of the problems seen through the lens of the New Frontier and the Great Society. There had been a naive public faith that new programs of government intervention would quickly bear fruit. Results failed to meet expectations. Advance slowed as injustices were reduced to ones less shockingly visible, as moral issues became clouded by the complexity of problems, as economic conditions turned less favorable, and as conflicts of interest intensified. Analysts concluded that the future was not sanguine. The circumstances of the 1960s had been unusually conducive to change and were not apt to be duplicated.[42]

If the contention is correct that unlike the situation during the "Second Reconstruction," the maximum level of federal force sustainable in the 1870s (conceivably *any* amount of direct coercion) could not have broken southern white resistance, there still remains a space open for the possibility of a happier outcome of Reconstruction in the nineteenth century had Lincoln lived to extend the Louisiana policy of "consent *and force.*" Unlike Congress, or Grant as president, Lincoln was usually adept at persuasion and skillful in using those sanctions available to him. He had demonstrated his ability to wield the power of patronage and of military appointment. He could have been expected to exercise with equal skill the extraordinary power he held by virtue of office and of legislation to grant pardons to those subject to penalty under the Confiscation Act of 1862. In the process of reconstructing state governments Lincoln could have been counted on to safeguard presidential authority from the kind of erosion that occurred under his successor. Although at war's end he might have remained for some time "the Confederates' chief villain,"[43] and never acquired the popularity Andrew Johnson established in the South, Lincoln could scarcely have become for white southerners, as did "Radical" Republicans, the symbol of the alien, the fanatic, the self-righteous, and the vindictive. And Lincoln would have enjoyed the advantage of timing lost to Republicans by the 1870s.

Lincoln's presidential style, at odds with that forthrightness that stands high in twentieth-century criteria for presidential leadership, was not inappropriate to the situation he faced. The manner in which he unveiled the crucial, controversial element of his Reconstruction policy—some measure of suffrage for blacks—was designed to crystallize support and minimize opposition. At the time only the most minimal suffrage proposal could command an intraparty consensus; this was all that he asked, actually less than his supporters had sought in Louisiana. Yet he managed to open the door to future enfranchisement for more blacks than the relatively few, Union soldiers and the "very intelligent," whose qualifications he commended. In phrasing that avoided a definite formulation of either means or goal he suggested the desirability of a fuller franchise, one that would meet what "the colored man" "desires." In the same address he stated that "the sole object of the government" was to get the secession states back into "their proper practical relation with the Union" and asked that "all join in doing the acts necessary" to restore them. He refrained from defining the "acts necessary." To counter criticism that he had set up the reconstructed state government, Lincoln minimized his role in Louisiana, but he did not disavow his authority as commander in chief to shape the Reconstruction process.[44] By virtue of that power he had just sent General Banks back to New Orleans with military authority to perform an essentially civil mission—to promote the kind of Unionist government and racial policy the administration desired.

Although his statements could be otherwise interpreted, Lincoln's purpose, like that of his party, went beyond the readmission of the secession states. In early 1865 he was in an excellent position to implement a larger purpose by combining a minimum of direct force with a maximum use of other means of asserting the power and influence of the presidency. Lincoln's election victory the previous November had greatly strengthened his hand with Congress and with the northern public. Final military victory could only have increased the public esteem and congressional respect he had won. In the summer and fall that followed, Lincoln would have found additional support in a mounting sense of indignation in the North as reports from the South confirmed warnings that the freedom of blacks would be in peril if left in the hands of southern whites. A widespread perception of injustice can be a powerful political force, as indeed it became in 1866.[45]

It would have been uncharacteristic of Lincoln not to have recognized the opportunity. In his pragmatic fashion, advancing step by step as events permitted, with caution but when necessary with great boldness, it is just possible that Lincoln might have succeeded in making a policy of basic citizenship rights for blacks "acceptable to those who must support it, tolerable to those who must put up with it."[46] The challenge to presidential leadership was formidable. If any man could have met the challenge, that man was Lincoln.

Had Lincoln in the course of a second term succeeded in obtaining a far broader consent from the white South to terms that would satisfy northern Republican opinion than did Congress in 1867–1869, ultimate victory in the battle over the ex-slave's status as free man would not necessarily have followed. There would still have been the need to build institutions that could safeguard and expand what had been won—laws that the courts would uphold, an economy offering escape from poverty and dependency, a Union-Republican party in the South recognized by its opponents as a legitimate contestant for political power. The opportunities open to Lincoln for institutionalizing gains made toward equal citizenship irrespective of color were limited.

A fatal weakness of Reconstruction, constitutional historians have argued, arose from the constitutional conservatism of Republican lawmakers, particularly their deference to the traditional federal structure embodied in the Constitution. This led them to preserve the primacy of state responsibility for the rights of citizens, thereby denying to the national government effective power to protect the rights of blacks. It has been contended that Reconstruction required "a major constitutional upheaval," that it "could have been effected only by a revolutionary destruction of the states and the substitution of a unitary constitutional system."[47] Part of the argument is unassailable. The new scholarship has demolished the old stereotype of Republican leaders as constitutional revolutionaries. They had, indeed, been waging a war for Constitution as well as for nation with every intent of maintaining both. And the concern of Republicans for state and local government was no superficial adulation of the Constitution; it was deeply rooted in their commitment to self-government. Yet unlike Democrats who denounced as unconstitutional any amendment to the Constitution that enlarged federal authority at the expense of the states, Republicans did not uphold states'-rights federalism without qualification. They believed that they had found a way to protect freedmen in their new citizenship status by modifying, rather than destroying, the traditional federal structure.

What is questionable in the case against "respect for federalism" as fatally compromising Reconstruction is the assumption that the states'-rights federalist approach to the problem made a solution impossible. Not all scholars would agree. Some believe that the Reconstruction amendments needed only to have been more carefully framed. Others hold that as written they were adequate to the task. The Supreme Court, of course, seemed to disagree, overturning much of the legislation Congress passed under the amendments. Beginning with the Slaughterhouse decision of 1873, which did not directly affect blacks but carried ominous implications for them, a Republican Court handed down a series of constrictive decisions described in retrospect as "vacuous" and as "a major triumph for the South." Concern to preserve the functions of the states strongly influenced those decisions. Some authorities hold that without destroying federalism the Court could have devised a workable new division of authority between state and nation that would have enabled the latter to protect the rights of blacks against violation by either states or individuals. The Court did not foreclose all avenues of congressional action to protect black rights. However, by 1875 when it rendered the first adverse decision directly relating to the national enforcement effort, further legislation to meet the Court's criteria of adequacy was politically impossible because of the strength in Congress of the Democratic political opposition.[48]

The Supreme Court seemed to have denied to congressional Reconstruction much needed legitimacy and legal sanctions. Without them, it is questionable that the Reconstruction effort could have been successfully defended during the postemancipation decades. The Court's narrow interpretation of which civil rights pertained to national as distinct from state citizenship added to the difficulties the Court had raised for the exercise of power to protect rights recognized as subject to the nation's authority. The decisions presented monumental obstacles to the enforcement of black rights. Better drafted amendments, laws, and indictments, more resourceful judicial reasoning, or less concern in the early decisions for technicalities might have avoided or remedied them.[49] Lincoln's presence was unlikely to have increased those possibilities directly. Yet had he been president in the immediate post-Appomattox period he might have succeeded in dissipating southern resistance, in unifying Republicans on the preconditions for restoration, and in inducing reconstructed state governments to accept those conditions—a tall order. The resulting climate of opinion could have led the Court to play a positive role in the nineteenth-century Reconstruction effort. A possibility, but a very tenuous possibility.

Similarly circumscribed was any potential role for Lincoln in helping shape economic developments to assure freedmen an escape from poverty and dependence. No explanation for the tragic outcome of the postwar decades for black America has been more generally accepted in modern scholarship than that Reconstruction failed because the national government did not provide land for the freedman. The thesis has been sharply challenged, and the challenge has not been met. The work of historians and economists in exploring afresh the roots of poverty, particularly of black poverty, in the postbellum South afford some relevant perspectives. Between

1974 and 1979 six book-length studies appeared with significant bearing on the problem of black poverty, and others were in progress; conference papers and published articles also reflected the vigor of scholarly interest in the question.[50]

No consensus has developed either as explanation for the continuing dependence and poverty of southern blacks or as an analysis of the potential economic effect of land distribution. However, four of five econometricians who addressed the latter question concluded that grants of land, while desirable and beneficial, would not have solved the predicament of the freedmen and their children. Robert Higgs has written that "historians have no doubt exaggerated the economic impact of such a grant." Gavin Wright holds that "the tenancy systems of the South cannot be assigned primary blame for Southern poverty," that a more equitable distribution of land "would not have produced dramatic improvements in living standards" or "generated sustained progress." In their book, *One Kind of Freedom*, Roger Ransom and Richard Sutch appear to accept what Heman Belz has characterized as the "new orthodoxy" of the historians, but they dramatically qualified that position in a subsequent paper. They argued that confiscation and redistribution would have resulted in little improvement in the postbellum situation, which they characterize as one of economic stagnation and exploitation, unless accompanied by federally funded compensation for landowners thereby providing liquid capital for reinvigorating agriculture and possibly developing manufactures.[51] This retrospective prescription is restrained as compared to the requirements outlined by twentieth-century experts who seek land distribution as an avenue out of rural poverty. They see successful land reform as requiring supplementary government programs providing credit, seed and fertilizer distribution, marketing facilities, rural and feeder transportation, pricing mechanisms affecting both what the farmer buys and what he sells, technical research, and agricultural education.[52]

More than a land program was needed to insure the freedman's economic future. Although areas of land with high fertility prospered, it seems doubtful that income from cotton between the close of the war and the turn of the century, even if equitably distributed, could have sustained much beyond a marginal level of existence for those who worked the cotton fields whether as wage earner, cropper, tenant, or small owner. And the lower South because of its soils and climate, as Julius Rubin has convincingly shown, had no viable alternative to cotton as a commercial crop until the scientific and technological advances of the twentieth century.[53] Nor could nonmarket subsistence farming offer much by way of material reward. The "more" that was needed can be envisaged in retrospect, and was glimpsed by contemporaries, but it is not clear how it could have been achieved. Gavin Wright has concluded that the postbellum South "required either a massive migration away from the region or a massive Southern industrial revolution." Both in the North and the South there was enthusiasm for promoting southern industry, but only the future could reveal how elusive would be that "New South" of ever-renewed expectations. Despite scholarship, new and old, there is no certain explanation of why the South failed to catch up with the North. If historians and economists should agree upon a diagnosis, it is unlikely that they will uncover a remedy that could have been recognized and implemented a century ago. The heritage of slavery most certainly will be part of the diagnosis. It left behind an underdeveloped, overwhelmingly rural economy tied to the world market and bereft of adequate foundations for rapid economic growth. Recovery and growth had to be attempted in a period of initial crop disasters, of disadvantage for primary products in terms of world trade, and by the mid-1870s of prolonged and recurrent economic crises.[54] There were high hopes for southern industrialization in the 1880s, but the effort substantially failed. With opportunity drastically limited in the South and industry expanding in the North, there was yet no great out-migration of blacks until the twentieth century. The reasons for this also are not altogether clear. Neither the restraints placed on southern agricultural labor by law and custom nor the discrimination blacks faced in the North is sufficient explanation. The ways in which European immigrants blocked black advance deserve further study, as does the attitude of blacks themselves both toward leaving the South and toward the unskilled, menial labor that alone might have afforded them large-scale entry into the northern labor market.[55]

Lincoln was a man of his age. The concepts and perceptions then dominant, although not unreasonable on the basis of past experience, were inadequate to meet the challenge of transforming the South. Postwar expectations were buoyant. King Cotton was expected to regain his throne with beneficent results for all. Freed from the incubus of slavery, the South would be reshaped after the image of the bustling North, with large landholdings disintegrated by natural forces, village and schoolhouse replacing plantation quarters, internal improvements and local industry transforming the economy. The former slave would share the bright future through diligence and thrift, and the forces of the marketplace.[56] There were, of course, dissenters, both radicals like George W. Julian and Thaddeus Stevens who would confiscate the great estates and conservatives such as those cotton manufacturers, by no means all, who would perpetuate the plantation in some form.[57] Neither had sufficient influence at war's end to shape national policy. Republican leaders who did make postwar policy would have reached beyond prevailing concepts of self-help, the law of supply and demand, and the danger of "class legislation" to enact a modest land program had not President Johnson vetoed it with an appeal to all the economic verities of the day.[58]

In the interest of the emancipated, Lincoln could have been expected to approve and encourage such deviations from the doctrinaire. And it would have been completely out of character for Lincoln to have exercised his power of pardon, as did President Johnson, with ruthless disregard for the former slave's interest and justifiable expectations. Indeed, there are intimations that Lincoln considered using that power to obtain from former masters grants of land for former slaves.[59] Whatever support the national government might have given to the freedman's quest for land would have been a psychological boon, more symbol than substance of equal citizenship and independence, but not without some economic advantage. A land program more effective than the southern homestead act was a real possibility, lost due to President Johnson's opposition. With Lincoln, a Whiggish heritage, as well as humanity and a sense of responsibility for the emancipated, reinforced a pragmatic approach to the relationship between government and the future of the freedmen. Nor was he inhibited by the anxiety felt by many, including Thaddeus Stevens, over the unprecedented debt incurred in fighting the war. In early 1865 he calmly contemplated adding to the war's cost by indemnifying southerners for property seized and not restored.[60] Whatever sums Congress might have appropriated to finance land purchase for freedmen could only have helped alleviate the South's postwar paucity of capital and credit. Its economic recovery would also have benefited from the lesser turbulence of the immediate postwar years had there been no war between president and Congress. Limited gains would have been possible and probable, but there existed neither the power nor the perception necessary to forestall the poverty that engulfed so many southerners, black and white, during the last decades of the nineteenth century.

There were limits to the possible. Yet the dismal outcome for southern blacks as the nation entered the twentieth century need not have been as unrelieved as it was in fact. More than a land program, the civil and political rights Republicans established in law, had they been secured in practice, could have mitigated the discrimination that worsened their condition and constricted whatever opportunities might otherwise have existed for escape from poverty. Moreover, the extraordinary effort black men made to vote— and to vote independently in the face of white cajolery, intimidation, and economic pressure—strongly suggests that for the emancipated to cast a ballot was to affirm the reality of freedom and the dignity of black manhood.[61]

The priority Republicans gave to civil and political rights in their fight to establish a meaningful new status for ex-slaves has been too readily discounted by historians. Small landholdings could not have protected blacks from intimidation, or even from many forms of economic coercion. They would not have brought economic power. In the face of overwhelming white opposition, they could not have safeguarded the new equality of civil and political status. Where blacks voted freely, on the other hand, there was always the potential for sharing political power and using it as a means to protect and advance their interests. There is considerable evidence that this did happen. Local officials elected by black votes during the years of Republican control upheld blacks against planters, state legislators repealed Black Codes, shifted the burden of taxation from the poor, granted agricultural laborers a first lien on crops, increased expenditures for education. Eric Foner has concluded that at least in some areas Republican Reconstruction resulted in subtle but significant changes that protected black labor and prevented planters from using the state to bolster their position. Harold D. Woodman's study of state laws affecting agriculture confirms the generalization that a legislative priority of the Redeemer governments was passage of measures to give landowners greater control over the labor force. By the end of the century legal bonds had been so tightened that as prosperity returned to cotton culture neither cropper nor renter but only their employer was in a position to profit. In a study of rural Edgefield County, South Carolina, Vernon Burton has found that black voting made possible real gains in economic position and social status between 1867 and 1877. Howard Rabinowitz's examination of the urban South discloses that Republican city governments brought blacks a greater share of elected and appointed offices, more jobs in construction work, in fire and police departments.[62] And beyond immediate gains, black votes meant support for educational facilities through which blacks could acquire the literacy and skills essential for advancement.

Security for black civil and political rights required acceptance by white southerners. An acquiescence induced by a judicious combination of force and consent needed for its perpetuation reinforcement by self-interest. The most effective vehicle of self-interest would have been a Union-Republican party able to command substantial continuing support from native whites. The Republican party that gained temporary dominance through the congressional legislation of 1867 enfranchising blacks failed to meet the test of substantial white support. Despite a strong white following in a few states, its scalawag component from the start was too limited to offset the opposition's attack on it as the party of the black man and the Yankee. And white participation diminished as appeals to race prejudice and sectional animosity intensified.

The potential for a major second party among southern whites existed in the aftermath of Confederate defeat. The Democratic party was in disarray, discredited for having led the South out of the Union and having lost the war. Old Whig loyalties subsumed by the slavery issue had nonetheless endured; southern unionism had survived in varying degrees from wartime adherence to the Union to reluctant support of the Confederacy. Opposition to Jefferson Davis' leadership and willingness to accept northern peace terms had grown as the hope for southern victory diminished. Such sources of Democratic opposition overlapped with the potential for ready recruits to Union-Republicanism from urban dwellers, from men whose origins had been abroad or in the North, from those whose class or intrasectional interests created hostility to the dominant planter leadership of the Democracy.[63] A "New South" of enterprise and industry presented an attractive vision to many a native son. And there were always those who looked to the loaves and the fishes dispensed from Washington.

Had party recruitment and organization, with full presidential support, begun at the end of hostilities and escaped the period of confusion and bitterness that thinned the ranks of the willing during the conflict between Johnson and Congress, the result could have been promising.[64] Greater white support and the accession of black voters by increments might have eased racial tension and lessened deadly factionalism within the party. Lincoln's political skill and Whig background would certainly have served party-building well, as would the perception of presidential policy as one of moderation and reconciliation. The extent to which southern whites did in fact support the Republican party after 1867 despite its image as Radical, alien, and black dominated, an image that stigmatized and often ostracized them, suggests the potency of a common goal, or a common enmity, in bridging the chasm between the races.

Even under the guidance of a Lincoln, the building of a permanent biracial major party in the South was by no means assured. A broad enduring coalition of disparate elements would face the necessity of reconciling sharply divergent economic interests. Agricultural workers sought maximum autonomy, more than bare necessities, and an opportunity for land ownership while planter-merchants strove to control labor and maximize profit. The burden of increased taxation to meet essential but unaccustomed social services, particularly for blacks, meant an inescapable clash of class and racial interests.[65] Concessions by the more privileged were especially difficult in a South of limited available resources and credit, impoverished by war and enmeshed in inflated costs, crop disasters, and falling cotton prices. By the mid-1870s a nationwide depression intensified regional problems. Efforts to promote a more varied and vigorous economy by state favor, credit, and appropriation became a political liability as the primary effect appeared to be the proliferation of civic corruption and entrepreneurial plunder.

Outside the South a vigorous Republican party and two-party system managed to endure despite the clash of intraparty economic interests. A similar development in the South faced the additional and more intractable conflict inherent in the new black-white relationship. Within the Republican party that took shape after 1867, factionalism often cut between blacks and carpetbaggers, on the one hand, and scalawags on the other; but there was also a considerable amount of accommodation, not all of it from blacks. A study of the voting record of eighty-seven Republicans, fifty-two of them native whites, who served in the North Carolina House of Representatives in the 1868 to 1870 session shows scalawags trailing carpetbaggers and blacks in voting on issues of Negro rights and support for public schools, yet compiling a positive overall record, a score of 61.2 and 55.9 respectively. On the few desegregation questions that came to a roll call, however, only a small minority of native whites voted favorably. In Mississippi when the black-carpetbagger faction gained control, they quietly ignored the platform calling for school integration even though black legislators were sufficiently numerous and powerful to have pressed the issue. Black officeholding was a similar matter where fair treatment held danger, and black leaders often showed restraint. Such issues were explosive. They not only threatened the unity of the party but undermined its ability to attract white votes or minimize opposition demagoguery and violence.[66] A Lincolnian approach to building an interracial party would have diminished the racial hazard, but could hardly have eliminated it.

The years of political Reconstruction, to borrow an apt phrase from Thomas B. Alexander's study of Tennessee, offered no "narrowly missed opportunities to leap a century forward in reform."[67] Not even a Lincoln could have wrought such a miracle. To have secured something less, yet something substantially more than blacks had gained by the end of the nineteenth century, did not lie beyond the limits of the possible given a president who at war's end would have joined party in an effort to realize "as nearly as we can" the fullness of freedom for blacks.

Possible is not probable. To the major obstacles must be added the hazards disclosed by the Louisiana story. Lincoln's Louisiana policy had been compromised by Banks' blunders of execution and attacked by Durant and fellow Radicals in part because they distrusted Lincoln's intent. The effective implementation of a president's policy by his surrogates is a problem to plague any administration. Distrust by those otherwise allied in a common goal pertained more distinctively to the man and his style of leadership. Yet Radical distrust of Lincoln may also have reflected dilemmas inherent in presidential leadership—the need for candor and for persuasion, for vision and for practicality, for courage and for flexibility, for heeding while leading a national consensus.[68] Obscured by his characteristic self-effacement, after his own fashion Lincoln as president was both lion and fox. Not all Radicals misjudged him. In 1864 and early 1865, William Lloyd Garrison came to the defense of Lincoln and his Louisiana policy. At a stormy meeting of the Massachusetts Anti-slavery Society in January 1865 with Banks and the president under harsh attack and black suffrage a central issue, "Mr. Garrison expressed his entire confidence in the integrity of Mr. Lincoln." About two weeks later, and after the passage of the Thirteenth Amendment, Garrison had occasion to write Lincoln.[69] His letter included a like expression of trust: "As an instrument in his hands, you have done a mighty work for the freedom of millions who have so long pined in bondage in our land—nay, for the freedom of all mankind. I have the utmost faith in the benevolence of your heart, the purity of your motives, and the integrity of your spirit. This I do not hesitate to avow at all times. I am sure you will consent to no compromise that will leave a slave in his fetters."

PART FOUR

The Second Reconstruction and the Changing Historiography of the South

CHAPTER ELEVEN

Ella Lonn

*Pioneer Woman Historian
of Civil War and Reconstruction*

By the time of its tenth birthday, the Southern Historical Association, an organization widely perceived as an embodiment of sectional self-consciousness and pride, had chosen to bestow its highest honor upon a woman, a northerner, and a Republican. Ella Lonn (1878–1962) made for herself a recognized, respected place in the historical profession during her twenty-seven years as a member of the Department of History of Goucher College (1918–1945). In the fall of 1944 when I arrived there Ella Lonn was in the city, on leave of absence, guarded by an older sister, Emma, from any distraction that might break her concentration upon research and writing. I was told that not even the president of the college could get through to her directly by telephone! On one occasion she was reputed to have been overlooked by the guard and locked up for the night in the Library of Congress. Her characteristic intensity is illustrated by another story. Late one afternoon a colleague met her hurrying along Charles Street. Miss Lonn stopped just long enough to say that she had suddenly realized she had to have some food and was headed for a cafeteria. She had been too busy to think of eating lunch—or breakfast!

Fellow faculty members recall her as absorbed in research, so hardworking as to evoke awe, unrelentingly serious, and driven by a conviction of the immeasurable importance of history. I should like to sketch for you something of her life before she arrived at Goucher, but there is time only to say that she was born in 1878 at LaPorte in the northwestern corner of Indiana, the daughter of a Swedish immigrant who had arrived there on the eve of the Civil War, in his early twenties with the trade of tanner. He reached "the plane of affluence" through "industry, determination and ambition," to quote the city historian.[1] Like her father, Ella was a civic-minded Republican possessed of "industry, determination, and ambition."

Her appointment to the Goucher faculty in 1918 came through a teachers' agency in Chicago. She was not actively seeking another academic position, according to the agent's letter, but "I incline to think you could get her as there is not much chance for a woman at Grinnell." Ella Lonn was more than pleased to receive an appointment in the Department of History at Goucher (she had been reduced at Grinnell to teaching German only), but she was not happy with the status offered her—an instructorship with an annual salary of $1,400. She was a woman of forty, with more than eleven years of teaching experience, five at the college level and with the rank of assistant professor. Her first book, *Reconstruction in Louisiana after 1868*, had been published that spring by C. P. Putnam's Sons. She had spent two post-doctoral years in England, Germany, and France doing research and studying at the University of Berlin and at the Sorbonne (1912–1914).

She was described in 1918 by those who wrote Goucher's president in her behalf as "an able public speaker. While not commanding in appearance, her subject matter and the way she presents it, always win and hold the attention of her audience," "a real scholar," "brim full of energy, an untiring worker."[2]

Ella Lonn's professional reputation rests upon six books: *Reconstruction in Louisiana; Desertion during the Civil War,* 1928; *Salt as a Factor in the Confederacy,* 1933; *Foreigners in the Confederacy,* 1940; *The Colonial Agents of the Southern Colonies,* 1945; and *Foreigners in the Union Army and Navy,* 1951, written six years after her retirement, when she was approaching seventy-three. Although we tend to identify her with Reconstruction history and the "Dunning School," and her Louisiana study shares the latter's virtues and limitations, note that four of the six volumes deal with the Civil War—though not with its battles except incidentally—and that a fifth is a study in colonial and British history. After extending her Ph.D. dissertation for publication, she never returned to Reconstruction as a focus for research. In addition to her books, Ella Lonn published a few articles, many reviews, and thirty-four sketches in the *Dictionary of American Biography.*

The qualities that scholars found most notable in her books were thoroughness and fairness. These characteristics can be captured in the phrases of reviewers: "so fair minded and careful a scholar"; "an extensive and careful search. . . . Dr. Lonn has made another monograph on this subject unnecessary"; "tirelessness of research and thoroughness of scholarship. Nothing short of amazing . . ."; "a definitive work. . . . Sound conclusions are based on facts stated and interpreted without bias."³ "Exhaustive" and "meticulous" were other adjectives used. Perhaps the most convincing evidence of the quality of her scholarship is the fact that every one of her six volumes, including the *Colonial Agents,* has been republished and is now in print. The praise of reviewers, with its concentration on her industry and impartiality, might suggest that her work was of high competence but pedestrian and unimaginative. On the contrary, she showed marked originality in the choice of topics and had a keen eye for the colorful and the specific although she kept it subordinated to her concept of writing history as a "sober treatise."⁴

Ella Lonn's choice as president of the Southern Historical Association was a recognition of her scholarship. Her sex was irrelevant, it played no role either for or against her. The male leaders of the SHA accepted and valued her, in the words of Thomas D. Clark, as "a studious, objective, no nonsense scholar." In those of E. Merton Coulter, "She was not a 'twice-told-tale' historian; she 'plowed virgin ground.'"⁵ Although she was not one of the three women among the eighteen "founding fathers," she participated importantly in the opening session of the very first annual meeting in 1935.⁶ Subsequently she served on most of the major committees of the association.

Leaders of the SHA who knew her remember Ella Lonn as gentle in nature, modest, somewhat retiring, feminine but not feminist, with "no cause to promote such as woman's rights."⁷ Like the picture I carried away from Goucher in the mid-1940s, their portrait is inadvertently misleading. During her years in Baltimore Ella Lonn was not retiring nor did she shun causes. Her public lectures made her well known. Some years she gave as many as forty, for special ceremonies at the local high schools, for the Goucher alumnae, the Baltimore College Club, women's clubs, men's clubs, local teachers associations, a state convention of nurses, the Maryland Committee for Representative Government, the League of Women Voters, the International League of Peace and Freedom, the League of Nations Association (for which she also directed a speakers' bureau), plus political lectures, each election "presented without partisan bias." In subject, her addresses and civic activity were far-ranging, from a twenty-eight page pamphlet on the need for conserving from pollution the products of Chesapeake Bay to an analysis of the Kellogg Peace Pact. She continued to be active in local public and political affairs even after her retirement. At the time of her death, six years after leaving Baltimore for Florida, the Baltimore *Sun* remembered her with a lengthy account noting stands she had taken publicly from 1919 through the 1950s.[8] The label "a conservative in politics," I suspect, was a more adequate description of her later than of her early involvement in public affairs.

Unlike many college professors of her day who attained recognition, Ella maintained an active continuing contact with secondary teachers in order to encourage high standards in the high schools. Her interest in civic affairs resulted in a 242-page book published in 1921 by the League of Women Voters on *The Government of Maryland*. Its first chapter was entitled "Woman's Share in Politics." Another of her concerns was "Americanization." Her point of view was that "Americanization" should first of all involve the native born in learning about "our immigrant peoples. . . . We have been brought reluctantly to admit what the immigrants from Northern and Western Europe have added. . . . But we seem averse to admit that it is the spade of the Italian and of the Pole which has built most of our railroads in the West, that it is the patient labor of the Slav before our blazing furnaces and in our mines which has so rapidly developed our natural resources."[9]

As a professional, Ella Lonn was an active member of the AHA and the AAUP, but her outstanding contribution in the 1920s was to the American Association of University Women. She was a keynote speaker at the annual conference in 1923, a delegate to the International Federation of University Women in Norway in 1924, and from 1925 to 1929 (1924–1928?) chairman of the standing Committee on Recognition, a critically important and arduous responsibility that she once termed "truly a labor of love." At that time the AAUP had appointed a Committee W, composed of seven women and four men, on the Status of Women in College and University Faculties, which made a preliminary report in 1921 but delayed another until three years later. Meanwhile in her 1923 address Ella Lonn succinctly summarized their preliminary report and then presented the results of a supplementary inquiry that she had made singlehandedly. She had analyzed seventy university catalogues, sent out 202 questionnaires, and both raised and answered the critical question that the AAUP committee did not face even in its second report: "What are we, as individuals, and as an association, able to do to improve this situation [the unsatisfactory status of women]?"[10]

Her answer included financial support to women for advanced graduate training and publication of their scholarly articles, a standing committee "to watch the situation closely," and an exchange of faculty members between men's and women's colleges. Other remedies that she tried to implement in passing upon the applications of colleges and universities for recognition by the AAUW were "a fair proportion" of faculty appointments for women "not merely [those] in the instructors' rank to do the drudgery," impartial promotion, a reasonable burden of teaching hours, justice in regard to salary, opportunity for administrative posts other than that of "a glorified chaperon or house-mother," representation on policy-making committees, and on boards of trustees! Although in the 1923 address she cautioned women against "undue impatience and ill-timed efforts," she concluded by answering those men "who may think that we women are needlessly impatient." She did so with the words of a young woman who was leaving the university at which she had taught for several years "without other reward for hard work than more hard work: 'I am leaving. I am so sick of seeing the honors all go to the men on every occasion that I cannot endure it longer.'"[11]

Ella Lonn's commitment to the recognition of women was not apparent in her scholarly work except peripherally, but her interest in the foreign-born is clearly reflected there, as is her concern with peace and reconciliation. In her *Foreigners* she set out to undermine impressions "cherished" by southerners "that their soil was the freest from the tread of foreign races," that their native sons had been "overwhelmed by hordes of European-born Federal soldiers and European mercenaries." She thought recognition of the part played by the foreign-born in the life of the Confederacy had been too long delayed.[12] In her *Salt* she found evidence of the wanton destruction of war, "the dreadful futile waste."[13] Her preface to *Desertion* asserts that to look desertion squarely in the face "is to see more of the truth about war and should be another step in the direction of peace." James G. Randall thought it would "debunk" war in general and the Civil War in particular.[14] For her presidential address, Ella Lonn chose the topic "Reconciliation between the North and the South." She analyzed those developments since 1900 that were unifying the two sections, identified the areas that she saw as still divisive, and asserted a faith that had permeated and dignified her career. The association, and other organizations like it, she affirmed, by the search for truth and by its dissemination could remove the last obstacles to reconciliation. "The search for the truth is steadily uncovering new facts which often require revision of old conceptions. This revision is of the utmost importance, not only to historians, but also to society."[15]

Her open intellectual attitude, suggested by that quotation and evident in her evaluation of the work of others, did not extend to the revisionism in Reconstruction history that now outdates, though it does not displace, the work of the Dunning school. At the annual meeting of the association in 1940, a few months after the publication of Howard K. Beale's "On Rewriting Reconstruction History," a "Round Table on Reconstruction" brought together Francis B. Simkins and a number of scholars who had written classic Dunning studies. Simkins welcomed a reopening of seemingly closed issues. He pointed out that Reconstruction had been condemned because it defied the southern concept of caste, that scholars "need not accept" the traditional opinion of the Negro's inferiority. Some Dunningites, notably Mildred Thompson, indicated that they would make changes to accommodate the new perspective. In the report of the session, Ella Lonn's contribution was summarized in one sentence: "Professor Ella Lonn of Goucher College in an informed discussion effectively defended the fine work that has been done on Reconstruction in the various states."[16]

There is no obvious explanation for the inconsistency between her generally receptive attitude toward the new and her unwillingness to accept a fresh evaluation of Reconstruction. Possibly, it was related to her coming of age while memories of the Civil War were still very much alive. A few cracks in her impersonal armour suggest that she had struggled on her own "Road to Reunion" and found in history the guide that led her, a northerner reared in a belief in the rightness of the northern cause, to a sympathetic understanding of the South. Also, she was the daughter of an immigrant who had achieved success and exemplified civic responsibility. Central to her account of Reconstruction was shock at the corruption, malfunctioning of government, and heavy tax burden that she found in Louisiana during the years of Radical Reconstruction. Yet to her credit, she had recognized that the responsibility for corruption cut across race and class.[17] Her racial attitude is not clearly revealed. "Race" was a term she often used loosely as a synonym for nationality or ethnic identification. There is nothing that I have found to indicate that she believed blacks innately inferior. Her minor writings indicate an undisguised admiration for Thomas Garrett of Wilmington, Delaware, whose home served as a refuge for slaves seeking freedom, and also for Frederick Douglass. She saw Douglass as a "striking, colorful" participant in "one of the most significant movements in American history, a man who despite his color rose by his own efforts and forceful personality" to be a leader of his race and "recognized as an outstanding American." Why then her defensive stance? Perhaps because of her fundamental intellectual assumptions and the nature of her training as an historian. They made it difficult for her to recognize the weight of the irrational in human behavior. They led her to believe that "exhaustive monographic study, undertaken on virgin ground with a conscientious effort to avoid any bias whatsoever, could result only in truth." What I am suggesting is that for Ella Lonn historical truth could not be a "twice-told-tale" without jeopardizing the basic verities upon which she had built her scholarly and her public life.

CHAPTER TWELVE

From Emancipation to Segregation
National Policy and Southern Blacks

In the early 1960s, the point of departure for this accounting of the state of writings on southern history, two revolutions were approaching a climax—the revolution in Reconstruction historiography and the revolution in black civil rights. Only yesterday the nation had been aroused and challenged by the historic school desegregation decision of the Supreme Court, by the Montgomery bus boycott, the sit-ins, the freedom rides, Little Rock, the electric cattle prods of Birmingham, the march on Washington inspired by Martin Luther King, Jr. Just ahead lay the wide-ranging Civil Rights Act of 1964, the biracial march from Selma (joined before it reached Montgomery by a contingent of historians),[1] and the crucial Voting Rights Act of 1965. Then came Watts, followed by similar black explosions in other cities of the West and North. Added to all this during the last half of the 1960s were the angry proud cries of "black power."

In its own way, the revolution in Reconstruction historiography was equally dramatic. It shattered generally accepted stereotypes long considered authenticated by the impressive research of the Dunning school historians.[2] This revolution, like the civil rights movement, had been in process for some time. In 1940 when Howard K. Beale challenged established views, he could cite for support the work of W. E. B. Du Bois, Vernon L. Wharton, Horace Mann Bond, Francis B. Simkins, and others. Nearly two decades later, in 1959, Bernard A. Weisberger's influential appraisal "The Dark and Bloody Ground of Reconstruction Historiography" appeared in the *Journal of Southern History*. After its publication the denigration of "carpetbaggers," "scalawags," Negro freedmen, and the work of the Reconstruction legislators in the southern states no longer would carry unquestioned scholarly authority. The changing climate of Reconstruction historiography was confirmed by John Hope Franklin's *Reconstruction After the Civil War* and David Donald's revision of J. G. Randall's *The Civil War and Reconstruction*, both published in 1961. The two books consolidated the victory of revisionism in dealing with events in the South and foreshadowed major reinterpretations of northern policy.[3]

By the early 1960s, the racial assumptions that had girded the older view of Reconstruction, though apparently still pervasive among white southerners generally, no longer bound the historians who were writing and reviewing southern history.[4] For them, the old orthodoxy had been discredited; the scholarly revolution, however, was suspect. The effect of the civil rights movement was both to accelerate and to compromise the new historiography. Shaken by the demolition of a structure of interpretation long accepted as sound, historians feared that revisionists were replacing the old construct with another equally vulnerable. To the shock of destruction was added unease over the moral implications of the new viewpoint, as if value judgments were inappropriate to the historian's task and somehow escapable, even in the midst of a great national struggle to right racial injustice. Thus Vernon Wharton, from whom commendation and encouragement might have been expected in view of his own early revisionist study, *The Negro in Mississippi* (1947), gave only grudging recognition to the new views in his examination of Reconstruction historiography for *Writing Southern History* (1965). Wharton emphasized the paucity of basic research since 1940 and the danger that reinterpretation was becoming a simplistic reversal of the role of saints and sinners, villains and heroes. The following year, Thomas J. Pressly was cautioning those historians who opposed racial discrimination to examine with particular rigor findings that coincided with their convictions. In 1970, Larry Kincaid rendered a blanket indictment of recent writings on Reconstruction politics as "Republican apologias." Shortly thereafter, David Donald, several of whose essays had been seminal for the reconstruction of Reconstruction politics, expressed concern that "bleeding-heart liberalism" was afflicting "too many historians . . . [with] the delusion that good causes can only be advocated by good men with good motives."[5]

The civil rights and black power movements, together with the changed perception of race from which they drew strength, did have significant influence upon historiography, upon its perspective, the subject matter with which it dealt, and the conclusions at which it arrived. However, the interplay of events and historical writing was not so obvious as first appearance might suggest. The timeliness of some influential studies was little more than coincidence. The mood and central concerns of the contemporary scene were varied and changing—from civil rights to Vietnam, Watergate, the economy, from hope and exhilaration to disillusionment, reproach, bitterness, uncertainty. This did not make for a new orthodoxy, nor was it conducive to beatification. As early as 1960 the most likely candidates for sainthood, the Radicals, were charged with abandonment of the Negro; before the end of the decade, the pejorative term *betrayal* attained the status of common currency in the vocabulary of Reconstruction.[6] Moreover, there were more fundamental, though unarticulated, reassurances against the dire forebodings about the course of revisionism. An acute awareness that discredited concepts of race had distorted the old synthesis did not in fact constitute reverse bias. And historians engaged in reexamining the record continued to honor the traditional canons of their profession that underscored complexity and enjoined integrity, as well as diligence, in the pursuit and use of evidence. Their major works were well received by the profession. Revisionist essays and articles aroused more dissent, but the controversies they stirred were generally accepted as a necessary and constructive part of the process of pursuing an understandable and undistorted past.

Moreover, historians dealing with the politics and consequences of emancipation were responsive to developments within their craft, particularly those that seemed to promise immunization against subjectivity. In an effort to find answers to intractable questions of politics, power, and intent, they turned to quantitative techniques, impersonal data, and collective biography.[7] They were numbered among the pioneers of the "new political history" with its emphasis upon ethnicity, localism, and party systems.[8] They made use of social science concepts, undertook sophisticated community and urban studies, and sought a comparative perspective.[9] Their efforts contributed to the flowering of black history with its focus on blacks as active shapers of history.[10] The "historiographical whirlwind" of the 1970s did not pass them by, though a contrary conclusion might be inferred from the account of contemporary historical writing undertaken for the American Historical Association and published in 1980. That volume found no place in its table of contents or even in its index for Civil Rights, Civil War, Emancipation, Freedmen, Race or Racism, Radical Republicans, Reconstruction, Redemption, or Segregation.[11] For all their receptivity to new approaches and techniques, historians of the emancipation and postemancipation decades continued to affirm rather than repudiate the centrality of politics and law as elements of power. They concerned themselves with related ideology, interests, issues, motives, and leadership.[12] They helped reinvigorate constitutional-legal history and pursued justice at the local level in order to determine the bounds of the former slave's freedom. Not even the contentious reexamination of the postemancipation economy has ignored political power implemented through courthouse and statehouse or abdicated at the national level.[13] And while the "presidential synthesis" was presumably discredited as superficial, revisionist historians of Reconstruction were establishing the importance of President Andrew Johnson's role in obstructing social change.

A handful of books published from 1960 through 1964 shifted the focus of the revisionist revolution from the South to the nation's capital and further north.[14] They linked Reconstruction to the antislavery movement and pushed back its chronological beginning to the first years of the Civil War. Previously, the generally accepted view of the conflict over national policy toward the seceded South had been one of Radicals as vindictive conspirators, of Andrew Johnson as a flawed but genuine statesman, and of identity between his policy—and his enemies (i.e., the Radicals)—and those of Lincoln. Except for conceding sincere concern on the part of a few righteous impractical idealists, the historiography still dominant in the 1950s had reduced to a nonissue, a mere rhetorical cover for other objectives, the question of the emancipated Negro's status as a free man.[15]

The composite picture derived much of its strength from Howard K. Beale's *The Critical Year* (1930). His work supplemented rather than discredited that of the Dunningites, for Beale had not yet questioned their view of a postwar South prostrate under military rule and "negro supremacy." With impressive scholarship, he had extended the Beardian concept of the Civil War as economic revolution to the postwar struggle between Johnson and Congress. In the election of 1866 he saw the triumph of northern business interests through campaign techniques that made the democratic process a mockery. Radical Republicans had skillfully used "claptrap" and emotion to obscure the real (i.e., economic) issues; as a result, it had been impossible for the electorate to know the truth or to vote wisely. The result ushered in the Age of Big Business. Reinforcing the hostile portrait of the Radicals were four books published from 1928 to 1930 that brightened Andrew Johnson's image. Two were sympathetic biographies, and the others were dramatic accounts of the period as an era of tragedy and hate. Of similar effect was T. Harry Williams' *Lincoln and the Radicals*, which appeared a decade later.[16]

The first part of the composite picture to be discredited was Beale's economic interpretation. Three historians who cannot be classified as Reconstruction revisionists, Robert P. Sharkey, Stanley Coben, and Irwin Unger, each published studies in 1959 that collectively destroyed Beale's assumption of a community of interest among northern businessmen and between them and the Radicals. Moreover, President Johnson was found to have enjoyed substantial support from the North's economic elite and the Radicals among the leaders of organized labor. Only by implication did one of the three, Stanley Coben, call for a fresh examination of the motivation and aims of Radical Reconstruction, and even he did not hazard an interpretation to replace the one he helped shatter.[17] The Beard-Beale thesis never regained respectability, but there has been a remarkable power of persistence in the assumption that economic interests or forces must somehow constitute the primary explanatory element in accounting for what the nation did, and omitted to do, in respect to former slaves.[18]

The revisionists of the early 1960s did major damage to the Beard-Beale explanation by supplanting it. They provided an answer to Coben's implicit query: if the Reconstruction conflict was not over economic interests, what was it all about? The answer that their work suggested coincided with the spirit of the times: at stake in the political contention over readmission of the seceded states had been the status of the freedmen and, by racial identity, the status of all Afro-Americans. The revisionists brought back to center stage in the drama of Reconstruction the issue of the future of the slave—his release from bondage and the nature of his freedom. Involvement in that issue, as some of their work suggested and later studies confirmed, had not been confined to the few but had extended to the electorate of the free states, both North and West.[19] The claim to civil rights and human dignity for—and by—blacks in the name of justice and a more perfect Union linked the 1860s and the 1960s. A changed conception of the past became evident as the terms *First Reconstruction* and *Second Reconstruction* gained wide usage to denote two great national efforts on behalf of black rights. And for a fleeting moment, both past and present seemed to dispel disillusion with the democratic process, a disillusionment Beale had voiced and the Dunningites had implied.

While the Coxes and Brock had been explicit in identifying the rights of blacks as central to the conflict between the president and the Republican Congress, McKitrick's account, with its delineation of Andrew Johnson as "outsider," its emphasis upon the importance of symbolism, and its suggestion of a moderate compromise, was more ambiguous. Indeed, a hostile critic could commend McKitrick "for not bleeding at the pores over phony moralities or beating his breast in the modern manner about democracy." Yet appearing as it did in the midst of the civil rights revolution, *Andrew Johnson and Reconstruction* became identified with the thesis "the true issue . . . of Reconstruction was the status of the Negro in American society."[20] Both James McPherson, in *The Struggle for Equality,* and Willie Lee Rose, in *Rehearsal for Reconstruction,* revealed the integrity and continuing vitality of the antislavery commitment to black freedom and black advancement. The Coxes had arrived at the conclusion that the unnegotiable issue between President Johnson and the Republican leadership was citizenship for blacks, with immediate recognition of equal civil rights except suffrage.

In a review of the Rose and McPherson volumes, David Brion Davis accepted in respect to the abolitionists an implication of the revisionists' work not confined to the antislavery vanguard, namely, that a revolution had been attempted. And he identified a key problem. He held it "imperative for us to know what went wrong."[21] Explanations already had been offered and many more were to follow, yet almost two decades later, no answer commanded consensus among historians. Indeed, by then, there were those who held that no revolution had been intended. A second question emerged, similarly intractable and at this writing but partially resolved. With the publication of Leon Litwack's *North of Slavery* in 1961, it was evident that scholarship had demolished the illusion, if ever it existed, of an antebellum North free of race prejudice. During the 1960s and 1970s an outpouring of historical writing on white racial attitudes and race relations, quantitatively the most verifiable impact of contemporary concerns upon historical inquiry, kept that reality highly visible.[22] In this context the complementary question to What went wrong? was How did it happen that a race-conscious white North, where (to use Lincoln's words) "not a single man of your [the black] race is made the equal of a single man of ours," set black slaves free and then made all blacks the equal of whites before the law and at the ballot box? The difficulty of this critical question has been compounded by semantics. In the terminology of the 1960s, the aim of the revolution attempted in the 1860s became "racial equality" rather than equality of civil rights irrespective of race. All white racial attitudes falling short of the 1960s standard tended to become homogenized under the undifferentiated label of "racism."

The northward direction of revisionist writings stimulated investigation of an apparently more manageable set of queries centering on the congressional Radicals and their relationship to fellow Republicans. In the discredited orthodoxy, Radicals had been the policy makers, using conspiracy and manipulation. McKitrick, the Coxes, and Brock all gave to moderates the critical role in the break with President Johnson. Meanwhile, Harold Hyman had called attention to the influence of army generals who had become radicalized, and David Donald had pointed out the near unanimity of the Republican vote on Reconstruction measures.[23] The new tool of roll-call analysis seemed to offer the possibility of settling once and for all who the Radicals were, their motives and interests, their divergence and convergence with other Republicans, and whether party had been more important than faction or geographic bloc in determining policy.

The first major reexamination of the Radicals was not based upon the new methodology. In *The Radical Republicans* (1969), Hans Trefousse reestablished their critical importance, at least through the war years, in moving the Republican party toward the elimination of slavery and the recognition of civil rights for blacks. He saw these goals as shared by President Lincoln, who was politically astute enough to implement them. In the face of President Johnson's opposition and the magnitude of the postwar problem, their influence diminished and was finally lost when the Senate failed to convict in the impeachment trial. As in his earlier biography of Benjamin Wade, Trefousse exposed race prejudice among friends of the Negro without painting them as hypocrites or diminishing their achievements. A notable reinterpretation of Edwin M. Stanton and a growing number of biographies of Republican congressional leaders provided an additional dimension to revisionism.[24]

Roll-call analysis found impressive application in Michael Les Benedict's detailed legislative study, *A Compromise of Principle* (1974). As a synthesis and extension of revisionism, as well as a fusion of traditional and new research methods, Benedict's work commanded universal respect. However, his identification and classification of Radicals and other Republicans did not settle that problem once and for all. Of greater significance in the development of Reconstruction historiography was a different question Benedict raised: Was congressional Reconstruction policy "in any true sense radical"? His work was read as answering the question in the negative. Benedict effectively demonstrated that Reconstruction legislation and amendments were the result of compromise, compromise that rejected the more extreme, or radical, proposals. He implied much more, but not unambiguously. His study, he warned, by concentrating on differences *among* Republicans offered "a somewhat distorted picture," for it directed attention away from the "immense" difference between Republicans and their adversaries, President Johnson and the Democrats. The latter involved a difference in principle that the former did not.[25] The warning was little heeded. By the mid-1970s the view that Radical Reconstruction had not been radical, with the implication that it should have been, appeared dominant, though not without challenge.[26] And by then, in-depth study of the nature and extent of the societal change that followed upon emancipation was only beginning.

In 1975, Richard N. Current observed that categorizing Reconstruction congressmen by roll-call analysis had reached the point of diminishing returns. Yet there was to be one more major effort, Allan Bogue's *The Earnest Men* (1981), the culmination of work begun much earlier. It is an exhaustive, technically sophisticated study of voting and rhetoric in the Civil War Senate, but its findings are limited. They indicate that Radicals in the Senate were less racist, less scrupulous about constitutional restraints, and more vengeful than their Republican colleagues. Bogue believes such distinctions within the party important, taking issue with historians who emphasize the basic agreement among Republicans. Yet he does not deny a Republican consensus on goals, or the importance of party, or the difference between parties. Nor does his division of all Republicans into two categories, radical and nonradical (he uses the small *r*), settle the question of Radical identity. A faint echo of Beard and Beale is evident in his observation that the Radicals' readiness to extend national at the expense of state power was "certainly such as to gratify the industrialist interested in untrammeled development of the nation's economic potential." And by focusing on a problem that arose out of the old orthodoxy, Bogue appears to sound a retreat from the centrality in historical writing since the early 1960s of race attitudes and the black man's status.[27]

Since roll-call analysis could not definitely settle the question of who were the Radicals or deal with the problem of whether Republican party unity or intraparty differences were of greater historical significance, it is not surprising that the new technique proved incapable of establishing the motivation of Republican congressmen generally. It did, however, show conclusively a high degree of Republican consistency toward legislation favorable to blacks.[28]

Historical writings, both traditional and methodologically innovative, made increasingly apparent a significant divergence in respect to race issues and attitudes between Republicans and northern Democrats. The racist stigma so readily attached to Republicans of the 1860s by scholars writing in the midst of the civil rights struggles of the 1960s has been significantly qualified in light of divergent party behavior. The degree of Republican support for emancipation, and then for the protection and rights of blacks, contrasted sharply with the record of their political opponents at the state as well as the national level. Recognition of this party difference relates to the basic riddle—how had race-prejudiced northern whites come to make blacks their equals in both the law and the franchise? Sophisticated quantitative techniques applied to election returns at the local level when fused with other types of evidence and analysis, including the ethnocultural, have made it possible to explore with remarkable subtlety and precision the interrelations between party and constituency on issues affecting the status of blacks. To date, the outstanding example is Phyllis F. Field's *The Politics of Race in New York* (1982). Her work and that of Robert Dykstra, John Rozett, and Michael McManus, when combined with other recent studies less technical in their approach, have clarified important components of the riddle.[29]

The riddle itself has many dimensions. Not surprisingly, in the writings of the past two decades, there has been disagreement, major but often latent, over the question of whether Republicans during the war and the postwar years had used blacks for party (or national) advantage or had used party (and national policy) to advance the condition of blacks.[30] Debate crystallized over one aspect of the disagreement, the issue of why Republicans supported equal suffrage. The view that they did so in order to maintain the party's political power, shorn of its Beard-Beale economic component, appeared credible. Few would dispute the basic assumption that the purpose of a major party was to obtain or retain political power. The history of the Republican party, though brief, conformed to that norm; and by the 1960s, historians had unearthed convincing evidence that made Republican action suspect—a pervasive race prejudice in the free states and its existence within the party's leadership and ranks. Yet the interest-of-party view was open to challenge. Advocacy of equal suffrage in the face of pervasive prejudice could be presumed to carry immediate political risk, and the potential ultimate gain for Republicans from impartial suffrage was not obvious and assured.[31] Although the studies cited here bear upon the disagreement over motivation, particularly as to the extension of suffrage, their conclusions are tentative and qualified.

A consensus appears to be emerging, however, in respect to certain aspects of the riddle of black advancement and white prejudice—the importance of party, of national issues at the state level, and of the dynamics of party attitude toward race issues. Through the 1860s, Republican sentiment became progressively more well disposed; static analysis cannot explain Republican behavior. While Democrats, with only minor deviation, were united against problack legislation, the Republican party was divided sufficiently to jeopardize its political fortunes. In advancing the cause of blacks, Republican political leaders safeguarded the interest of party by a variety of strategies. They manipulated the timing and wording of issues and justified the party's commitment to blacks by uniting it with patriotism, with animosity toward slavery and the South, and with loyalty to party. It now appears that party identification with efforts to improve the status of blacks was indispensable, though not always sufficient, for their success. This evolving historiographic recognition of the critical role of party carries no necessary corollary as to motive. Neither does it establish a greater influence of party on constituency than of constituency on party, since hazard to party on issues of black status lay not in a majority but in a minority of northern Republican voters. In short, the role of party illuminates but cannot solve the riddle if viewed solely as an instrument for formulating strategy and evoking loyalty.

The significance of state studies that examine the relationship between party and constituency on race issues does not diminish the importance of the national arena. Three books by Herman Belz, sharply focused upon congressional action and constitutional theory, added significantly to revisionism. They linked Reconstruction to emancipation and in doing so offered a distinctive explanation for the Republican party's identification with black rights. In *Reconstructing the Union* (1969), Belz pushed back the chronological beginning of Reconstruction to 1861 by showing that Congress deliberately refrained from pledging noninterference with the institution. He also highlighted Lincoln's commitment to emancipation in his Reconstruction Proclamation and confirmed the contention that Lincoln and the Radicals were in basic agreement, capable of jointly resolving the Reconstruction dilemma. In *A New Birth of Freedom* (1976), Belz started with the assumption that congressional emancipation began as a measure of military expediency. He then followed the process and reasoning through which emancipation became a commitment beyond expediency, culminating in the guarantees of citizenship and civil rights embodied in the Civil Rights Act of 1866 and the Fourteenth Amendment. His third book, *Emancipation and Equal Rights* (1978), argued that Republicans held a constitutional concept of republicanism as a nonmonarchical government based upon popular consent and participation, a concept incompatible with slavery that led to emancipation and equal citizenship for blacks.[32] In other words, Belz presented an inherently logical explanation for the Republican party commitment to black civil equality. It had resulted from a process of interaction between events from 1861 through 1866 and basic political concepts, those of self-government and of the inherent natural rights of free persons.

In upholding black civil rights during the Second Reconstruction, the Supreme Court both utilized constitutional-political scholarship and ensured continuing attention to the constitutional amendments of the 1860s and their judicial interpretation during the postemancipation decades.[33] Attack on segregation was paramount in the mid-twentieth-century civil rights movement in and out of court, but the issues, both historical and contemporary, went beyond Jim Crow. Segregation by the 1950s had become intolerable as a "badge of servitude," the blatant symbol of the distance between reality and the equal citizenship and human rights of free men that the Republican party had sought to secure by legislation and constitutional amendment in the 1860s.

Ironically, while the law Republicans had framed became the basis for the Court's belated defense of black rights, the dominant view of their work as interpreted by constitutional historians during the 1960s and 1970s was one of fundamental inadequacy because it had failed to revolutionize the federal structure of American government. First presented briefly but brilliantly by Alfred H. Kelly in comments during a 1965 conference on Reconstruction, the thesis was incorporated by Harold Hyman in his impressive examination of the impact of war and Reconstruction upon the Constitution, and ably developed by Michael Les Benedict and Phillip Paludan.[34] The criticism may have arisen from apprehension over the outcome of the Second Reconstruction as much as from the thicket of constitutional argument over the intent and scope of the emancipation amendments. Even as they were being cleared of the old charge of flagrant disregard for Constitution and courts,[35] Republican congressional leaders stood reindicted for the offense of a constitutional conservatism so devoted to traditional state-oriented federalism as to have foredoomed the former slaves' rights as free men and citizens. There were dissenting voices, none more insistent among younger scholars in the field than that of Robert Kaczorowski, who characterized constitutional change as indeed revolutionary. He held that legal authority under the Thirteenth and Fourteenth amendments was sufficient for national action to protect civil rights, that such authority was intended, exercised, and generally recognized until the Supreme Court's 1873 decision in the Slaughterhouse cases.[36]

The charge of constitutional conservatism, with its emphasis upon continuity, fed a negative judgment on the Republican Reconstruction effort reached on a number of other counts by historians writing in the late 1960s and 1970s. Yet disparagement met resistance from constitutional historians, including those identified with the criticism of Republicans as constitutional conservatives. Thus it was Paludan who answered the most scathing historical verdict on the war and emancipation to appear in print during the two decades under review. Despite the constricting effect of federalism, Benedict has shown that the Waite Court of the 1870s and 1880s recognized that power to protect civil rights had been given to Congress under the postwar amendments. According to his analysis, the justices in their *dicta* left a heritage that preserved, rather than repudiated, that power. And Hyman, in a fresh synthesis of mid-nineteenth-century constitutional development written in collaboration with William Wiecek, presented the Thirteenth Amendment as a sufficient constitutional base for national authority to make secure an expansive concept of civil rights. The work of Belz has generally emphasized the positive in terms of the magnitude of the constitutional change that transformed the legal status of blacks and nationalized civil rights.[37]

Ambivalence and outright clash of attitude mark historical writings dealing with the origin, nature, and execution of national policy toward southern blacks. Rehabilitation of Republican policy makers at the hands of revisionists of the early 1960s was eclipsed but not obliterated. With the climax of the civil rights and the historiographic revolutions coinciding in time, attention naturally focused on the problem of What went wrong? And as study after study exposed the pervasiveness of northern race prejudice in the Civil War era and the failure even of antislavery men to meet the standard of "full" equality for blacks, the inference that "racism" had been the fatal contaminant of the nation's first civil rights effort found wide acceptance. Within the work of a single historian, the most striking example of ambivalence and the darkening historiographic mood can be found in two widely read essays. C. Vann Woodward, in "Equality: The Deferred Commitment," identified equality as a third aim that emerged during the Civil War and became a formal commitment in the Civil Rights Act of 1866. Some years later, he repudiated "the third war aim" and, in "Seeds of Failure in Radical Race Policy," reduced the impetus for the Civil Rights Act of 1866 to little more than a desire to prevent southern blacks from bursting in hordes upon the North. Yet he concluded: "It is, nevertheless, impossible to account fully for such limited successes as the Second Reconstruction can claim without acknowledging its profound indebtedness to the First."[38]

The revisionists of the early 1960s focused attention on Andrew Johnson, leaving unchallenged for a time the interpretation of Lincoln then generally accepted by academic scholars. In contrast to the "Lincoln legend," it portrayed a reluctant emancipator, forced by the pressure of political and military necessity into issuing an Emancipation Proclamation that set no slave free. Lincoln's Reconstruction policy was applauded for its generosity to the (white) South, its opposition to the harsh and revolutionary designs of the Radicals, and its aim of restoring the Union quickly with "the Southern people [allowed] to solve their own race problem."[39] Most authorities did not discount as mere politics Lincoln's moral stance against slavery; Fehrenbacher's 1962 study of Lincoln in the 1850s was notably persuasive. Yet Richard Hofstadter's searing prose retained its corrosive force, particularly his assertion that the Emancipation Proclamation "had all the moral grandeur of a bill of lading." Scholarship had undermined Lincoln as emancipator and friend of freedom despite the fact that Richard Current had emphasized Lincoln's role in the passage of the Thirteenth Amendment and his ability to outgrow racial prejudices, and Benjamin Quarles, in his evenhanded *Lincoln and the Negro,* had added convincing evidence that in personal relations with blacks Lincoln respected their dignity as persons. It is not surprising that one of the earliest syntheses of Reconstruction revisionism, and undoubtedly the most influential, presented a wartime president who never transcended race prejudice, an enemy of slavery but "not quite the friend of the Negro," a man who embraced his destiny as liberator with reluctance, a skillful politician looking to build a Republican party in the South although that meant white southerners would be free to govern black men subject only "to certain minimum requirements of fair play."[40]

The temper of the civil rights movement, its acute racial sensitivities, its celebration of the "clean, straight tracks of radical reform," its "scorn for the devious ways of statecraft" further darkened Lincoln's already tarnished image. As historians continued to uncover the shocking extent and power of white race prejudice in the Civil War generation and as White Citizens Councils invoked the authority of Lincoln in defense of segregation, Lincoln's denials in the 1850s that he intended or favored political and social equality between the races became familiar and damning quotations. They threatened to transform the image of Lincoln the emancipator into Lincoln the symbol of white America's injustice to black America. Fanned by the defiant spirit of the black power movement, the charge of "white supremacist" made by Lerone Bennett, Jr., in *Ebony* caught fire. The accusation evoked scholarly, thoughtful scrutiny from white historians. Significantly, the response most sympathetic and sensitive to Lincoln left him only a "stepfather," faulted for want of moral indignation in the face of systematic discrimination against free Negroes. In the 1960s and 1970s it was difficult for white historians to reconcile Lincoln's role "with our own consciences" (to use the words of Robert Johannsen) or to ignore the challenge as ahistorical.[41]

Ironically, what first appeared conclusive documentary proof that Lincoln by 1864 did in fact wish a reconstruction based "upon the principle of civil and political equality of both races," a letter to James S. Wadsworth included in the authoritative *Collected Works of Abraham Lincoln*, proved vulnerable, a suspect document that could not be authenticated. Although its exposure was countered by other evidence that Lincoln was tending toward the Radical position on black suffrage, the long-dominant view of Lincoln's conservatism in respect to Reconstruction and race issues was reinforced. Indeed, as late as 1979, in appraising Peyton McCrary's careful study of wartime Reconstruction in Louisiana in which he concluded that Lincoln at the time of his death was moving to align himself with Radical policy, one reviewer objected that "this contradicts the conclusion of all other reputable scholars." One "other reputable scholar" immediately took exception.[42]

In fact, by the end of the 1970s a strong crosscurrent was evident in Lincoln historiography. Originating in David Donald's essays challenging the adversarial relationship between Lincoln and the Radicals, later confirmed in his biography of Charles Sumner, the new perspective was effectively developed by Hans Trefousse. His study of the Radicals, subtitled *Lincoln's Vanguard for Racial Justice*, made a strong case for similarity of basic aim and mutual reinforcement without glossing over the strains that surfaced between Lincoln and the Republican vanguard. It was Herman Belz who identified Lincoln's marginal notations on proposed new legislation that would have substantially enacted the provisions of the vetoed Wade-Davis reconstruction bill adding recognition of Louisiana and black suffrage. He concluded that Lincoln agreed, though reluctant to accept universal as distinct from limited suffrage. David Donald also found evidence of Lincoln's readiness to accept the compromise proposal, including the requirement that voting be without racial discrimination. In *With Malice Toward None*, the first book to challenge the preeminence of Benjamin Thomas' 1952 life as a one-volume biography of Lincoln, Stephen Oates incorporated these fresh perspectives and findings. In subsequent essays he explicitly stated and expanded the sympathetic view of Lincoln's emancipation and Reconstruction policies suggested in the biography.[43] Then in *Lincoln and Black Freedom* (1981), LaWanda Cox reexamined the presidential role, its exercise and the limits of its potential in the destruction of slavery and the attempt to establish equal citizenship. Lincoln emerged as a determined, though circumspect, emancipator and friend of black civil and political rights, consistently striving to obtain what was possible in the face of constitutional restraints, political realities, and white prejudice. Whether the crosscurrent becomes the mainstream remains with future historical writings.[44]

By the mid-1970s the negative thrust of racially sensitive accounts challenged not only the image of Lincoln as friend of freedom but the very concept of emancipation as a meaningful reality. Federal policy toward southern blacks as implemented by the army and the Freedmen's Bureau was presented as irreparably flawed and counterrevolutionary in intent. The indictment went far beyond the too frequent incidence of harsh, prejudiced, or unfeeling treatment of blacks by Union officers and men. It charged a deliberate purpose to prevent fundamental social and economic change and to ensure instead continuity of white control, black subordination, and a functioning plantation economy. The yearly contract-labor system introduced by the army and inherited by the Freedmen's Bureau was seen as precluding a radical postwar change in the status of former slaves. This view, first presented in a 1971 article by J. Thomas May, gained wide acceptance, strengthened by the publication two years later of Louis Gerteis' book on federal policy toward southern blacks and by the work of William Messner and C. Peter Ripley.[45] Evidence to support the argument was drawn primarily from army policy in the Mississippi Valley and especially in occupied Louisiana.[46]

The army as such, especially its professional nucleus, never enjoyed a reputation as the black man's friend and champion. On the other hand, the Freedmen's Bureau, though essentially a military organization, was so regarded for a brief historiographic interlude. The availability to scholars of the manuscript records of the Freedmen's Bureau, made possible by the establishment of the National Archives in the 1930s, opened a rich resource with almost unlimited potential for the study of emancipation and the early postwar South. By the mid-1950s the first fruits of research in the records included several articles and a general history of the bureau that remains the standard account, though reflecting Beale's view of the Radicals using the Negro and the bureau for political and economic exploitation of the South.

The more revisionist of the articles challenged the characterization of bureau operations in the older orthodoxy as partisan, corrupt, oppressive of white southerners, the source of racial antagonism and labor unrest. And O. O. Howard, the bureau's head, was portrayed as conscientiously striving, in the face of President Johnson's covert opposition and the hostility of southern whites, to safeguard the freedmen and to bring into being a genuine freedom that upset the established norm of race relationships. Support for the more sympathetic evaluation of the bureau found reinforcement in two major studies of the 1960s, John A. Carpenter's biography of O. O. Howard and Martin Abbott's examination of bureau activities in South Carolina.[47]

The Freedmen's Bureau was no sooner redeemed from old hostile stereotypes than it was subjected to the demanding racial standards of the late 1960s and found wanting. The most influential voice in discrediting Howard and the bureau was that of William McFeely. He presented Howard as a man of self-deceptive piety who, out of concern for his future as a professional army officer, followed the directives of President Johnson rather than resign his post to help the political opposition expose the president's proplanter, antiblack policy. According to McFeely, General Howard had for a time the power and resources to achieve a fundamental change in the status of blacks but instead capitulated to the president (his commander in chief) and delivered black labor into the hands of the planters. The effect was "to preclude rather than promote Negro freedom." Howard alone was not at fault. McFeely saw the ultimate source of the bureau's failure to effect social change in the South in the unwillingness of northerners "to prescribe similarly for the nation as a whole," that is, to create the prerequisites for mobility of the poor, both white and black, North and South.[48]

The stern and sweeping judgments pronounced against army, Freedmen's Bureau, and national policy have evoked reappraisals more subtle and more charitable than those conditioned by the temper of the 1960s. Although these voices are not dominant, there is a growing recognition that even as the immediate aims of the bureau and of southern planters coincided, their long-range goals in respect to the status of the freedmen fundamentally differed. And with increasing challenge to the concept of continuity in the social pattern of southern agriculture and recognition of the freedmen's role in initiating family share tenancy or sharecropping, the conclusion at which Ronald Davis arrived for the Natchez district could prove to have more than local validity. He found that "army and bureau policy enabled district freedmen to resist gang labor and planter determination of their working conditions."[49]

Despite contradictory instances often cited, the presence of a bureau agent may have served to erode planter control and nourish black assertiveness more often than has been recognized. No consensus is in sight, but Donald Nieman's careful study of bureau efforts, and failures, to provide security for blacks against white violence, oppressive employers, and unequal treatment before the law makes clear that a fair judgment on the work of the bureau must take account of the constraints under which it labored and the wide range of responses from its state officers and local agents.[50] Fair judgment will also require an ability to stand aside from twentieth-century repugnance toward assumptions prevalent in nineteenth-century benevolence, namely, that blacks emerging from slavery required tutelage in diligence, thrift, and family responsibility if they were to act responsibly as free men in a free society and garner the fruits thereof. And fair judgment cannot be based upon an unexamined assumption of the inherent conservatism, in the sense of hostility to social change, of the effort to bring stability and renewed productivity to a society disorganized by war, defeat, and the destruction of its "peculiar institution."

Impatience with white paternalism and the ideology of free labor has affected no aspect of recent writings on emancipation more negatively than that dealing with the education of freedmen, once considered the most constructive legacy of the northern effort to refashion southern society. In this field the darker mood of Reconstruction revisionism has been intensified by a parallel revisionism in educational history generally, one that sees American education as "shaped by cultural homogeneity" and functioning to service, and to secure acquiescence in, "an inegalitarian social structure." Varying in tone from restraint to stridency, four books published from 1978 through 1981 exemplify the dominant trend. Their criticism includes accommodation by northern teachers to southern white racism, insensitivity to black desire for independence from all white control, cultural imperialism, use of education to discipline and subjugate black labor, and betrayal of black freedom by choosing the "placebo" of education over the option of "direct means to black power . . . confiscation, expanded military protection, social planning, and an abandonment of laissez-faire social theory."[51] Although not in the ascendancy, the more sympathetic view of earlier revisionism must still be reckoned with, especially as presented in James McPherson's scholarly, racially sensitive account of the continuing effort of abolitionists and their offspring to assist blacks in the struggle for equality, *The Abolitionist Legacy* (1975).[52] While there is no dispute as to the short-term failure of schooling to revolutionize race relations or to achieve widespread social mobility for blacks and while other areas of agreement exist as well, the difference in the two perspectives is fundamental. Northern support for freedmen's education is seen by the one as expanding, by the other as constricting, black freedom.

By the early 1970s, one judgment on Reconstruction policy was so generally accepted that Herman Belz challenged it as the "new orthodoxy," with little more effect than Don Quixote's assault upon the windmill. It holds that Reconstruction failed because it did not provide land for the freedmen. The assumptions usually present, explicit or implied, are that confiscation with land redistribution to freedmen was a policy option and that landownership would have provided a basis for black well-being, equality, and power more sturdy than the grant of suffrage and equality before the law. Unlike the attribution of Reconstruction failure to northern racism, this explanation took firm root without anything comparable to the outpouring of scholarship on mid-nineteenth-century white racial attitudes and race relations. The desire of freedmen for land, however, was well established as was the reasonableness of their expectation of a supportive government policy. Since Belz's challenge, grounds for skepticism have found their way into print, but there have been no comprehensive studies of how contemporaries, particularly Republicans, saw the issue of confiscation and land grants, why no land program was put in place, or what economic and political consequences could have been expected.[53] Comparisons have been made with postemancipation in other agrarian areas, and some southern communities with a high degree of black proprietorship have been studied. Such measuring rods, by their very nature, can be only suggestive, but they do raise serious doubt that the effect of landownership in alleviating rural black poverty in the South would have been more than minimal. Nor is it clear, except for the pride of ownership, that the psychological and social satisfactions associated with black communities derived from title to the land rather than from a racial separateness that permitted some degree of escape from white dominance.[54]

One redoubt on the battleground of Reconstruction historiography captured by the revisionists of the early 1960s appears to be firmly held. White violence against blacks has been stripped of justification and recognized as a causal factor of immense importance in delimiting postwar freedom for southern blacks. The manuscript records of the Freedmen's Bureau yielded the evidence that destroyed the older orthodoxy. In a telling article published in 1962, John Carpenter established from reports of bureau agents the reality of numerous atrocities in 1865 and 1866, before freedmen were enfranchised. He saw the outrages as impetus for congressional Reconstruction policy. Drawing upon the manuscript records and published reports of the attorney general's office, Everette Swinney discredited the prevailing view that the Enforcement Acts of 1870–1871 were unwarranted, harsh, and iniquitous. These fresh directions culminated in Allen Trelease's comprehensive *White Terror* (1971), a study of Klan violence in the Reconstruction years from 1866 through 1872.[55] National policy decisions to protect southern blacks stand justified. Tragically, effective protection did not follow upon legislative decision. No historical accounting for that failure has yet been convincingly comprehensive, evenhanded, and discerning.[56]

A major though not necessarily an ultimate responsibility for protecting the freedmen rested with the three postwar presidents. Historians have tended, at least in their generalizations, to favor more impersonal factors as explanation, yet Johnson, Grant, and Hayes have each been found wanting. C. Vann Woodward's study of the settlement of the disputed election of 1876, *Reunion and Reaction*, continues to be the centerpiece for interpretation of Hayes's southern policy, one that ended the use of military force to uphold Republican regimes. Although Woodward himself stated that Grant, not Hayes, deserved whatever "of the credit or blame" attached to the new policy and that it came as a response to widespread public sentiment in the North, *Reunion and Reaction* has appeared a damning confirmation of a shabby bargain to exchange political and economic favors at the expense of southern blacks, the epitome of abandonment and betrayal. William Gillette, in *Retreat from Reconstruction*, developed the case against Grant; he also disclosed the magnitude of difficulty inherent in the task Grant attempted. Calling for a reconsideration of President Grant's role, Richard Current has characterized Grant as "in a certain respect, one of the greatest, if not the greatest of all presidents. . . . None of the others carried on such a determined struggle, against such hopeless odds," to protect all citizens and give reality to the Fourteenth and Fifteenth Amendments.[57] As for Andrew Johnson, the revisionists of the early 1960s indicated his opposition to equal citizenship for blacks and suggested that not only states'-rights principles but ineptness of political leadership, ambition, and race prejudice affected his course as president. It remained for Hans Trefousse and Michael Les Benedict in their studies of impeachment to show Johnson's deliberate obstruction of Republican Reconstruction. Trefousse argues that the president's opposition was effective, so weakening the congressional program that the result was defeat of the Reconstruction effort and victory for white supremacy in the South.[58]

In criticizing national policy and its implementation, historians have seen southern blacks as victims, which indeed they were; but blacks were not only victims. They were also active participants and shapers, and to some extent winners, in the history of emancipation and its aftermath. A vigorous and challenging aspect of present historiography is the retrieval and interpretation of the black or Afro-American experience from the early years of the Civil War, through the period of Republican party control in southern states, and beyond. This effort, while gathering momentum from the black power and black studies movements, has built upon a sturdy foundation of early scholarship by black historians and a few whites.[59] For example, state studies of Negroes during Reconstruction and after, pioneered by the black historian Alrutheus A. Taylor and followed by the more widely noted volumes by Vernon Wharton in 1947 and George Tindall in 1952, had emphasized the positive role of blacks in the economy and in politics. The early works had also called attention to black life and developing institutions, to education, the church, the black press, the Freedman's Savings Bank, associations for mutual support and sociability, even to black geographic mobility. More recent state accounts continue the pattern they set, and these aspects of black life have received further attention in both state and special studies.[60] Innovative, and particularly noteworthy, is the extensive research published since the 1960s on the black family. This work exemplifies the increased use of manuscript census returns and related sources for aggregate data that illuminate the lives of the inarticulate. Other innovations in black history are the mapping of urban geography, the use of twentieth-century slave narratives and contemporary oral recollections, and the perceptive analysis of folklore expressed in tales and song. Although additional investigation can be expected, the result to date is a positive picture of black initiative and achievement in building institutions that provided autonomy, support, and opportunity for leadership, in short, a community infrastructure far more developed and varied than was possible under slavery.[61]

While state accounts of the Negro continue to advance our knowledge of black history and race relations, a recent historiographic trend may prove even more enlightening, namely, localized studies of city, town, county, or district. This approach has already resulted in several significant volumes: Howard Rabinowitz's comparative study of race relations in Atlanta, Montgomery, Nashville, Raleigh, and Richmond; Robert Engs's account of black Hampton, Virginia; Eric Anderson's of North Carolina's black second congressional district (a predominantly political study); and John Blassingame's *Black New Orleans,* the only one of the four that fails to include politics. The focus of Ronald Davis's study of the Natchez district and Crandall Shifflett's of Louisa County in the Virginia tobacco country is the changing economic-class structure. Only segments have been published of two comprehensive local studies, one by Vernon Burton of Edgefield, South Carolina, a predominantly though not overwhelmingly black rural county with a village, and the other by Frank Huffman of Clarke County, Georgia, with an agrarian economy, the town of Athens, and a population roughly half black and half white.[62]

Since the South, the black South as well as the white, was not monolithic, more such investigations are needed. Localized studies can lead to important generalizations, a notable example being Rabinowitz's conclusion that in many areas of black urban life, segregation constituted an improvement over previous exclusion. But a focus upon locality, as on state or institution, carries the hazard of fragmentation; the challenge is to create a dynamic synthesis. The black encounter with freedom in the South during the half century from emancipation to the great exodus had a coherence and drama yet to be captured by the historian. The conventional time span of Reconstruction is inhibiting, as is the "static image" of blacks during the decades that followed, an image fractured since George Tindall criticized it twenty years ago, but not replaced.[63]

Economic aspects of the black postemancipation experience fall outside the bounds of this essay, but the division of labor in this volume should not be interpreted to reflect the trend in historical literature. On the contrary, recent work increasingly recognizes and pursues the intimate relationship between political and economic condition, between each and the nature of black institutions and black identity. Thus important treatments of the black family and household can be found in the essentially economic studies by Ronald Davis and Crandall Shifflett. Harold Woodman's interest in the transformation of the southern economy has led him to examine state law, while Donald Nieman's concern with law and local justice has necessitated close attention to the conditions of labor. J. Morgan Kousser, in reexamining southern politics, has linked the legalized suffrage restrictions of the 1890s and 1900s to the curtailed availability for blacks of educational facilities and leadership roles. And Eric Foner's account of strikes by the rice workers of South

Carolina indicates an intimate relationship between black participation in politics and black labor militancy, or at least its chance for some degree of success.[64]

Emancipation was a central dynamic of southern history, forcing a reconstruction of southern society of which Reconstruction after the Civil War was but an episode. The destruction of slavery, indeed the very prospect of its destruction, was momentous for southerners, both white and black. The consequences for the class structure and the economy of the South are matters of lively dispute, dealt with elsewhere in this volume. The immediate impact of emancipation upon those caught in the experience has been first of all a challenge to historical discovery. To a degree that would have appeared impossible only two decades ago, the response of the presumed mute, the former slaves—their acts, their thoughts, their words—are being recaptured with dramatic vividness. Leon Litwack's widely acclaimed success in doing so in his *Been in the Storm So Long* (1979) was based upon the sensitive, perceptive use of a wide array of primary sources, but most especially the interviews with former slaves conducted principally by WPA workers in the 1930s. Made readily available in several series totaling forty-one volumes edited by George P. Rawick, *The American Slave: A Composite Autobiography*, these recollections include many references to events during and after the war.[65]

Sources in the National Archives contemporary with the emancipation experience, and too extensive for the capacity of the individual researcher or editor, have been thoroughly canvassed by the Freedmen and Southern Society Project. Under the direction of Ira Berlin and his associates, forty thousand documents illuminating black life during the early years of freedom (1861 through 1867) have been culled from twenty-two record groups, including those of the Freedmen's Bureau. A substantial proportion preserves the words of former slaves, in letters often dictated, in depositions, testimony, and joint statements. An extensive selection will be printed in *Freedom: A Documentary History of Emancipation*, the first volume published being *The Black Military Experience* (1982), and the entire collection will be made available on microfilm. Introductory essays designed to indicate the historical context of the published documents also include fresh and challenging interpretations of the black experience. The series as a whole seeks to examine how black men and women sought "to enlarge their freedom and secure their independence from those who would dominate their lives."[66]

From these works and others focused on the early years of emancipation some conclusions are emerging. As Peter Kolchin was the first to argue, this period, though overshadowed in historiography by the years of Republican control in the South, significantly affected the shape of a new social order for blacks. Litwack eschewed overt generalization but made convincing the diversity of individual black response, and the editors of *Freedom* similarly are alert to variations, especially those related to time and place. While the myth of the loyal slave was laid to rest in the 1930s by Bell I. Wiley, recent writings underscore the eagerness for freedom and establish the former slave's ability to recognize and assert the rights of free men against arbitrary authority and injustice through protest, appeal, and use of those legal channels available to him. At the same time most slaves appear to have embraced freedom with pragmatic caution and wariness of whites. The active role taken by those who joined the ranks of the Union army or fled from bondage as the army advanced made them parties to their own liberation and to that of their fellows. Black men in blue uniforms saw themselves as liberators.[67]

Attention to early emancipation and to black institutions has not diminished the interest in black politics and black political leaders. Indeed, the editors of *Freedom* argue that the war years politicized former slaves who served in the military, and the call for suffrage by blacks in the South as well as in the North before Congress acted suggests a continuum of black political activity. Biographical studies of political leaders, individual and collective, as books and as articles, have multiplied since 1970.[68]

The outstanding biography of a southern black leader of the postemancipation decades, the only one to leave an extensive collection of private papers, might at first glance appear an exception to the predominantly political focus, for its subject concentrated his effort on black education and at least publicly renounced black politics. Yet Booker T. Washington, as presented by Louis Harlan, his biographer and the editor of his papers, as well as by August Meier in his study of Negro social thought, was a profoundly political figure, seeking and wielding power including that of political patronage.[69] Washington was also a complex and elusive character, both as a personality and as a leader of his race. Scholars continue to write about him and to disagree.[70] One of the most interesting, and perhaps unanswerable, questions recent differences raise is whether Washington diminished or enhanced racial pride and solidarity. However judged as a race leader, this man who came "up from slavery" attained extraordinary influence during a period when white resistance had drastically narrowed the opening for black talent in the South created by national policy in the 1860s.

The subjects of most biographical treatment are black political leaders in the obvious sense, those who held national, state, or local office or who exerted influence within the party. A significant beginning has been made in extending black political history into the post-Reconstruction years, although most writings center on the period of Republican control when blacks exercised a substantial degree of direct political power throughout the former Confederacy. The main thrust of biography has continued to liberate blacks in politics from the defamation and distortion of the old orthodoxy that pictured them as ignorant, propertyless, venal men, lording it over former masters or manipulated by self-serving white carpetbaggers and scalawags. So completely have these misconceptions been destroyed that biography, especially collective biography, has now become an instrument of political analysis. The identification of local leaders is serving not primarily to rescue them from obscurity but to illuminate the political process. Recent writings include some sharp criticism of individual and collective black leadership and of historians for having lavished praise without examining achievements.[71]

The most challenging study of black politics during Reconstruction is Thomas Holt's *Black Over White* (1977). Combining quantitative analysis and traditional research, Holt established the predominance of black political power in the Republican party and legislature of South Carolina and then held blacks accountable for the failure of Republicanism and Reconstruction, at least in the state. He argued that division among black legislators had been fatal. Using correlations between voting record and social origins, he concluded that the most important reasons for intraracial cleavage were color and social class. Propertied mulattoes, some freeborn and others skilled former slaves, who constituted a bourgeois elite with overrepresentation among legislators, lacked the perception to meet the urgent needs of darker-skinned agricultural workers. With this thesis of black class-color responsibility for failure, though foreshadowed by August Meier, Holt presented a distinctive and provocative class interpretation.[72] There has been increasing emphasis during the 1970s upon class rather than race as an explanation for "what went wrong," but historians who favor class have been largely concerned with conflict of interest between planter and agrarian worker, or between planter and southern merchant or industrialist. Interestingly, the major critique of Holt's conclusions has come from another young black historian, Armstead Robinson, whose own views center on conflict of class interest within each race, across racial lines, and between what he sees as the equalitarianism of the Republican party in the South and its subservience to economic conservatism in the North.[73]

Holt's bold thesis constitutes a challenge to historians who accept the primacy of white class interests, to those who give greater weight to white racism, and to all who attribute major responsibility to northern rather than to southern wielders of power. However, in other respects, Holt's work is in the mainstream of scholarship in that it seeks to determine the social characteristics of southern black leaders, their relationship with their constituencies, and the reasons for the excessive factionalism within southern Republicanism. Distinctions of color can be expected to figure in future writings, perhaps even more importantly, in view of the arresting studies of miscegenation and mulattoes by Joel Williamson and Gary Mills.[74]

Using Holt's social analysis as a basis of comparison, Edmund Drago in a study of Georgia black politicians has found a markedly different leadership in that state, less affluent, less well educated, with fewer mulattoes and fewer free men than freedmen. Like South Carolina's black leaders, they failed to use the full potential of their political power but for different reasons. According to Drago, Georgia's blacks turned to black ministers for political leadership, and their religious conviction led them to be unduly conciliatory and deferential, although they later learned from bitter experience to be more aggressive and black oriented. Another distinctive perspective on the collapse of Republicanism is offered by John Matthews for Georgia and Ted Tunnell for Louisiana. Each holds that disillusionment of blacks with Republican performance, not intimidation and terrorism, explains the Democratic victories. This reflects discredit upon white Republicans rather than black. Euline Brock has gone further than any other revisionist historian in criticism of a black leader. She sees Thomas W. Cardozo, Mississippi's black superintendent of education, as a gifted man who failed his race because of his class arrogance, his ambition, and his lack of scruple in increasing his personal fortune.[75]

Howard Rabinowitz, in editing *Southern Black Leaders of the Reconstruction Era* (1982), has undertaken "to examine how blacks gained, maintained, and finally lost power." Five congressmen, five state or local leaders, and four collective biographies are included in the volume. Fortunately several essays outrun the chronological boundaries of Reconstruction, of which the most provocative are by Michael Chesson on Richmond's black councilmen from 1871 to 1896 and by Eric Anderson on James O'Hara of North Carolina, a congressman in the 1880s but, more important, chairman of his county board of commissioners from 1874 to 1878 (in North Carolina, redemption is dated from 1870 or 1874). In the "Afterword," August Meier undertakes the difficult assignment of formulating "tentative conclusions." To more obvious generalizations about origin and diversity of the leadership group he adds the judgment that for black political leaders, a base in the black community was essential but not sufficient. To exercise significant influence or hold high office, they needed the cooperation of whites in general or an alliance with a particular white leader or faction. On the ground that present knowledge is inadequate for generalization, Meier sidesteps an answer to the critical question of whether a gulf in social origins between leaders and their black constituencies compromised the interest of the latter. He does, however, point out that blacks operating in a white-dominated world were under more than the usual constraints of American politics, which of themselves necessitated compromise.[76]

August Meier's caution is understandable, yet these studies and others separately published suggest a more positive evaluation of black political leaders even while acknowledging "ambiguities" (to use Meier's term) between their personal ambitions, or class status, and service to the race. More often than not, they were able, practical men, skillful in the art of politics, or soon becoming so. Within the limits open to them, most of these black leaders established creditable and meaningful records in terms of the interests of their black constituencies. It is undoubtedly true that some leaders served primarily as symbols, but a symbol of status and acceptance is not inconsequential to a people subjected to insult and intent on guarding their dignity. In legislative bodies, some served by articulating protest against white discrimination and injustice, offering remedial proposals and fighting repressive measures. Again, protest and proposals are not to be dismissed as irrelevant. Others, especially local leaders, obtained results insignificant in terms of the large issues of race and economic structure but of immediate consequence to their people. Richmond's black councilmen stopped the practice of grave robbing in black cemeteries; those of Atlanta obtained a sidewalk in front of the AME church and prevented Atlanta University from being bisected by a thoroughfare; those of Jacksonville, Florida, secured the appointment of a black police commissioner; Tennessee black legislators gained an annual appropriation for training black teachers and opened to Negroes state institutions for the blind and the deaf.[77]

On the basis of what is known of black politics in the 1880s and 1890s, it appears that members of the second generation of black political leaders were sufficiently effective to have helped trigger their own undoing, the white racist reaction that led to the displacement of partial by total disfranchisement and the hardening of de facto into legal segregation. Nor can the functioning of blacks in politics be determined without considering their behavior as voters. For a people without prior political experience, their response in the years immediately following enfranchisement was remarkable—in extent of participation, in courage when faced with physical or economic hazard, in independence asserted against the advice of former masters and, on occasion, against a deeply felt loyalty to the party of emancipation. Like most of their leaders, the black electorate seem generally to have been "their own men." Where black leaders continued to exercise political influence in the 1880s, it suggests that black voters, rather than lapsing into confusion and apathy after redemption, responded whenever an avenue remained open to some measure of power or meaningful self-assertion.[78]

J. Morgan Kousser has made striking contributions and ventured further than any historian since C. Vann Woodward in generalizing about post-Reconstruction or New South politics. At least in its first fruits, his work was not primarily concerned with blacks and Republican politics; yet it carries important implications for both. Kousser holds invalid several widely accepted concepts, the idea of a solid South after 1877, white Republican betrayal of blacks, black passivity after Hayes's inaugural, and lower-class-white responsibility for black disfranchisement. He sees black progress in the 1880s and 1890s as having threatened white and Democratic party supremacy, thereby helping to precipitate Jim Crow legislation and to complete black disfranchisement. In demonstrating the major impact of the last round of voting restrictions, he has also shown that blacks and their white allies had made a significant difference in southern politics after redemption. The conclusion of his 1980 article on the Kentucky school-fund referendum is a challenge to those "historians who have neglected to distinguish degrees of racism among southern whites or failed to note that, outside the Deep South at least, blacks in the post-Reconstruction era were neither powerless nor friendless." The substance of the article deals with the approval in 1882 by Kentucky voters of a substantial increase in property taxes for whites in order to finance a 300 percent increase in state expenditures for the education of black children.[79]

For the earlier period, Eric Foner has raised related challenging issues. He has called attention to the unique, dramatic quality of postemancipationism in America as the only instance where blacks soon after freedom exercised a real measure of political power. Unlike the sequel to slavery in other countries, in the South during Reconstruction he sees the polity as the scene of battle between former master and former slave to determine the degree of economic and social autonomy for the freed.[80] These fresh perspectives can be expected to relieve the bleak historiographic outlook dominant since the late 1960s that saw only the limits of northern action and the dismal continuities between black slavery and black freedom. There are other indications as well, some mentioned earlier, that the writings of the next decade will find less imbalance between the negatives and the positives of emancipation, both with respect to black experience and national policy. A straw in the wind is the reappearance of the term *revolution* in scholarly writings on the post-emancipation South for purposes other than to deny its existence.

By the turn of the century, or shortly thereafter, the southern states by law had closed and bolted the door to political influence and publicly acknowledged dignity opened to blacks through emancipation and Reconstruction. A half century later, even as the civil rights revolution was gathering momentum, disfranchisement and segregation seemed to most southerners part of a natural immutable order. The first target of revolt was Jim Crow. In *The Strange Career of Jim Crow,* a series of lectures delivered at the University of Virginia in 1954, published in 1955, and reissued in a revised edition in 1966, C. Vann Woodward produced a tract for the times that was also a history of such quality as to remain for three decades the point of departure for scholarly discourse, controversy, and research on the origins and history of segregation. To convince his fellow southerners that "proscription, segregation and disfranchisement" were not immutable, he showed that for more than two decades after Reconstruction, there had existed a degree of fluidity and tolerance in relations between the races unthinkable for later generations. He implied that an alternate pattern to Jim Crow might have developed and explained the South's "capitulation to racism" in the 1890s by a concurrent decline of restraints both external (northern) and internal (southern), by aggression arising from frustration, and by a general crescendo of white racism.[81]

The extent to which *The Strange Career* helped undermine southern white resistance to change is a question impossible to answer, but it can be said with some assurance that its result for historical writing was remarkably fruitful. Woodward accepted much of the new scholarship it stimulated, even where it modified his own. Investigation centered upon the origins of segregation, the impact of emancipation, and the reality of an alternative racial solution.[82] An additional dimension was added when Rabinowitz showed that in terms of some social services, segregation was a distinct advance over total exclusion and had black support. He also shifted attention to the question of why southern whites in the 1890s felt it necessary to substitute de jure for the widespread de facto segregation, and he offered a tentative hypothesis. A new generation of blacks unconditioned by slavery was sufficiently aggressive, especially in resisting local white policemen, to arouse white fears. More recently, David Donald has argued the inadequacy of all previous explanations for the deterioration of race relations in the 1890s and presented a white generational theory. Southern whites who as young men had experienced the dual traumas of the Civil War with defeat and of emancipation with the conduct of former slaves seen as betrayal had reordered their lives and their social order on the basis of sharecropping, Democratic party supremacy, and the subordination of blacks. Fearful that their successors would not perpetuate their achievements, in their fifties they sought to ensure the future by codifying into law racial segregation and disfranchisement.[83]

Although Donald dismissed out of hand the possibility that black restiveness and self-assertion triggered the change, the work of historians dealing with black political activity in the 1880s suggests a need to develop and test the black generational thesis. However generational explanations, white or black, may fare in the give and take of scholarly exchange, they seem less likely to replace than to supplement Woodward's analysis. More vulnerable is the implication in *The Strange Career* that southern whites of their own volition might have reversed the course of race relations. Before the 1890s, the de facto segregation prevalent in many areas indicated a broadly based white determination to keep the Negro "in his place." Nonetheless, Woodward's central argument, that there was a relative openness in the post-Reconstruction decades as compared with what followed, remains valid and has been strengthened by Kousser's analysis of southern politics.

Like revisionist writings on Reconstruction, the historiographic consequences of *The Strange Career* indicate how exaggerated were fears that emotional commitment to the civil rights revolution would result in simplistic history, merely a role reversal of saints and sinners. It is true that the presentism of a generation of scholars fostered some distortions. While elevating few to sainthood, it found a superabundance of sinners. In seeking explanation, it tended to diminish the role of the South and to exaggerate that of the North.[84] And by concentrating on Jim Crow, the priority of their own generation, historians both diverted attention from the political substance of power and gave undue weight to integration as a criterion for moral judgment upon white allies of blacks in the mid-nineteenth century. Fortunately the historical profession is self-healing.

This is not to imply that specific issues still very much in contention, and key questions for which there are no satisfactory answers, will be readily resolved. Nor is reconciliation in sight for major elements of explanation that too often contend as adversaries: race versus class, continuity versus change, individualism versus community. In addition, there is increasing evidence of significant variation associated with locality. The repeated calls for a grand new synthesis to replace the discredited Dunningite-Beard-Beale orthodoxy may reflect a yearning for the impossible. The racial bias that falsified but unified old accounts of "The Tragic Era" is gone. Nostalgia for a return of the Beard-Beale thesis in modernized garb is evident and may be answered, but universal acceptance cannot be expected for a holistic economic interpretation. Reconstruction itself, as time period or as concept, is an obstacle to effective synthesis. As the former, it has burst the boundaries that once contained its beginning and its end. As a concept, it invites disunity, for it can as reasonably be interpreted as reconstruction of the Union or as reconstruction of southern society. Finally, Reconstruction has so long reflected white perspectives that it will be difficult to transform it into a vehicle of history that fulfills John Hope Franklin's call for a synthesis that includes "the whole range of the freedmen's experience."[85] Perhaps the time has come to discard Reconstruction as an organizational category in favor of emancipation—its anticipation, its complexity, and its consequences.

NOTES

Introduction

1. Eric Foner, *Reconstruction: America's Unfinished Revolution, 1863–1877* (New York: Harper and Row, 1988).
2. Telephone interview with LaWanda Cox, July 30, 1995.
3. The research culminated in *The Social Ideas of American Educators* (Washington, D.C., 1935).
4. LaWanda Cox to August Meier, November 21, 1981; copy in the possession of the author.
5. Dorothea Lange and Paul Schuster Taylor, *An American Exodus: A Record of Human Erosion* (New York: Reynal and Hitchcock, 1939).
6. William B. Hesseltine and Louis Kaplan, "Women Doctors of Philosophy in History: A Series of Comparisons," *Journal of Higher Education* 14 (1943): 255; Jacqueline Goggin, "Challenging Sexual Discrimination in the Historical Profession: Women Historians and the American Historical Association, 1890–1940," *American Historical Review* 97 (June 1992): 769–802.
7. The articles are "Tenancy in the United States, 1865–1900: A Consideration of the Agricultural Ladder Hypothesis," *Agricultural History* 18 (July 1944): 97–105 and "The American Agricultural Wage Earner, 1865–1900: The Emergence of a Modern Labor Problem," *Agricultural History* 22 (April 1948): 95–114.
8. Cox, "American Agricultural Wage Earner," 114.
9. LaWanda Cox and John H. Cox, "General O. O. Howard and the 'Misrepresented Bureau,'" *Journal of Southern History* 19 (November 1953): 427–50.
10. LaWanda Cox, "The Promise of Land for the Freedmen," *Mississippi Valley Historical Review* 45 (December 1958): 413–40.
11. See, for example, Kenneth M. Stampp, *The Era of Reconstruction, 1865–1877* (New York, 1965), esp. 126–31; William S. McFeely, *Yankee Stepfather: General O. O. Howard and the Freedmen* (New Haven, 1966); Carol K. Rothrock Bleser, *The Promised Land: The History of the South Carolina Land Commission* (Columbia, S.C., 1969); Louis Gerteis, *From Contraband to Freedman: Federal Policy toward Southern Blacks, 1861–1865* (Westport, Conn., 1973); Edward Magdol, *A Right to the Land: Essays on the Freedmen's Community* (Westport, Conn., 1977); Eric Foner,

"Thaddeus Stevens, Confiscation, and Reconstruction," in *The Hofstadter Aegis: A Memorial* (New York, 1974), Stanley Elkins and Eric McKitrick, eds., 154–83; Herman Belz, "The New Orthodoxy in Reconstruction Historiography," *Reviews in American History* 1 (March 1973): 106–12.

12. The essay clearly recognized the tension between Republican policy makers and northern entrepreneurs, arguing that the land program "grew out of a deliberate legislative search for a plan that would . . . foil the selfish design of northern speculators," who hoped to gain control of confiscated land and produce cotton with a labor force of dependent former slaves. LaWanda Cox, "The Promise of Land," 440.

13. LaWanda Cox and John H. Cox, *Politics, Principle, and Prejudice, 1865–1866* (New York: Free Press, 1963), 232.

14. LaWanda Cox, *Lincoln and Black Freedom: A Study in Presidential Leadership* (Columbia: University of South Carolina Press, 1981).

15. LaWanda Cox, *Lincoln and Black Freedom*, 156–84; LaWanda Cox, "From Emancipation to Segregation: National Policy and Southern Blacks," *Interpreting Southern History: Essays in Honor of Sanford W. Higginbotham*, ed. John B. Boles and Evelyn Thomas Nolan (Baton Rouge: Louisiana State University Press, 1987), 199–253.

16. LaWanda Cox and John H. Cox, "Negro Suffrage and Republican Politics: The Problem of Motivation in Reconstruction Scholarship," *Journal of Southern History* 33 (August 1967): 303–30; LaWanda Cox, *Lincoln and Black Freedom*, 156–84; LaWanda Cox, "From Emancipation to Segregation."

17. LaWanda Cox, "From Emancipation to Segregation," 253.

Chapter 1. Tenancy in the United States, 1865–1900

1. This paper was presented under the title, "Tenancy: A Step Toward Farm Ownership? (1865–1900)," at the session of the Agricultural History Society with the American Historical Association in New York City on December 29, 1943.

2. Ernest L. Bogart, *Economic History of the American People*, 520–21 (2nd ed.; New York, 1935).

3. Harold U. Faulkner, *American Economic History* 394 (5th ed.; New York, 1943).

4. Edward C. Kirkland, *A History of American Economic Life* (New York, 1939), 476.

5. For examples, see Henry C. Taylor, *Agricultural Economics*, 238–69 (New York, 1919); William Ten Haken, "Land Tenure in Walnut Grove Township, Knox County, Illinois," *Journal of Land and Public Utility Economics* 4 (1928): 13–24, 189–98; Carl F. Wehrwein, "The 'Agricultural Ladder' in a High Tenancy Region," *Journal of Land and Public Utility Economics* 7 (1931): 67–77; John D. Black, ed., "Research in Agricultural Land Tenure: Scope and Method," published by Social Science Re-

search Council, *Bulletin* 20 (1933); and H. C. M. Case, "Work and Plans of the North Central Regional Land Tenure Committee," *Journal of Farm Economics* 25 (1943): 258-68.

6. For examples, see W. J. Spillman and E. A. Goldenweiser, "Farm Tenantry in the United States," U.S. Department of Agriculture, *Yearbook* 1916: 321-46; William J. Spillman, "The Agricultural Ladder," *American Economic Review Supplement* 9 (1919): 170-79; and L. C. Gray, and others, "Farm Ownership and Tenancy," U.S. Department of Agriculture, *Yearbook* 1923: 507-600.

7. See the author's *Agricultural Labor in the United States, 1865-1900, with Special Reference to the South.*

8. *Senate Executive Document* 53 (1864): 110, 38th Cong., 1st sess., "Preliminary . . . and . . . Final Report of the American Freedmen's Inquiry Commission."

9. For example, see *House Executive Document* 70 (1864): 4-5, 39th Cong., 1st sess., "Freedmen's Bureau."

10. Editorials in *National Anti-Slavery Standard,* May 26, July 16, 1866.

11. New York *Tribune,* December 14, 1869, 4.

12. New York *Times,* January 29, 1870, 4.

13. U.S. Industrial Commission, *Report* 10: 507 (Washington, 1901).

14. U.S. Bureau of the Census, 1900, Agriculture, 5:cix.

15. Ibid., 6:409; Robert P. Brooks, *The Agrarian Revolution in Georgia, 1865-1912* (Madison, Wis., 1914), 88; Eugene C. Brooks, *The Story of Cotton* (Chicago, 1911), 207; and Charles W. Burkett and Clarence H. Poe, *Cotton: Its Cultivation, Marketing, Manufacture, and the Problems of the Cotton World* (New York, 1906), 39-41.

16. Ernest L. Bogart and Charles U. Thompson, *The Industrial State, 1870-1893,* in *Centennial History of Illinois* (Springfield 1920), 4:234, 237.

17. Hallie Farmer, "The Economic Background of Frontier Populism," *Mississippi Valley Historical Review* 10 (1924): 418, 419.

18. Iowa Bureau of Labor Statistics, *Biennial Report* 1890-91, 53.

19. Arthur F. Bentley, *The Condition of the Western Farmer* (Baltimore, 1893), 31, 43, Solon J. Buck, *The Granger Movement* (Cambridge, Mass., 1913), 23, and *The Agrarian Crusade* (New Haven, 1920), 19-21; Farmer, "Economic Background of Frontier Populism," 419; Harold E. Briggs, "The Development of Agriculture in Territorial Dakota," *Culver-Stockton Quarterly* 7 (1931): 8; and "Grasshopper Plagues and Early Dakota Agricuiture, 1864-1876," *Agricultural History* 8 (1934): 57; Herbert S. Schell, "The Grange and the Credit Problem in Dakota Territory," *Agricultural History* 10 (1936): 63; Everett Dick, *The Sod-House Frontier, 1854-1890* (New York, 1937), 96; and John D. Hicks, *The Populist Revolt* (Minneapolis, 1931), 21.

20. John E. Briggs, "The Grasshopper Plagues in Iowa," *Iowa Journal of History and Politics* 13 (1915): 370.

21. Addison E. Sheldon, *Land Systems and Policies in Nebraska* (Lincoln, 1936), 106–7; Bentley, *Condition of the Western Farmer*, 62.

22. *House Miscellaneous Document* 5 (1879), 46th Cong., 2d sess., "Investigation by a Select Committee of the House of Representatives Relative to the Causes of the General Depression in Labor and Business . . .," 21, 366.

23. Farmer, "Economic Background of Frontier Populism," 421.

24. Raymond C. Miller, "The Background of Populism in Kansas," *Mississippi Valley Historical Review* 11 (1925): 477.

25. Dick, *Sod-House Frontier*, 97.

26. U.S. Department of Agriculture, Bureau of Statistics, n.s., *Report* 18 (1885): 29.

27. Ibid., 26. See also Romanzo Adams, "Agriculture in Michigan: A Sketch," Michigan Political Science Association, *Publications* 3:23 (Ann Arbor, Mich., 1899).

28. Herman C. Nixon, "The Populist Movement in Iowa," *Iowa Journal of History and Politics* 24 (1926): 5.

29. Based on the census. The Iowa counties were Butler, Fremont, Grundy, Ida, Mills, Poweshiek, and Scott. The Illinois counties were Christian, Ford, Grundy, Livingston, Logan, Madison, Marshall, Mason, Piatt, and St. Clair.

30. *American Historical Review* 41 (1936): 652–81.

31. Bentley, *Condition of the Western Farmer*, 67–68.

32. "Land Policy and Tenancy in the Prairie Counties of Indiana," *Indiana Magazine of History* 35 (1939): 1–26; "Land Policy and Tenancy in the Prairie States," *Journal of Economic History* 1 (1941): 60–82; and "The Role of the Land Speculator in Western Development," *Pennsylvania Magazine of History and Biography* 66 (1942): 314–33. Roy M. Robbins, *Our Landed Heritage*, 271–76 (Princeton, N.J., 1942), considers the extent of tenancy and the controversy over landlordism in the 1880s. See also, David M. Ellis, "Land Tenure and Tenancy in the Hudson Valley, 1790–1860," *Agricultural History* 18 (April 1944): 75–82.

33. Sheldon, *Land Systems*, 302.

34. Ibid., 107–8.

35. E. A. Goldenweiser and Leon E. Truesdell, "Farm Tenancy in the United States," U.S. Bureau of the Census, *Census Monograph* 4 (1924): 23–24, 90.

36. Based on the U.S. Bureau of the Census, 1890, "Report on Farms and Homes," 216.

37. "Farm Tenantry in the United States," 323.

38. Goldenweiser and Truesdell, "Farm Tenancy," 83–101; John D. Black and R. H. Allen, "The Growth of Farm Tenancy in the United States," *Quarterly Journal of Economics* 51 (1937): 400.

39. Wisconsin Bureau of Labor and Industrial Statistics, *Biennial Report*, 1895–96, 67–85, 108.

40. For examples, see Spillman, "The Agricultural Ladder," and Goldenweiser and Truesdell, "Farm Tenancy."

41. L. C. Gray, and others, "Farm Ownership and Tenancy," 560–61; George H. Von Tungeln, "Some Observations on the So-called Agricultural Ladder," *Journal of Farm Economics* 9 (1927): 94–106.

42. Black, "Research in Agricultural Land Tenure," 7; Black and Allen, "Growth of Farm Tenancy," 407.

43. New Jersey Board of Agriculture, *Annual Report*, 1888–89, 599.

44. U.S. Industrial Commission on Immigration, *Report* 15: 528, 530, 531, 547 (Washington, D.C., 1901).

45. Ohio Bureau of Labor Statistics, *Annual Report*, 1879, 255–57.

Chapter 2. The American Agricultural Wage Earner, 1865–1900

1. This article presents a segment of an extensive historical study on farm labor in the United States. At least two topics here mentioned, namely the role of wage labor in the transition from slavery to tenancy and the later relationships of southern laborers and landowners, are being dealt with separately.

2. Outstanding examples are the work of Carey McWilliams and Paul S. Taylor; even Carleton Parker and Paul Brissenden, whose studies of the Industrial Workers of the World are now classics, were economists rather than historians.

3. In 1869 the national average expenditure was $116.65, so that the counties shown had averages of $350 or more. In 1899 the corresponding figures were $64 and $192. If these sums seem small, it should be recalled that they are averages based upon all farms, many of which undoubtedly spent nothing at all for farm labor.

4. For a map of the average cash expenditure for farm labor per farm hiring labor in 1929, see J. C. Folsom and O. E. Baker, *A Graphic Summary of Farm Labor and Population*, U.S. Department of Agriculture, *Miscellaneous Publication* 265 (1937): 16.

5. The six states are South Carolina, Georgia, Florida, Alabama, Mississippi, and Louisiana. These states plus Virginia, West Virgnia, North Carolina, Texas, Tennessee, Kentucky, and Arkansas constitute the entire South. U.S. Bureau of the Census, 1870, *Census Reports* 1:720–65, 3:812; and U.S. Bureau of the Census, 1900, *Census Reports* 2:505, 510–49. Tenants were classified as farmers, not as farm laborers.

6. *Appletons' Annual Cyclopaedia . . . 1880*, 482.

7. U.S. Bureau of the Census, 1900, *Census Reports* 6:302–4.

8. Ibid., 304–13; F. S. Earle, "Development of the Trucking Interests," U.S. Department of Agriculture, *Yearbook*, 1900, 441–42; William H. Taylor, "The Influence of Refrigeration on the Fruit Industry," ibid., 574–80; Wells A. Sherman, *Merchandising Fruits and Vegetables* (New York, 1928), 23.

9. U.S. Department of Agriculture, *Report*, 1869, 447; ibid., 1870, 267; A. Oemler, "Truck Farming," ibid., 1885, 584, 607–8; Earle, "Trucking Interests," 439–40; Sherman, *Merchandising Fruits and Vegetables*, 31; U.S. Bureau of the Census, 1900, *Census Reports* 6:339.

10. Philip Alexander Bruce, *The Rise of the New South* (Philadelphia, 1905), 64–71; U.S. Bureau of the Census, 1900, *Census Reports*, 6:304–5, 311.

11. U.S. Interstate Commerce Commission, *Extracts from the Evidence and Proceedings in the Matter of Charges for the Refrigeration of Fruits and Vegetables* . . . (Chicago, 1905), 86.

12. U S. Department of Agriculture, *Report*, 1870, 266.

13. Ibid., 1865, 243–49, 252. However, by 1885 farmers on Long Island were abandoning market gardening for dairying. Ibid., 1885, 583.

14. Ibid., 1871, 144.

15. Clarence Irving Hendrickson, *An Economic Study of the Agriculture of the Connecticut Valley: A History of Tobacco Production in New England*, Connecticut Agricultural Experiment Station, *Bulletin* 174 (Storrs, 1931); Elizabeth Ramsey, *The History of Tobacco Production in the Connecticut Valley* in Smith College Studies in History 15, no. 3–4 (Northampton, Mass., 1930); Fred A. Shannon, *The Farmer's Last Frontier; Agriculture, 1860–1897* (New York, 1945), 245–54; Harold Fisher Wilson, *The Hill Country of Northern New England* (New York, 1936); Edward H. Jenkins, *Connecticut Agriculture* (reprint from *History of Connecticut*, New Haven, 1926); Carl R. Woodward and Ingrid N. Waller, *New Jersey's Agricultural Experiment Station, 1880–1930* (New Brunswick, N.J., 1932).

16. Oemler, "Truck Farming," 585.

17. New York Bureau of Labor Statistics, *Annual Report*, 1892, 1:221.

18. U.S. Industrial Commission, *Report, House Document* 179, 57th Cong., 1st sess. (1900–1902), 10:403. For other references to this method of hiring immigrant farm laborers, see ibid., 10:83, 11:520; Connecticut Board of Agriculture, *Annual Report*, 1883, 127; Massachusetts Board of Agriculture, *Annual Report*, 1884, 103; New Jersey Board of Agriculture, *Annual Report*, 1888, 597.

19. U.S. Industrial Commission, *Report*, 15:518–22, 526; U.S. Department of Agriculture, *Report*, 1870, 256; and its *Wages of Farm Labor in the United States; Results of Nine Statistical Investigations, from 1866 to 1892, with Extensive Inquiries concerning Wages from 1840 to 1865* (Division of Statistics, *Report*, misc. ser., 4, Washington, 1892), 26–27, 28; New Jersey Board of Agriculture, *Annual Report*, 1888, 517, 523, 542, 550, 574, 596.

20. Massachusetts Bureau of Statistics of Labor, *Annual Report*, 1870–71, 155, 159–61. This report prompted the editorial, "The Labor Question in Massachusetts," in *The Nation* 12 (June 8, 1871): 398.

21. Massachusetts Bureau of Statistics of Labor, *Annual Report*, 1871–1872, 33–34.

22. Massachusetts Bureau of Statistics of Labor, *Compendium of the Census of Massachusetts: 1875*, 232–33; and its *Annual Report*, 1878, 180.
23. Ibid., 1870–1871, 157.
24. Ibid., 156.
25. Massachusetts Board of Agriculture, *Annual Report*, 1868, 151.
26. Maine Board of Agriculture, *Annual Report*, 1881, 79.
27. Connecticut Board of Agriculture, *Annual Report*, 1887, 310–11.
28. Massachusetts Board of Agriculture, *Annual Report*, 1891, 415.
29. U.S. Industrial Commission, *Report* 11:89.
30. Ibid., 10:321.
31. Ibid., 885.
32. Pennsylvania Board of Agriculture, *Agriculture of Pennsylvania*, 1886, 50.
33. *Cultivator and Country Gentleman* 38 (April 3, 1873): 220.
34. Connecticut Board of Agriculture, *Annual Report*, 1883–84, 105.
35. Maine Board of Agriculture, *Annual Report*, 1889–90, 140.
36. There are a number of studies dealing with the history of California farm labor; see Paul S. Taylor and Tom Vasey, "Historical Background of California Farm Labor," *Rural Sociology* 1 (September 1936): 281–95; California State Relief Administration, Division of Special Surveys and Studies, *Migratory Labor in California* (San Francisco, 1936); Carey McWilliams, *Factories in the Field* (Boston, 1939); Varden Fuller, "The Supply of Agricultural Labor as a Factor in the Evolution of Farm Organization in California," in U.S. Congress, Senate Committee on Education and Labor, *Violations of Free Speech and Rights of Labor, Hearings . . . 76th Congress, 3rd session . . . Part 54: Agricultural Labor in California* (1940), 19778–19898; Stuart Jamieson, *Labor Unionism in American Agriculture*, U.S. Bureau of Labor Statistics, *Bulletin* 836 (1945): 43–192.
37. U.S. Department of Agriculture, *Monthly Reports*, 1874, 101; McWilliams, *Factories in the Field*, 50–56.
38. California State Agricultural Society, *Transactions*, 1870–71, 15–17, 83. On large landholdings and how they were acquired, see McWilliams, *Factories in the Field*, 12–25.
39. California Bureau of Labor Statistics, *Biennial Report*, 1883–84, 121.
40. In 1886 it was estimated that seven-eighths of the labor in vineyards and orchards was Chinese. California Bureau of Labor Statistics, *Biennial Report*, 1885–86, 46.
41. 44th Cong., 2d sess., *Senate Report* 689 (ser. 1734, Washington, 1877), 437, 443, 570, 579–80, 591, 1094.
42. Ibid., 40, 75, 458, 561, 570, 750, 751, 781, 786, 1027.
43. Ibid., 307, 781, 905, 1033–34.
44. California State Agricultural Society, *Transactions*, 1886, 201.
45. California Chief Executive Viticultural Officer, *Annual Report*, 1882–84, 28.

46. Fuller, "The Supply of Agricultural Labor . . . in California," 297.

47. California Bureau of Labor Statistics, *Biennial Report*, 1895–96, 102; Jamieson, *Labor Unionism*, 50–54.

48. California State Board of Horticulture, *Biennial Report*, 1901–1902, 274.

49. Ibid., 281.

50. Jamieson, *Labor Unionism*, 48, 50, 53, 56.

51. J. Frank Dobie, *A Vaquero of the Brush Country* (Dallas, 1929), xi–xii.

52. Robert M. Barker, "The Economics of Cattle-Ranching in the Southwest," *American Monthly Review of Reviews* 24 (September 1901): 312, Edward Everett Dale, *The Range Cattle Industry* (Norman, Okla., 1930), 64–65, 128; Louis Pelzer, *The Cattlemen's Frontier* (Glendale, Calif., 1936), 166; J. Orin Oliphant, "The Cattle Herds and Ranches of the Oregon Country, 1860–1890," *Agricultural History* 21 (October 1947): 229–30.

53. Dobie, *A Vaquero of the Brush Country*, 91.

54. Ernest Staples Osgood, *The Day of the Cattleman* (Minneapolis, Minn., 1929), 104, 148, 150; Robert S. Fletcher, *Organization of the Range Cattle Business in Eastern Montana*, Montana Agricultural Experiment Station, *Bulletin* 265 (Bozeman, 1932), 20–22, 39; Clara M. Love, "History of the Cattle Industry in the Southwest," *Southwestern Historical Quarterly* 20 (July 1916): 11–12; Owen Wister, "The Evolution of the Cow-Puncher," *Harper's Magazine* 91 (September 1895): 616.

55. Ruth Allen, *Chapters in the History of Organized Labor in Texas*, University of Texas, *Publication* 4143 (Austin, 1941), 33–41.

56. Reginald Aldridge, *Life on a Ranch* (New York, 1884), 215–18; letter to the editor, *The Nation* 41 (September 17, 1885): 237; H. M. Taylor, "Importance of the Range Industry," U.S. Bureau of Animal Industry, *Annual Report*, 1885, 324; Dale, *The Range Cattle Industry*, 62, 74.

57. Dale, *The Range Cattle Industry*, 23–24; Shannon, *The Farmer's Last Frontier*, 222.

58. Allen, *Chapters in the History of Organized Labor in Texas*, 35–36, 38.

59. Philip Ashton Rollins, *The Cowboy* (New York, 1936), 34.

60. Dale, *The Range Cattle Industry*, 122; Douglas Branch, *The Cowboy and His Interpreters* (New York, 1926), 157; Barker, "The Economics of Cattle-Ranching in the Southwest," 313; letter to editor, "The Cattle Business," *The Nation* 41 (August 27, 1885): 173; Pelzer, *The Cattlemen's Frontier*, 159, 163.

61. Branch, *The Cowboy and His Interpreters*, 11; Barker, "The Economics of Cattle-Ranching in the Southwest," 313; Everett Dick, "The Long Drive," Kansas State Historical Society, *Collections* 17 (Topeka, 1928): 50; Pelzer, *The Cattlemen's Frontier*, 246; Paul I. Wellman, *The Trampling Herd* (New York, 1939), 235.

62. William C. Holden, *The Spur Ranch* (Boston, 1934), 90–106.

63. U.S. Bureau of the Census, 1900, *Census Reports* 5:ccvi, ccxiv. In the western division, all but about 4 percent of the sheep were raised on livestock ranches

78. U.S. Industrial Commission, *Report* 10:846, 850; *Wages of Farm Labor* (1892), 51.

79. Letter to the editors in *Cultivator and Country Gentleman* 47 (January 19, 1882): 46.

80. Briggs, "Early Bonanza Farming," 34.

81. White, "The Business of a Wheat Farm," 543.

82. U.S. Industrial Commission, *Report* 10:934.

83. White, "The Business of a Wheat Farm," 543.

84. The best study of migratory harvest labor is D. D. Lescohier, *Harvest Labor Problems in the Wheat Belt*, U.S. Department of Agriculture, *Bulletin* 1020 (1922). See also Paul S. Taylor, "Migratory Farm Labor in the United States," U.S. Bureau of Labor Statistics, *Monthly Labor Review* 44 (March 1937): 538–39. A conservative estimate of the number of men from outside Kansas needed for its harvest in 1920 was 20,000; in 1919, an exceptional year, the number was nearer 100,000. Kansas Board of Agriculture, *Biennial Report*, 1919–20, 205.

85. Everett Dick, *The Sod-House Frontier, 1854–1890* (New York, 1937), 291.

86. U.S. Industrial Commission, *Report* 11 (1892): 81; *Wages of Farm Labor*, 7.

87. *Wages of Farm Labor* (1892), 53.

88. Since the wage maps are based upon an average for the total number of farms, they do not reveal all areas where atypical farm labor was important. For example, the map for 1899 does not show the most important potato-raising county (Aroostook, Me.), the county with most acres in onions (Hardin, Oh.), the leading strawberry areas (Sussex, Del.; Anne Arundel, Md.; Berrien, Mich.), the important cranberry county of Barnstable, Mass., nor the chief Florida orange county (Orange). Although a majority of the twenty-five counties producing in excess of $400,000 worth of miscellaneous vegetables are indicated on the map, a considerable percentage of them are missing. U.S. Bureau of the Census, 1900, *Census Reports* 6:283, 288, 293, 608–10, 612, 708.

89. *Wages of Farm Labor* (1892), 7; U.S. Industrial Commission, *Report* 11: 87, 91.

90. In other regions also, including Illinois, Michigan, Missouri, and Colorado, cities were utilized as a source of agricultural labor. *Wages of Farm Labor* (1892), 21–22, 43, 52; U.S. Industrial Commission, *Report* 10:533; U.S. Bureau of the Census, 1900, *Census Reports* 6:307.

91. James H. Blodgett, *Wages of Farm Labor in the United States: Results of Twelve Statistical Investigations, 1866–1902*, U.S. Department of Agriculture, Bureau of Statistics, *Bulletin*, misc. ser. 26 (1903), 33; U.S. Industrial Commission, *Report* 10:320, 11:90–91.

92. New Jersey Board of Agriculture, *Annual Report*, 1889–90, 491.

93. U.S. Industrial Commission, *Report* 10:133–34.

whereas in the states to the east a third were on farms not specializing in livestock.

64. Harold E. Briggs, "The Early Development of Sheep Ranching in the Northwest," *Agricultural History* 11 (July 1937): 174; Carl C. Rister, *The Southwestern Frontier, 1865–1881* (Cleveland, Oh., 1928), 284; Rupert N. Richardson and Carl C. Rister, *The Greater Southwest* (Glendale, Calif., 1934), 376–77.

65. Richardson and Rister, *Greater Southwest*, 371, 373–75; Charles W. Towne and Edward N. Wentworth, *Shepherd's Empire* (Norman, Okla., 1945), 305–33.

66. Briggs, "The Early Development of Sheep Ranching," 162, 166, 174; Towne and Wentworth, *Shepherd's Empire*, 134–35. Profits in the industry were high.

67. Towne and Wentworth, *Shepherd's Empire*, 175, 273–74; Richardson and Rister, *Greater Southwest*, 375.

68. U.S. Bureau of the Census, 1900, *Census Reports* 5:ccv.

69. Towne and Wentworth, *Shepherd's Empire*, 275.

70. Ibid., 135, 296, 298–300; Briggs, "The Early Development of Sheep Ranching," 171; Richardson and Rister, *The Greater Southwest*, 375.

71. Jamieson, *Labor Unionism*, 9, 221–22, 225.

72. The best secondary accounts are Harold E. Briggs, "Early Bonanza Farming in the Red River Valley of the North," *Agricultural History* 6 (January 1932): 26–37; and John Lee Coulter, "Industrial History of the Valley of the Red River of the North," North Dakota State Historical Society, *Collections* 3:529–672 (Bismarck, 1910). The most important contemporary accounts are William Godwin Moody, *Land and Labor in the United States* (New York, 1883), and his "The Bonanza Farms of the West," *Atlantic Monthly* 45 (January 1880): 33–36; and William Allen White, "The Business of a Wheat Farm," *Scribner's Monthly* 22 (November 1887): 531–48. See also U.S. Department of Agriculture, *Report*, 1873, 278, and for a recent summary, Shannon, *The Farmer's Last Frontier*, 154–61.

73. *House Miscellaneous Document* 5 (ser. 1928, 1879), 46th Cong., 2d sess., 21.

74. W. A. Peffer, *Agricultural Depression; Causes and Remedies . . . Report . . . to the Senate Committee on Agriculture and Forestry . . .*, 53rd Cong., 3rd sess., *Senate Report* 787, ser. 3288, Washington, 1894, 5.

75. U.S. Industrial Commission, *Report* 10:851. Cf. Shannon, *The Farmer's Last Frontier*, 160. Although the peak prosperity of bonanza farming was reached by 1890, a sampling of Red River counties indicates that large farms increased in number between 1890 and 1900 and that the average size of farms likewise increased both in that decade and in the succeeding one. There was a marked expansion of tenancy.

76. Peffer, *Agricultural Depression*, 26–27; Briggs, "Early Bonanza Farming," 33; Coulter, "Industrial History," 577.

77. Letter in *Cultivator and Country Gentleman* 47 (January 19, 1882): 46; White, "The Business of a Wheat Farm," 543; Coulter, "Industrial History," 578, 590; Briggs, "Early Bonanza Farming," 34.

94. S. W. Fletcher, *The Strawberry in North America* (New York, 1917), 73–74, and *Strawberry-Growing* (New York, 1917), 164; Harry Schwartz, *Seasonal Farm Labor in the United States* (New York, 1945), 51.

95. F. G. Mather, "On the Boundary Line," *Harper's Magazine* 49 (August 1874): 337; Wilson, *The Hill Country of Northern New England*, 161–62; U.S. Industrial Commission, *Report* 10:402.

96. U.S. Industrial Commission, *Report* 11:80, 788–89.

97. Blodgett, *Wages of Farm Labor*, 33.

98. *Wages of Farm Labor* (1892), 34; U.S. Industrial Commission, *Report* 15:503.

99. *Wages of Farm Labor* (1892), 48, 50.

100. Family labor became general in California with the coming of the Mexicans in great numbers during World War I. However, even in the 1880s women and children were in demand in the hopyards, vineyards, and berry fields. California Bureau of Labor Statistics, *Biennial Report*, 1883–84, 10.

101. The U.S. Industrial Commission found evidence that in the South children as young as six years of age picked cotton and boys of ten became plowmen. "This child labor on farms is not confined to negro children." *Report* 10:xx.

102. See nn. 17, 20, 21, 22, and 100 above; U.S. Industrial Commission, *Report* 15:524 (N.Y.), 526 (N.J.), 554 (Del.). For the use of children in the tobacco harvest of the Connecticut Valley, see Ramsey, *History of Tobacco Production*, 173–74.

103. U.S. Bureau of the Census, 1900, *Census Reports* 6:307.

104. U.S. Department of Agriculture, *Progress of the Beet-Sugar Industry in the United States in 1905, Report* 82, 11–13 (1906). By 1900 the beet-sugar industry was well established in California, Nebraska, Utah, and Michigan, and factories elsewhere marked its beginning in a number of other states including Colorado. Except in California where production began in the 1870s, beet sugar was largely a development of the 1890s.

105. Iowa Bureau of Labor Statistics, *Biennial Report*, 1890–91, 50. The estimate of forty-two local and county farm alliances was 46 percent of the children employed and sixty days of school lost. Ibid., 54.

106. Missouri Bureau of Labor Statistics, *Annual Report*, 1880, 274–75.

107. In 1890 the foreign born were 9 percent of all farm laborers; in 1900 they were 7.1 percent. Cf. Shannon, *The Farmer's Last Frontier*, 361–62.

108. See nn. 18 and 19 above.

109. 38th Cong., 1st sess., *Senate Miscellaneous Document* 106 (ser. 1177, 1864), 1.

110. 38th Cong., 2d sess., *Senate Miscellaneous Document* 13 (ser. 1210, 1865), 5. Congress authorized contract labor in 1864.

111. For the movement to import Chinese coolies to replace Negroes on the southern plantations, see Bert James Loewenberg, "Efforts of the South to Encourage Immigration, 1865–1900," *South Atlantic Quarterly* 33 (October 1934): 363–85; and

Roger W. Shugg, *Origins of Class Struggle in Louisiana* (University, La., 1939), 254–55.

112. Massachusetts Bureau of Labor Statistics, *Annual Report*, 1870–71, 157. See also the arguments for Chinese labor in the U.S. Department of Agriculture, *Report*, 1870, 572–76. In 1901 and 1902 the desirability of Chinese labor and of the discontinuance of restrictive legislation was upheld in the discussions of the meeting of the New Jersey Board of Agriculture. *Report*, 1901, 33; ibid., 1902, 350. For the Chinese in California agriculture, see nn. 40–42 above.

113. U.S. Department of Agriculture, *Monthly Reports*, 1873, 92. In 1869 the average wage in Pennsylvania for farm labor employed by the year with board was $18.05. Ibid., 1870, 7.

114. Ibid., 1873, 93; *Cultivator and Country Gentleman* 37 (February 29, 1872): 132; *American Agriculturist* 32 (October 1873): 366. A law against contract labor was passed in 1885, and additional legislation in 1887 and 1891 strengthened its provisions.

115. Massachusetts Board of Agriculture, *Annual Report*, 1884, 103; Missouri Bureau of Labor Statistics, *Annual Report*, 1880, 259–65; U.S. Department of Agriculture, Bureau of Statistics, *Wages of Farm Labor* (*Report*, n.s., 18, 1885), 26, and *Wages of Farm Labor* (1892), 48; U.S. Industrial Commission, *Report* 11:90, 101. An important figure in the public life of Tennessee complained that "our young Negro men are becoming tramps, and moving about over the country in gangs to get the most remunerative work." Ibid., 95.

116. U.S. Industrial Commission, *Report* 11:79–80.

117. *American Agriculturist* 49 (April 1890): 218; *Cultivator and Country Gentleman* 43 (November 14 and December 19, 1878): 723, 803–4, 44 (January 8 and 23, 1879): 20, 51–52.

118. For fuller treatment, see LaWanda F. Cox, "Tenancy in the United States, 1865–1900; A Consideration of the Validity of the Agricultural Ladder Hypothesis," *Agricultural History* 18 (July 1944): 97–105.

119. U.S. Industrial Commission, *Report* 10:7.

120. Ibid., 256–57. A prominent Minnesota farmer maintained that it was almost impossible for a young man to go in debt for a farm home at current prices. "If he does so, it is almost impossible for him within his natural life to become a free man; that is get out of debt and own a farm." Ibid., 710.

121. Ohio Board of Agriculture, *Annual Report*, 1891, 399.

122. Iowa State Agricultural Society, *Annual Report*, 1898, 407–8. See also ibid., 1896, 505–7; New York Bureau of Labor Statistics, *Annual Report*, 1897, 646.

123. *Wages of Farm Labor* (1885), 26, 27; U.S. Department of Agriculture, Division of Statistics, *Report of the Statistician*, n.s., *Report* 51 (1888), 183; and ibid., n.s., *Report* 73 (1890), 200, 207.

124. Wisconsin Bureau of Labor and Industrial Statistics, *Biennial Report*, 1895–96, 67–85, 108.

125. George K. Holmes, a statistician at the U.S. Department of Agriculture, said: "This is the lowest-paid labor of all the great occupation groups in this country, and the income would hardly seem sufficient to provide subsistence for a family." U.S. Industrial Commission, *Report* 10, 153.

126. George K. Holmes, *Wages of Farm Labor: Nineteenth Investigation . . .* , U.S. Department of Agriculture, Bureau of Statistics, *Bulletin* 99 (1912). In the following discussion the wage rates as given in this report are used except that those for 1866, 1869, and 1874/5 are reconverted to currency values. This can be done accurately for state figures but only approximately for national averages.

127. T. M. Adams, *Prices Paid by Vermont Farmers for Goods and Services and Received by Them for Farm Products, 1790–1940; Wages of Vermont Farm Labor, 1780–1940*, Vermont Agricultural Experiment Station, *Bulletin* 507 (Burlington, 1944).

128. U.S. Department of Agriculture, *Monthly Reports*, 1867, 4.

129. Unlike the national averages, Vermont farm wages showed a continuing increase from 1866 to 1869, a drop in the early 1870s (for which nationwide figures are not available), and the recovery in the early 1880s became a decline by 1885 (perhaps reflecting a relatively smaller amount of industrial competition for labor). The 1869 high point for Vermont farm wages (both day and month) was not again reached until 1913; although monthly wages with board almost reached the 1866 figure of $24.88 (which was slightly higher than that of 1869) in 1905 at $24.00 and slightly exceeded the 1866 rate by 1910. Adams, *Prices Paid by Vermont Farmers*, 88–89.

130. The index of farm wages is from the U.S. Bureau of Labor Statistics, *History of Wages in the United States from Colonial Times to 1928*, *Bulletin* 604 (1934): 227, which is based on the U.S. Department of Agriculture 1912 farm-wage report. The index figures of this bulletin for 1866, 1869, and 1874/5, based upon wages converted into gold, have been recomputed to represent the approximate actual currency wages paid. The index of nonagricultural labor is from the same source. Ibid., 521. Where the farm wages were gathered in the spring of the year, and are designated as of two years, the index number of nonfarm wages for each year is given unless they were identical. The base for the farm-wage index is 1910–1914, for the nonfarm index, 1913.

131. For similar conclusions, see Wesley C. Mitchell, *Gold, Prices, and Wages under the Greenback Standard* (Berkeley, Calif., 1908), 223.

132. The index of nonfarm wages is from Alvin H. Hansen, "Factors Affecting the Trend of Real Wages," *American Economic Review* 15 (March 1925): 32. The index of real wages for farm labor is computed from Hansen's index of the cost of living and the index of money wages presented above. Because no national cost-of-living index

computed exclusively for farm labor is available, the real-wage index presented here is only an approximation.

133. Adams, *Prices Paid by Vermont Farmers*, 97.

134. For a discussion of the factors affecting wage rates, see the U.S. Department of Agriculture, *Monthly Reports*, 1867, 8–9; and its *Wages of Farm Labor in the United States: Results of Eleven Statistical Investigations, 1866–1899*, Division of Statistics, *Bulletin* (misc. ser., 22, 1901), 34.

135. For trends in farm prices, see Frederick Strauss and Louis H. Bean, *Gross Farm Income and Indices of Farm Production and Prices in the United States, 1869–1937*, U.S. Department of Agriculture, *Technical Bulletin* 703 (1940).

136. Missouri Bureau of Labor Statistics, *Annual Report*, 1880, 266.

137. Ohio Bureau of Statistics of Labor, *Annual Report*, 1879, 1479–81; Michigan Bureau of Labor and Industrial Statistics, *Annual Report*, 1885, 185; ibid., 1895, 233; Kansas Bureau of Labor and Industry, *Annual Report*, 1893, 676; Nebraska Bureau of Labor and Industrial Statistics, *Biennial Report*, 1897–98, 274; North Dakota Department of Agriculture and Labor, *Biennial Report*, 1891–92, 124.

138. 46th Cong., 2d sess., *House Miscellaneous Document* 5 (ser. 1928, 1879), 22, 23; Moody, "The Bonanza Farms of the West," 41; Illinois Department of Agriculture, *Transactions*, 1879, 461; U.S. Industrial Commission, *Report* 11:130, 132.

139. The drop in farm wages during the depression years is discussed in U.S. Department of Agriculture, Division of Statistics, . . . *The Rate of Wages and Labor . . .* (*Special Report* 43, 1882), 11, and *Wages of Farm Labor* (1901), 7; U.S. Industrial Commission, *Report* 11:128–29.

140. For the decrease in man requirements in the production of farm crops, see Hadley Winfield Quaintance, *The Influence of Farm Machinery on Production and Labor* (Ithaca, N.Y., 1904); Leo Rogin, *The Introduction of Farm Machinery in Its Relation to the Productivity of Labor* . . . (Berkeley, Calif., 1931); Shannon, *The Farmer's Last Frontier*, 140–44.

141. U.S. Department of Agriculture, *Report*, 1890, 314; *Report* 73 (1890): 202; *Wages of Farm Labor* (1892), 45.

142. *Wages of Farm Labor* (1885), 29; *Report* 51 (1888), 176; *Wages of Farm Labor* (1892), 48, 51, 52, 53.

143. *Wages of Farm Labor* (1885), 29; *Report* 73 (1890): 202.

144. See n. 140 above. The most marked decrease in the manhours necessary for production was in grains and hay.

145. Crops not fed to livestock. U.S. Bureau of the Census, 1900, *Census Reports* 5:cxxviii. In 1939 farms with products valued at $10,000 or more were 1 percent of all farms but accounted for 31 percent of the total cash expenditure for labor. Farms with value of products at $4,000 or more constituted 5.2 percent of all farms and paid more than 50 percent of the wage bill. U.S. Department of Commerce and Department of Agriculture, *Analysis of Specified Farm Characteristics for Farms Classified*

by Total Value of Products, Technical Monograph (1943), 97; Louis J. Ducoff, *Wages of Agricultural Labor in the United States*, U.S. Department of Agriculture, *Technical Bulletin* 895 (Washington, 1945), 20.

146. For the census data used in this paragraph, see U.S. Bureau of the Census, 1900, *Census Reports* 5:xliv, lxix, cxxviii, cxxix. Of the large farms, 57 percent were other than livestock farms.

Chapter 3. The Promise of Land for the Freedmen

1. Grants-in-aid from the Social Science Research Council and the American Philosophical Society helped make possible the research upon which this article is based.

2. *National Republican* (Washington, D.C.), March 4, 1865, 2; *United States States at Large* 13 (1863–65), 507–9.

3. Walter L. Fleming, "Deportation and Colonization: An Attempted Solution of the Race Problem," in *Studies in Southern History and Politics: Inscribed to William Archibald Dunning* (New York, 1914), 3–30; Charles H. Wesley, "Lincoln's Plan for Colonizing the Emancipated Negroes," *Journal of Negro History* 4 (Washington, D.C., January 1919), 7–21; N. A. N. Cleven, "Some Plans for Colonizing Liberated Negro Slaves in Hispanic America," *Journal of Negro History* 9 (January 1926): 35–49; James G. Randall, *Lincoln the President: Springfield to Gettysburg* (New York, 1945–1946), 2:137–41.

4. For example, see bill introduced by Sen. James H. Lane of Kansas to settle Negroes in Texas. *Cong. Globe*, 38th Cong., 1st sess., 672–75 (February 16, 1864).

5. Ibid., 570 (February 10, 1864).

6. H.R. 51, with additions and deletions, 38th Cong., 1st sess., House Papers (National Archives).

7. Remarks of Martin Kalbfleisch and James Brooks, both Democrats of New York, *Cong. Globe*, 38th Cong., 1st sess., 573, 760, 763 (February 10, 19, 1864).

8. Ibid., 570, 573, 774–75 (February 10, 23, 1864).

9. Ibid., 2798 (June 8, 1864).

10. Later changed to read, "under such regulations as the commissioner and such freedmen shall agree." Ibid., 38th Cong., 2d sess., 80 (December 20, 1864).

11. Ibid., 38th Cong., 2d sess., 2798 (June 8, 1864).

12. Ibid., 38th Cong., 2d sess., 3331 (June 28, 1864).

13. Ibid., 38th Cong., 2d sess., 563–64 (February 2, 1865).

14. Ibid., 38th Cong., 2d sess., 766–67 (February 13, 1865).

15. Ibid., 38th Cong., 2d sess., 961 (February 22, 1865). Italics mine.

16. See remarks of senators James W. Grimes and John P. Hale, ibid., 958–59, 984–85 (February 21, 22, 1865).

17. Washington dateline, New York *Herald*, February 23, 1865.

18. Ibid.; "Review of the Week," Springfield *Daily Republican*, February 25, 1865, 2; Washington correspondent, *National Anti-Slavery Standard* (New York), March 4, 1865; "Mack" (Washington correspondent), Cincinnati *Daily Commercial*, February 28, 1865. "Mack" was pleased, criticizing "Sumner's pet scheme" as contemplating "a sort of serfdom" and paving the way for corruption in cotton stealing and cotton speculation.

19. It was so characterized in the House. *Cong. Globe*, 38th Cong., 2d sess., 1402 (March 3, 1865).

20. Italics mine.

21. The search has been extensive, but not exhaustive, for the subject is an elusive one. It is, of course, possible that some contemporary source may hold a more explicit statement than any we have found.

22. Edward L. Pierce, *Memoir and Letters of Charles Sumner* (Boston, 1893–1894), 4:178n; Pierce to Sumner, April 7, 1864, Sumner Papers (Harvard University Library).

23. *Cong. Globe*, 38th Cong., 1st sess., 568–69 (February 10, 1864).

24. Ibid., 573 (February 10, 1864).

25. Edward L. Pierce, *The Negroes at Port Royal: Report to Hon. S. P. Chase* (Boston, 1862), 24–28.

26. For the Sea Islands experiment, see Pierce's *Report to Chase* and his *Enfranchisement and Citizenship: Addresses and Papers*, ed. by A. W. Stevens (Boston, 1896); *Extracts from Letters of Teachers and Superintendents of the New England Educational Commission for Freedmen* (4th ser., Boston, 1864); Guion G. Johnson, *A Social History of the Sea Islands, with Special Reference to St. Helena Island, South Carolina* (Chapel Hill, 1930), 154–90; Henry Lee Swint, *The Northern Teacher in the South, 1862–1870* (Nashville, 1941); Laura J. Webster, *The Operation of the Freedmen's Bureau in South Carolina* (Smith College Studies in History 1, nos. 2 and 3: Northampton, Mass., 1916); George R. Bentley, *A History of the Freedmen's Bureau* (Philadelphia, 1955), 5–12.

27. Edward S. Philbrick to LeBaron Russell, June 15, 1863, Edward Atkinson Papers (Massachusetts Historical Society); "Selections from the Testimony," Appendix to Special Report No. 3, in "Revenue System of the United States," *House Exec. Docs.*, 39th Cong., 1st sess., no. 34, pt. 2 (ser. 1255), 16–19.

28. For general accounts of southern Negroes under Union control, see Bell I. Wiley, *Southern Negroes, 1861–1865* (New Haven, 1938), 175–259; John Eaton, *Grant, Lincoln, and the Freedmen* (New York, 1907), 1–235; Oliver O. Howard, *Autobiography of Oliver Otis Howard* (New York, 1908), 2:163–93; Thomas W. Knox, *Camp-Fire and Cotton-Field* (New York, 1865), 336 *et seq.*; Walter L. Fleming, "Forty Acres and a Mule," *North American Review* 182, 721–37 (May, 1906); Paul S. Pierce, *The Freedmen's Bureau: A Chapter in the History of Reconstruction* (Iowa

City, 1904), 1–33; Vernon L. Wharton, *The Negro in Mississippi, 1865–1890* (Chapel Hill, 1947), 23–47; Bentley, *History of the Freedmen's Bureau*, 1–29. See also the annual "Report of the Secretary of the Treasury," for 1862, 1863, and 1864, particularly the last (*House Exec. Docs.*, 38th Cong., 2d sess., no. 3 [ser. 1222], 26–27, 294–350).

29. *War of the Rebellion: A Compilation of the Official Records of the Union and Confederate Armies* ser. 1, vol. 34, pt. 2 (128 vols., Washington, 1880–1901), 227–31; Frank Moore, ed., *The Rebellion Record* (New York, 1862–1868), 7:480; Fred H. Harrington, *Fighting Politician: Major General N. P. Banks* (Philadelphia, 1948), 104–10.

30. See Banks's letter to William Lloyd Garrison, January 30, 1865, printed in *Liberator* (Boston), February 24, 1865, 30. For the continuance of the system under Gen. Stephen A. Hurlbut and continued local attacks, see Thomas W. Conway, General Superintendent of Freedmen, New Orleans, to Edwin M. Stanton, March 25, 1865, Records of the Bureau of Refugees, Freedmen, and Abandoned Lands (National Archives).

31. James McKaye, *The Mastership and Its Fruits; The Emancipated Slave Face to Face with His Old Master: A Supplementary Report to Hon. Edwin M. Stanton, Secretary of War* (New York, 1864); also largely reprinted in *National Anti-Slavery Standard*, July 23, 1864. See also John G. Sprout, "Blueprint for Radical Reconstruction," *Journal of Southern History* 23 (February 1957): 25–44 (Lexington, Ky.).

32. James E. Yeatman, *Report on the Condition of the Freedmen of the Mississippi, Presented to the Western Sanitary Commission, December 17, 1863* (St. Louis, 1864); and his *Suggestions of a Plan of Organization for Freed Labor and the Leasing of Plantations along the Mississippi River under a Bureau or Commission To Be Appointed by the Government* (St. Louis, 1864).

33. See n. 28 above; also L. Thomas to E. D. Townsend, July 29, 1864; John Eaton to C. W. Foster, August 12, 1864; Foster to Thomas, August 12, 1864, in Records of the Bureau of Refugees, Freedmen, and Abandoned Lands; Lincoln to Thomas, February 28, 1864; Roy P. Basler, ed., *Collected Works of Abraham Lincoln* (New Brunswick, 1953–1955), 7:212.

34. Eaton to Lincoln, June 13, 1864, Records of the Bureau of Refugees, Freedmen, and Abandoned Lands. Enclosed are detailed, printed "Rules and Regulations for the Employment of Freedmen, and Instructions to Superintendents, Department of the Tennessee and State of Arkansas." The rules even specify the kind and amount of weekly rations employers must provide laborers and their families.

35. Eaton, *Grant, Lincoln, and the Freedmen*, 145–49, 168–72, 222–31.

36. Reports from the Springfield *Republican* reprinted in *National Anti-Slavery Standard*, November 3, 7, 1864; Springfield *Republican*, January 6, 18, 21, 1865.

37. American Freedmen's Inquiry Commission, "Preliminary Report Touching the Condition and Management of Emancipated Refugees, Made to the Secretary of

War," June 30, 1863, and "Final Report," May 15, 1864, *Senate Exec. Docs.*, 38th Cong., 1st sess., no. 53 (ser. 1176), 14–15, 109–10; Sproat, "Blueprint for Radical Reconstruction," *Journal of Southern History* 23 (February 1957): 25–44.

38. For example, Pierce, *Negroes at Port Royal*, 28; Yeatman, *Suggestions of a Plan*, 7; Salmon P. Chase, "Letter of the Secretary of the Treasury, January 25, 1863," *Senate Exec. Docs.*, 37th Cong., 3d sess., no. 26 (ser. 1149), 1, 5–6; Sumner, *Cong. Globe*, 37th Cong., 3d sess. (January 26, 1863), 508; John Murray Forbes to Sumner, January 17, 1863, Sumner Papers; Philbrick, in Sarah Forbes Hughes, ed., *Letters and Recollections of John Murray Forbes* (Boston, 1899), 2:70–71; Joseph Parrish, *The "Negro Question"* (Philadelphia, 1864), 7; Lydia Maria Child, *The Freedmen's Book* (Boston, 1865), 272. The United States Commission for the Relief of the National Freedmen sent President Lincoln a resolution asking that freed slaves be given as soon as possible "a legal and quiet possession of adequate land for their residence and support," received February 5, 1864. Papers of Abraham Lincoln (Manuscript Division, Library of Congress).

39. *Liberator*, February 24, 1865, 30.

40. Eaton, *Grant, Lincoln, and the Freedmen*, 155.

41. Ibid., 134, 163–65, 209–10; Knox, *Camp-Fire and Cotton-Field*, 320–21; Wharton, *Negro in Mississippi*, 38–41; Report of Col. Samuel Thomas, Vicksburg, *House Exec. Docs.*, 39th Cong., 1st sess., no. 70 (ser. 1256), 265–66; Papers relating to Turner and Quitman Plantation, referred by War Department, June 13, 1865, Records of the Bureau of Refugees, Freedmen, and Abandoned Lands.

42. Chaplain Asa S. Fiske so stated in recommending Eaton for the position of commissioner of the Freedmen's Bureau. Fiske to Lincoln, March 4, 1865; Fiske to Stanton, March 8, 1865 (misdated February 8), Records of the Bureau of Refugees, Freedmen, and Abandoned Lands; Eaton, *Grant, Lincoln, and the Freedmen*, 225.

43. This abbreviated account is based upon extensive materials, including sources cited in n. 26 above and Saxton's report to Stanton, December 30, 1864, *Official Records*, ser. 3, vol. 4, 118–20, 1022, 1025–26; "Report of the Secretary of War, 1862," *House Exec. Docs.*, 37th Cong., 3d sess., no. 1 (ser. 1159), 18–19; Letter of the Secretary of the Treasury, January 25, 1863, transmitting report of A. D. Smith, tax commissioner, *Senate Exec. Docs.*, 37th Cong., 3d sess., no. 26; debates on S. 458, *Cong. Globe*, 37th Cong., 3d sess., 508–9 (January 26, 1863); "President Lincoln's Instructions to Tax Commissioners, September 16, 1863," *House Exec. Docs.*, 40th Cong., 2d sess., no. 146 (ser. 1337); Records of the South Carolina Direct Tax Commission, Treasury Department, and related Treasury Records (National Archives).

44. For a copy of the orders see "Report of the Commissioner of the Bureau of Refugees, Freedmen, and Abandoned Lands, December 1865," *House Exec. Docs.*, 39th Cong., 1st sess., no. 11 (ser. 1255), 10–11.

45. *Memoirs of General William T. Sherman* (2d ed., New York, 1899), 2:250; Frank A. Flower, *Edwin McMaster Stanton* (Akron, 1905), 298.

46. Testimony, "Impeachment of the President," *House Reports*, 40th Cong., 1st sess., no. 7 (ser. 1314), 116.

47. Beecher's account and the minutes were published in the New York *Daily Tribune*, February 13, 1865. See also Stanton to Garrison, February 17, 1865, William Lloyd Garrison Papers (Boston Public Library).

48. Benjamin F. Butler to Sumner, February 5, 1865, Sumner Papers.

49. Editorial, New York *Herald*, January 31, 1865; editorial, New York *Daily Tribune*, January 30, 1865; editorial, Springfield *Daily Republican*, January 30, 1865. There was a sharp controversy over the segregation aspect of the order, to which the *Tribune* and other of the more radical freedmen's friends took exception.

50. Fleming, "Forty Acres and a Mule," *North American Review* 182 (May 1906): 728.

51. Joseph P. Thompson to Oliver O. Howard, May 20, 1865, Howard Papers (Bowdoin College Library).

52. *National Freedman* (New York), March 1, 1865, 43–44; *National Republican* (Washington), February 27, 1865, 2.

53. *National Freedman*, March 1, 1865, 48. In addition, it endorsed the encouragement of white emigrants from the North, and an accompanying resolution expressed approval of the Freedmen's Bureau if it be "administered by a man of far-reaching wisdom."

54. See the sketch by Paul L. Haworth in *Dictionary of American Biography* (New York, 1928–36), 10:245–46; George W. Julian, *Political Recollections, 1840 to 1872* (Chicago, 1884); Grace Julian Clarke, *George W. Julian* (Indianapolis, 1923); Paul W. Gates, "Federal Land Policy in the South, 1866–1888," *Journal of Southern History* 6 (August 1940): 305–6; Julian Journal, Julian Papers (Indiana State Historical Society). Julian's defeat in 1870 was attributed to the influence of an "army of rapacious land lobbyists." *National Anti-Slavery Standard*, March 12, 1870.

55. In debate on the bill, H.R. 276, *Cong. Globe*, 38th Cong., 1st sess., 1187, 2251 (March 18 and May 12, 1864).

56. William Whiting, *War Powers under the Constitution of the United States* (43rd ed., Boston, 1871), 465, 469–78.

57. Samuel S. Cox, Democrat of Ohio, *Cong. Globe*, 38th Cong., 1st Sess., 709 (February 17, 1864).

58. McKaye, *The Mastership and Its Fruits*, 36–37.

59. *Cong. Globe*, 38th Cong., 1st sess., 519 (February 5, 1864).

60. Ibid., 3327 (June 28, 1864).

61. Ibid., 38th Cong., 2d sess., 688–94 (February 9, 1865); Julian, *Political Recollections*, 245. See also Whiting, *War Powers*, 409.

62. *Cong. Globe*, 38th Cong., 2d sess., 1026 (February 24, 1865).

63. The unfriendly members were Sen. Waitman T. Willey of West Virginia and Representative James S. Rollins of Missouri; the other members were senators Henry

Wilson of Massachusetts and James Harlan of Iowa and representatives Robert C. Schenck of Ohio and George S. Boutwell of Massachusetts.

64. *Cong. Globe,* 38th Cong., 2d sess., 1125 (February 27, 1865).

65. Bentley, *History of the Freedmen's Bureau,* 49. The characterization of the final report of the Freedmen's Inquiry Commission as a reflection of the "businessman's attitude" (ibid., 47) is misleading. The reaction against government supervision of Negro labor was widespread among the Negro's friends. See discussion above; also Chaplain J. H. Fowler to Garrison, February 24, 1865, from Beaufort, S.C., printed in *Liberator,* March 17, 1865. Fowler urged for the "victims of slavery," land, justice, and treatment as men; "leave the rest to God and nature." Those who had rented and bought land for themselves, he wrote, had done better than those under the supervision of white agents; they "don't want superintendents."

66. John and LaWanda Cox, "General O. O. Howard and the 'Misrepresented Bureau,'" *Journal of Southern History* 19 (November 1953): 440–42.

67. Based on files of *Liberator* and *National Anti-Slavery Standard;* see especially the first editorial after the *Standard* was taken over by the Phillips faction, May 27, 1865.

68. This analysis is based in considerable part upon the editorials of the *Commercial and Financial Chronicle* (New York), vols. 1–12 (July 1865–June 1871).

69. Edward Atkinson, *Cheap Cotton by Free Labor, by a Cotton Manufacturer* (Boston, 1861); his "Cotton Manufacture," in Boston Board of Trade, *Ninth Annual Report* (Boston, 1863), 105–11; his letter to the editors, *Boston Daily Advertiser,* January 4, 1864, clipping in Atkinson Papers; his "Future Supply of Cotton," *North American Review* 98 (April 1864): 477–97; Harold F. Williamson, *Edward Atkinson: The Biography of an American Liberal, 1827–1905* (Boston, 1934), 3–32. For an account of the plantation venture in the Mississippi Valley sponsored in 1864 by Atkinson, see Albert W. Kelsey, *Autobiographical Notes and Memoranda 1840–1910* (Baltimore, 1911), 67–90.

70. Forbes to Saxton, January 16, 1863, Forbes to Sumner, January 17, 1863, Sumner Papers; Hughes, ed., *Letters and Recollections of John Murray Forbes,* 2:70, 181.

71. See remarks of Grimes, Hale, and Lane, *Cong. Globe,* 38th Cong., 2d sess., 958–59, 984–85 (February 21 and 22, 1865).

72. James W. Grimes of Iowa, James Harlan of Iowa, Timothy O. Howe of Wisconsin, Henry S. Lane of Indiana, Lyman Trumbull of Illinois, James R. Doolittle of Wisconsin.

73. Three years earlier in the debate on the confiscation bill Senator Trumbull had frankly stated: "There is a very great aversion in the West—I know it to be so in my state—against having free negroes come among us. Our people want nothing to do with the negro. . . . [They] ask 'What will you do with them; we do not want them set free to come in among us.'" *Cong. Globe,* 37th Cong., 2d sess., 944 (February 25, 1862).

74. American Union Commission Circular, November 9, 1864; Petition of the Refugee Relief Commission of Ohio, n.d., 38th Cong., 1st sess., House Papers; *Report to the Contributors to the Pennsylvania Relief Association for East Tennessee* (Philadelphia, 1864).

75. Joseph P. Thompson to Howard, May 20, 1865, Howard Papers. Thompson, the influential and antislavery pastor of the New York Church of the Broadway Tabernacle and president of the American Union Commission, stated that he had taken to Washington a memorial that he had drawn and the commission adopted, that it was diligently circulated among members of both Houses and referred to Representative Schenck of the House Committee on Military Affairs, and that this action "led to the framing of a bill embodying the main features of the memorial"—i.e., the report of the second conference committee that became law. Schenck had introduced a brief bill to establish a bureau under the War Department for both refugees and freedmen, which he held preferable to the first conference committee's bill on the grounds that it aided white refugees as well as freedmen and that it was less detailed. He opposed a "vast" department and feared a long pupilage for the Negro that would create a state of dependence. Schenck was a member of the second conference committee that drafted the final version of the Freedmen's Bureau bill, and his influence and that of the memorial is obvious. There was nothing in Schenck's bill or remarks, however, to suggest more than temporary use of the lands. Unfortunately, the memorial of the American Union Commission, which he presented on February 2, 1865, was not printed in the *Globe* and despite intensive search has not been uncovered in the papers of the House or Senate. It would be of interest to know whether the memorial suggested a land allotment program such as that embodied in the law. However, nothing in Thompson's account nor in the American Union Commission's Circular of November 9, 1864, nor in his address to the commission's meeting February 12, 1865, indicates that such was the case, although in the latter Thompson characterized large landholdings as "the radical vice . . . of our Southern society," a system of society that "the war is upheaving." American Union Commission, *Speeches of Hon. W. Dennison, Postmaster-General, Rev. J. P. Thompson, D.D., President of the Commission, Col. N. G. Taylor of East Tennessee, Hon. J. R. Doolittle, U.S. Senate, Gen. J. A. Garfield, M.C. in the Hall of Representatives, Washington, Feb. 12, 1865* (New York, 1865), 21–22.

Chapter 4. Lincoln and Black Freedom

1. This essay is based upon my *Lincoln and Black Freedom: A Study in Presidential Leadership* (Columbia: University of South Carolina Press, 1981) and my essay "From Emancipation to Segregation: National Policy and Southern Blacks," in *Interpreting Southern History: Essays on the Recent Historical Literature in Honor of*

S. W. Higginbotham, ed. John B. Boles and Evelyn T. Nolen (Baton Rouge: Louisiana State University Press, 1986).

2. For citations to the quotations from Randall, Hofstadter, Stampp, and Current, and their views generally, see "From Emancipation to Segregation," nn. 42, 43, 44. The last quotation is from Vincent Harding, *There Is a River: The Black Struggle for Freedom in America* (New York: Harcourt, Brace, Jovanovich, 1981), 236.

3. Benjamin P. Thomas, *Abraham Lincon: A Biography* (New York: Alfred A. Knopf, 1952), 407.

4. Robert Johannsen, "In Search of the Real Lincoln, or Lincoln at the Crossroads," *Journal of the Illinois State Historical Society* 61 (1968): 23.

5. Richard N. Current, *The Lincoln Nobody Knows* (New York: McGraw Hill, 1958), 36.

6. Wendell Phillips to Ann Phillips, March 31, 1862, Blagden Papers, Houghton Library, Harvard University, printed in part in Irving H. Bartlett, *Wendell and Ann Phillips: The Community of Reform, 1840–1880* (New York: W. W. Norton, 1982), 52–53.

7. Roy P. Basler, ed., Marion Dolores Pratt and Lloyd A. Dunlap, asst. eds., *The Collected Works of Abraham Lincoln* (New Brunswick, N.J.: Rutgers University Press, 1953–55), 5:146. Any subsequent Lincoln quotation from *The Collected Works of Lincoln* that is readily located by date or occasion will not be noted.

8. Flanders to Lincoln, January 16, 1864, Abraham Lincoln Papers, Library of Congress, microfilm ed. 1959.

9. Basler, *Collected Works of Lincoln*, 6:364–65.

10. Richard Nelson Current, *Speaking of Abraham Lincoln: The Man and His Meaning for Our Times* (Urbana: University of Illinois Press, 1983), 164.

11. Basler, *Collected Works of Lincoln*, 8:248.

12. Ibid., 2:501.

13. Ibid., 2:256.

14. Ibid., 2:537.

15. Frederick Douglass, *Life and Times of Frederick Douglass Written by Himself* (rpt. of 1892 rev. ed., New York: Crowell-Collier, 1962), 360–61.

16. Basler, *Collected Works of Lincoln*, 5:372.

17. Ibid., 7:483.

18. Ibid., 7:243; Hahn to W. D. Kelley, June 21, 1865, New York *Times*, June 23, 1865, reprinted from the Washington *Chronicle*.

19. Basler, *Collected Works of Lincoln*, 7:486.

20. New Orleans *Tribune*, May 23, 1865.

21. Clipping of an address at Tremont Temple, Boston, in Nathaniel P. Banks Papers, Library of Congress.

22. New Orleans *Tribune*, April 25, 1865.

23. Banks to Preston King, May 6, 1865, Andrew Johnson Papers, Library of Congress.

24. From a headline in the *Maryland Union*, October 20, 1864, quoted in Charles Lewis Wagandt, *The Mighty Revolution: Negro Emancipation in Maryland, 1862–1864* (Baltimore: Johns Hopkins University Press, 1964), 260.

Chapter 5. Andrew Johnson and His Ghost Writers

John H. Cox, co-author.

1. William A. Dunning, "A Little More Light on Andrew Johnson," Massachusetts Historical Society, *Proceedings* (Boston), 2d ser., vol. 19 (1905), 395–405. Dunning was going through the Johnson Papers, then but recently acquired by the Library of Congress. All material from the draft messages used in this paper is from vols. 1 and 2 of Johnson's messages in the Johnson Papers.

2. In his diary, Welles noted his objections to both bills and stated that the president had asked him to study the Freedmen's Bureau bill and that he had given the president his views on the civil rights bill. Howard K. Beale (ed.), *Diary of Gideon Welles Secretary of the Navy under Lincoln and Johnson* (New York, 1960), 2:431–33, 460.

3. An undated note from Senator Cowan, filed in the Johnson Papers under date of February 19, 1866, reads: "Herewith you will find a paper from which you may glean an idea or two—I think it is well considered—and I would not fear to stand on any position assumed."

4. Senator Cowan did not vote on the original measure; both he and Senator Doolittle supported the president's veto.

5. Thomas Ewing to Johnson, March 15, 1866, Johnson Papers; also copy in Ewing Papers (Manuscript Division, Library of Congress).

6. Joseph S. Fullerton to Johnson, February 9, 1866, Johnson Papers.

7. For the comparative study of the official messages we have used the texts as published in Edward McPherson, *A Political Manual for 1866* (Washington, 1866), 68–72 and 74–78. The quotations, however, are from the official version of the messages as published in *Senate Journal*, 39th Cong., 1st sess., 168–73 and 279–85.

8. McPherson, *Political Manual*, 74.

9. Entries for January 6, March 2, 1867, and July 1, 3, 1868, shorthand diary of William G. Moore, Johnson Papers.

10. Fullerton to Johnson, February 12, 1866, ibid.

11. Speech in reply to the Virginia Delegation, February 10, 1866, newspaper clipping, ibid.; also printed in McPherson, *Political Manual*, 56–58.

12. Italics ours.

13. We are indebted to Mr. Nathan Behrin, Pittman expert, for transcribing the shorthand notation.

14. Filed under March 27, 1866, Johnson Papers.

15. Stanbery to Johnson, April 20, 1866, ibid.

16. Thomas Ewing, Jr., wrote his father, March 25, 1866, that "it is reported" that Stanbery was preparing the message. At first, the son considered the contents of the bill unobjectionable. See also his letter of March 26, 1866, Ewing Papers.

17. George Reed, ed., *Bench and Bar of Ohio* (Chicago, 1897), 1:84–87.

18. Entry of August 15, 1868, transcript of Moore Diary, Johnson Papers.

19. *Independent* (New York), July 19, 1866.

20. New York *Times,* March 28, 1866.

21. Ibid., April 23, 1866.

22. Letter of April 25, 1866, Ewing Papers.

23. New York *Daily Tribune,* July 18, 1866.

24. Beale, ed., *Diary of Gideon Welles,* 2:487.

Chapter 6. Civil Rights

John H. Cox, co-author.

1. There was also some opposition to the civil rights bill from Republican Conservative leaders. Senator Cowan urged a veto on the ground that otherwise "they" would be able to claim power to do anything, including granting the right of suffrage. Cowan to Johnson, March 23, 1866, Andrew Johnson Papers, Library of Congress. Secretary Welles prepared a five-page argument against the bill; see LaWanda Cox and John H. Cox, "Andrew Johnson and His Ghost Writers: An Analysis of the Freedmen's Bureau and Civil Rights Veto Messages," *Mississippi Valley Historical Review* 48 (December 1961): 474, 477.

2. Morgan to Johnson, March 19, 1866, Johnson Papers.

3. Blair to Johnson, March 18, 1866, ibid.

4. Beecher to Johnson, March 17, 1866, ibid.

5. Cox to Johnson, March 22, 1866, ibid.

6. Weed to Seward, March 25, 1866, ibid.

7. The note is filed under date of March 27, 1866, ibid.

8. See Cox, "Andrew Johnson and His Ghost Writers," 474–77, 479.

9. Messages, Johnson Papers.

10. The official message was a slightly edited composite of three working papers, Seward's, Henry Stanbery's, and Secretary Welles'. Cox, "Andrew Johnson and His Ghost Writers," 473–77.

11. This passage appeared in no one of the three drafts.

12. In these points, the message followed Stanbery's draft.

13. This passage appeared in no one of the three drafts. For the text of the official message, we have used Edward McPherson, *A Handbook of Politics for 1866* (Washington, 1866), 74–78.

14. Morgan to I. Sherman, April 2, 1866, Edwin D. Morgan Papers, New York State Library.

15. Morgan to H. H. Van Dyck, March 31, 1866, ibid.

16. Morgan to Seward, March 26, 1866; see also his two notes of March 2, 1866, William Henry Seward Papers, University of Rochester Library.

17. Endorsement on Morgan to Seward, March 26, 1866, ibid.

18. W. G. Moore (of the president's staff) to Seward, March 26, 1866, ibid.

19. Howard K. Beale, ed., *The Diary of Gideon Welles* (New York, 1960), 2:463–64.

20. Morgan to R. Balcom, April 3, 1866; see also Morgan to Weed, April 4, 1866, Morgan Papers.

21. Weed to Morgan, April 6, 1866, ibid.

22. Morgan to Weed, April 8, 1866, Thurlow Weed Papers, University of Rochester Library.

23. Morgan to J. Jay, May 16, 1866; see also Morgan to G. Dawson, May 19, 1866, Morgan to H. H. Van Dyck, May 19, 1866, Morgan Papers.

24. *Cong. Globe*, 39th Cong., 2d sess., 1761 (April 4, 1866).

25. New York *Herald*, March 17, 1866.

26. Ibid., March 28, 1866.

27. Dawes to wife, March 31, 1866, Henry L. Dawes Papers. Dawes voted to override the veto.

28. Some devoted advocates of civil rights for the freedmen, notably John Bingham, questioned the constitutional basis for the Civil Rights Act. Bingham voted against the bill for that reason, and is generally recognized as the father of the civil rights provisions of section one of the Fourteenth Amendment.

29. See Eric L. McKitrick, *Andrew Johnson and Reconstruction* (Chicago, 1960), 350–52, 356–57.

30. Even after the vetoes, there was much sentiment for conciliation. Especially after the formulation of what was to become the Fourteenth Amendment, there was hope that Johnson might give the moderates an alternative to opposition. See Thomas Ewing, Jr., to his father, April 12, 1866, Thomas Ewing Papers; *Diary of Gideon Welles*, 2:527; New York *Times*, June 14, 15, 1866.

31. Cowan to Johnson, March 23, 1866, Johnson Papers.

32. Cochrane to Johnson, Jan. 23, 1866, Johnson Papers.

33. Baber to Johnson, March 29, 1866, Johnson Papers; Baber to Doolittle, February 28, 1866, March 29, 1866, James R. Doolittle Papers, Historical Society of Wisconsin; Baber to Seward, March 30, 1866, Johnson Papers.

34. Houston to Johnson, April 5, 1866, Johnson Papers.

35. W. A. Newell to Johnson, April 9, 1866, ibid. Evidence of popular support for civil rights legislation can be found in other private papers as well. For example, Gen. O. O. Howard, head of the Freedmen's Bureau, received a letter from an associate who was at the time in New York City. It read: "You may be sure the veto of the Civil Rights Bill stirred up even the old conservatives of this city. Mr. Raymond had letters

from many, stopping the Times, whom he had not anticipated would turn against him. Will you get a new Bureau Bill. I hope so and think it can be done. There is no mistake as to the reaction among the *people*, and the President must yield." J. W. Alvord to Howard, April 17, 1866, O. O. Howard Papers, Bowdoin College Library.

36. J. Warren to Seward, February 24, 1866, Seward Papers.
37. E. G. Cook to Seward, April 20, 1866, ibid.
38. F. Vinton [?] to Morgan, April 7, 1866, Morgan Papers.
39. S. Osgood to Morgan, April 18, 1866, ibid.
40. O. D. Swan to Morgan, May 3, 1866, ibid.
41. H. Day to Morgan, May 8, 1866, ibid.
42. Springfield *Republican,* March 28, 1866.
43. Ibid., April 4, 1866.
44. Clipping, scrapbook, Johnson Papers.
45. Clipping, ibid.
46. These generalizations are based primarily upon the extensive press clippings on the civil rights veto, ibid.
47. Before the opening of Congress in December 1865, Schuyler Colfax, Speaker of the House, made a speech that was widely regarded as a statement of majority Republican opinion. He abjured any inflexibility of policy, spoke warmly of what the president had already accomplished in securing commitments from the southern states, but made clear that some additional assurances were considered necessary. The first of these, and indeed the only one that was substantive, was that "the Declaration of Independence be recognized as the law of the land" by the protection of the freedmen in their rights of person and property including the right to testify. He made no mention of suffrage for the Negro nor of any punitive action against the South. For text of speech, see New York *Times,* November 19, 1865.
48. Clipping from a Buffalo paper, March 29, 1866, scrapbook, Johnson Papers.
49. Chicago *Evening Journal,* March 28, 1866, ibid.
50. See Stanley Coben, "Northeastern Business and Radical Reconstruction: A Reexamination," *Mississippi Valley Historical Review* 46 (June 1959): 67–90; Robert P. Sharkey, *Money, Class and Party: An Economic Study of Civil War and Reconstruction* (Baltimore, 1959); Irwin Unger, "Business Men and Specie Resumption," *Political Science Quarterly* 74 (March 1959): 46–70. Howard K. Beale's study made much of economic issues, but his findings showed that they had not been central to the political campaign of 1866. Johnson's failure to make them such, Beale considered "a fatal error in political judgment." *The Critical Year: A Study of Andrew Johnson and Reconstruction* (New York, 1930), 299.
51. Letters in the Johnson Papers indicate this support, see those of August Belmont, March 24, 1866, A. J. Drexel, May 3, 1866, Alexander T. Stewart, June 18, 1866; also reports of business support in the letters of W. G. Smith, March 2, 1866

(Buffalo), J. B. Hussey, March 3, 1866 (New York), W. J. Hilton, March 7, 1866 (Albany), R. B. Carnahan, March 16, 1866 (Pittsburgh), G. W. Morgan, July 14, 1866 (Ohio), D. S. Seymour, Nov. 8, 1866 (Troy).

52. In the Samuel Tilden Papers there are printed letters outlining the arrangements, including a seating chart for the dinner, and itemizing the expenses with assessments. Tilden's share of the cost was $145.38. Smythe, Johnson's appointee as Collector of the Port, feared the plans for Johnson's New York visit would give the impression that "a *few* are to get hold of you" and advised the president to stop at the Fifth Avenue Hotel, rather than Delmonico's, to "give '*the people*'" a better opportuniy to see him. Smythe to Johnson, August 25, 1866, Johnson Papers.

53. New York *Times*, September 2, 1866.

54. Wilson to Johnson, March 3, 1866, Johnson Papers.

55. McKitrick, *Andrew Johnson and Reconstruction*, 19 n. 2.

56. The roll call came on a motion to table the resolution. McPherson, *Political Manual for 1866*, 110–11.

57. Ibid., 109.

58. Ibid., 113; compare the vote, 81.

59. On the meaning of "Radical," compare McKitrick, *Andrew Johnson and Reconstruction*, 53–67. The Chicago *Tribune*, the leading Radical newspaper, had some revealing comments. Before the Republican convention of 1860, it identified the "more radical" wing of the party as a body of men "somewhat in advance of the party's creed," zealous, honest and possibly impractical, who recognized that they had no power to interfere with slavery in the states but still hoped "that the election of a Republican President will in some way tend to the crippling of the institution they hate." In 1866, the *Tribune* defined as the vestige of slavery "all discrimination against freedmen." Until these be removed, it held that the South would not be at peace with itself or with the North. Chicago *Tribune*, February 6, 1860, February 16, 1860, and clipping on Freedmen's Bureau veto, scrapbook, Johnson Papers.

60. See the quotations cited above, nn. 5, 6, 32, 43.

61. Benjamin Kendrick, *Journal of the Joint Committee of Fifteen on Reconstruction* (New York, 1914), 251–52.

62. T. Barry to Grider, March 8, 1866, Johnson Papers.

63. *State and Union*, April 5, 1866, scrapbook, ibid.

64. *Constitutional Union*, March 28, 1866, ibid.

65. Clipping on civil rights veto, ibid.

66. Boylestown *Democrat*, February 27, 1866, ibid.

67. Wayne County [Ohio] *Democrat*, ibid.

68. See LaWanda Cox and John H. Cox, *Politics, Principle, Prejudice, 1865–1866: Dilemma of Reconstruction America* (New York, 1963), ch. 8.

69. Portland *Press*, Scrapbook, Johnson Papers.

70. For the texts of the messages we have used McPherson, *Political Manual for 1866*.

71. See Cox, *Politics, Principle, Prejudice*, ch. 3, fnn. 29, 30, 31; ch. 5, fnn. 18, 21, 22, 25; ch. 10, fn. 3.

72. *Diary of Gideon Welles* 2:369.

73. Ibid., 374.

74. Springfield *Republican*, September 30, 1865.

75. *Diary of Gideon Welles* 2:431.

76. Ibid., 394.

77. James L. Sellers, "James R. Doolittle," *Wisconsin Magazine of History* 17 (December 1933): 176; (March 1934): 287–88, 293, 302–3.

78. Doolittle to Johnson, September 9, 1865, Johnson Papers.

79. J. C. G. Kennedy to Doolittle, March 9, 1866; notes for speech, March or April 1866, Doolittle Papers.

80. Doolittle to wife, Mary, November 11, 1866, ibid.

81. Sellers, "James R. Doolittle," 26–27.

82. Messages, Johnson Papers. See Cox, "Andrew Johnson and His Ghost Writers," 463.

83. Cowan to Johnson, March 23, 1866, Johnson Papers.

84. McPherson, *Political Manual for 1866*, 80.

85. Quoted in B. J. Pershing, "Senator Edgar A. Cowan, 1861–1867," *Western Pennsylvania Historical Magazine* 4 (October 1921): 229–30.

86. Ibid.

87. *Speech of Hon. Edgar Cowan of Pennsylvania on Executive Appointments and Removal, Delivered in the Senate of the United States, May 9, 1866* (Washington, 1866), 13.

88. Dixon to Johnson, October 8, 1865, Johnson.

89. Mark Howard, *Despotic Doctrines Declared by the United States Senate Exposed; and Senator Dixon Unmasked* (Hartford, 1863), 8.

90. From the Toledo *Commercial*, in Ellen Ewing Sherman, comp., *Memorial of Thomas Ewing of Ohio* (New York, 1873), 123.

91. Ewing Papers.

92. Speech in reply to a toast, published in *An Appeal to the Senate to Modify Its Policy and Save from Africanization and Military Despotism the States of the South* (printed by order of the National Democratic Resident Committee; Washington D.C., 1868).

93. Messages, Johnson Papers. See Cox, "Andrew Johnson and His Ghost Writers," 475, 477–79.

94. *Diary of Gideon Welles* 3:4.

95. Charles Warren, *The Supreme Court in United States History* (rev. ed.; Boston, 1937), 2:603.

96. J. G. Randall and David Donald, *The Civil War and Reconstruction* (rev. ed.; Boston, 1961), 24. Maurice G. Baxter, *Orville H. Browning: Lincoln's Friend and Critic* (Bloomington, Indiana, 1957), 19–20, 67–69.

97. For Browning's wartime position, see Baxter, *Orville H. Browning*, 119–20, 141–43, 148.

98. National Union Club Documents, *Speeches of Hon. Edgar Cowan, Hon. Jas. R. Doolittle, Hon. Hugh McCulloch, Letter of Hon. O. H. Browning and an Address by a Member of the Club; also the Condition of the South: A Report of Special Commissioner B. F. Truman* (Washington, 1866), 21–22; *Diary of Gideon Welles* 2:534, 638.

99. Baxter, *Orville H. Browning*, 228, 245–56.

100. Joseph Schafer, "Alexander W. Randall," *Dictionary of American Biography* 15:344–45.

101. Ibid.; H. A. Tenney and David Atwood, *Memorial Record of the Fathers of Wisconsin* (Madison, 1880), 134–35.

102. Clark S. Matteson, *The History of Wisconsin* (Milwaukee, 1892), 303.

103. *Diary of Gideon Welles* 2:534, 608–9, 617–18, 628; 3:64, 83.

104. Hugh McCulloch, *Men and Measures of Half a Century: Sketches and Comment* (New York, 1889), 518.

105. Mobile *Times*, October 24, 1865, reprinted in New York *Herald*, November 2, 1865.

106. *Diary of Gideon Welles*, vols. 3, 4.

107. Ibid., 2:394.

108. McCulloch, *Men and Measures*, 381; *Diary of Gideon Welles* 2:531, 534.

109. McCulloch, *Men and Measures*, 515–18.

110. Campbell to Johnson, August 21, 1865, Johnson Papers.

111. Campbell to Johnson, January 22, 1866, ibid.

112. Campbell to Johnson, May 1, 1866, ibid.

113. The possible importance of the death of his wife was suggested to us by Prof. Glyndon G. Van Deusen, who has a very special knowledge of the Seward Papers.

114. See Cox, *Politics, Principle, Prejudice*, ch. 2, fn. 28.

115. *Diary of Gideon Welles*, vols. 3, 4.

116. Ibid., 2:534–35, 608–10. In the Seward Papers are two documents, one of which suggests that between the overriding of the civil rights veto and the call for the Philadelphia Convention, Seward was trying to obtain a reasonable compromise on an amendment; the other indicates an unyielding position on the part of the president during the same period. The first is a copy of House Bill 543, for restoring the states lately in insurrection, submitted by Stevens for the Committee on Reconstruction April 30, 1866. In his own hand, Seward made changes and additions that would have softened the proposal but left intact the provisions for protecting civil rights. The second is a copy dated May 28, 1866, of the constitutional amendment suggested the previous January by the president that provided only for representation according to

voters and direct taxation based on the value of property. On its reverse side is noted the following:

No amendment to the Constitution, or laws passed by Congress, as conditions precedent to the admission by Congress of loyal Representatives.

Representation from the several States should be left where the Constitution now places it.

No committals to any plan or proposition which may be made, while incomplete, and before thorough consideration by the President.

Note particularly the first statement. It is in marked contrast to Seward's proposal on the April bill that when any state should ratify the amendment, its senators and representatives would be admitted (after taking the required oaths of office).

117. Messages, Johnson Papers. See Cox, "Andrew Johnson and His Ghost Writers," 461.

118. Beale, *The Critical Year*, 400–402.

119. Welles says that Seward's endorsement of the message in cabinet meeting was "formal not from the heart, but yet not against it." *Diary of Gideon Welles* 2:628.

120. Letters of criticism from old friends, some written in anger, more in sorrow, are preserved in the Seward Papers. See letters to Seward from J. Warren, February 24, 1866; C. C. Royce, March 10, 1866; I. A. Gates, April 16, 1866, July 17, 1866; E. G. Cook, April 20, 1866; A. Conkling, May 4, 1866; L. M. Bond, May 24, 1866; R. Balcom, July 13, 1866; W. G. Bacon, July 16, 1866; D. C. Gamble, July 18, 1866; G. Hall, July 19, 1866; S. M. Hopkins, July 22, 1866; J. Henderson, July 27, 1866; C. L. Wood, July 29, 1866; G. Dawson to F. W. Seward, July 14, 1866, July 18, 1866; Seward to Ryerson, April 30, 1866; Seward to Conkling, May 7, 1866; Seward to Balcom, July 14, 1866; Seward to Hopkins, July 25, 1866. The coldness of lifelong friends broke Weed. Sarah Pellet to Seward, March 6, 1869, Seward Papers.

121. A. F. Kinnaird to Weed, December 30, 1865, Weed Papers.

122. Unidentified member of the House of Representatives, quoted in C. L. Wood to Seward, July 29, 1866, Seward Papers. For Seward's public position in May, see his Corning Hall, Auburn, speech, draft, and printed copy, ibid.

The failure of the Philadelphia Convention to organize a third party did not indicate that this goal was abandoned. One reason for postponement was the desire to win support from Republican ranks, which was essential to victory and also to the creation of a new party that would be more than a rejuvenation of the Democratic party under another label. Republicans were saying that no idea could be "more crazy than that of getting up a new Union party. There was nothing to be furnished from the Republican side but leaders, and the Democrats are not such d——d fools as to supply all the rank and file" without demanding leadership also. Unidentified member of the House of Representatives, quoted in C. L. Wood to Seward, July 29, 1866, ibid.

Raymond's curiously contradictory account of his interview with Johnson prior to the Philadelphia Convention is of interest in this connection. While Raymond opposed a third party and the president agreed that the convention should not attempt to organize one, Raymond yet reported his impression that the president was eager to gain a foothold in the South and to lay the foundation for a *"National"* party that would absorb the Democratic party of the North and West and all of the Union party except the Radicals. Raymond commented that this seemed to him a desirable object! "Extracts from the Journal of Henry J. Raymond (edited by his son), 4th paper: The Philadelphia Convention of 1866," *Scribner's Monthly* 20 (June 1880): 276–77; see also John A. Krout, "Henry J. Raymond on the Republican Caucuses of July, 1866," *American Historical Review* 33 (July 1928): 839.

123. This fact is clearly evident from the correspondence in the S. L. M. Barlow Papers, Huntington Library.

124. Even so restrained a man as John Sherman wrote in early July 1866: "I almost fear he [Johnson] contemplates civil war." J. Sherman to W. T. Sherman, July 8, 1866, Rachel Sherman Thorndike, ed., *The Sherman Letters, Correspondence Between General and Senator Sherman from 1837–1891* (New York, 1894), 276.

125. Italics added. Draft, Seward to Seymour, October 14, 1868, Seward Papers.

126. See Cox, *Politics, Principle, Prejudice,* ch. 4, fn. 49, and ch. 8, fnn. 47–56.

127. New York *Times,* March 26, 1866.

128. See above, nn. 22 and 23.

129. New York *Times,* July 30, 1866, June 15, 1866, and McKitrick, *Andrew Johnson and Reconstruction,* 358.

130. Raymond's letter to the committee requesting him to run again for Congress, September 15, 1866, in Augustus Maverick, *Henry J. Raymond and the New York Press* (Hartford, 1870), 175–84. See also Raymond's address of February 1866, at Cooper Institute, in ibid., 175–84.

131. *Diary of Gideon Welles* 2:534, 618; 3:251.

132. "Extracts from the Journal of Henry J. Raymond: The Philadelphia Convention," 278–79; McKitrick, *Andrew Johnson and Reconstruction,* 411.

133. Edward McPherson, *Handbook of Politics for 1868* (Washington, 1869), 241. Raymond drafted the resolutions after hearing those proposed by William B. Reed of Pennsylvania, Governor Sharkey of Mississippi, and Senator Cowan, all of which he considered too prosouthern. "Extracts from the Journal of Henry J. Raymond: The Philadelphia Convention," 278.

134. Maverick, *Henry J. Raymond,* 189. See also Raymond's address to the convention in *The Proceedings of the National Union Convention Held at Philadelphia, August 14, 1866* (pamphlet, n.p., n.d.), 12–13.

135. Raymond to R. Balcom, July 17, 1866, in Maverick, *Henry J. Raymond,* 173–74.

136. New York *Times*, October 11, 1866, November 12, 1866.

137. J. Sherman to W. T. Sherman, May 16, 1865, April 23, 1866, *The Sherman Letters*, 251, 270; see also John Sherman, *Recollections of Forty Years in the House, Senate and Cabinet: An Autobiography* (Chicago, 1895), 1:364, 366–67, 369.

138. J. Sherman to W. T. Sherman, October 26, 1866, *The Sherman Letters*, 278.

139. *Diary of Gideon Welles* 2:448. For Trumbull's repudiation of the president after the civil rights veto, see above, n. 24.

For Grimes, see William Salter, *The Life of James W. Grimes, Governor of Iowa, 1854–1858 and Senator of the United States, 1859–1869* (New York, 1876), 75, 392; F. I. Herriott, "James W. Grimes versus the Southrons," *Annals of Iowa* 15 (July 1926): 325–27; Fred B. Lewellen, "Political Ideas of James W. Grimes," *Iowa Journal of History and Politics* 42 (October 1944): 383–95.

For Fessenden, see Francis Fessenden, *Life and Public Services of William Pitt Fessenden* (Boston, 1907), 1:283–87; 2:29–32, 34–35, 65–66, 314–15; and William A. Robinson, "William Pitt Fessenden," *Dictionary of American Biography* 6:348–50.

For Trumbull, see Horace White, *The Life of Lyman Trumbull* (Boston, 1913), 277; also Arthur H. Robertson, "The Political Career of Lyman Trumbull," M.A. thesis, University of Chicago, 1910, 37–39, 56, 59, 75. Robertson's study indicates that Trumbull's prewar view of the race problem included colonization and the conviction that Negroes could not be placed upon an equal social or political position with whites. However, by the winter of 1865–66, there can be no doubt of Trumbull's deep sense of national responsibility for the freedmen nor of his sincerity in fighting to secure for them equal rights, short of suffrage and office holding.

140. George H. Porter, *Ohio Politics During the Civil War Period* (New York, 1911), 210–13; Homer C. Hockett, "Jacob Dolson Cox," *Dictionary of American Biography* 4:476–78; Jacob Dolson Cox, *Military Reminiscences of the Civil War* (New York, 1900), 1:157–63; James Rees Ewing, "Public Services of Jacob Dolson Cox," Ph.D. diss., Johns Hopkins University, 1902, 8, 14–15; William C. Cochran, *General Jacob Dolson Cox: Early Life and Military Services* (pamphlet, Oberlin, Ohio, 1901), 10–13.

141. Cox to Johnson, March 22, 1866, Johnson Papers.

142. Cox to Johnson, June 21, 1866, ibid.

143. Ewing, *Public Services of Jacob Dolson Cox*, 15.

144. Printed in William Dudley Foulke, *Life of Oliver P. Morton* (Indianapolis, 1899), 1:449.

145. Ibid., 434, 455; James, *Framing of the Fourteenth Amendment*, 29, 200. See also Governor Morton's message of November 1865, in W. H. Schlater (of the president's staff) to Johnson, November 12, 1865, Johnson Papers.

146. Foulke, *Life of Oliver P. Morton* 1:466–67; McKitrick, *Andrew Johnson and Reconstruction*, 309–10.

147. Compare Beale, *The Critical Year,* 106–7, 121–22, 178, 180, 184–86.

148. See above, nn. 4–9, 20–23, 27, 31, 49.

149. McPherson, *Handbook of Politics for 1868,* 102.

150. Compare McKitrick, *Andrew Johnson and Reconstruction,* 443.

151. New York *Herald,* September 19, 1866.

152. Cox to Marble, October 9, 1866, Manton Marble Papers. See also Barlow to R. Taylor, October 26, 1866, Barlow Papers.

153. Barlow to R. Johnson, October 24, 1866, Barlow Papers.

154. Barlow to T. J. Barnett, September 27, 1866, ibid.

155. Browning to W. H. Benneson and H. V. Sullivan, October 13, 1866, printed in New York *Times,* October 24, 1866. See also the earlier public statement of Democratic and Conservative members of Congress to the effect that the "dignity and equality of the States" must be preserved, including "the exclusive right of each State to control its own domestic concerns"; published in the New York *Herald,* July 4, 1866.

156. Professor Beale erroneously assumed that Seward's unidentified draft message had been prepared by Johnson and had reflected his views. *The Critical Year,* 400–403.

157. Doolittle to Browning, November 8, 1866, Doolittle Papers; see also James, *Framing of the Fourteenth Amendment,* 178, and McKitrick, *Andrew Johnson and Reconstruction,* 464–65, especially fn. 38.

158. Weed to Seward, November 24, 1866, Seward Papers. By the end of February, Weed was apprehensive of congressional reconstruction proposals and uncertain of the best presidential tactics; Weed to Seward, February 21, 1867, ibid.

159. P. W. Bartley to Johnson, November 9, 1866, Johnson Papers.

160. S. Smith to Johnson, November 10, 1866, ibid.

161. T. S. Seybolt to Johnson, November 8, 1866; F. A. Aiken to Johnson, November 26, 1866, ibid.

162. New York *Times,* October 31, 1866, November 3, 9, 12, 17, 19, 1866, December 4, 27, 31, 1866.

163. *Diary of Gideon Welles* 3:78.

164. Ibid., 232.

165. New York *Times,* November 14, 1867; McKitrick, *Andrew Johnson and Reconstruction,* 498.

166. See Cox, *Politics, Principle, Prejudice,* ch. 5, 95–106.

167. Of the sixty-five votes that Johnson obtained on the first ballot for the presidential nomination of the Democratic party in 1868, all but four were from southern delegates. Charles H. Coleman, *The Election of 1868: The Democratic Effort to Regain Control* (New York, 1933), 164, 208.

168. J. Sherman to W. T. Sherman, July 8, 1866, *The Sherman Letters,* 276. For Trumbull's reaction see *Cong. Globe,* 39th Cong., 1st sess., 1761 (April 4, 1866); and C. H. Ray to M. Blair, April 10, 1866, enclosure in Blair to Johnson, April 15, 1866,

Johnson Papers. A digest and explanation of the bill, unsigned, but in Trumbull's handwriting, is in the Johnson Papers; see Cox, "Andrew Johnson and His Ghost Writers," 473.

169. Fessenden to Morgan, June 26, 1867, Morgan Papers. The distrust, of course, involved party as well as principle. By mid-1866, it was widely believed that Johnson intended to bring the Democracy back into national power and ascendancy, and that he had deliberately sought to wreck the party that had elected him.

Chapter 7. Negro Suffrage and Republican Politics

John H. Cox, co-author.

1. The First Reconstruction Act, passed over President Andrew Johnson's veto March 2, 1867, and the Fifteenth Amendment, passed by Congress February 26, 1869, and declared ratified March 30, 1870. In 1860 the only states with equal suffrage for Negroes were Maine, New Hampshire, Vermont, Massachusetts, and Rhode Island. New York permitted Negroes with a $250 freehold estate to vote. By 1869 the following northern states had been added to the above list: Nebraska, Wisconsin, Minnesota, and Iowa.

2. A. Caperton Braxton, *The Fifteenth Amendment: An Account of Its Enactment* (Lynchburg, Va., n.d.). The foreword is dated April 30, 1934.

3. Ibid., 7.

4. Ibid., 16–17, 24, 33–38, 41, 47.

5. Ibid., 56–57, 58.

6. Ibid., 78.

7. Ibid., 46.

8. Ibid., 59.

9. Ibid., 47–48.

10. John Mabry Mathews, *Legislative and Judicial History of the Fifteenth Amendment* (Baltimore, 1909).

11. Ibid., 35.

12. Ibid., 12, 22, 32, 36.

13. For a comment on their treatment of Reconstruction, see Bernard Weisberger, "The Dark and Bloody Ground of Reconstruction Historiography," *Journal of Southern History* 25 (November 1959): 446–47; Alan D. Harper, "William A. Dunning: The Historian as Nemesis," *Civil War History* 10 (March 1964): 54–66; Kenneth M. Stampp, *The Era of Reconstruction, 1865–1877* (New York, 1965), 3–23.

14. William Archibald Dunning, *Reconstruction, Political and Economic, 1865–1877* (New York, 1907), 111.

15. Ibid., 94, 174, 135.

16. James Ford Rhodes, *History of the United States from the Compromise of 1850*

to the Final Restoration of Home Rule at the South in 1877 (New York, 1907–1910), 6:200–201 (c. 1906).

17. Ibid., 5:522 (c. 1904).

18. Ibid., 6:30.

19. The paper was not published, but an abstract, together with some indication of the discussion that followed, appeared in Massachusetts Historical Society, *Proceedings*, 2d ser. (Boston, 1905), 18:465–67; (1906), 6:34–37.

20. Rhodes, *History* 7:168.

21. Ibid., 170.

22. Abstract of paper on "Negro Suffrage and Reconstruction," Massachusetts Historical Society, *Proceedings*, 2d ser., 18:466–67.

23. Ibid., 19:37; Rhodes, *History* 7:174.

24. Abstract of paper on "Negro Suffrage and Reconstruction," Massachusetts Historical Society, *Proceedings*, 2d ser., 19:37.

25. Ellis Paxson Oberholtzer, *A History of the United States Since the Civil War* (New York, 1917–1937), 1:484–85.

26. Walter Lynwood Fleming, *Sequel of Appomattox: A Chronicle of the Reunion of the States* (New Haven, 1919), 169–70.

27. We borrow the phrase from Willard Hays's study in historiography, "Andrew Johnson's Reputation," East Tennessee Historical Society, *Publications* 32 (1960): 18.

28. Claude G. Bowers, *The Tragic Era: The Revolution After Lincoln* (Cambridge, 1929), 7, 13–15, 99, 151–54.

29. Ibid., 214–15.

30. George Fort Milton, *The Age of Hate: Andrew Johnson and the Radicals* (New York, 1930), 216, 219, 225; quotations are from pp. 216 and 225.

31. Ibid., 649–50.

32. J. G. Randall, *The Civil War and Reconstruction* (Boston, 1937), 799.

33. J. G. Randall and David Donald, *The Civil War and Reconstruction* (2d ed., Boston, 1961), 641.

34. Howard K. Beale, *The Critical Year: A Study of Andrew Johnson and Reconstruction* (New York, 1930), 173–95.

35. Ibid., 173–74.

36. Ibid., 146–47.

37. Ibid., 187, 194–95.

38. Charles H. Coleman, *The Election of 1868: The Democratic Effort to Regain Control* (New York, 1933), 18–24, 48–54.

39. Ibid., 369–70.

40. Ibid., 363, 377–78.

41. Ibid., 13.

42. Important were the unpublished Harvard doctoral dissertation (1954) of Leslie H. Fishel, Jr., parts of which appeared as "Northern Prejudice and Negro Suffrage,

1865–1870," *Journal of Negro History* 39 (January 1954): 8–26, and "The Negro in Northern Politics, 1870–1900," *Mississippi Valley Historical Review* 42 (December 1955): 466–89; Emma Lou Thornbrough, *The Negro in Indiana: A Study of a Minority* (Indianapolis, 1957); Louis Ruchames, "Race, Marriage, and Abolition in Massachusetts," *Journal of Negro History* 40 (July 1955): 250–73; C. Vann Woodward, "Equality: America's Deferred Commitment," *American Scholar* 27 (Autumn 1958): 459–72.

43. John Hope Franklin's *Reconstruction: After the Civil War* (Chicago, 1961) consolidates and extends this revisionism. For an earlier summation, see Howard K. Beale, "On Rewriting Reconstruction History," *American Historical Review* 45 (July 1940): 807–27.

44. For examples, see John and LaWanda Cox, "General O. O. Howard and the 'Misrepresented Bureau,'" *Journal of Southern History* 19 (November 1953): 427–56; John A. Carpenter, "Atrocities in the Reconstruction Period," *Journal of Negro History* 47 (October 1962): 234–47.

45. LeRoy P. Graf, "Andrew Johnson and the Coming of the War," *Tennessee Historical Quarterly* 19 (September 1960): 208–21; Eric L. McKitrick, *Andrew Johnson and Reconstruction* (Chicago, 1960); LaWanda and John H. Cox, *Politics, Principle, and Prejudice, 1865–1866: Dilemma of Reconstruction America* (New York, 1963).

46. Two germinal and widely reprinted articles were those by Bernard De Voto, "The Easy Chair," *Harper's Magazine* 192 (February 1946): 123–26, and by Arthur Schlesinger, Jr., "The Causes of the Civil War: A Note on Historical Sentimentalism," *Partisan Review* 16 (October 1949): 969–81.

47. For present-day sympathy with the abolitionists, see Martin Duberman, ed., *The Antislavery Vanguard: New Essays on the Abolitionists* (Princeton, 1965); and for a criticism of overly simplified approaches to motivation, see Duberman's own essay, "The Northern Response to Slavery," ibid., 406–13.

48. This is evident in Charles H. Wesley, "The Participation of Negroes in Anti-Slavery Political Parties," *Journal of Negro History* 29 (January 1944): 32–74; Leon F. Litvack, *North of Slavery: The Negro in the Free States, 1790–1860* (Chicago, 1961); Howard H. Bell, "Negro Emancipation in Historic Retrospect: The Condition and Prospects of the Negro as Reflected in the National Convention of 1864," *Journal of Human Relations* 11 (Winter 1963): 221–31; and August Meier, *Negro Thought in America, 1880–1915: Racial Ideologies in the Age of Booker T. Washington* (Ann Arbor, 1963).

49. Particularly noteworthy were Hans L. Trefousse, "Ben Wade and the Negro," *Ohio Historical Quarterly* 68 (April 1959): 161–72, and Ira V. Brown, "William D. Kelley and Radical Reconstruction," *Pennsylvania Magazine of History and Biography* 85 (July 1961): 316–29.

50. For example, see the emancipation centennial issue of the Illinois State Historical Society, *Journal* 56 (Autumn 1963).

51. The quotations and paraphrase are from Carl N. Degler, *Out of Our Past* (New York, 1959), 211; W. R. Brock, *An American Crisis: Congress and Reconstruction, 1865–1867* (London, 1963), 302–3; Stampp, *Era of Reconstruction,* 12–13, 214–15.

52. Stampp, *Era of Reconstruction,* 98–102; quotations are on pp. 101 and 102.

53. Brock, *An American Crisis,* 75.

54. Ibid., 62, 180–81; the quotation is on p. 62.

55. Cox and Cox, *Politics, Principle, and Prejudice,* especially ch. 10.

56. Fishel, "Northern Prejudice and Negro Suffrage," 11; Fishel, "Negro in Northern Politics," 466; Thornbrough, *Negro in Indiana,* ix–x, 251–52; Litwack, *North of Slavery,* 62, 80, 90–91.

57. James M. McPherson, *The Struggle for Equality: Abolitionists and the Negro in the Civil War and Reconstruction* (Princeton, 1964), viii.

58. Ibid., 430–31.

59. David Donald, *The Politics of Reconstruction, 1863–1867* (Baton Rouge, 1965), 12, 26–28, 82; quotations are from pp. 28 and 82. The first part of the assumption is explicitly stated as a hypothesis; the second part is implicit throughout.

60. Ibid., 17.

61. Stampp, *Era of Reconstruction,* 92–94, 141–42. The most striking example is Edgar A. Toppin, "Negro Emancipation in Historic Retrospect: The Negro Suffrage Issue in Postbellum Ohio Politics," *Journal of Human Relations* 11 (Winter 1963): 232–46.

62. Revisions in the manuscript made after its completion as a doctoral dissertation softened the original statement of the author's views but did not materially alter them. Compare *The Right to Vote: Politics and the Passage of the Fifteenth Amendment* (Baltimore, 1965) with "The Power of the Ballot: The Politics of Passage and Ratification of the Fifteenth Amendment," unpublished Ph.D. diss., Princeton University, 1963, especially the preface and the first and last chapters.

63. Italics ours. Gillette, *Right to Vote,* 165.

64. Ibid., 41–43, 89–90, 160, 163; quoted passages are on pp. 43 and 160.

65. Ibid., 115, quoting *World* editorial of April 1, 1870.

66. For the election of 1868, see Coleman, *Election of 1868,* 363. Calculations for the other years are based upon the electoral vote as given in W. Dean Burnham, *Presidental Ballots, 1836–1892* (Baltimore, 1955), 888–89. In 1872, Republicans had 286 electoral votes and would have held a substantial majority without the 6 southern states and the 2 border states that were included in the total. Republicans could have won in 1876 without the 19 contested votes of Florida, Louisiana, and South Carolina had they retained either New York (35 votes) or both Connecticut (6) and Indiana (15). In the elections of 1880, 1884, 1888, and 1892, the Republican candidate gained no electoral votes from any former slave state. In 1884, as in 1876, either the New York vote or a combination of those of Indiana and Connecticut would have won the election for the Republicans. In 1892 the electoral count was 277 Democratic,

145 Republican, and 22 Populist. Republicans needed an additional 78 votes for a majority, which could have come from New York (36), Illinois (24), Indiana (15), and Connecticut (6). The party kept Pennsylvania and Ohio (except for one vote); it had not held New Jersey (10 votes) since 1872.

67. More than a simple majority would have been necessary to retain control of Reconstruction in the face of President Johnson's vetoes and to pass the Fifteenth Amendment. Johnson supporters welcomed Negro suffrage as an issue on which they expected to redress their 1866 defeat. Doolittle to Browning, November 8, 1866, quoted in Cox and Cox, *Politics, Principle, and Prejudice*, 230.

68. All local and state election returns, except presidential votes, are from the *Tribune Almanac*. Some percentages are there given; more have been calculated. We are indebted to Stuart Horn, doctoral candidate at the City University of New York, for his assistance in compiling statistical data.

69. Fishel, "Northern Prejudice and Negro Suffrage," 24.

70. The other two states where equal suffrage was defeated were Wisconsin and Michigan.

71. Dixon Ryan Fox, "The Negro Vote in Old New York," *Political Science Quarterly* 32 (June 1917): 252–75; Litwack, *North of Slavery*, 80–84. Fishel has also linked the defeat of the suffrage proposal and the Democratic victory in New York. "Northern Prejudice and Negro Suffrage," 20. See also, Gillette, *Right to Vote*, 115, n. 18.

72. Aaron M. Powell's report of Sen. Henry Wilson's statement, *National Anti-Slavery Standard*, June 13, 1868, cited in McPherson, *Struggle for Equality*, 421. Sen. Oliver Morton wished the amendment passed and ratified quickly because he feared its effect if the issue hung over the elections of 1870 and 1872. Henry Wilson estimated that the struggle to make the Negro an equal citizen had cost the Republican party a quarter of a million votes. In an eloquent reply to the charge that the amendment was only an effort to maintain power and the spoils of office, Wilson pointed out that there was "not to-day a square mile in the United States where the advocacy of the equal rights and privileges of those colored men has not been in the past and is not now unpopular. . . . The public man or the political party that honestly and zealously espouses their cause will continue to be misunderstood, misrepresented, and maligned. . . . I fear it will be so in some portions of the country for years to come." *Cong. Globe*, 40th Cong., 3d sess., 672 (January 28, 1869), quoted in part in Braxton, *Fifteenth Amendment*, 55.

73. Stampp, *Era of Reconstruction*, 106–7.

74. Sumner to Bright, May 27, 1867, in Edward L. Pierce, *Memoir and Letters of Charles Sumner* (Boston, 1894), 4:319.

75. Brock, *American Crisis*, 192–95; Donald, *Politics of Reconstruction*, 73–75.

76. Local elections did, of course, have consequences for senators, who were elected by state legislatures; and a shift of political fortune in a critical state was al-

ways of national interest. However, the Fifteenth Amendment was not generated from local politics. The argument of political expediency implies political profit in national elections.

77. See n. 66 above and n. 79 below.

78. The percentage of Negroes in the population as compared with the percentage margin of victory in 1872 follows: Connecticut, 1.8 percent with 2.4; New York, 1.2 percent with 3.1; Pennsylvania, 1.9 percent with 12.1; New Jersey, 3.4 percent with 4.4; Ohio, 2.4 percent with 3.2; Indiana, 1.5 percent with 3.2; Illinois, 1.1 percent with 6.2. The Negro percentage is from Gillette's convenient chart, *Right to Vote,* 82; the percentage of the Republican vote was calculated from the election figures in Burnham, *Presidential Ballots,* as was that of 1868 and 1876.

79. Before 1872: New Jersey in 1860 (in part), 1864, and 1868, and New York in 1868. After 1872: Connecticut, New York, and Indiana in 1876 and 1884; New Jersey in 1876, 1880, and 1884.

80. The four were the Second District in New Jersey, the First in Ohio, the Sixth in Indiana, and the Thirteenth in Illinois. This conclusion is based upon an inspection of election returns as reported in the *Tribune Almanac,* comparing the margin of victory for Democratic winners in 1868 with an approximation of the number of potential Negro voters estimated as one-fifth of the Negro population in the counties comprising each district. Population figures were taken from the *Ninth Census of the United States, 1870* (Washington, 1872). Districts where Republican candidates were seated as the result of a contest were not counted as Democratic even though a Democratic majority was shown in the *Tribune Almanac* election returns.

81. That Negroes were responsible for the increase in the Republican vote cannot, of course, be proved but appears highly probable; similarly, the explanation for the larger Democratic vote is inference. The Republican vote in Alexander County with a Negro population of 21.73 percent rose from 656 to 804 (37.8 to 45.6 percent); in Pulaski with a Negro population of 27.4 percent from 543 to 844 (46 to 55.59 percent). The three counties showing an increase in the number of Democratic votes were Jackson (Republican votes increased there also), Massac, and Pulaski.

82. Districts lost were the Sixteenth Pennsylvania, the Third and Fourth Ohio, and the Seventh Indiana. Districts retained were the Second Connecticut, the Eleventh and Twelfth New York, the Third, Fifth, Tenth, and Thirteenth Pennsylvania, the Fourth New Jersey, the Second, Sixth, Seventh, Fourteenth, and Sixteenth Ohio, and the Fourth Indiana.

83. This tentative conclusion is based upon Republican victories in at least four of the five congressional elections before 1870. The winner in 1860 had to be estimated on the basis of the county vote because district boundaries were changed in 1862. In only one of the seven had the margin of Republican victory in 1866 been less than five hundred. This district, the Fifth in Philadelphia, may have needed Negro votes for victory in 1870 despite its Republican record. Together with it, the Thirteenth in

Pennsylvania and the Fourth in Indiana had slim majorities in 1870. In the latter two, however, the margin decreased as compared with 1868, making it unlikely that Negro enfranchisement helped more than it hurt the Republican candidates.

84. In every one of the seven close Ohio districts, the majority vote had been against the state's Negro suffrage amendment in 1867. Their congressmen, however, supported Negro suffrage, all having voted for the First Reconstruction Act of March 1867, and also for Negro suffrage in the District of Columbia on January 18, 1866, and again on December 14, 1866. These men, each of whom served both in the Thirty-ninth and Fortieth Congresses (1865–69) were Rutherford B. Hayes, Robert C. Schenck, William Lawrence, Reader W. Clarke, Samuel Shellabarger, Martin Welker, and John A. Bingham.

85. The Tenth District in Pennsylvania, made up of Lebanon and Schuylkill counties, had a Negro population of 458, or about 90 potential voters. The Republican margin increased by 404 votes. The Fourth District in New Jersey had a larger Negro population, but the incumbent's margin jumped from 79 to 2,753.

86. The Republican incumbent lost in 1868 by 322 votes but contested the outcome and was seated. In 1870 another Republican won by 500 votes. There were 2,623 Negroes, somewhat more than 500 possible voters, of whom some would have qualified under the old freehold requirement.

87. One in New York (Queens); three in Pennsylvania (Chester, Delaware, Franklin); eight in New Jersey (Cape May, Cumberland, Salem, Camden, Mercer, Monmouth, Somerset, Bergen); ten in Ohio (Meigs, Gallia, Pike, Ross, Brown, Clinton, Fayette, Clark, Greene, Paulding); five in Indiana (Clark, Floyd, Spencer, Vanderburgh, Marion); and seven in Illinois (Alexander, Jackson, Gallatin, Massac, Pulaski, Randolph, Madison). The three urban centers with the largest aggregate number of Negroes in 1870 did not meet the 5 percent criterion and are not included. Leslie Fishel has compiled a revealing table showing Negro and foreign-born urban population: table 2, appendix 3-b, "The North and the Negro, 1865–1900: A Study in Race Discrimination," unpublished Ph.D. diss., Harvard University, 1954. For the three cities with more than 5,000 Negroes, the comparative figures in 1870 were:

	Colored	Foreign-born	Total
Philadelphia	22,147	183,624	674,022
New York	13,072	419,094	942,292
Cincinnati	5,900	79,612	216,239

88. Twelve counties showed an increase in both the number and percentage of Republican votes in 1870 as compared with 1868; in nine of these, Republicans also made a better showing than in 1866. In 1876 twelve counties had a higher percentage of Republican votes than in 1868. Of these, eight were identical with counties showing marked gains in 1870. The eight, with an indication of their pre-1870 party

record, are: in New Jersey, Camden (R), Mercer (D/R), and Somerset (D); in Ohio, Pike (D) and Ross (D/R); in Indiana, Clark (D); in Illinois, Alexander (D) and Pulaski (D/R). The two clear instances of contested counties turning Republican in 1870 and remaining Republican were Mercer in New Jersey and Pulaski in Illinois, the former with a Negro population of 5.1 percent and the latter with 27.3 percent.

89. Brock, *American Crisis*, ch. 5; Donald, *Politics of Reconstruction*, ch. 3.

90. Gillette, *Right to Vote*, 50, 57–58, 71, 77; Mathews, *Legislative and Judicial History*, 36, 44–46.

91. Brown, "William D. Kelley and Radical Reconstruction," Hans L. Trefousse, *Benjamin Franklin Wade: Radical Republican from Ohio* (New York, 1963); Ernest A. McKay, "Henry Wilson and Reconstruction: The Anatomy of a Radical," an unpublished paper prepared for a graduate seminar at Hunter College and preliminary to a biography in process as a doctoral dissertation at New York University.

92. Republican support in Kansas was the weakest, with the 1867 referendum gaining only 54.3 percent of the vote for the party's candidate for governor the previous year. In the 1867 defeat for Negro suffrage in Minnesota, the proposal had the support equal to 78.7 percent of those voting for the Republican governor. The 1865 vote on the constitutional proposal in Connecticut amounted to 64 percent of the vote for the Republican candidate for governor; that in Wisconsin, to 79 percent of the Republican gubernatorial vote. New York rejected equal suffrage in 1869 with supporters equaling 60 percent of the 1868 Republican vote for governor and 80 percent of the party's 1869 vote for secretary of state.

93. For the pre-1860 record, see Emil Olbrich, *The Development of Sentiment on Negro Suffrage to 1860* (Madison, Wis., 1912). Recent state studies of outstanding merit are Leslie H. Fishel, Jr., "Wisconsin and Negro Suffrage," *Wisconsin Magazine of History* 46 (Spring 1963): 180–96, and Ira V. Brown, "Pennsylvania and the Rights of the Negro, 1865–1887," *Pennsylvania History* 28 (January 1961): 45–57.

94. The technique used by Edward L. Gambill, Glenn M. Linden, and David Donald to identify Radicals and Moderates on the basis of their voting records in Congress could be adapted to clarify the position of Republicans with respect to the Negro. See Donald, *Politics of Reconstruction*, appendix; Gambill, "Who Were the Senate Radicals?" *Civil War History* 11 (September 1965): 237–44; Linden, "'Radicals' and Economic Policies: The Senate, 1861–1873," *Journal of Southern History* 32 (May 1966): 189–99. Conventional sources and methodology have not been exhausted. A number of recent scholarly biographies shed little light on motivation because they have not sharply defined the problem and analyzed their subjects' attitudes toward the Negro and racial equality.

95. *Cong. Globe*, 39th Cong., 1st sess., 311 (January 18, 1866); Edward McPherson, *Hand Book of Politics for 1868* (Washington, 1868), 115. The total vote was 116 yeas, 54 nays, and 12 not voting.

96. New York *Times*, September 27, 1865.

Chapter 8. General O. O. Howard and the "Misrepresented Bureau"

John H. Cox, co-author.

1. The research upon which this article is based was made possible by grants-in-aid from the Social Science Research Council and the American Philosophical Society, and originated in an inquiry concerning the freedman as a farm laborer.

2. E. B. Ward to Gen. O. O. Howard, October 2, 1868; Howard to Ward, October 7, 1868; Howard to a Gentleman in Virginia, March 27, 1868, in O. O. Howard Papers (Bowdoin College Library).

3. The materials examined were voluminous and included the entire file of the central office (the Assistant Adjutant General). All records of the Bureau of Refugees, Freedmen, and Abandoned Lands are deposited in the National Archives. An excellent preliminary checklist was prepared in 1946 by Elizabeth Bethel, Sara Dunlap Jackson, and Lucille Pendell. Unless otherwise indicated, all manuscripts cited in this article are in the Records of the Bureau.

4. For example, Gen. J. G. Foster to Howard, November 21, 1866; Gen. Wager Swayne to Maj. S. C. Greene, September 15, 1866; Gen. P. H. Sheridan to Howard, December 27, 1865; E. W. Hickman to President Johnson, with endorsements, September 13, 1865; Mrs. C. Forshey to Johnson, referred November 17, 1865, with endorsements; A. F. Pratt to A. W. Randall, with endorsements, September 9, 1866.

5. The standard accounts are Paul S. Peirce, *The Freedmen's Bureau: A Chapter in the History of Reconstruction* (Iowa City, 1904), and Laura J. Webster, *The Operation of the Freedmen's Bureau in South Carolina* (Smith College *Studies in History* 1, nos. 2–3 [Northampton, 1916]). Neither is based upon the manuscript records, nor have the leading authorities on Reconstruction utilized these materials. The most notable and comprehensive study to appear based upon the manuscripts is Elizabeth Bethel, "The Freedmen's Bureau in Alabama," *Journal of Southern History* 14 (1948): 49–92. Other studies that use these records include Henry L. Swint, *The Northern Teacher in the South, 1862–1870* (Nashville, 1941); George R. Bentley, "The Political Activity of the Freedmen's Bureau in Florida," *Florida Historical Quarterly* 28 (1949–1950): 28–37; Thomas B. Alexander, "Ku Kluxism in Tennessee, 1865–1869," *Tennessee Historical Quarterly* 8 (1949): 195–219; Thomas B. Alexander, *Political Reconstruction in Tennessee* (Nashville, 1950); W. A. Low, "The Freedmen's Bureau and Education in Maryland," *Maryland Historical Magazine* 47 (1952): 29–39; William T. Alderson, Jr., "The Freedmen's Bureau and Negro Education in Virginia," *North Carolina Historical Review* 29 (1952): 64–90; and Claude Elliott, "The Freedmen's Bureau in Texas," *Southwestern Historical Quarterly* 56 (1952–1953): 1–24. See also the abstract of George R. Bentley's dissertation, "A History of the Freedmen's Bureau," in University of Wisconsin, *Summaries of Doctoral Dissertations* 10 (Madison, 1950): 307–9, and for current research, American Historical As-

sociation, *List of Doctoral Dissertations Now in Progress at Universities in the United States, October 1952* (Washington).

6. War Department, BRFAL, circular no. 22, December 22, 1865.

7. Ibid., no. 5, May 30, 1865. See also Howard to Gen. A. Baird, November 9, 1866.

8. Captain A. W. Shaffer to Howard, June 13, 1866. For a readily available source account of the trials of a bureau officer, see John William de Forest, *A Union Officer in the Reconstruction* (New Haven, 1948), especially ch. 4.

9. For example, Gen. J. S. Fullerton to Howard, July 23, 1865; Gen. F. D. Sewall to Howard, December 15, 1866.

10. For example, Gen. C. B. Fisk to Howard, December 9, 1865; Col. O. Brown to Howard, April 3, 1866; Gen. E. Whittlesey to Howard, May 15, 1866; Gen. A. Baird to Howard, July 7, 1866; Whittlesey to Howard, February 25, 1867.

11. Gen. S. Thomas to assistant commissioners, August 6, 1866.

12. Howard to Gen. J. B. Kiddoo, August 21, 1866, in Howard Papers.

13. A statement of an acting assistant commissioner made in requesting a military guard and a clerk to assist each of his subordinates. Enclosure in Gen. R. K. Scott to Howard, July 9, 1866.

14. H. W. Beecher to E. M. Stanton, May 3, 1865, in Howard Papers.

15. Howard to Chaplain T. W. Conway, May 25, 1866, ibid.

16. Sewall to Gen. J. T. Sprague, July 1, 1867.

17. Howard to G. Whipple, May 18, 1866, in Howard Papers.

18. Howard to Gen. D. E. Sickles, April 5, 1866.

19. Gen. U. S. Grant endorsement, July 9, 1866, on instructions of Howard, June 12, 1866; Gen. G. H. Thomas to Howard, December 1, 1866.

20. Gen. A. P. Ketchum to A. A. Bradley, September 14, 1866.

21. War Department, BRFAL, circular no. 4, December 10, 1866; M. Woodhull, Assistant Adjutant General, to Fisk, February 27, 1866.

22. This authority was granted in the law continuing the bureau.

23. Howard to the president, April 14, 1866. The order is in War Department, BRFAL, circular no. 2, April 10, 1866.

24. Howard to Colonel Morrow, May 1, 1866.

25. In other studies we shall present fuller documentation and analysis of this phenomenon.

26. Proceedings and findings in the trials of Whittlesey, Mann, Seely, Wickersham, Rosekrans, and Glavis, in Courts Martial Records (National Archives).

27. Fisk to Howard, September 10, 1866, in Howard Papers. The newspaper clipping was enclosed in the letter.

28. Howard to S. Thomas, September 12, 1866, ibid.

29. S. Thomas to Howard, September 9, 1866, ibid.

30. For example, Swayne to Howard, October 2, November 28, December 30,

1865; Gen. D. Tillson to Howard, November 1, 1865; Brown to Howard, December 9, 11, 1865; Howard to Brown, December 12, 1865; Fisk to Howard, December 19, 1865; Col. T. W. Osborne to Howard, December 30, 1865.

31. S. Colfax to Howard, September 7, 1866, in Howard Papers.

32. Howard to Colfax, September 11, 1866, ibid.

33. S. Thomas to Howard, September 5, 1866, ibid.

34. Howard to T. W. Conway, May 25, 1866, ibid.

35. Howard to G. F. Morgan, September 14, 1866, ibid.

36. Howard to H. B. Cadbury, March 26, 1866, ibid.

37. Howard to W. E. Dodge, August 6, 1866, ibid.

38. Howard to J. R. Sypher, August 30, 1866, ibid.

39. Howard to Fisk, August 27, 1866, ibid.

40. Unidentified New York newspaper clipping, in Howard Scrapbook, no. 2, 121, ibid.

41. Howard to Grant, November 30, 1867.

42. Whittlesey, circular letter, November 28, December 18, 1867.

43. Howard to Gen. O. Brown, December 1, 1868; Howard to Gen. N. A. Miles, November 5, 1867; Howard to J. R. Shepherd, January 25, 1867.

44. Howard to Conway, June 14, 1866, in Howard Papers.

45. See below, n. 83.

46. Howard to the Secretary of War, September 25, 1869.

47. Baird to Howard, May 25, 1866, in Howard Papers.

48. Baird to Howard, June 6, 1866.

49. Howard to Gen. A. C. Gillem, July 18, 30, 1867; Gillem to Howard, July 25, 27, 1867; Whittlesey to Gillem, August 7, 1867; Howard to Gillem, August 8, September 11, 1867.

50. Howard to Gillem, August 8, 1867.

51. Howard to Gen. W. P. Carlin, August 10, 1867; Whittlesey to Brown, December 2, 1867; Howard to Col. C. C. Sibley, June 3, 1868.

52. Oliver O. Howard, *Autobiography of Oliver Otis Howard* (New York, 1907), 2:424.

53. Webster, *Freedmen's Bureau in South Carolina*, 149.

54. Report of the Joint Committee on Reconstruction, *House Reports*, 39th Cong., 1st sess., no. 30 (serial no. 1273), pt. 2, 249.

55. J. M. McKim to Howard, January 9, 1866, in Howard Papers.

56. See Howard's account (*Autobiography* 2:317) of his statement to a Negro delegation early in 1866.

57. B. F. Rice to Howard, June 21, 1867; Sewall to Rice, June 27, 1867.

58. Sewall to Sibley, June 10, 1867.

59. Sewall to Howard, May 13, 1867, in Howard Papers.

60. G. Mallery to Sewall, July 11, 1868, with endorsement and notation.

61. Howard to Gen. J. A. Mower, May 24, 1867, in Howard Papers.

62. Howard to Scott, December 11, 1867; G. Pillsbury to Howard, December 12, 1867.

63. Scott to Howard, December 23, 1867.

64. Bethel, "The Freedmen's Bureau in Alabama," 81; Howard to Gen. J. Hayden, January 22, 1868; Hayden to Howard, January 27, 1868; Whittlesey to Hayden, March 2, 1868. For Howard's earlier decision that an officer nominated for Congress must be relieved of bureau office, see Swayne to Howard, December 26, 1867; Howard to Swayne, December 28, 1867; and Bethel, "The Freedmen's Bureau in Alabama," 76–77.

65. Howard to Capt. E. H. Weirman, September 16, 1868.

66. Sewall to J. E. Bryant, June 26, 1867; B. F. Whittemore to Howard, October 21, 1867, with endorsement of Gen. R. K. Scott; Whittlesey to Whittemore, October 25, 1867. Whittemore was backed strongly by local supporters, the Freedmen's Aid Society, and the American Missionary Association in seeking reappointment as special agent in charge of schools in eastern South Carolina. The assistant commissioner praised him highly but pointed out that his candidacy for office would reflect adversely upon the bureau.

67. The extent and nature of these activities have never been subjected to systematic examination and analysis. The best account is in Bethel, "The Freedmen's Bureau in Alabama," 72–82. Bentley in his "The Political Activity of the Freedmen's Bureau in Florida" does not consider motives and accepts a number of the basic assumptions challenged in this article.

68. Compare Hilary A. Herbert, ed., *Why the Solid South?* (Baltimore, 1890), 16, and Peirce, *Freedmen's Bureau*, 164. The Herbert volume is often cited as authority. It was written by a group of southern congressmen and dedicated to "the Business Men of the North," with the intention of reassuring them of the desirability of southern investments provided there was no further northern interference in the South on the "mistaken" assumption that the Negro required protection.

69. Howard to G. M. Dodge, June 15, 1868; Annual Report of General Howard, October 14, 1868, in *House Exec. Docs.*, 40th Cong., 3d sess., no. 1, vol. 3, pt. 1 (ser. no. 1367), 1016–60.

70. Howard to C. W. Nelson, September 23, 1868, in Howard Papers.

71. Howard to Brown, December 1, 1868.

72. War Department, BRFAL, circular no. 5, May 30, 1865.

73. Howard to Scott, March 2, 1867; Howard to Gov. J. L. Orr, March [?], 1867; Sewall to Sprague, July 1, 1867.

74. War Department, BRFAL, circular no. 5, May 30, 1865.

75. S. Thomas to Swayne, May 19, 1866.

76. Howard to Swayne, August 28, September 20, 27, 1866; Howard to Stanton, August 28, September 27, 28, 1866; Ketchum to Tillson, October 6, 1866; Ketchum

to Col. J. Bomford, October 9, 1866; Ketchum to Scott, October 20, 1866; Howard to Tillson, November 16, 1866, in BRFAL Records; Howard to Brown, October 1, 1866; Howard to Tillson, November 13, 1866, in Howard Papers.

77. O. Brown, address to the freedmen of Virginia, received at bureau headquarters, June 29, 1865.

78. The statement is not meant to disregard the various limitations upon that jurisdiction. The extent of the bureau's judicial powers is a complicated subject that cannot be presented here. Similarly, other powers mentioned in this paragraph were more qualified than this brief summary might seem to suggest.

79. Howard to Brown, December 1, 1868.

80. Howard to Secretary of War, November 19, 1869.

81. Howard, *Autobiography* 2:203; Howard to J. A. Peters, July 24, 1871, in Howard Papers.

82. Howard to assistant commissioners, June 14, 1865, Howard to officers and agents in South Carolina, Georgia, and Florida, October 23, 1865.

83. Sprague to Howard, October 4, 1865; Woodhull to Sprague, October 9, 1865; Woodhull to Osborne, October 10, 1865; Osborne to Howard, November 30, 1865; Woodhull to O. Jennings, October 20, 1865; Tillson to Gov. J. Johnson, October 25, 1865; Woodhull to Tillson, November 1, 1865, in BRFAL Records; Howard to a Gentleman in Virginia, March 27, 1868, in Howard Papers.

84. Howard to Gen. E. M. Gregory, March 3, 1866.

85. Gen. T. J. Wood to Howard, September 27, 1866.

Chapter 9. The Perception of Injustice and Race Policy

At the time the prelude was written Professor Cox expected to be able to complete the study. The essay on Freedmen's Bureau agent James McGogy (which follows) was written and the research on a second bureau agent, William Leidtke, was finished. Additional case studies were projected for selected Republican leaders and newspapers through the 1890s to explore the usefulness of the thesis as an element of explanation for the retreat from the nation's Reconstruction commitment.

1. LaWanda Cox and John H. Cox, *Politics, Principle, and Prejudice: 1865–1866* (New York: Free Press, 1963).

2. LaWanda Cox and John H. Cox, "Negro Suffrage and Republican Politics: The Problem of Motivation in Reconstruction Historiography," *Journal of Southern History* 33 (August 1967): 303–30.

3. The most influential of these volumes is Leon F. Litwack, *North of Slavery: The Negro in the Free States, 1790–1860* (Chicago: University of Chicago Press, 1961). For other citations, see LaWanda Cox, "From Emancipation to Segregation: National Policy and Southern Blacks," in John B. Boles and Evelyn Thomas Nolan, eds., *Inter-*

preting Southern History: Historiographic Essays in Honor of Sanford W. Higginbotham (Baton Rouge: Louisiana State University Press, 1987), 208–9, n. 22.

4. Edmond N. Cahn, *The Sense of Injustice: An Anthropocentric View of Law* (New York: New York University Press, 1949), 13.

5. I am especially indebted to the anthropologist G. Elaine Roccio of Wayne State University for her cogent analysis of the relationship between the genetically given need-for-nurture and the development of a sense of justice built upon the recognition of the legitimate expectations of others. Letter to author, July 20, 1976. I also found relevant a wide range of psychological writings beginning with the conflicting views of Sigmund Freud in *Civilization and Its Discontents,* Eric H. Erickson in *Childhood and Society* and *Insight and Responsibility,* and Eric Fromm in *Escape from Freedom* and including accounts of moral judgment, altruism, prosocial behavior, emergency intervention, and the psychology of justice by, among others, Jean Piaget, Lawrence Kohlberg, Martin L. Hoffman, Ervin Staub, Lauren G. Wispe, and Melvin J. Lerner. Several publications are noteworthy: "Positive Forms of Social Behavior," *Journal of Social Issues* 28 (Summer 1972), and "The Justice Motive in Social Behavior," ibid., 31 (Summer 1975); David J. De Palma and Jeanne M. Foley, eds., *Moral Development: Current Theory and Research* (New York: John Wiley, 1975); Nancy Eisenberg, ed., *The Development of Prosocial Behavior* (New York: Academy Press, 1982); and Raymond J. Corsini, *Encyclopedia of Psychology* (New York: John Wiley, 1984).

6. See Martin Hoffman, "Development of Prosocial Motivation: Empathy and Guilt," in Eisenberg, ed., *Development of Prosocial Behavior,* 275–95; Melvin J. Lerner, "The Justice Motive: Some Hypotheses as to Its Origins and Forms," *Journal of Personality* 35 (March 1977): 14.

7. For example, see Ervin Staub, "Social and Prosocial Behavior: Personal and Situational Influences and Their Interactions," in Staub, ed., *Personality: Basic Aspects and Current Research* (Englewood Cliffs, N.J.: Prentice Hall, 1980), 272–78.

8. LaWanda Cox, *Lincoln and Black Freedom: A Study in Presidential Leadership* (Columbia: University of South Carolina Press, 1981), 218, n. 45.

9. See Zick Rubin and Letitia Anne Peplau, "Who Believes in a Just World?" *Journal of Social Issues* 31 (Summer 1975): 65–87; Lerner, "The Justice Motive," 1–52.

10. For early South Bend, Mary Clarke Coquillard, *Alexis Coquillard—His Time: A Story of the Founding of South Bend, Indiana* (South Bend, 1931). Population and agricultural data are from the U.S. Bureau of the Census, 1860. In 1860, 1,368 persons, 7.7 percent of Cass County population, were reported "Free colored," almost 70 percent of them classified as "Mulatto," the rest as "Black."

11. Kate [Farber] to Mary, November 2, 1955, letter in possession of Diane Kingdon, great granddaughter of McGogy's brother, Elija K., who kindly gave me a copy. I am indebted to Eric L. Mundell, Reference Librarian of the Indiana Historical Society Library, for information on the McGogy family from the 1850 census of La-

Porte (town) and for reference to McGogy senior in the St. Joseph County records, and in Thomas Edward Howard, *A History of St. Joseph County* (Chicago, 1907).

12. The most revealing details of the first marriage are in an affadavit of Daniel H. McGogy, a younger brother, made February 9, 1906, James F. McGogy Pension File XC 966 734. A copy of the marriage license is in the records of the county clerk's office in LaPorte, reference to which was found for me by Dorothy Rowley, LaPorte County Historian and Associate Curator of the LaPorte County Historical Society. As was customary at the time, it included no such personal data as residence or occupation and, uncharacteristically, left blank the space provided for name of clergyman. Personal descriptions of McGogy are in his army records, R.G. 94, National Archives.

13. *History of Page County, Iowa* (Des Moines, 1880), 676; Muster Rolls, Company D, 48th Indiana Infantry, McGogy's compiled service record, National Archives, Record Group 94 (hereinafter NA, RG); affadavit of James McGogy, March 26, 1891, in his pension file. For the record of the company and regiment, and the campaigns in which they participated, see Frederick H. Dyer, *Compendium of the War of the Rebellion* (Des Moines, 1908), 1137–38; Earl Schenck Meiers, *The Web of Victory: Grant at Vicksburg* (New York, 1955), 36–39, 109–15, 137, *et seq.*; T. N. Dupuy and C. G. Dupuy, *The Compact History of the Civil War* (New York, 1962), 234–37, 240–45; Mark Mayo Boatner, *The Civil War Dictionary* (New York, 1959), 176–77, 428–29, 871–76; Logan Esarey, *History of Indiana from Its Exploration to 1922; Also an Account of St. Joseph County by John B. Stoll* (Dayton, Ohio, 1922), 2:136–37; Timothy E. Howard, *A History of St. Joseph County, Indiana* (Chicago, 1907), 1:722.

14. John D. Winters, *The Civil War in Louisiana* (Baton Rouge, La., 1963), 183–95; John Y. Simon, ed., *The Papers of Ulysses S. Grant* (Carbondale, Ill., 1979), 8:20–132, 485–524; Samuel E. Snure, "The Vicksburg Campaign as Viewed by an Indiana Soldier," *Journal of Mississippi History* 19 (October 1957): 263–69.

15. McGogy's presence or absence from his company, as well as his appointment and muster into the black regiment, are recorded in his compiled service record, Company D, 48th Indiana Infantry and Company B, 50th U.S. Colored Troops, NA, RG 94.

16. Simon, ed., *Grant Papers*, 8:215; [Thomas Eaton] *Report of the General Superintendent of Freedmen, Department of the Tennessee and State of Arkansas for 1864* (Memphis, 1865), 10; Ira Berlin, et al., eds., *Freedom: A Documentary History of Emancipation, 1861–1867*, ser. 1, vol. 1: *The Destruction of Slavery* (Cambridge, U.K., 1985), 261–62; Dudley Taylor Cornish, *The Sable Arm: Negro Troops in the Union Army, 1861–1865* (New York, 1966), 142–45, 232–33; Ira Berlin, et al., eds., *Freedom: A Documentary History of Emancipation, 1861–1867*, ser. 2: *The Black Military Experience* (Cambridge, U.K., 1982), 116–19, 518.

17. Winters, *Civil War in Louisiana*, 189–90; L. Thomas to Edwin M. Stanton, *Official Records of the War of the Rebellion* (Washington, 1880–1901), ser. 3, vol. 3, 121 (hereinafter cited as *OR*).

18. John Eaton, *Grant, Lincoln, and the Freedmen: Reminiscences of the Civil War* (New York, 1907; rpt. ed., 1969), 55; Cornish, *Sable Arm*, 112–26; L. Thomas to Stanton, April 12, 1863, *OR*, ser. 3, vol. 3, 121; "Prejudice" section in *Report of the General Superintendent of Freedmen*, 7.

19. Richard H. Sewell, *Ballots for Freedom: Antislavery Politics in the United States, 1837–1860* (New York, 1976), 181–83; Emma Lou Thornbrough, *The Negro in Indiana: A Study of a Minority* (Indianapolis, 1957), 33–133. See also Eugene H. Berwanger, *The Frontier Against Slavery: Western Anti-Negro Prejudice and the Slavery Extension Controversy* (Urbana, Ill., 1967), 30–59, and Leon F. Litwack, *North of Slavery: The Negro in the Free States, 1790–1860* (Chicago, 1961), 66–72.

20. Marion Clinton Miller, "The Antislavery Movement in Indiana," Ph.D. diss., University of Michigan, 1938, 99, 106, 222–23, 256; Jasper Packard, *History of La-Porte County Indiana and Its Townships, Towns and Cities* (La Porte, 1876), 209, 238, 247, 251–52, 280, 431; *History of LaPorte County, Indiana* (Chicago, 1880), 197; *History of St. Joseph County, Indiana* (Chicago, 1880), 547–53.

21. *History of St. Joseph County*, 572.

22. Ibid., 618–26; Thornbrough, *Negro in Indiana*, 112–14.

23. In the state as a whole, only 16 percent of the vote on the Negro exclusion provision was negative while 32 percent of the votes cast in La Porte and 47 percent in St. Joseph were against exclusion. Calculated from the figures in Charles Kettleborough, *Constitution Making in Indiana* (Indianapolis, 1916), 2:617–18.

24. *Report on the Debate and Proceedings of the Convention for the Revision of the Constitution of the State of Indiana, 1850* (Indianapolis, 1850), 1:78, 228–30, 241, 455–58, 615–17; 2:1817–18; William H. Smith, *Schuyler Colfax: The Changing Fortunes of a Political Idol* (Indianapolis, 1952), 31–34; Miller, "Antislavery Movement in Indiana," 121.

25. *History of St. Joseph County*, 548–50; O. J. Hollister, *Life of Schuyler Colfax* (New York, 1886), 61–65, 119–23, 132–33; Miller, "Antislavery Movement in Indiana," 240.

26. Packard, *History of La Porte County*, 242. Similarly, in retrospect the anonymous author of the 1880 *History of St. Joseph County* identified with those who had lived "to glory in the triumph of their cause, to see the last vestiges of slavery swept away, and all men equal before the Constitution and the laws of their country." *History of St. Joseph County*, 626.

27. Record of Events, July to August 31, September and October 1863, Company B, 50th U.S. Colored Troops, NA, RG 94; Dyer, *Compendium*, 1732; report of Col. Charles A. Gilchrist, March 9, 1864, *OR*, ser. 1, vol. 12, pt. 1, 395–400.

28. Peter F. Walker, *Vicksburg: A People at War, 1860–1865* (Chapel Hill, 1960), 212–20; *Report of the Superintendent of Freedmen*, 94–95; Eaton, *Grant, Lincoln, and the Freedmen*, 97, 104, 131–36.

29. Swayne to O. O. Howard, July 24, 1865, *Records of the Assistant Commissioner*

for Alabama, Bureau of Refugees, Freedmen, and Abandoned Lands, National Archives Microfilm Publication M-809, roll 2. (Hereinafter BRFAL, Ala., AC.) The chronology of McGogy's career with the bureau has been reconstructed primarily from his service records and from special orders issued by the assistant commissioner. See BRFAL, Ala., AC, roll 17.

30. McGogy to Miller, August 19, 1865, BRFAL, Ala., AC, roll 6.

31. During the visit Swayne both saw the president and testified before the Congressional Joint Committee on Reconstruction. Swayne to O. O. Howard, February 14, October 4, 1866, O. O. Howard Papers, Bowdoin College Library; Swayne to O. O. Howard, March 9, 1866, BRFAL, Ala., AC, roll 3.

32. New York *Times,* December 19, 1902, 9, December 21, 1902, supplement, 2; Thomas M. Spaulding, "Wager Swayne," *Dictionary of American Biography,* 18: 240–44; Alonzo Tuttle, "Noah Waynes Swayne," ibid., 239–40. There is no consensus among historians as to Swayne and his record as assistant commissioner. See Kenneth B. White, "Wager Swayne: Racist or Realist?," *Alabama Review* 31 (April 1978): 92–109; John B. Myers, "The Freedmen and the Law in Post-Bellum Alabama, 1865–1867," ibid., 23 (January 1970): 56–69; Elizabeth Bethel, "The Freedmen's Bureau in Alabama," *Journal of Southern History* 14 (February 1948): 49–92, esp. 57–58, 80–81; Donald G. Nieman, *To Set the Law in Motion: The Freedmen's Bureau and the Legal Rights of Blacks, 1865–1868* (Millwood, N.Y., 1979), 17–20, 92–94, 157, 175–76, 199, 219; Sarah Woolfolk Wiggins, *The Scalawag in Alabama Politics* (University, Ala., 1977), 11–12, 15, 20–21; Peter Kolchin, *First Freedom: The Response of Alabama's Blacks to Emancipation and Reconstruction* (Westport, Conn., 1972), 5–7, 66–67, 158–59; William S. McFeely, *Yankee Stepfather: General O. O. Howard and the Freedmen* (New Haven, 1968), 77–78; George R. Bentley, *A History of the Freedmen's Bureau* (Philadelphia, 1955), 66, 130, 196–99; Walter L. Fleming, *Civil War and Reconstruction in Alabama* (New York, 1905), 315, 429; Gail Snowden Hasson, "The Medical Activities of the Freedmen's Bureau in Reconstruction Alabama, 1865–1868," Ph.D. diss., University of Alabama, 1982, 39–52.

33. The quote is the characterization of Swayne by the prerevisionist historian Walter L. Fleming who also wrote that "General Swayne showed no bias except the natural bias of one who did not understand the people, and who had no sympathy with any of the southern social or political principles." *Civil War and Reconstruction in Alabama,* 315 n. 3, 420.

34. Circular No. 5, May 30, 1865, with approval of the president, June 21, *Selected Series of Records Issued by the Commissioner, Bureau of Refugees, Freedmen, and Abandoned Lands,* National Archives Microfilm Publication M-742, roll 7 (hereinafter cited as BRFAL, LS); Swayne to Robinson, September 13, 1865; letter of advice to assistant commissioners, June 14, 1865, BRFAL, Ala., AC, Ala., roll 1, 17.

35. Swayne to O. O. Howard, October 9, 1865, BRFAL, Ala., AC, roll 2. During his first six months in Alabama, from July 24, 1865 through January 31, 1866, Swayne

sent Howard weekly reports that provide a vivid, intimate, and detailed picture of his efforts, problems, and attitudes. Swayne was handicapped by incredible bureaucratic red tape and the constant shifting or muster out of officers and troops, limitations effectively presented in Kenneth B. White, "Black Lives, Red Tape: The Alabama Freedmen's Bureau," *Alabama Historical Quarterly* (Winter 1981): 241–58. However, White's contention that bureaucratic mismanagement precluded success is an overstatement.

36. Italics added. This analysis is based on Swayne's weekly reports and related letters, especially those to Governor Parsons, to local officials, and to General Woods, and his printed annual report of October 31, 1866, all in BRFAL, Ala., AC, rolls 1 and 2; General Orders, September 15, 1865, BRFAL, Ala., AC, roll 17; and Nieman, *To Set the Law in Motion*, 5–8, 17–20. See also the citiations in n. 39, below.

37. Swayne to O. O. Howard, July 24, 31, 1865, BRFAL, Ala., AC, roll 2; Swayne to Parsons, July 29, 1865, *Registers and Letters Received by the Commissioner, Bureau of Refugees, Freedmen, and Abandoned Lands*, National Archives Microfilm Publication M-752, roll 17 (hereinafter cited as BRFAL, LR).

38. Swayne to O. O. Howard, August 4, 1865 (telegram), BRFAL, LR, roll 17; Swayne to Howard, August 7, 1865, BRFAL, Ala., AC, roll 2.

39. For President Johnson's and General Howard's attitude toward black testimony and equal rights, see LaWanda Cox and John H. Cox, *Politics, Principle, and Prejudice, 1865–1866: Dilemma of Reconstruction America* (New York, 1963), 167–69, 195–203 and Donald G. Nieman, "Andrew Johnson, the Freedmen's Bureau, and the Problem of Equal Rights," *Journal of Southern History* 44 (August 1978): 399–420. See also, Nieman, *To Set the Law in Motion*, 5–8; Bentley, *History of the Freedmen's Bureau*, 65–68; and for Swayne, White, "Wager Swayne," 95–98; Myers, "Freedmen and the Law," 56–57, 67.

40. Swayne to Parsons, July 31, August 1, 1865, Swayne to Howard, August 21, 1865, BRFAL, Ala., AC, rolls 1, 2; Kolchin, *First Freedom*, 7.

41. Swayne to Parsons, August 11, 1865, BRFAL, Ala., AC, roll 2.

42. Ibid.

43. Swayne to Howard, August 14 (telegram), August 14 (letter), August 16 (telegram), BRFAL, LR, roll 17; Swayne to Howard, August 21, 1865, BRFAL, Ala., AC, roll 2.

44. Ibid.

45. Report of the assistant commissioner of Alabama, 1866, 4, 24, BRFAL, Ala., AC, roll 2. See also Swayne's testimony of March 9, 1866, *Report of the Joint Committee on Reconstruction at the First Session of the Thirty-ninth Congress* (Washington, 1866), 139, 141, in which he also linked nonvoting to injustice, but more discreetly. Suffrage for blacks was a politically sensitive issue, with a majority of Republicans not yet convinced of its appropriateness or necessity.

For Swayne's indignation over unequal justice and outrages, and his attempt to enlist local magistrates in an effort to stimulate white public opinion in support of "civil justice [in] its fullest and most equitable operation without distinction of color," see Swayne to Sir, September 9, 1865, Swayne to Judge Robert Dougherty, September 9, 1865, BRFAL, Ala., AC, rolls 1, 2.

Swayne's comprehensive General Orders No. 14 to agents on their duties, September 15, 1865, instructed them to monitor the fairness of civil proceedings and promptly report cases of evident denial of justice. They were also to arrange "with a reliable justice of the peace" to have his office near that of the bureau in order to ensure action upon complaints. BRFAL, Ala., AC, roll 17.

46. Swayne ended his October 1866 report: "Secession had its origin and life in Slavery; when liberty is made complete, we shall have ground for faith in perpetual Union." BRFAL, Ala., AC, roll 17.

47. General Orders No. 14, September 15, 1865, BRFAL, Ala., AC, roll 17.

48. Kerr to Swayne, January 21, 1866; McGogy to Swayne, June 15, 1866; Swayne to Steadman, June 16, 1866, BRFAL, Ala., AC, rolls 8, 19, 1.

49. McGogy to Kinsman, May 23, 1866, BRFAL, Ala., AC, roll 8.

50. B. Williams to Robert Patton, May 9, 1866; H. P. Clayton to Patton, June 6, 1866; Pardons and Petitions, drawer 73, governor's correspondence, Alabama Department of Archives and History. I am indebted to Tim Johnson of Montgomery for locating these and other relevant communications in the Alabama Archives.

51. McGogy to Kinsman, May 23, 1866, BRFAL, Ala., AC roll 18.

52. Ibid.

53. McGogy to Cadle, June 4, 1866, BRFAL, Ala., AC, roll 18.

54. Houghey to Swayne, May 17, 1866; McGogy to Cadle, June 4, 1866, BRFAL, Ala., AC, roll 18.

55. Swayne to Howard, weekly reports, November 1865, BRFAL, Ala., AC, roll 2.

56. Swayne to Howard, June 16, 1866, BRFAL, Ala., AC, roll 1. Swayne's response to the commission was restrained, Swayne to Fullerton, June 13, 1866, ibid. This paragraph and the preceding one are based primarily upon the bureau records and Nieman, *To Set the Law in Motion*, 108–21, 135–41. See also Cox and Cox, *Politics, Principle, and Prejudice*, chs. 9 and 10; Nieman, "Andrew Johnson, the Freedmen's Bureau, and Equal Rights;" Kaczorowski, "Revolutionary Constitutionalism in the Era of the Civil War and Reconstruction," *New York University Law Review* 61 (November 1986): esp. 890–95, 903–6; Bentley, *History of the Freedmen's Bureau*, 125–35; Kaczorowski, *Politics of Judicial Interpretation*, 27–37, 43; and the articles by Bethel, Myers, and White cited in n. 32 above. White's characterization of Swayne as a pragmatic racist, naively insensitive to the depths of white racism, is a serious distortion.

57. Swayne to Howard, June 25, 1865, BRFAL, Ala., AC, roll 1.

58. Mostyn to Cadle, February 1, 1866, BRFAL, Ala., Greenville, letters sent, vol. 123, NA; Porter to Mostyn, February 22, 1866; Porter to Cadle, April 13, 1866;

Porter to Swayne, April 28, June 4, 1866, BRFAL, Ala., AC, roll 8; Swayne to Howard, June 20, 1866, BRFAL, Ala., AC, roll 1; Seawell to President Johnson, June 18, 1866, with endorsements, BRFAL, LR; Bethel, "Freedmen's Bureau in Alabama," 59.

For Seawell and Porter, see Daniel Michael Jackson, "Red Hills and Piney Woods: A Political History of Butler County, Alabama, in the Nineteenth Century," Ph.D. diss., University of Alabama, 1985, 202, 204, 205–6, 217–18, 227, 228, 238–40, 252, 254, 257; John Buckner Little, *History of Butler County, Alabama, 1815 to 1885* (Cincinnati, 1885; rpt., 1971), 114–20. Porter was born in Charleston, South Carolina, and spent part of his adult life there.

59. Porter to Swayne, February 7, 1866; Porter to Cadle, February 10, 15, 1866; Porter to McGogy, July 11, 1866, BRFAL, Ala., AC, roll 8; Hasson, "Medical Activities of the Freedmen's Bureau," 135–36, 150–55, 221.

60. Porter to Swayne, April 28, 1866; Steinbeg to Kinsman, June 3, 1866, BRFAL, Ala., AC, rolls 8, 9; notes on Mostyn and Steinberg, John A. Carpenter Papers, Schomburg Center for Research in Black Culture, New York Public Library.

61. Arthur to Swayne, June 18, 1866; Porter to Swayne, May 16, June 22, 1866, BRFAL, Ala., AC, rolls 19, 8; Swayne to Crenshaw, June 22, 1866; Swayne to Howard, June 25, 1866; Swayne to Steinberg, June 25, 1866, BRFAL, Ala., AC, roll 1; Markle to Kinsman, June 22, 1867, BRFAL, Ala., AC, roll 12; notes on Mostyn and Steinberg, Carpenter Papers.

62. Swayne endorsement, July 13, 1866, on Seawell to President Johnson, June 15, 1866, BRFAL, LR.

63. This summary is based upon Alabama bureau records from June 1866 to February 1867, both in manuscript and on microfilm. For quotations, Swayne's General Orders No. 14, September 15, 1865, BRFAL, Ala., AC, roll 17; McGogy to Kinsman, July 3, 1866, BRFAL, Ala., Greenville, LS, vol. 123, NA.

64. McGogy to Kinsman, June 27, 1866; Kinsman to McGogy, June 28, 1866, BRFAL, Ala., AC, rolls 8, 1.

65. McGogy to Conyngham, September 11, 1866 (roll 8); Kinsman to McGogy, September 14, 1866 (roll 1); McGogy to Kinsman, September 21, 1866 (roll 8); McGogy to Conyngham, October 11, 1866 (roll 8); BRFAL, Ala., AC; McGogy to Markle, Oct. 5, 1866, BRFAL, Ala., Greenville, LS, vol. 123, NA; McGogy's annual report, October 31, 1866, BRFAL, Ala., AC, roll 18; Hasson, "Medical Activities of the Freedmen's Bureau," 151–55.

66. McGogy to Kinsman, June 20, 1866 (roll 8); Kinsman to McGogy, June 21, 1866 (roll 1), BRFAL, Ala., AC.

67. McGogy to Buckley, July 16, 24, August 8, 15, 22, September 13, October 20, 1866; McGogy to Hildreth, July 23, 1866, BRFAL, Ala., Greenville, LS, vol. 123, NA.

68. McGogy to Porter, August 17, 1866; McGogy to Buckley, November 10, 19, 28, 30, 1866; and two letters of January 23, 1867, BRFAL, Ala., Greenville, vols. 123, 124, NA; McGogy to Kinsman, December 17, 1866, BRFAL, Ala., AC, roll 8.

69. McGogy to Kinsman, November 22, 1866 (roll 8); Kinsman to McGogy, November 23, 1866 (roll 1), BRFAL, Ala., AC.

70. Two letters from McGogy to Kinsman, November 22, 1866, BRFAL, Ala., AC, roll 8.

71. McGogy to Cadle, August 23, 1866 (roll 8); Kinsman to McGogy, August 24, 1866 (roll 1), BRFAL, Ala., AC.

72. McGogy to D. Parmer, September 12, 1866; McGogy to Conyngham, September 12, 1866, BRFAL, Ala., Greenville, LS, vol. 123, NA. For General Orders No. 44, see Nieman, *To Set the Law in Motion*, 141–43.

73. McGogy to Kinsman, September 26, 1866; McGogy's annual report, October 31, 1866; Markle to McGogy, August 23, September 18, 1866, with endorsements; McGogy to Kinsman, December 18, 20, 1866, BRFAL, Ala., AC, roll 8; McGogy to Judge Bolling, December 12, 1866; McGogy to Conyngham, December 21, 1866, BRFAL, Ala., Greenville, LS, vol. 124, NA.

74. This and the following paragraphs are based on the copybooks of letters sent from the Greenville office from June 20, 1866 through January 26, 1867; for the quotations, see McGogy to Porter, June 30, 1866; McGogy to Cook, January 26, 1867, BRFAL, Ala., Greenville, LS, vols. 123, 124, NA. Errors in grammar and spelling in quoted passages have been indicated by *sic;* the office copies quoted here appear to be in McGogy's handwriting but might have been written by a clerk.

75. McGogy to Bolling, September 26, 28, 1866, BRFAL, Ala., Greenville, LS, vol. 123, NA.

76. McGogy to Lietle, July 18, 1866; McGogy to Payne, July 19, 1866, BRFAL, Ala., Greenville, LS, vol. 123, NA.

77. McGogy to Cook, November 12, 1866; McGogy to Trawick, October 6, 1866, BRFAL, Ala., Greenville, LS, vol. 124, 123, NA.

78. McGogy to Kinsman, January 4, 1867 (roll 12); Kinsman to McGogy, January 7, 1867 (roll 1), BRFAL, Ala., AC.

79. Italics added. McGogy to Kinsman, January 11, 1867, BRFAL, Ala., AC, roll 12. See also McGogy to Cook, January 26, 1867, BRFAL, Ala., Greenville, vol. 124, NA. McGogy vigorously protested vagrancy arrests to Intendant Cook but there is no evidence they were effective.

80. Kinsman to McGogy, January 14, 1867, BRFAL, Ala., AC, roll 1. Though McGogy read the *Advocate* piece as unjustified, malicious attack upon himself, the reports may have had some foundation in the actions of his superintendent at the Garland colony. Some days after the *Advocate* story, McGogy was informed "by reliable sources" that Markle had received "for two persons furnished Mr. Verday out of the colony" the sum of seven dollars. McGogy at once sent his clerk assistant to take over affairs at the colony, writing Markle that his employment with the bureau would end in two days unless he was able "to convince this office by letter that the above charges

are incorrect." McGogy to Markle, January 17, 1867, BRFAL, Ala., Greenville, LS, vol. 124, NA.

81. McGogy to Kinsman, Jan. 23, 1867, BRFAL, Ala., AC, roll 12.

82. There were other charges against Hicks, including interference with the freedmen's school, on which he was apparently not convicted. McGogy to Kinsman, December 17, 30, 1866; McGogy to Conyngham, December 28, 1866; Porter to Swayne, December 31, 1866, BRFAL, Ala., AC, roll 8; Greenville *Advocate,* December 27, 1866. I am indebted to Judy Taylor of Greenville for the December 27 newspaper items.

83. Porter to Swayne, December 31, 1866, BRFAL, Ala., AC, roll 8; notes on Roderick Theune, Carpenter Papers; Hasson, "Medical Activities of the Freedmen's Bureau," 69.

84. Walter L. Fleming, the prerevisionist historian, so characterized General Meade in *The Civil War and Reconstruction in Alabama,* 497–98. See also James E. Sefton, *The United States Army and Reconstruction, 1865–1867* (Baton Rouge, La., 1967), 114, 125–26, 183–84; Bentley, *History of the Freedmen's Bureau,* 196–97; Bethel, "Freedmen's Bureau in Alabama," 74–75, 80–81.

85. This paragraph and the one that follows are based upon McGogy's correspondence with his bureau superiors. Many such letters are in the published microfilm records and in the unfilmed field records, but some are available only in the latter. For quotations, see McGogy to Kinsman, February 6, 21, 1867, BRFAL, Ala., AC, roll 12; McGogy to Groves, February 25, 1867, BRFAL, Ala., Talladega, LS, vol. 165, NA.

86. For quotations, McGogy to Kinsman, February 12, 15, 16, 19, 1867, BRFAL, Ala., AC, roll 12.

87. McGogy to Kinsman, February 16, 1867, BRFAL, Ala., AC, roll 12; McGogy to Groves, February 16, 1867; McGogy to Browning, February 26, 1867, BRFAL, Ala., Talladega, LS, vol. 165, NA.

88. McGogy to Conyngham, April 4, 1867; McGogy to Kinsman, June 22, 1867; McGogy to Arthur, January 10, 1868; McGogy to Sharkly, February 1, 1868, BRFAL, Ala., Talladega, LS, vol. 165, NA.

89. Kinsman to ten agents, June 22, 1867, BRFAL, Ala., AC, roll 2; McGogy to Kinsman, July 1, 6, 1867, BRFAL, Ala., Talladega, LS, vol. 167, NA.

90. McGogy to Kinsman, July 13, 1867, BRFAL, Ala., Talladega, LS, vol. 165, NA.

91. McGogy to Kinsman, July 17, 23, 1867; McGogy to Sims, July 10, 1867; McGogy to Sheriif, July 15, 1867; McGogy to Dorsey, July 17, 1867, BRFAL, Ala., Talladega, LS, vol. 165, NA.

92. Kinsman to McGogy, July 16, August 2, 1867 (roll 2); McGogy to Kinsman, July 29, 1867; McGogy's affadavit of August 1, 1867, with endorsements (roll 12), BRFAL, Ala., AC.

93. McGogy affadavit of August 1, 1867 (roll 12); McGogy to Sharkly, May 11, 1868 (roll 14), BRFAL, Ala., AC.

94. McGogy to Sharkly, May 11, 1868, BRFAL, Ala., AC, roll 14. Customarily correspondence with the general commanding went through his adjutant, although there are several letters to McGogy from Swayne. Undoubtedly, the headquarters staff exercised considerable authority and discretion over routine matters.

95. McGogy to Sanderson, September 11, 1868, with endorsements of September 15, 17, 1868, BRFAL, Ala., AC, roll 14.

96. Registers of letters received, BRFAL, Ala., AC, roll 4; registers of letters received, BRFAL, LR, roll 10.

97. McGogy's monthly report, August 3, 1867, BRFAL, Ala., AC, roll 18.

98. McGogy to Conyngham, April 9, 1867; McGogy to Kipp, May 16, 1867; McGogy to King, June 26, 28, 1867, BRFAL, Ala., Talladega, LS, vol. 165, NA; McGogy, Special Order No. 1, June 25, 1867, BRFAL, Ala., AC, roll 12.

99. McGogy to Kipp, July 23, August 17, 1867; McGogy to Kinsman, September 2, 1867, BRFAL, Ala., Talladega, LS, vol. 165, NA; McGogy to Kinsman, September 23, Oct. 17, 1867 (roll 12); Kinsman to McGogy, September 6, Oct. 15, 1867 (roll 2); McGogy to Kinsman, December 3, 1867 (roll 18), BRFAL, Ala., AC.

100. McGogy to Buckley, March 22, May 2, 13, June 8, 24, September 3, 1867; McGogy to Fister, August 26, 1867, BRFAL, Ala., Talladega, LS, vol. 167, NA.

101. McGogy to Buckley, September 3, 1867; McGogy to Silsby, October 19, 1867, BRFAL, Ala, Talladega, LS, vol. 165, NA.

102. McGogy's monthly reports, December 3, 1867, March 2, 30, May 1, 1868, BRFAL, Ala., AC, roll 18.

103. McGogy to Sharkly, May 16, 1868, with endorsements of May 21 and June 3, 1868, BRFAL, Ala., AC, roll 14; McGogy to Buckley, August 20, 1867, BRFAL, Ala., Talladega, LS, vol. 165, NA. On the Talladega normal school, see Joe M. Richardson, "To Help a Brother On: The First Decade of Talladega College," *Alabama Historical Quarterly* 37 (Spring 1975): 19–37, and his *Christian Reconstruction: The American Missionary Association and Southern Blacks, 1861–1890* (Athens, Ga., 1986), 128–31. See also Kolchin, *First Freedom*, 89–91. Swayne originally asked McGogy to negotiate a lease of the Baptist college building but the trustees would only sell. Obtaining the deed was a complicated affair. McGogy to Kinsman, March 7, 1867, McGogy to Conyhngham, April 11, 1867, BRFAL, Ala., AC, roll 12.

104. McGogy to Kinsman, June 5, December 24, 1867 (roll 12), Jan. 4, 1868 (roll 14); McGogy's monthly report of July 5, 1867 (roll 18), BRFAL, Ala., AC; McGogy to Kinsman, August 27, 1867, BRFAL, Ala., Talladega, LS, vol. 165, NA.

105. Edward McPherson, *A Handbook of Politics for 1868* (Washington, D.C., 1868), 319; for the bureau and military reconstruction, see Nieman, *To Set the Law in Motion*, ch. 6, with specific references to Alabama, 199, 203, 206, 214, 219.

106. McGogy to Solicitor, Coosa County, March 25, 1867; McGogy to Kinsman, May 30, 1867; McGogy to judge of probate, Clay County, October 28, 1867; McGogy to justice of the peace, Calhoun County, January 13, 1868; McGogy to Judge Marsden, Shelby County, March 9, 1868, BRFAL, Ala., Talladega, LS, vol. 165; Marsden to McGogy, March 12, 1868, BRFAL, Ala., Talladega, LR.

107. McGogy to Kinsman, June 5, October 21, 1867 (roll 12); McGogy's monthly report, March 30, 1868 (roll 18), BRFAL, Ala., AC; McGogy to Hamlin, June 4, 1867; McGogy to Goodwin, October 16, 1867; McGogy to Patterson, October 22, 1867; McGogy to Sherill, October 25, 1867; McGogy to Autra, October 31, 1867; McGogy to Jackson, December 7, 1867; McGogy to Stone, May 16, 1868, BRFAL, Ala., Talladega, LS, vols. 165, 166, NA.

108. McGogy's monthly reports of November 2, 1867, December 3, 1867, December 24, 1867 (roll 18); McGogy to Kinsman, December 24, 1867, January 1, 1868 (roll 14), BRFAL, Ala., AC; McGogy to justice of the peace, Calhoun County, January 13, 1868, BRFAL, Ala., Talladega, LS, vol. 165, NA.

109. McGogy to Kinsman, June 5, 1867 (roll 12); McGogy to Hamlin, January 4, 1868 (roll 14), BRFAL, Ala., AC; McGogy to Hamlin, June 4, 1867, BRFAL, Ala., Talladega, LS, vol. 165, NA. McGogy's comment to Judge Hamlin may have reflected less his own attitude than an effort to enlist the judge's racial assumptions on the side of justice for the freedmen. Elsewhere in his communications with southern whites on behalf of blacks a note of irony appears.

110. McGogy to Sharkly, January 30, 1868, BRFAL, Ala., AC, roll 14.

111. McGogy to Sharkly, January 30, 1868 (roll 14); Sharkly to McGogy, February 7, 1868 (roll 2), BRFAL, Ala., AC; McGogy to commanding officer, Jacksonville, January 14, 1868; McGogy to judge of probate, Clay County, January 16, 1868, BRFAL, Ala., Talladega, LS, vol. 165, NA.

112. O. O. Howard to Hayden, January 22, 1868 (roll 14); Hayden to Howard, January 27, 1868 (roll 2), BRFAL, Ala., AC; Bethel, "Freedmen's Bureau in Alabama," 81.

113. McGogy to Sims, February 5, 1868, BRFAL, Ala., Talladega, LS, vol. 165, NA; McGogy to Sharkly, February 6, 1868, two letters with enclosures and endorsements (roll 14), Sharkly to McGogy, February 10, 1868 (roll 2), BRFAL, Ala., AC.

114. Hayden's endorsement on McGogy to Sharkly, February 6, 1868, BRFAL, Ala., AC, roll 14.

115. Whittlesey endorsement on McGogy to Sharkly, February 6, 1868, BRFAL, Ala., AC, roll 14. McGogy had responded to the censure by stating that he believed that he was acting within the jurisdiction of his office but would endeavor in the future to conform strictly to the discharge of his duty.

116. McGogy to Kinsman, August 19, 1867, BRFAL, Ala., Talladega, LS, vol. 165, NA. On removals in Alabama, see Fleming, *Civil War and Reconstruction in Alabama*, 483, and Sefton, *U.S. Army and Reconstruction*, 125–26, 144–47.

117. Shouse to McGogy, March 21, 1868, with endorsements, BRFAL, Ala., Talladega, LR, NA; McGogy to Houston, March 21, 1868, BRFAL, Ala., Talladega, LS, vol. 165, NA.

118. McGogy to Sharkly, March 30, 1868, with Sharkly's endorsement, BRFAL, Ala., Talladega, LR, NA.

119. Ibid.

120. McGogy's monthly reports, March 30, 1868, May 1, 1868, June 2, 1868, BRFAL, Ala., AC, roll 18; McGogy to Lt. Johnson, March 30, 1868; McGogy to Williams, April 29, June 12, 1868; McGogy to probate judge, St. Clair County, June 10, 1868, BRFAL, Ala., Talladega, LS, vol. 165, NA; Lt. Johnson to McGogy, April 7, 1868; Williams to McGogy, April 27, May 22, 1868, BRFAL, Ala., Talladega, LR, NA.

121. McGogy to Sharkly, March 9, 1868 (roll 14); McGogy's monthly reports of March 30 and May 1, 1868 (roll 18), BRFAL, Ala., AC.

122. McGogy's monthly report of May 1, 1868, ibid.; McGogy to Wood, April 28, 1868, BRFAL, Ala., Talladega, LS, vol. 166, NA.

123. For Gardner and for political developments in Butler County, the work of Michael J. Daniel is indispensable and evenhanded. See his "Samuel Spring Gardner, A Maine Person in Alabama," *Maine Historical Society Quarterly* 23 (Spring 1984): 151–76; and his dissertation cited above, "Red Hills and Piney Woods"; also notes on Gardner in the Carpenter Papers and Gardner's monthly report, June 1, 1868, BRFAL, Ala., AC, roll 18.

124. Gardner to Hayden, January 30, 1868 (roll 14); Sharkly to Gardner, February 3, 1868 (roll 2), BRFAL, Ala., AC; Daniel, "Red Hills and Piney Woods," 220–31, "Samuel Spring Gardner," 158–60.

125. Gardner's monthly reports of June 1, 1868, July 3, 1868 (roll 18); Gardner to Sharkly, July 13, 14, 28, 1868 (roll 14), BRFAL, Ala., AC; Daniel, "Red Hills and Piney Woods," 231–38; Daniel, "Samuel Spring Gardner," 161; Gardner's testimony, *Report of the Joint Committee on Outrages* (Montgomery, Ala., 1868), 15.

126. McGogy's monthly report, September 3, 1868, BRFAL, Ala., AC, roll 18; the quotation from the *Advocate* is cited in Daniel, "Red Hills and Piney Woods," 239, see also 240–41.

127. Beecher to McGogy, November 5, 1868, BRFAL, Ala., Greenville, LR, NA; "Report of the Secretary of War, November 20, 1868," *House Executive Docs.*, 40th Cong., 3d sess., vol. 3, pt. 1, xxv, 74–82, 122–23; Sefton, *U.S. Army and Reconstruction*, 213–17, 230–31.

128. McGogy to Smith, September 4, 1868; John A. Hart to Smith, September 4, 12, October 17, 1868; R. M. Reynolds to Smith, September 5, 1868; Gardner to Smith, September 24, 1868, governor's correspondence, Alabama Archives.

129. Daniel, "Samuel Spring Gardner," 162–63; Daniel, "Red Hills and Piney Woods," 241–46; for testimony, see *Report on Outrages*, 16–18, 29–30, 52; Gardner to Smith, September 24, 1868, governor's correspondence, Alabama Archives.

130. Hart to Smith, October 17, 1868, ibid.; McGogy to Beecher, October 18, 1868, BRFAL, Ala., Greenville, LS, vol. 126, NA; McGogy's monthly report, November 5, 1868 (roll 18); Beecher to Howard, November 10, 1868 (roll 2), BRFAL, Ala., AC; *Report on Outrages,* 52–57; Daniel, "Red Hills and Piney Woods," 242–43; Bethel, "Freedmen's Bureau in Alabama," 85–86.

131. Daniel, "Samuel Spring Gardner," 164–69; Daniel, "Red Hills and Piney Woods," 251–60.

132. McGogy's monthly report, November 5, 1868, BRFAL, Ala., AC, roll 18.

133. Italics added. McGogy to Miller, November 28, 1868, governor's correspondence, Alabama Archives; McGogy to Beecher, November 28, 1868 (roll 14); McGogy's monthly report, December 4, 1868 (reel 18); Beecher to Howard, December 10, 1868 (roll 2), BRFAL, Ala., AC.

134. McGogy's monthly report, December 4, 1868, BRFAL, Ala., AC, roll 18.

135. I am indebted to Mimi C. Jones, Senior Reference Archivist of the Alabama Department of Archives and History for locating references to McGogy in the 1870 census schedules and in the 1869 Montgomery tax records.

136. McGogy to Beecher, November 7, 1868, BRFAL, Ala., Greenville, LS, vol. 126, NA; lease, McGogy to M. J. Farrow, December 18, 1867, conveyances, book 2 (index), book 19, 427–29, Judge of Probate Records, Montgomery County Courthouse. I am indebted to Nancy Weems of Montgomery for locating the lease and also the deed of sale for McGogy's plantation.

137. Ibid.

138. Lien, Isaac Parker to McGogy, May 7, 1870, conveyances, 546–47, Judge of Probate Records, Elmore County Courthouse.

139. Deed, James F. and Mary McGogy to Sancho Hails, October 14, 1869, State of Indiana, Sullivan County, recorded in book 1 of deeds, 518, Judge of Probate Records, Montgomery County Courthouse; Montgomery County Tax Book 1869: Real Estate and Personal Property (McGogy); Tax Book 1870: Land Subject to Taxation (Hails), Alabama Archives; Lawrence N. Powell, *New Masters: Northern Planters During the Civil War and Reconstruction* (New Haven, 1980), 22, 145–46, 151.

140. The account of McGogy's years in Iowa is based primarily upon documents in his pension file, news of his death and burial published in the Shenandoah *World,* especially that of November 29, 1904, and the biographical sketch in *History of Page County, Iowa* (Des Moines, 1880), 676. For locating Iowa materials, I am indebted to Karen J. Laughlin, Reference Librarian, Iowa State Historical Department and to Mary Lou Holdridge, Acting Director, Shenandoah Public Library.

141. Letter dated March 31, 1904, copy in McGogy's pension file.

142. For news reports of the celebrations, see Page County *Democrat,* August 6, 1870, August 5, 1871, August 8, 1872, August 7, 1873, August 6, 1874; Clarinda *Herald,* July 14, 1880, August 5, 1885, August 11, 1886; "Colored Folks Held Big August 4 Celebrations" and "Underground Railway Center 4 Miles North of Clarinda,"

in *Clarinda Centennial: Thrills of a Century, 1853–1953* (Clarinda, 1953); *Page County, Iowa History, Compiled and Written by the Works Progress Administration in the State of Iowa* (Clarinda, 1942), 40; Leona Nelson Bergman, *The Negro in Iowa* (Iowa City, 1969); for population statistics, John A. T. Hull, *Census of Iowa for 1880* (Des Moines, 1883), 212–13; for black churches, *Biographical History of Page County, Iowa* (Chicago, 1890), 346.

The WPA account states that as many as ten thousand to fifteen thousand attended the celebrations but that hardly seems credible. During the post–Civil War years the black leader who managed the celebrations was Dr. Thomas Gordon Jones, described by Clarinda's 1953 centennial committee as "a tall and slender man who wore on his cheeks the stylish sideburns of the period." When his wife died at age ninety-nine in Omaha, the Clarinda newspaper ran a two-column story with a picture of the couple entitled "In Remembrance of Aunt Eliza Jones." Why August 4 was chosen for the celebrations is not clear. Perhaps it was because of weather appropriate for an outdoor celebration and because blacks in Iowa had from the 1850s celebrated emancipation in the West Indies in August. In the early 1930s, blacks began leaving Clarinda in order to find employment and very few black families still reside there.

For a search of the extant local newspapers of the 1870s and 1880s, and for other information about blacks in Clarinda, I wish to thank Mrs. Betty Winter of Clarinda. Helpful assistance was also given by David Hudson of the University of Iowa Libraries and by Prof. Robert Dykstra, the leading authority on Iowa's nineteenth-century race policies.

143. Shenandoah *World*, November 29, 1904.

144. No knowledge of McGogy's Freedmen's Bureau sevice has survived in the family papers or oral tradition. For changing attitudes toward race in Iowa, see Robert R. Dykstra, "Iowa: 'Bright Radical Star,'" *Radical Republicans in the North: State Politics During Reconstruction*, James C. Mohr, ed. (Baltimore, 1976); Dykstra, "The Issue Squarely Met: Toward an Explanation of Iowans' Racial Attitudes, 1865–1868," *Annals of Iowa*, 3d ser., 57 (Summer 1984): 430–50; Dykstra, *Bright Radical Star: Black Freedom and White Supremacy on the Hawkeye Frontier* (Cambridge, Mass., 1993).

Chapter 10. Reflections on the Limits of the Possible

1. Howard K. Beale, ed., *The Diary of Gideon Welles* (New York, 1960), 2:281; Albert Mordell, ed., *Civil War and Reconstruction: Selected Essays by Gideon Welles* (New York, 1959), 192–93; Charles H. McCarthy, *Lincoln's Plan of Reconstruction* (New York, 1901), 426; "Impeachment of the President: Testimony," 40th Cong., 1st sess., *House Report*, No. 7: 401, 403–4; Roy P. Basler, ed., *The Collected Works of Abraham Lincoln* (New Brunswick, N.J., 1953–55), 8:404.

2. LeRoy P. Graf and Ralph W. Haskins, eds., *The Papers of Andrew Johnson* (Knoxville, Tenn., 1967–), 5:18 (October 4, 1861), 229 (March 22, 1862), 536 (July 4, 1862).

3. Albert Castel, *The Presidency of Andrew Johnson* (Lawrence, Kas., 1979), 28–29; Sarah W. Wiggins, *The Scalawag in Alabama Politics, 1865–1881* (University, Ala., 1977), 5–17; Francis B. Simkins and Robert H. Woody, *South Carolina during Reconstruction* (Chapel Hill, N.C., 1932), 39–42. Historians have not as yet undertaken the laborious work in the manuscript census to determine with certainty the antebellum wealth and slave ownership of members of the constitutional conventions and legislatures and of officeholders during 1865 and 1866.

4. Beale, ed., *Diary of Gideon Welles* 2:11, 305, 307.

5. My analysis of Stanton's Reconstruction proposals and subsequent changes is based upon a comparative study of two versions of the May 9, 1865, executive order for Virginia and four versions of what evolved into the May 29, 1865, proclamation for North Carolina available in the microfilmed Johnson Papers; various accounts by Gideon Welles—his original diary entries, the revised diary, his letter to Andrew Johnson of July 27, 1869 (Beale, ed., *Diary of Gideon Welles* 2:281–82, 291, 294, 301–3, 304, 393–95; 3:714–24), his essay on "Lincoln and Johnson" originally published in *The Galaxy*, April and May 1872 (Mordell, ed., *Civil War and Reconstruction*, 190–213); the testimony of Stanton and of Grant in 1867 before the House Judiciary Committee considering impeachment ("Impeachment of the President: Testimony," 400–406, 826–36); and the exhaustively researched biographies of Stanton by Benjamin P. Thomas and Harold M. Hyman (*Stanton: The Life and Times of Lincoln's Secretary of War* (New York, 1962), 306, 357–58, 402–4, 438–39, 444–46) and of Welles by John Niven (*Gideon Welles: Lincoln's Secretary of the Navy* (New York, 1973), 491–92, 497–99, 501–5, 508–12).

I have been unable to locate the original Stanton proposal that combined Virginia and North Carolina nor his revised executive order for North Carolina except for its heading. To the printed heading has been pasted three separate sheets of handwritten manuscript, followed by a printed sheet that itself is three pieces pasted together, and lastly a final sheet of handwritten manuscript. I am indebted to Paul T. Heffron, acting chief, Manuscript Division, Library of Congress, for the careful inspection of the document to determine its composition.

Without the two missing documents it is not possible to determine with certainty whether the change from military to civilian governor was made at the May 9 cabinet meeting or earlier, but it would appear to have been made subsequent to Lincoln's death. Similarly there is some uncertainty about the suffrage provision, or rather the lack of one, in the paper Stanton prepared for Lincoln. Stanton testified that he left the matter blank, a statement Welles contested but on the basis of Stanton's second proposal, the one of May 9, Welles was not certain as to the content of the first that he had only heard read. Welles had a copy of the printed proposal dated May 9 for an executive order covering North Carolina only, but it cannot be found in any collection of his papers and was probably destroyed in a fire. The earlier paper that Lincoln saw is apparently still extant although not available to scholars.

The official executive order for Virginia differed from Stanton's version in omitting the provision in respect to volunteers for occupation duty in the South but retained the preceding part of the sentence that read: "That the Secretary of War assign such Assistant Provost Marshal General, and such Provost Marshals in each district of said State as he may deem necessary." A like statement was not included, however, in the North Carolina and subsequent proclamations. Another difference worth noting is that Johnson's proclamations dropped all reference to the secretary of war but enjoined every other member of the cabinet by specific reference to proceed to reestablish the functions and laws under his jurisdiction. What seems to have happened is that Johnson transformed a temporary framework, within which Lincoln intended to develop the substance of Reconstruction, into a "plan" that Johnson treated as itself the substantive settlement between North and South. This has been obscured by loose usage of the term "plan" and by a necessarily heavy reliance upon Welles' accounts, which were biased by his own extreme states'-rights views, his strong aversion to military control, and his defense of President Johnson.

Niven has suggested that Welles' influence may have been decisive in Johnson's decision to make no concession on suffrage, that had Welles spoken for limited black suffrage the outcome might have been different. Hyman sees the question of centralized control of the provost marshal corps as a matter of army organization and command authority rather than one of presidential policy.

I am indebted to both Professor Niven and Professor Hyman for help in my fruitless attempt to locate the missing documents, and also to the staff of the Huntington Library, the Connecticut Historical Society, the manuscript division of the University of Rochester Library, the manuscript division of the Library of Congress, and the Military Archives Division of the National Archives.

6. Cuthbert Bullitt to Johnson, May 5, 1865; Wells to Johnson, May 22, 1865, July 3, 1865; Cottman to Johnson, June 5, 1865, Johnson Papers; Wells to his wife, May 23, 1865, Weems Collection, LSM.

For Johnson's ambition, see introductions to each volume of *Papers of Andrew Johnson;* LaWanda Cox and John H. Cox, *Politics, Principle, and Prejudice, 1865–1866: Dilemma of Reconstruction America* (New York, 1963), 95–106; Castel, *Presidency of Andrew Johnson,* passim, esp. 29, 227; James E. Sefton, *Andrew Johnson and the Uses of Constitutional Power* (Boston, 1980), 52, 59, 71–72, 74, 114, 124.

7. For Johnson's race attitudes, see Cox and Cox, *Politics, Principle, and Prejudice,* 151–71; Hans L. Trefousse, *Impeachment of a President: Andrew Johnson, the Blacks, and Reconstruction* (Knoxville, Tenn., 1975), 3–16; David W. Bowen, "An-

drew Johnson and the Negro," *East Tennessee Historical Society Publications* 40 (1968): 28–49, and his dissertation of the same title.

8. I am indebted to James Gutmann and Ernest Nagel for reassurance on this point and for the following citations: Sidney Hook, *Reason, Social Myths, and Democracy* (New York, 1940), 216–20; Paul Edwards, ed., *The Encyclopedia of Philosophy* (New York, 1967), 2:392–93 (H. B. Acton); Frederick Engels, *Dialectics of Nature* (Moscow: Progressive Publishers, 1964), 83–91; W. H. Johnston and L. G. Struthers, trans., *Hegel's Science of Logic* (London, 1961), 1, 386–90.

9. *Papers of Andrew Johnson*, 1:135; 2:355, 477; 3:62, 162–65, 277, 336–38, 495–96; 5:535.

10. Ibid., 5:233. See also his address of April 23, 1862, ibid., 328.

11. Wendell Phillips to Ann Phillips, March 31, 1862, Blagden Papers, Houghton Library, Harvard University, printed in part in Bartlett, "New Light on Wendell Phillips."

12. *Papers of Andrew Johnson*, 1:136; 2:477; 3:319–20, 328–29.

13. Ibid., 5:4. William T. M. Riches, "The Commoners: Andrew Johnson and Abraham Lincoln to 1861," Ph.D. diss., University of Tennessee, 1976; Bowen, "Andrew Johnson and the Negro," and his forthcoming "Andrew Johnson, Governor of Tennessee," in the governors of Tennessee series; Cox and Cox, *Politics, Principle, and Prejudice*, 153, 162–63. Cf. Sefton, *Andrew Johnson*, 126–27, who accepts the arguments advanced in Johnson's Freedmen's Bureau veto message as evidence that Johnson held an "equality of expectations" for black advancement by honest effort.

14. For Johnson's impact especially upon the Freedmen's Bureau and the army, see John and LaWanda Cox, "General O. O. Howard and the 'Misrepresented Bureau,'" *Journal of Southern History* 19 (Nov. 1953): 435–39; William S. McFeely, *Yankee Stepfather: General O. O. Howard and the Freedmen* (New Haven, 1968), 241, 246–55; Donald G. Nieman, *To Set the Law in Motion: The Freedmen's Bureau and the Legal Rights of Blacks, 1865–1868* (Millwood, N.Y., 1979), 4–8, 18–20, 119–21 and his "Andrew Johnson, the Freedmen's Bureau, and the Problem of Equal Rights, 1865–1866," *Journal of Southern History* 44 (Aug. 1978): 399–420; Michael Perman, *Reunion Without Compromise: The South and Reconstruction, 1865–1868* (Cambridge, U.K., 1973), 98–102; Otto H. Olsen, ed., *Reconstruction and Redemption in the South* (Baton Rouge, La., 1980), 17–19.

15. Phillip S. Paludan, *A Covenant with Death: The Constitution, Law, and Equality in the Civil War Era* (Urbana, Ill., 1975), 42, n. 33.

16. Basler, *Collected Works* 8:404.

17. Ibid., 207, 402.

18. Basic revisionist studies of the break between President Johnson and Congress are Eric L. McKitrick, *Andrew Johnson and Reconstruction* (Chicago, 1960); Cox and Cox, *Politics, Principle, and Prejudice;* W. R. Brock, *An American Crisis: Congress*

and Reconstruction, 1865–1867 (New York, 1963); and Trefousse, *Impeachment*. For recent summations, see Patrick W. Riddleberger, *1866: The Critical Year Revisited* (Carbondale, Ill., 1980) and Castel, *Presidency of Andrew Johnson*. The latter includes a critique of revisionism and hails a new "conservative revisionist" trend in Reconstruction scholarship (222–30).

19. Olsen, ed., *Reconstruction and Redemption*, 5, 168. For southern reaction and strategy, Perman, *Reunion Without Compromise;* for Unionist disfranchisement and "scalawag" usage, Wiggins, *Scalawag in Alabama Politics*, 19–21, 28–34, 37; for excellent accounts of confusion, division, and realignment at the state level, William C. Harris, *Presidential Reconstruction in Mississippi* (Baton Rouge, La., 1967), esp. 28–45, 248, and Carl H. Moneyhon, *Republicanism in Reconstruction Texas* (Austin, Tx., 1980), esp. 24–41, 44–55. See also Gordon B. McKinney, *Southern Mountain Republicans, 1865–1900: Politics and the Appalachian Community* (Chapel Hill, N.C., 1978), 30.

20. An amendment at least as strong as the Fourteenth in its protection for blacks would probably have been hammered out and ratified with the cooperation of the president. Indeed, section two, which sought to resolve the problems created by the demise of the three-fifths compromise and the controversy over black enfranchisement, in all likelihood would have been strengthened by a more direct provision for black suffrage. Cf. Don E. Fehrenbacher's essay in Cullom Davis et al., eds., *The Public and the Private Lincoln: Contemporary Perspectives* (Carbondale, Ill., 1979), 124; Kenneth M. Stampp, *The Era of Reconstruction, 1865–1877* (New York, 1965), 215; Castel, *Presidency of Andrew Johnson*, 228.

21. Some measure of black political influence survived Redemption and the compromise of 1877 until the turn of the century. Eric Anderson, *Race and Politics in North Carolina, 1872–1901: The Black Second* (Baton Rouge, La., 1981); Robert F. Engs, *Freedom's First Generation: Black Hampton, Virginia, 1861–1890* (Philadelphia, 1979); Thomas Holt, *Black over White: Negro Political Leadership in South Carolina during Reconstruction* (Baton Rouge, La., 1977); Arnold H. Taylor, *Travail and Triumph: Black Life and Culture in the South Since the Civil War* (Westport, Conn., 1976), ch. 1; Charles Vincent, *Black Legislators in Louisiana during Reconstruction;* John W. Blassingame, *Black New Orleans, 1860–80* (Baton Rouge, La., 1976); Peter Kolchin, *First Freedom: The Responses of Alabama's Blacks to Emancipation and Reconstruction* (Westport, Conn., 1973); Joe M. Richardson, *The Negro in the Reconstruction of Florida, 1865–1877* (Tallahassee, Fla., 1965); Joel Williamson, *After Slavery: The Negro in South Carolina During Reconstruction, 1861–1877* (Chapel Hill, N.C., 1965); Vernon L. Wharton, *The Negro in Mississippi, 1865–1890* (Chapel Hill, N.C., 1947); Alrutheus A. Taylor, *The Negro in Tennessee, 1865–1880* (Washington, D.C., 1941).

22. David Donald, *Charles Sumner and the Coming of the Civil War* (New York, 1960), x.

23. Italics added. The original version was presented at the Thirteenth International Congress of Historical Sciences held in Moscow in August 1970 and first printed as a pamphlet for participants and then reprinted in 1973 as part of a volume of the collected papers of the Congress. The revised version was delivered at the Symposium on Southern History at the University of Mississippi, September 1976, and printed under the title "The Price of Freedom," in David G. Sansing, ed., *What Was Freedom's Price?* (Jackson, Miss., 1978), 93–113.

24. For a graphic description of the setting of Lincoln's April 11 address, and the response to it, see Stephen B. Oates, *With Malice Toward None: The Life of Abraham Lincoln* (New York, 1977), 460–62.

A commitment comparable to that of the mid-twentieth century was not altogether lacking in the 1860s for a number of abolitionists attacked the concept of racial inequality on the basis of biblical authority and logic. See James M. McPherson, *The Struggle for Equality: Abolitionists and the Negro in the Civil War and Reconstruction* (Princeton, N.J., 1964), 136–53.

The economic implications of the civil-political equalitarianism of the mid-nineteenth century differed from those of the equalitarianism of the late twentieth century, particularly as to the obligations of government, but neither have embraced the goal of a complete equality of condition. For a stimulating examination of the nature and history of the concept of equality in the United States, see J. R. Pole, *The Pursuit of Equality in American History* (Berkeley, Calif., 1978).

25. George M. Fredrickson, "After Emancipation: A Comparative Study of the White Responses to the New Order of Race Relations in the American South, Jamaica, and the Cape Colony of South Africa," in Sansing, ed., *What Was Freedom's Price?*, 71–92; Peyton McCrary, "After the Revolution: American Reconstruction in Comparative Perspective," paper presented at the annual meeting of the American Historical Association, New York, December 28, 1979.

For other comparative studies relevant to postemancipation, George M. Fredrickson, *White Supremacy: A Comparative Study in American and South African History* (New York, 1982), esp. 179–238 and his "Comparative History," in Michael Kammen, ed., *The Past Before Us: Contemporary Historical Writing in the United States* (Ithaca, 1980), 465–70. Work in progress by Peter Kolchin on Russia and by Stanley Engerman on the West Indies will yield further comparative insights. See the latter's comments in Engerman and Eugene D. Genovese, eds., *Race and Slavery in the Western Hemisphere* (Princeton, N.J., 1975), 495–526, and Kolchin's "In Defense of Servitude: American Proslavery and Russian Proserfdom Arguments, 1760–1860," *American Historical Review* 85 (Oct. 1980): 809–27.

26. Jerome Blum, *The End of the Old Order in Rural Europe* (Princeton, N.J., 1978), 429–41; see also Daniel Chirot, *Social Change in a Peripheral Society* (New York, 1976) and his "The Growth of the Market and Servile Labor Systems in Agriculture," *Journal of Social History* (Winter 1975): 67–80.

27. George Beckford, *Persistent Poverty: Underdevelopment in Plantation Economies of the Third World* (New York, 1972), xxvi, and his "Toward an Appropriate Theoretical Framework for Agricultural Development Planning and Policy," *Social and Economic Studies* 17 (Sept. 1968): 233–42. For Jamaica, Gisela Eisner, *Jamaica, 1830–1930: A Study in Economic History* (Manchester, 1961); Philip D. Curtin, *Two Jamaicas: The Role of Ideas in a Tropical Colony, 1830–1865* (New York, 1970). For Guiana, Alan H. Adamson, *Sugar without Slaves: The Political Economy of British Guiana, 1838–1904* (New Haven, 1972); Jay R. Mandle, *The Plantation Economy: Population and Economic Change in Guyana, 1838–1960* (Philadelphia, 1973); Michael Moohr, "The Economic Impact of Slave Emancipation in British Guiana, 1832–1852," *Economic History Review* 2d. ser., 25 (November 1972): 588–607. See also Sidney Mintz, *Caribbean Transformations* (Chicago, 1974); Woodville K. Marshall, "Notes on Peasant Development in the West Indies Since 1838," *Social and Economic Studies* 17 (Sept. 1968): 252–63; W. F. Wertheim, "Asian Society: Southeast Asia," and "Economy, Dual" in *International Encyclopedia of the Social Sciences* (New York, 1968), 1:423–38; 4:495–500. The Galbraith quotation is from *The Nature of Mass Poverty* (Cambridge, Mass., 1979), 133.

28. For calling the São Paulo comparison to my attention, I am indebted to Patricia Mulvey, fellow member of the Political History Group of the Institute for Research in History.

29. Florestan Fernandes, *The Negro in Brazilian Society* (New York, 1969), his "Immigration and Race Relations in São Paulo," in Magnus M. Morner, ed., *Race and Class in Latin America* (New York, 1970), 122–42, and his "Beyond Poverty: The Negro and the Mulatto in Brazil," in Robert Brent Toplin, ed., *Slavery and Race Relations in Latin America* (Westport, Conn., 1974), 277–97; Toplin, introduction and "Abolition and the Issue of the Black Freedman's Future in Brazil," ibid., 253–76; Arthur F. Corwin, "Afro-Brazilians: Myths and Realities," ibid., esp. 385–400; Donald Coes, "Brazil," in W. Arthur Lewis, ed., *Tropical Development, 1880–1913* (Evanston, Ill., 1970), 100–113; Charles Wagley, *An Introduction to Brazil* (New York, 1963), 74–79; Carl N. Degler, *Neither Black nor White: Slavery and Race Relations in Brazil and the United States* (New York, 1972); Thomas H. Holloway's recent study, *Immigrants on the Land: Coffee and Society in São Paulo, 1886–1934* (Chapel Hill, N.C., 1980), provides an effective analysis of how the coffee plantation economy in its heyday made possible viable family farm ownership for many immigrants who started life in Brazil as penniless farm workers.

30. For a perceptive review of the literature on prewar racism in the North, particularly among Republicans, see Kenneth M. Stampp, "Race, Slavery, and the Republican Party of the 1850s," in his *The Imperiled Union: Essays on the Background of the Civil War* (New York, 1980), 105–35. For the distinction between the race attitudes of President Johnson's supporters and opponents, Cox and Cox, *Politics, Principle, and Prejudice,* 211–28.

Daniel Chicot argues that an ideology equivalent to racism, one that insists laborers are culturally inferior to masters, has been used to justify enduring peasant poverty where masters and serfs are of common ethnic origin and color, "Growth of the Market and Servile Labor Systems in Agriculture," 75.

31. A helpful introduction to these concepts can be found in the articles of the *International Encyclopedia of the Social Sciences* on "Prejudice: The Concept," by Otto Klineberg; "Prejudice: Social Discrimination," by J. Milton Yinger; and "Race Relations: Social Psychological Aspects," by Thomas F. Pettigrew.

32. For a selection of relevant documents, 1869–1891, and interpretive comment, LaWanda Cox and John H. Cox, eds., *Reconstruction, the Negro, and the New South* (Columbia, S.C., 1973), 105–207. On the Liberal Republicans, Richard A. Gerber, "Liberal Republicanism, Reconstruction, and Social Order: Samuel Bowles as a Test Case," *New England Quarterly* 45 (September 1972): 393–407; Patrick W. Riddleberger, "The Break in the Radical Ranks: Liberals vs. Stalwarts in the Election of 1872," *Journal of Negro History* 44 (April 1959): 136–57; John G. Sproat, *"The Best Men": Liberal Reformers in the Gilded Age* (New York, 1971), 29–44. For antislavery men who embraced the "let-alone" policy toward the South, James M. McPherson, "The Antislavery Legacy: From Reconstruction to the NAACP," in Barton J. Bernstein, ed., *Towards a New Past: Dissenting Essays in American History* (New York, 1969), 131–45, and his *The Abolitionist Legacy: From Reconstruction to the NAACP* (Princeton, N.J., 1975), 24–34, 81–94. For the effort to enact an enforcement bill in the 51st Congress, Richard E. Welch, Jr., "The Federal Elections Bill of 1890: Postscript and Prelude," *Journal of American History* 52 (December 1965): 511–26. See also J. Morgan Kousser, *The Shaping of Southern Politics: Suffrage Restriction and the Establishment of the One-Party South, 1880–1910* (New Haven, Conn., 1974), 18–33, in which the view of the national Republican record is compatible with that expressed here, and William Gillette, *Retreat from Reconstruction, 1869–1879* (Baton Rouge, La., 1979), which passes a much harsher judgment upon northern Republican leadership. Further light on the reasons for Republican retreat can be expected in a forthcoming study by Michael Les Benedict. A thoughtful overview of Reconstruction as an aborted revolution can be found in James M. McPherson, "Reconstruction: A Revolution Manque," reprinted in Allen F. Davis and Harold D. Woodman, *Conflict and Consensus in Early American History* (Lexington, Mass., 1984), 413–25.

33. William Gillette makes a strong case for the desegregation Civil Rights Bill as a factor in the overwhelming Republican defeat of 1874, but does not claim that it was the only cause. *Retreat from Reconstruction,* 246–58.

34. C. Vann Woodward, "Yes, There Was a Compromise of 1877," *Journal of American History* 60 (June 1973): 221–22; Stanley P. Hirshson, *Farewell to the Bloody Shirt: Northern Republicans & the Southern Negro, 1877–1893* (Gloucester, Mass., 1968), 45–59; Vincent P. DeSantis, *Republicans Face the Southern Question: The*

New Departure Years, 1877–1897 (Baltimore, 1959), 99–101; Gillette, *Retreat from Reconstruction*, 333–34.

35. Lawrence Grossman, *The Democratic Party and the Negro: Northern and National Politics, 1868–92* (Urbana, Ill., 1976); Joel H. Silbey, *A Respectable Minority: The Democratic Party in the Civil War Era, 1860–1868* (New York, 1977), 27–28, 80–83, 190–93, 199–203, 209, 232, 241–42.

36. For the use of violence, Allen W. Trelease, *White Terror: The Ku Klux Klan Conspiracy and Southern Reconstruction* (New York, 1971). Many state and more general studies have recounted the various techniques of white southern resistance. A recent noteworthy effort to examine the potential for success or failure of Republicanism in the post–Civil War South is Olsen, ed., *Reconstruction and Redemption*. The editor's introduction is perceptive, informed, and provocative.

37. Eugene Genovese, "Re-examining Reconstruction," *New York Times Book Review*, May 4, 1980, 9, 40; Perman, *Reunion Without Compromise*, esp. 14; Gillette, *Retreat from Reconstruction*, 76–185 (the quotations are from pp. 171–72).

38. I have found particularly helpful P. H. Partridge, *Consent and Consensus* (New York, 1971). See also Carl Joachim Friedrich, *Man and His Government: An Empirical Theory of Politics* (New York, 1963), 159–79, and his *Tradition and Authority*; David Lockwood, "Some Remarks on 'The Social System,'" *British Journal of Sociology* 7 (1956): 134–46; Samuel Du Bois Cook, "Coercion and Social Change," in J. Roland Pennock and John W. Chapman, eds., *Coercion* (Chicago, 1972), 107–43, and Robert Paul Wolff, "Is Coercion 'ethically neutral'?" ibid., 144–47; Hannah Arendt, "Authority," in *Between Past and Future* (New York, 1968), 99–141; and articles in the *International Encyclopedia of the Social Sciences* on "Consensus: The Concept of Consensus," by Edward Shils; "Power," by Robert A. Dahl; and "Sanctions," by A. L. Epstein.

Ralf Dahrendorf in developing a conflict-coercion theory first affirmed and then repudiated the compatibility of consensus and conflict. In his *Essays in the Theory of Society* (Palo Alto, Calif., 1968), 127–28, 149–50.

39. Everette Swinney, "Suppressing the Ku Klux Klan: The Enforcement of the Reconstruction Amendments, 1870–1874," Ph.D. diss., University of Texas, 1966, 233–35, 300–301, 317; Gillette, *Retreat from Reconstruction*, 25–55, 104–65.

40. The quotation is from Gillette, ibid., 102. Swinney puts the number of troops occupying the South at from 12,000 to 13,000 in 1867–68 and about 5,000 in 1870–72, "Suppressing the Ku Klux Klan," 190.

41. *Annual Reports of the Attorney General of the United States, 1957–1972*; U.S. Commission on Civil Rights, *The Federal Civil Rights Enforcement Effort: A Report* and their *The Voting Rights Act: Ten Years After: A Report* (Washington, D.C., 1985); Sar A. Levitan, William B. Johnston, Robert Taggart, *Still a Dream: The Changing Status of Blacks since 1960* (Cambridge, Mass., 1975), 267–92, 331–55;

Neil R. McMillen, "Black Enfranchisement in Mississippi: Federal Enforcement and Black Protest in the 1960s," *Journal of Southern History* 43 (August 1977): 351–72.

42. U.S. Commission on Civil Rights, *The Federal Civil Rights Enforcement Effort: One Year Later*, xii; Levitan, *Still a Dream*, 349–55. See also *The Unfinished Business: Twenty Years Later: A Report Submitted to the U.S. Commission on Civil Rights by its Fifty-one State Advisory Committee*, September 1977, 4–5.

43. The characterization is from Michael Davis, *The Image of Lincoln in the South* (Knoxville, Tenn., 1971), 63.

44. Basler, *Collected Works*, 8:401–4. Lincoln's remarks in reference to black suffrage have been interpreted as a commitment to leave the decision to the states, as a matter of right. In fact, he avoided the issue of authority. Gideon Welles was very influential, but clearly in error, in identifying Lincoln's views with those of Andrew Johnson and his own.

45. The practical impact of an aroused sense of injustice, the conditions that evoke it and those that restrain it, deserve more attention than they have received from historians. For suggestive discussions of the sense of justice and injustice directed primarily to the concerns of political and legal theorists, see Edmond N. Cahn, *The Sense of Injustice: An Anthropocentric View of Law* (Bloomington, Ind., 1949), 13–27, and his article "Justice" in the *International Encyclopedia of the Social Sciences*, 8:346–47; Giorgio del Vecchio, *Justice, An Historical and Philosophical Essay* (New York, 1982), 77–81; Carl J. Friedrich and John W. Chapman, eds., *Justice* (New York, 1974), 30 (Friedrich), 191–97 (Iredell Jenkins).

Circumstances in the post–Civil War period suggest that a sense of injustice to have an important political impact requires the arousing of public attention and indignation and a general perception that something can be done to remedy the injustice. Also important would seem to be reinforcement by linkage to other concerns of party and nation, and a minimum of conflict with such interests.

46. The quotation was a general statement, not one used in the context of Lincoln's leadership. Richard E. Neustadt, *Presidential Power: The Politics of Leadership from FDR to Carter* (New York, 1980), 135.

James MacGregor Burns faults Lincoln as opportunistic, expedient, cautious, and orthodox to a degree that blocked the federal action necessary to carry out the nation's moral commitment to the freedmen. Though Lincoln was skillful in using those "transactional" aspects of leadership Burns demeans, he also exemplified the "transforming" leadership Burns most admires. *Leadership*, 391–92, 429–30. Otto H. Olsen presents Lincoln as leader of revolution, "Abraham Lincoln as Revolutionary," *Civil War History* 24 (September 1978): 213–24.

47. Alfred H. Kelly, in Harold M. Hyman, ed., *New Frontiers of the American Reconstruction* (Urbana, Ill., 1966), 52–56; Hyman, *A More Perfect Union* (New York, 1973), 414–553 (esp. 438–41, 447–48, 477, 490); Michael Les Benedict, "Preserving

the Constitution: The Conservative Basis of Radical Reconstruction," *Journal of American History* 61 (June 1974): 65–90; Paludan, *Covenant with Death*, 1–60, 274–82. The first part of the quotation is from Paludan, the second from Kelly.

48. Robert J. Harris, *The Quest for Equality: The Constitution, Congress and the Supreme Court* (Baton Rouge, La., 1960), 24–56, 82–108; Laurent B. Frantz, "Congressional Power to Enforce the Fourteenth Amendment against Private Acts," *Yale Law Journal* 73 (July 1964): 1353–84; Mark DeWolfe Howe, "Federalism and Civil Rights," Massachusetts Historical Society, *Proceedings* 77 (1965), 15–27; Alfred Avins, "The Ku Klux Klan Act of 1871: Some Reflected Light on State Action and the Fourteenth Amendment," *Saint Louis University Law Journal* 11 (Winter 1967): 331–81; John Anthony Scott, "Justice Bradley's Evolving Concept of the Fourteenth Amendment from the Slaughterhouse Cases to the Civil Rights Cases," *Rutgers Law Review* 25 (Spring 1971): 552–69; Charles Fairman, *Reconstruction and Reunion, 1864–1884, Part 1* (New York, 1971), 1354, 1359, 1387–88; Robert J. Kaczorowski, "Searching for the Intent of the Framers of the Fourteenth Amendment," *Connecticut Law Review* 5 (Winter 1973): 368–98, and his two papers on civil rights during Reconstruction presented at the annual meetings of the Southern Historical Association, 1973, and the Organization of American Historians, 1975; Charles W. McCurdy, "Legal Institutions, Constitutional Theory, and the Tragedy of Reconstruction," *Reviews in American History* 4 (June 1976): 210–11; Belz, *Emancipation and Equal Rights* (New York, 1978), 120–25, 129–39. The characterization as "vacuous" is from Fairman, that of "a major triumph for the South" from Harris.

49. Michael Les Benedict has made a persuasive case for the Supreme Court under Chief Justice Morrison R. Waite (1873–1888) as having gone a long distance in its obiter dicta toward reconciling federalism with broad congressional power to protect and extend black rights. "Preserving Federalism: Reconstruction and the Waite Court," *Supreme Court Review* (1978): 39–79.

50. The challenge to the land thesis was made by Herman Belz in "The New Orthodoxy in Reconstruction Historiography," *Reviews in American History* 1 (March 1973), 106–13.

The six books referred to are Stephen J. DeCanio, *Agriculture in the Postbellum South: The Economics of Production and Supply* (Cambridge, Mass., 1974); Robert Higgs, *Competition and Coercion: Blacks in the American Economy, 1865–1914*; Ransom and Sutch, *One Kind of Freedom*; Mandle, *The Roots of Black Poverty*; Jonathan M. Wiener, *Social Origins of the New South: Alabama, 1860–1885* (Baton Rouge, La., 1978); and Gavin Wright, *The Political Economy of the Cotton South: Households, Markets, and Wealth in the Nineteenth Century* (New York, 1978). See also Edward Magdol, *A Right to the Land: Essays on the Freedmen's Community* (Westport, Conn., 1974); Claude F. Oubre, *Forty Acres and a Mule: The Freedmen's Bureau and Black Land Ownership* (Baton Rouge, La., 1978); Daniel A. Novak, *The Wheel of Servitude* (Lexington, Ky., 1974); and Dwight B. Billings, Jr., *Planters and* the Making of a "New South": Class, Politics, and Development in North Carolina, 1865–1900 (Chapel Hill, N.C., 1979).

Agricultural History devoted two entire issues to the southern economy, those of April 1975 (49) and January 1979 (53) and Explorations in Economic History used its January 1979 issue (16) for publication of papers from a symposium at Duke University on issues raised by Ransom and Sutch, One Kind of Freedom. Sansing, ed., What Was Freedom's Price? is a collection based upon a symposium held in 1976 at the University of Mississippi. A number of relevant papers were presented at the St. Louis Conference on the First and Second Reconstructions, February 1978, organized by members of the Department of History, University of Missouri–St. Louis. Major articles have been published by Journal of Southern History 42 (November 1977): 523–54, Harold D. Woodman, "Sequel to Slavery: The New History Views the Postbellum South," and by American Historical Review 84 (October 1981), 970–1006, Jonathan M. Wiener, "Class Structure and Economic Development in the American South, 1865–1955," with comments by Higgs and Woodman.

There are sharp differences in approach and analysis in the recent scholarship. Ransom and Sutch emphasize merchant monopoly; Wright, the world demand for cotton; Mandle, a continuing plantation economy; Wiener, the persistence of large landholdings and the political power of planters; Higgs, black economic advances and the limitations attributable to racial coercion; DeCanio, agricultural labor as not technically "exploited" but disadvantaged by lack of land and capital; Woodman, the emergence of a peculiarly southern type of working class in agriculture.

51. Higgs, Competition and Coercion, 77–80, 93; Wright, Political Economy of the Cotton South, 177–80, and his "Freedom and the Southern Economy," Explorations in Economic History 16 (January 1979): 106; Ransom and Sutch, One Kind of Freedom, 80, and their "The Economic Reorganization of the Post-Emancipation South," paper presented at the Conference on the First and Second Reconstructions. Cf. DeCanio, Agriculture in the Postbellum South, 223, 239–40, and his "Accumulation and Discrimination in the Postbellum South," Explorations in Economic History 16 (April 1979): 202–4.

There is also a growing doubt as to whether having obtained landownership blacks could have maintained it. See Willie Lee Rose in What Was Freedom's Price?, 12–14; Manning Marable, "The Politics of Black Land Tenure, 1877–1915," Agricultural History 53 (January 1979): 142–52; Leo McGee and Robert Boone, eds., The Black Rural Landowner; Endangered Species (Westport, Conn., 1979). For studies with somewhat more positive implications for the success of black landownership, see Carol K. R. Bleser, The Promised Land: The History of the South Carolina Land Commission, 1869–1890 (Columbia, S.C., 1969), 140–56, and James T. Currie, Enclave: Vicksburg and Her Plantations, 1863–1870 (Jackson, Miss., 1980), 83–145; but cf. Norman L. Crockett, The Black Towns (Lawrence, Kas., 1979). See also Janet Sharp Hermann, The Pursuit of a Dream (New York, 1981), esp. 195–245. My own misgivings about the adequacy of a land program to solve the problem of black poverty go back many decades when a comparative study of tenure, 1870–1900, in selected antebellum plantation counties disclosed the atypically high black landownership in Beaufort County, South Carolina, yet the area was one of marked poverty. See my Ph.D. diss., University of California, 1941, "Agricultural Labor in the United States, 1865–1900, with Special Reference to the South."

52. Beckford, *Persistent Poverty*, 224–27; Doreen Warriner, *The Economics of Peasant Farming* (New York, 1965), xxxii, and her *Land Reform in Principle and Practice* (New York, 1969), vi, 427–36; Michael P. Todaro, *Economic Development in the Third World: An Introduction to Problems and Policies in a Global Perspective* (New York, 1977), 227–28.

53. Julius Rubin, "The Limits of Agricultural Progress in the Nineteenth-Century South," *Agricultural History* 49 (April 1975): 362–73. The cotton South was, of course, only one of several southern economies but the focus upon it is reasonable in view of the concentration of blacks in cotton production.

The classic study of cotton production in the South is M. B. Hammond, *The Cotton Industry: An Essay in American Economic History* (New York, 1966; rpt. ed.). See also Harold D. Woodman, *King Cotton and His Retainers: Financing and Marketing the Cotton Crop of the South, 1800–1925* (Lexington, Ky., 1968), 334–59; Fred A. Shannon, *The Farmer's Last Frontier: Agriculture, 1860–1897* (New York, 1945), 110–17, 415; Ransom and Sutch, *One Kind of Freedom*, 188–92; Wright, *Political Economy of the Cotton South*, 158–84, and his "Cotton Competition and the Post-Bellum Recovery of the American South," *Journal of Economic History* 34 (September 1974): 610–35; Robert L. Brandfon, *Cotton Kingdom of the New South: A History of the Yazoo Mississippi Delta from Reconstruction to the Twentieth Century* (Cambridge, Mass., 1969), 21, 114–39.

The immediate postwar years were disastrous for cotton growers and had far-reaching consequences. See Lawrence N. Powell, *New Masters: Northern Planters During the Civil War and Reconstruction*, 145–50; Currie, *Enclave*, 156–63; Cox and Cox, eds., *Reconstruction, the Negro, and the New South*, 331–36.

54. The quotation is from Gavin Wright, "One Kind of Freedom," *The Civil Liberties Review* (May/June 1978): 49. He has called attention to the high fertility rates of the rural population that transformed the region from one of labor scarcity to one of labor surplus. "Freedom and the Southern Economy," 106, and *Political Economy of the Cotton South*, 160. For his view of the relationship between the slave plantation economy and that of the postbellum South, ibid., 3–176; see also Douglass C. North, *The Economic Growth of the United States, 1790–1860* (Englewood Cliffs, N.J., 1961), 4–7, 12–33, 153–55.

C. Vann Woodward's attribution of the South's industrial backwardness to a colonial status in relation to the Northeast long dominated historical interpretation, *Origins of the New South, 1877–1913*, 291–320. For a summation of challenges to this view prior to the 1970s, Sheldon Hackney, "*Origins of the New South* in Retrospect," *Journal of Southern History* 38 (May 1972): 208–13.

For radical approaches to underdevelopment as an aspect of a capitalist world order, E. J. Hobsbawm, *The Age of Capital, 1848–1875* (New York, 1975), 27–71, 189–211; Immanuel Wallerstein, *The Modern World System: Capitalist Agriculture and the Origins of the European World Economy in the Sixteenth Century* (New York, 1974), 29–39, his "Dependence in an Interdependent World: The Limited Possibilities of Transformation within the Capitalist World Economy," *African Studies Review* 17 (April 1974): 1–26, and his "The Rise and Future Demise of the World Capitalist System: Concepts for Comparative Analysis," *Comparative Studies in Society and History* 16 (September 1974): 387–415; James D. Cockcroft, Andre Gunder Frank, and Dale L. Johnson, *Dependence and Underdevelopment: Latin America's Political Economy* (New York, 1972).

The starkest explanation for the plight of the cotton South, particularly that of its black workers, was made in passing by the distinguished economist W. Arthur Lewis in discussing the factoral terms of trade. He argues that the disadvantage of tropical countries in the yield per acre of foodstuffs resulted in a standard of living that made available in the second half of the nineteenth century a vast reservoir of Indian and Chinese labor "willing to travel anywhere to work on plantations for a shilling a day." Since cotton as a commercial staple could be grown in the tropics, the American South, even with its higher yields per acre, could not have competed with tropical cotton except by exploiting black labor: "American blacks earned so little because of the large amount of cotton that would have flowed out of Asia and Africa and Latin America at a higher cotton price." *The Evolution of the International Economic Order*, 14–20.

55. The study of black migration underway by William Cohen should fill an important gap in our understanding of the lack of a sizable out-migration. He has kindly confirmed the implication of his published article that physical coercion or involuntary servitude do not go very far in accounting for the lack of a black movement to the North. Cohen to Cox, April 11, 1980; William Cohen, "Negro Involuntary Servitude in the South, 1865–1940: A Preliminary Analysis," *Journal of Southern History* 42 (February 1976): 31–60. See also Harold D. Woodman, "Post–Civil War Southern Agriculture and the Law," *Agricultural History* 53 (January 1979): 319–37; Mandle, *Roots of Black Poverty*, 71–83; cf. the extreme interpretation presented by Novak, *Wheel of Servitude*. I found suggestive the accounts of black employment opportunities in Elizabeth H. Pleck, *Black Migration and Poverty: Boston, 1865–1900* (New York, 1979) and in David A. Gerber, *Black Ohio and the Color Line, 1860–1915* (Urbana, Ill., 1976) and also references to black reluctance to migrate in Engs, *Freedom's First Generation*, 116–17, and in Vernon Burton, "Ungrateful Servants? Edgefield's Black Reconstruction: Part 1 of the Total History of Edgefield County, South Carolina," Ph.D. diss., Princeton University, 1976), 131–57. See also two recent studies,

Stanley Lieberson, *A Piece of the Pie: Blacks and White Immigrants Since 1800* (Berkeley, 1980), 30–47, 298–325, 328–38; and David M. Johnson and Rex R. Campbell, *Black Migration in America: A Social Demographic History* (Durham, N.C., 1981), 43–70, 86.

Why blacks did not leave the South for public lands in the North is a special aspect of the problem. Geographically, Kansas was the most obvious and available destination. Robert G. Athearn believes that the consequence of the great unplanned millenarian black exodus to that state in 1879–1880 was to block further migrations that might have been assimilated if made gradually on a more limited scale. No intensive study has been made of how those blacks fared who obtained a foothold on the public lands of the Great Plains, a harsh environment for homesteaders, black or white. Athearn, *In Search of Canaan: Black Migration to Kansas, 1879–1880* (Lawrence, Kas., 1979); Nell Irvin Painter, *Exodusters: Black Migration to Kansas after Reconstruction* (New York, 1977). For black settlements in Kansas and Oklahoma, see Crockett, *Black Towns*.

56. Willie Lee Rose has limned these attitudes with understanding and tolerance, *Rehearsal for Reconstruction* (Indianapolis, 1964), 211–16, 228–29. See also Eric Foner, *Politics and Ideology in the Age of the Civil War* (New York, 1980), 100–112, and his *Free Soil, Free Labor, Free Men: The Ideology of the Republican Party Before the Civil War* (New York, 1970), 11–18, 29–34; Carl R. Osthaus, *Freedmen, Philanthropy, and Fraud: A History of the Freedman's Savings Bank* (Urbana, Ill., 1976), 1–20, 221–25; Nieman, *To Set the Law in Motion*, 53–59; Daniel T. Rodgers, *The Work Ethic in Industrial America, 1850–1920* (Chicago, 1978), 14–22.

The break-up of the large landed estates was generally assumed to be a natural and inevitable process. Gen. James Wadsworth told the Freedmen's Inquiry Commission that confiscation and redistribution of southern land was unnecessary because "natural causes would bring it about." American Freedmen's Inquiry Commission, Testimony, National Archives. See also Lawrence N. Powell, "The American Land Company and Agency: John A. Andrew and the Northernization of the South," *Civil War History* 21 (December 1975): 305–6, and his *New Masters*, 43–44.

Two studies suggest to me that had economic conditions in the postwar South developed as anticipated, and with the new civil-political status of blacks sustained, the expectations for black advancement at least in urban areas would not have been unrealistic. Engs, *Freedom's First Generation;* Frank J. Huffman, "Old South, New South: Continuity and Change in a Georgia County, 1850–1880," Ph.D. diss., Yale University, 1974. Also suggestive is the study by Donald L. Winters, *Farmers Without Farms: Agricultural Tenancy in Nineteenth-Century Iowa* (Westport, Conn., 1978), which finds that despite the difficulties northern farmers faced in the last decades of the nineteenth century, tenancy remained a stepping stone to land ownership for a significant number. Cf. LaWanda Cox, "Tenancy in the United States, 1865–1900:

A Consideration of the Validity of the Agricultural Ladder Hypothesis," *Agricultural History* 18 (July 1944): 97-105.

57. George W. Julian, not Thaddeus Stevens, took the lead in trying to obtain homesteads for blacks. Edward Atkinson, the most articulate spokesman for the northern cotton industry, championed small farms. For a recent study of Stevens' role, see Eric Foner, "Thaddeus Stevens, Confiscation, and Reconstruction," reprinted in *Politics and Ideology*, 128-49.

58. The significance of the land provisions of the vetoed Freedmen's Bureau bill, first pointed out in my 1941 dissertation and subsequently in McFeely, *Yankee Stepfather*, 228-31, has not generally been recognized by historians with the recent exception of Eric Foner, *Politics and Ideology*, 140. For relevant documents and comments, Cox and Cox, eds., *Reconstruction, the Negro, and the New South*, xxviii-xxx, 31-47, 315-26.

59. See LaWanda F. Cox, *Lincoln and Black Freedom: A Study in Presidential Leadership* (Columbia, S.C., 1981), 28 n.43. Gen. James Wadsworth, after his conference with Lincoln on returning from the valley inspection tour, testified that he did not think confiscation was the policy of the government "unless it becomes necessary to do it to carry out the policy of emancipation." American Freedmen's Inquiry Commission, Testimony, National Archives.

In 1864 Lincoln indicated a willingness to sign a bill providing for permanent forfeiture of real property, although in 1862 he had forced Congress on threat of a veto to limit forfeiture under the second Confiscation Act to the lifetime of the owner. The circumstances surrounding this major reversal of policy suggest that it was prompted by consideration for the freedmen. I hope elsewhere to examine the episode in some detail. Also of potential significance for the freedmen's future was an exception to restoration of property rights in Lincoln's amnesty proclamation (but not in Johnson's) "where rights of third parties shall have intervened." Similarly, Lincoln's support of John Eaton's effort at Davis Bend to promote the development of an independent black yeomanry is especially suggestive in view of the analysis of Eaton's purpose by Stephen Joseph Ross in "Freed Soil, Freed Labor, Freed Men: John Eaton and the Davis Bend Experiment," *Journal of Southern History* 44 (May 1978): 213-30; Lincoln to Eaton, February 10, 1865, Basler, *Collected Works* 8:274.

60. John G. Nicolay and John Hay, *Abraham Lincoln* (New York, 1890-1904), 10:123.

61. The recollections of former slaves confirm that black voting was "an act of defiance to the local white community," i.e., a rejection of white norms for black subordination. Paul D. Escott, *Slavery Remembered: A Record of Twentieth-Century Slave Narratives* (Chapel Hill, N.C., 1979), 153-54.

62. Foner, *Politics and Ideology*, 114-20, 123-24; Woodman, "Post-Civil War Southern Agriculture and the Law," 329, 333-34, 336-37; Burton, "Ungrateful Ser-

vants?" and his "Race and Reconstruction: Edgefield County, South Carolina," *Journal of Social History* 12 (Fall 1978): 31–56; Howard N. Rabinowitz, *Race Relations in the Urban South, 1865–1890* (New York, 1978), 264–66, 279–81; see also Kousser, *Shaping of Southern Politics*, 14, 37, his "Progressivism—For Middle-Class Whites Only: North Carolina Education, 1880–1910," *Journal of Southern History* 46 (May 1980): 179–85, 191–92, and Anderson, *Race and Politics in North Carolina*, 315–30, 335. In contrast, Holt in *Black over White*, 148–79, sees black political leaders as failing black labor because of bias arising from their class, color, and origins.

63. For southern Whigs, Confederate dissidents, and scalawags see Charles Grier Sellers, Jr., "Who Were the Southern Whigs," *American Historical Review* 59 (January 1954): 335–46; Thomas B. Alexander, "Persistent Whiggery in the Confederate South, 1860–1877," *Journal of Southern History* 27 (August 1961): 305–29; John V. Mering, "Persistent Whiggery in the South: A Reconsideration," *South Atlantic Quarterly* 69 (Winter 1970), 124–43; Wilfred B. Yearns, *The Confederate Congress* (Athens, Ga., 1960), 218–35; Thomas B. Alexander and Richard E. Beringer, *The Anatomy of the Confederate Congress* (Nashville, 1972), 337–44; David Donald, "The Scalawag in Mississippi Reconstruction," *Journal of Southern History* 10 (November 1944): 447–60; Allen W. Trelease, "Who Were the Scalawags," ibid., 29 (November 1963): 445–68; "Communications," from Donald and Trelease, ibid., 30 (May 1964): 253–57; Warren A. Ellem, "Who Were the Mississippi Scalawags," ibid., 38 (May 1972): 217–40; "Communication" from Trelease and Ellem, ibid., vol. 38 (November 1972): 703–6; Otto H. Olsen, "Reconsidering the Scalawags," *Civil War History* 12 (December 1966), 304–20; Richard O. Curry, "The Civil War and Reconstruction, 1861–1877: A Critical Overview of Recent Trends and Interpretations," ibid., 10 (September 1974): 230–33; Elizabeth S. Nathans, *Losing the Peace: Georgia Republicans and Reconstruction, 1865–1871* (Baton Rouge, La., 1968), esp. vi–vii, 225–27; Wiggins, *Scalawags in Alabama Politics*, esp. 128–35; Gordon B. McKinney, "Southern Mountain Republicans and the Negro, 1865–1900," *Journal of Southern History* 41 (November 1975): 493–516, and his *Southern Mountain Republicans*, 3–61; James Alex Baggett, "Origins of Scalawag Leadership in the Upper South," paper presented at the annual meeting of the Southern Historical Association, Atlanta, 1979, and his "Origins of Early Texas Republican Party Leadership," *Journal of Southern History* 40 (August 1974): 441–54; Moneyhon, *Republicanism in Reconstruction Texas*.

64. Cox, *Lincoln and Black Freedom*, 154–55. Peter Kolchin in a study of southern congressmen, 1868–1872, has concluded that carpetbaggers were the driving element within reconstruction governments and that a predominantly scalawag delegation was a sign of Republican weakness. "Scalawags, Carpetbaggers, and Reconstruction: A Quantitative Look at Southern Congressional Politics, 1868–1872," *Journal of Southern History* 45 (February 1979): 63–76.

65. William C. Harris has argued that despite the exaggeration of Redeemers and

their apologists, the tax burden imposed by Republicans was heavy given the hard times and led to a genuine taxpayer revolt that helped topple the Republican regime in Mississippi. *The Day of the Carpetbagger: Republican Reconstruction in Mississippi* (Baton Rouge, La., 1979), 626–33, and in Olsen, ed., *Reconstruction and Redemption*, 93–97.

66. Allen W. Trelease, "Republican Reconstruction in North Carolina: A Roll-Call Analysis of the State House of Representatives, 1868–70," *Journal of Southern History* 42 (August 1976): 319–44; Olsen, ed., *Reconstruction and Redemption*, 28, 35–36, 38–43 (Jerrel H. Shofner on Florida), 59–60 (Wiggins on Alabama), 85–86 (Harris on Mississippi), 120–25 (Jack P. Maddex on Virginia), 173–75, 189 (Olsen on North Carolina); Gillette, *Retreat from Reconstruction*, 190–258; McKinney, *Southern Mountain Republicans*, 41, 43–44, 49–50, 54–56, 60, 131–41; Moneyhon, *Republicanism in Reconstruction Texas*, 71–72, 98, 118–19, 138, 155–58, 168–70, 178–79, 182, 195–96.

For a fresh perspective on segregation as an advance over exclusion, see Rabinowitz, *Race Relations in the Urban South*, part 2. No less principled a Radical than Albion W. Tourgee considered Charles Sumner's Civil Rights bill with its provision for desegregated schools a "blister-plaster.... It will be like the firebrands between the tails of Samson's foxes." Cox and Cox, eds., *Reconstruction, the Negro, and the New South*, 125–26.

67. Thomas B. Alexander, "Political Reconstruction in Tennessee, 1865–1870," in Richard O. Curry, ed., *Radicalism, Racism, and Party Realignment: The Border States during Reconstruction* (Baltimore, 1969), 77.

68. On Louisiana, see Cox, *Lincoln and Black Freedom;* on leadership dilemmas, Ross Clayton and William Lammers, "Presidential Leadership Reconsidered: Contemporary Views of Top Federal Officials," *Presidential Studies Quarterly* 8 (Summer 1978): 239–40, 242–43, 244.

Had Banks returned to New Orleans from Washington when Lincoln first asked him to do so, there would have been little likelihood of a "counter-revolution" in Louisiana during Lincoln's lifetime whether or not Michael Hahn would then have sought escape from the governorship by election as senator. This was the act that, in Banks' absence, opened the gates of power for the Kennedy-Cottman-Wells men. The opposition to the Free State government, which Durant had done so much to arouse and continued to nurture, was, of course, an important factor both in Hahn's discomfiture as governor and in Banks' protracted stay in Washington.

69. *Liberator,* February 3, 1865, 18; McPherson, *Struggle for Equality,* 298–99; Walter M. Merrill, ed., *Let the Oppressed Go Free, 1861–1867: The Letters of William Lloyd Garrison* (Boston, 1971–1981), 5:258.

Chapter 11. Ella Lonn

1. Rev. E. D Daniels, *A Twentieth Century History and Biographical Record of LaPorte County, Indiana* (Chicago, 1904), 720-22.

Her mother was the daughter of early settlers at LaPorte, "an omniverous reader" who organized her family as they grew up "into a little reading circle . . . (to which the maid was invited). One winter was devoted to Scott, another to Hawthorne, another to American poets, etc." Faculty Records, Office of the President, Goucher College.

From kindergarten through high school Ella Lonn's education was in the public schools of LaPorte. She attended the University of Chicago, graduating in 1900 Phi Beta Kappa with special honors in history and political science. For six and a half years she taught high school history, English, and German in Iowa and Indiana. From 1908 to 1911 she was a graduate student at the University of Pennsylvania, obtaining there her M.A. and Ph.D. Most of her classes were with either Edward P. Cheyney in English and British colonial history or with Herman V. Ames, professor of American constitutional history and dean of the Graduate School of Arts and Sciences. Ibid.; University of Pennsylvania, Ella Lonn's Graduate Record Sheet.

2. Faculty Records, Office of the President, Goucher College.

3. Milledge L. Bonham, Jr., review of *Reconstruction in Louisiana* in *Mississippi Valley Historical Review* 5 (December 1918): 366-68; Charles W. Ramsdell, review of *Salt as a Factor in the Confederacy* in *American Historical Review* 39 (July 1934): 753-54; Bell I. Wiley, review of *Foreigners in the Confederacy* in *Journal of Southern History* 6 (November 1940): 561-63; O. P. Chitwood, review of *Colonial Agents of the Southern Colonies* in *American Historical Review* 51 (October 1945): 133-34.

In her pursuit of evidence and her determination to be even-handed, Ella Lonn could be forthright to the point of tactlessness. See the exchange of letters in July 1917 between her and Henry Clay Warmoth, controversial governor of Louisiana during Reconstruction, in Warmoth Papers, Southern Historical Collection, University of North Carolina Library. Compare her subsequent assessment of Warmoth in *Reconstruction in Louisiana after 1868* (rpt., Peter Smith, Gloucester, Mass., 1967), 52, 78-79, 90, 93, and in her sketch of Warmoth for the *Dictionary of American Biography*.

4. Ella Lonn, *Foreigners in the Union Army and Navy* (Baton Rouge, La., 1951), 172. See ch. 8, "Life at the Works" in her *Salt as a Factor in the Confederacy* (rpt., University of Alabama Press, [1965]), her review of Bell I. Wiley, *Life of Jonny Reb* in *Journal of Southern History* 9 (August 1943): 420-21, and his review of her *Foreigners, loc. cit.*

5. Thomas D. Clark to author, April 1, 1980; E. Merton Coulter to author, April 4, 1980; Walter B. Posey to author, April 2, 1980.

6. There was one formal paper, by Charles W. Ramsdell on problems in the writing of the history of the Confederacy, and Ella Lonn was the chief discussant. Not only

were her remarks well received, Ramsdell had mentioned just five titles as excellent monographic studies of the type required. Two of the five were Ella Lonn's. William C. Binkley, "Report of the First Annual Meeting," *Journal of Southern History* 2 (February 1936): 70-71.

7. Coulter to author, April 4, 1980.

8. Miss Lonn spent a month in 1924 at Geneva sitting in with sessions of the Assembly and Council of the League of Nations, and in 1928 she was present at Dr. Stresemann's arrival in Paris and outside the French foreign office for the signing of the Kellogg Peace Pact in order to see and hear at first hand the French reaction. Faculty Records, Office of the President, Goucher College; *Who Was Who in America* 6:252; *Conservation of the Products of the Chesapeake Bay*, prepared by Ella Lonn under the auspices of the Central (Baltimore) District of the Maryland Federation of Women's Clubs [Baltimore, 1924]; Ella Lonn, "The Kellogg Peace Pact," *Maryland Club Woman* (February 1929): 5, 20-28.

9. See her "A Course in Methods of Teaching the Social Studies in High Schools," *Historical Outlook* 15 (December 1924): 387-91; "Making Geography Attractive to History Students," *Proceedings of the Association of History Teachers of the Middle States and Maryland* 29 (1931): 47-58; *Problems in Americanization: A Course of Suggested Readings for Native Born Americans*, under the auspices of the Women's Civic League [Baltimore, 1920]; "Women's Colleges and Americanization," *Bulletin of Goucher College* (April 1920): 3-14 [quotation from pp. 7-8].

Miss Lonn was president of the Maryland History Teachers Association, 1934-35, and of the Middle States Association of History and Social Science Teachers, 1936-37. For eight years she chaired the citizenship committee of the Women's Civic League and for a briefer period headed the citizenship division of the Baltimore Federation of Women's Clubs and served on a similar committee created by the Maryland State Superintendent of Education.

10. She was a member of the AAUP from 1922 until her death in 1962, and from 1936 through 1947 chaired the association's committee on admission of members. Marie Welebir, administrative secretary, AAUP, to author, May 15, 1980.

For her work with the AAUW see Marion Talbot and Lois Kimball Mathews Rosenberry, *The History of the American Association of University Women 1881-1931* (Boston, 1931), 202; Ella Lonn, "Academic Status of Women on University Faculties," *Journal of the American Association of University Women* 17 (January 1924): 5-11; Ella Lonn, "The Work of Recognition," ibid. 20 (January 1927), 33-36. Cf. "Preliminary Report of Committee W on Status of Women in College and University Faculties," American Association of University Professors, *Bulletin* 7 (October 1921): 21-32 and "Second Report of Committee W on the Status of Women in College and University Faculties," ibid. 10 (November 1924): 65-73.

11. Lonn, "Academic Status of Women," and "The Work of Recognition." Her questionnaires had revealed a widespread perception that women were not as pro-

ductive as research scholars as were men. Her response was "not yet. We women must produce more research of a uniformly high caliber on *worth-whiley* subjects," undaunted by the knowledge that "the rewards of scholarship are greater for a man than for a woman, as even good work seldom wins promotion or new calls for us." She conceded that women more than men yielded "to the temptation of dissipating our energies with social, civic, and philanthropic work." "Academic Status of Women," 10. Her reference to administrative opportunities other than that of "a glorified chaperon" probably reflects dissatisfaction with her first post-doctoral appointment, at Fargo College, North Dakota, where she not only taught history but was dean of women for one year, 1911–1912.

12. Ella Lonn, *Foreigners in the Confederacy* (rpt., Peter Smith, Gloucester, Mass., 1965), vii, 1.

13. Lonn, *Salt as a Factor in the Confederacy*, 202–4, 226.

14. Ella Lonn, *Desertion During the Civil War* (rpt., Peter Smith, Gloucester, Mass., 1966), v; copy, J. G. Randall to E. P. Cheyney, April 9, 1928, J. G. Randall Papers, Library of Congress. *Desertion* was originally published by the American Historical Association through its revolving fund for publication. See Randall's review of *Desertion* in *American Historical Review* 34 (July 1929): 860–61.

15. "Reconciliation between the North and the South," *Journal of Southern History* 13 (February 1947): 3–26 (quotation from p. 14).

16. The words "need not accept" were used in the summary of the session and were not necessarily those of Simkins. A. B. Moore, "Report of the Sixth Annual Meeting," ibid., 7 (February 1941): 68. Thomas D. Clark still recalls the session; Clark to author, April 1, 1980.

17. *Reconstruction in Louisiana*, 36, 68, 88; Ella Lonn, review of Willie M. Caskey, *Secession and Reconstruction of Louisiana* in *Journal of Southern History* 5 (May 1939): 268–69. Miss Lonn was not, however, alert to race and class prejudice and their distortion of source material.

Chapter 12. From Emancipation to Segregation

1. Walter Johnson, "Historians Join the March on Montgomery," *South Atlantic Quarterly* 79 (Spring 1980): 158–74.

2. Dunning's own work is presented as being less racist, and also less scholarly, than his reputation by Philip R. Muller in "Look Back without Anger: A Reappraisal of William A. Dunning," *Journal of American History* 61 (September 1974): 325–38. Black historians, lacking a white supremacist bias and concerned to undermine the denigration of blacks, were revisionist from the start of their participation in American historical scholarship. See Daniel Savage Gray, "Bibliographical Essay: Black Views on Reconstruction," *Journal of Negro History* 58 (January 1973): 73–85; Rayford W. Logan, "Carter G. Woodson: Mirror and Molder of His Time, 1875–1950,"

Journal of Negro History 58 (January 1973): 1-17; and *Negro History Bulletin* 13 (May 1950): especially the tribute to Woodson by John Hope Franklin.

3. Howard K. Beale, "On Rewriting Reconstruction History," *American Historical Review* 45 (July 1940): 807-27; Bernard A. Weisberger, "The Dark and Bloody Ground of Reconstruction Historiography," *Journal of Southern History* 25 (November 1959): 427-47; John Hope Franklin, *Reconstruction After the Civil War* (Chicago: University of Chicago Press, 1961); J. G. Randall and David Donald, *The Civil War and Reconstruction* (Boston: Heath, 1961).

4. Although not without exception, the generalization is based upon an examination of the articles and reviews in the *Journal of Southern History* 1963-65; Carl N. Degler, "The South in Southern History Textbooks," *Journal of Southern History* 30 (February 1964): 52-53; and other evidence. The last major work on Reconstruction to be totally unreconstructed was E. Merton Coulter, *The South During Reconstruction, 1865-1877* (Baton Rouge: Louisiana State University Press, 1947). For comment on its generally favorable reception and a critique, see John Hope Franklin, "Whither Reconstruction Historiography?" *Journal of Negro Education* 17 (Fall 1948): 446-61.

5. Vernon L. Wharton, *The Negro in Mississippi, 1865-1890* (Chapel Hill: University of North Carolina Press, 1947), and "Reconstruction," in Arthur S. Link and Rembert W. Patrick, eds., *Writing Southern History: Essays in Historiography in Honor of Fletcher M. Green* (Baton Rouge: Louisiana State University Press, 1965), 295-315; Thomas J. Pressly, "Racial Attitudes, Scholarship, and Reconstruction: A Review Essay," *Journal of Southern History* 32 (February 1966): 92-93; Larry Kincaid, "Victims of Circumstance: An Interpretation of Changing Attitudes Toward Republican Policy Makers and Reconstruction," *Journal of American History* 47 (June 1970): 62; David Donald, Review of Bonadio's *North of Reconstruction,* in *Journal of American History* 48 (September 1971): 472-73. For Donald's early revisionism, see his "The Scalawag in Mississippi Reconstruction," *Journal of Southern History* 10 (November 1944): 447-60; "The Radicals and Lincoln," in his *Lincoln Reconsidered: Essays on the Civil War Era* (New York: Knopf, 1956), 103-27; "Why They Impeached Andrew Johnson," *American Heritage* 8 (December 1956), 20-25, 102-3; and "Devils Facing Zionwards," in Grady McWhiney, ed., *Grant, Lee, Lincoln, and the Radicals: Essays on Civil War Leadership* (Evanston, Ill.: Northwestern University Press, 1964), 72-91.

6. Patrick W. Riddleberger, "The Radicals' Abandonment of the Negro During Reconstruction," *Journal of Negro History* 45 (April 1960): 88-102; August Meier, "Negroes in the First and Second Reconstructions of the South," *Civil War History* 13 (June 1967): 114-30.

7. For early examples, David Donald, *The Politics of Reconstruction, 1863-1867* (Baton Rouge: Louisiana State University Press, 1965); and Edward L. Gambill, "Who Were the Senate Radicals?" *Civil War History* 11 (September 1965): 237-44;

for later, more sophisticated usage, J. Morgan Kousser, "Progressivism—For Middle Class Whites Only: North Carolina Education, 1880–1910," *Journal of Southern History* 46 (May 1980): 169–94; and Allan G. Bogue, *The Earnest Men: Republicans of the Civil War Senate* (Ithaca: Cornell University Press, 1981). A monumental undertaking is that of Richard L. Hume to analyze the delegate composition and voting record of all the state constitutional conventions of congressional Reconstruction. See his articles in *Florida Historical Quarterly*, especially "Membership of the Florida Constitutional Convention of 1868: A Case Study of Republican Factionalism in the Reconstruction South," *Florida Historical Quarterly* 51 (July 1972): 1–21; "The Arkansas Constitutional Convention of 1868: A Case Study in the Politics of Reconstruction," *Journal of Southern History* 39 (May 1973): 183–206; "Carpetbaggers in the Reconstruction South: A Group Portrait of Outside Whites in the 'Black and Tan' Constitutional Conventions," *Journal of American History* 44 (September 1977): 313–30; "The Membership of the Virginia Constitutional Convention of 1867–1868: A Study of the Beginnings of Congressional Reconstruction in the Upper South," *Virginia Magazine of History and Biography* 86 (October 1978): 461–84; and "Negro Delegates to the State Constitutional Conventions of 1867–69," in Howard N. Rabinowitz, ed., *Southern Black Leaders of the Reconstruction Era* (Urbana: University of Illinois Press, 1982), 129–53. For a lucid, informed plea for a quantitative approach to black history, Thomas Holt, "On the Cross: The Role of Quantitative Methods in the Reconstruction of the Afro-American Experience," *Journal of Negro History* 61 (April 1976): 158–72.

8. See Robert P. Swierenga, ed., *Beyond the Civil War Synthesis: Political Essays of the Civil War Era* (Westport, Conn.: Greenwood Press, 1975), especially the editor's introduction (xi–xx) and the essay by Joel H. Silbey, "The Civil War Synthesis in American Political History" (3–13).

9. For an example of effective use of a theoretical concept, J. William Harris, "Plantations and Power: Emancipation on the David Barrow Plantations," in Orville Vernon Burron and Robert C. McMath, Jr., eds., *Toward a New South? Studies in Post–Civil War Southern Communities* (Westport, Conn.: Greenwood Press, 1982), 246–64. For innovative nonpolitical urban studies, John W. Blassingame, *Black New Orleans, 1860–1880* (Chicago: University of Chicago Press, 1973); and James Borchert, *Alley Life in Washington: Family, Community, Religion, and Folklife in the City, 1850–1970* (Urbana: University of Illinois Press, 1980). For the comparative approach to postemancipation, C. Vann Woodward, "The Price of Freedom," in David G. Sansing, ed., *What Was Freedom's Price?* (Jackson: University Press of Mississippi, 1978), 93–113; George M. Fredrickson, "After Emancipation," in Sansing, ed., *What Was Freedom's Price?*, 71–92; and *White Supremacy: A Comparative Study in American and South African History* (New York: Oxford University Press, 1981); Thomas C. Holt, "'An Empire Over the Mind': Emancipation, Race, and Ideology in the British West Indies and the American South," in J. Morgan Kousser and James M.

McPherson, eds., *Region, Race, and Reconstruction: Essays in Honor of C. Vann Woodward* (New York: Oxford University Press, 1982), 283–313; and Eric Foner, *Nothing But Freedom: Emancipation and Its Legacy* (Baton Rouge: Louisiana State University Press, 1983).

10. Two studies that have received critical acclaim are Thomas Holt, *Black Over White: Negro Political Leadership in South Carolina during Reconstruction* (Urbana: University of Illinois Press, 1977); and Leon F. Litwack, *Been in the Storm So Long: The Aftermath of Slavery* (New York: Knopf, 1979). Recognition is also due August Meier for his contributions to black history not only as productive scholar but as editor of the University of Illinois Press series Blacks in the New World. His major special study within the time span of this essay appeared in 1963, *Negro Thought in America, 1880–1915: Radical Ideologies in the Age of Booker T. Washington* (Ann Arbor: University of Michigan Press).

11. The footnotes are somewhat more generous in recognizing work in the field. Michael Kammen, ed., *The Past Before Us: Contemporary Historical Writing in the United States* (Ithaca: Cornell University Press, 1980).

12. The affirmation is implicit in their work; for an explicit statement, see Eric Foner, *Politics and Ideology in the Age of the Civil War* (New York: Oxford University Press, 1980), 3–12.

13. Harold M. Hyman, *A More Perfect Union: The Impact of the Civil War and Reconstruction on the Constitution* (New York: Knopf, 1973), and "Law and the Impact of the Civil War: A Review Essay," *Civil War History* 14 (March 1968): 51–59; William Cohen, "Negro Involuntary Servitude in the South, 1865–1940: A Preliminary Analysis," *Journal of Southern History* 42 (February 1976): 31–60; Harold D. Woodman, "Post–Civil War Southern Agriculture and the Law," *Agricultural History* 43 (January 1979): 319–37; and see Harold D. Woodman's essay in this volume.

14. Eric L. McKitrick, *Andrew Johnson and Reconstruction* (Chicago: University of Chicago Press, 1960); LaWanda F. Cox and John H. Cox, *Politics, Principle, and Prejudice, 1865–1866: Dilemma of Reconstruction America* (New York: Free Press, 1963); W. R. Brock, *An American Crisis: Congress and Reconstruction, 1865–1867* (New York: St. Martin's Press, 1963); James M. McPherson, *The Struggle for Equality: Abolitionists and the Negro in the Civil War and Reconstruction* (Princeton: Princeton University Press, 1964); Willie Lee Rose, *Rehearsal for Reconstruction: The Port Royal Experiment* (Indianapolis: Bobbs-Merrill, 1964).

An important link between revisionism facing North and the earlier revisionism facing South was John Hope Franklin's concept of developments under Johnson ("Reconstruction: Confederate Style," ch. 3 of *Reconstruction After the Civil War*). David Donald's essays on impeachment and on Lincoln and the Radicals (see n. 5) were seminal, as were the Coxes' articles published in the 1950s on O. O. Howard and the Freedmen's Bureau and on the promise of land for the freedmen (see nn. 47, 53).

15. The most important dissent, W. E. Burghardt Du Bois, *Black Reconstruction:*

An Essay Toward a History of the Part Which Black Folk Played in the Attempt to Reconstruct Democracy in America, 1860–1880 (New York: Harcourt, Brace, 1935), had little impact on white historiography in part because of its Marxist orientation. Analyses of writings on Reconstruction have been numerous. In addition to those by Weisberger, Wharton, Pressly, and Kincaid, see T. Harry Williams, "An Analysis of Some Reconstruction Attitudes," *Journal of Southern History* 12 (November 1946): 469–86; Willard Hays, "Andrew Johnson's Reputation," *East Tennessee Historical Society Publications* 31 (1959): 1–31 and 32 (1960): 18–50; Albert Castel, "Andrew Johnson: His Historiographical Rise and Fall," *Mid-America* 45 (July 1963): 175–84; Staughton Lynd, "Rethinking Slavery and Reconstruction," *Journal of Negro History* 50 (July 1965): 198–209; B. P. Gallaway, "Economic Determinism in Reconstruction Historiography," *Southwestern Social Science Quarterly* 46 (December 1965): 244–54; Harold M. Hyman, ed., *The Radical Republicans and Reconstruction, 1861–1870* (Indianapolis: Bobbs-Merrill, 1967), xvii–lxviii; James E. Sefton, "The Impeachment of Andrew Johnson: A Century of Writing," *Civil War History* 14 (June 1968): 120–47; Eric L. McKitrick, ed., *Andrew Johnson: A Profile* (New York: Hill & Wang, 1969), vii–xxii; Richard O. Curry, "The Civil War and Reconstruction, 1861–1877: A Critical Overview of Recent Trends and Interpretations," *Civil War History* 20 (September 1974): 215–38; and Albert Castel, *The Presidency of Andrew Johnson* (Lawrence: Regents Press of Kansas, 1979), 218–30.

16. Howard K. Beale, *The Critical Year: A Study of Andrew Johnson and Reconstruction* (New York: Harcourt, Brace, 1930), esp. 1–9; Robert W. Winston, *Andrew Johnson: Plebeian and Patriot* (New York: H. Holt and Co., 1928); Lloyd P. Stryker, *Andrew Johnson: A Study in Courage* (New York: Macmillan, 1929); Claude G. Bowers, *The Tragic Era: The Revolution after Lincoln* (New York: Blue Ribbon Books, 1929); George Fort Milton, *The Age of Hate: Andrew Johnson and the Radicals* (New York: Coward-McCann, 1930); T. Harry Williams, *Lincoln and the Radicals* (Madison: University of Wisconsin Press, 1941).

17. Robert P. Sharkey, *Money, Class, and Party: An Economic Study of Civil War and Reconstruction* (Baltimore: Johns Hopkins Press, 1959), esp. 279–82, 287–311; Stanley Coben, "Northeastern Business and Radical Reconstruction: A Reexamination," *Mississippi Valley Historical Review* 46 (June 1959): 67–90; Irwin Unger, "Business Men and Specie Resumption," *Political Science Quarterly* 74 (March 1959): 46–70; and *The Greenback Era: A Social and Political History of American Finance, 1865–1879* (Princeton: Princeton University Press, 1964), esp. 3–9. See also Gallaway, "Economic Determinism in Reconstruction Historiography."

18. Patrick W. Riddleberger attempted to synthesize Beale's work and that of the revisionists in *1866: The Critical Year Revisited* (Carbondale: Southern Illinois University Press, 1979). See also August Meier, "An Epitaph for the Writing of Reconstruction History?" *Reviews in American History* 1 (March 1981): 82–87; and my

discussion later of the army, the Freedmen's Bureau, education for freedmen, the land question, and the various class interpretations of the "failure" of Reconstruction.

19. A recent study that strikingly illustrates the point is Eugene H. Benwanger, *The West and Reconstruction* (Urbana: University of Illinois Press, 1981), esp. 3–12. See also James C. Mohr, *The Radical Republicans and Reform in New York during Reconstruction* (Ithaca: Cornell University Press, 1973), and Mohr, ed., *Radical Republicans in the North: State Politics During Reconstruction* (Baltimore: Johns Hopkins University Press, 1976).

20. Cox and Cox, *Politics, Principle, and Prejudice*, 195–232; Brock, *An American Crisis*, 14, 18–23, 85–92, 248–49; McKitrick, *Andrew Johnson and Reconstruction*, 21–41, 334–35, 409–10, 421, 442–43; William B. Hesseltine, Review of McKitrick's *Andrew Johnson and Reconstruction*, in *Journal of Southern History* 27 (February 1961): 111; Castel, *The Presidency of Andrew Johnson*, 222.

21. David Brion Davis, "Abolitionists and the Freedmen: An Essay Review," *Journal of Southern History* 31 (May 1965): 167.

22. A pathbreaking article was Leslie H. Fishel, Jr., "Northern Prejudice and Negro Suffrage, 1865–1870," *Journal of Negro History* 39 (January 1954): 8–26. The most influential general works were Leon F. Litwack, *North of Slavery: The Negro in the Free States, 1790–1860* (Chicago: University of Chicago Press, 1961); Winthrop D. Jordan, *White over Black: American Attitudes Toward the Negro, 1550–1812* (Chapel Hill: University of North Carolina Press, 1968); and George M. Fredrickson, *The Black Image in the White Mind: The Debate on Afro-American Character and Destiny, 1817–1914* (New York: Harper and Row, 1971). Other studies of special import for the Civil War era included Eugene H. Berwanger, *The Frontier Against Slavery: Western Anti-Negro Prejudice and the Slavery Extension Controversy* (Urbana: University of Illinois Press, 1967); V. Jacque Voegeli, *Free but Not Equal: The Midwest and the Negro During the Civil War* (Chicago: University of Chicago Press, 1967); James A. Rawley, *Race and Politics: "Bleeding Kansas" and the Coming of the Civil War* (Philadelphia: Lippincott, 1969); Forrest G. Wood, *Black Scare: The Racist Response to Emancipation and Reconstruction* (Berkeley: University of California Press, 1968); and David A. Gerber's fine state study, *Black Ohio and the Color Line, 1860–1915* (Urbana: University of Illinois Press, 1976).

23. Harold M. Hyman, "Johnson, Stanton, and Grant: A Reconsideration of the Army's Role in the Events Leading to Impeachment," *American Historical Review* 46 (October 1960): 85–100; Donald, "Devils Facing Zionwards," in McWhiney, ed., *Grant, Lee, Lincoln, and the Radicals*, 79–80.

24. Hans L. Trefousse, *The Radical Republicans: Lincoln's Vanguard for Radical Justice* (New York: Knopf, 1969), *Ben Butler: The South Called Him BEAST!* (New York: Twayne Publishers, 1963), *Benjamin Franklin Wade: Radical Republican from Ohio* (New York: Twayne Publishers, 1963), and *Carl Schurz: A Biography* (Knox-

ville: University of Tennessee Press, 1982); Fawn M. Brodie, *Thaddeus Stevens: Scourge of the South* (New York: Norton, 1959); Benjamin P. Thomas and Harold M. Hyman, *Stanton: The Life and Times of Lincoln's Secretary of War* (New York: Knopf, 1962); Charles A. Jellison, *Fessenden of Maine: Civil War Senator* (Binghamton, N.Y.: Syracuse University Press, 1962); Norma L. Peterson, *Freedom and Franchise: The Political Career of B. Gratz Brown* (Columbia: University of Missouri Press, 1965); Mark M. Krug, *Lyman Trumbull: Conservative Radical* (New York: A. S. Barnes, 1965); Richard S. West, Jr., *Lincoln's Scapegoat General: A Life of Benjamin F. Butler, 1818–1893* (Boston: Houghton Mifflin, 1965); David Donald, *Charles Sumner and the Rights of Man* (New York: Knopf, 1970); Ernest McKay, *Henry Wilson: Practical Radical, A Portrait of a Politician* (Port Washington, N.Y.: Kennikat Press, 1971); Richard H. Abbott, *Cobbler in Congress: The Life of Henry Wilson, 1812–1875* (Lexington: University Press of Kentucky, 1972); Gerald S. Henig, *Henry Winter Davis: Antebellum and Civil War Congressman from Maryland* (New York: Twayne Publishers, 1973); Robert F. Horowitz, *The Great Impeacher: A Political Biography of James M. Ashley* (New York: Brooklyn College Press, 1979); James Pickett Jones, *John A. Logan: Stalwart Republican from Illinois* (Tallahassee: University Presses of Florida, 1982).

25. Michael Les Benedict, *A Compromise of Principle: Congressional Republicans and Reconstruction, 1863–1869* (New York: Norton, 1974), 14. See also his "Racism and Equality in America," *Reviews in American History* 6 (March 1978): 18–20.

26. See Peter Kolchin, "The Myth of Radical Reconstruction," *Reviews in American History* 3 (June 1975): 228–35.

27. Except as a technical achievement, the place of the book in the mainstream of Reconstruction historiography is unclear, for Bogue's caveats are numerous and his conclusions guarded. Bogue, *The Earnest Men,* esp. 98–124, 296–341 (quotation on p. 333).

28. Glenn M. Linden, "A Note on Negro Suffrage and Republican Politics," *Journal of Southern History* 36 (August 1970): 411–20, and *Politics or Principle: Congressional Voting on the Civil War Amendments and Pro-Negro Measures, 1838–1869* (Seattle: University of Washington Press, 1976).

29. Phyllis F. Field, *The Politics of Race in New York: The Struggle for Black Suffrage in the Civil War Era* (Ithaca: Cornell University Press, 1982), and "Republicans and Black Suffrage in New York State: The Grass Roots Response," *Civil War History* 21 (June 1975): 136–47; Robert R. Dykstra, "Iowa: 'Bright Radical Star,'" in Mohr, ed., *Radical Republicans in the North,* 167–93; John M. Rozett, "Racism and Republican Emergence in Illinois, 1848–1860: A Re-Evaluation of Republican Negrophobia," *Civil War History* 22 (June 1976): 101–15; Michael J. McManus, "Wisconsin Republicans and Negro Suffrage: Attitudes and Behavior, 1857," *Civil War History* 25 (March 1979): 36–54. Through a sophisticated statistical analysis of voting behavior, Dale Baum, *The Civil War Party System: The Case of Massachusetts, 1848–1876*

(Chapel Hill: University of North Carolina Press, 1984), has established the primary importance of antislavery together with "middling" wealth in forging and sustaining the Republican majority in Massachusetts until the mid-1870s. For more traditional accounts, Cox and Cox, *Politics, Principle, and Prejudice,* 211–28; Eric Foner, *Free Soil, Free Labor, Free Men: The Ideology of the Republican Party Before the Civil War* (New York: Oxford University Press, 1970), 261–300, 333; Mohr, *The Radical Republicans and Reform in New York,* 202–70; Richard H. Sewell, *Ballots for Freedom: Antislavery Politics in the United States, 1837–1860* (New York: Oxford University Press, 1976), esp. viii, 321–42; Richard Paul Fuke, "Hugh Lennox Bond and Radical Republican Ideology," *Journal of Southern History* 45 (November 1979): 569–86; Berwanger, *The West and Reconstruction,* esp. 5–6, 102–84, 202–8; LaWanda F. Cox, *Lincoln and Black Freedom: A Study in Presidential Leadership* (Columbia: University of South Carolina Press, 1981), 161–64.

For fresh perspectives on the Democratic party that take into account racial attitudes and tactics, Jean H. Baker, *Affairs of Party: The Political Culture of Northern Democrats in the Mid-Nineteenth Century* (Ithaca: Cornell University Press, 1983); Joel H. Silbey, *A Respectable Minority: The Democratic Party in the Civil War Era, 1860–1868* (New York: Norton, 1977); Lawrence Grossman, *The Democratic Party and the Negro: Northern and National Politics, 1868–92* (Urbana: University of Illinois Press, 1976). See also Edward L. Gambill, *Conservative Ordeal: Northern Democrats and Reconstruction, 1865–1868* (Ames: Iowa State University Press, 1981); and Jerome Mushkat, *The Reconstruction of the New York Democracy, 1861–1874* (Rutherford, N.J.: Fairleigh Dickinson University Press, 1981).

30. The sharp dichotomy is, of course, an overstatement, but even when viewed as a matter of emphasis, the disagreement is fundamental.

31. The challenge was made in LaWanda Cox and John H. Cox, "Negro Suffrage and Republican Politics: The Problem of Motivation in Reconstruction Historiography," *Journal of Southern History* 33 (August 1967): 303–30. See also Cox and Cox, eds., *Reconstruction, the Negro, and the New South* (Columbia: University of South Carolina Press, 1973), xiv–xix. For the most authoritative conflicting view, William Gillette, *The Right to Vote: Politics and the Passage of the Fifteenth Amendment* (Baltimore: Johns Hopkins Press, 1965), and in the 1969 paperback edition, the added epilogue (166–90). For comment, Curry, "The Civil War and Reconstruction," 227.

32. Herman Belz, *Reconstructing the Union: Theory and Policy During the Civil War* (Ithaca: Cornell University Press for the American Historical Association, 1969), *A New Birth of Freedom: The Republican Party and Freedmen's Rights, 1861 to 1866* (Westport, Conn.: Greenwood Press, 1976), and *Emancipation and Equal Rights: Politics and Constitutionalism in the Civil War Era* (New York: Norton, 1978). See also the Belz revision of *The American Constitution: Its Origin and Development,* by Alfred H. Kelly and Winfred A. Harbison (6th ed.; New York: Norton, 1983), 299–371.

33. See Alfred H. Kelly, review of H. J. Graham's *Everyman's Constitution*, in *Journal of Southern History* 35 (May 1969): 290–92; and Charles R. Black, Jr., *Brief for Appellants: Brown v. Board of Education of Topeka* . . . (rpt.; New York: Supreme Printing, 1954), foreword and pt. 2 (pp. 67–188). For citations to relevant historical and legal scholarship, see Harold M. Hyman and William M. Wiecek, *Equal Justice Under Law: Constitutional Development, 1835–1875* (New York: Harper and Row, 1982), 552–53; Belz, *Emancipation and Equal Rights*, 160–61; Kelly, Harbison, and Belz, *The American Constitution*, 799–800; and footnotes in Michael Les Benedict, "Preserving Federalism: Reconstruction and the Waite Court," *Supreme Court Review* 1978: 39–79.

34. See Alfred H. Kelly's comments on Hyman's paper in Harold M. Hyman, ed., *New Frontiers of the American Reconstruction* (Urbana: University of Illinois Press, 1966), 51–57; Hyman, *A More Perfect Union*, 438–41, 447–49; Michael Les Benedict, "Preserving the Constitution: The Conservative Basis of Radical Reconstruction," *Journal of American History* 41 (June 1974): 65–90; Phillip S. Paludan, *A Covenant with Death: The Constitution, Law, and Equality in the Civil War Era* (Urbana: University of Illinois Press, 1975), 1–60, 274–82.

35. Stanley I. Kutler, "Reconstruction and the Supreme Court: The Numbers Game Reconsidered," *Journal of Southern History* 32 (February 1966): 42–58, and *Judicial Power and Reconstruction Politics* (Chicago: University of Chicago Press, 1968).

36. Robert J. Kaczorowski, *The Politics of Judicial Interpretation: The Federal Courts, Department of Justice and Civil Rights, 1866–1876* (New York: Oceana Publications, 1985), "Searching for the Intent of the Framers of the Fourteenth Amendment," *Connecticut Law Review* 5 (Winter 1972–73): 368–98, and two papers on civil rights during Reconstruction presented at the annual meetings of the Southern Historical Association, Atlanta, Georgia, November 1973, and the Organization of American Historians, Boston, Massachusetts, April 1975. From a different perspective, Peyton McCrary, like Kaczorowski, presents emancipation-postemancipation developments as revolutionary ("The Party of Revolution: Republican Ideas About Politics and Social Change, 1862–1867," *Civil War History* 30 [December 1984]: 328–50).

37. John S. Rosenberg, "Toward a New Civil War Revisionism," *American Scholar* 38 (Spring 1969): 250–72; the response of Phillip S. Paludan, "The American Civil War: Triumph through Tragedy," *Civil War History* 20 (September 1974): 239–50; Rosenberg, "The American Civil War and the Problem of 'Presentism': A Reply to Phillip S. Paludan," *Civil War History* 21 (September 1975): 242–53; Paludan, "Taking the Benefits of the Civil War Issue Seriously: A Rejoinder to John S. Rosenberg," *Civil War History* 21 (September 1975): 254–60; Benedict, "Preserving Federalism"; Hyman and Wiecek, *Equal Justice Under Law*, 386–438; Kelly, Harbison, and Belz, *The American Constitution*, 328–44, 362–71. For another way in which Reconstruc-

tion legislators strengthened federal jurisdiction in the interest of civil rights, see William M. Wiecek, "The Great Writ and Reconstruction: The Habeas Corpus Act of 1867," *Journal of Southern History* 36 (November 1970): 530–48.

38. C. Vann Woodward, "Equality: The Deferred Commitment," in *The Burden of Southern History* (Baton Rouge: Louisiana State University Press, 1960), 69–87, and "Seeds of Failure in Radical Race Policy," in *American Counterpoint: Slavery and Racism in the North-South Dialogue*, ed. C. Vann Woodward (Boston: Little, Brown, 1971), 159–60, 163–83 (quotation on p. 183).

39. J. G. Randall, *The Civil War and Reconstruction* (Boston: Heath, 1937), 483–96, 498, 507–8, 706–7, *Lincoln, the President: Springfield to Gettysburg* (New York: Dodd, Mead, 1946), 2:126, 130–32, 137–39, 141–42, 150, 157–58, 164–65, 181–82; Randall and Richard N. Current, *Lincoln, the President: Last Full Measure* (New York: Dodd, Mead, 1955), 2–6, 27–28, 33; Randall, *Lincoln and the South* (Baton Rouge: Louisiana State University Press, 1946), 81–161; Benjamin P. Thomas, *Abraham Lincoln: A Biography* (New York: Knopf, 1953), 333, 356–57, 359, 405–7, 438 (quotation on p. 407). For a more positive assessment by Randall of Lincoln as emancipator, see his *Lincoln: The Liberal Statesman* (New York: Dodd, Mead, 1947), 192–97.

For two decades Randall was recognized as the leading Lincoln authority in academe, and for an even longer period Thomas' book, which owed much to Randall, was characterized as the best one-volume biography of Lincoln. Randall's views were challenged largely by those outside the ranks of professional historians. In keeping with what appeared the paramount problem of Randall's time, he saw greatness in Lincoln's design for a generous peace. On the peacemaker image, see also Frank L. Owsley, "A Southerner's View of Abraham Lincoln," in Harriet Chappell Owsley, ed., *The South: Old and New Frontiers: Selected Essays of Frank Lawrence Owsley* (Athens: University of Georgia Press, 1969), 223–34. For comment on Randall's place in historiography, Benjamin P. Thomas, *Portrait for Posterity: Lincoln and His Biographers* (New Brunswick, N.J.: Rutgers University Press, 1947), 275–84; David M. Potter, *The Lincoln Theme and American National Historiography, an Inaugural Lecture Delivered Before the University of Oxford* . . . (Oxford, Eng.: Clarendon Press, 1948), 22–24; Don E. Fehrenbacher, *The Changing Image of Lincoln in American Historiography* (Oxford, Eng.: Clarendon Press, 1968), 17–18; and Mark E. Neely, Jr., "The Lincoln Theme Since Randall's Call: The Promises and Perils of Professionalism," *Papers of the Abraham Lincoln Association* 1 (1979): 10–18, 23–29, 59.

40. Don E. Fehrenbacher, *Prelude to Greatness: Lincoln in the 1850s* (Stanford: Stanford University Press, 1962); Richard Hofstadter, *The American Political Tradition and the Men Who Made It* (New York: Knopf, 1948), 92–134 (quotation on p. 131); Richard N. Current, *The Lincoln Nobody Knows* (New York: Hill and Wang, 1958), 214–36; Benjamin Quarles, *The Negro in the Civil War* (Boston: Little, Brown, 1953), 134–36, 140, 251–55, and *Lincoln and the Negro* (New York: Oxford

University Press, 1962), 194–208, 217–24; Kenneth M. Stampp, *The Era of Reconstruction, 1865–1877* (New York: Knopf, 1965), 24–49 (quotations on pp. 35, 48).

41. Fehrenbacher, *The Changing Image of Lincoln*, 21–22 (quotations on p. 21); Ludwell H. Johnson and Fawn M. Brodie, letters to the editor, *New York Times Book Review*, September 23, 1962, 50–51; Lerone Bennett, Jr., "Was Abe Lincoln a White Supremacist?" *Ebony* 23 (February 1968): 35–38; Herbert Mitgang, "Was Lincoln Just a Honkie?" *New York Times Magazine*, February 11, 1968, 35; Robert F. Durden, "A. Lincoln: Honkie or Equalitarian?" *South Atlantic Quarterly* 71 (Summer 1972): 281–91.

For restrained but negative references to Lincoln's position on black rights in scholarly literature, Litwack, *North of Slavery*, 276–77; McPherson, *The Struggle for Equality*, 23–25, 241; Voegeli, *Free but Not Equal*, 169; Berwanger, *The Frontier Against Slavery*, 136–37; James A. Rawley, *Turning Points of the Civil War* (Lincoln: University of Nebraska Press, 1966), 132–33, 139, 143, and *Race and Politics*, 197–99, 255–56, 258, 268–69; Fredrickson, *The Black Image*, 91, 165–67; Don E. Fehrenbacher, "Lincoln and the Constitution," in Cullom Davis et al., eds., *The Public and the Private Lincoln: Contemporary Perspectives* (Carbondale: Southern Illinois University Press, 1979).

For careful consideration of Lincoln's racial attitudes, Don E. Fehrenbacher, "Only His Stepchildren: Lincoln and the Negro," *Civil War History* 20 (December 1974): 293–310; George M. Fredrickson, "A Man But Not a Brother: Abraham Lincoln and Racial Equality," *Journal of Southern History* 41 (February 1975): 39–58, and his comment in Davis et al., eds., *The Public and the Private Lincoln*, 95–98. See also Robert W. Johannsen, "In Search of the Real Lincoln, Or Lincoln at the Crossroads," *Journal of the Illinois State Historical Society* 41 (Autumn 1968): 229–47 (quotation on p. 237); Christopher N. Breiseth, "Lincoln and Frederick Douglass: Another Debate," *Journal of the Illinois State Historical Society* 68 (February 1975): 9–26; Richard K. Fleischman, "The Devil's Advocate: A Defense of Lincoln's Attitude Toward the Negro, 1837–1863," *Lincoln Herald* 81 (Fall 1979): 172–86; Richard N. Current, "Lincoln, the Civil War, and the American Mission," in Davis et al., eds., *The Public and the Private Lincoln*, 143–46; and Curry, "The Civil War and Reconstruction," 220–24.

Otto H. Olsen has presented Lincoln as revolutionary, risking war for an ideal, but the ideal at stake he identifies as the free-labor ideology and structure of an expanding capitalism, holding that slavery's violation of the "rights of the enslaved was of secondary concern to Lincoln," "Abraham Lincoln as Revolutionary," *Civil War History* 24 (September 1978): 213–24 (quotation on p. 217).

42. Ludwell H. Johnson, "Lincoln and Equal Rights: The Authenticity of the Wadsworth Letter," *Journal of Southern History* 32 (February 1966): 83–87 (quotation on p. 84), and "Lincoln's Solution to the Problem of Peace Terms, 1864–1865," *Journal of Southern History* 34 (November 1968): 576–86; Harold M. Hyman, "Lin-

coln and Equal Rights for Negroes: The Irrelevancy of the 'Wadsworth Letter,'" *Civil War History* 12 (September 1966): 258–66; Johnson, "Lincoln and Equal Rights: A Reply," *Civil War History* 13 (March 1967): 66–73; Peyton McCrary, *Abraham Lincoln and Reconstruction: The Louisiana Experiment* (Princeton: Princeton University Press, 1978); Joe Gray Taylor, Review of McCrary's *Abraham Lincoln and Reconstruction*, in *American Historical Review* 84 (October 1979): 1161–62; Harold M. Hyman, in "Communications," *American Historical Review* 85 (April 1980): 504–5.

A related area of historical controversy is Lincoln on colonization, how long he favored it, and the degree to which his support was a strategy to counter opposition to emancipation rather than a solution of the race problem. See Voegeli, *Free but Not Equal*, 45; Fehrenbacher, "Only His Stepchildren," 307–8; G. S. Boritt, "The Voyage to the Colony of Lincolnia: The Sixteenth President, Black Colonization, and the Defense Mechanism of Avoidance," *Historian* 37 (August 1975): 619–32; Mark E. Neely, Jr., "Abraham Lincoln and Black Colonization: Benjamin Butler's Spurious Testimony," *Civil War History* 25 (March 1979): 77–83; Gary R. Planck, "Abraham Lincoln and Black Colonization: Theory and Practice," *Lincoln Herald* 72 (Summer 1970): 61–77; Jason H. Silverman, "'In Isles Beyond the Main': Abraham Lincoln's Philosophy on Black Colonization," *Lincoln Herald* 80 (Fall 1978): 115–22. For additional writings on the subject, see citations in the Silverman article.

43. Trefousse, *The Radical Republicans*, and see also his *Lincoln's Decision for Emancipation* (Philadelphia: Lippincott, 1975); Belz, *Reconstructing the Union*, 252–55, and "Origins of Negro Suffrage During the Civil War," *Southern Studies* 17 (Summer 1978): 115–30; Donald, *Charles Sumner and the Rights of Man*, 196–97; *cf.* Cox, *Lincoln and Black Freedom*, 36–37, 119–21; Stephen B. Oates, *With Malice Toward None: The Life of Abraham Lincoln* (New York: Harper and Row, 1977), *Our Fiery Trial: Abraham Lincoln, John Brown, and the Civil War Era* (Amherst: University of Massachusetts Press, 1979), 61–85, "Toward a New Birth of Freedom: Abraham Lincoln and Reconstruction, 1854–1865," *Lincoln Herald* 82 (Spring 1980): 287–96, and *Abraham Lincoln: The Man Behind the Myths* (New York: Harper and Row, 1984), 93–119, 136–47. See also David Lightner, "Abraham Lincoln and the Ideal of Equality," *Journal of the Illinois State Historical Society* 75 (Winter 1982): 289–307; and Eugene H. Berwanger, "Lincoln's Constitutional Dilemma: Emancipation and Black Suffrage," *Papers of the Abraham Lincoln Association* 5 (1983): 25–38.

44. Cox, *Lincoln and Black Freedom*, 3–43, 142–84. Other recent historiographic developments may reinforce the negative image. The important and basically valid view of blacks as active shapers rather than passive recipients of history has sometimes been used to overemphasize the need for black manpower as the explanation for the emancipation proclamations and to fault Lincoln as friend of freedom because as such he became a symbol that robbed blacks of credit for "setting themselves free" (Vincent Harding, *There Is a River: The Black Struggle for Freedom in America*

[New York: Harcourt Brace Jovanovich, 1981], 214, 231-37, 254-57 [quotation on p. 236]). A sharply different perspective, one in which the impersonal forces of modernization doom slavery, carries a hazard of reducing to insignificance the way in which the institution was legally destroyed and the role of Lincoln in that process.

A third approach that can carry negative implications is that of putting Lincoln "on the analyst's couch" (to borrow a title from Richard O. Curry). In seeking explanations for Lincoln's actions in respect to the Union and slavery in his subconscious filiopiety, filial rebellion, or narcissistic search for immortality, psychohistorians demean both the public man and the issues of slavery and black freedom. George B. Forgie, *Patricide in the House Divided: A Psychological Interpretation of Lincoln and His Age* (New York: Norton, 1979); Charles B. Strozier, *Lincoln's Quest for Union: Public and Private Meanings* (New York: Basic Books, 1982); Dwight G. Anderson, *Abraham Lincoln: The Quest for Immortality* (New York: Knopf, 1982).

Two preeminent Lincoln authorities appear ambivalent toward the newer scholarship that presents as positive Lincoln's record on race and Reconstruction. Don E. Fehrenbacher, "The Anti-Lincoln Tradition," *Papers of the Abraham Lincoln Association* 4 (1982): 20-28; Richard N. Current, "Lincoln the Southerner," in *Speaking of Abraham Lincoln: The Man and His Meaning for Our Times* (Urbana: University of Illinois Press, 1983), 150-52, 164-66. See also Current, *Northernizing the South* (Athens: University of Georgia Press, 1983), 52-53.

In a remarkable explication of his changing views on Lincoln, Stampp has repudiated his earlier judgment of Lincoln as a reluctant emancipator. That the negative assessment still carries credence, however, is evident in the Fortenbaugh Memorial Lecture delivered at Gettysburg in November 1983 by David Brion Davis. Kenneth M. Stampp, *My Life with Lincoln,* Bernard Moses Memorial Lecture, March 1, 1983 (Berkeley: Graduate Division, University of California, 1983); Davis, *The Emancipation Movement* (Gettysburg: Gettysburg College, 1983), 20-21.

45. J. Thomas May, "Continuity and Change in the Labor Program of the Union Army and the Freedmen's Bureau," *Civil War History* 17 (September 1971): 245-54; Louis S. Gerteis, *From Contraband to Freedman: Federal Policy Toward Southern Blacks, 1861-1865* (Westport, Conn.: Greenwood Press, 1973); William F. Messner, "Black Violence and White Response: Louisiana, 1862," *Journal of Southern History* 41 (February 1975): 19-38, "Black Education in Louisiana, 1863-1865," *Civil War History* 22 (March 1976): 41-59, and *Freedmen and the Ideology of Free Labor: Louisiana, 1862-1865* (Lafayette: University of Southwestern Louisiana, 1978); C. Peter Ripley, *Slaves and Freedmen in Civil War Louisiana* (Baton Rouge: Louisiana State University Press, 1976). A similar view, but one sympathetic to the white South, can be found in Theodore Brantner Wilson, *The Black Codes of the South* (University: University of Alabama Press, 1965), esp. 57-60, 142, 145, 147, 149.

46. For an evenhanded treatment of the labor system in wartime Louisiana under Gen. Nathaniel P. Banks, see McCrary, *Abraham Lincoln and Reconstruction*,

135–58; see also Cox, *Lincoln and Black Freedom,* 131–34. Important for an evaluation of federal policy is the role of John Eaton and his assistant, Samuel Thomas, in the establishment of a black community at Davis Bend, Mississippi. *Cf.* accounts by Gerteis, *From Contraband to Freedman,* 175–81; Steven Joseph Ross, "Freed Soil, Freed Labor, Freed Men: John Eaton and the Davis Bend Experiment," *Journal of Southern History* 44 (May 1978): 213–32; James T. Currie, *Enclave: Vicksburg and Her Plantations, 1863–1870* (Jackson: University Press of Mississippi, 1980), 83–144; and Janet Sharp Hermann, *The Pursuit of a Dream* (New York: Oxford University Press, 1981), 37–105.

Broader studies of the army's role during and after the war are suggestive, especially that of Joseph G. Dawson III, *Army Generals and Reconstruction: Louisiana, 1862–1877* (Baton Rouge: Louisiana State University Press, 1982). See also his "General Phil Sheridan and Military Reconstruction in Louisiana," *Civil War History* 24 (June 1978): esp. 150–51; Marvin R. Cain, "A 'Face of Battle' Needed: An Assessment of Motives and Men in Civil War Historiography," *Civil War History* 28 (March 1982): esp. 22–25; Kenneth E. St. Clair, "Military Justice in North Carolina, 1865: A Microcosm of Reconstruction," *Civil War History* 11 (December 1965): 341–50; and James E. Sefton, *The United States Army and Reconstruction, 1865–1877* (Baton Rouge: Louisiana State University Press, 1967), which has been characterized as antirevisionist in perspective.

47. George R. Bentley, *A History of the Freedmen's Bureau* (Philadelphia: University of Pennsylvania Press, 1955), viewed the bureau as arousing white racial hostility that seriously hurt the freedmen; W. A. Low, "The Freedmen's Bureau and Civil Rights in Maryland," *Journal of Negro History* 37 (July 1952): 221–47; John Cox and LaWanda Cox, "General O. O. Howard and the 'Misrepresented Bureau,'" *Journal of Southern History* 19 (November 1953): 427–56; John A. Carpenter, *Sword and Olive Branch: Oliver Otis Howard* (Pittsburgh: University of Pittsburgh Press, 1964); Martin Abbott, "Free Land, Free Labor, and the Freedmen's Bureau," *Agricultural History* 30 (October 1956): 150–56, and *The Freedmen's Bureau in South Carolina, 1865–1872* (Chapel Hill: University of North Carolina Press, 1967).

48. William S. McFeely, *Yankee Stepfather: General O. O. Howard and the Freedmen* (New Haven: Yale University Press, 1968), 5, and "Unfinished Business: The Freedmen's Bureau and Federal Action in Race Relations," in Nathan I. Huggins, Martin Kilson, and Daniel M. Fox, eds., *Key Issues in the Afro-American Experience,* (New York: Harcourt Brace Jovanovich, 1971), 2:5–25 (quotation on p. 23). For other generally unfavorable accounts of the bureau's work, see Kenneth B. White, "Wager Swayne: Racist or Realist?" *Alabama Review* 31 (April 1978): 92–109; James Oakes, "A Failure of Vision: The Collapse of the Freedmen's Bureau Courts," *Civil War History* 25 (March 1979): 66–76; Todd L. Savitt, "Politics in Medicine: The Georgia Freedmen's Bureau and the Organization of Health Care, 1865–1866," *Civil War History* 28 (March 1982): 45–64; Gaines M. Foster, "The Limitations of Federal

Health Care for Freedmen, 1867–1868," *Journal of Southern History* 48 (August 1982): 349–72; and Thomas D. Morris, "Equality, 'Extraordinary Law,' and Criminal Justice: The South Carolina Experience, 1865–1866," *South Carolina Historical Magazine* 83 (January 1982): 15–33. See also Howard Ashley White, *The Freedmen's Bureau in Louisiana* (Baton Rouge: Louisiana State University Press, 1970).

49. Foner, *Politics and Ideology*, 100–112; Richard Paul Fuke, "A Reform Mentality: Federal Policy Toward Black Marylanders, 1864–1868," *Civil War History* 22 (September 1976): 214–35; Paul A. Cimbala, "The 'Talisman Power': Davis Tillson, the Freedmen's Bureau, and Free Labor in Reconstruction Georgia, 1865–1866," *Civil War History* 28 (June 1982): 153–71; Harris, "Plantations and Power," and Ralph Shlomowitz, "The Squad System on Postbellum Cotton Plantations," both in Burton and McMath, eds., *Toward a New South?*, 246–80; Shlomowitz, "'Bound' or 'Free'? Black Labor in Cotton and Sugarcane Farming, 1865–1880," *Journal of Southern History* 50 (November 1984): 569–96; Ronald L. F. Davis, *Good and Faithful Labor: From Slavery to Sharecropping in the Natchez District, 1860–1890* (Westport, Conn.: Greenwood Press, 1982), 58–83, 105–6, 192–96 (quotation on p. 192), and "Labor Dependency Among Freedmen, 1865–1880," in Walter J. Fraser, Jr., and Winfred B. Moore, Jr., eds., *From the Old South to the New: Essays on the Transitional South* (Westport, Conn.: Greenwood Press, 1981), 155–65; and William Cohen, *Black Mobility and the Transformation of the Southern Labor System* (forthcoming).

50. Donald G. Nieman, *To Set the Law in Motion: The Freedmen's Bureau and the Legal Rights of Blacks, 1865–1868* (Millwood, N.Y.: KTO Press, 1979). See also Barry A. Crouch, "The Freedmen's Bureau and the 30th Sub-District in Texas: Smith County and Its Environs During Reconstruction," *Chronicles of Smith County, Texas* 11 (Spring 1972): 15–30; Rebecca Scott, "The Battle over the Child: Child Apprenticeship and the Freedmen's Bureau in North Carolina," *Prologue* 10 (Summer 1978): 101–13; James Smallwood, "Charles E. Culver, a Reconstruction Agent in Texas: The Work of Local Freedmen's Bureau Agents and the Black Community," *Civil War History* 27 (December 1981): 350–61; and William Cohen, "Black Immobility and Free Labor: The Freedmen's Bureau and the Relocation of Black Labor, 1865–1868," *Civil War History* 30 (September 1984): 221–34.

John A. Carpenter before his death had identified 2,441 agents of the Freedmen's Bureau and compiled for each a data sheet consisting of forty-five categories pertaining to the man's background, bureau assignment, attitudes, and performance. These data, when made available to the profession, as is Mr. Carpenter's intent, will be an invaluable resource for many purposes, not the least of which is a more comprehensive understanding of the bureau's functioning in the field.

51. Marvin Lazerson, Review of Nasaw's *Schooled to Order*, in *American Historical Review* 86 (October 1981): 909; Donald Spivey, *Schooling for the New Slavery: Black Industrial Education, 1868–1915* (Westport, Conn.: Greenwood Press, 1978), ix–x,

3–44; Jacqueline Jones, *Soldiers of Light and Love: Northern Teachers and Georgia Blacks, 1865–1873* (Chapel Hill: University of North Carolina Press, 1980); Ronald E. Butchart, *Northern Schools, Southern Blacks, and Reconstruction: Freedmen's Education, 1862–1875* (Westport, Conn.: Greenwood Press, 1980), quotations on pp. 74, 202; Robert C. Morris, *Reading, 'Riting, and Reconstruction: The Education of Freedmen in the South, 1861–1870* (Chicago: University of Chicago Press, 1981). See also Keith Wilson, "Education as a Vehicle of Racial Control: Major General N. P. Banks in Louisiana, 1863–64," *Journal of Negro Education* 50 (Spring 1981): 156–70; and Lois E. Horton and James Oliver Horton, "Race, Occupation, and Literacy in Reconstruction Washington, D.C.," in Burton and McMath, eds., *Toward a New South?*, 135–51.

52. James M. McPherson, *The Abolitionist Legacy: From Reconstruction to the NAACP* (Princeton: Princeton University Press, 1975), and "White Liberals and Black Power in Negro Education, 1865–1915," *American Historical Review* 75 (June 1970): 1357–86. See also John W. Blassingame, "The Union Army as an Educational Institution for Negroes, 1862–1865," *Journal of Negro Education* 34 (Spring 1965): 152–59; Howard N. Rabinowitz, "Half a Loaf: The Shift from White to Black Teachers in the Negro Schools of the Urban South, 1865–1890," *Journal of Southern History* 40 (November 1974): 565–94; Sandra E. Small, "The Yankee Schoolmarm in Freedmen's Schools: An Analysis of Attitudes," *Journal of Southern History* 45 (August 1979): 381–402; and William Preston Vaughn, *Schools for All: The Blacks and Public Education in the South, 1865–1877* (Lexington: University Press of Kentucky, 1974), a major study concerned primarily with the issue of integration.

Northern and bureau efforts to promote black education in the upper South have generally been treated with sympathy. See W. A. Low, "The Freedmen's Bureau in the Border States," in Richard O. Curry, ed., *Radicalism, Racism, and Party Realignment: The Border States During Reconstruction* (Baltimore: Johns Hopkins Press, 1969), 245–64; Larry Wesley Pearce, "The American Missionary Association and the Freedmen in Arkansas, 1863–1878," *Arkansas Historical Quarterly* 30 (Summer 1971): 123–44, 242–59; Richard Paul Fuke, "The Baltimore Association for the Moral and Educational Improvement of the Colored People, 1864–1870," *Maryland Historical Magazine* 46 (Winter 1971): 369–404; Joe M. Richardson, "The American Missionary Association and Black Education in Civil War Missouri," *Missouri Historical Review* 49 (July 1975): 433–48; Roberta Sue Alexander, "Hostility and Hope: Black Education in North Carolina during Presidential Reconstruction, 1865–1867," *North Carolina Historical Review* 53 (April 1976): 113–32; and Philip Clyde Kimball, "Freedom's Harvest: Freedmen's Schools in Kentucky After the Civil War," *Filson Club Historical Quarterly* 54 (July 1980): 272–88.

Ironically, a recent theme in the "revisionist" class-emphasis historiography of education, namely, that the self-activity of former slaves deserves major credit for the origin and development of freedmen's education, may inadvertently undermine the education-for-subordination thesis. See James D. Anderson, "Ex-Slaves and the Rise of Universal Education in the New South, 1860–1880," in Ronald K. Goodenow and Arthur O. White, eds., *Education and the Rise of the New South* (Boston: G. K. Hall, 1981), 1–25. For educational historiography, see Harvey Neufeldt and Clinton Allison, "Education and the Rise of the New South: An Historiographical Essay," in Goodenow and White, eds., *Education and the Rise of the New South*, 250–93.

53. Herman Belz, "The New Orthodoxy in Reconstruction Historiography," *Reviews in American History* 1 (March 1973): 106–13; Cox and Cox, eds., *Reconstruction, the Negro, and the New South*, xxviii–xxx; Willie Lee Rose, "Jubilee and Beyond: What Was Freedom?" in Sansing, ed., *What Was Freedom's Price?*, 12–14; Manning Marable, "The Politics of Black Land Tenure, 1877–1915," *Agricultural History* 53 (January 1979): 142–52; Cox, *Lincoln and Black Freedom*, 175–78.

Attention had been directed to national land policy affecting the South and the freedmen by Paul Wallace Gates, "Federal Land Policy in the South, 1866–1888," *Journal of Southern History* 6 (August 1940): 303–30; LaWanda Cox, "The Promise of Land for the Freedmen," *Mississippi Valley Historical Review* 45 (December 1958): 413–40; Rose, *Rehearsal for Reconstruction;* and McPherson, *The Struggle for Equality*. Subsequent special studies: Carol K. Rothrock Bleser, *The Promised Land: The History of the South Carolina Land Commission, 1869–1890* (Columbia: University of South Carolina Press, 1969); Christie Farnham Pope, "Southern Homesteads for Negroes," *Agricultural History* 44 (April 1970): 201–12; Warren Hoffnagle, "The Southern Homestead Act: Its Origins and Operation," *Historian* 32 (August 1970): 612–29; Herman Belz, "The Freedmen's Bureau Act of 1865 and the Principle of No Discrimination According to Color," *Civil War History* 21 (September 1975): 197–217; Lawrence N. Powell, "The American Land Company and Agency: John A. Andrew and the Northernization of the South," *Civil War History* 21 (December 1975): 293–308; Robert F. Horowitz, "Land to the Freedmen: A Vision of Reconstruction," *Ohio History* 86 (Summer 1977): 187–99; Claude F. Oubre, *Forty Acres and a Mule: The Freedmen's Bureau and Black Land Ownership* (Baton Rouge: Louisiana State University Press, 1978).

54. J. W. Cooke, "Stoney Point, 1866–1969," *Filson Club Historical Quarterly* 50 (October 1976): 337–52; Charles Nesbitt, "Rural Acreage in Promise Land, Tennessee: A Case Study," in Leo McGee and Robert Boone, eds., *The Black Rural Landowner—Endangered Species: Social, Political, and Economic Implications* (Westport, Conn.: Greenwood Press, 1979), 67–81; Norman L. Crockett, *The Black Towns* (Lawrence: Regents Press of Kansas, 1979); Hermann, *The Pursuit of a Dream*, esp. 219–45; Elizabeth Rauh Bethel, *Promiseland: A Century of Life in a Negro Community* (Philadelphia: Temple University Press, 1981); Crandall A. Shifflett, *Patronage and Poverty in the Tobacco South: Louisa County, Virginia, 1860–1900* (Knoxville: University of Tennessee Press, 1982). By 1900 an amazing 88 percent of all black heads of household in Louisa County owned land, but Shifflett sees

landownership as bringing neither economic well-being nor independence from white dominance. For citations to earlier accounts of black communities, see Bethel, *Promiseland*, 273 n. 1, 274 n. 12.

55. John A. Carpenter, "Atrocities in the Reconstruction Period," *Journal of Negro History* 47 (October 1962): 234–47; Everette Swinney, "Enforcing the Fifteenth Amendment, 1870–1877," *Journal of Southern History* 28 (May 1962): 202–18; Allen W. Trelease, *White Terror: The Ku Klux Klan Conspiracy and Southern Reconstruction* (New York: Harper and Row, 1971). William Gillette, *Retreat from Reconstruction, 1869–1879* (Baton Rouge: Louisiana State University Press, 1979), deals with enforcement efforts during the Grant administration. See also Herbert Shapiro, "Afro-American Responses to Race Violence During Reconstruction," *Science and Society* 36 (Summer 1972): 158–70. Episodes of violence have been examined in a number of articles published after *White Terror*, most recently, Barry A. Crouch, "A Spirit of Lawlessness: White Violence; Texas Blacks, 1865–1868," *Journal of Social History* 18 (Winter 1984): 217–32. And a comprehensive study of violence as an instrument of southern counterrevolution has recently appeared, George C. Rable, *But There Was No Peace: The Role of Violence in the Politics of Reconstruction* (Athens: University of Georgia Press, 1984). The Federal Elections Bill of 1890, the so-called Force Bill, was rescued from unmerited opprobrium by Richard E. Welch, Jr., "The Federal Elections Bill of 1890: Postscript and Prelude," *Journal of American History* 52 (December 1965): 511–26.

56. Cox, *Lincoln and Black Freedom*, 165–71, has suggested that coercion alone without a substantial degree of consent from southern whites, was an inadequate means to secure black civil and political rights in view of the national tradition of government based upon consent and of opposition to military authority. See also Wilbert H. Ahern, "Laissez Faire vs. Equal Rights: Liberal Republicans and Limits to Reconstruction," *Phylon* 40 (March 1979): 52–65; and George C. Rable, "Bourbonism, Reconstruction, and the Persistence of Southern Distinctiveness," *Civil War History* 29 (June 1983): 135–53, and *But There Was No Peace*. Further light on the problem can be expected from Michael Les Benedict's *Let Us Have Peace: Republicans and Reconstruction, 1869–1880* (New York: Norton, forthcoming).

57. C. Vann Woodward, *Reunion and Reaction: The Compromise of 1877 and the End of Reconstruction* (Boston: Little, Brown, 1951), 9–10 (quotation on p. 10); Introduction and Vincent P. De Santis, "Rutherford B. Hayes and the Removal of the Troops and the End of Reconstruction," both in Kousser and McPherson, eds., *Region, Race, and Reconstruction*, xxvii–xxviii, 417–50, challenge Woodward's interpretation; Richard N. Current, "President Grant and the Continuing Civil War," in David L. Wilson and John Y. Simon, eds., *Ulysses S. Grant: Essays and Documents* (Carbondale: Southern Illinois University Press, 1981), 8. William S. McFeely, in *Grant: A Biography* (New York: Norton, 1981), deals only briefly with Grant's southern policy (416–25). See also George Rable, "Republican Albatross: The Louisiana

Question, National Politics, and the Failure of Reconstruction," *Louisiana History* 23 (Spring 1982): 109–30.

58. Hans L. Trefousse, *Impeachment of a President: Andrew Johnson, the Blacks, and Reconstruction* (Knoxville: University of Tennessee Press, 1975); Michael Les Benedict, *The Impeachment and Trial of Andrew Johnson* (New York: Norton, 1973). On Johnson's obstructionism, see also Donald G. Nieman, "Andrew Johnson, the Freedmen's Bureau, and the Problem of Equal Rights, 1865–1866," *Journal of Southern History* 44 (August 1978): 399–420, and *To Set the Law in Motion*. For the way in which southern leaders took advantage of Johnson's policy, see Michael Perman, *Reunion Without Compromise: The South and Reconstruction, 1865–1868* (New York: Cambridge University Press, 1973).

Two recent brief volumes on Andrew Johnson tend to avoid or minimize the question of his impact as president upon the quality of freedom for southern blacks. Castel, *The Presidency of Andrew Johnson;* James E. Sefton, *Andrew Johnson and the Uses of Constitutional Power* (Boston: Little, Brown, 1980). LeRoy P. Graf and Ralph W. Haskins, as editors of *The Papers of Andrew Johnson* (6 vols. to date; Knoxville: University of Tennessee Press, 1967–), present in their introductions the most informed and convincing analysis of Andrew Johnson now available, but the series has not yet reached the years of his presidency.

59. For black historiography, see n. 2; and George B. Tindall, "Southern Negroes Since Reconstruction: Dissolving the Static Image," in Arthur S. Link and Rembert W. Patrick, eds., *Writing Southern History: Essays in Historiography in Honor of Fletcher M. Green* (Baton Rouge: Louisiana State University Press, 1965), 337–61; John Hope Franklin, "Reconstruction and the Negro," and August Meier, "Comment on John Hope Franklin's Paper," both in Hyman, ed., *New Frontiers*, 59–86; I. A. Newby, "Historians and Negroes," *Journal of Negro History* 54 (January 1969): 32–47; Eugene D. Genovese, "The Influence of the Black Power Movement on Historical Scholarship: Reflections of a White Historian," *Daedalus* 100 (Spring 1970): 473–94; August Meier, "Benjamin Quarles and the Historiography of Black America," *Civil War History* 26 (June 1980): 101–16, and "Review Essay: Whither the Black Perspective in Afro-American Historiography?" *Journal of American History* 70 (June 1983): 101–5; Willie Lee Rose, *Slavery and Freedom*, ed. William W. Freehling (New York: Oxford University Press, 1982), 90–111; August Meier and Elliott Rudwick, "J. Franklin Jameson, Carter G. Woodson, and the Foundations of Black Historiography," *American Historical Review* 89 (October 1984): 1005–15, and *Black History and the Historical Profession* (Urbana: University of Illinois Press, 1986).

60. Alrutheus A. Taylor, *The Negro in South Carolina During the Reconstruction* (Washington, D.C.: Association for the Study of Negro Life and History, 1924), *The Negro in the Reconstruction of Virginia* (Washington, D.C.: Association for the Study of Negro Life and History, 1926), and *The Negro in Tennessee, 1865–1880* (Washing-

ton, D.C.: Associated Publishers, 1941); Wharton, *The Negro in Mississippi;* George Brown Tindall, *South Carolina Negroes, 1877–1900* (Columbia: University of South Carolina Press, 1952); Joel Williamson, *After Slavery: The Negro in South Carolina During Reconstruction, 1861–1877* (Chapel Hill: University of North Carolina Press, 1965); Joe M. Richardson, *The Negro in the Reconstruction of Florida, 1865–1877* (Tallahassee: Florida State University, 1965). See also Frenise A. Logan, *The Negro in North Carolina, 1876–1894* (Chapel Hill: University of North Carolina Press, 1964); Margaret Law Callcott, *The Negro in Maryland Politics, 1870–1912* (Baltimore: Johns Hopkins Press, 1969); Lawrence D. Rice, *The Negro in Texas, 1874–1900* (Baton Rouge: Louisiana State University Press, 1971); and James M. Smallwood, *Time of Hope, Time of Despair: Black Texans During Reconstruction* (Port Washington, N.Y.: Kennikat Press, 1981).

Special studies include Clarence E. Walker, *A Rock in a Weary Land: The African Methodist Episcopal Church During the Civil War and Reconstruction* (Baton Rouge: Louisiana State University Press, 1982); W. Harrison Daniel, "Virginia Baptists and the Negro, 1865–1902," *Virginia Magazine of History and Biography* 76 (July 1968): 340–63; Robert L. Hall, "Tallahassee's Black Churches, 1865–1885," *Florida Historical Quarterly* 58 (October 1979): 185–96; Daniel F. Littlefield, Jr., and Patricia Washington McGraw, "The Arkansas Freeman, 1869–1870—Birth of the Black Press in Arkansas," *Phylon* 40 (March 1979): 75–85; Allen W. Jones, "The Black Press in the 'New South': Jesse C. Duke's Struggle for Justice and Equality," *Journal of Negro History* 64 (Summer 1979): 215–28; Carl R. Osthaus, *Freedmen, Philanthropy, and Fraud: A History of the Freedman's Savings Bank* (Urbana: University of Illinois Press, 1976); Nell Irvin Painter, *Exodusters: Black Migration to Kansas after Reconstruction* (New York: Knopf, 1977); Robert G. Athearn, *In Search of Canaan: Black Migration to Kansas, 1879–80* (Lawrence: Regents Press of Kansas, 1978); and Anne S. Lee and Everett S. Lee, "The Health of Slaves and the Health of Freedmen: A Savannah Study," *Phylon* 38 (June 1977): 170–80.

61. John W. Blassingame, "Before the Ghetto: The Making of the Black Community in Savannah, Georgia, 1865–1880," *Journal of Social History* 6 (Summer 1973): 463–88; Armstead L. Robinson, "Plans Dat Comed from God: Institution Building and the Emergence of Black Leadership in Reconstruction Memphis," in Burton and McMath, eds., *Toward a New South?,* 71–102. On the black family, see Peter Kolchin, *First Freedom: The Responses of Alabama's Blacks to Emancipation and Reconstruction* (Westport, Conn.: Greenwood Press, 1972), 56–78; Blassingame, *Black New Orleans,* 79–105, 236–41; Elaine C. Everly, "Marriage Registers of Freedmen," *Prologue* 5 (Fall 1973): 150–54; C. Peter Ripley, "The Black Family in Transition: Louisiana, 1860–1865," *Journal of Southern History* 41 (August 1975): 369–80; Herbert G. Gutman, *The Black Family in Slavery and Freedom, 1750–1925* (New York: Pantheon, 1976), 363–450; William Harris, "Work and the Family in Black Atlanta, 1880," *Journal of Social History* 9 (Spring 1976): 319–30; James Smallwood, "Eman-

cipation and the Black Family: A Case Study in Texas," *Social Science Quarterly* 57 (March 1977): 849–57; Edmund L. Drago, "Sources at the National Archives for Genealogical and Local History Research: The Black Household in Dougherty County, Georgia, 1870–1900," *Prologue* 14 (Summer 1982): 81–88; Davis, *Good and Faithful Labor*, 169–84; Shifflett, *Patronage and Poverty*, 84–98. Of closely related interest, Claudia Goldin, "Female Labor Force Participation: The Origin of Black and White Differences, 1870 and 1880," *Journal of Economic History* 37 (March 1977): 87–108. The history of black women in the South during the postemancipation decades has received only incidental attention, but more can be expected. See Sharon Harley and Rosalyn Terborg-Penn, eds., *The Afro-American Woman: Struggles and Images* (Port Washington, N.Y.: Kennikat Press, 1978); and John E. Fleming, "Slavery, Civil War and Reconstruction: A Study of Black Women in Microcosm," *Negro History Bulletin* 38 (August–September 1975): 430–33.

Newer techniques are exemplified in John Kellogg, "The Formation of Black Residential Areas in Lexington, Kentucky, 1865–1887," *Journal of Southern History* 48 (February 1982): 21–52; Borchert, *Alley Life in Washington;* Paul D. Escott, *Slavery Remembered: A Record of Twentieth-Century Slavery Narratives* (Chapel Hill: University of North Carolina Press, 1979), 119–75; Lawrence W. Levine, *Black Culture and Black Consciousness: Afro-American Folk Thought from Slavery to Freedom* (New York: Oxford University Press, 1977).

62. Howard N. Rabinowitz, *Race Relations in the Urban South, 1865–1890* (New York: Oxford University Press, 1978), contains a good deal more on black life than the title suggests; Robert Francis Engs, *Freedom's First Generation: Black Hampton, Virginia, 1861–1890* (Philadelphia: University of Pennsylvania Press, 1979), Eric Anderson, *Race and Politics in North Carolina, 1872–1910: The Black Second* (Baton Rouge: Louisiana State University Press, 1981); Davis, *Good and Faithful Labor;* and for the Natchez district, see also Michael Wayne, *The Reshaping of Plantation Society: The Natchez District, 1860–1880* (Baton Rouge: Louisiana State University Press, 1983); Shifflett, *Patronage and Poverty;* Orville Vernon Burton, "The Rise and Fall of Afro-American Town Life: Town and Country in Reconstruction Edgefield, South Carolina," in Burton and McMath, eds., *Toward a New South?*, 152–92, and "Race and Reconstruction: Edgefield County, South Carolina," in Edward Magdol and Jon L. Wakelyn, eds., *The Southern Common People: Studies in Nineteenth-Century Social History* (Westport, Conn.: Greenwood Press, 1980), 211–37; Frank J. Huffman, Jr., "Town and Country in the South, 1850–1880: A Comparison of Urban and Rural Social Structures," in Magdol and Wakelyn, eds., *The Southern Common People*, 239–51. The intersection of urban and black studies promises to be continuingly fruitful; see Steven W. Engerrand, "Black and Mulatto Mobility and Stability in Dallas, Texas, 1880–1910," *Phylon* 39 (September 1978): 203–15; and Joanne Wheeler, "Together in Egypt: A Pattern of Race Relations in Cairo, Illinois, 1865–1915," in Burton and McMath, eds., *Toward a New South?*, 103–34. On the other

hand, several outstanding area studies give disappointingly little attention to blacks: David L. Carlton, *Mill and Town in South Carolina, 1880–1920* (Baton Rouge: Louisiana State University Press, 1982); Steven Hahn, *The Roots of Southern Populism: Yeoman Farmers and the Transformation of the Georgia Upcountry, 1850–1890* (New York: Oxford University Press, 1983); Lacy K. Ford, "Rednecks and Merchants: Economic Development and Social Tensions in the South Carolina Upcountry, 1865–1900," *Journal of American History* 71 (September 1984): 294–318. Two important state studies have appeared too late for comment. Barbara Jeanne Fields, *Slavery and Freedom on the Middle Ground: Maryland during the Nineteenth Century* (New Haven: Yale University Press, 1985); and Roberta Sue Alexander, *North Carolina Faces the Freedmen: Race Relations During Presidential Reconstruction, 1865–67* (Durham: Duke University Press, 1985).

63. Tindall, "Southern Negroes Since Reconstruction," in Link and Patrick, eds., *Writing Southern History*, 338–39. A topically fragmented but useful general account of postemancipation southern blacks is Arnold H. Taylor, *Travail and Triumph: Black Life and Culture in the South Since the Civil War* (Westport, Conn.: Greenwood Press, 1976).

64. Woodman, "Post–Civil War Southern Agriculture and the Law," 319–37; Nieman, *To Set the Law in Motion*, 33–71; J. Morgan Kousser, *The Shaping of Southern Politics: Suffrage Restriction and the Establishment of the One-Party South, 1880–1910* (New Haven: Yale University Press, 1974), 228–29, 248–50; "A Black Protest in the 'Era of Accommodation': Documents," *Arkansas Historical Quarterly* 34 (Summer 1975): 155, "Progressivism—For Middle-Class Whites Only," and "Making Separate Equal: Integration of Black and White School Funds in Kentucky," *Journal of Interdisciplinary History* 10 (Winter 1980): 399–428; Foner, *Nothing But Freedom*, ch. 3. See also Jerrell H. Shofner, "Militant Negro Laborers in Reconstruction Florida," *Journal of Southern History* 39 (August 1973): 397–408; and Charles L. Flynn, Jr., *White Land, Black Labor: Caste and Class in Late Nineteenth-Century Georgia* (Baton Rouge: Louisiana State University Press, 1983), esp. 84–114 on the role of law. Mark W. Summers, *Railroads, Reconstruction, and the Gospel of Prosperity: Aid under the Radical Republicans, 1865–1877* (Princeton: Princeton University Press, 1984), links southern railroad development to the political fortunes of southern Republicanism. On the recent revival of interest in the economic and class aspects of Reconstruction, see Michael Les Benedict, "The Politics of Prosperity in the Reconstruction South," *Reviews in American History* 12 (December 1984): 507–14.

65. Litwack, *Been in the Storm So Long*, xiii; George P. Rawick, *From Sundown to Sunup: The Making of the Black Community* (Westport, Conn.: Greenwood Publishing Corp., 1972), xv–xviii. Use of the forty-one volumes edited by Rawick has been facilitated by the publication of Donald M. Jacobs, ed., *Index to "The American Slave"* (Westport, Conn.: Greenwood Press, 1981).

66. Ira Berlin, Joseph P. Reidy, and Leslie S. Rowland, eds., *Freedom: A Documen-*

tary History of Emancipation, 1861–1867. Selected from the Holdings of the National Archives of the United States, ser. 2, *The Black Military Experience* (New York: Cambridge University Press, 1982), quotation on p. xxii. On the Freedmen's Bureau records, see Barry A. Crouch, "Hidden Sources of Black History: The Texas Freedmen's Bureau Records as a Case Study," *Southwestern Historical Quarterly* 83 (January 1980): 211–26.

67. Kolchin, *First Freedom*, xix; Berlin, Reidy, and Rowland, eds., *The Black Military Experience*, esp. 1–34, 183–97, 433–42; Escott, *Slavery Remembered*, 119–44; Barry A. Crouch. "Black Dreams and White Justice," *Prologue* 6 (Winter 1974): 255–65; Robert H. McKenzie, "The Shelby Iron Company: A Note on Slave Personality after the Civil War," *Journal of Negro History* 58 (July 1973): 341–48; Bobby L. Lovett, "The Negro's Civil War in Tennessee, 1861–1865," *Journal of Negro History* 61 (January 1976): 36–50; Martin Abbott, "Voice of Freedom: The Response of Southern Freedmen to Liberty," *Phylon* 34 (December 1973): 399–405; Edmund L. Drago, "How Sherman's March Through Georgia Affected the Slaves," *Georgia Historical Quarterly* 57 (Fall 1973): 361–75; Paul D. Escott, "The Context of Freedom: Georgia's Slaves During the Civil War," *Georgia Historical Quarterly* 58 (Spring 1974): 79–104; William C. Hine, "The 1867 Charleston Streetcar Sit-ins: A Case of Successful Black Protest," *South Carolina Historical Magazine* 77 (April 1976): 110–14; Clarence L. Mohr, "Before Sherman: Georgia Blacks and the Union War Effort, 1861–1864," *Journal of Southern History* 45 (August 1979): 331–52; John T. O'Brien, "Reconstruction in Richmond: White Restoration and Black Protest, April–June 1865," *Virginia Magazine of History and Biography* 89 (July 1981): 259–81; Victor B. Howard, *Black Liberation in Kentucky: Emancipation and Freedom, 1862–1884* (Lexington: University Press of Kentucky, 1983).

68. Okon Edet Uya, *From Slavery to Public Service: Robert Smalls, 1839–1915* (New York: Oxford University Press, 1971); Victor Ullman, *Martin R. Delany: The Beginnings of Black Nationalism* (Boston: Beacon Press, 1971); Edwin S. Redkey, comp. and ed., *Respect Black: The Writings and Speeches of Henry McNeal Turner* (New York: Arno Press, 1971); James Haskins, *Pinckney Benton Stewart Pinchback* (New York: Macmillan, 1973); Peggy Lamson, *The Glorious Failure: Black Congressman Robert Brown Elliott and the Reconstruction in South Carolina* (New York: Norton, 1973); Peter D. Klingman, *Josiah Walls: Florida's Black Congressman of Reconstruction* (Gainesville: University Presses of Florida, 1976); Loren Schweninger, *James T. Rapier and Reconstruction* (Chicago: University of Chicago Press, 1978); Charles Vincent, *Black Legislators in Louisiana During Reconstruction* (Baton Rouge: Louisiana State University Press, 1976).

Articles are an important supplement to book-length studies: David C. Rankin, "The Origins of Black Leadership in New Orleans During Reconstruction," *Journal of Southern History* 40 (August 1974): 417–40; Walter J. Fraser, Jr., "Black Reconstructionists in Tennessee," *Tennessee Historical Quarterly* 34 (Winter 1975):

362–82; Barry A. Crouch, "Self-Determination and Local Black Leaders in Texas," *Phylon* 39 (December 1978): 344–55; Joe M. Richardson, "Jonathan C. Gibbs: Florida's Only Negro Cabinet Member," *Florida Historical Quarterly* 42 (April 1964): 363–68, and "Francis L. Cardozo: Black Educator During Reconstruction," *Journal of Negro Education* 48 (Winter 1979): 73–83; Edwin S. Redkey, "Bishop Turner's African Dream," *Journal of American History* 54 (September 1967): 270–90; William C. Harris, "James Lynch: Black Leader in Southern Reconstruction," *Historian* 34 (November 1971): 40–61; Kenneth Eugene Mann, "Blanche Kelso Bruce: United States Senator Without a Constituency," *Journal of Mississippi History* 38 (May 1976): 183–98; James W. Leslie, "Ferd Havis: Jefferson County's Black Republican Leader," *Arkansas Historical Quarterly* 37 (Autumn 1978): 240–51; Charles E. Wynes, "T. McCants Stewart: Peripatetic Black South Carolinian," *South Carolina Historical Magazine* 80 (October 1979): 311–17; Bess Beatty, "John Willis Menard: A Progressive Black in Post–Civil War Florida," *Florida Historical Quarterly* 59 (October 1980): 123–43; Charles Vincent, "Aspects of the Family and Public Life of Antoine Dubuclet: Louisiana's Black State Treasurer, 1868–1878," *Journal of Negro History* 46 (February 1981): 26–36; Samuel Shapiro, "A Black Senator from Mississippi: Blanche K. Bruce," *Review of Politics* 44 (January 1982): 83–109; William C. Hine, "Black Politicians in Reconstruction Charleston, South Carolina: A Collective Study," *Journal of Southern History* 49 (November 1983): 555–84.

Black political leaders also figure in state histories of Reconstruction, of the Republican party, and of the Negro (see n. 62; and citations in the essay by Joe Gray Taylor in this volume). A useful collection by authorities on state politics of the period is Otto H. Olsen, ed., *Reconstruction and Redemption in the South* (Baton Rouge: Louisiana State University Press, 1980). They shift the focus of explanation for the failure of southern Republicanism to the South. So does Loren Schweninger, "Black Citizenship and the Republican Party in Reconstruction Alabama," *Alabama Review* 29 (April 1976): 83–103. On the other hand, in a defense of southern Republican congressmen, Terry L. Seip has added yet another charge against northern Republicans, namely, that they failed to give their southern colleagues the political and economic support essential to sustain them and southern Republicanism in power. See his *The South Returns to Congress: Men, Economic Measures, and Intersectional Relationships, 1868–1879* (Baton Rouge: Louisiana State University Press, 1983).

69. Louis R. Harlan, *Booker T. Washington: The Making of a Black Leader, 1856–1901* and *Booker T. Washington: The Wizard of Tuskegee, 1901–1915* (New York: Oxford University Press, 1972, 1983); Harlan et al., eds., *The Papers of Booker T. Washington* (13 vols.; Urbana: University of Illinois Press, 1972–84); Harlan, "Booker T. Washington in Biographical Perspective," *American Historical Review* 75 (October 1970): 1581–99, "The Secret Life of Booker T. Washington," *Journal of Southern History* 37 (August 1971): 393–416, and "Booker T. Washington and the *Voice of the*

Negro, 1904–1907," *Journal of Southern History* 45 (February 1979): 45–62; Meier, *Negro Thought,* 100–18. See also Willard B. Gatewood, "William D. Crum: A Negro in Politics," *Journal of Negro History* 53 (October 1968): 301–20; and Emma Lou Thornbrough, *T. Thomas Fortune: Militant Journalist* (Chicago: University of Chicago Press, 1972).

70. See Arvarh E. Strickland, "Booker T. Washington: The Myth and the Man," *Reviews in American History* 1 (December 1973): 559–64; Lawrence J. Friedman, "Life 'in the Lion's Mouth': Another Look at Booker T. Washington," *Journal of Negro History* 59 (October 1974): 337–51; Allen W. Jones, "The Role of Tuskegee Institute in the Education of Black Farmers," *Journal of Negro History* 60 (April 1975): 252–67; Alfred Young, "The Educational Philosophy of Booker T. Washington: A Perspective for Black Liberation," *Phylon* 37 (September 1976): 224–35; Don Quinn Kelley, "Ideology and Education: Uplifting the Masses in Nineteenth Century Alabama," *Phylon* 40 (June 1979): 147–58, and "The Political Economy of Booker T. Washington: A Bibliographic Essay," *Journal of Negro Education* 46 (Fall 1977): 403–18.

71. John Hosmer and Joseph Fineman, "Black Congressmen in Reconstruction Historiography," *Phylon* 39 (June 1978): 97–107; Euline W. Brock, "Thomas W. Cardozo: Fallible Black Reconstruction Leader," *Journal of Southern History* 47 (May 1981): 183–206; Holt, *Black Over White,* and "Negro State Legislators in South Carolina during Reconstruction," in Rabinowitz, ed., *Southern Black Leaders,* 223–46.

72. For Louisiana a similar, though weaker, case has been made for the political relevance of intraracial class differences. David C. Rankin, "The Impact of the Civil War on the Free Colored Community of New Orleans," *Perspectives in American History* 11 (1977–78): 379–416, and "The Origins of Negro Leadership in New Orleans during Reconstruction," in Rabinowitz, ed., *Southern Black Leaders,* 162, 169–73; Ted Tunnell, "Free Negroes and the Freedmen: Black Politics in New Orleans During the Civil War," *Southern Studies* 19 (Spring 1980): 5–28. Meier, "Negroes in the First and Second Reconstructions," 119–20, argued that the Negro elite was most concerned with civil rights and the franchise; the black masses with landownership.

73. The latter assumption apparently reflects the influence of David Montgomery, who argues in *Beyond Equality: Labor and the Radical Republicans, 1862–1872* (New York: Knopf, 1967) that southern Republicanism was an indirect casualty of northern industrialists' concern for controlling northern labor. Armstead L. Robinson, "Explaining the Failure of Democratic Reform in Reconstruction South Carolina," *Reviews in American History* 8 (December 1980): 521–30, "Beyond the Realm of Social Consensus: New Meanings of Reconstruction for American History," *Journal of American History* 68 (September 1981): 276–97, and "Plans Dat Comed from God," in Burton and McMath, eds., *Toward a New South?,* 88–99. For a fresh distinctive explanation of Republican factionalism, see Lawrence N. Powell, "The Poli-

tics of Livelihood: Carpetbaggers in the Deep South," in Kousser and McPherson, eds., *Region, Race, and Reconstruction*, 315–47.

74. Joel Williamson, *New People: Miscegenation and Mulattoes in the United States* (New York: Free Press, 1980), esp. 75–91; Gary B. Mills, "Miscegenation and the Free Negro in Antebellum 'Anglo' Alabama: A Reexamination of Southern Race Relations," *Journal of American History* 68 (June 1981): 16–34.

75. Edmund L. Drago, *Black Politicians and Reconstruction in Georgia: A Splendid Failure* (Baton Rouge: Louisiana State University Press, 1982); John M. Matthews, "Negro Republicans in the Reconstruction of Georgia," *Georgia Historical Quarterly* 60 (Summer 1976): 145–64; T. B. Tunnell, Jr., "The Negro, the Republican Party, and the Election of 1876 in Louisiana," *Louisiana History* 7 (Spring 1966): 101–16 (he has repudiated that conclusion in Ted Tunnell, *Crucible of Reconstruction: War, Radicalism, and Race in Louisiana, 1862–1877* [Baton Rouge: Louisiana State University Press, 1984], 212 n. 4); Brock, "Thomas W. Cardozo," *Journal of Southern History* 47 (May 1981): 183–206.

76. Rabinowitz, ed., *Southern Black Leaders*, esp. xi–xx, 393–405 (quotations on pp. xviii, 393).

77. Ibid., 212–13, 318–19; Edward N. Akin, "When a Minority Becomes the Majority: Blacks in Jacksonville Politics, 1887–1907," *Florida Historical Quarterly* 43 (October 1974): 123–45; Joseph H. Cartwright, "Black Legislators in Tennessee in the 1880s: A Case Study in Black Political Leadership," *Tennessee Historical Quarterly* 32 (Fall 1973): 265–84. See also Elizabeth Balanoff, "Negro Legislators in the North Carolina General Assembly, July 1868–February 1872," *North Carolina Historical Quarterly* 49 (Winter 1972): 22–55; Ruth Currie McDaniel, "Black Power in Georgia: William A. Pledger and the Takeover of the Republican Party," *Georgia Historical Quarterly* 62 (Fall 1978): 225–39; James T. Moore, "Black Militancy in Readjuster Virginia, 1879–1883," *Journal of Southern History* 41 (May 1975): 167–86; Allen W. Trelease, "Republican Reconstruction in North Carolina: A Roll-Call Analysis of the State House of Representatives, 1868–1870," *Journal of Southern History* 42 (August 1976): 330, 341; George W. Reid, "Four in Black: North Carolina's Black Congressmen, 1874–1901," *Journal of Negro History* 64 (Summer 1979): 229–43 and n. 68.

78. See Holt, *Black Over White*, 4, 206; Joseph H. Cartwright, *The Triumph of Jim Crow: Tennessee Race Relations in the 1880s* (Knoxville: University of Tennessee Press, 1976); William F. Cheek, "A Negro Runs for Congress: John Mercer Langston and the Virginia Campaign of 1888," *Journal of Negro History* 52 (January 1967): 14–34; Eugene J. Watts, "Black Political Progress in Atlanta: 1868–95," *Journal of Negro History* 59 (July 1974): 268–86; William Warren Rogers and Robert David Ward, "'Jack Turnerism': A Political Phenomenon of the Deep South," *Journal of Negro History* 57 (October 1972): 313–32; William J. Cooper, Jr., "Economics or Race:

An Analysis of the Gubernatorial Election of 1890 in South Carolina," *South Carolina Historical Magazine* 73 (October 1972): 209–19; Peter D. Klingman and David T. Geithman, "Negro Dissidence and the Republican Party, 1864–1872," *Phylon* 40 (June 1979): 172–82; Loren Schweninger, "Alabama Blacks and the Congressional Reconstruction Acts of 1867," *Alabama Review* 31 (July 1978): 182–98. I have not attempted to review here the literature on populism as it relates to blacks. See Harold D. Woodman, "Economic Reconstruction and the Rise of the New South, 1865–1900," *Interpreting Southern History: Historiographical Essays in Honor of Sanford W. Higginbotham,* John B. Boles and Evelyn Thomas Nolen, eds. (Baton Rouge: Louisiana State University Press, 1987), 254–307.

79. Kousser, *The Shaping of Southern Politics,* 11, 14–29, 36–37, 43–44, 228–29, "Post-Reconstruction Suffrage Restrictions in Tennessee: A New Look at the V. O. Key Thesis," *Political Science Quarterly* 88 (December 1973): 655–83, "Separate but not Equal: The Supreme Court's First Decision on Racial Discrimination in Schools," *Journal of Southern History* 46 (February 1980): 17–44; "A Black Protest in the 'Era of Accommodation,'" "Progressivism—For Middle Class Whites Only," "Making Separate Equal," quotation on p. 424, and review of Anderson's *Race and Politics in North Carolina,* in *Journal of Southern History* 48 (February 1982): 123–25. See also Gordon B. McKinney, "Southern Mountain Republicans and the Negro, 1865–1900," *Journal of Southern History* 41 (November 1975): 493–516.

80. Eric Foner, "Reconstruction Revisited," *Reviews in American History* 10 (December 1982): 91–92. The emergence of southern legal history as a distinctive field of scholarship also promises new insight into postemancipation developments. See Edward L. Ayers, *Vengeance and Justice: Crime and Punishment in the Nineteenth-Century American South* (New York: Oxford University Press, 1984), 141–84; and David J. Bodenhamer and James W. Ely, Jr., eds., *Ambivalent Legacy: A Legal History of the South* (Jackson: University Press of Mississippi, 1984), 3–29, 80–86.

81. C. Vann Woodward, *The Strange Career of Jim Crow* (2d rev. ed.; New York: Oxford University Press, 1966), 64, 67.

82. For Woodward's response to subsequent scholarship, see his *Strange Career of Jim Crow,* "The Strange Career of a Historical Controversy," in *American Counterpoint,* 234–60, review of Rabinowitz's *Race Relations in the Urban South,* in *Journal of Southern History* 44 (August 1978): 476–78, and foreword to Howard N. Rabinowitz, *Race Relations in the Urban South* (Urbana: University of Illinois Press, 1980), ix–x. For other evaluations of the literature on segregation, see Joel Williamson, ed., *The Origins of Segregation* (Boston: Heath, 1968); August Meier and Elliott Rudwick, "A Strange Chapter in the Career of 'Jim Crow,'" in Meier and Rudwick, eds., *The Making of Black America: Essays in Negro Life and History, The Black Community in Modern America* (New York: Atheneum, 1969), 2:14–19; Howard N. Rabinowitz, "From Exclusion to Segregation: Southern Race Relations, 1865–1890," *Journal of American History* 63 (September 1976): 325–50, and *Race Relations*

(1980): 331; Kousser and McPherson, eds., *Region, Race, and Reconstruction*, xxv–xxvii. For the continuing vitality of *The Strange Career* as a stimulus, see John W. Cell, *The Highest Stage of White Supremacy: The Origins of Segregation in South Africa and the American South* (Cambridge, Eng.: Cambridge University Press, 1982). Delaware's race relations, at least as to disfranchisement, apparently were not typical. See Amy M. Hiller, "The Disfranchisement of Delaware Negroes in the Late Nineteenth Century," *Delaware History* 13 (October 1968): 124–53.

83. Rabinowitz, *Race Relations* (1980), esp. 332–39; David Herbert Donald, "A Generation of Defeat," in Fraser and Moore, eds., *From the Old South to the New*, 3–20.

Even more recently, Joel Williamson has linked *de jure* disfranchisement and segregation to southern white male sexual appetites and attitudes toward white womanhood. Under the explosive pressure of economic depression, white men set in motion a vicious scapegoating of the black man by racist radicals. This was expressed in restrictive legislation as well as in racial violence. According to Williamson, the laws found support from racist conservatives who sought to protect blacks, from Democrats who desired to disenfranchise their political opponents, and from a reforming impulse that would purify de facto disfranchisement by eliminating the necessity for fraud and intimidation. They completed a cultural separation between blacks and whites (*The Crucible of Race: Black-White Relations in the American South Since Emancipation* [New York: Oxford University Press, 1984], 115–18, 134–35, 224–58, 305–23, 513–17).

84. A shift of attention from North to South appears to be accelerating. In a strikingly original analysis of southern politics, Michael Perman finds the white South moving to accept the essentials of Reconstruction until the Republican victory of 1872 led their opponents to embrace the politics of race and blacks to increased assertiveness within the Republican party. Ted Tunnell highlights the inescapable contradictions facing a Republican party that sought both its own survival and a biracial society but also faults Louisiana's white Republican leaders for lack of the commitment and daring needed to mobilize blacks in militant resistance to white terrorism. Dan Carter's account of the failure of southern white conservative leaders during presidential Reconstruction, without absolving them from responsibility, implies that failure was inevitable, given the chaos of the postwar South, the confusion of politics, the obsessive white fears rooted in racial assumptions of the proslavery argument, and the persistence of the southern sense of honor. Michael Perman, *The Road to Redemption: Southern Politics, 1869–1879* (Chapel Hill: University of North Carolina Press, 1984), esp. chps. 5–6; Tunnell, *Crucible of Reconstruction*, 160–72, 212–18; Dan T. Carter, *When the War Was Over: The Failure of Self-Reconstruction in the South, 1865–1867* (Baton Rouge: Louisiana State University Press, 1985).

85. John Hope Franklin, "Mirror for Americans: A Century of Reconstruction History," *American Historical Review* 85 (February 1980): 11.